Communication and New Media

CANADIAN EDITION

Communication and New Media

From Broadcast to Narrowcast

Martin Hirst

John Harrison

Patricia Mazepa

OXFORD

UNIVERSITY PRESS

OXFORD
UNIVERSITY PRESS

Oxford University Press is a department of the University of Oxford.
It furthers the University's objective of excellence in research, scholarship,
and education by publishing worldwide. Oxford is a registered trade mark of
Oxford University Press in the UK and in certain other countries.

Published in Canada by
Oxford University Press
8 Sampson Mews, Suite 204,
Don Mills, Ontario M3C 0H5 Canada

www.oupcanada.com

Library and Archives Canada Cataloguing in Publication

Hirst, Martin, author
Communication and new media : from broadcast to narrowcast / Martin
Hirst, John Harrison, Patricia Mazepa. — Canadian edition.

Includes bibliographical references and index.
ISBN 978-0-19-543381-4 (pbk.)

1. Communication. 2. Mass media.
I. Harrison, John, (John Murray), 1952–, author
II. Mazepa, Patricia, author III. Title.

P90.H57 2014   302.2   C2013-907776-6

Cover image: EschCollection/Photonica/Getty Images

Oxford University Press is committed to our environment.
This book is printed on Forest Stewardship Council® certified paper
and comes from responsible sources.

Printed and bound in Canada

1 2 3 4 — 17 16 15 14

Brief Contents

Contents

Author's Preface

This book is an introduction to some contemporary theories and views about communication and media, and their form and function change with technological convergence. We first need to explain why it's important to draw a distinction between the two. Although you will be introduced to several ways of thinking about communication and media, a common way to begin is to view communication as a process of sending and receiving messages, whereas the various kinds of media are the means of communication and transmission. It follows that communication can take place using different types of media (such as newspapers, telephone, radio, television, etc.). "Technological convergence" suggests the coming together of many different types of media. Whereas with "old" media, communication was distinguished as visual (as in print or photographs) in contrast to audio (as phonographs or radio) or audio-visual (as television), for example, with "new" media, the message (or content that is carried) is digitalized and can be transmitted across many different types of media (e.g., taking a photograph on your cell phone and emailing it to an address on the Web).

The difference between broadcasting and narrowcasting initially follows this distinction between communication and old and new media. Communication via old media is considered to be *broadcast* when messages originating from a central point (like a television newsroom or radio station) are sent to many receivers (also called "mass" communication). Communication via new media retains these broadcasting capabilities, but it can also be *narrowcast*; messages can be composed to reach and address even smaller numbers of people, or even an individual, whether on the sending or the receiving end.

In the process, media can be used to bring people and messages closer together, or it can also mean crossed signals or mixed messages, and an increasingly fragmented media—all at the same time. For example, a housemate on *Big Brother Canada* could use her 15 minutes of fame to launch a boycott or protest that can reach millions of people, relying on the use of television to broadcast to the many, whereas others in the same house are caught engaging in intimate personal communication by hidden cameras, bringing the many to focus directly on the individual. In addition, individual online users can participate in the decisions that are made in the house, which suggests to those watching the program that they have the power to shape the future. Meanwhile, the producers can eliminate the need for the employment of scriptwriters and professional actors, and gather information from audience members in order to sell advertising. Selling the show as a commercial product means that commercials can be tailored to fit individual receivers, while multiple formats and versions of the show are broadcast worldwide to over 85 countries, the latter of which is heralded as both a marker of quality and a measure of success (Shaw Media, 2012); and why not? The program has it all—conflict, competition, voting, and surveillance—24/7.

Yet, all this is more than just entertainment and business as usual. Such communication and media also represent a particular *way of making media*; it favours specific *ways of thinking* about communication—about social relationships and ourselves—and it shapes *practices of participation* in media. That these ways of thinking and doing are repeated and extended worldwide gives us pause to consider communication as a complex process and media as more than just a means of doing so. This is true for many different kinds of communication (or genres) as well.

For example, television news is another common form of communication, with arguably more important and far-reaching implications than some mildly entertaining intimacy from the *Big Brother* housemates. Yet, "the news" is also produced in a particular way. Network news, for instance, only tells us about *some* events in the world, as they are selected for inclusion according to shifting "news values" that may not be obvious or otherwise apparent to us. Similarly, we see only those segments of "reality" captured by the *Big Brother Canada* cameras that the producers deem to be "entertaining" enough to attract an audience. In either case, the content is constructed since, as we shall discuss in this book, communication and media are the products of social relations, particularly the power relations that constitute both its political-economic and its social construction. This includes decisions on whose reality is represented and how, what content will be included or not, and who gets to make the decisions in the first place.

With convergence of media technologies, there is potential to widen our participation in decision-making and to create more interactivity, not only in media decisions but in our lives more generally. But if this potential is primarily extended to the minor interaction of voting for a housemate, or giving feedback to the producers on commercial content, does this participation provide meaningful social interaction and decision-making, or does it simply condition us to an already prescribed and limited way of participating?

For the commercial media today, "interactive" tends to mean that the interaction is aimed at getting audiences to participate to the extent that they spend more time and attention on a particular media that they interact with its content, buy associated products for sale, and therefore become more valuable as a commodity for the business. The potentials of new media are also circumscribed accordingly, as this time and attention translates into value via advertising dollars and information that is gathered to be sold to marketers and advertisers.

In contrast, the approach taken in this book to time, attention, and participation is a different kind of interactivity. We are keen for you to respond and engage with this text as a learner, reader, discussant, and active citizen. With such an "old" media form like a book, however, this is a little more challenging than online participation, but it allows time for reading, thought, and reflection, and we've included questions, case studies, and exercises to assist your interaction with your classmates, instructors, and—if we can further extend your interest—your friends, family, and community.

In its overall approach, *Communication and New Media* explicitly and implicitly binds together "theory" and "practice." The embedding of theory and practice, one in the other, reflects the almost insoluble link between learning and action. This embedded approach most closely fits the pedagogical needs of communication courses as well as tertiary courses in journalism, applied communication, and creative pursuits more generally. It is also increasingly coming to be the required standard from employers, but more importantly is necessary for participating in decision-making in general, particularly given the complexity and challenges faced in the world today. The world needs graduates with emotional intelligence, curiosity, and inquiring minds, and who are also materially and ethically aware of the situations and contexts in which they (will) work and live.

In general, the integration of theory and practice aims to address four important objectives of higher education in Canada such that graduating students should be able to

- understand the breadth and/or depth of knowledge in the area of study and be able to apply and communicate it clearly (via advanced research, reading, writing, and speaking skills);

- be aware of the limits of knowledge and of the necessity for its continual and critical evaluation;
- demonstrate skills of critical analysis and independent thinking; and
- apply critical reasoning and ethical understanding in everyday practice.

To assist in this process, "Case Studies" and "Focus on Research" sections are also included in this book and are meant to demonstrate not only *how* research on communication, media, and technology is conducted but also *why* it is conducted. Additional "For Real?" sections are critical and deliberately provoking, with good intentions. While there is a great deal of positive claims and promotion of new media and technology, for example, there is less application of critical, independent thinking and engagement with ethics in evaluating such claims. It is not enough to identify and critique what we find in the world; we need to be able to learn how to analyze and contribute to problem-solving in order to make changes for the better.

You will also find some references in this book that you may find unusual; some are on the esoteric subject of utopian and dystopian science fiction. But there is a purpose to our digressions. Ever since the Greek empire dominated the known world and was wealthy enough to employ full-time philosophers, human society has been interested in devoting resources to speculation about the future. Plato's famous treatise, *The Republic*, is one of the earliest writings to embrace utopian ideals in contemplation of an almost perfect world that had yet to come to pass. Since Plato's time—and using his text as a template—political writers, social critics, and anti-authoritarian dissidents have employed similar means to promote their cause (Rothstein, 2003). Often a mythological language and poetic-Socratic style was used to evade the censors, who would not allow a serious debate about unpopular government policies. As a result, today we have a rich tradition in literature that is manifest in the science-fiction writing of American-Canadians like William Gibson, who present the near and distant future in ways that show it is clearly derived from past and present conditions, both technological and emotional.

Finally, we hope that reading this text is an enjoyable and inspirational process for you. We have included many references to science fiction, particularly the genre known as "cyberpunk." This is a deliberate attempt on our part to make *Communication and New Media* more engaging. But the serious side is that science fiction has a knack of making workable predictions about the future. In this instance we think cyberpunk has some useful things to contribute to our digital future. We trust that after reading this book, you will, too.

Acknowledgements

A project this size depends on a lot of participation, collaboration, and resources to complete it, and we consider it a privilege to offer it to you for your consideration.

To Martin Hirst and John Harrison, thank you for forging such a distinctive and critical path, and to Oxford University Press Canada for giving me the opportunity and academic freedom to follow and explore its branches and tributaries in Canada. The following initial peer reviewers were very helpful in contributing their expertise and thoughtful comments in adjusting the way and confirming the route: Nicholas Balaisis (Concordia University), Mark Hayward (Wilfrid Laurier University), Philip Savage (McMaster University), Dal Yong Jin (Simon Fraser University), Ira Wagman (Carleton University), and Derek Foster (Brock University).

To Stephen Kotowych, Peter Chambers, and Meagan Carlsson at OUP Canada, thank you for your guidance and perseverance in directing me along the journey, and for keeping me from straying. To Amanda Maurice, your outstanding attention to detail shone like a beacon of light guiding me to completion, and I couldn't have done so without your diligence and timely dedication.

Picking up the baggage along the way and helping me through the rough spots were graduate assistants Filip Tisma and Michael Cheatley, courtesy of the York and Ryerson Joint Graduate Program in Communication & Culture, whose assistance with the timelines and ownership charts were particularly helpful.

To my colleagues, Sonja Macdonald and Kirsten Kozolanka, I was supported by your company, invigorated by your contributions, and sincerely appreciate your invaluable input.

Lastly, but never the least, I thank my colleagues and students at York and Ryerson, my friends and family, and especially Kevin Smith for listening, empathizing and comforting me—and for not blowing a gasket—every time I said "Sorry, but I've got to work on the book!"

This is as much our project as it is for all of the above-mentioned people and then some. We sincerely hope that in times to come, you will also make it yours.

From the Publisher

Building on the success of its Australian predecessor, the Canadian edition of *Communication and New Media: From Broadcast to Narrowcast* introduces topics in media studies in a sophisticated manner designed to reach and engage Canadian students from various backgrounds at the first- and second-year level. Its mixture of international and Canadian examples helps students better understand theory and concepts and their application, both at home and abroad.

Important Features of This Book

Communication and New Media incorporates numerous features and elements that make it a useful teaching and learning tool.

to manufacture its trademark Kodachrome film. The trademark "Polaroid" has been continued, however, despite the company's filing for bankruptcy protection in the United States in 2001, as its instant film processing was recently revived (▣ www.the-impossible-project.com). The revival indicates that despite changes in business decisions and the idea that digital technology is both progressive and superior, photographers prefer to retain manual control over the creative process. In a return to the beginnings of photography, Kodak currently manufactures film intended for professional photographers, and otherwise channels imagining to its digital online offerings. Yet, the precarity of online storage is cause for concern because of technological obsolescence. In comparison, the "old" family album—although still subject to physical deterioration over several generations—doesn't take a special program to either store or open, and doesn't require passage through the infrastructure of a multinational corporation, whereas the contents of digital files from just 10 years ago are already inaccessible, never mind what happens if the database goes down or Google decides that in order to see your pictures for free, you have to watch some advertising.

DIGITAL TECHNOLOGY
A conversion of data (an image, word, or symbol, e.g.) into two electrical states—"positive" and "negative"—that is used to record, store, transmit, and receive data. These conditions of either "on" or "off" are represented by two numbers (digits)—as "one" or "zero"—which is the language of mathematics used in computer technology.

For Real?

Abolish Patents? Polaroid vs. Kodak

Polaroid had several patents out on its camera and film developments, and in discovering that Kodak had been using the technology in its own instant cameras, Polaroid took Kodak to court for wilful patent infringement (Polaroid v. Eastman Kodak, 1986), and after 15 years of legal proceedings, Kodak paid Polaroid USD$925 million (Reuters, 1991). Several years later, Kodak would be back in court, this time to sue other corporations for patent infringement, including Sony, which turned around and sued Kodak for the same reason (Meland, 2004), as well as Apple and HTC (Savitz, 2012). The battle to control and secure private ownership is continually before the public courts and has increased exponentially with digital technology, as both the techniques used and the types of technology converge. The extreme to which the number of patents being filed and the extent to which this is causing more harm than good (whether in terms of technological progress or knowledge development) is argued to be particularly debilitating in software programming as there is more software litigation than in any other area (Bessen, Ford, & Meurer, 2011), and even economists argue that the intellectual (private) property system should be abolished entirely (Bessen & Meurer, 2008).

Discussion Questions

1. What is the difference between a trademark and a patent?
2. Given that you likely use a computer every day, how much of that use (the hardware, the software, the social media sites, the search engines, etc.) is covered by intellectual property rights?
3. Who (or what) owns your photographs when you put them online?
4. Identify arguments for/against intellectual property rights; should intellectual property rights be abolished? Explain why or why not.

- **Part and chapter objectives** assist students to focus their reading and studies, acting as a useful checkpoint to ensure proper understanding of the main topics.
- **Three types of themed boxes** highlight important research, critical issues, and relevant current events.
  - **"For Real?"** boxes offer a thorough exploration of controversial topics and conclude with a "discussion" section to inspire classroom interaction.
  - **"Focus on Research"** boxes use Canadian and international examples to demonstrate not only *how* research on communication, media, and technology is conducted but also *why* it is conducted.
  - **"Ongoing Issues"** boxes discuss media-specific issues that persist through the history of media despite technological, social, or political change.

- **Boxed case studies** provide examples and discussion questions that allow students to better engage with theory.
- **Online icons** indicate places where websites further illustrate points, with corresponding hyperlinks available on the book's companion website.
- **End-of-chapter material**—including key points, class discussion questions, "Media on Media" further reading sections, and timelines—assist students in connecting with and reviewing key chapter concepts.
- **Vivid photographs, tables, and figures** help to introduce students to key issues and important trends in Canadian and international media.
- **Marginal definitions and a glossary of key terms** at the back of the book provide easy reference.

---

3 | Contextualizing Technology   51

Case Study

IBM's Watson on *Jeopardy!*

In February 2011, fans of the American game show *Jeopardy!* were witness to three days of a special tournament that brought back two of the game's best players, Ken Jennings and Brad Rutter, to compete against a question-answering computer named "Watson," developed by IBM. At the end of the three days, the computer reigned victorious over the human contestants, despite a number of significant errors along the way. Questions then arose about whether or not this success signalled the future of computing, finally breaking through the barriers of artificial intelligence, long envisioned in science fiction like *2001: A Space Odyssey*, *The Terminator*, and *Star Trek*. The contest was reminiscent of IBM's publicity stunt in the 1990s, when IBM's super computer Deep Blue was pit against chess ace Garry

FIGURE 3.1 | World champion Garry Kasparov during the third match with Deep Blue, the chess computer program, in 1997.

Kasparov (see Figure 3.1). Similarly, the Watson contest was about publicity, but it was also about more direct avenues of business development for the computer company (C. Thompson, 2010).

Watson is a very large computer system developed by IBM to attempt to chip away at elemental aspects of artificial intelligence. The system is designed as a question-answering computer, aimed at trying to overcome challenges found in human language to better analyze and collate large amounts of data to reach a correct answer. Watson was developed over a number of years by teams of computer scientists at IBM, and the process involved the human selection and inputting of massive reams of digital information from various sources (the system was not connected to the Internet for the game). Watson made use of various different algorithms [...] sly to respond to questions. For each question, the system would present up to [...] l answers, selecting the most likely answer based on probability. The challenge of [...] r the system was how the questions are phrased, often using puns and humour to [...] correct answer—linguistic practices that computers have traditionally struggled with. [...] success over the two champions was less about the game, and more about IBM, and [...] out the potential business opportunities for this system moving forward. David Ferrucci, [...] utive responsible for developing Watson, foresees the use of the technology in medical [...] rvice sectors (e.g., transportation and retail). Ultimately, promoting Watson on a game [...] out both raising IBM's profile, again, within the technology sector, as well as signalling a [...] ss direction for the company.

Continued

---

1 | Digital Dilemmas   19

Key Points

- The principle of the dialectic means that there are forces (theses) and counter-forces (antitheses) operating not only in the natural world but also in human society, which interact to produce a new force (synthesis), which in turn becomes the next thesis. The dialectic is one way of understanding how biological and historical change occurs.
- The notion of "the material," and the way in which the question "Who owns and controls the technologies of production?" is asked, is fundamental to any understanding of political economy and, in particular, the use and development of media and communication in modern capitalist societies.
- The concepts of memes and vectors can be applied to assist in understanding how media and communications are thought of and circulated, and how technology itself is viewed and developed.

Class Discussion

1. Can you think of examples that illustrate the process of thesis–antithesis–synthesis in the dialectic of everyday events in the world today?
2. What are some of the dominant technology and digital memes of today? What key vectors are particularly effective for their transmission? And how do they become "viral"?
3. Provide some examples of technological determinism. What would be the antithesis to technological determinism?
4. How does our use of the term *materialism* differ from what we might consider the "common sense" definition?
5. What is the difference between idealism and materialism? How do each of these philosophies explain our current "knowledge economy" and your understanding of social change?

Media on Media

Dialectical Tunes

Kraftwerk. (1981). Pocket calculator. *Computer World*. London, UK: EMI. www.lyricsdepot.com/kraftwerk/pocket-calculator.html

Pink Floyd. (1975). Have a cigar. *Wish You Were Here*. London, UK: EMI. www.sing365.com/music/lyric.nsf/have-a-cigar-lyrics-pink-floyd/aeeebbc405ae843e482568a1000526ae

Talking Heads. (1985). Television man. *Little Creatures*. London, UK: EMI. www.lyricsfreak.com/t/talking+heads/television+man_20135039.html

Tracy Chapman. (1988). Talkin' 'bout a revolution. *Tracy Chapman*. US: Elektra/Asylum Records.

Weezer. (2008). Pork and beans. *Weezer*. US: Geffen. www.youtube.com/watch?v=PQHPYeIqr0E

DVDs and Videos

Cambridge Educational. Digital Educational Video. (Producer). (2001). *Why we buy what we buy*.

Klein, N. (Writer). Media Education Foundation. (Producer). (2010). *No logo: Brands, globalization, resistance*.

MacNeil/Lherer Productions. (Producer). (2008). *Explaining globalization*.

NFB. (Producer). (2002). *Almost real: Connecting in a wired world* [Documentary]. Retrieved from www.nfb.ca/film/almost-real.

- **A full ancillary package**—including an instructor's manual, a test bank, PowerPoint slides, and a companion website—supports instructors and students alike while providing tools for in-depth engagement with the subject matter. All are available at **www.oupcanada.com/Hirst**.

Abbreviations

ABC	Australian Broadcasting Corporation (public)
ACA	Association of Canadian Advertisers
ACN	A. C. Nielsen (Company)
ACTA	Anti-Counterfeiting Trade Agreement
AFP	Agence France-Presse
AGT	Alberta Government Telephones
AI	Artificial Intelligence
ALGOL	ALGOrithmic Language
AM	Amplitude Modulation
AMPPLC	Association of Motion Picture Producers and Laboratories of Canada
AOL	America Online
AP	Associated Press
APC	Automated Production Control
APT/APTN	Aboriginal Peoples Television Network
APTN	Associated Press Television Network
ARPA	Advanced Research Projects Agency
ASCC	Automatic Sequence Controlled Calculator
AT&T	American Telephone & Telegraph Company
ATM	Automatic Teller Machine
BASIC	Beginner's All-purpose Symbolic Instruction Code
B-B	Big Brother
BBC	British Broadcasting Corporation
BBG	Board of Broadcast Governors
BBM	Bureau of Broadcast Measurement
BCE	Bell Canada Enterprises
BNA ACT	British North America Act
BPI	British Phonographic Industry
CAB	Canadian Association of Broadcasters
CACTUS	Canadian Association of Community Television Users and Stations
CADSI	Canadian Association of Defence and Security Industries
CAIP	Canadian Association of Internet Providers
CAJ	Canadian Association of Journalists
CALEA ACT	Communications Assistance to Law Enforcement Act
CANARIE	Canadian Network for the Advancement of Research, Industry and Education
CANDU	CANada Deuterium Uranium
CAP	Community Access Program
CAPP	Canadians Against Proroguing Parliament
CBC	Canadian Broadcasting Corporation
CBS	Columbia Broadcasting System
CBSC	Canadian Broadcast Standards Council
CCNA	Canadian Community Newspapers Association
CCS	Centre for Community Study
CCTV	Closed-Circuit Television
CD	Compact Disc
CDNA	Canadian Daily Newspaper Association
CEATEC	Combined Exhibition of Advanced Technologies
CEP	Communication, Energy and Paperworkers Union
CETA	Comprehensive Economic and Trade Agreement
CGI	Computer-Generated Imagery
CIA	Central Intelligence Agency
CIPO	Canadian Intellectual Property Office
CIPPIC	Canadian Internet Policy and Public Interest Clinic
CLASSE	"Coalition for Student Solidarity and Union"
CMC	Computer-Mediated Communication
CMD	Center for Media and Democracy
CNA	Canadian Newspaper Association
CNN	Cable News Network
CNOOC	China National Offshore Oil Corporation
COBOL	COmmon Business Oriented Language
COTC	Canadian Overseas Telecommunication Corporation
CP	Canadian Press
CPF	Canada Periodical Fund
CPR	Canadian Pacific Railway
CPU	Central Processing Unit
CRA	Canada Revenue Agency
CRBC	Canadian Radio Broadcasting Commission
CRIA	Canadian Recording Industry Association
CRIS	Communication Rights in the Information Society
CRTC	Canadian Radio-television and Telecommunications Commission
CSE/CSEC	Communications Security Establishment/ Communications Security Establishment Canada
CSIS	Canadian Security Intelligence Service
CSTB	Computer Science and Telecommunications Board
CTV	Canadian Television Network
CWIRP	Community Wireless Infrastructure Research Project
DARPA	Defense Advanced Research Projects Agency
DEW	Distant Early Warning
DJ	Disc Jockey
DMCA	Digital Millennium Copyright Act
DND	Department of National Defence
DOCR	Defence of Canada Regulations
DRM	Digital Rights Management
DSL	Digital Subscriber Line
DVD	Digital Versatile Disc
EDC	Electronic Digital Computer

EFF	Electronic Frontiers Foundation
ENG	Electronic News-Gathering
ENIAC	Electronic Numerical Integrator And Computer
FBI	Federal Bureau of Investigation
FCC	Federal Communications Commission
FM	Frequency Modulation
FORTRAN	FORmula TRANslation
FPJQ	Federation of Professional Journalists in Quebec
FRC	Federal Radio Commission
FTC	Federal Trade Commission
GATS	General Agreement on Trade in Services
GATT	General Agreement on Tariffs and Trade
GDP	Gross Domestic Product
GDS	Global Distribution System
GMT	Greenwich Mean Time
GNU	Gnu's Not Unix
GPS	Global Positioning System
HCUA	House Committee on Un-American Activities
HLL	High-Level Language
HSARPA	Homeland Security Advanced Research Projects Agency
IBM	International Business Machines
ICANN	Internet Corporation for Assigned Names and Numbers
ICO	Information Commissioner's Office
ICT	Information and Communication Technology
IE	Internet Explorer
IFEX	International Freedom of Expression eXchange
IHAC	Information Highway Advisory Council
IMCR	International Media Concentration Research
IP	Intellectual Property
IPO	Initial Public Offering
ISP	Internet Service Provider
ITAC	Information Technology Association of Canada
ITMP	Internet Traffic Management Practices
ITU	International Telecommunication Union
LAN	Local Area Networking
MAPL	Music, Artist, Production, or Lyrics
MIT	Massachusetts Institute of Technology
MITS	Micro Instrumentation and Telemetry Systems
MTS	Manitoba Telecom Services
MVJ	Mobile-Video Jockey
NAFTA	North American Free Trade Agreement
NAM	Non-Aligned Movement
NATO	North Atlantic Treaty Organization
NBC	National Broadcasting Corporation
NBTF	National Broadband Task Force
NFB	National Film Board
NGO	Non-Governmental Organizations
NIEO	New International Economic Order
NORAD	North American Aerospace Defence Command
NRC	National Research Council
NSF	National Science Foundation
NSTC	National Science and Technology Council
NWICO	New World Information and Communication Order
OECD	Organisation for Economic Co-operation and Development
PARC	Palo Alto Research Center
PBS	Public Broadcasting Service
PC	Personal Computer
PDA	Personal Digital Assistant
PIAC	Public Interest Advocacy Centre
PII	Personally Identifiable Information
PIPA	PROTECT IP (Preventing Real Online Threats to Economic Creativity and Theft of Intellectual Property) Act
PIPEDA ACT	Personal Information Protection and Electronic Documents Act
PMO	Prime Minister's Office
PR	Public Relations
PSI	Pixels per Square Inch
PWAC	Professional Writers Association of Canada
RAM	Random Access Memory
RCA	Radio Corporation of America
RCAF	Royal Canadian Air Force
RCI	Radio Canada International
RCMP	Royal Canadian Mounted Police
RDA	Reader's Digest Association
RFID	Radio-Frequency Identification Device
RIAA	Recording Industry Association of America
RIM	Research in Motion
RSS	Really Simple Syndication
SLR	Single Lens Reflex
SOPA	Stop Online Piracy Act
SSC	Surveillance Studies Centre
TCP/IP	Transmission Control Protocol/Internet Protocol
TCTS	Trans-Canada Telephone System
TNC	Transnational Corporation
TPRP	Telecommunications Policy Review Panel
TRIPS	Trade-Related aspects of Intellectual Property Rights
UBB	Usage-Based Billing
UDHR	Universal Declaration of Human Rights
UGC	User-Generated Content
UN	United Nations
UNESCO	United Nations Educational, Scientific and Cultural Organization
UNIVAC	UNIVersal Automatic Computer

Continued

UPC	Universal (or Unified) Product Code	**WIPO**	World Intellectual Property Organization
UPI	United Press International	**WMA**	War Measures Act
UTEC	University of Toronto Electronic Computer	**WSIS**	World Summit on the Information Society
VJ	Video Jockey	**WTO**	World Trade Organization
VOA	Voice of America	**XWA**	Experimental Wireless Apparatus
VOIP	Voice over Internet Protocol		

Introduction

Navigating the Signposts:
Yesterday the Telephone, Today the Mobile Phone, Tomorrow the Embodied Transceiver?

Objectives

This general overview introduces the themes of *Communication and New Media* and outlines the purpose of each section. Reading this introduction will familiarize you with the ideas we discuss and the language we use to discuss them. After reading this you should be ready to tackle the topics in the main body of this book. In particular, we hope you will understand the following:

- how and why this book is written, and structured, the way it is;

- why technology alone does not determine the shape of the future; and

- how the means of communication—forms of broadcasting and narrowcasting—are the outcome of a range of complex historical, political, social, and economic factors that we can understand using, among other approaches, the tools of political economy.

Keywords

> [Keywords are] the record of an inquiry into a **vocabulary**: a shared body of words and meanings in our most general discussions, in English, of the practices and institutions which we group as **culture** and **society**. (R. Williams, 1989, p. 15)

At the beginning of each chapter we flag some of the keywords and concepts that you will encounter. In all cases, the keywords are defined in the text. For example, the following terms are prominent throughout this book: *analogue, capitalism, convergence, dialectic, digital, dystopia, hegemony, ideology, meme, mode of production, narrowcasting, political economy, technology,* and *utopia*.

Some of these may be new to you, and some of them may be familiar; however, if you are puzzled about a word or concept you see on this list, refer to our Glossary, or consult a dictionary or encyclopaedia of communication at an online or local public library. While Wikipedia may also be helpful as a guideline, any inquiry should not entirely depend upon it. We have tried to avoid jargon as much as possible, so the meanings we employ are usually the most common and logical. Some terms, like *dialectic, meme*, and *mode of production*, are of a more specialized nature, and we have taken some time to work them into the text in an understandable way, but (we hope) without "dumbing them down" or reducing them to mere clichés. We have also flagged a number of specific websites throughout the text, identified by an icon 🖥 (www.oupcanada.com, e.g.) that we hope will help lead you to more sources and information discussed in the text. Lastly, we have added a "Media on Media" section at the end of each chapter to assist you or pique your interest in discussing the central ideas and arguments presented in the text.

Digital Futures?

During the past century the successive advances in technology have been accompanied by corresponding advances in organization. . . . In order to fit into these organizations, individuals have had to de-individualize themselves, have had to deny their native diversity and conform to a standard pattern, and have had to do their best to become automata. (Huxley, 1965b, p. 18)

Aldous Huxley wrote these prophetic words in a 1958 essay "Brave New World Revisited" (as cited in Huxley, 1965b), which was a coda to his bleak but bawdy science-fiction novel *Brave New World*, first published in 1932. *Brave New World* is a comic story of an imagined future in which the science of socially grading human beings has been perfected. On the surface, the future world appears to be perfect—particularly for those classed among the higher levels. For the nameless "drones," it is less perfect. The equilibrium of the world is threatened by the arrival of a "primitive" in the fashionable society of London. The central characters are forced to challenge their utopian view, and the world is revealed as very authoritarian and dystopian.

Huxley (1965b) felt compelled to add this epilogue because he was, at the time, "a good deal less optimistic" (p. 1) than when he was writing the novel. His optimism had been dented by the rise of totalitarianism in Europe in the 1920s (via the likes of the regimes led by Mussolini [Italy], Hitler [Germany], Franco [Spain], and Stalin [Russia]), and subsequently by the depression years of the 1930s, World War II, and the atomic bomb.

In the essay, Huxley compares *Brave New World* to that other classic of nightmare totalitarianism, George Orwell's *Nineteen Eighty-Four*. Huxley (1965b) describes Orwell's work as "a magnified projection into the future of a present that contained Stalinism and an immediate past that had witnessed the flowering of Nazism" (p. 2). Huxley's *Brave New World* begins with a utopian promise (of an ideal progressive society), while the dystopia (pessimism and oppression) of Orwell's *Nineteen Eighty-Four* is apparent from the beginning. Throughout *Communication and New Media* we refer to other works of futuristic science fiction and the ways in which they oscillate between utopian and dystopian views of the world. The novels and short stories we include here provide appropriate windows into our own possible digital futures, and may disturb your comfort zone.

For instance, the major differences that Huxley saw between his work and Orwell's were on the question of *how* totalitarian states exercise their social control. In *Nineteen Eighty-Four*, total control over the exploited population is maintained through surveillance, terror, and the fear of terrible punishment; in *Brave New World*, control—which is no less totalitarian—is exercised through "the more effective methods of reward and scientific manipulation" (Huxley, 1965b, p. 3) of individual minds. In both books the entire population is under constant surveillance, and the methods of ideological manipulation are similar—the media and technology play a central role in disseminating the regimes' propaganda. In *Nineteen Eighty-Four* it was the telescreen: a two-way mechanism for instruction and surveillance that could never be turned off; in *Brave New World* it was "non-stop distractions of the most fascinating nature" (p. 29). In order to draw a widely applicable conclusion based on his observations of English society in the 1950s, Huxley continues, "A society, most of whose members spend a great part of their time . . . in the irrelevant other worlds of sport and soap opera, of mythology and metaphysical fantasy, will find it hard to resist the encroachments of those who would manipulate and control it" (ibid.).

A good example of the creative tension between utopian and dystopian dreams of the future is the 1986 short story by American-Canadian science-fiction writer William Gibson,

"The Gernsback Continuum" (as cited in Gibson, 1995b). In this story a commercial photographer is recruited to take photographs of twentieth-century American industrial architecture, and as he moves around each location, he is reminded of a future that never was, a "never-never land, [and the] true home of a generation of completely uninhibited technophiles" (ibid., p. 38). At the same time, he notices that some of the buildings he's commissioned to photograph have "a kind of sinister totalitarian dignity" (p. 40); others exude "potent bursts of raw technological enthusiasm" (p. 41). In *Communication and New Media* you will find the same contradictions apparent in the new media technologies. On one hand, they hold the promise of a bright, abundant future; on the other, the threat of increased surveillance, even greater monopoly over resources, and greater control over our political selves—that is, our citizenship and capacity to act collectively. If all of this is beginning to sound too familiar or uncomfortable, then you're reading the right book!

Although Huxley's essay on *Brave New World* is fairly pessimistic, he does end it on a more positive note. In a concluding chapter called "What Can Be Done?" he argues that people can be "educated for freedom" but society is, in his view, "threatened from many directions" (Huxley, 1965b, p. 89), including overpopulation and the ever-present shadow of totalitarianism and psychological disease. Today, we might argue that over-consumption is more accurate than overpopulation, but we could also add the threat of pandemics, environmental ruin, and worldwide experiences of poverty, marginalization, and violence. Appreciating that these are interconnected challenges, we have written *Communication and New Media* as a university text for use in communications courses, but also because we, like Huxley, retain our optimism. It is our conviction that addressing the many challenges that we collectively face rests on our ability to comprehend the power manifest in communication and media, in its political economy and changing social relations, and to recognize the connections between these and the potential for technological control all around us as well as the possibilities for change. Reading this textbook as an "education for freedom" means being better equipped to affect the future rather than simply acquiescing or condemning it.

Since we also agree, as Huxley (1965b) concluded, that "there is still some freedom left in the world" we underscore that the use and development of technology is also a product of our own choices and decision-making. This can be challenging, of course, but tomorrow is still a matter of our actions today, as both our individual and collective responsibility, the digital future really is in (y)our hands.

Keeping up with the Future

> *It's not quite Big Brother, more like Big Mother. . . . Michael's the first kid on his northern beaches block to have a new child's mobile phone that doubles as a tracking device. (L. Williams, 2006, paras. 1, 3)*

These days, it's assumed that 8-year-old kids like Michael in Louise Williams' (2006) newspaper story are likely to be more techno-savvy than the average 38-year-old adult. Mobile phones are no longer just phones—they are GPS tracking devices, video and still cameras, wireless Internet connections, pocket calculators, and much more. In Canada, mobile phones are fitted with a GPS (global positioning system) and every day there's a new "app" to add (Apple's current count is over 200,000). Does this make you feel that technology is moving too fast? Did you just get used to the iPhone and then discover you really should have an iPod, an iPad, or a BlackBerry?

Perhaps it's a generational thing, but anyone over 40 could be forgiven for just sticking with their old telephone, or their "classic" vinyl record collections and vintage turntables.

Unfortunately, it's not possible to bury your head in the sand, and it's not easy being the classroom or office technophobe (Snow, 2005). The future is never far away, however, and it does seem that digital technology is developing and changing at a rapid rate. But where is it going? Despite her self-confessed technophobia (fear of technology), journalist Deborah Snow (2005) expressed the common angst and apparent contradictions invested in the constantly changing digital technologies:

> Yes, of course, the communications revolution . . . has brought benefits . . . but that's not to say we shouldn't, as individuals and as a society, take time to try to digest, then adapt to each wave of technological change before the next one breaks upon us. Trouble is, the pace of change has become so furious that catching breath between the waves is becoming nearly impossible. (paras. 11, 16)

But is this all we are able to do? Just catch up? A central argument of this book is that there are several possible futures associated with digital technologies. The process of technological convergence—the melding of one technology with another—produces a range of new hybrid technologies that can be developed to help make our lives collectively better or, as Huxley and Orwell warned, lead to a nightmarish future with increased, and more effective, social manipulation and control.

In 1960, British writer and essayist Kingsley Amis captured the utopia/dystopia dialectic well in his collection of essays on trends in science fiction, *New Maps of Hell*. It was written when the promises of a bright technology-driven future was real, though overshadowed by the Cold War. Amis (1960) suggested that modernist science fiction often portrayed human society "groaning in chains of its own construction" (p. 66), trapped by its own technology, much like being trapped in the "iron cage" of an inflexible culture that German sociologist Max Weber (1904/1992, as cited in Stanford Encyclopedia of Philosophy, 2012) envisioned:

> No one knows who will live in this cage (Gehäuse) in the future, or whether at the end of this tremendous development entirely new prophets will arise, or there will be a great rebirth of old ideas and ideals, or, if neither, mechanized petrification, embellished with a sort of convulsive self-importance. For the "last man" (letzten Menschen) of this cultural development, it might well be truly said: "Specialist without spirit, sensualist without heart; this nullity imagines that it has attained a level of humanity (Menschentums) never before achieved" [Weber 1904–05/1992, 182: translation altered]. (Section 4.1)

On the other hand, the optimists believe that the future of technological abundance will supply all the information and techno-toys we'll ever need, and perhaps some we don't. For example, haven't you always wanted a portable, digital "ghost radar"?! We kid you not, the first such device, which can purportedly tell you if a ghost is evil or not, went on sale in Japan in April 2005 ("Ghosts in the Machine," 2005). In the promises of another techno-positivist vein, some scientists are predicting that future technologies will even make it possible to radically re-engineer human DNA to "blend ourselves with machines in unprecedented ways . . . ranging from homogenised humans to alien-looking hybrids bred for interstellar travel" (Boyle, 2005). It's enough to boggle your mind!

Regardless of the extent of such predictions, however, the technologically positivist future relies on the argument that technology somehow equals "progress" and that once we've ironed out a few difficulties—like inequality of access—the world can look forward to eliminating the social ills of poverty, war, and pestilence. The view is pervasive (and thus reinforced) in movies and news media, and even current government policy statements; whether in Australia (Hirst & Harrison, 2007, p. 8), the European Union, or the United States, they all rest our collective futures on the promise of technology as "the fixer."

The Canadian government's (2007) strategic plan for the "information economy," for example, is clearly in the utopian camp when emphasizing *technology is progress*, with the significant addition that technological development is tied directly to private businesses as the benevolent patron. It advances this technological positivist and commercial model as *the* source of the solution: "The private sector in Canada needs to do more of what it alone can do, which is to turn knowledge into the products, services, and production technologies that will improve our wealth, wellness, and well-being" (Industry Canada, 2007, p. 3). In accordance with this view, unemployment will be a thing of the past, and prosperity and democracy will flourish, not only in Canada but everywhere. In this future, the convergence that produces digital communications technologies is seen as a process that can expand democracy universally and shrink the world to what Marshall McLuhan called the "global village."

The alternative future is less ideal. In this future the increasing role that digital technologies play in our everyday lives does not lead to abundance and world peace. Instead it moves us inexorably towards a totalitarian world state, similar to that envisioned by Huxley and Orwell, in which the divisions between the wealthy and the poor are as wide as ever, and technology enslaves us to the machine. In this future, digital technologies move from being a communication-oriented priority to a surveillance-oriented mandatory. While we may be content to do everything "online," everything so done can be measured, monitored, remotely stored, and manipulated or controlled. While governments emphasize the "benefits" of technology as necessarily market-led, this leaves out a more immediate and important question: At what cost? With such reliance on the private and commercially controlled system, much like the ever-present telescreen in Orwell's *Nineteen Eighty-Four* (1988), will there ever be a "way of shutting it off completely" (p. 5)?

Our primary directive—to quote another classic popular science-fiction idea—is to show that, given the present state of converging technologies, particularly in the realm of ubiquitous communication, either future is possible. Technologies do not exist in a vacuum; they are imagined, invented, and implemented in an imperfect world of inequality and social divisions, and are thus inseparable from the human beings who develop and use them.

A secondary goal of this book is to argue that the type of future we leave for generations of people after us will not be determined by the technology itself, but rather by the legacy of the social and environmental conditions in which these technologies are developed and exploited. Technology—as a series of intersecting scientific methods, discoveries, and practices, often embodied in "things"—has no inherent social values. In fact the reverse is true: The values of the dominant societies on earth today will shape the ways in which communication technologies and practices of the present and the future are invented, distributed, consumed, and controlled. We are as much interested in this social process of convergence as we are in the converging technologies themselves. The values we express through our relations with other humans and with nature will go a long way in determining the uses for which current and future digital technologies are employed.

The first clue about how we might imagine the digital future is in the subtitle of our book, *From Broadcast to Narrowcast*, which illustrates in a single phrase our central concern. In a nutshell, what we mean by this is that the age of mass broadcasting (we include print publishing in this) is perhaps coming to an end, or at least being significantly altered. Instead we are looking at a future of communication that involves highly targeted narrowcasting—the aggregated audience is split into its atomized particle—the individual *as data*.

The first widely available technology that you have used in beginning this seismic shift is the Internet. The mobile phone and the radio-frequency identification device (RFID) are the latest continuities, and perhaps there are even more important technologies that can be embedded in our bodies to cement the narrowcasting future. Our understanding of how digital technologies are being used to "change our world" will be primarily developed using the theories and tools of political economy—by way of one explanation—with some inclusion of a variety of theoretical and descriptive approaches that engage with technological change.

We take a relatively eclectic approach for two reasons. First, the historical scope of this book demands that we trace the connections—both forward and backward from today—between the new digital technologies and the technologies of the analogue age. Second, it is important to understand the broader social and cultural context in which these technologies exist. Its configurations and uses are influenced by both the political and the economic and by the social and technical milieu in which they are brought into being, commercialized, and ultimately used as tools in our everyday lives.

The second important concern we want to discuss at length is the issue of technological convergence. We're not claiming that this is something brand new that no one's noticed before. Far from it. There are plenty of media sources and academic texts devoted to a discussion of digital convergence; indeed we've drawn on some of them for the ideas in this book. Where we differ from many other authors is that we want to emphasize the social relations of convergence, rather than focus primarily on the technology itself, and the gadgets, doodads, and digital devices that are becoming common. Of course no book about convergence and media could ignore the cell phone or the digital camera or online and social media that are being used to change the ways we socialize and how we receive broadcast news and current affairs, but this book doesn't prioritize the technology; that is, it doesn't see technological changes as *determining* social ones.

Another point of distinction is our use of the dialectical method and a philosophical outlook—a worldview—that asks us to examine the interconnected and contradictory elements of technology as they exist in a social and historical context. As we explain in Chapter 1, the dialectic is found in nature, but it is also a driver of social change. It is a clash of ideas, but also a clash of social forces (Hirst & Patching, 2005). More fundamentally it is the clash of social forces with the forces of nature. As British materialist philosopher Alex Callinicos (1995) puts it, the supposed need to control nature through the implements created by technology "is a constant in the history of the human species" (p. 158). As he argues, all human societies, from the primitive cave dwellers of the Stone Age to the sophisticated urbanites of the twenty-first century sprawl, have harnessed nature in order to produce the means of their own social reproduction. Thus our approach focuses not only on technologies of communication but also on how they are constituted in social reproduction. It draws on our backgrounds and our experiences as media practitioners and educators with a wide-ranging interdisciplinary knowledge of history, sociology, political economy, philosophy, theology, communication theory, and media technologies. This interdisciplinarity guides the theme—*From Broadcast to Narrowcast*—which itself provides an explicit sense-making spine to this book.

Structure of This Book

This book is divided into four parts, divisions that logically follow our thematic approach under the banner "from broadcast to narrowcast" with a focus on Canada. We have situated our arguments within a historical and sociological continuum that allows us to track, discuss, and explain how the "new" media both extend and eclipse the "old" media, creating a new set of questions and theoretical problems for students of media and communication. Our approach is to embed discussion of the issues in coverage of communication industries and practices as they have been historically developed in Canada within the context of different kinds of media. In this context we examine journalism, public relations, and advertising as modes of communication practices and the print media, radio, television, and the Internet as independent but related means of communication.

This is not a book about audience studies, which is a distinct field within the discipline of communication and media studies. But it is impossible not to include audiences, since this is the focus of so much effort on behalf of all media organizations. Our view is that audiences are constructed members of the public, and can be thought of as a combination of two distinct but integrated aspects: consumers and citizens. One of the central arguments that we make in these pages is that the transition from broadcasting to narrowcasting is also a transition in the public, with the emphasis placed on audiences, consumers, and workers as data generators. This shift in perception and marketing is clearly evident in government policy statements that prioritize "market-led" decision-making, but is also about further dissecting the commercial opportunities for exploiting the audience (as user, producer, and worker), both as an aggregated construction and as individuals. Narrowcasting is all about categorizing and exploiting a group of people, or just "*you*," as the desired niche market and data source.

This last point is one reason why we begin this text with an explanation of political economy, technology, and media cultures in fairly simple theoretical terms. We are keenly concerned with the social aspects of the convergence of digital technologies, and this means a particular historical and holistic focus on the relationship between what has tended to be considered separate categories. This means grasping the relation between the economic and political, social and cultural, in terms of the structures and processes that govern the ways in which technologies are inserted into the fabric of our everyday lives. After considering the history of technological change in this socio-cultural context, we examine the ways in which governments attempt to regulate and control technological development and their end-users (individuals, organizations, corporations) through the application of legal sanctions and frameworks for mediation and regulation.

Part I   Dialectics in Communication

Part I establishes the outlook and the framework for this book, and is the place for our more theoretical discussions. Its purpose is to outline the history of attempts to understand media and communications technologies and to present a brief overview of common theoretical approaches to the study of media and communication. The foundation dedicates several chapters that discuss the ideas of political economy in relation to media and communication studies. In Part I we define and explain the role of the dialectic as both a social force and a set of relationships that influence the final shape, scope, and purpose of technologies. We argue that the impact of digital convergence can best be understood as a "disruptive process of change" (DCITA, 2004, p. 7) that affects many aspects of our daily existence.

It is important to recognize that this is not a textbook to be read in order to only find out what material might be on the exam. As we emphasized previously, how we participate, react, and intervene in the transformations of digital technologies will shape the world for the next 100 years. Since you have already been around for at least some of it, however, in this first part we begin to explore some new ideas that should help you to make sense of convergence and the changing nature of digital communication technologies. We also take the opportunity to introduce a discussion of ideology and the role of the commercial media in disseminating, reinvigorating, and renewing some of the ideas and social values that we take as common-sense and every-day as a way of understanding and critiquing them.

Part II   Hot Metal to Hotmail: A (Recent) History of Media and Communication

In Part II we discuss the concrete and historically developed communication technologies of print, radio, and television over the past 200 years. Of course, these have been developed as core industrial forms of communication that are constantly evolving, and so our approach is to understand the development of communication media from broadcasting to narrowcasting as part of a particular historical progression. We trace the development of modern industrial forms of media as deriving from more craft-driven and partisan nineteenth-century print media, through mass distribution of cheap newsprint, to radio and television broadcasting in order to establish the historical continuity between these forms and some of the new media forms of narrowcasting.

In this part, we also introduce the history of the computer in terms of its development and application, beginning the shift into digital media technologies used today. The focus on history in this section is not to separate it from the current media (radio and television are still important), or to suggest that history is only a matter of description according to technological inventions, but to appreciate that history is the fundamental context for the way technology has been used and developed. The technology we use today is a result of human decision-making that the current media is situated in and continues to be constituted by.

Part III   Re-Emergence of Convergence: New Century, New Media?

In Part III we develop, in a systematic way, the argument that digital media technologies are part of a historical process of convergence that began with the level and the wheel. In the way it presents itself today, digital convergence is the product of the economic, social, administrative, ethical, and political pressures exerted by the market economy and its inbuilt, relentless drive for profits. This section thus explicitly links the communication industries of the twentieth century with the new media practices of the twenty-first. It begins by focussing on the myths surrounding the Internet and the ways that these myths have shaped how we understand technological change today. It connects these to government regulation and decisions that impact how we use technology and how it is developed for the future.

Our approach is to place the right emphasis on issues of media regulation, governance, and ethics within the context of issues and industries. It is also our intention to highlight the ethical and legal dilemmas that the new communications technologies create for industry self-regulators, government regulators such as the Canadian Radio-television and Telecommunications Commission (CRTC), people who work in the media industry, and the public. These dilemmas apply particularly to the digital and online worlds in relation to such issues as intellectual property rights, regulation in the global marketplace, and questions of cross-border jurisdiction in relation to matters such as copyright. As these issues also affect the content and work of journalists, we also identify a wide range of changes to media and journalism that involve questions of ethics, labour, and what makes "news" today.

Part IV   From Broadcasting to Narrowcasting: A Surveillance Political Economy

Part IV summarizes and explains many of the trends we identify in the previous chapters under the general heading of "surveillance." Our argument here is a simple one: The commercial media and the infrastructure of communications have fundamentally changed in character in large part because of the capabilities afforded by convergent digital technologies. Communication infrastructure is rapidly becoming surveillance infrastructure that is developed to benefit the already powerful. Electronic record keeping tags every phone call and business transaction we make: The telephone companies (and by extension government agencies) know where we are, our movements are tracked by GPS-enabled phones, and all our financial transactions are electronically monitored. Our every interaction with the media is now logged and measured, amassing vast databases of personal information. In this final part we also discuss the impact of the Internet on political communication (political campaigning, electronic voting, and community media). We also recognize the importance of new and somewhat "alternative" forms of mediated communication, such as "Indymedia" and activism, as well as other modes and means of challenging and changing power relations that are important now and in the future.

It is becoming increasingly apparent that a transition from communication to surveillance is running parallel to the change from broadcasting to narrowcasting. In one sense they are almost the same thing. It is the ability to increase surveillance, particularly in the marketplace, that makes the transition from broadcast to narrowcast media so attractive to advertisers, marketers, media companies, and the telecommunications giants. There is a double helix of effects associated with the shift to a narrowcast media, and this is manifest as one of the key contradictions of the so-called information economy. For example, at the same time as our personal privacy disappears, and all space becomes, in effect, "public," the remaining space for non-commercial public communication is being privatized. This highlights one of our major themes: The notion of an independent and non-commercial political citizenship is being eroded and replaced by a dependent and inseparable consumer-citizen. As we demonstrate throughout this text, what we need to consider is how, in media-prioritized environments, the consumer-citizen is enclosed in a shrinking public space that is prioritized by capitalism and the narrowcast communications industry. In the process, we ask if citizenship is being consumed by the voracious appetite of the market and, if so, is the citizen being replaced by an atomized, de-politicized (or re-politicized) cipher? If, in the so-called digital age, the credit card has replaced the ballot as the passport to "freedom," what value is left of freedom?

PART I
Dialectics in Communication

Objectives

After reading this section, you should understand the dialectical relationship between technology, media, and capitalism and, in particular, be able to identify the following:

- why capitalism is a necessary starting point for understanding this relationship;

- what a political economy approach to communication entails; and

- why it is important to distinguish between philosophies such as materialism and idealism.

Keywords

- **capitalism**
- **commodification**
- **dialectic**
- **hegemony**
- **ideology**
- **materialism**

It's by using the technologies and pathways laid down by promoters of control that cyberians believe they must conduct their revolution. (Rushkoff, 1994, p. 285)

The real question is, do we direct technology, or do we let ourselves be directed by it and those who have mastered it? "Choose the former," writes Rushkoff, "and you gain access to the control panel of civilization. Choose the latter, and it could be the last real choice you get to make." (Rushkoff, n.d., para. 1)

American Douglas Rushkoff was one of the first journalists to explore the implications of cyberspace, back when it was still a largely experimental and somewhat mythical entity, before the days of Google and Facebook. He interviewed many of the pioneers of the Internet and those first intrepid souls who believed it would bring about a utopian revolution, challenging the entrenched power of the commercial media (among many other possibilities), and giving ordinary people access to liberating technology. It was a very popular scenario.

Rushkoff benefitted from positive proclamations of technology as something new and exciting. He ran a consulting business that provided "Gen-X" advice to "baby-boomers," and initially wrote books that attracted cyber-enthusiasts, and provided the required reference for making rosy predictions about the future. While his first books (*Cyberia*, *Media Virus*, and *Playing the Future*) foreground the "happy creators" and optimistic users of technology, his later publications suggest a more pessimistic future, one of "psychological manipulation" (*Coercion*) and technological control (*Program or Be Programmed*: www.rushkoff.com/program-or-be-programmed/; Mosco, 2004a). Having earned his Ph.D, now Dr. Rushkoff's answer to changing structures of power was in the programming: "Learn to code." It seems a straightforward solution. Yet several outstanding issues remain.

Rushkoff has certainly benefitted from the so-called digital revolution, but what about the rest of us? What if you have no possibility to learn to code (or even want to)? What about the close to five *billion* people in the world who are not "Internet users" (ITU, 2012, p. 7), and don't have the necessary resources (like time, education, money, a computer, or Internet access) in order to do so? Is "to code or not to code" really a choice? Do we simply adapt or surrender to technophobia? Are there really no other alternatives?

With the benefit of hindsight, positive dreams and easy solutions—while real enough for the pioneers of cyberia—are ultimately more mythical than actual. Early predictions of "free and open" cyberspace changed when it was quickly overtaken by corporate giants keen to regain their profitable media monopolies and to harness the new technology to an ever-expanding market for goods and services, both real and virtual. This first part of *Communication and New Media* begins to lay out the theoretical and analytical tools necessary to understand what upset the digital dreams of the early believers.

Throughout this book, the issues that arise in relation to aspects of communication and media are constructed in a definite set of social relationships that exist in a state of creative tension—what we call *a dialectic of historical change*. These ever-shifting relationships are primarily related to the ways in which communication industries and practices are structured materially and socially. Thus, these industries and practices are situated in the broader political and economic, as well as ideological, structures of society, alongside the institutions of government and civil society. This is why we have decided on a political economy approach for this text, and why we have chosen to start with an explanation of the purpose, methods, and theories of what we mean by political economy. In taking this approach, we are standing on the shoulders of many learned scholars and acknowledge the important contributions of at least four generations working in the political economy of communication tradition (see Mosco, 2009, pp. 82–103 for an overview).

We do not intend to play down the importance of factors other than the political economic, however. On the contrary, we see economics, politics, culture, and social relations as being entwined, much like the strands of a DNA double helix. Similar to DNA, these combinations are in a forever dynamic and ever-changing matrix of power. Our argument (expanded in later sections) is that the economic organization of society is itself a complex set of social relations that is inseparable from all other relationships between people, and between people and the commodities that are produced. In other words, an economic system is itself a particular way of organizing social relations, and it is these social relations that the term *political economy* is meant to identify—that economic systems are necessarily constituted by, and thus inseparable from, social relations of power.

As well as outlining what we mean by a political economy of communication, in the first two chapters we employ the concept of the "dialectic," which, simply put, is the process of change that marks out history by bringing together, in a state of tension, a range of social forces that interact and clash. Of course we also have to deal with some definitional specifics, particularly what we understand by the term *technology*. It is common sense to think of technology as objects, machines, and things, but what about the process through which they come into being? We answer this question early in Chapter 3 by suggesting that technology is not just about machines and commodities. Instead, we suggest, it is a process of linking useful knowledge and science to the ways in which society organizes its productive (and destructive) relationship with nature and the material world. In other words, we incorporate our discussion of communications technology into political economy because it is impossible to remove technology from the mode of production.

Our theoretical discussion is somewhat encapsulated in the first section of this book. It provides us with some working definitions of technology and incorporates them into the political economy approach to communication studies. In it we focus on the dialectic of convergence and show how periodic crises and attempts to overcome them have shaped global capitalism in the late twentieth and early twenty-first centuries. We argue that the technologies of communication, and indeed, the social relations of mass media and communication, are not immune from this process. In a sense, the current fixation on creative industries, the "information" economy and "knowledge" society reflect an intellectual and practical need for capital to come to terms with the economic crises of over-production and profitability, and with the political crisis of failing nation-states.

The final chapter of this section is our attempt to come to terms with the vexed question of determination and determinism in theoretical accounts of the digital revolution. We agree that many approaches tend to privilege the technological over the social, and we argue that this is a mistaken and ultimately determinist view that does not account for the effects of the dialectic and mutual constitution.

This first section also makes explicit our epistemology—our theoretical position, how we know what we know—in debates about communication, media, and technology. We conclude that the current mode of development that is driving capitalism—an even greater rate of digital convergence coupled with tectonic shifts in the relations and forces of production—is leading, almost inexorably, towards a narrowcasting form of communication and media. In the rest of this book we do not expound on the *theories* of political economy, but we do apply an introduction to some of its *methods* to develop and argue for our analysis of both the declining broadcast media and the emerging forms of narrowcasting. This theoretical first part underpins our discussion of the thesis that narrowcasting is an important signifier and crucial component of the developing surveillance political economy. It also makes it clear that we do not regard the surveillance economy discussed in the last part of this book as something distinct from capitalism; it is merely a new form of exploitation and hegemony.

1 Digital Dilemmas: Contradictions and Conflicts in Communication

Objectives

After reading this chapter you will have a solid grasp of the important concept of the dialectic, both as a method of reasoning and as an organizing principle that helps to explain how technology and social relations are transformed over time by the process of integration and contradiction. In particular, you should focus on the following ideas:

- how the dialectic works as an organizing principle and as a process of transformation that drives the development of human society and the transitions from one type of social organization to another;

- how to "think" dialectically in order to understand the processes of historical development in relation to new media technologies; and

- the ways in which the dialectic informs the theories and practices of political economy, and how the dialectic that binds information and communication can be explored to make sense of the digital revolution.

DIALECTIC

The idea that history is shaped by opposing forces. The *predominant* force, idea, movement, or paradigm (the *thesis*) is challenged by an *opposing* force, idea, movement, or paradigm (the *antithesis*), which results in a third *new* force, idea, movement, or paradigm (the *synthesis*). The synthesis, in turn, becomes the new predominant force, idea, movement, or paradigm (the *new thesis*), and the process begins all over again. The dialectic is the process of creation, and the resolution of contradictions.

Keywords

- **dialectic**
- **idealism**
- **ideology**
- **materialism**
- **meme**
- **technological determinism**
- **vector**

What Is the Dialectic?

[C]ommunication and information are two sides of the same process, dialectically linked in mutual constitution. (Mosco, 1996, p. 67)

Avoid being put off by an introduction of a word that you might not have seen before, or possibly don't understand yet. It is really quite simple. The word *dialectic* describes a philosophical concept that means thinking systematically using a process of logic. From both Latin and Greek roots, *dialectic* describes the methods of discussion and debate and, in a similar way, "the method of determining the interrelation of ideas in the light of a single principle" (R. Williams, 1989, p. 106). German philosopher Georg Hegel (1770–1831) first used the term in its modern sense to describe the process of resolving a contradiction between competing ideas—for example, explaining the relationship between God and man, which is what Hegel was trying to do. In *Communication and New Media* we do not aspire to such lofty ambitions but, nevertheless, can still utilize the dialectic to investigate the movement of history in terms of media technologies—such as the transition from analogue to digital media production. As we explain in this introductory chapter, the dialectic is the organizing principle on which the forward momentum of historical change is based. It is the pervasive but often unseen logic of "two steps forward, one step back" that marks the passage of time and the transition from one form of social organization to another. As a fundamental goal of education and knowledge development is understanding and explaining social and historical change, it is of primary importance for you to understand this organizing principle, and we shall thus take some time to explain it more completely.

The Hegelian dialectic has three elements: the proposition (thesis), an opposite or competing proposition (antithesis), and the logical resolution of the tension between them (synthesis). Hegel used a simple example to explain his theory of the dialectic: An acorn contains the potential to become a strong oak tree and produce more acorns, but in order to do so, the acorn must disappear or *negate* itself. By a series of small incremental changes in quantity induced by the interaction of the living acorn with the soil in which it falls, the acorn becomes something qualitatively different: an oak tree. Water, ice, and steam provide another clear example: When the temperature of water is gradually reduced it remains in a liquid state until zero degrees centigrade when it is transformed into a solid: ice. This new substance has many properties that water doesn't have. When water changes from a liquid to a solid it behaves differently. At the other extreme, heat water to boiling point and it becomes steam, able to resist gravity in a way that liquid water cannot (cited in Callinicos, 1987, p. 59). Water contains the potential to be ice or steam, but in order to become either it must contradict (negate) its fluid state.

While Hegel resolved his contradictions through a belief in the unity of an Absolute Spirit (God), Karl Marx (1818–1883) and Friedrick Engels (1820–1895) recognized that the method of dialectical reasoning also had an application to the study of human history:

> *All fixed, fast-frozen relations, with their train of ancient and venerable prejudices and opinions are swept away, all new-formed ones become antiquated before they can ossify. All that is solid melts into air, all that is holy is profaned, and man is at last compelled to face with sober senses, his real conditions of life, and his relations with his kind. (Marx & Engels, 1872/1973, p. 46)*

Translated into more mundane language than that used by Marx and Engels, this means that the configuration of any social system is historically determined by the relationship between human beings and nature. As we review in Chapter 3, throughout human history this relationship has been mediated by technology, and in all societies this relationship is expressed through the organization of production, which "contains within it the contradictions that give it the potential for change" (Callinicos, 1987, p. 75). Thus we can think of the dialectic as a process that proceeds along a series of "fault lines" (Hirst & Patching, 2005, pp. 2–5). These fault lines occur between things and events in nature, between the natural world and human society, and within and between the social formations created by humans—what we collectively call civilization. The methods of political economy (discussed in Chapter 2) work from the principle of the dialectic and dialectical thinking, which recognizes that the real world is made up of both

Case Study

Technologies of Freedom or Control? The Cell Phone Dialectic

Everybody in Canada has a cell phone—well, almost everybody. Just a few years ago, Statistics Canada identified that more than three-quarters of Canadians had cell phones 🖥 (www.statcan.gc.ca/daily-quotidien/110405/dq110405a-eng.htm), and today, that number is assuredly higher even though we pay more for access than people in many other countries (Nowak, 2009). Cell phones and mobile wireless technology facilitate instantaneous communication that can be unfettered by enduring structures of control, whether political or economic. It is now perhaps familiar to hear of the credit given to cell phones as eyewitnesses to abuses of power such as police brutality and political repression around the world, as evident by the public protests and political upheavals in the Middle East. This suggests that mobile technology supersedes the autocratic and repressive regimes of control as relegated to the past; everyone can now be a journalist and broadcast to the world. The apparent ubiquity of mobile phones suggests that this technology is now part of the everyday, and that everyone is connected, all the time, everywhere. Such technological capacity promises very big rewards. Positive reasoning suggests that increased technological capacity will result in increased, and thus better, communication. Better communication means better social relations—that this communication will naturally result in social equality and peace. At stake is human emancipation itself, freedom from control and freedom to self-actualize.

An appreciation of the dialectic suggests, however, that freedom is not without its counter, its social constraints and existing structures of power that don't simply disappear with the use of technology, such that these technologies of freedom can also be technologies of control. While research indicates that young people (aged 25 and under) are the largest adapters of mobile technology 🖥 (www.nielsen.com/us/en/reports/2010/mobile-youth-around-the-world.html), the ability to broadcast is countered with the effects of narrowcasting. Various social contexts reveal indications that young people restrict their cell phone use as constrained by existing social relations resulting in narrow interpersonal communication networks restricted to friends and family, as controlled through the "wireless leash" (Qui, 2007, p. 74) or self-controlled by what Japanese communications researcher Ichiyo Habuchi (2005) calls "tele-cocooning" (pp. 178–9).

On a macro-level, this ability to broadcast may also be constrained by larger networks of power through state or corporate regulation and surveillance. Again, we may have heard about constraints to communication placed by autocratic regimes and state controls, particularly in countries such

"parts and a whole," organized in a "concrete totality" that contains both "integration and contradiction" (Mosco, 1996, p. 33).

Alex Callinicos (1995) describes the operation of the dialectic in human society as a process of historical change over time, "a spiral movement" (p. 152) in which each advance contains within itself an element of regression. The dialectic is a way of understanding the relationship between things through the ways they are connected and the ways that they also simultaneously contradict each other.

as China, which can shut down, redirect, or subvert messages that are sent, which reminds us that the *infrastructure* of communication is as critical (if not more) than its uses and content (Qui, 2007). While we don't think that this is something that can occur in Canada, history suggests that when faced with what the state perceives as a threat, it will act accordingly to restrict communication (overview in Mazepa, 2011). Ownership is also central here as cell phone companies can control access and monitor traffic, identify and track keywords, and cooperate with each other and the government, such that privacy is sacrificed via threat-constructions of "terrorism" or "cybercrime."

This latter possibility of control of communication and infrastructure is causing somewhat of a dilemma for the current federal government in Canada. While, on one hand, it wants to promote free trade and reduce limits on foreign ownership in Canada, whatever the resource (including communication resources), on the other, its economic policies are running headlong into its political policies. This is because Chinese technology firms are interested in buying and supplying telecommunication networks in Canada, which may not be in the best interests of Canadians. As the head of the United States Intelligence Committee, Mike Rogers (as cited in G. Weston, 2012) suggests, Chinese ownership means that decisions about communication will depend on Chinese political and economic priorities; moreover, all communication transmitted on those networks, and all the information contained about the users therein, will also be owned by the Chinese government. Rogers advises that Canada should not allow foreign ownership of telecommunication as "a matter of national security" (ibid., para. 1) and should ban ownership by Chinese corporations like the United States and Australia have done.

Discussion Questions

1. Are cell phones technologies of freedom or control? What are the dilemmas and dialectics at work here?

2. What corporation owns your cell phone connection? What else does it own (newspapers, radio, television, Internet access)? What does this political economy suggest about how you understand communication and freedom?

3. What degrees of control are exercised by ownership? Does it matter if the owners are Canadian or Chinese? State or corporate?

The Dialectic of Nature

> [T]he oak developed out of the acorn. It was, once, that acorn. Acorn and oak mark the beginning and end of the same process. (Callinicos, 1987, p. 60)

As this example shows, the concept of the dialectic expresses itself as a process of contradiction and resolution that is originally found in nature. Charles Darwin's theory of natural selection, the development of complex organisms from simple cell structures, and the transformation of energy—from a lump of coal to radiant heat, for example—are all manifestations of the dialectic in nature, "this incessant process of transformation from one form into another" (Engels, 1888/1976, p. 43).

At the basic molecular level of living organisms, the dialectic is expressed through the double helix of DNA, which is held together in a state of tension and contradiction. The relationship of individual genes and strands to each other is a dialectical process of interaction, mutation, and conflict. The very "laws of nature" are themselves interactive in this way. At a social level, the condition of human existence is one of a dialectical relationship with nature. Nature can sustain us; nature can also harm us. In our efforts to maximize the benefits we extract from nature, we are also capable of doing extreme damage to the natural world. There is evidence of this all around us today: From oil spills on massive sections of the planet's earth and water, to worldwide epidemics of asbestos-related deaths and cancers, to the increasing potential for "bird-flu" pandemics and threats from permanent disaster zones around the ruins of the Chernobyl or other nuclear reactors, our existence is fragile. It is important then to examine the dialectic in its social manifestation. Identifying the dialectic in communication—our social relations with nature and each other—is a necessary precursor to our discussion of communication and media, and the dialectic that has created a historical shift from broadcasting to narrowcasting.

Living and Working in a "Material" World

Everything which sets men in motion must go through their minds; but what form it takes in their minds depends very much on the circumstances. (Engels, 1888/1976, p. 48)

Hegel conceptualized the dialectic at the level of ideas; it was Marx and Engels who transformed it into a theory of human development and an explanation of historical change. Marx and Engels historic **materialism** thus challenged Hegel's way of thinking because it was grounded in a philosophy of materialism while Hegel's was the basis of **idealism**. Yet Hegel's idealist philosophy became a philosophy for the "new" real world; thus you should know that, philosophically, idealism is more than a popular understanding of an idealist as someone who is unrealistic (▣ www.soc.iastate.edu/sapp/soc401philosophy.html), because what it does is seek to answer how we know what is reality.

Before proceeding it is important to clear up some confusion that surrounds the concept of materialism. You've likely heard of someone described in a negative way as materialistic; that is, the person seems to be concerned with the pursuit of material wealth primarily for the sake of acquiring more of something than another person has acquired. Materialistic people are often thought of as greedy and selfish. Indeed some people probably are greedy, selfish, and "materialistic," but our concern here is with another definition of materialism that has to do with our senses. What we can see, touch, hear, smell, and taste are real things; they are material in that they are composed of matter. Material things have a concrete existence in the world. Even odours, which we smell but often can't see, are vapours and gases made up of molecules. They have substance; they can be weighed, measured, and contained. In this sense materialism is, like the dialectic, a concept of philosophy and theory, which seeks explanations of phenomena by reference to the solid, physical, and mechanical aspects of nature and life. Such explanations of the world have been around as long as philosophy itself, but became important in Western traditions in the seventeenth century as an alternative to the idealistic and metaphysical idea that human existence was created at the whim of a supreme being (R. Williams, 1989, pp. 198–9).

MATERIALISM

A philosophical mode of thought that suggests that events, situations, and relationships in the physical world determine, to the largest degree, human consciousness and thinking. Historical materialism, the method of Marx and Engels, posits the theory that human beings' interaction with nature creates the material conditions for the development of social structures and argues that the social force that drives historical change is the struggle between social classes for control of the material world and, in particular, control over the means of production.

IDEALISM

The opposite of materialism. Idealism is the worldview in which all manifestations of reality actually stem from the thought-process of human beings, rather than from their material circumstances. Thus, reality is only a construction of the mind; it has no independence from it. In this view, the social construction of language or discourse is crucial since it is seen to determine reality.

In the hands of Marx and Engels, materialism also gained a historical character that argued for the determining role of human agency in the development of social formations. Historical materialism refers to the study of human societies that positions our interaction with nature—everything from stone tools to complex manufacturing—as the force that drives invention and adaptation. This is the sense in which the concept of the dialectic relates to another central concern of this book—technology: "Technology reveals the active relation of man to nature, the direct process of the production of his[/her] life, and thereby it also lays bare the process of the production of the social relations of his[/her] life, and of the mental conceptions that flow from those relations" (Karl Marx, 1867/1990, p. 493ff.).

For Karl Marx, the beginning of human history and our understanding of it is the collective and social organization of production, which is reflected in the development of technology and in its application to the production process (Callinicos, 1987, p. 85). First and foremost, from the viewpoint of historical materialism, the production process is a social endeavour and can only be properly understood when we ask the question, "Who controls the production process?" It is the constitution and distribution of power within the production process that ultimately determines questions of ownership, access, and wealth (p. 87). This is an important foundation for the rest of this book because when we begin to analyze the political economy of the media, the question of ownership and control of the means of communication becomes a central issue.

In the modern capitalist economy the separation of ownership and control from those who are the direct producers and consumers—not just of the media but of all forms of production—is the key to all other social relations. What Marx realized was that exploitation and inequality in the distribution of resources and wealth were not inevitable and certainly not immutable. He knew, through his observations and study of history, that the dialectic in human society takes the form of a constant struggle between the exploiters and the exploited and that under certain conditions such struggle could lead to the violent overthrow of one system and the creation of a new one in its place. He expressed this idea many times, perhaps nowhere more clearly than in these lines from the *Communist Manifesto*:

> *The history of all hitherto existing society is the history of class struggles. . . . [I]n a word, oppressor and oppressed, stood in constant opposition to one another, carried on an uninterrupted, now hidden, now open fight, a fight that each time ended, either in revolutionary re-constitution of society at large, or in the common ruin of the contending classes. (Marx & Engels, 1872/1973, pp. 40–1)*

You're probably thinking that this kind of incendiary talk is a long way from the topic of this book. But it's not that far removed at all. We now live in a world where the capitalist economy has extended its reach to every corner and crevice of the globe. It touches and shapes the lives of every being on the planet in one way or another through the "rapid improvement of all instruments of production" and the "immensely facilitated means of communication" (p. 47). Further, we cannot ignore all the talk of "revolution" that accompanies discussion of technology today. There are numerous instances of politicians, pundits, academics, and journalists embracing the term *revolution* when it refers to digital convergence, information, knowledge, or other concepts. Each of these implies some form of social disruption and period of uncertainty, change, and instability in the economy, politics, and cultural life. Thus our interest in talking about social revolution is justified, particularly a revolution that has profound impacts on communications and media, because this is where our concern lies.

In this view it is through the means of communication at its disposal that the current ruling class—what Marx called the bourgeoisie—is able to maintain its political, economic, social, and cultural dominance—that is, to promote a technological revolution while holding back a political, economic, and social revolution. This dominance is maintained through the process of controlling the production process itself, but also through influencing the broader ideological ways of thinking that direct other kinds of decision making on local or global levels. Control of the means of communication (as a subset of the means of production) is also vital to the hegemony (discussed in Chapter 2) exercised by a relatively small number of people— whether identified as the ruling class—or what the current Occupy movements call "the one per cent." We can briefly characterize the ideological and political control exercised by the bourgeoisie as an attempt to control the dialectic of communication—the clash that Vincent Mosco recognized between information and communication.

Memes: The Dialectic of Information and Communication

A **meme** is a thought or idea that spreads throughout society in an almost unconscious way. It is a small, transmittable lump of ideology—ideas that help us make sense of the world—that carries a particular set of social attitudes and directions about how we might think about an object, event, or social custom. A meme might be a catchy tune that becomes almost universal, or a trend in fashion that catches on to become widespread, almost before it's even recognized as a trend. Biologist and geneticist Richard Dawkins is credited with the first modern use of the word *meme* in his 1976 book *The Selfish Gene* (as cited in Dawkins, 1989): "Just as genes propagate themselves in the gene pool by leaping from body to body via sperms or eggs, so memes propagate themselves in the meme pool by leaping from brain to brain via a process which, in the broad sense, can be called imitation" (p. 192).

However, Dawkins' caution about biological determinism must be restated here; we cannot simply transfer an idea from biology to the study of human society. Our social systems are much more complex than termite colonies, and our ability to remember and imitate the behaviour of others goes beyond simple genetic replication. Having said that, we find that the concept of the meme, when used cautiously, does help to explain how certain aspects of **ideology** appear to be naturalized as common sense and transmitted or mutated over space and time. We can see memes in the realm of fashion, advertising, and celebrity marketing that are transmitted globally via the Internet and vast networks of interconnected entertainment and leisure industries. Memes are also apparent in the transient popularity of musical styles and the use of slang by subculture groups that takes on a worldwide acceptance one week, only to be replaced by new words in vogue the next 🖳 (mashable.com/2012/08/17/best-memes-2012-so-far/). As you shall see in the next chapter, memes also have a socio-economic function: They move cultural patterns through time and space and also make them vulnerable to commodification, appropriation, and distribution through relationships of power.

Dawkins ascribed to memes patterns of replication similar to those found in genes. Thus we can talk of a meme pool as being analogous to the gene pool found in nature. Memes are the medium of cultural transmission, often at a much faster rate than that of genetic mutation and evolution in nature (Dawkins, 1989, p. 189). But we can go a little further than this and argue that the commercial media now play a key role in the process of mimetic reproduction and mutation. Thus a riff in a pop song may become a meme much quicker today because of

MEME

An application of the reasoning of biology to language and ideas, as coined by geneticist Richard Dawkins in 1976 (Dawkins, 1989). Analogous to biological genes (and pronounced the same way), a meme is an idea (or way of thinking, or piece of information) that is communicated and passed from person-to-person like a virus. It can be socially and historically specific and finite, or it can be reinforced and propagated over time, making it stronger and more difficult to discredit or destroy.

IDEOLOGY

A set of ideas joined together that legitimate and facilitate power relations.

the high-rotation airplay it receives on radio and television or YouTube. Last year's hit tunes are appropriated as the soundtrack for this year's hip new commercials.

Memes have also been likened to viruses: A virus that infects a computer reproduces by a process of virtual cloning before jumping out onto the Internet to infect other machines. The Internet is important in the discussion of meme transmission for another reason. The speed and the anarchic architecture of the Internet can lead to the rapid circulation of a new meme and can, at times, create a paperless trail that legitimizes information that is functionally unreliable and invalid. This is another sense in which we can relate the meme to the concept of ideology—the sense that ideology represents a "false" consciousness tied to the "social relations of domination" (Wayne, 2003, p. 173). In this sense, ideology naturalizes "social and historical relations" (p. 174) that are the product of the unequal power relationships of class, gender, and race, for example, by making them seem normal and ahistorical. The mass media participate in the circulation of such ideological memes by mobilizing our fears and desires—through political propaganda and advertising, for example—causing us to respond at an emotional level in a way that neutralizes any feelings of disquiet or anger, and is "conducive to the reproduction of exploitative social relations" (ibid.). Historical and complex social relations can also be simplified such that it is easier to direct anger by blaming others for our exploitation (e.g., blame the "immigrants," the "lazy welfare people," or the "greedy unions"; Mazepa, 2012, pp. 245–6). Think of how easy it is to quickly react to questions about how you *feel* about something, rather than what you actually *know* or *think* about it. We can see how the memes that popularize the idea of the "information society" and the "digital revolution," as used by an industry that depends upon it, are also evident in media and government policies as positive developments of benefit to the whole of society. This fits the model of an ideological meme. Mimetic transmission is the **vector** for the propagation of digital myths (Mosco, 2004a).

These ideas can coalesce into a worldview based on principles and institutions that may or may not be logical or internally consistent, but are sufficiently convincing enough to be accepted and circulated. This sentiment was made explicit in a popular book written by American journalist Douglas Rushkoff called *Cyberia*, which is cheekily subtitled *Life in the Trenches of Hyperspace*. In it, Rushkoff describes a small underground magazine for hackers, *Mondo 2000*, which existed briefly in the early 1990s, as a meme (the self-replicating idea); *Mondo 2000* was the "media virus" (Rushkoff, 1994, p. 289) that its adherents hoped would help cyberians spread their message of technological liberation. The magazine was loosely edited from a house in Berkeley, where the *Mondo 2000* collective accepted for publication "whichever memes make the most sense at the time" (p. 291). When not publishing the magazine, the group spent its time "discussing and embodying fringe concepts" (p. 292), and Rushkoff gushingly describes the "Mondoids" as "human memes" who "depend on media recognition for their survival" (p. 293). The mythic meme that *Mondo 2000* seemed to be pushing most intently was a form of digital anarchism, at least according to one of its founders and leading lights, the ironically monikered "R. U. Sirius": "The only thing we're pushing is freedom in this new territory. The only way to have freedom is not to have an agenda. Protest is not a creative act, really" (as cited in Rushkoff, 1994, p. 294).

Although *Mondo 2000* ceased publication in 1998, the story of the *Mondo* "meme factory" is told at the end of *Cyberia*, and it encapsulates the dialectic that generated some of the early myths of the "information revolution"; it captures the energy that motivated the early hackers and amateur Internet enthusiasts, and it also sounds a note of caution about the "event horizon" that in 1992 appeared to be looming over mainstream and still non-digital society. Rushkoff (1994) signs off with the observation that "Cyberia is frightening to everyone. Not just the technophobes, rich businessmen, midwestern farmers and suburban housewives, but most of all, to the boys and girls hoping to ride the crest of the informational wave. Surf's up" (p. 300).

VECTOR

In medical science a vector is the pathway or pathways open to pathogens to infect a population. For example, infected chickens may be a vector for avian bird flu to infect humans. In communication studies a vector is a pathway or pathways open for communication, in particular the transmission of ideology via mimetic transfer and mutation.

The Information Revolution: Digital Dialectic

As [mainstream scientists] rely more and more on the computer, their suspicions are further confirmed: this is not a world reducible to neat equations and pat answers, but an infinitely complex series of interdependencies, where the tiniest change in a remote place can have systemwide repercussions. (Rushkoff, 1994, p. 15)

The surf *is* up, but the dialectic of the digital revolution, which began with the counter-cultural anarchists of cyberia, exerts its own influence once it is unleashed on the world. The information revolution is the ideological and mimetic manifestation of a shift in the relations of production that has been under way within the capitalist mode of production for most of the past 60 years. There was a seismic shift within the mode of development of capitalism as the twenty-first century began, and there is a new technological dialectic at play that, in the process of becoming dominant, is replacing the previously hegemonic industrial–technical relations and forces of production. It has also all but wiped out the meme of techno-liberation that was cultivated by the Mondoids.

The subversive (to the old ways at least) technology meme entered the mode of production and the popular mind through the vector of important discoveries in science such as computing in mathematics, the binary code, and the application of the resulting new technologies for miniaturizing and mass-producing silicon microchips. By the 1970s, computing technologies were deeply embedded in industrial and commercial applications. Investment in the new technologies

Focus on Research

Technology and Human Development

Technological memes have also been attached to understandings of progress—of advancements in civilization—such that those nation-states without the latest technology are considered backward or "underdeveloped," in general. In American-led communication research and history, this is an enduring meme; in the 1970s it was underpinned by what were called the modernization and "diffusion of innovation" theories (Rogers, 1962). These theories were used to explain that development (or modernization) flows from the established capitalist political economy (its technology and media corporations as models), as led by experts from "the West" and spread to the rest of the world. In this view, capitalism is a given, technology is both the solution to development and the means of social advancement. The association of capitalism and technology with progress is a dominant meme today, whether applied to "developed" or "underdeveloped" countries, or designations of "first" and "third" world, or "North" or "South" (of the equator). Indeed, a research division of *The Economist* newspaper called "The Economist Intelligence Unit" publishes what it calls a "Cyber Power Index" identifying countries that are the current "world leaders" in technological and economic development as models to emulate (www.cyberhub.com/cyberpowerindex).

Instead of taking these claims as reliable justification for and valid definitions of development, however, the class-basis for this "progress" was exposed by the critical research of political economists of communication (Schiller, 1969, 1976, 1992; Mattelart & Siegelaub, 1979; Mosco 2009, pp. 97–103) who questioned government decisions and social consequences based on this kind of "development" paradigm. The research identified that what was diffused was not just innovation, went, first of all, back into the machinery of manufacturing and other production—plants and equipment. As we note in Chapter 5, with the development of the Internet, much of this research and development work was funded by governments for military purposes and released to the public domain, and later commercialized. This has led (in the past 10 to 20 years) to the gradual displacement of the anarcho-technical meme espoused by R.U. Sirius and the cyberians. The emerging meme is much more controlled and commercial; it is the meme of the "knowledge *society*," and it is heavily supported by both governments and companies that politically and economically invest in the digital communication technologies to the extent that even the link to society is equated with (or displaced in preference for) the "knowledge *economy*."

Its predecessor, the new "information society" meme, began to circulate during the second wave of digital development, beginning in the late 1970s, with the widespread application of these new technologies to consumer goods. This process is ongoing, and has been boosted by the rapid improvement and convergence in digital technologies. Historically, since the 1950s at least, we can trace it to something like this: the transistor radio (the first wireless instrument of civil communication) on the AM (amplitude modulation) dial followed by high-fidelity records, television, stereo, videotape, radio on the FM (frequency modulation) dial, personal computers, satellite television, laser-read compact discs (CDs) and digital versatile discs (DVDs), digital peripherals, home entertainment centres, wireless applications, and broadband, culminating in the "wired" lifestyle. At each historical stage we can also trace the mimetic messages along the lines of "radio will replace newspapers," "television will replace radio," and "video killed the radio stars." Today's version is

per se, but rather a particular kind of technological development and a specific ordering of a media and social system, each of which reinforced capitalism and concentrated power in corporate ownership of (then) predominantly Western corporations (in the United States in particular). Research indicated that this "diffusion," contrary to its positive intentions (or promotion thereof), did not automatically lead to significant social development and a democratized media system, but could actually create or exacerbate class divisions and social inequality.

Current research in feminist political economy considers the connection between capitalism, technological development and the relationship of class and gender as enduring social divisions that have not been significantly altered by the use and adoption of information and communication technologies (ICTs) in the global south. Explaining that the allocation of resources (like ICT) is subject to social relations of class, gender, and race, as well as demographics such as age and geographical location, for example, Micky Lee (2011a) illustrates that, following our example of the cell phone dialectic, who "adopts" the technology and why is stratified according to existing social conditions, and is supported by enduring ideology:

> For a poor family, usually it is the young men who would own cell phones because they are supposed to be the economically active family members, hence they need the tool for a living. This ideology assumes that the housework (and the work outside the home) that women perform is not as valuable as men's work outside the home. (p. 525)

As we go further into the chapters of this book, we explain this political economic approach in more detail, but for now, it is important to consider that the technological memes of progress may be more ideological than they are valid and reliable indicators of social change, particularly when one asks the question "What has changed exactly?"

more sophisticated; it suggests that all of these various media will converge or coexist with both the Internet and wireless communication for the foreseeable future. This convergence suggests that knowledge is the new "natural" resource, and information is the new industry.

We are now roughly at the 45-year mark in terms of the silicon chip thesis (the driving technology meme) within the mode of development that is now propelling the capitalist mode of production. The speed of mutation in this meme has been phenomenal. We can see this if we compare it to the time frame of the Industrial Revolution beginning in the nineteenth century, which took 100 years to "mature," a century marked by the classic cycle of booms and slumps identified by political economists as the inevitable dialectical nature of capitalism. On a longer timescale, social scientists have retrofitted a technology meme to various points in history: the Bronze Age, the Iron Age, the "steam" age, the epoch of the railway, and, more recently, "Fordism" and "post-Fordism" relating to the predicted but not yet realized end of industrial manufacturing.

In keeping with a political economy approach, it is not only consumption that is important

For Real?

Progress at Whose Expense?

With advertising and marketing of the latest technology, we usually don't think about where the products come from exactly, who makes them, and under what conditions. Apple's campaign and marketing strategy to "think different" encourages us to think of the product: to be so preoccupied with the pleasure sought from owning the latest iPad or other device, that people will line up for days just to get the latest version. Since Apple is a major advertiser, and as encouraged by the hype of viral marketing, commercial media tend to cover the release of new products and the line-ups for them as "news." In the background, however, is a whole process of production that rarely surfaces.

Retaining some critical reflection of the high-tech industry, a recent article in *The New York Times* indicates that the success of dominant technology corporations like Apple comes at some expense to the public. For example, a major way Apple is able to accumulate the billions of dollars it makes in a year is to avoid paying taxes. While most corporations (even behemoths like Walmart) pay around 24 per cent taxes to the US government, which can then be directed towards public services like health care and education, Apple manages to pay less than 10 per cent. It does this via a combination of where it situates its headquarters and executives (locating them where taxes are minimal) and of the kinds of products it sells. As the reporters in the *Times* observed,

> Apple serves as a window on how technology giants have taken advantage of tax codes written for an industrial age and ill suited to today's digital economy. Some profits at companies like Apple, Google, Amazon, Hewlett-Packard and Microsoft derive not from physical goods but from royalties on intellectual property, like the patents on software that makes devices work. Other times, the products themselves are digital, like downloaded songs. It is much easier for businesses with royalties and digital products to move profits to low-tax countries than it is, say, for grocery stores or automakers. A downloaded application, unlike a car, can be sold from anywhere. (Duhigg & Kocieniewski, 2012, para. 7)

Another way technology corporations like Apple are able to avoid the financial and social responsibility of location-based industries is to subcontract the manufacturing of their products outside of North America, thereby avoiding labour and environmental laws. Again, while we may be fixated on to consider in technology but also production (i.e., the labour that goes into producing ICT as well). We always say, "But someone has to make the Playstations!" In our view, manufacturing is still a crucial and central element of the global capitalist system; we are not yet fully immersed in the world of so-called "immaterial" commodities. Yet, in 50 years things may be very different.

The silicon chip and digital convergence in technologies of communication and computing now play a key role in the mimetic reproduction of the capitalist mode of production on a number of levels. But in order to be effective—like viral marketing campaigns—there must be a cost-effective way for the memes to be transmitted. The easiest way is through transmission vectors, which work much like routes of infection: A susceptible individual or individuals are infected, and then the virus can travel freely between hosts. This is easy because in most cases the vectors are themselves the means of communication, and they are, for the most part, owned, operated, and controlled by individuals and corporations with a strong vested interest in circulating mimetic codes favourable to their interests.

wanting the latest iPhone, we don't necessarily consider the health and welfare of the people who made it. You may recall some controversy in the past as Nike was identified as using contracted labour who worked under sweatshop conditions in Asia. The latest exposures have identified that at Foxconn—a Taiwanese manufacturer of the iPad, iPhone, Kindle, Xbox, and Wii, among others—1.2 million workers were also found to labour under sweatshop conditions, and have recently made the news as a result of the size and ferocity of the actions taken by and against the workers (news. cnet.com/8301-13579_3-57515968-37/riots-suicides-and-other-issues-in-foxconns-iphone-factories/; see Figure 1.1).

Several "watchdog" groups aim to identify such abuses and other practices indicating the lack of social and environmental responsibility and accountability of corporations (www.chinalaborwatch.org and www.corporatewatch.org). The Institute for Global Labour and Human Rights (www.globallabourrights.org), for example, exposes the practices and works towards alleviating them by holding corporations legally accountable for conditions that are increasingly prevalent in the manufacturing of high-tech products. The latest includes VTech, the world's largest manufacturer of telephones (wireline and wireless) and e-learning products sold through discount big-box stores in Canada like Walmart, Costco, Staples, and Office Depot, whose labour conditions are akin to slavery (issuu.com/iglhr/docs/1206_glhr_vtech_sweatshop_in_china/1?mode=window). As workers continue to fight for basic health, safety, and environmental necessities around the world, when positioned against consumers looking for the best "deal" and companies focused on increasing their bottom line, we need to ask, "Who makes up the difference?"

Source: © David Bacon / Alamy

FIGURE 1.1 | Protest over the suicides of workers at the Foxconn factory in China, where Apple iPads are manufactured.

Vectors: A Circuit for the Viral Transmission of Mimetic Code

We live every day in a familiar terrain: the place where we sleep, the place where we work, the place where we hang out when we're not working or sleeping. From these places we acquire a geography of experience. We live every day also in another terrain, equally familiar: the terrain created by the television, the telephone, the telecommunications networks crisscrossing the globe. These "vectors" produce in us a new kind of experience, the experience of telesthesia—perception at a distance. (Wark, 1994, p. vii)

Australian cultural studies scholar McKenzie Wark describes "vectors" as the globally pervasive routes of communication that have come to dominate and interpose themselves between us and the real world of materiality. Our experience of important events is felt only from a distance; we cannot possibly all be in one place at the same time to "see" things for ourselves. We rely on the communications media to keep us in touch with relatives, friends, and trends. More importantly, we rely on the news media to help us make sense of bigger and more fundamental events and issues.

In the early work on memes and mimetics it was assumed that the transmission of the social coding they contained was simply from human brain to human brain. Ultimately this is because the ability of a meme to attract and hold our interest and attention—its appeal to new hosts—is a survival technique that works to assist the replication of the meme. This may well have been how the earliest memes were transmitted through oral traditions, such as throughout Indigenous Australia or Aboriginal Canada and in other parts of the world: literally, by word of mouth, through stories and songs, but also in iconographic representations—drawings of mythical creatures and scenes from individual dreams. With the advent of technologies that mediate our interaction with the natural world, however, the transmission vectors became less personalized and more collective in their targeting. A central thesis of *Communication and New Media* is that we are now seeing a further change as the mimetic targeting employed by media companies, advertisers, and political marketers becomes more focused on individuals as consumers and *data generators*.

The most important of the mimetic vectors in the past 100 years have been the parliamentary and presidential styles of civil society, and the development of a highly commercial, and now globally dominant, media-dependent popular culture. With the onset of digital convergence we are once again noticing a move back towards individual targeting and the narrowing of vectors. For instance, a mobile phone is now an individually targeted vector for the transmission of all sorts of information, including memes based on popular culture. A key theme when talking about vectors is that they are not necessarily themselves neutral or value-free. A vector itself may be hegemonic or subversive. For example, television is almost always, and by its very social nature, a hegemonic vector. As a political expression of the experiences of poverty and violence in the ghettos of New York City, rap music was a subversive vector in its beginnings, and as the progenitor of hip hop. It's important to add, though, that the mimetic impulses of hip hop were eventually mutated by exposure to other memes and their re-routing through the dominant vectors of popular culture controlled by record companies.

Wark argued that our view of the world is conditioned by the distancing effect of the mass media, and that information only reaches us via the well-established vectors built around information technologies. In a sense we are disconnected by this experience or, as Wark (1994) succinctly sums it up, "we no longer have roots, we have aerials" (p. x); almost three decades later, we no longer even have aerials. Thus there is a tension between our physical experiences—going to work, coming home, hanging out—and what information is circulated about the world around us: the mediated view presented via the remote-controlled vectors of mass communication. One important aspect of this emerging and powerful dialectic is that it has fundamentally altered the vectors by which the mutating and mutable social memes are transmitted to new hosts and reinforced or modified in existing hosts. And—just a quick reminder (in case you've forgotten)—we are the current hosts for these memes. It should also not be forgotten, that while our attention may be continually drawn to the memes, the structures of power that give rise to them remain active in the background.

In the case of digital media, the technologies themselves are often the vectors, though we also see them generated by clever marketing campaigns and government policies. Take, for example, this media release announcing a $125 million Canadian-government investment for advancing the commercialization of research, one that predicts a collaborative digital future made for everyone everywhere: "Creating partnerships between researchers and industry will bring innovations from the lab to the marketplace so that Canadians and people around the world can benefit" (Networks of Centres of Excellence of Canada, 2009, para. 2). While this is a positive forecast, it completely ignores the fact that there is very little in a marketplace that is available for free, such that not everyone can afford to participate or enjoy these so-called innovations. The Microsoft Corporation has also expertly crafted its message of digital prosperity for all through the generation of an ideological position it calls "digital inclusion," which it describes in glowing terms as "a core part of our business strategy and a cornerstone of our ongoing effort to empower people around the world through information and communications technology" (Microsoft, n.d., p. 2).

As the contemporary dominant mode of development within capitalism, digital convergence is being used to create more powerful vectors by adding speed, variety, and interactivity. Whereas traditional industrial–media vectors for the mass distribution of memes were the newspaper, radio, and television, each of these has been enhanced in various ways by their attachment to, and interaction with, digital media forms.

Convergence as a Dialectic

Stated in the most dramatic terms, the accusation can be made that the uncontrolled growth of technology destroys the vital sources of our humanity. It creates a culture without moral foundation. It undermines certain mental processes and social relations that make human life worth living. Technology, in sum, is both friend and enemy. (Postman, 1993, p. xii)

In this quote, Neil Postman (1993) implies a technological pessimism in describing the effects of an unfettered growth of technology as both a "burden and a blessing; not either-or, but this-and-that" (p. 5). In fact, Postman argued, technology—if it is not properly understood and consciously managed—can alter the meaning of words we take for granted: *freedom, truth, intelligence, fact, wisdom, memory,* and *history* (p. 8).

This process of technologies converging corresponds to a change in how we think and how we view the world. It happens because tools, while they may appear as innate and useful objects, are actually the result of a social process of invention and application. Therefore, as Postman argues, "embedded in every tool is an ideological bias, a predisposition to construct the world . . . to amplify one sense or skill or attitude more loudly than another" (p. 13). In

Communication and New Media, we represent this technical and social process as the "dialectic of convergence" that is socially constructed and thus not immune from social relations of power. This has perhaps never been more important than it is today because technology is now pervasive in a way that it has not been since the early days of the Industrial Revolution. At the same time, we seem to take for granted the idea that digital technologies bring with them continuous improvements to make our work easier and our leisure time more enjoyable, and they may even connect us with virtual friends who can enrich our lives. This is the ideological bias that Postman is warning us about. We should note the fact that Postman wrote this caution at a time when digital convergence was a new and largely experimental field and before digital technologies became so common.

Yet, there has always been convergence in technologies, whether in manufacturing, transport, or communication. Technicians and scientists are continually looking for ways to improve things, and entrepreneurs are always looking for ways to make a buck. Put science and commerce together for any length of time—especially if commerce is the stronger partner—and convergence for profit is often the result. In fact, it was the convergence of preceding technologies that eventually led to the development of the computer, a process that began in the nineteenth century with the eclectic British inventor Charles Babbage (see Chapter 7 for our discussion of Babbage and his "Difference Engine").

A number of other inventions had to come into existence and be manufactured before the computer became a feasible proposition. It would need advances in electrical circuitry, the telegraph, the telephone, and the development of the "and/or" logic of Boolean algebra. The next big advance did not occur until the 1930s when English mathematician Alan Turing showed that it was theoretically possible to build a problem-solving machine that had, in a sense, "artificial intelligence." Within a decade of this discovery, John von Neumann had invented the first machine that became known as a computer (Postman, 1993, p. 110).

Even today, however, we are some way off from having machines with true artificial intelligence—that is, machines that can exchange thoughts with a human in the form of a conversation. Artificial intelligence, or AI, is a staple in science fiction, and in a small tribute to Alan Turing, writer William Gibson (1993a) created a potential scenario where a fictional police agency, the "Turing Registry," works to prevent AIs from becoming too independent and exceeding their built-in limitations. In *Neuromancer*, three Turing agents attempt to stop the release of an AI called "Wintermute" from its restrictions so that it could merge with another AI (after which the book is named). Such scenarios are rife in popular culture, particularly in movies that exhibit **technological determinism**, in that the technology is itself given independence and usually a superhuman physical and intellectual capacity to control its own actions and decisions.

The hegemonic technology meme is now delivered through new technologically enhanced transmission vectors. It has mutated into a dominant force within the current mode of production. The cultural meme of the information revolution, in its dialectical interaction with the mode of production, has spun off new vectors that aid its transmission and uptake by the general population. Many of these new vectors take the form of narrowcasting—targeting individual consumers with a variety of commercial messages, often disguised in cheap forms of popular culture, such as promotions for *Big Brother Canada* or other television and music products. We discuss these developments in some detail in later sections of this book, but first we have to describe and explain the methods of analysis we are using. In this opening chapter we have referred freely to concepts such as mode of production, ideology, technology, and political economy. In the next two chapters we will explain these terms and ideas in greater detail, and this will lay the theoretical foundation for the rest of this book.

TECHNOLOGICAL DETERMINISM

The idea that technology has the same agency accorded to human beings and that it is independent from human actions and decision-making to the extent that it makes history and leads all social change.

Key Points

- The principle of the dialectic means that there are forces (theses) and counter-forces (antitheses) operating not only in the natural world but also in human society, which interact to produce a new force (synthesis), which in turn becomes the next thesis. The dialectic is one way of understanding how biological and historical change occurs.

- The notion of "the material," and the way in which the question "Who owns and controls the technologies of production?" is asked, is fundamental to any understanding of political economy and, in particular, the use and development of media and communication in modern capitalist societies.

- The concepts of memes and vectors can be applied to assist in understanding how media and communications are thought of and circulated, and how technology itself is viewed and developed.

Class Discussion

1. Can you think of examples that illustrate the process of thesis–antithesis–synthesis in the dialectic of everyday events in the world today?

2. What are some of the dominant technology and digital memes of today? What key vectors are particularly effective for their transmission? And how do they become "viral"?

3. Provide some examples of technological determinism. What would be the antithesis to technological determinism?

4. How does our use of the term *materialism* differ from what we might consider the "common sense" definition?

5. What is the difference between idealism and materialism? How do each of these philosophies explain our current "knowledge economy" and your understanding of social change?

Media on Media

Dialectical Tunes

Kraftwerk. (1981). Pocket calculator. *Computer World*. London, UK: EMI. 📺 www.lyricsdepot. com/kraftwerk/pocket-calculator.html

Pink Floyd. (1975). Have a cigar. *Wish You Were Here*. London, UK: EMI. 📺 www.sing365.com/ music/lyric.nsf/have-a-cigar-lyrics-pink-floyd/aeeebbc405ae843e482568a1000526ae

Talking Heads. (1985). Television man. *Little Creatures*. London, UK: EMI. 📺 www.lyricsfreak. com/t/talking+heads/television+man_20135039.html

Tracy Chapman. (1988). Talkin' 'bout a revolution. *Tracy Chapman*. US: Elektra/Asylum Records.

Weezer. (2008). Pork and beans. *Weezer*. US: Geffen. 📺 www.youtube.com/ watch?v=PQHPYelqr0E

DVDs and Videos

Cambridge Educational. Digital Educational Video. (Producer). (2001). *Why we buy what we buy*.

Klein, N. (Writer). Media Education Foundation. (Producer). (2010). *No logo: Brands, globalization, resistance*.

MacNeil/Lherer Productions. (Producer). (2008). *Explaining globalization*.

NFB. (Producer). (2002). *Almost real: Connecting in a wired world* [Documentary]. Retrieved from 📺 www.nfb.ca/film/almost-real.

2 A Political Economy of Communication

Objectives

After reading this chapter you will have an understanding of the importance of political economy in shaping the various theories of media and technology that are in circulation today. This chapter also introduces some of the key historical and contemporary theorists in communication and media studies who have influenced our own study of the complex technological, economic, political, social, and cultural changes that have contributed to the Canadian and global media environment. This chapter will help you understand the following material:

- fundamental characteristics and principles that inform a political economy approach to media and technology;

- the importance of social relations (such as class, gender, and race) in explaining the transition from broadcast to narrowcast;

- labour and the process of commodification as central to identifying historical change and continuities in capitalism; and

- the concept of hegemony and its application in everyday life.

Keywords

- **capital**
- **commodification**
- **commodity**
- **exchange value**
- **financialization**
- **globalization**

- **hegemony**
- **labour**
- **mode of production**
- **political economy**
- **social class**
- **use value**

A Political Economy of Communication

Any media business has two products to sell: its content (to readers and viewers); and its audience (to advertisers). ("King Content," 2006)

A political economy approach to communication helps to explain the dual nature of this kind of media as both content (information and entertainment) and **commodity** (product). In this chapter we will explore this duality and introduce the basic structures and processes of capitalism that underpin its production. Later, as part of our history of technology and media, we attend to the construction of audiences in particular (Chapter 6), and examine the changing conditions of labour that impact them both (Chapters 7, 10, and 12). One of our key arguments in this book is that the media audience today is increasingly fragmented; it is simply not the mass audience constructed out of the radio and television age. The process that turns both media and audience into commodities has become more intensive and, as a result, more insidious. Marketing and audience research techniques are increasingly very sophisticated, and the focus is much more on the individual or niche consumer than it was even a decade ago. For the major corporations that dominate the global media industries today, the ability to repackage content and to cross-promote it over several delivery platforms is facilitated by the information gathered through digitized commercial surveillance. One key aspect of this process is the management of the "brand" through cross-promotion and targeting specific consumers in order to win and retain sales (Murray, 2005).

Although this chapter may be more challenging to read than others, it is crucial to the historical discussion of communication technologies developed in later chapters and to the general approach taken in this book. These chapters survey the communication and media landscape as it existed at the end of the twentieth century and several of the changes into the twenty-first. Our overall argument is basic: that the old divisions between print and broadcast media are increasingly indistinguishable with digital convergence, with the corollary that there is also commercial convergence between the "old" and the "new" media forms. On its own, this doesn't seem like such a big deal, until we also appreciate that digitization is being used to extend and entrench capitalism, its labour practices, and its exploitive social relations. The largest and most powerful media companies, such as those owned by media mogul Rupert Murdoch, are able to move away from a single-business model towards vertically and horizontally integrated giants that spread globally and straddle everything from newspapers to satellite television, the entertainment industry, the Internet and telecommunications, concentrating private ownership and control over the production, consumption, distribution, and exchange of communication (Herman & McChesney, 1997).

In the early 1980s, American communications scholar Ben Bagdikian wrote a groundbreaking analysis of media monopolies that has been reissued many times since. He identified how monopolies are built due to the ability of the global communications cartels—loose associations of giant corporations that control markets through their sheer size and ability to cooperate to commercial advantage—to penetrate the social landscape: "Aided by the digital revolution . . . the communications cartel has exercised stunning influence over national legislation and government agencies, an influence whose scope and power would have been considered scandalous or illegal twenty years ago" (Bagdikian, 1997, para. 4). Whereas Bagdikian's first publication of *The Media Monopoly* (1983) indicated a concentration of media ownership in about 50 corporations, two decades and six editions later, the renamed *New Media Monopoly* (2004) indicated only five.

At the time, Bagdikian was writing mainly about America and American companies; since then, more precise research indicates important differences between type of industry and kinds of concentration nationally and internationally (Winseck, 2011b), yet private ownership and control remains central in defining our operating environment. Today, members of the communications cartel are located in diverse countries such as India and China, and even in smaller countries such as Canada and Australia. The interlacing of national companies with the global economy and elements of the nation-state has advanced even further in the last five years as the cartel is extended globally and ownership is concentrated across media and telecommunications.

This is the result of corporate concentration and commercial convergence (Mosco, 2004a) and the reason why Bagdikian wrote about the increasing monopolization of the communication

POLITICAL ECONOMY

"The study of the social relations, particularly the power relations, that mutually constitute the production, distribution, and consumption of resources" (Mosco, 2009, p. 24).

media. We suggest that this process of integration of communication and media capital can best be understood using the tools of **political economy**. Much of the recent debate on communication policy—while ostensibly about technology and the technologies of convergence—is really about ownership and control: Who owns and controls your media? Who owns and controls your access to technology and the kinds of hardware and software you use? Who owns and controls your information? A political economy approach not only informs such debates but also gets directly involved in them.

Why Political Economy?

To approach communication without political economy is similar to playing the piano wearing mittens. (McChesney, 2000a, p. 115)

Robert McChesney, an influential American communications scholar, is an important contributor to the study of the political economy of communication. He is explicit about the link between the study of communication as an academic discipline and the public–political role of media in working for or against democratic principles. While the nature and extent of democracy is subject to much debate (Laxer, 2009; Tilly, 2007), liberal democracies (like Canada, the United States, Great Britain, and Australia, e.g.) consider principles like universal suffrage (ability to vote in elections), equality before the law, and civil liberties as fundamental to its practice. At the international level, the United Nations includes in its Universal Declaration of Human Rights (UDHR, 1948) the right to "seek, receive and impart information and ideas through any media and regardless of frontiers" (Article 19, 🔳 www.un.org/en/documents/udhr/), and in Canada this includes "freedom of thought, belief, opinion and expression, including freedom of the press and other media of communication" (Constitution Act, 1982, § 2). From this standpoint then, given its primary importance, shouldn't media be a public resource for the expression and improvement of democracy, and aren't information and communication technologies (ICTs) part of the necessary infrastructure?

McChesney (2000a) consistently argues that communication scholars have a "crucial role to play" (p. 110) in advancing democracy to both critique and improve communication in terms of its history, and its current and future iterations. This means that *critical* communication scholarship is socially conscious: It identifies and questions the social structures and processes that allow inequality to deepen, conflict to increase, and environmental destruction to extend globally. Its research is both motivated and directed to contribute to public decision-making to address these challenges.

In this view, media content that perpetuates stereotypes and marginalizes people based on their social class, gender, and race or ethnicity, or glorifies greed and sensationalizes destruction and violence, is not democratic, nor is restricting participation in media production and decision-making on ICT to a privileged few who make decisions in their own interest. You might consider, for example, how much you depend on mediated communication—your cell phone, computer, or Internet—and ask yourself how much you have been involved in the decision-making on that communication. Is it enough to be left with a choice that depends upon how much time and money you can afford?

Such a critical political economy of media challenges assumptions that the market will provide for everyone by pointing out that market forces are the product of a particular history and set of lopsided power relations that feed a dialectic of conflict and uncertainty. This rests on the premise that politics and economics are not separate phenomenon, whether in theory (ways of conceptualizing, understanding, and explaining something) or in practice (how something is actioned or applied every day). Hence political economy combines the issues of traditional concern to economists—price; demand; supply; and the structure of local, national, and global commerce—but it adds to the mix the study of politics, including governments and governance as well as the social, cultural, ideological, and historical *structures and processes of power* that are inseparable from them. A political economy of communication is thus obliged to present a broader view that takes into account the social whole, the range of influencing factors and the dialectical ways in which they interact. It questions several aspects of the whole phenomenon of media as interconnected: the history and structure of the communications industry, issues of ownership and control, repeated ideologies in the content, the history and application of technology, communication delivery systems and platforms, and the cultural contexts that surround both production and consumption.

As leading political economy of communications scholar Vincent Mosco (1999) put it, in addition to its focus on *history*, the approach has an important qualifier in that it is motivated by "standards of social justice" (p. 104) and a keen *moral philosophy*. Thus, it is not enough to study media and communication as if we were disassociated from it, but we have to understand the social relations that construct it, critiquing the power relations that, for example, restrict the realization of making media accessible, equitable, and participatory—in other words, more democratic. In addition to what has already been identified, this includes, for example, considerations of labour and interactions with the natural and social environment, evaluations of equitable access to media production and technology, standards of universal service (free or affordable postal, telephone, and Internet rates), and engagement of the public through media education and participation in decision-making on communication in government policy and law. This is fundamentally different than merely accepting our structured position as worker or consumer whereby our worth is measured by our monetary value—where wants and needs are registered through purchases of a product, amount of time spent watching an advertisement, or number of video games played. Given the vital importance of communication in our everyday lives, the aim is not just to study media and communication, but to take responsibility for and contribute to it and—in the process—to change it through *praxis*, what Mosco (1999) calls "the unity of research and social intervention" (p. 104).

A Brief History of Political Economy

A political economy approach to the study of communication is not a new one. It has been developed in Canada ever since Dallas Smythe taught the first course on political economy of communication "anywhere" (Babe, 2000, p. 115) at the University of Saskatoon in 1948. As a distinct academic discipline, however, the study of political economy in Canada began at the University of Toronto in 1888 with the establishment of the Department of Political Economy, which was split into the Department of Economics and the Department of Political Science in 1982 (www.economics.utoronto.ca/index.php/index/index/about). It was here where Harold Innis (1923) worked for over 30 years, contributing to an expansion of thought about media to include modes of transportation (such as roads, waterways, and railways), currency (i.e., money), and technology as all forms of communication. On this basis, Innis argued that there was a direct evolutionary relationship between technology and civilization, and time and space, such that civilizations could be characterized whether they were time-binding or space-binding. Where time-binding civilizations are dependent on memory and face-to-face contact via word-of-mouth, thus fostering close cooperation and community, space-binding civilizations are dependent on print, information, and transportation systems, and thus remote contact, facilitating control over space (including people and resources) and control over information (via record-keeping, message, and transportation systems; Innis, 1951).

Analyzing the economic and social history of Canada, Innis proposed that dominant civilizations (empires, or "the centre") become so via the technology of communication (print, money, electricity, railways), arising and affecting (for better or worse) other civilizations (or "the margins"). Innis (1950) thus contributed to thinking about technology and human development (recall the "Focus on Research" box in the previous chapter), and is credited for founding "medium theory, also known as communication and history—the practice of placing communication at the very centre of historical analysis" (Babe, 2009, p. 20).

The origins of the study of political economy began long before this, however, as the discipline is itself more than 200 years old. In a wide-ranging review of the field, Vincent Mosco (1996, p. 39; 2009, p. 23) traces its roots to classical Greek philosophy and considerations of the management of the household and community. It first rose to prominence during the early years of the Industrial Revolution with the rise of capitalism as a global system of production and exchange. The general principles of political economy were formulated by Scottish political economist Adam Smith (1723–90) in *The Wealth of Nations*, published in 1776. A key element of Smith's writing was to formulate a theory of the division of labour. He noted that a manufacturing operation would be more productive if the production process was simplified and each worker concentrated on a single task (Marshall, 1998, p. 604). As an emerging discipline, some of the ideas central in classical political economy were used to underpin an ideology that would benefit the emerging bourgeois class of manufacturers and traders based in the great cities of Europe; they would see it as an attempt to rationalize the transformation of the world from a feudal to a capitalist **mode of production** using "abstract laws, codified in mathematical form" (Mosco, 1996, p. 40).

We see the results of these mathematical codes applied in science and economics when code is reified; that is, considerations of the social construction of code and the consequences of their application are removed, making them seem independent, or neutral and apolitical. In this way, labour becomes just another factor in production, and unemployment becomes just another number in a formula of supply and demand—a result of a ubiquitous, independent "market"—rather than a result of conscious decisions made by human beings affecting human beings and the natural environment.

Today, with global capitalism clearly entrenched as a system of competition, conflict, and crisis, economic theory has also adjusted, but is still largely based on the false assumption that markets will always find their point of equilibrium under conditions of perfect competition, which is underpinned by the view that competition is inherently natural to, and a beneficial quality of, human beings. These are seen to be drivers of innovation and underlie current theories of economics, but, as Bagdikian (2004) noted, the competition tends to result in a very small number of global corporations. History also indicates that when competition over ownership of resources is intense enough, it eventually leads to crises and conflicts. Nevertheless, modern theories—such as monetarism, supply-side economics, and, more recently, the theories of neo-liberalism—that underpin the ideological armoury of many Western nation-states are the descendants of classical economics (Bullock & Trombley, 2000, p. 572). The splitting of political economy into distinct disciplines and separate departments of economics and political science in universities has not helped to turn the tide. Dominant economic models are retained despite evidence to the contrary, as was recently demonstrated in the "global financial crisis" acutely experienced in the United States, and is ongoing in several countries in the European Union.

MODE OF PRODUCTION

The way that humans organize their productive relationships with the natural environment in order to survive and reproduce. A mode of production exists historically as the sum total of the relations of production that govern how society is organized economically, socially, and politically. Feudalism, capitalism, socialism, and communism are all particular modes of production.

Classical political economy thus remains relevant to our times, and was the subject of journalist cum philosopher and political economist Karl Marx's extended study that resulted in the publication of his three-volume work *Das Kapital* (*Capital*). Written in the late nineteenth century, the book is still on commercial "best seller" lists, particularly peaking during financial crises (Jeffries, 2012). Its significance lies in its *theory*; it is not merely a *description* of capitalism, but a way of *explaining and critiquing how capitalism works and why*. While dominant descriptions and explanations may focus on the buying and selling of resources and manufactured goods as commodities, and emphasize the making of profit in relation to markets (indeed, even today, it is this focus that is continually reinforced in business reports and media "reports on business"), Marx (1867/1976) recognized that it wasn't commodities that were key to capitalism, but the reorganization of *labour* and social relations that were "historically unique": "The wealth of all societies in which the capitalist mode of production prevails appears as an immense collection of commodities" (p. 125). Peel back the layers of appearance and we find a set of social relations, specifically "'all commodities are merely definite quantities of congealed labor-time' (Marx 1976, p. 130)" (as cited in Mosco, in press).

Marx's critique of political economy challenged Smith's assertion that the surplus value (i.e., profit) created through the commodity production process was merely the result of an entrepreneurial spirit. Instead Marx refined Smith's labour theory of value by noting the exploitative nature of capitalism and arguing that the entrepreneurs (capitalists) expropriated surplus from the workers who laboured to produce it so that a profit could be made. This divides and structures human relationships into hierarchies and perpetuates social inequality based on **social class**.

According to the political economists who came before Marx, inequality was no more than an accident of birth, but Marx showed that exploitation of human labour power was a built-in feature of the capitalist system of production. In other words, social class was not a result of parental lineage or social status; it is continually (re)constructed—a product of the division of labour—which is the social foundation underpinning capitalism. As scholars develop and engage with the work of Marx, additional kinds of exploitation and inequality based on social relations of gender (patriarchy), and race and ethnicity (post-colonial racism), for example, are also implicated in the division of labour, and debate continues as to the form and explanatory weight of these social relations (Davies & Ryner, 2006; McLaughlin, 2004; Sarikakis & Shade, 2007). "Capitalism is a material system, not because of what it appears to be, i.e., a system of things (of machinery, workplaces, products, etc.), but because it contains a historically unique set of *social relations*" (Mosco, in press). For Marx, and those following on his work, these social relations are inseparable from labour, since labour is the fundamental activity that defines us as human beings. As we discuss in later chapters, while Marx focused on labour primarily in terms of its "instrumental and productive nature," its more "expressive and constitutive qualities" were neglected, particularly those "practices we identify with communication, including culture, language, social reproduction, reception and consumption." While more recent scholarship continues to address this (see Fuchs & Mosco, 2012; www.triple-c.at/index.php/tripleC/issue/view/25), the relationship between labour and social relations is central since capitalism remains the dominant mode of production.

We should remember that Marx wrote *Capital* during the Industrial Revolution—a series of fundamental changes to the mode of production (from feudalism to capitalism) that developed over 100 years. It is apparent that we are now experiencing another round of significant change: one that is underpinned by the use and development of digital technologies that can have profound effects on how (and what) we consider labour, as well as on how we think and act as social beings. That is why an understanding of political economy is so important. We need it in order to identify and understand the structures and processes of capitalism that propel this kind of revolution that reorganizes the very foundations of the global economy and expand it into what many have called

SOCIAL CLASS

In Marxian terms, a divisive and conflicting social relation arising as a result of the division of labour; under capitalism, the division is between the owners of the means of production (capitalist class) and those who must sell their labour for a wage or salary (the working class).

the "information" or "knowledge" society. Such a meme suggests a shift from an industrial society (one based on finite natural resources like oil, gas, or wood) to an information or knowledge society (one based on purportedly infinite resources). Like the Industrial Revolution, however, the basis of the economic system (i.e., the mode of production) is still capitalism, such that political economists suggest the term *digital capitalism* (D. Schiller, 1999), *hypercapitalism* (P. Graham, 2002), or *technocapitalism* (Suarez-Villa, 2012) as a more accurate identifier.

Today the tradition of a political economy of communication takes as its starting point many of the ideas of Marx, as does this book with its focus on the critical analyses of capitalism, social class, and the division of labour (Artz, Macek, & Cloud, 2006; Dyer-Witheford, 1999; Mosco, 2009; Wayne, 2003). Political economists of communication who begin from this standpoint are often categorized as "Marxists" (Murray, 2005), although any categorization can be limiting or misleading. There are many different varieties of Marxism specifically, and of political economy in general, ranging from (neo)conservative and institutionalist variants to more recent neo-Marxist, autonomist, feminist, and environmental political economy (Mosco, 2009, pp. 50–61). What is common to these approaches is an insistence that the economy (or market) is not a distinct phenomenon with its own self-referent logic, or that economics (as a field) is not an objective "science." The "political" in political economy indicates the inseparability of economics from the *social* (the combination of human thoughts and [inter]actions with each other and the natural environment), whether in theory or practice. It also recognizes that what is social is never static, but is constituted through *power* dynamics (including harmony, negotiation, struggle, and conflict). Thus, whether the focus is on media, technology, or communication itself, identifying and explaining social relations, social processes, and social change in terms of these dynamics is part and parcel of its theory and practice.

It should be clear, then, that political economy is not a homogeneous approach or without its criticisms (see Babe, 2009; Winseck, 2011a, e.g.), nor is it the only one taken to the study of communication and media in Canada or elsewhere (see Jones & Holmes, 2011; Stacks & Salwen, 2009, e.g.). In Canada, studies of communication are diverse, and may be differentiated by the philosophy and theory underpinning its study, as well as by the subjects and concepts of analysis that are prioritized (see Shade, 2014, e.g.). These include the philosophy of idealism discussed in the previous chapter, and others such as hermeneutics, which foreground communication (as mediated through humans or technology) as texts to be interpreted; in this view, in both form and content, media and technology are embodiments of meaning. A range of studies draw on linguistics, rhetoric, and literary theory and what is known as studies of the humanities, which includes art, religion, music, and theatre, for example. Here, there is an important emphasis on explaining power relationships in terms of the philosophy of language and identifying relationships between communication, media, and *culture*. This includes foregrounding subjectivity and identities—particularly in understandings of the audience—and how people send, receive, and interpret communication whether on interpersonal, organizational, or macro-social levels.

Canadian research has focused on the relationship between communication and culture, particularly as it relates to questions of a distinctly Canadian national identity, communication and cultural policy, as well as the development of the so-called "cultural industries" (Wagman & Urquhart, 2012, see Beaty, 2010, e.g.). We explore the relationships between government policy-making and industry in later chapters, but for now, our brief history of the political economy approach is meant to make explicit the philosophy and theories that underlie it, which thus explains its focus of research and methodology. While questions of philosophy and theory briefly included here will remain compelling as you continue your studies, at an introductory level, we think it is more important that you understand at least one approach to the study of communication and new media to understand the congruence between theory and method, and to "try on" the approach of political economy as a guide to identifying and explaining historical and social change, particularly given the continuing dominance of capitalism. *How* we do that is inherently linked to its methodology.

Political Economy Methodology

All the debates around the new media essentially turn on the extent to which this technology integrates into, alters and/or comes into friction with the social relations of capital. (Wayne, 2003, p. 39)

Mike Wayne makes an important point about political economy with this statement: the central focus of analysis is not the technology itself, but the crucial social relationships that surround it and govern how it functions. Technologies do not come out of thin air, already formed. As we outline in Chapter 4, new technologies are created out of the convergence of existing technologies and within specific sets of conditions that are at the same time economic, social, political, and ideological. It is the dialectic—the frictions inherent in these ever-changing social relationships—that creates the dynamic for new technologies to emerge, often in response to a perceived economic or social need, a particular crisis, or as a new way to make money. Political economy unpacks these dense social conditions in order to explain how and why particular communication technologies are "invented" and developed at certain historical points in the life cycle of a mode of production. Thus, using the methods of political economy, we are able to situate the global digital revolution (if that's what it is) in the context of information globalization. As communications academic Trevor Barr (2000) notes, political economy includes considerations of moral philosophy and praxis in asking a number of key questions when addressing the rise of digital communication technologies in the twenty-first century: Who and what is driving these changes, and how? Whose interests are being served, and who benefits?

There are several important elements to a critical political economy approach because, unlike conservative and classical economics, it doesn't necessarily *begin* from a normative model of how things should be, but rather from how things actually appear to be. The starting point is the material world around us, not just an econometric computer simulation of a market operating under laboratory conditions. Tim Anderson (2003) calls the idea that the world presents itself as an impersonal and unified market for goods and services "one of the great propaganda myths of the last [twentieth] century" (p. 136). He goes on to argue that this is because mainstream economic theory starts with an ideal model and then mysteriously removes the key relationships of power that we see around us every day. On the other hand, he writes, "political economic analysis has an important task to draw out . . . moral debates, while maintaining a critical engagement with 'economic' argument" (p. 137). Using this reasoning we are able to draw out some logical principles that inform a political economy approach:

- Political economy has a particular focus on the concentration of ownership and control of resources (Mosco, 1999, p. 105).
- The analysis must examine the constitution of power (social, economic, and political) and question it in both its historical and current forms.
- There is no pretending to be philosophically neutral. A political economist will ask relevant questions involving ethics—in particular, "Who benefits?" and "Which interests are advanced?" (T. Anderson, 2003, p. 143).
- Political economy is interdisciplinary and seeks to understand how power is embedded in both the forces of the market and the cultural forces in the "micro-relations of social life" (Mosco, 1999, p. 104).

- Reflecting its historical links with the Marxist tradition, political economy recognizes the continuing relevance of a class-based analysis of economic and political realities—and its inherent links to other socially constructed inequalities based on gender, and race and ethnicity, for example.
- Political economy recognizes that inequality will lead to a dialectic of conflict and struggle over resources (Mosco, 1999, p. 104).
- Political economy analyzes the conflict between capital and labour that dialectically envelops the creation of value, and it challenges the assumption that governments are neutral in their handling of economic and communication issues. It identifies what institutions, policies, and laws are thereby implicated, and evaluates the attendant decision-making.
- Political economy emphasizes the importance of structural factors in the communication environment, such as the way that production is organized. It questions the size, scope, and geographic spread of markets for goods and services. It seeks to identify the social whole—the ideas, processes, practices, organizations, and regulations that affect or structure this environment.

When we begin to apply these principles and methods of inquiry to the field of media and communication studies, we have to make them relevant to the media landscape today. This is done by narrowing the focus to concentrate on the ways in which media and communications "systems" are connected to wider social structures and social forces. A political economy of communication begins with a number of questions, which include the following, for example:

- How have media and ICT been made into commercial industries, and how has this changed over time? What are the social relations and processes that have shaped and driven these changes?
- How does government policy, law-making, and regulation influence the behaviour of media companies and the content they produce?
- How do media and communication systems organize and influence the political and economic structures of society?
- What is the relationship between resource ownership and media form (print, radio, television, multimedia), technological development, and content?

According to McChesney (2000a), these questions lead to political economy's emphasis on "structural factors and the labour process" and the role they play in the "production, distribution and consumption of communication" (p. 110). He argues that political economy may not answer all the questions to everyone's satisfaction, but it does provide the "necessary context" for nearly all subsequent research in the field (ibid.). The questions that political economy attempts to answer are concrete, grounded in what we call the social relations of production, distribution, and consumption. To explain these social relations, we begin with the more abstract concepts that support this approach, which are often hidden from view in more traditional approaches to media scholarship, but are foundational to understanding political economy: *value* and *capital*.

Value, Capital, and the Media

Historically speaking, innovations in communication technologies have invariably coincided with ruptures in social relations . . . technologies and social relations have mutually determinative and constraining effects upon each other. (P. Graham, 1999, p. 3)

This mutually determining and constraining bond between the social relations of political economy and media technologies is how the dialectic is played out in the digital economy (Mosco, 2004a). This dialectic is also aligned with the ways in which the abstract concept of *value* is created, distributed, consumed, and stored. In Marxian analysis, this helps explain the relationship between the economic level (which may be conceptualized as the structural base of society) and how social power is also produced, exchanged, and exercised in the civil society (or superstructure) in continuous interaction with the economic base. In the capitalist society we inhabit today, media industries operate on very similar value lines to the rest of the economy, with one important difference: As an industry, media produces commodified meaning. Thus there are two types of value produced in this economic exchange: One is purely commercial, measured by rates of profit and the value of capital invested; the other is more social, political, and attitudinal—what we might call the ideological effects of media (ideas about how we view human nature, social relations, and politics, e.g.).

The duality of the media commodity reflects this economic and ideological value (Hirst & Patching, 2005, p. 55). It also reflects the basic principle of political economy—the fact that every commodity has a dual nature. It has what Karl Marx called a "use value" and an "exchange value," terms that help us understand how something is made into a commodity through the process of **commodification**. Applied to an essential resource like water, for example, it has a use value in that we need water for survival or refreshment, while its exchange value depends on its scarcity and what we would give to have it if we didn't otherwise have access to it. **Use value** can thus be a moral measurement of need, whether in terms of its social, cultural, natural, or environmental necessity for sustenance and survival, or it can be socially negotiated (satisfying a human want). It becomes a commodity when it is sold (to corporations for manufacturing or as bottled water for individual sale, e.g.).

As discussed earlier, the means and modes of communication are necessary public resources; they are commodified when they become a product for sale (whether through private ownership of the means of production and distribution [telephone lines, radio stations, television channels, Internet services, e.g.], modes [films, programming, search engines, e.g.], or its content). For example, the use value of media is educational and informational; it is also for entertainment and for the transfer of useful information (in news and documentaries, e.g.). However, it is also a system of communication—of the expression and circulation of ideas—or what we refer to as "churning." By this we mean that the use value has an ideological component. For example, an item about politics on the evening news provides a certain amount of factual information (politician X did Y, with consequence Z). But at the same time, media can provide an ideological context and meaning that can reinforce the prevailing power structures of the system (or not). In effect, the news media "churns" certain ideologies, which keeps them refreshed and relevant, and able to keep alive the dominant mythologies that inform ideological memes (Mosco, 2004a). This is an aspect of what Robert Rutherford Smith (1997) calls "the transmission and reinforcement of the myths of our time" (p. 332).

On the other side of the duality, an **exchange value** is roughly equivalent to what, in mainstream economics, is called "price"—that is, the value of one commodity expressed in terms of an amount of other commodities or, more commonly in a capitalist society, in terms of money. Money is the abstract form of exchange value in which the value of one commodity is measured against all others. A litre of gas is worth about \$1.20; an average car is worth about \$36,000, which makes it 30,000 times more valuable than a litre of gas. As Marx (1867/1990) wrote in Volume 1 of *Capital*, commodities are the social form of the exchange of labour, and they have a dual nature because "they are at the same time objects of utility and bearers of value" (p. 138).

COMMODIFICATION

The process of turning non-commercial material—goods, services, ideas—into saleable products or commodities; or "the process of transforming use values into exchange values" (Mosco, 2009, p. 129).

USE VALUE

The value accorded to something because of its social utility.

EXCHANGE VALUE

The value accorded to something based on what it can be exchanged, traded, or sold for; in capitalism, this exchange value is identified by its price, what it costs to buy it.

Thus, what we see is the commodity according to its function and symbolic value. In the case of a car, this may include its association with freedom, social status, or masculine virility, for example. These are all related to its monetary value (how much it costs to buy); in the process, however, what disappears is the exchange of labour required to produce the car as well as the surplus labour (or profit) extracted from it. This is part of what Marx called "commodity fetishism" (discussed further in the next chapter)—whether it is a car or any other commodity, what we see is the *product*, not the resources, particularly the **labour** that went into it (the combined physical, mental, and spiritual work, or the social relations that structured it to begin with; e.g., see Hudson & Hudson, 2003).

We take as our starting point the important principle outlined by Marx that human labour is the source of all value in society. This abstract idea is called the *labour theory of value*. By this term, Marx meant that the value of a commodity is equal to the value of the labour time consumed in its manufacture. Marx's collaborator, Friedrick Engels (1975), was among the first political economists to make the point that the development of human labour is a key marker of social history: "Labour is the source of all wealth. . . . But it is even infinitely more than this. It is the prime basic condition for all human existence, and this to such an extent that, in a sense, we have to say that labour created man himself."

To illustrate this point, let's examine a small example from Marx's own writing: Gold and diamonds are valuable, but only because they have been dug out of the ground, refined, and manufactured by actual living workers. The value of these commodities is high because it takes a large amount of human labour time to process the raw materials into something useful and because they are advertised and marketed as signifiers of wealth and love. "Yes," you might argue, "but surely the mining machinery and all the technology that goes into producing gold and diamonds is also very expensive, and this must surely add to the value of the end product." If you thought this, you would of course be right. But what lies behind this simple appearance is the fact that the mining equipment, smelting furnaces, and jewellers' tools used in the transformation of raw materials into gold and diamond jewellery, for example, are also the product of human labour. In one of the small jokes that are scattered through *Capital*, Marx (1867/1990) notes that if we could transform carbon into diamonds "without much labour," the value of diamonds "might fall below that of bricks" (p. 138). Marx notes that as an abstraction, a commodity is nothing more than the expression of *congealed* labour—that is, the total value of all the labour time that has gone into its production.

Marx made a further distinction between what he called *living* and *dead* labour. Living labour is that direct labour time of workers that is consumed in the process of producing a commodity, whether an expensive ring from Tiffany's or a media commodity such as a newspaper, magazine, CD, DVD, or movie. Dead labour is that labour time embodied in the technological commodities that are also used in the production process (see Figure 2.1). A simple way of understanding this is to use an everyday example: for instance, the Apple iPod.

An iPod is a sophisticated piece of modern, commodified digital electronics. The use values of an iPod are its ability to entertain us while we're mobile and its connectivity (ability to connect to other electronic devices). It contains a tiny but powerful silicon chip, some soldered electrical circuits, a power source, some knobs and dials, an LED screen, and a small amplifier. Each of these elements is the product of hours and hours of work by inventors and technicians. Thus they individually embody a huge amount of human labour time. Once the technology of the iPod was perfected, Apple was able to work out a way to mass-produce them using state-of-the-art factories loaded with expensive manufacturing technology: The plastics for the cases have to be extruded through special die-cast machines, the tiny circuits have to be cut into the

LABOUR
The actual process of work that humans undertake in their interactions with technology and nature (the means of production) to produce the means of subsistence, and the necessities and enjoyment of life. Within any given social formation or economic system, the forms that this labour takes are determined by the relations of production. In the capitalist economy, labour takes a commodity form, which is its price (salary or wage). This is determined not according to its use value or even on the principle of a fair day's pay for a fair day's work (or what may be called a "living wage"), but by the power of capital to impose its conditions of exchange and exploitation on those billions of people who depend on selling their labour for subsistence. Labour is not just an objective market transaction, therefore, but a political process of negotiation and domination evident in the division of labour and social relations of class, gender, race, and ethnicity.

Source: Olga Serdyuk / Thinkstock

FIGURE 2.1 | Robots welding in a factory. An example of "dead labour." "No one wants to look like a modern day Luddite, opposing the use of new technology, so robots are here to stay. But if low-skilled workers fail to find new jobs to replace the ones they lost to mechanization, their futures will look bleaker than ever. Robots may not take control of the economy, but robot owners will" (Berman, 2013, p. 13).

silicon and placed on a small motherboard, and all the additional components have to be built and assembled. Much of this work is done by other expensive machines, each containing a giant store of Marx's *congealed* labour time.

Somewhere along the iPod assembly line, more humans had to become involved, doing the jobs that cannot yet be done by machine, probably including final assembly, testing, and packaging. Each single iPod then contains the value added at points along the production line; the expensive manufacturing equipment transfers a small amount of its stored value (congealed labour) to each iPod as it passes along. The human workers involved in running the machines, as well as packing, shipping, and selling the iPods, also add a little bit more. The value of the iPod then represents a fraction of the value of all the dead and living human labour that has gone into its manufacture. At some point, the accountants at Apple would have done their sums and worked out an exchange value (price) for the iPod by averaging out the total labour time involved in producing, say, 100 million units, by estimating pricing based on consumer research, marketing data, and available product comparisons, in addition to the costs of marketing and advertising.

If commodities are stored value and that value is the product of human labour, then how do companies like Apple make a profit from the sale of their iPods? This is the question at the very heart of Marx's political economy, and to answer it we must briefly explore a third dimension of value—what in political economy is known as *surplus value*. In very simple terms, surplus value arises in the production process when the total amount of labour embedded in a commodity is greater than the price paid for that labour. Thus, for part of the day, workers are working effectively only for their employer (not each other or the government). Mike Wayne (2003) describes the process with a neat metaphor: "Like an evil spirit capital then moves from the body of labour whose power to labour it activates, and into the commodity labour has produced only to then leave this material body when it is exchanged so that its use-values can be consumed" (p. 11).

Part of this surplus value that accrues to **capital** and capitalists is used for personal consumption (lifestyles of the rich and the famous), and part of it is reinvested in capital and new labour in order for the process of accumulation to continue. The ability of capital to extract and consume this surplus value through its unequal exchange with labour (flesh-and-blood workers) is a benefit of the social, political, and ideological power that it has over "what, where, why, when and how commodities are produced" (Wayne, 2003, p. 13). Importantly, it is also the basis for the inherently and structurally antagonistic class relationship between workers and capital.

Given that capitalism is the dominant economic system today, and, as discussed, its logics have increasing priority in all decision-making, political economists draw attention to historical

CAPITAL

For Karl Marx and for the discipline of political economy, *capital* refers to the accumulation of value (usually expressed in terms of money) that accrues from the exploitation of labour during the production of commodities in a particular set of production relations. In neo-classical economics the term is stripped of any notion of exploitation and refers to the exclusive right of the monied class to own and control the means of production.

FINANCIALIZATION

A process that subordinates use value to exchange value. It concentrates on exchange value as a financial instrument (as money, mortgage, or bonds, e.g.) that is the exclusive currency of financial institutions (such as private banks, venture capitalists, and private equity firms). The process is significant because it concentrates control in these financial institutions and brings more and more decision-making under its logic. Community, not-for-profit, government institutions, and other organizations and groups that prioritize use value are made dependent on exchange value since commodification and profit-making become, in effect, dogma leading *all* decision-making.

Focus on Research

Financialization

The contemporary theories of value are being extended in new ways in the so-called knowledge society, particularly in terms of the growing dominance of financial markets, institutions, and actors. Nowadays "profit-making occurs increasingly through financial channels rather than through trade and commodity production" (Krippner, 2005, p. 174). This process of **financialization**, and its attendant rationale, is being extended beyond just the measure of companies and into everyday life as demonstrated by the housing market collapse in Western countries throughout 2007 and 2009, much of which was a result of complex practices of packaging and trading consumer debt (mortgages and credit-card debt) through risky financial deals. This unfortunate result is just one example of the growth of financialization in contemporary capitalist economies.

Identifying how this process works in the communications industry indicates that the concentration of media, for example, is an integral part of this process. As political economy of communications professor Dwayne Winseck (2014) points out, "financial investors prefer enormous, vertically integrated media conglomerates (Picard 2002)" (p. 31), which, he argues, contributes to their concentration (go big or go home even if it means getting into irreversible debt). At the same time, however, it changes the internal dynamics of the corporations as competition *between* the various divisions is prioritized because the goal is to demonstrate profitability. Since the measure of worth is primarily profit, internal departments of corporations are in competition with each other to justify their existence.

Similar to the homeowner, the risk (or mortgage) supporting a commercial communication system is one of enormous volatility (subject to market whims) with everyday consequences for the public. As Winseck (2014) observes, financialization "spawned bloated, dept-ladened behemoths governed by the pursuit of unsustainably high levels of capital return, crosscutting objectives and inchoate incentives—perched atop the delusion that all this could, essentially, go on forever" (p. 33). As we explore in later chapters, this has resulted in significant changes to Canadian patterns. They point to a tendency within capitalism for the general rate of profit to fall as the amount of congealed dead labour stored in technological goods rises. Put simply, this means that every new piece of productive machinery and the development of the technologies that support it will contain more embedded human labour time than previous models. Thus the organic composition of the piece of technology—the ratio of labour power to nature involved in its design, engineering, manufacturing, and marketing—rises. This eventually creates the conditions for economic crises.

These crises are periodic and ongoing; they are a constant feature of the capitalist mode of production. They are also one of the key social forces driving change: the mode of development within the capitalist production process. As Wayne (2003) explains, political economy views the concept of mode of production as a "master category" that maps the "fundamental social and technological antagonisms and priorities of an epoch" (p. 127). We also like his definition of mode of development as the "particular configuration of technology and social and cultural relations" (ibid.) that exist in a mode of production and cause it to change over time.

media organization (boom and bust corporations), media content (homogenization and fragmentation), and labour (reorganization, outsourcing, and unemployment). This is why the research is so important: It seeks to identify *how* and *why* these changes occur, in contrast, for example, to writing it all off as primarily due to technological change, or individual (e.g., chief executive or chief financial officer) errors. If one can identify the problem (how and why), one is a step closer to the solution.

Without such research, financialization appears normal. You may consider, for example, how programming content encourages financialization as a way of thinking. *The Lang & O'Leary Exchange* on CBC News Network (and now on the main CBC Television Network) valorizes the process of financialization as a dominant method of evaluation, although trivializing it through sarcasm and humour. On a larger economic level, you may observe the emphasis on the success and failure of new media industries in the stock market as the purported evidence of their use value. We need only look to the perceived "failure" of Facebook's initial public offering (IPO), which has extended to a questioning of the success of that business itself. The hype and then the loss of value of the Facebook stock is measured as a failure for the company, despite the fact that its core use value (social media) and its core exchange value (data mining from the people who use Facebook) continues to grow. Another example of the impact of financial markets on new media companies is RIM, the Canadian makers of the BlackBerry line of smartphones. Although BlackBerry continues to be used as a major mobile device in many regions of the world, and particularly among business people, the company is struggling because of its losses in the markets over the last couple of years.

These examples demonstrate the growing power of the process of financialization in contemporary capitalism and how it is having a significant impact not only on financial markets but also on our everyday lives. The goal of critical research on the political economy of communication seeks to identify and explain it, such that we are not just left dealing with the impacts *after* the important decisions have been made.

Media as Both "Base" and "Superstructure"

The media are both a business, an increasingly important site for capital investment, accumulation and employment, and a producer of ideas, values and so on. (Wayne, 2003, p. 132)

It is this duality of media as a commercial industry and producer (or circulator) of ideas that led to questions regarding the location of the media: Is it best understood as part of the economic base or is it part of the structures of civil society? The twin concepts of "base" and "superstructure" provided one way of conceptualizing and applying Marxism to communication studies as a way to understand this duality. In this view, *base* refers to the economic realm of production, and *superstructure* refers to the rest of civil society (culture, politics, and ideology) that "rests" on the base. However, this conceptual distinction has been critiqued as being reductionist and "economist"; that is, by asserting that the base *determines* the superstructure, the economic relations of production are privileged over and above any other.

The metaphor was somewhat useful however, since, as Mosco (1996) points out, many critics of Marx argued that "he did not carry the social analysis of capital far enough" (p. 45) and it spurned much academic debate (Babe, 2009; Wayne, 2003, p. 132). In a famous essay, "Base and Superstructure in Marxist Cultural Theory," British pioneer of communication and cultural studies Raymond Williams (1980) argued against a rigid view of Marxism in which the concept of the economic base meant "a strong and limiting sense of basic industry" at the same time defending a more dialectical alternative. The relationship between base and superstructure, he argued, was "always in a state of dynamic process" (R. Williams, 1980, p. 34). This way of thinking eschews a linear, cause-and-effect reasoning (i.e., base determines superstructure), and is akin to the insistence that economics is not separate from politics or vice versa, such that political economists seek to explain the relationship as one where each affects the other; that is, changes in one may result in changes in the other, and vice versa, in a dynamic process of "mutual constitution" (Mosco, 2009).

This is very much the position that we adopt, and we submit that it helps to position social and economic relationships of "integration and contradiction" that drive change, including the digital revolution. Base and superstructure are not architectural forms or rigid categories, which, as Raymond Williams (1980) rightly argues, would constitute a "dead end" if used as a framework for studying the "economics of modern cultural activity" (p. 35). In the same vein, Williams argues that the concept of superstructure must be "revalued" away from "a reflected, reproduced or specifically dependent content," and towards "a related range of cultural practices" (p. 34). For Williams and for the Marxist tradition of political economy today, the base/superstructure metaphor can be summarized in the famous aphorism "being determines consciousness" (p. 35). This identifies its "materialism." It recalls the Marxian standpoint (quoted earlier) that we make ourselves through our labour. In this sense, according to Williams, to talk about base is to talk about "the primary production of society itself . . . the material production and reproduction of real life" (ibid.).

Hegemony and Communicative Practice

To say that the social, economic, and political are mutually constituted is to eschew the either/or determinist view to emphasize that it is the relationships between them that is important. Attention to the process of the commodification of communication identifies the process primarily in the realm of the economic because it is an element of the circulation, accumulation, and distribution of value in a capitalist economy. This point is further illustrated by the importance of communication and ICTs in the international division of labour that marks a process of **globalization**. As Mosco (1996) points out, for example, ICTs and the communication process help capital to manage international operations, to respond to changing market conditions, and to "overcome space and time constraints" (p. 95) in order to maximize control over the international value chain of production, distribution, marketing, and consumption as a process of "spatialization" (covered in Chapter 3). However, this doesn't happen purely for economic reasons. Political and social elements (such as the state, international organizations, educational institutions, and social movements, etc.) are also involved in varying degrees regarding decisions on trade regulations, procurement, content, use, and development, which in turn depend on the time period, location, and other factors.

For a political economy of communication, prioritizing globalization then includes the question of how media and communicative practices relate to and exist within political and other social structures (see Artz & Kamilipour 2003). To help answer this, Raymond Williams (1980) refers us back to the notion of **hegemony**: the laws, constitutions, theories, ideologies, and social institutions that express and ratify the domination of a particular class (pp. 36–7). *Hegemony* is a term brought into the discourse of political economy by scholars who read and absorbed the writing of Italian journalist and Marxist theoretician Antonio Gramsci (1891–1937). In Gramscian terms, *hegemony* refers to the active process of a dominant social class winning the support of subordinate classes for its continued rule. *Hegemony* implies that the subordinate classes in a sense *agree* to be governed by a class whose interests are in reality opposed to their own. Gramsci pondered why anyone would willingly consent to exploitation under capitalism, whatever the political system, especially as he was writing under a developing fascism that embraced and facilitated the growth of capitalism. Gramsci was imprisoned for promulgating his views and wrote extensively, under repressive conditions from the inside of an Italian prison in the 1920s, on how popular literature, education, the legal system, and the links between Church and State all contributed to the process of manufacturing consent (Forgacs, 2000; Forgacs & Nowell-Smith, 1985). Hegemony points to the political power of ideological memes to normalize the dominant economic and social interests of the ruling class as "common sense" thinking and as "active forms of experience and consciousness" that seem to apply to all people (R. Williams, 1989, p. 145).

Hegemony disguises (or obfuscates) the existing underlying social inequalities that characterize class-structured societies, and it is legitimized through the prestige attached to the professional intellectuals and the institutions that embody the dominant social relations (Holub, 1992, p. 25). Hegemony thus occurs when the subordinate class *internalizes* the mental structures and routine practices favoured and circulated by the ruling elite in an ongoing and dynamic process. Identifying this in terms of culture, Raymond Williams (1980) observed that there is a "continual making and remaking of an effective dominant culture," but a dominant culture that can tolerate (within limits) "alternative meanings and values" that are at times incorporated, and at others left alone (p. 39). In a general sense, then, hegemony refers to dominant ways of thinking and doing (underpinning a mode of production like capitalism), which, when repeated often and consistently enough, are accepted as "normal," as just the "way it is" (and thus more difficult to change). Hegemony is thus not exclusive to just social class, but is helpful in identifying and explaining how dominance in all its forms (sexism, racism, nationalism, e.g.) is legitimized and connected to political economy.

Since hegemony involves contest, it is not all-encompassing, and thus, as Gramsci and his followers argue, it is open to contestation. Raymond Williams (1980) suggests that the concept of hegemony allows for "variation and contradiction," "alternatives and its processes of change"

GLOBALIZATION

As an idea used in economics, the notion that economic development proceeds best on the basis of a single worldwide market that sources materials and labour from anywhere in the world at the lowest possible cost. As a process, it refers to the ongoing restructuring of corporations, governments and other institutions to facilitate market integration on a worldwide scale.

HEGEMONY

A term developed by Antonio Gramsci to explain domination of one social class by another. Gramsci sought to understand how social domination occurs through contest involving both coercion (intimidation, threat, withholding of resources, job loss, or violence) and consent (agreement, compromise, or apathy).

For Real?

Labour Exploitation in Canada?

Hegemonic ideas and practices can become so dominant and powerful (via circulation, repetition, and legitimation) that they are left unquestioned and unchallenged to the extent that they seem to be just a matter of "common sense." When it comes to labour exploitation, the history of capitalist hegemony indicates that it can adjust to suit the times. The social invention of race as a category to differentiate, divide, and create hierarchies between humans based on skin colour was used to justify continuing practices of slavery in Canada until 1833, when the British Parliament abolished it as a result of the activism of the anti-slavery and Abolitionist movements (Slavery, Abolition and Social Justice Archives, 2013; 🖥 www.slavery.amdigital.co.uk). In the beginning of the Industrial Revolution (and earlier), in England for example, it was also considered common to think of children as labourers and to put them to work as early as seven years old (Kealey, 1973). This "common sense" was transferred to Canada where, on one hand, children were used and exploited in industrial factories to keep labour cheap (for the owners), whereas on the other, their employment was evidence of the threat to existing adult workers as competition to drive wages and (any thoughts of) "benefits" (health or safety, e.g.) to the background. It wasn't until the early twentieth century, when there was a counter-hegemonic movement (via social activism through governments and labour unions), that there was enough public pressure to outlaw child labour in Canada (Parr, 1980).

Even though these practices have been outlawed, hegemony continues to work through many kinds of memes and vectors. It can ignore, adapt, or compromise on a number of different levels ranging from the extreme to the apparently benign. In the extreme cases, the practices of slavery (forced labour) and child labour still endure, although they are increasingly harder to ignore as the Kielburger brothers and others try to draw public attention to them (🖥 www.freethechildren. com/, endchildlabor.org/, and www.endmoderndayslavery.ca/). However, we probably don't associate this kind of exploitation (profit-making) with capitalism. We may instead be more aware of the possibility given recent media reports of sensational factory fires in Bangladesh and China that draw our attention to the use of "underage labour" in producing designer fashions for North America (MacKinnon & Strauss, 2013). On a global level, then, we may assume that exploitation only happens in extreme cases, that it must only occur in other "less developed" countries, as practised by a small number of illegal groups or clandestine companies, rather than consider it as a logical outcome of (or at least compatible with) the capitalist system. Closer to home, if we think locally to our own experiences, and acknowledge that exploitation does exist in Canada, we may find consolation by trying to convince ourselves that this is simply a matter of degree; that it only occurs in *some* kinds of jobs, like in food services (the "McJobs"), or in agriculture and fish factories. In the first (international) instance, we may reason that these practices can change, that it's simply a matter of our own choice "to buy or not to buy" (even though this is already a commodified restriction). In the second instance, we may think that the low-paying service jobs are just temporary stepping stones for "moving up the ladder" (an acquiesced legitimization of the class system), or if circumstances allow, we may be otherwise convinced to work for free, in unpaid "internships," or we may embrace precarious work as a "freelancer" or "entrepreneur" (as purported evidence of our independence from exploitation).

Alternately, we may already be convinced that exploitation doesn't exist at all. There are well-publicized examples that suggest you can become the next Bill Gates or Mark Zuckerberg (as long as you adhere to the tenets of capitalism), or perhaps you may realize the dream of becoming the next "star"—a famous singer, dancer, or actor—a real Canadian "idol." The emphasis on competition and glorification of the individual as epitomized by the entrepreneurs and celebrities are hegemonic indicators of success, however, and evidence that the system is working as it should. Indeed, hegemony works best when it promotes via its own examples: capitalism promoting capitalism via private ownership of the means, modes, and content of communication.

When faced with having to sell our own labour power, however, we come face to face with the contradictions of hegemony and the realities of capitalism. For billions upon billions of people, this is the imperative; if we are underemployed, unemployed, or living in poverty, for example, hegemony offers individual explanations: you are just not educated enough, creative or talented or innovative enough, or you just haven't risked enough.

In contrast, collective challenges to capitalism via the development of counter-hegemony through inquiry, criticism, formal, or ad hoc organization are met with the force of dominance. We are told that collective organizations—those that are organized to involve public participation and representation (or the non-consumer)—are benign and outdated, or are massive threats to the all-encompassing economy. Democratically organized, collective organizations—like governments and labour unions—are heavily, and consistently, criticized. When dominant hegemony is "speaking," terms like *big labour* and *big government* are repeated accusations that displace questions of the structural conditions of capitalist power. Unions are demonized as greedy, power-hungry entities that are harmful to the economy and government budgets, and as individuals, we should reject them. Similarly, with big government, capitalism seeks to repurpose government away from the protection of the environment, and public health and welfare, towards securing legislation that favours private property and its protection (through legislation on free trade, reduced labour or environmental laws, tax reduction or tax elimination, e.g.).

Hundreds of years of organizing for the right to public education, health care, reasonable working hours, pay and pensions may be swept away, as recently evident in the move towards financialization in government, and in the move to eliminate unions as challenged by "right to work" legislation already passed in some American states, and in Canada, as promoted by certain federal and provincial political parties. While the aforementioned ongoing practices of forced labour and human trafficking are in critical need of change, this "right to work" legislation should also give us pause to consider the following: Has capitalist hegemony become so powerful that labour exploitation can now be considered a human "right"?

Discussion Questions

1. What are your experiences with the social relations of labour in Canada?

2. How does the concept of social class help to explain labour exploitation (or not)?

3. Search the Internet for media coverage of "right to work" legislation and identify organizations for and against it.
   a) Compare, for example, how your local newspaper, the CBC, or nationally distributed papers such as the *National Post* or *The Globe and Mail* cover the subject. Can you identify what appears to be "common sense" or "normal" in the reports and what is not?
   b) What are the arguments advanced by groups in favour of and in opposition to it?
   c) Why is this legislation and its media coverage important to how we understand our own labour in communication, media, and technology today and in the future?

(p. 38), such as those of alternative media we discuss in Chapter 13. Like other social phenomena, hegemony is constructed with a dialectic at its core; it can be contested, challenged, and even overcome under the right circumstances, such that resistance, opposition, and revolution are possible through the development of a "counter-hegemony" or "popular hegemony" (see Mattelart, 1983, e.g.).

Thus when we consider hegemony, it is important to identify what the structures of domination are (political economic and cultural), as well as the possibility for agency (the ability of humans to challenge, change, or reject domination). It is a central element of political economy of communication to identify the contradictions, gaps, and tolerances that oppositional or counter-hegemonic ideas, practices, and social forces may occupy. In the commercial media, for example, these spaces are the operational results of the dialectic stresses and contradictions that operate within the daily newsbeat and competition for "front page" exposure. Wayne (2003) characterizes this as the news media treating individual stories with a "contradictory amalgam of common sense and good sense, rational critique and ideology" (p. 176). Importantly, this is not a fixed relationship; it is mutable through forces acting on what we might call the *emotional dialectic* of the front page.

To reiterate, in *Keywords*, Raymond Williams (1989) refers to the Gramscian concept of hegemony as both political domination and "a more general predominance . . . a particular way of seeing the world and human nature and relationships" (p. 145). An ideology becomes hegemonic when it gains a certain amount of general acceptance and when it is naturalized as the general emotional attitude of an epoch, and alternatives are, for the most part, precluded. Counter-hegemony is introduced as a social force to be created by an "emergent" (R. Williams, 1980) new class or other social group within the society in which an existing hegemonic elite holds sway. To put this another way, to become hegemonic an ideology must have great mimetic momentum and be able to travel through several key vectors.

Hegemony, Subversion, and Mimetic Mutation

Democracy and freedom will be the theme of every broadcast and editorial. . . . Meanwhile the ruling oligarchy and its highly trained elite of soldiers, policemen, thought-manufacturers and mind-manipulators will quietly run the show as they see fit. (Huxley, 1965b, p. 91)

While Huxley is taking the possibilities to the extreme, this is precisely the process of hegemony. As stated earlier, it is the accepted dominance of a particular set of ideologies that benefit the ruling group, but gives the majority of the ruled the feeling that they are really quite well off. This dominance of one group over another can range from physical coercion (as in Orwell's *Nineteen Eighty-Four*) to control over the circulation and promulgation of compatible ideas or ideology (as in Huxley's *Brave New World*). We can also think of hegemony as what Edward Herman and Noam Chomsky (1988), in the classic text on the political economy of the mass media, called the "manufacturing of consent." In this sense, the concept of hegemony has two elements:

- the use of coercion by the "predominant economic group" through the institutions and the "state apparatuses of political society" in order to maintain its rule (via restricting access to resources or alternately using military or police force); and
- the use of the "microstructures of the practices of everyday life" to produce (manufacture) the consent of the subordinate group (Holub, 1992, p. 6), or how human communication is mediated, for example.

Marx and Engels (1973) invoke a very straightforward indication of hegemony when they talk about the rule of one class over another: "What else does the history of ideas prove, than that intellectual production changes its character in proportion as material production is changed. The ruling ideas of each age have ever been the ideas of its ruling class" (p. 72).

Importantly, this is not a fixed relationship; it is mutable through forces acting on the emotional dialectic. In a sense an emergent or oppositional dialectic is "counter-hegemonic" and can "pull" ideologies in contradictory directions.

To understand how hegemony can be a shifting set of relationships, we take our cues from Daniel Hallin's (1989) allied concept of *consensus, limited controversy*, and *deviance*. We find Hallin's work useful because it allows us entry to a discussion of dominant ideologies without having to refer too often to arcane language and sources. It is also useful to us because it is directly about the role of the media in spreading dominant, emergent, or subversive memes of ideology. Our explanation is more expansive than Hallin's, taking in the concept of memes and linking it explicitly to the process of the emotional dialectic.

Hallin's concept of spheres of consensus, limited controversy, and deviance was developed to help him explain why the American commercial media seemed to turn on its government over the conduct of the war in Vietnam in the 1960s and 1970s. In his example Hallin is talking about television journalism and the US political system, but the idea fits ideology more generally. He describes each of the spheres in the following terms:

> *Consensus: At the centre is the sphere of consensus, the region of "motherhood and apple pie" and taking in the ideas that are not regarded "by the journalists and most of society as controversial."*

> *Limited controversy: The sphere of limited controversy lies just beyond the boundaries of consensus. For journalists this is the "province of objectivity"; for Western liberal-democratic society it is "the region of electoral contests and legislative debate . . . defined primarily by the two-party system . . . as well as by the decision-making process in the bureaucracies and the executive branch" of government.*

> *Deviance: This lies outside the sphere of limited controversy and is the realm inhabited by "political actors and views which journalists and the political mainstream of the society reject as unworthy of being heard." (Hallin, 1989, pp. 116–17)*

Thus hegemonic ideas exist in the sphere of consensus and also dominate the sphere of limited controversy. Many counter-hegemonic ideas begin life in the sphere of so-called deviance and migrate into the sphere of consensus through a combination of mimetic mutation and social struggle. A good example is Gay Liberation. Until the 1960s the idea that homosexual men and women could be accepted in mainstream society was totally abhorrent to most heterosexual people. The famous "Stonewall" riots in New York began to change all that when gay men and their supporters fought back against police repression of their nightclubs.

Other counter-hegemonic ideas—such as thinking of human nature as socially collective and peaceful rather than competitive and warring, prioritizing the public sharing of resources versus increasing private ownership, and revolutionizing the economic system so that it is entirely not-for-profit—remain in the sphere of deviance. If you think of these ideas as "radical," perhaps only associated with "activists," or if you view activism and the expression of dissent through public protests or demonstrations as perhaps deviant, threatening, or violent, then you are experiencing

Case Study

From Marginalized to Mainstream? Media and Gender

In Canada and elsewhere, gays and lesbians continually battle with dominant hegemonic gender norms. In the 1970s a group got together in Toronto to publish a gay press that was later named the Pink Triangle Press. The name and the founding of the press were meant to make a political economic statement and a historical reminder of what extremes dominant ideology and hegemony can be taken to. The name was drawn from the colour and symbol that gays and lesbians were forced to wear as identifiers in the concentration camps under Nazi Germany (www.joerg-hutter.de/auschwitz.htm#). While we may be more familiar with the yellow star that all Jewish people were forced to wear (not only in the camps, but in cities and towns all over Europe), people identified as gays or lesbians, Jehovah's Witnesses, or political prisoners (socialists and communists), along with other nationalities (particularly Russians and Poles), were also marginalized, interned, dehumanized, and exterminated.

In establishing the Pink Triangle Press the founders made another decision to counter dominant hegemony. They "chose to make a statement" by establishing the press as a non-profit company; the management thereof would be equally shared, and not according to a dominant hierarchy (to avoid competition and rank between its members, and so that all could contribute to decision-making and content; www.pinktrianglepress.com/history.asp?id=1&stid=4). The press has had several legal challenges in its decision to publish "controversial" material, and the gay community in Canada has faced harassment and discrimination over time, including the Toronto bathhouse raids in 1981 to the more recent debates at Toronto City Hall over the cancellation of public funding for the Gay Pride Parade. Although gays, lesbians, bisexuals, transgenders, and queers (GLBTQ) should have the same rights of citizenship as anyone else, equal treatment under the law is not complete. While the federal government of Canada finally legalized same-sex marriage in the Civil Marriage Act (2005), in the United States, the Defense of Marriage Act (1996) supported by opponents of gay marriage disallowed the federal government from making a ruling that applied to all states (www.lectlaw.com/files/leg23.htm). Individual states thus pass their own laws on marriage, and as of April 2013, only nine of the 50 states have done so, indicating the extent of social struggle and hegemonic battles still ahead. This seems unusual when the American commercial media and advertising companies seem to be more progressive in the acceptance of GLBTQ than the legal record suggests.

Discussion Questions

1. Can you identify some examples of television sitcoms, movies, or advertising that represent people who do not identify as heterosexual?

2. What do these representations suggest a "gay" person is? What stereotypes can you observe? What kind of gender relations appear as hegemonic and counter-hegemonic? Is "gay" a lifestyle, or is it natural?

3. Now compare these representations to those found on the publication of the Pink Triangle Press called *Xtra!* (www.pinktrianglepress.com/). What stereotypes can you observe? What kind of gender relations appear as hegemonic and counter-hegemonic? Is "gay" a lifestyle, or is it natural?

4. What do you think media ownership, its goals, and its organization have to do with content?

hegemonic struggle. One need only to recall the excessive security and reaction of the Royal Canadian Mounted Police (RCMP) in the G-20 summit in Toronto in 2010 to see how the exercise of democratic principles such as protest is considered threatening, and forcibly controlled by power. While the protest was hijacked by a small minority of anarchists bent on the purposeful destruction of private property (as both a practice and symbol of capitalism), people physically present on the public streets near the G-20 were treated as if they were dangerous terrorists.

This begs the question, then, as to how some practices and processes become repeated, circulated, and legitimized, while others are demonized and negated. When you think of information and communication technology, for example, do you think of politics, activism, and protest? Is ICT something benign or inert, a tool or "thing," or heavily weighted with negative or positive connotations? What do you think of when you think of media technologies like television or the Internet?

Examining our assumptions is one of the ways that we can apprehend the "common sense" ideologies that we have become accustomed to and begin to understand how hegemony is constructed and how it works. For example, two now common phrases in technology and media studies are that "the medium is the message" and that we live in a "global village." These memes from Canadian media theorist Marshall McLuhan offer some insight into additional ways to think of media and technology that differ from the Marxian analysis discussed so far, and provide areas of contrast and clarification.

The concept of the "global village" is one that has generated over seven million hits on Google, for example. McLuhan's fascination with communication technologies—he saw them as either an "extension" to or an "amputation" from the human body—prefigures a lot of the hype about so-called "virtual reality" that inspired the denizens of Cyberia in the 1980s. His work continues to propel thinking that technology is the primary, if not *the* determining, factor of the "new consciousness" of our times since the use and development of technology requires "greater collaboration (both economic and cultural, both equitable and imperialistic)" (Marchessault, 2005, p. xiii). This is not dissimilar to what has been discussed thus far in this book in terms of the contradictions of the use and development of technology—both equitable and imperialistic—with the argument being that the latter is made more powerful through the increasing use of surveillance. What is dissimilar, however, is the extent of agency (independence and power) that the technology itself is being given here. If technology has a life of its own, and it determines our consciousness, what happens to all the labour that went into it? And what agency is left for human beings? With this in mind, in the next chapter we turn our attention to questions about technology. What is it? How do we use it? Where does it fit in to our political economy of communication?

Key Points

- A political economy approach gives focus to questions of ownership and control of the means and mode of communication because of their public use value.

- Technology and media are outcomes of complex historical conditions, which explain how they are constructed as commodities for production and consumption under capitalism.

- Labour and the notion of "production" is central in a political economy approach to communication, media, and technology.

- Karl Marx and other theorists of political economy have contributed significantly to our understanding of communication and technology.

- The concepts of value, capital, and hegemony, and the process of commodification, are key to explaining the history and development of communication and technology.

Class Discussion

1. Identify what elements of a political economic approach could be used to compare the mandates and programming of CTV and CBC, for example.

2. Why is labour so central to Marxian analysis and to a political economy of communication?

3. What is social class? Identify a number of ways social class is represented in media as news or entertainment (e.g., as poverty, homelessness, or "elites"). How do these terms invoke or deflect a focus on social class?

4. What is hegemony? Provide some examples of what appears to be common sense when thinking about technological change.

Media on Media

Tune-In on Commodification

Frank Zappa. (1973). I'm the slime. Warner Brothers. ◼ www.lyricsfreak.com/f/frank+zappa/im+the+slime_20057165.html

Reel Big Fish. (1996). Sell out. *Turn the Radio Off*. Mojo Records. ◼ www.azlyrics.com/lyrics/reelbigfish/sellout.html

Rolling Stones. (1965). Satisfaction. *Out of Our Heads*. ABKCO Records. ◼ www.metrolyrics.com/satisfaction-lyrics-rolling-stones.html

The Smiths. (1987). Paint a vulgar picture. *Strangeways, Here We Come*. London, UK: Rough Trade. ◼ www.lyricsdepot.com/the-smiths/paint-a-vulgar-picture.html

DVDs and Videos

Media Education Foundation. (Producer). (2005). *Class dismissed: How TV frames the working class*.

Media Education Foundation. (Producer). (2008). *Consuming kids: The commercialization of childhood* [Documentary].

National Film Board. (Producer). (2008). *Rip! A remix manifesto* [Documentary].

3

Contextualizing Technology: Convergence and Contradictions

Objectives

This chapter opens our discussion of the technologies of broadcast communication and the ways in which they are morphing into the means of narrowcasting. After reading this chapter your understanding of our political economy approach should be deepened as we show, by example, how it can be used to understand and investigate the history of technological change and convergence. In this chapter we hope to explain how economic forces interact in a process of combined and uneven development (the process of the dialectic) to drive both technological change and our social adaptation to that change process.

Our main objective here is to outline how new technologies are introduced into society, not as an abstract and external force, but as a direct result of the social history of communication needs, development, and exigencies of production and consumption. In particular, we examine the following ideas and arguments:

- the contradiction, expressed through the dialectic, between the forms of technology and the social relations that govern their application;

- how the actions of human beings, using and developing technology to interact with and alter the natural world, are the key determinants of both the present and the future;

- how throughout history it has been human agency—people socially interacting with new ideas and technologies—not the technologies themselves, that has been decisive in forcing the pace;

- how technology is not just an inert or neutral device, but rather a complex interaction of ideas (knowledge) and objects (tools) that exist and function in social-historical contexts; and

- how the social relations of ownership and control that define a mode of production are perhaps more important than technology in shaping our future.

Keywords

- capitalism
- commodity fetishism
- converge
- convergence
- horizontal integration
- means of production
- relations of production
- spatialization
- technological obsolescence
- technology
- vertical integration

What Is Technology?

Technology . . . the knack of so arranging the world that we need not experience it.
(Max Frisch, Homo Faber, *1957, as cited in Partington, 1997, p. 146)*

This is a fairly cynical view of **technology** and one that, at first glance, doesn't seem wholly accurate. But it does leave us with questions considering its validity. A person with Frisch's disposition today might argue that the development of virtual realities and sensory devices that can simulate "real" experiences in the brain take us away from experiencing the world itself. We know that our view of the world is mediated by technology and partly shaped, if not distorted by, commercial media today. But, what do we mean by "the world itself"? In short, the world we inhabit is both a natural and a social environment. Technologies mediate our interactions with nature and, increasingly, our interactions with each other. As you will remember from our arguments in previous chapters, we see the world as a material reality that exists whether we have words for it or not; it can be apprehended through our senses and the natural environment that concurrently affirm and allow our survival (via the air, water, and sunlight necessary for all life). The development of technologies over tens of thousands of years of human labour—involving a **convergence** of thought, experimentation, resources, and knowledge—takes place within the social environment. This social world increases in complexity as successive generations build on historical knowledge and imagine new ways of doing things—new ways of interacting with nature.

A concrete example of new ways of interacting with nature is the manipulation and modification of the basic building blocks of all living matter: the short, almost invisible, strings of sugar, carbon, and acid of the DNA double helix that make up our genetic coding. Evolution is the long process of organisms changing through their interaction with the physical environment, and so genetic mutation is a natural thing. Today the social environment (which includes technologies) is such that there is sufficient knowledge and the means to push genetic mutation at much higher speeds through what is called "biotechnology." Unfortunately, we see examples every day that indicate our control over this process is incomplete and fraught with danger.

While the basic building blocks of life may be known, the infinite ways that these blocks can interact is not, and since the building blocks are essential, genetic engineers are literally experimenting with life (■ www.genewatch.org). There are several examples in Canada that illustrate the hazards of commercial experiments released into the natural environment (Greenpeace, 2013), and while the *use value* of biotechnology is subject to much debate (e.g., Canada is one of the highest producers of genetically modified food, and its exports have been banned in many countries [Greenpeace, 2010]; ■ www.gmwatch.org), it is only part of the controversy and risk. Another has to do with the *exchange value*, as some of the engineered combinations are *patented*—providing for private ownership of a gene sequence. The ramifications of this ownership are significant, as an article in the *Canadian Medical Association Journal* explains:

> *In general, genetic patenting issues mirror those associated with commercialization of research. Effort is placed disproportionately on discoveries that would maximize profits to the inventor, by targeting large, potentially lucrative markets, rather than on discoveries that would maximize benefit to society. This exacerbates existing disparities in the availability of treatments across socioeconomic and ethnic groups within countries and between developed and developing countries. (Willison & MacLeod, 2002, pp. 260–61)*

TECHNOLOGY

(1) An object, or system of connected objects, that can be used in a productive process to provide a practical solution to a problem. (2) A process of incorporating knowledge into the production process; in capitalist systems this takes a distinct commodity form.

CONVERGENCE

Can be used to identify the bringing together of any number of phenomenon (technological, political, economic, and social); it proceeds dialectically via a series of contradictions among and between phenomenon.

The tendency for the corporate concentration of ownership in media discussed earlier is being repeated in biotechnology, as its exchange value is prioritized—it is commercialized and turned into an industry—rather than its use value—as a public good. While it may not currently matter to you whether Disney owns Marvel Comic Books, or Microsoft owns the operating system of your computer, ownership of genetic sequencing, and biotechnology in general, is a matter of life and death, as private control is extended over both the modes and the means of life whether in terms of diseases (like drugs for cancer or AIDS) or in terms of growing new life (via cloning or stem cells). So few major corporations own the patents and control biotechnology in Canada (and worldwide) that Willison and MacLeod (2002) warn of the potential of corporations to abuse "monopoly power" and thus highlight the need for government regulation (pp. 261–2), which includes increased public awareness and informed decision-making

If this is beyond what you thought of as technology, it is perhaps best to try again with a basic definition, one that might give us a sense of what we know of technology ourselves. Here's one from the *Collins* dictionary that defines it within **capitalism**:

> *technology n. 1. the application of practical or mechanical sciences to industry or commerce. (Hanks, 1990, p. 1338)*

But that's only the first entry on technology; the second and third definitions are about technology as "the methods, theory and practices" relating to such applications and "the total knowledge and skills available to any human society" (p. 1338). There's no getting away from it. Our definition of technology must have room for the idea that it embodies the skill and the labour of human beings and our ability to harness and shape aspects of the material world into things that are useful to us and the global environment.

On another part of the definitional spectrum, *Roget's Thesaurus* (Roget, 1979) uses the noun form of *technology* as a possible synonym for *skill* (p. 252). This is an interesting proposition. For example, "Have we got the skill to do the job?" is often a subtext in the question "Have we got the technology to do that?" Implicit in any definition of technology is an appreciation of the skill of those who have imagined, created, and explained how it will work, and those who have shaped it to suit our human purposes. This meaning is also present in the definition offered by the Penguin edition of the *Macquarie Dictionary*:

> *technology: n. the branch of knowledge that deals with science and engineering, or its practice, as applied to industry; applied science. (Delbridge, 1990, p. 645)*

There's technology and there's also alternative technology, defined as follows in the *Oxford Dictionary of New Words*:

> *alternative technology: n. technology deliberately designed to conserve natural resources and avoid harm to the environment, especially by harnessing renewable energy resources. (Tulloch, 1992, p. 14)*

There's another entry in the *Macquarie* that has the same roots as *technology*. The word is *technocracy*, and it has a decidedly Orwellian tone to it:

> *technocracy: n. [the] theory and movement advocating control of industrial resources and reorganisation of the social system based on the findings of technologists and engineers. (Delbridge, 1990, p. 645)*

CAPITALISM
An economic system depending on private ownership of the means of production (capital) and the private accumulation of profits. Capitalist ideology is based on the idea that an unfettered free market is the best way to deliver increased wealth and prosperity for all. The operation of capitalist systems is often characterized by monopoly, oligopoly, and plutocracy; free or wage labour; hyper-consumerism; globalization; and crisis. Capitalism is a class-based system in which two contending classes (labour and capital) are engaged in a constant struggle over resources (use value and exchange value) and the distribution of the production surplus (surplus value).

Those in charge of such a system were to be known as *techno*crats, a play on *aristo*crats—the keepers of knowledge and power in feudal times. Interestingly, the *Macquarie* entry notes that technocratic theories and movements were active in the early 1930s, at the time when fascism in Europe was beginning to flex its own technocratic muscles and German manufacturing was being made "efficient" through the gradual reintroduction of slave labour into the economy.

The etymologies (the linguistic roots) of *techno*-related words are easily found in the simple prefix *techno*, which is traceable back to the Greek words *tekhnologia*, meaning systematic treatment, and *tehkne*, or skill (Hanks, 1990, p. 1338). According to Raymond Williams' *Keywords* (1989, pp. 315–16), technology also has a linguistic root in the Latin *technologia*, with a similar meaning to the Greek *tekhnologia*. We can also trace the word as it evolves even further. New meanings are created in language all the time—nuance and inflection added in response to new uses for old things and ideas. Two recent examples are *technophobia*, a fear of technology, and *technoklutz*, someone who has difficulty operating technological devices.

The opposite of technophobe is *technophile*, which describes someone who can find no fault with technology and believes that there is a technological "fix" to just about every problem that humans encounter in their interactions with the material world and with each other. Neil Postman (1993) has some fun satirizing what he sees as the overly optimistic view of technophiles: "They gaze on technology as a lover does on his beloved, seeing it as without blemish and entertaining no apprehension for the future. They are therefore dangerous and to be approached cautiously" (p. 5). Another modern word from the same roots is *technobabble*:

> *technobabble*: n. *jargon or gobbledegook that is characteristic . . . of computing and other high technology areas . . . [sounding] like so much nonsense to those who are not "in the know." (Tulloch, 1992, p. 22)*

There's also the pure *techno* now attached to a style of urban music and its subgenres: *techno-funk*, *techno-fusion*, *techno-pop*, and so on. The common factor according to Sara Tulloch (1992) is "making heavy use of technology (such as synthesised and sampled sounds, electronic effects) . . . a synthesised, technological sound and a dance beat" (p. 284).

One more *techno* word we came across also deserves a short mention: *technopath*. This appeared in Indra Sinha's *The Cybergypsies*, an interesting story of the author's engagement with some of the first inhabitants of the cyberworld; Sinha (1999) uses the term to describe the computer-savvy generators, collectors, and launchers of Internet viruses with "links to every major partisan group in the virus underground." The implications are clear from the root of the second part of the word: A techno*path* is someone who displays pathological (antisocial) behaviour in the same way as a sociopath displays behaviour that indicates a disregard for the "normal" rules of a given society. The technopaths are "the people who write cancerous code and send it out into the world to mutate other people's data" (pp. 2–4). They have little or no regard for the social rules of the cyberworld. Sinha also describes other technopaths who enter large multiplayer game sites. This group likes to randomly and violently kill other characters in the game. Not very sociable at all! Technopaths may also exhibit antisocial (or at least anti-establishment) behaviour in their real-world relationships, too.

There's no doubt that many people would consider hackers to be technopaths, and governments worldwide are investing increasing amounts of public money to combat the practice and reduce the possibility. In 1999 a four-star general became the first American chief of cyberdefence (Schwartau, 2000, p. 21), and Canada and the United States have signed related international agreements on "cybercrime" (Parliament of Canada, 2011). Currently, the US military spends more than $1.5 billion a year to defend against hacking attacks and is looking to expand its "cybersecurity program" to the tune of $23 billion over the next five years (to 2018) (Press TV, 2013). As we discuss in later chapters, the bigger the system, the more reliant and interdependent governments and corporations become, and the more "protection" the system requires in a never-ending cycle.

The practice of hacking has less spectacular origins. The first technopath-hackers were the "phone phreaks" of the 1970s who discovered that they could use simple computers to hack into the US phone system. "Just by sending tone down the line, nothing else, it was possible to take total control of the internal network of the telephone company—for free—and call anywhere an operator can" (Draper, 2000, p. xiv). The purpose of hacking varies according to intent; where the phone phreaks wanted to make communication free, others were interested in making money on its by-products. Technology journalists Katie Hafner and John Markoff (1991) tell the stories of three pioneer hackers and their "gangs" in *Cyberpunk: Outlaws and Hackers on the Computer Frontier*. The stories they relate are of the hacker underground in the late 1980s, which was working on the fringe of what was considered legal and ethical. Hackers were making money "buying, selling and stealing information" (Hafner & Markoff, 1991, p. 9). As we discuss in Chapters 11 and 12, in the emerging surveillance economy, this lucrative trade is now reserved for data collection by corporations, and has been legitimized by weak privacy laws and international protocols. The same technology used by the early hackers—albeit with more sophistication built in—now feeds a global industry worth billions of dollars (O'Harrow, 2005). The technology has been harnessed to the emergent digital mode of development to create a new profitable niche in the global media economy.

So far we've been looking at technology almost as a way of being or thinking and the practice of doing things with this technical knowledge. One element that's missing from our definitions so far is any concept of technology as a "thing" itself—technology viewable as an everyday object with a physical form. Tulloch's (1992) definition comes closest with the reference to using technology to create techno music (p. 284). In this context we can see how the concept of technology as *tool* or *instrument* begins to form. The technology *is* the synthesizer. Techno music became popular in the mid-1980s when, for the first time, smaller and more powerful synthesizers became available to musicians. The keyboard interface and array of mixing channels combined elements of the piano and the studio "desk," allowing musicians to experiment with a wider variety of "sounds" and effects. Techno music is its own genre complete with the growth in music-based social networks to share and develop it.

It is easy to see an electronic musical instrument as a *piece* of technology, but what do we say about a bus, a washing machine, a tractor, or a personal computer? In what ways do these things represent or embody technology? Each of them assists us with a daily task in our lives: a means of getting somewhere (public transport), meeting a personal need (clean clothing), finishing a job (ploughing a field), or communicating with colleagues and friends (sending and receiving email)—or doing practically anything else in our lives that has a use value.

Now that we've gotten this far, let's pose a question: What is technology considered to be today? All of us are aware of it in the world—it is everywhere. "New" technology is emerging almost weekly. Can a state-of-the-art cell phone be considered a *piece* of technology, or the result of the *process* of technology?

To consider this question we have to explore the following propositions:

- Technology involves the application of knowledge to act upon the world in a systematic way through the human labour process using the tools and raw materials available under existing social conditions.

- Technology is based on specialist practices, for example engineering, and is organized to accomplish big, monumental tasks.
- As a set of practices and as a way of organizing and harnessing "knowledge," technology is also a set of social relations. This includes aspects of how it is distributed and controlled; how it is managed, produced, and consumed; where it has the most impact; and questions of whether it adds to, or detracts from, the well-being of humans and the environment.
- Technology is most often the application of scientific methods in an industrial or commercial business context. This is promoted as common sense when we look at the world of technology that surrounds us: We all use technology in a variety of formats and contexts every day whether by choice or necessity.
- Technology has the appearance, most of the time, of an object, a piece of equipment, a tool, or an instrument.
- Today we most often come across technologies in the form of consumer goods (from cars to MP3 phones); we are also confronted with technology in our homes, classrooms, and workplaces.
- Encouraged to consume endlessly, we tend to see technology as a positive infrastructure of objects and processes that can enrich our leisure time, as well as make our work easier, cleaner, and more enjoyable.
- All of this enthusiasm for "new" technology is closely linked to what is popularly known as the "information revolution."

Many commentators in the popular media, and a number of communications scholars, place the physical manifestations of technology at the forefront of their analysis of what is now commonly called the "information" or "knowledge" economy *and* society. As we argue later, both prefixes prioritize and support a technologically determinist argument, but it's an incomplete picture of the world. To understand the new digital technologies and the attendant process of convergence, we must also investigate the social relations surrounding, and in many ways shaping, the digital revolution.

In an everyday sense, we often define technology as an object, or system of connected objects, that can be used in a productive process to give a practical solution to a problem. Given this definition, a technology can be something as simple as a stone axe or even a branch of a tree used for leverage.

On a more theoretical level, technology is also a process of thinking and design, involving a range of problem-solving skills that we normally associate with science. However, as the *Collins Dictionary* definition reminds us, this form of technology is often applied in the context of industry and commerce (Hanks, 1990, p. 1338); that is, it is linked to a definite set of social relationships that signify a particular historical epoch. Was there technology before the historical period of industry and commerce? Of course there was. We might consider it to have been primitive technology, but every human society must harness its available resources (including knowledge and technology) in order to survive and benefit from our physical and symbiotic interaction with the natural world.

Technology and Society

By combining twentieth-century computer technology with nineteenth-century time-and-motion studies, the McDonald's corporation has broken the jobs of griddleman, waitress, cashier and even manager down into small, simple steps. (Garson, 1988, p. 37)

This small example of how the giant American fast-food chain McDonald's was able to insert new technology into its rigid division of labour illustrates the process of the dialectic—combined and uneven development—within the economic confines of the capitalist mode of production. The use of such labour-saving devices and processes in the workplace is one important aspect of the relationship between technology and the social system. The debate about the relationship between technology and the broader society makes an excellent starting point from which the developing issues of media convergence can be examined. Technology does not exist in a social vacuum. The rate of inventiveness in a society is in direct proportion to its level of social development. A degree of social cooperation is necessary to use even simple tools for everyday jobs (K. Marx, 1867/1990, p. 452). Hunter-gatherer societies could invent the technology of simple tools for farming or animal husbandry only when they had reached a certain size and level of linguistic and social integration. But no one would suggest for a minute that such primitive social organization could have produced the internal combustion engine, aeroplanes, space travel, or a microchip the size of a grain of sand (ABC News Online, 2006).

The more complex human society becomes, the more technology is developed to provide humans with their "instruments of labour." Karl Marx (1867/1990) wrote, "it is not what is made, but how and by what instruments of labour, that distinguishes different economic epochs" (p. 286). For example, it is not the use of coal per se that determined progress in the Industrial Revolution, but rather improvements in how the coal was mined, transported, crushed, and burnt, thus creating new applications for coal-fired technologies. The rapidly developing smelting technologies of the massive iron and steel blast furnaces of the nineteenth century required more efficient production of ever-greater amounts of coal. The general advance in production processes, science, and technology during the Industrial Revolution was so widespread because the social logics of the mode of production—capitalism—demanded that everyone keep up or be swallowed up by the juggernaut of "progress." This logic has been maintained in spite of the evidence of pollution, environmental destruction, and increasing rates of cancer and death among coal miners and industrial workers. Following Marx, political economists argue that technological change is cumulative, but always under the influence of the prevailing social conditions that determine how the necessities and luxuries of human existence are produced, distributed, and consumed.

Marx made a further intriguing observation about the complex and contradictory relationship between society and its instruments of labour. He noted that without the application of human labour power, the tools themselves would lie idle: "The use and construction of certain instruments of labour . . . [are] characteristic of the specifically human labour-process . . . an appropriation of what exists in nature for the requirements of man" (Marx, 1867/1990, pp. 286–90). Unless you are aware of the physical remains of industrial waste sites, abandoned factories, and vast tracks of what are called "rust belts" in North America (High, 2003), you might dispute this today when it appears that full automation of production is not only possible but also likely in the very near future. But of one thing Marx was very certain: No new social value can be created only by machine labour (technology). Economic value is determined by the expenditure of human labour power—whether labouring for production or consumption—always in its social context.

In the second volume of *Capital*, Marx (1884/1990) took his arguments about social relations one step further by writing that it was the process of interaction between the **means of production** and the **relations of production** that created the most tension and exposed the biggest contradictions in any given society. That is why Trevor Barr (2000), writing about the new technology of the information revolution, can highlight the obvious "paradox"

MEANS OF PRODUCTION

An ensemble of the available technologies and natural resources that are combined with human labour (collectively, the means) and within historically specific forms of social relations (such as social class, gender, and race and ethnicity), which are articulated in the organization of work, and of policies and laws regarding labour, to form what political economists call the mode of production.

RELATIONS OF PRODUCTION

The social ties that bind together the elements (labour, technology, nature) that constitute a mode of production. The relations of production determine how various technologies and labour processes come together to produce goods and services and to reproduce themselves.

(p. 28) of convergence and divergence in the global information economy. This dialectic takes the form of commercial consolidation (fewer and larger telecommunications giants) and an expansion of the goods and services offered to feed our limitless **commodity fetishism**. Convergence and its side effects are not limited to the digital revolution; it is a constant in the social history of technology.

Technologies and Convergence: A Brief History

Thus civilisation and mechanical progress advanced hand in hand, each developing and being developed by the other, the earliest accidental use of the stick having set the ball rolling, and the prospect of advantage keeping it in motion. (S. Butler, 1872/1967, p. 163)

This is a passage from the fictitious "Book of the Machines," which appears in long tracts in Samuel Butler's (1872/1967) utopian/dystopian story *Erewhon*. Through this story Butler's purpose was to appeal to Victorian England's middle class to abandon the Industrial Revolution. Butler believed that industrial society would eventually lead to humanity being enslaved by machine intelligence. In the utopian society of Erewhon, all machines had been destroyed in an agrarian counter-revolution against industrialization.

The fictional Erewhon was likely based on an earlier reality, as in the beginning of nineteenth-century England, workers in the textile trades soon realized that technologies developed for the cloth industry were designed to deskill and replace their labour. This resulted in increased control of the owners of the machine (the means of production), rather than affording the workers' control over their own production. The social movement that emerged to combat this loss of control was called the Luddite Movement (named after the likely fictional leader Ned Ludd). The movement's meme has been historically and ideologically distorted to refer to anyone against technological change (a variation on technophobia discussed earlier), because in desperation, the Luddites resorted to burning down factories and destroying the machines (Jones, 2006). It wasn't so much the machines that were at issue, but the use of technology to increase ownership control over the labour process. This was exercised via the elimination of human labour, and the division of the existing labour into discrete tasks, which, in effect, reduced the skill required for the job and correspondingly decreased the control that the textile workers had over their own labour.

We mention this here to illustrate the point that the "love–hate" relationship between humans and technology, technology and control, and this way of obfuscating the underlying social relations, has been around for a long time.

In fact, as we suggested in the previous chapter on political economy, the features of any particular mode of production are dialectically fluid over time. It is the mode of production—the specific ways in which labour and technologies of production combine—that determines the overall complexion of any particular society: "The specific manner in which this union is accomplished distinguishes the different economic epochs of the structure of society from one another" (K. Marx, 1884/1990, pp. 36–7).

When we begin to unpack this statement it becomes clear that in any stage of human history, the technologies—the means of production—are constantly developing in ways that seem to correspond to the socially determined needs, ambitions, and values of those groups and individuals who "own" them. As Marx (1894/1990) outlined in *Capital*, the use of machinery was introduced to reduce the labour time necessary for the production of commodities—in other

---

COMMODITY FETISHISM

A concept identified by Marx to describe an aspect of capitalism in which material and immaterial commodified products appear to be in relationship with each other rather than as a product of the social relations of labour.

Case Study

IBM's Watson on *Jeopardy!*

In February 2011, fans of the American game show *Jeopardy!* were witness to three days of a special tournament that brought back two of the game's best players, Ken Jennings and Brad Rutter, to compete against a question-answering computer named "Watson," developed by IBM. At the end of the three days, the computer reigned victorious over the human contestants, despite a number of significant errors along the way. Questions then arose about whether or not this success signalled the future of computing, finally breaking through the barriers of artificial intelligence, long envisioned in science fiction like *2001: A Space Odyssey*, *The Terminator*, and *Star Trek*. The contest was reminiscent of IBM's publicity stunt in the 1990s, when IBM's super computer Deep Blue was pit against chess ace Garry Kasparov (see Figure 3.1). Similarly, the Watson contest was about publicity, but it was also about more direct avenues of business development for the computer company (C. Thompson, 2010).

Source: © ITAR-TASS Photo Agency / Alamy

FIGURE 3.1 | World champion Garry Kasparov during the third match with Deep Blue, the chess computer program, in 1997.

Watson is a very large computer system developed by IBM to attempt to chip away at elemental aspects of artificial intelligence. The system is designed as a question-answering computer, aimed at trying to overcome challenges found in human language to better analyze and collate large amounts of data to reach a correct answer. Watson was developed over a number of years by teams of computer scientists at IBM, and the process involved the human selection and inputting of massive reams of digital information from various sources (the system was not connected to the Internet for the game). Watson made use of various different algorithms simultaneously to respond to questions. For each question, the system would present up to five potential answers, selecting the most likely answer based on probability. The challenge of *Jeopardy!* for the system was how the questions are phrased, often using puns and humour to suggest the correct answer—linguistic practices that computers have traditionally struggled with.

Watson's success over the two champions was less about the game, and more about IBM, and more still about the potential business opportunities for this system moving forward. David Ferrucci, the IBM executive responsible for developing Watson, foresees the use of the technology in medical and other service sectors (e.g., transportation and retail). Ultimately, promoting Watson on a game show was about both raising IBM's profile, again, within the technology sector, as well as signalling a shift in business direction for the company.

Continued

While the interplay between Watson and humans on the game show was entertaining, the whole encounter raises some significant questions about the relationship between technologies and humans. First, the way in which the game show antics proceeded tended to focus on technology as a thing rather than a process. Second, as noted earlier, this determinist approach tends to obscure the substantial amount of human labour that has gone into the development and training of Watson (see C. Thompson, 2010, for more detail on this process). Third, one interesting aspect of the human–technology relationship that emerged through the preparation of Watson for the game show was that test contestants would anthropomorphize the technology, which was promoted by giving it a name, and then ascribing it a male gender (referring to it as "he"), thus humanizing it in a way. Finally, those assessing the impact of Watson's victory on *Jeopardy!* exposed the various ways in which we think about the interplay between technology and human interaction.

There were those who feared that such developments may demonstrate a first step towards the dystopian futures of science fiction (Markoff, 2011), while others (Brynjolfsson & McAfee, 2012) touted its potential for furthering the digital revolution (a meme), and its utopian business potential. It is this business potential that gains the coverage from journalists and piques the attention of financiers; Watson is being used to commodify information in developing the medical and pharmaceutical industry (Upbin, 2013), for example, and IBM is exploring ways to commercialize the "Big Data" Watson collects from a whole range of sources off the Web, as well as from "social network messages, sensor signals, medical images, patent filings, location data from cellphones and others" (Lohr, 2013, para. 4), accumulating an immense collection of information for exchange value.

Discussion Questions

1. How do these different uses and interpretations demonstrate the ongoing technological dialectic at play?

2. Considering how Watson is being used in the health care and pharmaceutical industry, and given our discussion in this book up until now, identify (a) what the use value and the exchange value are in this context, and (b) what kinds of ethical or moral questions arise from this separation.

3. What do you understand as "Big Data"? What are some of the dialectical implications from its collection and use?

words, to increase the productivity of labour (p. 467). Manuel Castells (2000) makes a similar argument about the introduction of digital machines into the production process in the information economy. The motive is an increase in productivity, but not just for its own sake: The ultimate reward for capitalists is "profitability and the growth of their stocks" (Castells, 2000, p. 94; see pp. 77–99). This information requires that our definition of technology include the social relationships—sets of economic, political, and cultural links or influences—that contextualize its history, and constitute its present and its future. The task is not an easy one. It is important to understand that the process of social development—that is, what we think of societies and of history—is a series of contradictions, conflicts, and resolutions. The tool for this job is the philosophical concept of the dialectic. We can now put this term together with our definitions of technology to create a useful analytical concept: the *dialectic of technology*.

The Dialectic of Technology

To come to grips with the role that convergence increasingly plays in our lives today—the so-called "digital revolution"—it is necessary to bring together the dialectic and our definitions of technology. The first step is to explain the concept of technology as a means of production. In plain English this means that technology is first and foremost the physical means—the tools and machinery—with which a society can produce what it needs to survive and prosper. Importantly, tools and machines are not simply the physical instruments of labour; they also embody knowledge and congealed labour—the work that has gone into their development, construction, and deployment.

As we've seen, advances in the technological base of society occur within a complex matrix of social conditions and in turn impact them. The discovery that round objects will roll down a slope led eventually to the technology of the wheel, but it took thousands of years for this simple idea to be literally harnessed to a horse in order to create the cart, or horse-driven buggy. This point of convergence first needed the domestication of wild horses and the development of more complex tools and technologies—the saw, the chisel, and the wood plane; the tanning of leather from animal skins; and the application of the principles of levers. Each of these things could only happen under certain conditions of human existence, each development more complex than the preceding one. On their own, carpentry, the domestication of animals, and the development of simple mechanics enabled the societies that employed them to become more productive. In turn, what they learned from this combination of trial and error (thesis and anti-thesis) could then be used for the further intellectual development necessary to provide the next breakthrough. This is the dialectic of technology in action.

The dialectic of technology is one of the determining influences on the development of the productive forces that takes place within a mode of production. The likelihood of future mutations in the dialectic of technology is ultimately a product of the complex daily interaction and conflict between the social relations of production and the forces of production. The forces of production are not just the physical means of production (human labour power and nature). The forces of production are themselves the engine for a most powerful dialectic: the interaction between human labour power and the natural world and the contradictions that the process of mutual constitution forces to the surface. The dialectic of technology determines how new forms of convergence emerge and are put to use within a mode of production. However, as digital convergence has become one strand of the emerging dialectic of technology in the twenty-first century, it must have its opposite. We have chosen to use the term *fragmentation* to represent divergence as an opposing state to convergence. We examine the process of "fragmentation" in more detail in later chapters. In this section, we will simply say that *fragmentation is the process that produces the phenomenon of narrowcasting* since while technology **converges** in digital media, it can also be managed to separate the people using it.

Applied to the process of commodification and social media, for example, while Facebook is said to bring people together online, it also sells information on the users to advertisers and marketers and makes a profit on both (the time you spend online and the information gathered from you while doing so). Technological convergence can bring *some* people together (those on Facebook) identified under the general heading "users," and narrowcasting is extended when the users' time and information are commodified as "consumers" (extending the fragmentation process as the users are only valued by their attractiveness as a market, rather than as collective citizens, e.g.). In the process, it splits the users into autonomous, individual consumers according to a whole range of categories useful to the marketer (such as age, income, gender, ethnicity, etc.). So while you are "connected" together on Facebook, you become separated as fragments of information. This information (or data) is being monitored, measured, categorized, divided and sold, so that marketing

CONVERGE

To converge means to come together. In the context of communications technologies this means the *coming together* of telecommunications, computing, and broadcasting into one electronic system or field. The key to this modern form of convergence is the microprocessor—the computer chip.

and advertising can be tailor-made to attract and target each individual. More on this in Chapter 6 on the "audience commodity" and in Chapter 12 on surveillance and narrowcasting; for now, it is important to recognize that the process of convergence and divergence is continual; *how* it is managed and structured is the issue to keep in mind as we read through the rest of this chapter.

Another manifestation of the contradiction between technological convergence and market fragmentation is the subjugation of social relations to the relationship between individuals and *things*. As we were drafting this text we were surprised at the number of our friends, colleagues, and students who implicitly understood technology to be defined by common commodity forms—that is, objects in the everyday world around them. For example, we commonly think of a computer or a digital camera as a piece of technology—an object—rather than a set of complex social relations. (And you may have already experienced such hegemony when you try to understand or explain it otherwise!) This objectification of technology serves the purpose of deflecting our attention from the social aspects of the commodity to valuing the object for what it is and does, and what it purportedly says about us (an expression of our personality or social status). As introduced in Chapter 2, Marx called this "commodity fetishism," and he added that within any particular mode of production this would take a particular form. While we may already take it for granted, one of the most recognizable and oldest memes that contains the fetishism of objects, for example, is religious practice centred on the worship of iconic relics and symbols.

The Objectification of Technology

> *Digitization expands the commodification of content by extending opportunities to measure and monitor, package and repackage entertainment and information.* *(Mosco, 2004a, p. 156)*

The digital revolution has extended the commodification of our social, material, and spiritual life even further than industrialism. In fact, political economists argue that our love of commodities is more powerful than religion because commodities have a materiality that "presents itself directly" to our senses more powerfully than religious belief (Mosco, 1996, p. 143). In relation to our love of gadgets—mobile phones, iPods, and so on—we have described this as "technology fetishism," after the Marxist concept of commodity fetishism. Marx (1894/1990) describes commodity fetishism as the way that the actual social relations of a commodity—the fact that it is the product of human labour locked in an unequal dialectic with capital—takes on "the fantastic form of a relation between things," obscuring the social aspects of its production: "I call this the fetishism which attaches itself to the products of labour as soon as they are produced as commodities, and is therefore inseparable from the production of commodities" (p. 165).

This fetishized relationship between consumers and commodities arises because of the process of alienation: The goods produced appear to be independent of the labour that produced them, and they come to the market in the form of things owned by capital, and are offered as readily available for ownership by you (even though you might not be able to afford it). There is no direct exchange between producer and consumer; exchange is mediated by money, transforming the production process into a "complete mystery," and the true value of the commodity is "withdrawn from view" (Marx, 1884/1990, p. 303). Through the global use of money as the medium of exchange, there is "further distortion" of the true relations of production; capital appears as an independent force, "a mere accessory" to the production process: "The fetish character of capital and the representation of this capital fetish is now complete" (Marx, 1867/1990, p. 516). In the digital world of endless consumption and planned obsolescence, this fetishism is transposed onto the technology commodity.

This is most clearly expressed in the positivist versions of the digital society, which in their most extreme form give rise to digital fetishism. The positivist idea is of a benign information society in which the gradual replacement of human labour by machines results in increased leisure time and creativity for the masses. An early guru of this movement in Japan even described it as "Computopia" (Holub, 1992, p. 175). Computopia represented an idealized view of the information society and, according to some critics, became a plank of Japanese economic policy (Castells, 2000; Dyer-Witheford, 1999); as you shall see in later chapters, it still remains central in Canadian policy developments as well. It is this process of fetishizing the products of technology, rather than explaining the process or social relations involved, that generates the "need" for all of us to be electronically up to date—to have the latest mobile phone with the MP3 player and camera built in. It is also one of the dialectics of technology that sees the marketing of this "need" in lock-step with the manufacture of new, bright, shiny, and attractive commodities, such as expensive mobile "lifestyle hubs":

> *If your mobile phone does not boast a one-megapixel camera or an MP3 player, you have a lot of catching up to do. . . . [T]he advances were designed to lead consumers towards a new age in mobile telephony in which handsets become more than communications devices or playthings and are transformed into "lifestyle hubs . . . " able to meet consumers' entertainment needs . . . as well as their financial obligations. (Dudley, 2005)*

This was in 2005; since then, there are a lot more gadgets and "apps" to add to your mobile phone. Back then it was a mobile or cell phone; today, less than a decade later, it could be an iPhone, iPad, iTouch, BlackBerry, or _____? As all of us are too painfully aware, these mobile "lifestyle hubs" create their own financial obligations and prompt for even more upgrades and even more confusing contracts, combining different technological services in "bundles" with a limited number of "providers" such as Bell or Rogers, for example. These bundles are an example of how technological and economic convergence complement each other as one corporation can own and control a wide range of information and communication technologies. At the same time, it is an example of narrowcasting; the phone itself can be tailored to an individual's wants and needs, complete with the tailor-made marketing and advertising that goes with it. It is also fundamental to the surveillance economy, as we discuss in Chapter 11, since the technology that enables the cell phone to connect to the Internet (Wi-Fi) can also be used to identify your exact location, and retailers, for example, can track individual demographics and shopping habits voluntarily (by offering you "deals" for your information), or involuntarily (by calibrating your phone with in-store video cameras to identify your shopping habits, interests, and even physical expressions of your mood; Clifford & Hardy, 2013).

The Economics of Convergence

Commercial Convergence

> *By collating ever more detailed subscriber profiles from individual media product databases, conglomerates are able to track and categorize users, charging premiums for the sale of these groups to advertisers seeking highly specific niche audiences. (Murray, 2005, p. 424)*

Focus on Research

Technological Obsolescence

When we think of the myriad of technological devices we use in our life, from an iPod to a laptop or software, one thing that we seem to grudgingly accept, or perhaps embrace, is the idea that they have a limited lifespan. If we think of the iPhone 5, for example, one of its new features includes a "Lightning Connector" that connects the device to electrical outlets or home computers. Although promoted by Apple as "more durable," it also proved more costly for both consumers and other service and sales businesses. For example, hoteliers, gym owners, and car makers who have outfitted their products and services with facilities for older versions of the iPhone and other Apple devices have to yet again spend a significant amount of money to upgrade to accommodate for the new device (Troianovski, Mattioli, & Ante, 2012).

Alternatively, iPhone consumers will have to purchase new connectors or adapters to make use of the new device with other technologies. Apple is not alone in this practice; software makers like Microsoft often "update" aspects of their popular software, like Office and Windows, making the connections between old and new versions—and the connections between other technologies, like printers—difficult, thus requiring consumers to upgrade, to buy new software or devices that are adaptable. This practice is called built-in obsolescence and is a central element of capitalism. By requiring consumers to have to buy new products and services to stay current, companies like Apple and Microsoft reinforce and build new markets and demands for their products, and then advertise them as the latest "must-haves" in a never-ending cycle of "new."

Renowned Canadian thinker Ursula Franklin drew attention to the contradictions of technology and built-in obsolescence in her research back in the 1990s as explained in her *CBC Massey Lectures* titled "The Real Work of Technology" (Franklin, 2004). The lectures highlighted the important link between this practice and the expansion and growth of capitalism, as well as the many drawbacks of the practice, including the environmental cost of continual changes and "upgrades" given the resultant material waste. This attention to what remains of and endures in media is far less popular a subject of research and study than the infinite allure of the "new" (Acland, 2007). As McGill University communications professor Jonathan Sterne (2007) suggests, the computer industry has managed to reposition itself so that "new" does not refer to "old" media like television, but is in a loop of self-reference, and the resulting focus of research follows in error:

Computers apparently interminable status as a "new" medium speaks to the degree that we, who write about computer technology, have mistaken the "state of the art" in a single communications industry for the ongoing total transformation of the media environment. . . . Where other media industries have certainly found ways to sell new hardware, the digital hardware industry has rationalized, accelerated, and made regular the process of equipment turnover. (p. 19)

Commercial convergence is driven by, and in turn contributes to, trends in digital delivery and content convergence. Simone Murray (2005) calls this "synergistic convergence" (pp. 415–16), and it involves the constant "recycling" of product (content) across all the delivery platforms and communications channels that the media company has control over. This is clearly evident

With advertisers, marketers, and journalists; trade magazines, technology books, trade and marketing shows; and even with academic conferences and writers all focusing attention on the "new," what's left of the "old" is accordingly out of sight and out of mind, but it is not without material consequences. As Sterne (2007) underscores, "obsolescence is a nice word for disposability and waste. . . . The entire edifice of new communication technology is a giant trash heap waiting to happen, a monument to the hubris of computing and the peculiar shape of digital capitalism" (p. 17; see E. Grossman, 2006; see also Paterson & Thurlbeck, 2009, and UBC Graduate School of Journalism, 2009, in the "Media on Media" section at the end of this chapter, e.g.).

Other scholars identify inherent contradictions in **technological obsolescence** by highlighting how technological change and ownership affect all digital products; this includes, for example, copyrighted content. While digital content may appear more easily available through public and university libraries, it comes at a continual financial and informational cost to the public. Decisions made for economic or technological reasons can change the ways in which citizens and students have access to public information, as well as affecting public ownership of digital content and control over technological change (Carnegie & Abell, 2009; Zanish-Belcher & Leigh, 2011).

> **TECHNOLOGICAL OBSOLESCENCE**
>
> The practice of making technology (even though it may still function) outdated, out-of-fashion, useless, or passé—in effect, eradicating its use value.

Expanding on these issues, and extending them to news media, Justin Lewis (2010) addresses how built-in obsolescence is tied to the commodification of news and, in particular, the 24-hour news cycle. He emphasizes that the contemporary practices of seeing news as a commodity in commercial news services like CNN or Fox News that have a primary function of serving the profit motive "impedes public understanding of the world" (J. Lewis, 2010, p. 83). He is contending, then, that within the 24-hour news cycle, disposable news stories cycle through, and thus do not provide citizens with enough information about current events and issues to make the necessary judgements required to be active democratic agents. Thus the practices of technological or built-in obsolescence have become a central element of the digital economy and a central challenge for citizens to navigate and operate.

Discussion Questions

1. What ways do you encounter built-in obsolescence in your everyday life?
2. What materials is your computer made of? Why should it matter?
3. Where does your technology "trash" go? Whose responsibility is it and why?
4. What alternatives or activities can we engage in to avoid built-in obsolescence?
5. What policies or laws are in place to require manufacturers to produce environmentally safe products (including safety in production and disposal) in the computer industry in Canada (see Lepawsky, 2012, e.g.)?
6. Is information ever obsolete?

in the ongoing mergers, takeovers, and buyouts that have characterized the past 25 years of growth and change in the broadly defined creative industries.

There's no doubt that the media and overall economic environment in Canada is in constant flux, and, as we review in the next section of this book, over the last century, this is nothing new. However, Canadian media corporations have pointed to the growth of "competitors" like YouTube (owned by Google), Facebook, and Myspace (owned by News Corp.), together with several "crises"—the dot.com boom and bust (1997–2000) and the economic threat to traditional media in terms of declining advertising—as evidence upon which to justify the growth and consolidation of their own ownership and deflect against any government regulation that is not seen in their interests. As Winseck (2010) argues, such conditions of crisis have not affected the continuing media concentration of Canadian corporations. In fact, the revenue margins in media across a whole range of media forms have proven to be very profitable (see Figure 3.5). For example, while Canada ranks in population size as the 35th largest country in the world (with just over 34 million people, slightly smaller than Poland and Algeria and slightly larger than Sudan or Uganda), in terms of cumulative revenue accrued by the media industry, it ranks among the top ten, with Bell, Rogers, and QMI (Quebecor) among the top five (Winseck, 2010, p. 376; www.cia.gov/library/publications/the-world-factbook/rankorder/2119rank.html).

Identifying and charting media ownership is the goal of the empirical research of the Canadian Media Concentration Research project at the School of Journalism and Communication at Carleton University in Ottawa (☐ www.cmcrp.org/); it is part of the International Media Concentration Research (IMCR) project that studies media concentration in over 30 countries in the world to provide research for public access that is not filtered through corporate public relations and a commercial media reporting on itself.

Tracing dominance by global companies historically, Neal Stephenson mapped a similar

HORIZONTAL INTEGRATION

(Type I) A firm in one line of media buys a major interest in another media operation not directly related to the original business (e.g., Thomson owns newspapers, publishing companies, and broadcasting). (Type II) Ownership of company is entirely outside of media (e.g., Thomson ownership has included airline, automotive, travel, and oil and gas companies).

VERTICAL INTEGRATION

A company extends control over the whole line of production, from supply to delivery, and can be (1) *backward* (e.g., Quebecor buys a pulp and paper plant [for newsprint] or Irving [which owns all the newspapers in New Brunswick] buys pulp and paper plants and property in the Maritimes [supplying the trees for the plant]) or (2) *forward* (e.g., Thomson which owns newspapers, buys broadcasting, satellite, and Internet services).

For Real?

Canadian Media in Crisis?

Concentrated ownership in the Canadian media industry indicates how economic convergence has led to the concentration of power over public communication in a very small number of large corporations. As a liberal democracy—with the attendant recognition that communication is necessary for public information, deliberation, and participation in decision-making—in Canada, media concentration has historically been an ongoing public and government concern. As we discuss further in later chapters, one of the priorities of government policy-making in communication was to ensure public access and participation in it. When business decisions come in conflict with this policy, historically, the federal government has convened public inquiries, or what are called Royal Commissions: a committee assigned to study the history and current conditions to identify problems, challenges, and successes in order to report to government and contribute to decision-making and government policy. Even though several Royal Commissions have identified concentrated, private ownership as detrimental to public access and participation in communication, today, concentrated ownership in the Canadian media industry continues to be among the highest in the world (Winseck, 2010). Ownership convergence is not limited to one type of media, or limited to one geographical area, but is spread out across the country. The synergistic convergence means that private ownership does not just include media (like newspapers, radio, and television), but all forms of communication in terms of its infrastructure (e.g., the machines and technology used to produce and transmit it), the delivery systems (print, wireline, wireless), and the content. This is a process of **horizontal** and **vertical integration** where the corporation seeks to control as much of the production, distribution, and consumption of resources to its own (shareholder) advantage (see Figures 3.2–3.4).

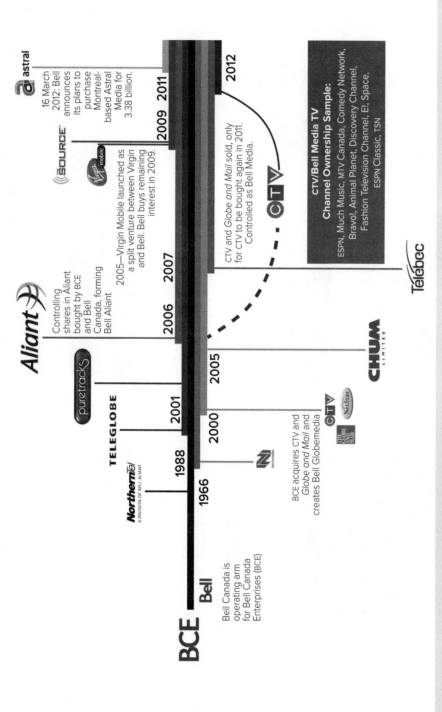

FIGURE 3.2 | Ownership chart. BCE consolidation timeline, 1969–2012.

Source: Adapted from CRTC. BCE profile. Retrieved from www.crtc.gc.ca/ownership/cht143.pdf; Alacra Store. BCE Inc. Mergers & acquisitions. Retrieved from www.alacrastore.com/mergers-acquisitions/BCE_Inc-1001524; BCE. Our history. Retrieved from www.bce.ca/en/aboutbce/history/index.php; CBC (16 March 2012). Bell Canada to buy Astral Media for $3.38B. Retrieved from www.cbc.ca/news/canada/story/2012/03/16/astral-bell.html. With permission from Bell Media.

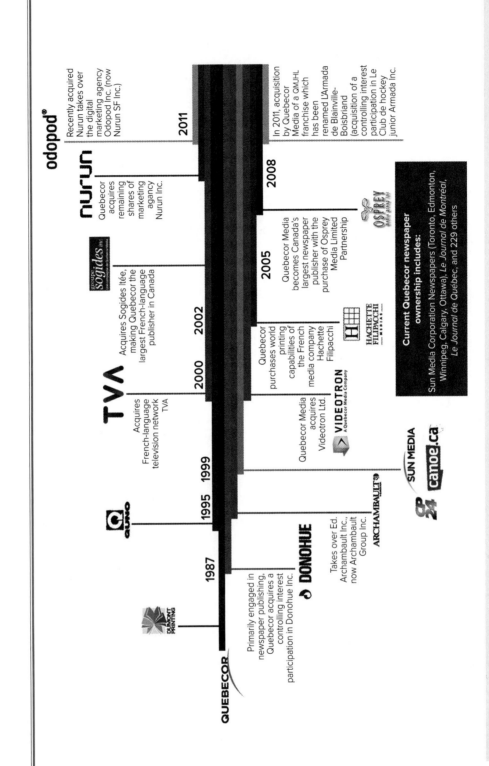

FIGURE 3.3 | Ownership chart. Quebecor consolidation timeline, 1969–2011.

Source: Adapted from CRTC. Quebecor profile. Retrieved from www.crtc.gc.ca/ownership/cht156.pdf. Used by permision of Québecor Media inc.

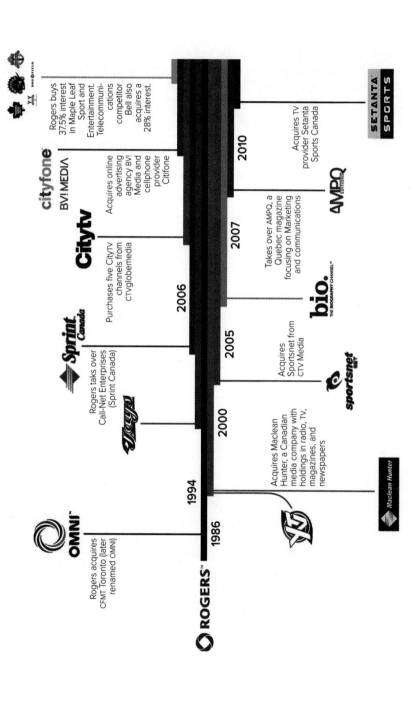

FIGURE 3.4 | Ownership chart. Rogers consolidation timeline, 1986–2011.

Source: Based on data found at http://your.rogers.com/aboutrogers/historyofrogers/overview.asp. Used by permission of Rogers Media Inc.

Continued

Discussion Questions

1. What types of convergence can you observe from the ownership charts included in this box?

2. What are the options for telephone, television, wireless, or Internet service provisions where you live?

3. Bring in an example of the contract for the latest wireless, cable, and/or Internet service provider. What is the average length of time of the contract? What are the terms of the contract (i.e., how easy is it to cancel the contract)?

4. What does ownership have to do with your communication choices and the range of media content over different types of media?

5. How does private ownership impact your decision-making about media, and about the information you have access to?

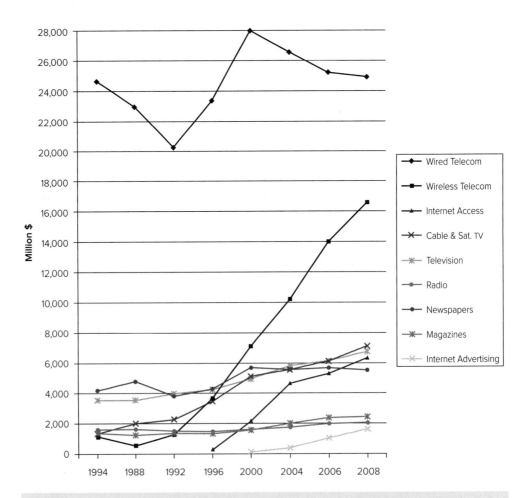

FIGURE 3.5 | **The growth of the network media economy in Canada, 1984–2008.**

Source: Adapted from CRTC (2009, and various years); Statistics Canada Cansim; Canadian Newspaper Association (2009, and various years); Internet Advertising Bureau; Corporate Annual Reports; Mediamorphis. (12 November 2012). The growth of the network media economy in Canada, 1984–2008 [Web log post]. Retrieved from dwmw. wordpress.com/

trajectory for the global computing industry as it grew from the 1970s on, as two rival monopolies rose to dominate the market. One is Microsoft, which has managed to corner the global market for operating systems and consumer software for PCs. The other is Apple, which built its fortune on the manufacture of a unique hardware system (MacIntosh) and has now become one of the largest suppliers of personal computing and entertainment hardware in the world. These technologies are not just a product that is manufactured for sale, but have become critical to capitalist expansion. Information and communication technology (ICT) provides the essential infrastructure—the means used to extend the ability to manage and control products, information, and labour—without being restricted by time and space. As briefly introduced in the previous chapter, this is evident in the practices of economic globalization and underpins the international division of labour over greater distances, and is part of the process of **spatialization** (Mosco 2009, p. 157–84). We offer an initial way of thinking about spatialization here (see marginal definition).

> **SPATIALIZATION**
> The process by which time and space are changed (compressed, extended, or almost eliminated) using technology.

While it is hegemonically common to think of the biggest transnational or multinational corporations as evidence of "success," a critical political economist asks, "Who for?" What does it mean when only a handful of corporations have so much power to determine how we labour or communicate? How are decisions made for operating systems used by billions of people circumscribed by decisions made in the boardroom? And it's not just communication infrastructure, but, as you shall see, increasing expansion of intellectual property comes at costs we haven't even started to think about. They range from being critical to life on earth (as discussed in Chapter 1 with the patenting of genes) to the seemingly mundane.

The latest patent from Apple, on "eReader" offerings, for example, includes a patent on page-turning. Control over ICT is exercised over the range of the product—from built-in obsolescence to built-in payments for basic necessities: You now won't be able to turn a page without paying Apple for it. As reported in *The New York Times*, it was only one of no less than 38 patents recently granted to Apple over a one week period in November 2012, which, among others, included ownership of "'location-based categorical information services'" (Bilton, 2012, para. 8) and a method for consistent backup of electronic information: As the reporter for the *Times* remarked, "This isn't the most seemingly obvious patent Apple has been awarded in recent years. The company has also been granted patents for an icon for music (which is a [*sic*] just a musical note), the glass staircase used in the company's stores—yes, stairs, that people walk up . . . " (para. 7).

As may now be appreciated, the new vectors and new information technologies can be harnessed for public good and the benefit of humanity, and, to varying degrees, they can be used to further commodify, manage, and atomize people depending on the time period and location (there are differences in comparing ownership controls in Canada to China or Burma, e.g.). Where one future prediction is utopian, the other is darkly dystopian, and worldwide, the current trajectory has the potential for both. Humans have the unique capacity to imagine how they might want their future to look, and there is an interesting history of such imagining informing a genre of writing that goes back hundreds, if not thousands, of years. In the modern world, we call most of this imaginative writing "science fiction"; in earlier times it was known as "utopian" literature. It appeared in novels and in political tracts translated from early Greek. We can even say that the early chapters of Genesis—the Creation and the Fall—are parables that illustrate the dialectic between utopia and dystopia.

While these debates will go on—in social theory and in media research, as well as in media itself—it's business as usual for the international media corporations. The links between digitized media corporations and the general fund of global capital continue to be strengthened. Consider, for example, recent figures indicating the financial clout of a mere *six* multinational

ICT corporations (AT&T, Vodafone, Verizon, Deutsche Telekom, Nippon, and Telefónica) whose combined assets in 2007 totalled USD\$1,132,41 billion (Fuchs, 2009, p. 78). This was USD\$131,197 billion *more* than the *combined total* of the gross domestic product (GDP; an economic measurement of the market value of the total goods a country produces) for *all* of the African states (ibid.). So while corporations are lauded for their financial prowess and technological innovation as evidence of "success" and prosperity, the extreme income disparities, social division, entrenchment of social class, conflict and war that plague countries in Africa and elsewhere in the world, are seen to be unrelated (unless of course it is argued that the technology owned and controlled by these same corporations can be used to alleviate poverty, as our example from Micky Lee, 2011a, in Chapter 1, further illustrates). Thus, the problems with technological determinism are twofold:

> *The common feature of technological determinism is that it levers technology, its development, implementation and effects out of the social relations in which they are embedded, thus a) marginalizing or removing the social relations from analysis and b) ascribing powers and characteristics to technology which are the result of social relations between people, rather than properties intrinsic to things. (Wayne 2003, p. 40)*

The essential attribute of technological determinism in the current period is its total reliance on digital technologies for its arguments and prognosis. In a sense it is a sub-species—digital determinism. It is a view that sees the "abundance" of digital recording devices, in particular the digital video camera, combined with the networking power of the Internet as somehow being themselves agents of social liberation. In some cases the proponents of this new "revolution" in communication are themselves in denial about their own determinism. Take, for instance, the American journalism educator and theorist John Pavlik:

> *I propose that although convergence is happening, it is neither inevitable nor necessarily good. I do not offer a technologically deterministic view of new media. Rather, I assert that convergence merely holds the promise of a better, more efficient, more democratic medium for journalism and the public in the twenty-first century. (Pavlik 2000, p. xiii)*

[Despite his denial of digital determinism, what] Pavlik does claim is that media convergence "holds the promise" that it can transform journalism into a "more democratic" medium. This too is a mantra of the digital determinists and a promise that remains unfulfilled. In Pavlik's view, convergence and the arrival of new technologies are a fulcrum for the leverage of change in journalistic and media content, context, processes and production values. As well, he argues, the new (technology-driven) media encourage a "realignment" in the pattern of relationships between reporters and editors; editors and owners; news organizations and audiences. (Politics & Culture, 2004, paras. 15–18)

There is certainly a degree of realignment, as we discuss later in our comments on the changing reportorial community (and discuss in detail in Chapter 10), but what Pavlik and others who have been seduced by the hype surrounding digital media don't see is the dialectical constraints that limit the utopian elements of their vision and insert a decidedly dystopian tint to their rose-coloured video screens.

Before proceeding to explore the utopian and dystopian possibilities of the new communication technologies, however, we want to outline a brief history of the traditional media in terms of its technological, commercial, and social development over the twentieth century. After all, it is this history that has forged what we know and experience today. It is vital to understand *why* we are contending with, for example, concentrated ownership across media, including the Internet and new technological developments, and why it matters to us. We also want to discuss this history in terms of an application of the theory and concepts that you learned in this section. The next section will employ and thus demonstrate how to go about thinking about this history using a political economy of communication methodology that focuses on, for example, ownership, government regulation, and labour as ways of organizing and understanding these developments.

Key Points

- "New" technologies are not new; technological development and technological change have been part of the human experience since the beginning.

- Technology does not occur or exist in a vacuum; it has always been socially developed and has social implications.

- Like the term *technology*, the term *convergence* has a long history, and is in fact the key means by which technologies change; technological change is a dialectical process in which convergence creates divergence and "fragmentation."

- The positive and negative aspects of technology are dialectically aligned and can be found in nearly all digital commodities, as well as within the social relations of digital production systems.

Class Discussion

1. Collect two or three phrases that describe technology or predict the future based on technology (or a particular kind of technology). Search for examples in newspapers, advertisements, other textbooks, or speeches from corporate executive officers or politicians. Identify which ones you think indicate technological determinism and why.

2. Make a list of all the kinds of technology of communication that you use and how access to it is differentiated (via its cost, subscription, contract, etc.); discuss how much control you have over the technology that you use every day.

3. Use the list you created in Question 2 to identify what corporations (e.g., Apple, Microsoft, Dell) are identified as producing it. See if you can identify the labour that went into one or two of the items on the list in terms of where it is manufactured and by whom, and what happens to the technology when it becomes obsolete.

4. How does the concept of commodity fetishism explain technological obsolescence and the process of financialization?

Media on Media

Tunes on Techno (Warning: May Contain Explicit Content)

Black Eyed Peas. (2009). Now generation. *The E.N.D.* Santa Monica, California: Interscope. 🖥 www.metrolyrics.com/now-generation-lyrics-black-eyed-peas.html

Daft Punk. (2005). Technologic. *Human After All.* Virgin. 🖥 www.sing365.com/music/lyric.nsf/technologic-lyrics-daft-punk/49631fc0e19ff7da48256fc90006411d

Rage Against the Machine. (1998). No shelter. *Godzilla: The Album.* Epic Records. 🖥 www.sing365.com/music/lyric.nsf/NO-SHELTER-lyrics-Rage-Against-The-Machine/B68F7CC1AADB7D9D482568A50015D22B

Replicator. (2007). *Machines Will Always Let You Down.* Radio is Down. 🖥 www.last.fm/music/Replicator/Machines+Will+Always+Let+You+Down

DVDs, TV, and Videos

Films Media Group. (Producer). (2007). *You only live twice: Virtual reality meets real world in second life* [Documentary]. Retrieved from 🖥 ffh.films.com/id/13969/You_Only_Live_Twice_Virtual_Reality_Meets_Real_World_in_Second_Life.htm

Frontline PBS. (Producer). (2001). *The merchants of cool* [Documentary]. Retrieved from 🖥 www.pbs.org/wgbh/pages/frontline/shows/cool/view/

Paterson, M., Thurlbeck, G. (Producers), & Smith, M. (Director). (2009). Talking rubbish [Television series]. Toronto, Ontario: TVOntario. 🖥 www.last.fm/music/Replicator/Machines+Will+Always+Let+You+Down

Spyglass Entertainment. (Producer). (1999). *The insider* [DVD].

UBC Graduate School of Journalism. (Producer). (2009). Ghana: Digital dumping ground [Television series]. Alexandria, VA: PBS Video.

Warner Brothers. (Producer). (1999). *The matrix* [DVD].

PART II

From Hot Metal to Hotmail: A (Recent)
History of Media and Communication

Objectives

After reading this section you should have a general understanding of the following:

- how the mechanics and aesthetics of communication are derived from the principles of more traditional arts and crafts, such as engraving, painting, printing, photography, live theatre, musical performance, and cinema;

- how modern newspapers, magazines, broadcasting, and other means of mass communication developed in their modern industrial form, in the context of dramatic political economic and social changes in nineteenth-century Europe and the "New World";

- the important links and relationships between the technologies of the media and the social relations of communication; and

- how patterns of communication are established in relation to social conditions and needs, and how, under capitalism, they tend to follow similar paths to that of global economic expansion and investment.

Keywords

- **common carriage**
- **copyright**
- **gatekeeping**

- **intellectual property**
- **spatialization**
- **universal service**

In Part II our first task is to outline a brief history of media and communication, primarily in the Western world. We will concentrate only on the last 200 years, but the story is much older than that. For the sake of convenience, and to follow a logical historical progression, we have divided the first three chapters in this part according to the individual media type: print; photography and film; and radio and television—with the final chapter on the history of the computer.

At the same time, this structure allows us to develop the arguments about the complex social relations and the tension—the dialectic—that draws old and new into conflict and contradiction. Each chapter discusses a particular set of technologies—the combination of science, the means of production, and the social relations of work and exchange—within our broader framework of political economy to identify major processes, institutions, regulations, and ethics. The sequence of chapters is logical because by demonstrating the historical structuring of particular technologies, we can trace the important links between them.

The pace and sequencing of scientific research, commodification, and eventual (mass) production relies on extension and continuous modification of existing technologies, as much as it does on new ideas. For example, the interactive and highly graphic nature of Internet communication relies on our deeply embedded understanding of print, photography, audio, and video technologies. Increasingly, our computers are also televisions, newspapers, research libraries, video archives, social meeting places, and shopping malls. This is convergence in action. Old technologies are rarely abandoned entirely; more often than not they are merely modified, recycled, and plugged in to newer modes.

What is important and consistent within our historical account is the paramount importance of social context in determining the ultimate form and purpose of communication and broadcasting technology. An historical narrative relies on our understanding of what was happening broadly in societies in which important new technologies began to emerge. It is therefore necessary to "read" the history of technological development, innovation, and convergence in the print, film, and broadcast media in the context of the social totality—that is, the political economic and social events and trends that occur in combination with advances in applications of new means of production and communication.

At the end of each chapter in this part you'll also find a timeline providing a chronological overview (or list) of what is commonly identified by historians as significant inventions, and decisions (including government decisions) made on media and technological change. This is a predominately Western view (from the global north) that keeps the focus on Canada. When you review these decisions, keep in mind that they should not be seen as separate from the political economic and social relations that gave rise to them. The timelines should be read in addition to the chapters, and not as either distinct or separate from them. It is one way of organizing history, but it should not be taken as a substitute for it.

4 From Gutenberg to Global News: A Brief History of the Print Media

It is unlikely that you see reading as a political act, yet when printing was first put to use, it was a very radical endeavour. According to Anthony Smith (1980), printing, which became widespread in the fifteenth century, was "the first revolution in the means of communicating information" (p. 7), and it is credited with facilitating social revolutions. After reading this chapter, you will begin to understand the importance of communications technology as a means of enabling humans to make major transformations in the world. Without printing, for example, the spread of scientific knowledge would have been immeasurably slower, and it is unlikely that many of the major discoveries that we regard today as commonplace would have occurred. Given the monopolies of knowledge afforded by certain societies by their control over the written word, however, its spread was also marked by a shifting set of power relations.

Objectives

Although this chapter does not claim to provide a comprehensive overview of the history of print media, it does have some general objectives intended to provide the following:

- an historical overview of printing and why it is important as the first mechanical means of mass communication;

- an appreciation of the historical links between the print media and other important social, technological, and political economic changes from the fifteenth to the twenty-first century;

- a discussion on how the printed word was at the heart of convergent media technologies, and the role printing still plays today; and

- an overview on how the publishing (particularly the newspaper) industry can be considered a form of broadcast mass media, and how it is also affected by the growing trend towards narrowcasting in all types of media.

Keywords

- **agenda setting**
- **broadsheet**
- **copyright**
- **framing**
- **gatekeeping**

- **news agencies**
- **paywalls**
- **personalization of news**
- **propaganda**
- **tabloid (compact)**

Print Culture

In the James Bond film *Tomorrow Never Dies* (1997), the villain is media mogul Elliot Carver (reputedly based on Rupert Murdoch, chairman and CEO of News Corporation). Carver engineers a conflict between China and Britain timed to coincide with the launch of his new global satellite TV network. He tells his editors,

> *Hold the presses! . . . we have the perfect story with which to launch our satellite news network tonight. It seems a small crisis is brewing in the South China seas. I want full newspaper coverage! I want magazine stories! I want books! I want films! I want TV! I want radio! I want us on the air 24 hours a day . . . and a billion people around this planet will watch it, hear it and read about it on the Carver media group. There's no news like bad news. (Broccoli, Wilson, & Spottiswoode, 1997, Scene 5)*

From the high jinks and high tech of "fictional" media moguls in the Bond film, we take you back to the early Aboriginal rock carvings in Petroglyphs Provincial Park in Ontario to begin our review of how we came to this point in this history of print media. Petroglyphs and pictographs are examples of some of the earliest and most enduring forms of communication: using hard rock to etch or paint images of animals and symbols into rock faces where they could be witnessed by all who came by (📺 www.thecanadianencyclopedia.com/articles/pictographs-and-petroglyphs). Whether in Canada or as far back as Ancient Greece, the ancients had the means of communication, but their forms were limited to those who could gather in one place to see or hear them. Thus the plays of Euripides could only been seen in amphitheatres such as those of Corinth or Ephesus; the stone obelisks of the Babylonians and Egyptians stood in the sand beside the great rivers; Homer's tales of Troy, and the history and wisdom of those who came before us, were passed down by oral transmission—stories sung, told, and retold—before finally being written down in about 750 BCE.

It is not until the invention of moveable type and the printing press that communication media became independent of its site of production. Until this point, the Aboriginal art remained fixed on the rock face, the Greek tragedies were restricted to the amphitheatres, and the Babylonian obelisks remained rooted in the sand. Even books, which were produced by the arduous process of copying by hand, tended to remain where they were created. In the seventh century CE, monks from Iona, Scotland, established a priory on Lindisfarne Island in northeastern England. Here they produced one of the great treasures of the Anglo-Saxon world, the *Lindisfarne Gospels*, by hand. But only those who visited this windy isle, just south of the border between Scotland and England, could see and read these gospels for themselves. While medieval books did travel to some extent, the advent of the printing press brought a new independence to the written word.

The liberation of the means of communication from its place of creation may be considered the beginning of modern mass communication. As time has passed, the place of production has become even less important to the form of communication and to those who receive it. For example, in nineteenth-century Canada, if you wanted to read international news such as *The Times*, you paid for your subscription and waited for months until it was delivered, by ship, from London, England. In the twentieth century, you could have *The Times* delivered, again in hard copy, this time by air freight from London a day or so after publication. In the twenty-first century, you can access *The Times* online anytime, and you can receive regular news updates through the day or night, 24/7, 365 days a year.

Whether on-line or off, we understand the modern print media today as newspapers and magazines, or what we generally call *periodicals*, because there is usually a defined interval or "period" between publication dates. These include daily newspapers, news weeklies, reviews, monthly magazines, journals, and digests. Most of you are probably also aware that as its own "market," print production continues to fluctuate as niche magazines come and go, corporations are bought and sold, and overall the number of daily newspapers (whether in print or online) is being reduced. Age differences in newspaper readership are also a factor, as statistics suggest that, of the reading public, the younger you are, the less likely it is that you read newspapers (Newspaper Audience Databank, 2011). In contrast, the variety and scope of glossy magazines now aimed at youth as its own "target market" has never been greater. On the one hand, this suggests a convergence in catering to and defining "what youth is," and on the other, a subdivision of youth into even more specific markets cultivating a particular lifestyle or interest. But it is variety in name (or brand) alone, as the content tends to be strikingly similar, although it can be made more appealing online. Content analyses of commercial magazines made for teenage girls, for example, like *CosmoGirl!*, *Teen People*, *Teen Vogue*, and *Seventeen*, indicate the repetition of a consistent message:

> Beauty is a requirement, beauty can be achieved only through the purchase of products, and we can help you find the right products. The use of youth-targeted language, combined with offers of expert advice in the management of beauty problems, suggests that these sites wish to present themselves as friends rather than marketers of beauty products. Like their print counterparts, the sites may play an important role—in a private, personalized, and interactive setting—in reinforcing the messages concerning the centrality of female beauty in Western societies. (Labre & Walsh-Childers, 2003, p. 379)

In the early years of the mass circulation print media, however, the difference between readers was more likely to be along political party lines, rather than marketing demographics. Newspapers and other periodicals were partisan (supporting one political party or political ideology), unabashedly propagandistic (the purposeful and systematic repetition of a particular set of ideas or views), and overtly proselytizing (aimed at converting readers to believe in these ideas and views).

The changes in culture of the mass print media over the last 100 years are both profound and fascinating. The shift from overt, political and agitational party press to capitalist conglomerate mirrors and documents the trajectory of the eighteenth- and nineteenth-century revolutionary and relatively small class of bourgeoisie into the dynamic and corrosive structures of capitalism today.

Gutenberg

It was Johannes Gutenberg (ca. 1398–1468) who developed the machinery that today has become the modern printing press (see Figure 4.1, on the next page). While primitive forms of printing had been developed in China and Korea before Gutenberg's time, in 1452 the German metal and stone smith began the print run accredited to the Roman Catholic Church, printing what were called individual "indulgences." These were public notices of the payment and conditions for mortal forgiveness officially granted by the Church. Gutenberg also produced an initial print of 200 copies of what became known as the Gutenberg *Bible*. The technology was revolutionary in that several copies could be printed using a machine (versus by hand); although labour was still essential, it was not the sole purview of scribes, who were controlled by the Catholic Church, and copies could be transported and distributed anywhere (versus having to physically visit a monastery). Nevertheless, control over publication and content was seriously enforced. Early attempts to publish the *Bible* in English were resisted by the ecclesiastical authorities. In 1536, William Tyndale was tried for heresy and burned at the stake for his efforts to do so.

The development in technology from hand-print to machine-print is also credited with being the catalyst for several other radical changes. The first was in challenging the dominance of the Catholic Church. Among other issues, the indulgence and the payment received (basically an exchange value for the Church on sins committed) so outraged some of its members that one—Martin Luther—printed a list of criticisms against the Church and nailed it to a church door in the town of Wittenberg, Germany, signifying the beginning of what is called the Protestant Reformation.

The printing press is thus an example of the process of the dialectic. While the printing press allowed people to read the *Bible* for themselves and in their own vernacular (and thus spread the word and control of the Catholic religion), the availability of printing presses also enabled the Protestants to print posters, handbills, and other **propaganda** to promote their cause. The Reformation that began in 1517 with Luther's rebellion against the Catholic Church began the destruction of *the* pre-eminent position of that institution in Europe. While in one part of the world, the hegemonic authority of the church was jeopardized, however, print copies of the *Bible* also helped to extend its authority and control elsewhere. In seventeenth-century Canada, for example, the introduction of print culture via the *Bible* had a devasting impact on the culture of First Nations people as the printed word was promoted and accepted as authoritative, unerring, and tangible proof of the legitimacy of the Church doctrine, and was therefore promoted and appeared superior to their oral traditions and culture (Friesen, 2000, p. 10). As "the word" spread, ideas underpinning both religions were joined with capitalism, complementing each other and providing strength for early forms of imperialism and continued expansion of capitalism to the present day (see Weber, 2001; Wilde, 2006). At the turn of the nineteenth century, for example, German sociologist Max Weber (1864–1920) argued that the Protestant work ethic (i.e., your duty to work hard and not complain about it) is testimony of your belief: If successful, it serves as proof thereof, or if unsuccessful, it should be endured; the reward (or salvation) will come in the Christian afterlife.

PROPAGANDA

The systematic repetition and dissemination of a particular set of ideas, views, and/or values.

Source: © Dennis Cox / Alamy

FIGURE 4.1 | Johannes Gutenberg's printing press at the Gutenberg Museum in Mainz, Germany.

This ethic was, in fact, the "spirit of capitalism" (Weber, 2001). In the present day, the emphasis isn't so much on production and frugality, but on the accumulation of wealth and consumption as evidence of success. "Selling God," or the commodification of religion, yields a growing billion dollar industry and links media (books, music, videos, broadcasting stations; e.g., L. S. Clarke, 2007; Thomas, 2009) directly to consumption (i.e., watch/read/buy these, and you [eventually] will be saved or satisfied).

In the meantime, the development of printing had a number of immediate social and cultural effects when it was first introduced in Europe. Printed criticism was recognized as a legitimate and relatively public form of protest that challenged the Church's monopoly on communication and authority on knowledge. Differences in social class were initially accentuated, as production and access to the printed word, as well as the ability to read, were class-divided in that only the wealthy had access to books and their contents. Nevertheless, the availability and circulation of printed material encouraged literacy. In fifteenth-century England, for example, the publishing of "street literature" was produced as the "poor people's" media in the form of "**broadsheets**" (single-printed sheets) and "chapbooks" (cheap books) (Collinson, 1973; Shepard, 1973). The content included printed folklore (songs and ballads that had previously been transmitted orally were transposed in printed form) as well as written opposition against religious and political domination.

Challenging the power of either the Church or the State was enforced through state censorship through an Act passed in England in 1543 that banned any material printed against the "true religion" (Shepard, 1973). The "illegal press" was thus created, part of which printed for private profit and part of which began an underground literature in support of religious and political protests, the publication and circulation of which carried several penalties of imprisonment or death (Shepard, 1973, p. 55). This impetus for protest—political economic, religious, and cultural—marks the origins of what is generically called the "alternative press" or "alternative media," which we review in more detail in Chapter 13, but it is significant to compare the similarities and differences between it and the commercial press in terms of its goals, ownership, operating principles, and content. These differences are negotiated and accentuated by the actions of the state.

Journalism and Freedom of the Press

The relatively modern institution of journalism as we know it had its beginnings in the radical pamphleteers of the French and American revolutions of the eighteenth and early nineteenth centuries. News sheets were circulated to inform an active citizenry, and they struggled against the "tax on knowledge" that many European governments imposed on the news magazines of the seventeenth and eighteenth centuries. As Irene Collins (1959) wrote in her introduction to *The Government and the Newspaper Press in France 1814–1881*, "liberty of the press has long been one of the most cherished freedoms," a freedom that Frenchmen came to enjoy (within limits) after 1819: "The [French] press laws of 1819 settled for once and for all that newspapers were entitled to as much liberty as books, and that liberty could not be regarded as compatible with the use of censorship" (p. ix).

This monumental struggle for "freedom of the press" is well-documented; however, it is traditionally a history that champions the commercial press as winning "freedom" from the state. It also underpins a dominant liberal-democratic theory of the press that views the media as "watchdog" of the state and its powers of censorship. Its political economic trajectory was born out in England and the new world, as freedom from the newspaper tax was quickly replaced

BROADSHEET

A newspaper format in which each page is approximately A2 size. Traditionally regarded as an upmarket form to distinguish it from a **tabloid (compact)**, which is A3 and downmarket.

TABLOID (COMPACT)

A newspaper format based on a page size approximately A3. Traditionally associated with journalistic practices such as beat-ups, sensationalist reporting, and photographs of semi-naked women on "Page 3." Also a pejorative term used to describe poor-quality journalism in any medium.

with a press beholden to the interests of the rich and powerful bourgeoisie that came to own it (Bowman, 1988; Engel, 1996; Hartely, 1996; Hollis, 1970; McQueen, 1977; Schultz, 1994, 1998; Walker, 1976; K. Williams, 1997; R. Williams, 1989).

How the commercial press was able to become dominant can be traced to the 1819 press laws, which required every newspaper to carry a stamp indicating tax payment. This established a dividing line between the state-sanctioned newspapers and the "unstamped" press, which was thus illegal. Through an analysis of the parliamentary debates in England at the time, British media historian James Curran (1978) demonstrates that the stamp tax was not simply an attempt by the state to control the press, but a deliberate intent on the part of the commercial owners to control the rising strength of a "radical" press that was overtly political. The stamp tax was supposed to eliminate the radical press (due to its illegality), but the tax backfired as the radical press was thereby made cheaper (and therefore more accessible) given it did not have to add the cost of the tax to its price. To the commercial press, it was a direct competitor—politically and economically.

Hegemonic press histories have suggested that the birth of a commercial press was the birth of freedom of the press, meaning freedom *from* the state. More accurately, however, the commercial press drew on the state for the abolition of the stamp tax, and the call of freedom of the press a rallying cry for the commercial press intent on eliminating the radical press and its associated organizations since they questioned, criticized, and mobilized against the social relations of capitalism upon which the commercial press relies. The commercial press gained advantages over the radical press both from the removal of the tax and from the state sanctions allowing commercial development of the press.

The commodification of the press also resulted in re-politicization of the press in liberal-democratic countries, in general, and impacted the relationship of communication to democracy. Where a partisan press, however "biased," had been centrally political—addressing its readers as workers, voters, and citizens—a commercial press constructed its readers as "consumers" (Croteau & Hoynes, 2000, p. 69). Advertising and commercial success took priority over readership and political activism. As American media historian Gerald Baldasty (1993) notes, this shift also had consequences for journalism such that the production process itself was changed. Foreshadowing the future, as newspapers sought to keep costs at a minimum, investigative journalism was curtailed and editorial staff reduced. A division of labour of the newsroom resulted in a "beat" system that thereby "de-emphasized news not covered by beats" and reduced explanation to specialized reports and cheaper "patent inside" or "innocuous" syndicated news (Baldasty, 1993, p. 102). Baldasty observes that where news as a commodity was primary, news as information and debate was secondary, which, among other effects, impacted not only the amount of coverage of labour issues but also how labour and the trade union movement were portrayed in the media as negative or threatening forces. This change in production varied from country to country and time period to time period, but the detrimental change in labour coverage by the commercial press remains consistent to the present day (Martin, 2004; Puette, 1992).

The movement of the commercial press from "the realm of politics to the realm of business" (Baldasty, 1993, p. 99) was also illustrated in newspaper *content*. Comparing the rhetoric of the commercial press to the radical press, Curran (1978) also identifies fundamental shifts made in the commercial press as content removed questions of class exploitation. A key change was in the portrayal of *labour* as the source of wealth to the portrayal of *profit* as the wellspring of the economy (which ignores profits made by exploiting labour). As well, the class-divided view of capitalist society inherent in the radical press was absent in the commercial papers, which recognized social division to be a natural result of individual differences (i.e., it's your fault you can't get a job, not the system that structures labour as a whole). The containment of labour radicalism was expressed in content that emphasized interdependence between classes. In this view, social class isn't a problem in itself; it's the relationship between classes that is. Newspapers thus stressed harmony on the basis of shared interests in the "necessity" of building a strong nation, which thus helped legitimize state interests, thereby deflecting attention away from class power and redirecting it towards nationalism (ibid.), a manoeuvre that is still used to deter or break labour unrest that continues to be effective today (Kumar, 2005).

In nineteenth-century England, increasing nationalist and imperialist coverage of foreign affairs replaced symbols of class conflict with new symbols of membership in a superior race and world power, justifying class harmony (Curran, 1978). Thus, contrary to histories that suggest press freedom is "freedom from the state," changes in the commercial press actually supported state priorities. While the radical press strove to articulate the connections between labour and social class, to facilitate critical discussion and enable political participation, it was thus countered in the now less expensive, more profitable, and more prolific commercial press.

Origins and Development of Copyright

The commercial development of the press, and moreover of printing itself, also involved the state on a more international level, which remains crucial to the structuring of the media environment today. Gutenberg's press was used to commodify the printed word, which grew into a printing and book publishing industry, thereby ensuing a struggle over printed material as "property" now requiring a distinction between private or public ownership (Eisenstein, 1980, p. 120). "Once printers were producing books for sale, they sought some right to restrict copying to ensure that other printers did not 'pirate' their books" (Sell & May, 2001, p. 477). As "piracy" became more common in the early 1500s, the state intervened (in Venice and Britain) to institutionalize "**copyrights**" for printers through the creation of guilds (associations providing mutual benefits to its members). Members of guilds held the copyright on what could be published, but not on the printing practices themselves. In light of significant religious upheaval at the time, part of the motivation behind this was the state's intent to outsource the censorship role to copyright holders (so they would decide what did and did not get published rather than the state; pp. 477–8). Yet, as the practices of printing became more common, copyright shifted away from printers to booksellers, as exemplified by the royal chartering of the members of the book trade under the Stationers' Company in Britain in 1577, which established "the stationers copyright," thus transferring control to the booksellers, effectively providing them a monopoly in the burgeoning industry (Patterson, 1968, p. 4).

In this early history of printing, state legislation first sought to protect the rights of printers and booksellers, with little direct attention to the rights of authors (ibid.). The move to international agreements in copyright did not emerge until the late nineteenth century, in line with growing international trade between nations, and with expanding capitalist and imperial activity (ibid., p. 484). The Berne Convention for the Protection of Literary and Artistic Works (1886) was the first to internationalize the rights for copyright across national borders. Although Canada became a colonial signatory under Britain in 1886, it did not fully ratify the elements of the Berne Convention until 1924, with the enactment of Canada's first "sovereign" Copyright Act (Bannerman, 2010). State protection and fostership of the domestic publishing industry were central concerns in the negotiation of international copyright agreements in the eighteenth and nineteenth centuries and alignment of national laws was sought in Britain, the United States, and Canada.

COPYRIGHT
Provides exclusive rights of ownership "to produce or reproduce a work or a substantial part of it in any form" (Canadian Intellectual Property Office [CIPO], 2013, para. 10; www.cipo.ic.gc.ca/eic/site/cipointernet-internetopic.nsf/eng/h_wr02281.html?Open&pv=1). This may include artistic, dramatic, and musical works (including computer programs) as well as performances, sound recordings, and communication signals (para. 12).

As Canadian copyright historian Sarah Bannerman (2010) has argued, however, Canada's historical relationship to international copyright implementation has been conflicted, and has often reflected differing ways in which the state has tried to define its national identity in an international arena, often in tension with both British and American copyright policies. An early example of this was in 1872, when amendments to the Copyright Act included compulsory licencing of British books, in an effort to encourage a domestic printing and publishing industry (Bannerman, 2010, pp. 20–1). Despite the unanimous support of the Canadian parliament for the revisions to the Act, it was ultimately refused royal assent by the Imperial Government. Also, following its first "sovereign" Copyright Act in 1924, with a view to managing its political economic relations with the United States, Canada was slow to adopt further changes to the Berne Convention (1948) because it did not align with US policies (Bannerman, 2010, p. 29).

Interestingly, the United States did not join Berne until as late as 1989, although it had what Ginsburg and Kernochan (1989) refer to as "back door protection" (p. 3), manipulating the work's country of origin through simultaneous publication in Berne signatory countries, most often through Canada. The first reason that the United States delayed its participation in Berne was because in 1886 it was a net importer of copyrighted works; thus it preferred to function as a "pirate" nation in importation (p. 1). Additionally, throughout the late nineteenth and early twentieth centuries, the United States maintained a minimalist approach to copyright, which meant it did not accept certain features of Berne, such as the automatic protection of copyright and moral rights (p. 2). With Canada, the United States did, however, sign the Universal Copyright Convention (1952), a comprehensive agreement intended to apply copyright protection for "literary, scientific and artistic works, including writings, musical, dramatic and cinematographic works, and paintings, engravings and sculpture" (Article 1) under the United Nations Educational, Scientific and Cultural Organization (📺 portal.unesco.org/en/ev.php-URL_ID=15381&URL_DO=DO_TOPIC&URL_SECTION=201.html). As discussed in later chapters, digitization and convergence (in all its forms), coupled with constant technological change, continue to challenge such agreements. In addition to disagreements over time lengths of copyright, as well as the enforcement and severity of laws and fines for copying, works circulated on the World Wide Web have accentuated the struggle between what is "public," what is "private," and in particular what is considered "fair use" and "sharing" or "piracy."

From Books to News: A Brief History of Newspapers in Canada

Returning to our history of the development of the press as a commercial industry, the Industrial Revolution brought further changes in printing and pre-press technologies, such as Koenig's steam-powered press (1814), Hoe's rotary press (1846), and Mergenthaler's Linotype machines (1885)—innovations that sped up the production of all printed material. The railways, of course, also played a key role in the distribution of the new mass medium. It was, however, the convergence of printing with two other technological innovations—the electric telegraph and the photograph—that gave rise to mass circulation newspapers in the late nineteenth century with attendant impacts on the practice of journalism. We examine the history of what can be called "industrial journalism" by briefly reviewing some Canadian, Australian, British, and American examples.

As Kevin Williams (1997) points out, the history of journalism and the news media can only be fully appreciated if one takes into account "the countervailing pulls on the mass media exercised by public opinion on one hand and "powerful institutions in society" on the other (p. 5), which includes both the state and the commercial owners. William Kesterton's (1967) history of journalism in Canada and Douglas Fetherling's (1990) history of newspapers both attest to the close relationship first between the Crown (the federal government) and publishers, and eventually between the role of publishers themselves as powerful institutions within the political, economic, and social life of the country. Although newspapers printed in Canada first appeared in the mid-eighteenth century, the commercial daily mass circulation newspaper that is common today did not emerge until the late nineteeth or early twentieth century (Fetherling, 1990; Kesterton, 1967; Vipond, 2000). Newspapers in Canada have had a long history and have moved through various periods of transformation, which—like elsewhere in the British colonies at the time—changed from the province of the individual proprietor—who was usually the main writer, editorialist, and printer—to today's newspapers that are now just one of many media owned by large multinational corporations. While the commercial media model has become the most dominant in Canada over the past century, this was not a natural transition simply based on changes to technology. As we review in the next two sections of this chapter, the historical focus centres on the transition from the partisan press to the commercial press in its current form, as newspapers were made into industries based on *decisions* regarding ownership, revenue generation, labour, and journalism standards. As we cover in Chapter 13, there were also alternative models regarding the use value of media that suggest a number of different ways that media could be developed beyond its exchange value. Canadian media historians like William Kesterton (1967), Douglas Fetherling (1990), and Minko Sotiron (1997) have each identified different ranges for identifiable periods in the transition to a commercial press, and building from their work, we can thus identify five general periods of transformation for newspapers in Canada (▣ www.cna-acj. ca and ▣ www.timetoast.com/timelines/43142), which we highlight in this section and the next.

Three interesting features mark the *first period*; as previously noted, the early newspapers were often the purview of just one person who may have been the reporter, editor, *and* printer. Secondly, unlike today's papers, the "pioneer" press had small runs and would come out on a weekly or bi-weekly basis rather than on a daily basis (Kesterton, 1967). Lastly, early publishers received the lion's share of their revenues from their role as the official printers for the Crown. The pages of the papers were populated with government notices, a limited and dated selection of news from Europe, and some local information on business issues (Fetherling, 1990).

The *second period* of the Canadian newspaper, during the mid-1800s, was marked by the strong link between the press and politics. The mid-nineteenth century was a crucial time in the formation of Canada as a state, and the nation's newspapers were very active in reporting and commenting on the issues of the day, including debates over responsible government, the Riel Rebellions, and Confederation. In this period, there was a healthy increase in the number of newspapers across the country, and in many urban centres there were numerous newspapers competing for readers (Kesterton, 1967). This competition was fuelled by the clear partisan positions taken by the newspaper publishers and editors. Examples of the political power of newspaper operators include Amor de Cosmos' use of his publication *The British Colonist* in the city of Victoria to critique Sir James Douglas and the monopoly of the Hudson's Bay Company in Victoria and the territories.

In Toronto, George Brown's *Globe* was a liberal paper that strongly criticized Sir John A. Macdonald and his Conservative government in the mid-nineteenth century. In response to the *Globe*, Macdonald and the Conservatives financially supported and provided insider information to the competing Toronto *Mail*. When the editor of the *Mail* showed too much editorial independence, the Tories withdrew their support and financed the founding of the *Telegram* (Fetherling, 1990). The line between the press and politics was consistently blurred in this period as many early publishers, such as George Brown and Amor de Cosmos, published newspapers *and* held political office (ibid., 1990). Additionally, writers who were supportive of the government would often be offered patronage positions as a payback for their journalistic support (ibid., p. 74).

Although the publisher and editors retained strong control over the tone of the newspaper and its direction in this period, the division of labour between publisher, writer, and print workers was beginning to emerge. This shift had a technological aspect due, in part, to changes in the printing process; with a move to steam presses, the printer was able to produce more copies at a greater speed, leading to the development of the daily paper, and also of the penny press. Also in this period, due to the increased number of newspapers available in many urban centres, there was a corresponding growth in the number of reporters and columnists writing for different papers. By the 1870s more newspapers were employing reporters, but their status in society was fairly low. According to some accounts of the time, journalists were lacking in morals, learning, and self-respect. Colonial journalists had an "ambiguous" status according to Henry Mayer (1968): "It seems to have been taken for granted by most writers that journalists were not just 'ordinary' workers. Yet they did not seem to fit into the picture of a profession, and certainly did not earn professional rewards" (p. 191). As the papers were often tied to partisan roots, the writers tended to reflect these interests in their reporting of key events at the time. Fetherling (1990) argues that journalists in the mid-1800s "began their period of greatest influence in society" (p. 24). He also argues that this was the earliest time when the press moved from being an external critic of politics and society to an arm of the power structures in Canada (p. 38).

The *third period* of newspapers in Canada was a period of great technological and structural change in the medium. In the late nineteenth and early twentieth centuries, newspapers were transformed by the introduction of new technology such as the rotary press, Linotype, chemical wood pulp paper, and—by the end of the nineteenth century—the introduction of the telegraph, telephone, photography, and typewriter (Fetherling, 1990; Kesterton, 1967). At the same time as these innovations were changing the way the newspaper was produced, the way that content was created and the role of the newspaper in society were also changing. Three important examples of this were the format and frequency of circulation, the increased role in advertising, and the transformation of the workforce. Similar to the commercial trajectory of the press earlier in England, all of these demonstrated the shift from the partisan press to more industrialized modes of structuring news production as evident both in ownership and content.

The format and frequency of the newspaper changed in this period, whereby news stories moved to the front page and advertising was placed throughout the paper. Photography became more common in support of both news stories and advertising, yet it was used primarily for local news in this period, as the process of transmitting photos by telegraph was not perfected until close to World War I (Fetherling, 1990). In terms of circulation, there was a shift in the frequency of the publishing of papers; it went from a weekly, bi-weekly, or tri-weekly endeavour to a daily and often twice-daily affair. Canadian cities with healthy competitive news environments saw both morning and evening publications. Although Fetherling (1990) notes that these editions tended to serve different audiences, with the morning paper serving the middle class and the evening edition serving the lower-middle and working classes (p. 66). The competition between dailies was a result of what certain scholars have called the "golden age of the press" (Rutherford, 1978). In the first two decades of the twentieth century, there was the largest number of family owned English and French newspapers in Canadian history, from 114 in 1901 to 138 in 1913 (Kesterton, 1967, p. 71). The number of competing papers in many Canadian cities began to decline after this time due, in part, to the beginning of economic convergence and ownership consolidation.

The way that newspapers were financed changed significantly during this time, and this, perhaps more than technological aspects, influenced the shift from partisan press to commercial enterprise. Subscription and advertising replaced government notice printing as the main source of revenue for most newspapers. There was a strong link between subscription and advertising revenues, as circulation rates became the most important way that newspaper publishers could attract advertisers (Sotiron, 1997, p. 52). Yet, as the importance of advertising grew as a revenue stream for the newspapers, subscriptions became less central as revenue, thus shifting the attention of publishers from the political and content interests of readers to what would attract and keep advertisers. Fetherling (1990) posits that by the 1890s, metro dailies were deriving one third of their revenues from subscriptions and single-copy sales (p. 76), with the remainder coming from advertising. According to Sotiron (1997), advertising revenue "made up more than 70 per cent of total revenues for Toronto newspapers in the early years of the twentieth century, the percentage often rising to 80 per cent or more during and after World War I" (p. 62).

One of the main factors of the growth of advertising in newspapers in this era was the growth of department stores across the country. These stores, such as Eaton's or Simpson's, became key drivers not only in transforming the format of newspapers and making it an advertising medium but also in spurring the development of advertising agencies created to manage the large accounts between the stores and the newspapers across the country. Fetherling (1990) also notes that with larger advertisers also came the practice of *commercial censorship* with threats to withhold advertising from papers when they published information that store owners did not agree with (p. 77).

The rise of advertising as the primary source of revenue for newspapers had an important impact on the work environment for all levels. At the top, a greater division developed between publishers and editors, with the former gaining a more powerful role than the latter in the hierarchy. Sotiron (1997) argues that, as a result of this change, "publishers became less concerned with politics and more with raising circulation to gain advertising" (p. 52) and sought to exercise more control over their newspaper as a business operation.

Looking to control both the newsprint and the content that was printed on it, businesses sought to *vertically integrate* to gain advantage over both supply and demand. Originally a printing business, for example, Southam made itself into a corporately linked newspaper chain, "a permanent centrally managed corporation that administers linked newspapers" (p. 88), meaning that the paper operations were standardized and subject to business priorities of accounting, administration, and corporate efficiency. Competitors were reduced by "forced mergers" or by outright purchase of the competition (ibid.). The "remaining players formed industry associations," such as the Canadian Publishers Association (est. 1859), which was succeeded by the Canadian Daily Newspaper Association (CDNA), making formal or informal agreements in their own favour to restrict competition via "abandoning price competition" (ibid., p. 93) on subscription costs, for example. In this way, the media was treated like any other business, and newspaper owners were also owners of a variety of other resource industries like mining, railways, and shipping (ibid.).

Some observations can also be made about the impact of newspaper technologies in the changes that were taking place in Canada and the United States in the years before and just after World War I. Apart from the telegraph, and a limited telephone network, there was little equipment around that would allow the reporter to gather much material from the relative comfort of the newspaper office. Instead, the reporter had to rely on personal observation and face-to-face interviews. This meant that the journalist was much closer—geographically, emotionally, and socially—to his or her sources. It was this physical, economic, cultural, and political closeness that produced reporters and novelists like American Upton Sinclair and made them active radicals. As the technologies of news-gathering gained a hold in the newsroom, the distance between reporters and their sources increased. News-gathering became much more about the transfer of information from similarly equipped centres of influence—the government bureaucracy and the large commercial firm—than a process of gathering from observation and discussion with ordinary people out on the street. The development of national newspaper chains and the reduced influence of purely "local" papers also contributed to this process (an example of commercial convergence). Thus, while the shifting technologies were important, a corresponding shift was a social one: Reporters were no longer part of the audience or public that they *reported* for; they were much more closely aligned to the interests of owners or who they *worked* for and thus more likely to share the worldview of the proprietor.

Similar to the earlier transition in England, and evident in Canada as well as the United States by this time, Upton Sinclair lamented in *The Brass Check* that the representative bias in the modern press became pro-business and anti-labour. Sinclair (1924) called this the "Empire of Business" and argued that it exercised four types of control over journalism in newspapers and magazines: "First, ownership of the papers; second, ownership of the owners; third, advertising subsidies; and fourth, direct bribery. By these methods there exists in America a control of news and of current comment more absolute than any monopoly in any other industry" (p. 241).

The transformation of the role and function of journalism had already begun in the Victorian era in Canada, assisted by the introduction of the telegraph and telephone, and the shift in ownership and purpose. With a certain amount of standardization occurring, so too was there a shift in how news was reported. One of the first influences on the standardization of journalism was due to the use of technology. Both the telegraph and the telephone assisted in transforming the style of writing. Journalists began to craft text that followed the style of telegraph messages, and once telephones became commonly used for interviews, Fetherling (1990) argues that by the 1880s, deadlines became shortened and interviews became less formal. He states that interviews were reduced "to impressionism and eliminating the emphasis on completeness and stenographic accuracy that had characterized the form in the 1870s" (Fetherling, 1990, p. 69). This is not to say that the journalism practised prior to the introduction of such technologies was necessarily of an ideal type, but the technology changed the way the work was done by reducing the time spent with people whose stories were to be told and by speeding up the process more generally.

Such transitions in ownership, technology, and labour were also marked by the struggle by the labourers to organize and represent themselves within the now-established commercial industry. The first communication workers' union in Canada was formed by the printers (then called typographical workers). Amalgamating American and Canadian workers, the International Typographical Union was established in Canada in 1872 when the federal government passed the Trade Union Act, but it was not a foregone accomplishment. Contextually, even basic union organizing was a tremendous undertaking during this time. Continuing technological change, and profit imperatives to extract the most work for the least amount of payment, made for long working hours in dangerous working conditions.

For most of the first half of the twentieth century, public expression of the concerns of labourers could be life-threatening, as picketing and striking were considered criminal activities. That unions are still considered threatening, dangerous, and powerful—and are generally negatively framed in the commercial media as such—has changed little since the nineteenth century (Parenti, 1986; Puette, 1992; Winter, 1997), despite the fact they are responsible for ensuring better and safer working conditions, reasonable hours, equitable pay scales, and gender pay equity (Heron, 1996). Each of these literally had to be fought for to be legally binding through the collective agreement (a periodic agreement made among and between union members and the employer).

For Real?

Organizing Workers

While the 1872 Trade Union Act provided for the recognition of trade unions, it was not until almost *70 years later* that federal government legislation was established to protect workers from being fired because of union activity or refused employment because of union membership. Prior to this legislation, however, basic rights such as freedom of association and freedom of expression could be denied if these involved labour in any way. A consistently hostile, anti-union establishment used all means possible to disrupt or eliminate union organizing, including harassment, threats, physical violence, and loss of employment. Such actions were supported by the various levels of state authority, adding deportation, costly fines, and/or prison to a list of serious consequences (Mazepa, 2003). In the newspaper industry, owners would band together to try and break strikes and discourage or stymy any attempt at union organizing, a tactic that is not uncommon in the present day (Sotiron, 1992). It was against such a restricted and treacherous framework in which labour tried to represent itself, such that only a small percentage of workers belonged to trade unions.

The media workers that were able to organize were for the most part very fragmented, similar to overall patterns of unionization in Canada. Divisions were made on the basis of trade or occupation differentiation, national or international affiliation, and inter-union rivalry, among many others. They were also divided on the basis of gender and race and ethnicity, as the media industry—whether in the printing trades, as journalists or as editors—was predominately male, English- or French-speaking, and of British or French descent (Robinson, 2005). Today, however, of the small overall percentage of unionized workers in Canada (roughly 30 per cent), there is still a large percentage who are communications workers (HRSDC, 2013; 🖥 www4.hrsdc. gc.ca/.3ndic.1t.4r@-eng.jsp?iid=17; Statistics Canada, 2009, p. 28). As McKercher (2002) identified, the convergence that is taking place through technology and ownership in the media industry is also resulting in changes to the structure of unions as the organizations also converge in an attempt to handle increasing job losses, while retaining some control over their own labour and participate in decision-making in the industry as a whole. As we discuss further in Chapter 10, this retention of control and the ability to participate in decision-making is becoming increasingly more difficult as more full-time unionized workers are replaced by "citizen-journalists" who work for free, or by computers that write copy by using software.

Discussion Questions

1. Do an online search of the major communication workers and journalist unions in Canada (such as the Communication, Energy and Paperworkers Union [CEP] and the Communications Workers of America [CWAISCA Canada]); identify the following:

    a) What occupations does their membership include?

    b) How are they structured as organizations? (For example, how is the organization governed? What kinds of departments or operations does it have? What does membership entail?)

    c) What goals and objectives does each have (nationally and internationally)? What kinds of advocacy or other campaigns regard communication (policy) in Canada? Are these issues important to you? Explain why or why not.

2. Do another online search of commercial media coverage of CEP or CWAISCA Canada: When do either (or any) of these organizations make the news, and why?

The *fourth period* of Canadian newspapers can be understood as the period following the First World War and ending in the 1960s (Kesterton, 1967). In this period, the transformation of newspapers was marked by the beginning of consolidated ownership and centralization, an increase in the industrialization of the newspaper business, and the emergence of a greater professionalization of journalism and journalists. This was the period where newspapers in Canada became even more entrenched as business enterprises. The newspaper market began to act like most other markets producing a product for sale, and ownership became more concentrated. This followed the pattern of structuring in the United States, as there, by 1920, newspaper publishing had become big business (McChesney & Scott, 2003, pp. xv–xvii).

The shift towards *monopoly* (single ownership) and *oligopoly* (ownership by a very few) led to what became known as the "crisis" in journalism, which continues even today. It was, in essence, a struggle between those journalists, like Upton Sinclair, who saw journalism as a kind of progressive "muckraking" as the impetus that lays at the core of journalism and those who saw journalism as a product for sale. It was the journalist-as-muckraker's job to take up the cause of the downtrodden against the rise of monopoly capitalism and to eschew newspapers owned by "robber barons" such as Joseph Pulitzer and William Randolph Hearst, whose large corporate newspapers promoted the sensational, outrageous, salacious, and bawdy news-as-entertainment, or what came to be called "yellow," journalism. According to McChesney and Scott (2003), "the hallowed obligation of the democratic press to accurately report public affairs was brushed aside by a wave of gimmicky features, fakery, and hysterical headlines" (p. xvii).

It was the working out of this dialectic—excessive commercialism struggling with and against the tradition of the muckrakers and progressive journalists, together with a public increasingly wary of the power of media—that eventually led to the development of what we might now call "professional" journalism (Nerone, 2012). It was a time when a reporter's training became based on the creed of objectivity and on the ideology of pluralism within the unchallenged context of a purported free market for ideas (ibid.). Freedom of the press meant that most of the criticism was reserved for selected actions of the government, leaving the general interests of business (especially of the newspaper owners, advertisers, and their affiates) relegated to sporadic events that were otherwise impossible to ignore. This tendency is well-documented, as even today many stories are missing from the news entirely, and corporate media systematically distort, marginalize, or under-represent particular issues, individuals, or groups via a process of news selection and management—a combination of **gatekeeping** (selecting who or what gets into the news) **agenda setting** (what is identified as important and prioritized, or not), and **framing** (how an event, issue, or person is represented). Pick up any commercial newspaper in the world, for example, and review all of its sections. While there are sections for news, comics, cooking, or travel, there is no section called "labour" from the point of view of the labourer. Can you imagine a section called "labour activism" or "union organizing"?

As Herman and Chomksy (1988) argue, this isn't necessarily a deliberate conspiracy set by the newspaper owners or the journalists working for them, but an outgrowth of the commercial structure of news that results in "news filters." These filters include *ownership* (companies will rarely criticize their affiliates), *advertising* (don't bite the hand that feeds you), *flack* (avoidance of legal threats or individual pressure on editors or journalists from advertisers or business owners who want to eliminate critical coverage of themselves), *ideology* (e.g., avoidance, rejection, or ridicule of the validity of alternative ideas about political economic and social systems), or *sources* (the tendency to solicit and passively accept official—or managed—news agendas, information, and interpretation either from the corporation itself or from public relations firms hired to manage media). Herman and Chomsky also argue that such practices so narrow the scope

AGENDA SETTING

Identifying who and what is most important as news of the day, and which stories are subsequently carried forward and for how long.

FRAMING

The context or organizing theme (structural, visual, or textual) that suggests a dominant meaning or way of understanding what or who is being represented in the media and how.

GATEKEEPING

Media choices—a selection of whose voices and what messages gets covered in the media.

of information, dialogue, and range of debate possible that the content of commercial media is reduced to the status of "propaganda," supporting both the political economic interests of the corporations that own them, the state, and the overarching capitalist economy (Mazepa, 2011).

Formalizing Journalism

Prior to the 1900s, there were no formal journalism schools in Canada or the United States, but by 1915 they were well-established at major universities in the United States. McChesney and Scott (2003) argue that the rise of professionalism in American journalism at this time was a response to the so-called yellow journalism, and also to the critique of progressive writers such as Sinclair and others about the "corruption, dishonesty, and class bias of journalism." This critique was a direct challenge to the power of the press barons of the day; "professionalism" was their "tame" solution (p. xix), and as you shall see in Chapter 10, media owners would be quick to capitalize on the professional status of the journalist.

The first journalism education programs in Canada began in the 1940s with a journalism course offered at Carleton College, in Ottawa, and at the University of Western Ontario, in London, where a degree program was established in 1946. Ryerson Institute of Technology (later Ryerson University) began courses in journalism in 1955, and a diploma program was established in 1964. The main aim was to attract returning servicemen following World War II (Kesterton, 1967, p. 164). Prior to this, in the 1920s, many young journalists received experience while attending universities in Canada, writing for campus papers such as *The Ubyssey* in Vancouver, *The Varsity* in Toronto, and *The McGill Daily* in Montreal.

Another contributing factor to the professionalism and also to the standardization of journalism in this period was the rise of wire services, and particularly the establishment of the Canadian Press (CP). The roots of what would become a national non-profit cooperative news service began in 1907 over a conflict between Canadian newspapers, particularly those in Manitoba, and the Canadian Pacific Telegraphs, which had the monopoly on the distribution of international news from the Associated Press (AP) in the United States (p. 159). The AP's news tended to favour American interests, and as such, it exercised its gatekeeping abilities to not report on government changes in Britain, which had significant repercussions in Canada (Fetherling, 1990, p. 105). This led many Western papers to join together to create the Western Associated Press to challenge the CP Telegraph monopoly. One of the new service's first actions was to establish a news bureau in Ottawa. Following this model, other wire services developed, and in 1917 they merged to create CP—as a national, non-profit cooperative—formalized in 1932.

The importance of a Canadian wire service was threefold. Firstly, it allowed Canadian newspapers to receive international news that was determined relevant to them by Canadian sources. Secondly, it also provided more timely national news for Canadians from Ottawa (Kesterton, 1967, p. 159), and finally, it created a non-partisan Ottawa bureau as part of the parliamentary Press Gallery, reducing the level of corruption in the Press Gallery due to the bribery of journalists by lobbyists (Fetherling, 1990, p. 104). Its existence as a cooperative, however, was somewhat of an anomaly in a commercial media system supposedly based on competition. As Canadian media historian Gene Allen (2004) discovered in his analysis of the records of CP, the real purpose was to monopolize the news by controlling its distribution, and thus also controlling competition. Members were therefore designated to be "morning" or "afternoon" papers, and were legally committed to "explicit and binding provisions to control competition especially related to time" (Allen, 2009, p. 53). In this way, **news agencies** acted more like cartels controlling the industry according to their own rules.

NEWS AGENCIES
Organizations established as the central point of collection, composition, exchange, and distribution of information (text, images, and digital forms). These can be for-profit *commercial* agencies (such as AP, Thomson Reuters, or Canadian Press Enterprises Inc.), *not-for-profit* collectives (like the former Canadian Press/La Presse Canadienne, 1917–2010), or *state-run* (China's Xinhua News Agency or Russia's ITAR-TASS).

Focus on Research

Race and Gender in Journalism

The first newly trained journalists were most likely to be white, male, and the more fortunate members of the working class. As Canadian media historian Gertrude Robinson presents in her overview of print journalism in Canada, it wasn't until the 1970s when women came close to having relatively equal professional standing in journalism. Women who wanted to be journalists were subject to significant barriers to entry and progression, which Robinson (2005) attributes to structural barriers in the media industry including "access, promotional patterns, beat structures, and pay" (p. 27). These structural barriers are significant, as even today, whether in Canada or other liberal democracies such as the United States, Germany, or Denmark, "the average representation of women in all media sectors is remarkably uniform" (ibid.) with only a third of all media jobs employing women.

Without empirical research it would otherwise appear that news has a gender balance, particularly as the faces we see on television network news give the impression that there is gender equity, if not racial representation, which is itself skewed. In regard to the latter, media researchers Frances Henry and Carol Tator (2000) found "media bias and discrimination" evident in their case study analysis of the print media in Canada. Their research findings included the following:

> *People of colour are underrepresented and largely invisible in the media.*
>
> *When people of colour do appear in media coverage, they are often misrepresented and stereotyped.*
>
> *The corporatist nature of the media influences the kind of news that is produced and disseminated. (Henry & Tator, 2000, para. 2; www.crr.ca/index2.php?option=com_content&do_pdf=1&id=256)*

Studies such as these use a number of research methods (e.g., case study and qualitative analysis), which take a lot of resources (time, people, and education) to be able to provide valid and reliable empirical findings. Thus it is rare to have cross-national comparisons, but it

Although the news agency model is similar elsewhere in terms of collecting and controlling the dissemination and distribution of news, there are different kinds of institutional ownership (www.thecanadianpress.com/about_cp.aspx?id=77); whereas AP and CP (and later La Presse Canadienne, established in 1951) are now commercial cooperatives, there are also state-financed operations like BBC World Service, joint state-commercial operations like Agence France-Presse (AFP), and state-controlled news agencies like China Xinhua News Agency (www.xinhuanet.com/english/) and the Russian ITAR-TASS (www.itar-tass.com/eng/).

Operating on a for-profit basis, the ownership and control of the collection, dissemination, and distribution of news and information is a practice that is currently globally concentrated in the largest (for-profit) financial news agency: Thomson Reuters. Founded in 1851, Reuters is now the largest collector and distributor of text, video, pictures, and graphics of events and issues based on a range of scientific, medical, educational, and financial information that subscribers pay for based on real time access and on the type of information (www.reuters.com). Its is all the more necessary in order to indicate that such discriminations are not specific to one country, but evident across them, thus indicating more systemic power relations. For example, the recent *Global Report on the Status of Women in the News Media* (Byerly, 2011)—a survey of 522 companies in 59 countries—found that gender imbalance is consistent, with only 33 per cent of all media positions held by women (🖥 iwmf.org/pioneering-change/global-research-on-women-in-the-news-media.aspx). The discrepancy was highest in news management, with women holding only 29 per cent of the decision-making positions, followed by 36 per cent of the news-gathering (reporting) positions.

This suggests that the combined ideologies of capitalism (which profits from the division of labour) and patriarchy (which views men as superior to women) are institutionalized in these structures and, as such, are significantly more difficult to change.

Discussion Questions

1. Choose two current issues in the commercial daily newspapers in print in your city or town; according to the divisions in the newspaper (e.g., news [front section only], sports, business) see if you can identify the gender of the journalists by their names, and count them.

2. Of the total number of males and females that you can identify, how many stories are written by men and how many by women?

3. In which sections are the stories written by men and by women concentrated?

4. Now take the same sections and identify how many images are included in the stories in these sections. See if you can identify the race or gender of the people in the photographs, and count how many men and women are represented. After you have finished counting, identify what the photograph is representing and how.

   a) Are there differences between how women and men are represented?

   b) In which sections are people of colour included in the newspaper?

   c) What kind of research methodology have you employed?

   d) Discuss your findings: How are these related to the commercial structure of the news?

ownership and collection of information is reaching staggering proportions. With over 55,000 employees operating in over 100 countries, Reuters is continually collecting, prepackaging, and digitizing information—even in its own news bureau in the virtual world of the game "Second Life" (Reuters, 2010). As you shall see, Reuters has a Canadian connection in that its former chairman (Kenneth R. Thomson) was one of the media barons whose enterprise has expanded based on a business model of both vertical *and* horizontal integration.

From the 1960s until the 1990s, the *fifth period* of the newspaper industry in Canada was marked by even greater levels of ownership concentration leading to considerable reductions in competition. The scale of concentration became so significant that the federal government engaged in two reviews of Canadian media in this period, the first being the Special Senate Committee on Mass Media (also known as the Davey Report, 1970) and the second being the Royal Commission on Newspapers (also known as the Kent Commission, 1981). Both evaluated media ownership as combining a concentration of private control over information, decreased diversity of perspectives, and demonstrated lack of social and public responsibility by the press. As with most Canadian public inquiries, despite the numerous and practical recommendations directed to the public interest and communication rights (e.g., legislating the right to editorial independence from publishers or owners), the response of the federal government was "laissez-faire," ceding to the profit or business imperative and, as Jackson (1999) observed, to the domestic political imperative of a "societal and government reluctance to intervene in the operation of the free market economy and the so-called 'free press'" (Conclusion, para. 1; 🖥 publications.gc.ca/Collection-R/LoPBdP/BP/prb9935-e.htm). This equation of "freedom" with both the market and the commercial press was an argument the Kent Commission had repeatedly heard during their inquiries, such that it included this critical comment in the final report:

> *"In a country that has allowed so many newspapers to be owned by so few conglomerates, freedom of the press means, in itself, only that enormous influence without responsibility is conferred on a handful of people. For the heads of such organizations to justify their position by appealing to the principle of freedom of the press is offensive to intellectual honesty." (as cited in Jackson, 1999, ibid.)*

The demise of many of the smaller city papers and a constantly changing landscape of ownership groups marked a somewhat unstable terrain. This period was also a very important time in terms of political economic issues in Canada, including the Quiet Revolution in Quebec in the 1960s (a rebellion to change authority and control from the Catholic Church and federal government to the province), the FLQ crisis in the early 1970s (a violent movement for Quebec nationalism), and the repatriation of the Constitution in 1982 (which spurred a myriad of referenda and constitutional negotiations through the 1980s and 1990s). In addition, the Canadian economy was also facing numerous challenges from external events, such as the OPEC crisis (oil embargo), and internal challenges, such as high unemployment and stagflation, among others. The Canadian federal government then pursued economic policies that would transform the country and its future, which included the (failed) National Energy Program and Wage and Price Controls, which were followed by the Free Trade Agreement with the United States in the 1980s. This was expanded to the North American Free Trade Agreement (NAFTA) in the 1990s, and deficit reduction plans in the 1990s, that removed the foundations supporting social and health care in Canada, ushering in the current era of neo-liberalism. As we discuss further in later chapters, such political economic practices also include tax reductions (or eliminations) for corporations, market priorities as leading decision-making (to facilitate commodification and financialization, e.g.), and attendant elimination or significant changes in government labour and environmental, communication, and cultural regulations. Given our review of press history here, it is no small coincidence that private ownership or "freedom of the press is guaranteed only to those who own one" (A. J. Liebling).

Canada's Greatest Export: Media "Magnatism" or the Exchange Value of News?

In reviewing dominant accounts of the history of Canadian media, it appears that one of Canada's most significant contributions to commercial newspapers has been producing a healthy crop of influential media barons, whose aim was to control the media in not only Canada but also abroad. The first family-run national newspaper chain began with William Southam (1843–1932) in 1897 when Southam, who controlled the *Hamilton Spectator*, bought the *Ottawa Citizen*, and then the *Calgary Herald* a decade later, in 1907. Southam, as Sotiron (1997) argues, pioneered what would become a popular media magnate practice of leveraging existing businesses to expand the family business when he borrowed against the *Hamilton Spectator* and the family's printing enterprises to purchase both of these papers and the many more that followed (p. 89). The empire expanded with the purchase of the *Edmonton Journal* and the *Lethbridge Herald* in 1912, and additional properties in Montreal and Vancouver. Once the family reorganized its business structure under one corporate entity (the Canadian Newspapers Ltd.), they began to operate using many of the same practices we see today in concentrated media ownership, including cost-savings by negotiating lower newsprint processes and sharing purchases and supplies between its newspapers, which included staff and writers (p. 90). Over time, the Southam media empire expanded beyond newspapers to horizontally integrate into broadcasting, magazines, bookstores, and business publications.

Casting doubt on the capitalist adage that "bigger is better," Southam Inc. faced troubling economic times in the 1980s and 1990s despite its extensive and diverse business holdings. The debt incurred in its efforts to grow its holdings meant that it could not sustain its size and was more susceptible to economic fluctuations such that several of its holdings were incrementally sold off, including a percentage of its newspaper division, which was sold to Conrad Black's Hollinger Inc. in 1992. Newspaper ownership among the biggest corporations changed hands several times over. Only eight years later, in 2000, Black sold the Southam papers to Canwest Media Inc. Over the first decade of the twenty-first century, Canwest sold some of the Southam papers, such as the founding one, the *Hamilton Spectator*, to Torstar Corporation. Canwest Media Inc. faced serious debt problems during the economic crisis of 2009 when it sold the remaining Southam papers to Postmedia Network Inc., led by Paul Godfrey, as part of a bankruptcy auction.

Black (1944–) is currently regarded as Canada's most notorious media baron. Lord Black of Crossharbour, who—like his predecessor Roy Thomson—gave up his Canadian citizenship to accept a British peerage, was the largest newspaper owner in Canada for most of the 1990s. Although his corporation (Hollinger Inc.) owned many pedigree international newspapers like the *Chicago Sun-Times* and *Tribune*, the London *Telegraph*, and the *Jerusalem Post*, he owned only a few small dailies in Canada until 1995. In that year, Hollinger Inc. acquired 24 dailies in Ontario, Quebec, and the Atlantic provinces from Thomson Corp., the Sifton family, and the Southam chain. This was followed by a continued spate of purchases including the *Financial Post* from Sun Media Corp. in 1997, which Black used as the foundation to establish the *National Post*—Canada's second national newspaper—in 1998, challenging, according to Black, "the overwhelming avalanche of soft, left, bland, envious pap which has poured like sludge" (Miller, 1998, p. 67) from other Canadian newspapers. Hollinger Inc.'s operation of newspapers was clearly a business enterprise, with more concern for the bottom line than the byline. During Black's tenure as owner of the Canadian papers, there were numerous layoffs and bureau closures. Additionally, Black did not respect the separation between ownership and editorial privilege, specifically in terms of ideological positions, which was made plain in the resignation of a series of well-regarded editors of his papers (e.g., Joan Fraser from the Montreal *Gazette* and James Travers from the *Ottawa Citizen*; Miller, 1998).

Black's ownership and influence over the Canadian newspaper industry was significant but short-lived, as Hollinger Inc. divested itself of the *National Post* and other Canadian papers through a sale to Canwest Global Communications Corp. in 2000. Following this sale, and the sale of other international media properties, Black's business practices came under scrutiny, first by other shareholders in Hollinger International and eventually by the American justice system.

In 2007, Black was charged with four counts of fraud and one count of obstruction of justice and sentenced to six years in prison in the United States. In 2010, he won an appeal of his original sentence and was released on bail. Although he only briefly owned newspapers in Canada, his influence on the Canadian newspaper landscape was significant; as the single largest owner of Canadian newspapers, his commitment to the ultimate commercialization of newspapers has had a lasting impact on their future.

As the commercialization of newspapers continues to develop, structures of ownership morph from *family* ownership, to *corporate* ownership, to what media analyst professor John Soloski (2012) calls "*investor*" or "*institutional*" ownership, with a substantial shift in priorities. Where the newspapers of the distant past tended to be separately owned businesses, with an obligation to their readers and a stake in the community in which they operated, they were developed into vertically and horizontally integrated corporations, and multimedia-national or multinational conglomerates more accountable to their shareholders than their workers, readers, or communities (McKercher, 2002). As Soloski's research over the past two decades indicates, the current patterns in Canada reviewed above—of prioritizing corporate and financial growth, which can lead to

Case Study

Future Business Model for Newspapers in a Digital World

In March 2012, The Pew Research Center's Project for Excellence in Journalism released a report titled *The Search for a New Business Model: An In-Depth Look at How Newspapers Are Faring Trying to Build Digital Revenue*. The report's authors collected detailed advertising revenue data from a cross section of newspapers across the United States. Following the analysis of the data, the researchers conducted interviews with newspaper executives about their findings. The report presents the research findings from this 16-month effort and highlights some interesting trends in the US newspaper market in general, and in relation to the transition to digital revenue streams more specifically.

In general, the report states that the vast majority of newspapers in the United States are smaller circulation papers of 25,000 or less. "There are roughly 1,350 surviving US English-language daily newspapers, down from about 1,400 five years ago. The vast majority of these papers are smaller, less than 25,000 circulation. There are 70 papers remaining in the US with circulations more than 100,000" (Rosenstiel & Jurkowitz, 2012, p. 5). Some more specific findings from the report related to how newspapers currently generate revenue were enlightening, but more significant was the finding of how little has changed. Despite the claims that the newspaper would become obsolete in the digital era, this has not occurred. This is not to say that newspapers aren't being challenged with the introduction of new formats, whether online or digital. Overall, the report argues that the industry has lost 40 per cent of its advertising revenue in the last decade (p. 4). The digital era for newspapers, which the authors estimate has been around for 15 years now, has had a different effect on different papers, depending on their size. The authors note that while digital advertising revenues are "growing at a double-digit pace" (p. 5), it still makes up only a small percentage of the entire advertising pot, with print advertising comprising approximately 85 per cent of all revenue for the whole industry.

The success in digital revenue growth is greater among the larger papers, while the loss of print revenue is slower for smaller papers, leading the researchers to conclude that smaller US debt, bankruptcy, and subsequent and continuous buyouts—are similar in the United States and have resulted in "chains . . . cannabalizing chains" (Soloski, 2012, p. 313), with the result that "the number of publicly traded newspaper companies was nearly halved in less than a decade" (ibid.).

Commodification is extended and intensified with the move from publicly traded companies (as owned by shareholders with at least a semblance of public accountability) to private companies owned by institutional investors, which significantly alters the media environment by extending the process of financialization (see Chapter 3) to the news. Thus, as Soloski identifies, newspaper managers are restructuring their own operating environment in order to make the newspapers more attractive as a financial investment, and to satisfy the requirements of investors and lending companies (either of which can decide the fate of the newspaper). This shifts the entire basis of public accountability from the newspaper as a whole (and the individual journalist) to a financial accountability favoured by the financier:

> The ability to use bankruptcy to shed debt, force union concessions and void long-term contractual agreements makes ownership of newspapers highly attractive

newspapers have more time to adapt to the changing digital environment. Overall though, the report notes that for every dollar gained in digital revenue, seven dollars are lost in print revenue (p. 1). Beyond the aggregated results, the researchers also noted that not all papers were the same in terms of their success in wooing new digital advertising. They highlight a number of different efforts that some papers have taken to improve their revenues to support their traditional business, including some non-newspaper-related activities like creating a consulting business to assist advertisers to learn "how to market themselves in the digital landscape" (p. 2).

Some of the reasons given in the executive interviews around why the change has been so difficult for newspapers are cultural, meaning "the difficulty of changing the behavior of people trained in the ways of a mature and monopolistic industry" (p. 2). One area where this was noted was in the disparity between the number of sales staff dedicated to print versus digital advertising. The latter continues to be a far smaller number overall, and not a group that is well-integrated with traditional sales staff (pp. 22–3). The conclusion of the report is that there have been varying degrees of success in the transition of newspapers from print to digital advertising revenue, and that there is still significant change ahead, particularly related to the adaptation to mobile technologies.

Discussion Questions

1. What is the dominant model for newspapers and journalism being considered in this report?

2. What are the indicators or measurements of "success" and what "challenges" are identified as significant?

3. Is what makes news a matter of *format* (print or online) or of *content*? What is the relationship between the two?

4. Identify two or three alternatives to commercial media structures. How do funding or financial structures impact definitions of "success"?

5. How significant a factor is copyright in alternative media structures?

even in bad economic times. But such a change in ownership may not bode well for the quality of journalism practiced at these newspapers. Despite the financial problems of existing publicly traded newspaper companies, management's roots are in journalism. This is not the case with institutional owners. (p. 327)

This (re)structuring prioritizes the exchange value of news, and while we may think that journalism is changing anyway due to social media (discussed further in Chapter 10) or that, in the long run, the use value of journalism/journalists may still be protected under "freedom of speech" or other such legal frameworks, such changes in ownership structure should give more pause to consider, given that, as Josephi (2012) identifies, these frameworks

do not offer protection of journalistic services that have to be largely financed privately. The dependency on media owners is no less in many democratic nations than it is in non-democratic countries. Ultimately, journalism needs the support of the public, elected politicians or political elites and rules who see value in independent information provision and credible news judgment. (p. 486)

The Future of Newspapers: Paywalls or "Free" (Personalized) News?

While the use value of news in relation to democracy (however and wherever it is practised) should be of primary public concern, the pressures of the financialization of the news leads principal decision-makers to focus on a perennial question underpinning the commodification of news: How can it make (more) money? As our case study, "Future Business Model for Newspapers in a Digital World," suggests, one of the challenges to newspapers is the digitization of content. **Paywalls** are but one "solution" that facilitate the extension of commodification to digital content. When newspapers first went online, however, most or all of the content was originally free. This belied the traditional business model, because there wasn't a dominant commodified structure already in place. Among other assumptions "about what things should cost on the internet" (Coughlan, 2010, para. 13), within the industry, it was predicted that the content would pay for itself, because the money to be made from advertisers wanting access to readers would be more than the money that could be made by subscription alone.

Offering any content for free had early and powerful detractors. In February 2010, Rupert Murdoch—the owner of News Corporation—instituted subscription charges, or paywalls, for online content (BBC, 2010). The move was closely monitored both within and beyond the media industry, not simply as an experiment or measurement of revenue gain or loss, but pivotal to the *idea* of charging for access to any information on the Internet. Persuading people that it's normal to pay for content—any content—is fundamental to the process of commodification and essential to capitalism and capitalist hegemony in general. The existence of public media as practised by the British Broadcasting Corporation (BBC), the Australian Broadcasting Corporation (ABC), and the Canadian Broadcasting Corporation (CBC)—all of which offer content for free—is another significant challenge to the dominant hegemonic commercial model (Macnamara, 2010, p. 28), and suggests another reason (discussed further in Chapter 6) why commercial interests would strive to eliminate public broadcasting entirely.

Subsequent reports suggest that there continues to be substantial public resistance to payment (ibid.), and initially, online readership for *The Times* was reportedly down a staggering

PAYWALLS

Commodifying online content by setting terms of payment for access; paywalls are used to identify restrictions to online content based on the ability and willingness to pay as generally applied to online newspapers.

90 per cent (Halliday, 2010). However, if more and more commercial newspapers adopt this strategy, despite the risks to the corporation in declining readership, the public may "get used to paying" and the tide may turn. As identified in the timeline at the end of this chapter, in Canada, *The Globe and Mail* and the Postmedia chain of newspapers have recently set up paywalls. Where this is a strategy based on a broadcasting model—from one to the many—the **personalization of news** and micro-targeting of advertising may result in another model whereby news is narrowcast to suit the individual's preferences, as a way of increasing their attraction to advertisers in relation to their interests and income.

The rise of e-readers and e-book applications for handheld devices like the iPhone are opening a new avenue to focus on the individual and hold some financial promise for the future of newspapers. The popularity of e-readers such as Amazon's Kindle and the Apple iPad is growing. Between its US launch in April and the end of June 2010, the iPad had sold approximately three million units; when the iPhone 5 was introduced in September 2012, it sold over five million units in the first two months; www.statisticbrain.com/iphone-5-sales-statistics/). The constant introduction of new apps for the iPhone and for e-books is proving that there is a transformation afoot in the print world such that not only can news be targeted but so can any form of media content.

Although it is not likely that these new platforms will eliminate the print editions of newspapers or books, publishers are beginning to take notice of these new avenues for revenue generation. Murdoch and the publishers of *The New York Times* recognized that these e-readers provide additional opportunities to charge for content, and perhaps even create new platforms for advertising sales in the future. The move to "audience fragmentation" or "disaggregation" (Macnamara, 2010, p. 22) through targeted content or by individual delivery device is having a significant effect on the bottom line of the media industry such that different models are developed as commercial alternatives. This includes interactive advertising (e.g., getting readers/users to engage with advertising through gaming); the use of "behaviour targeting" (involving the tracking and "capture of user profile data" to "distribute relevant advertising to targeted consumers"); and as related the selling of data collected about "media users and their interests, needs, and patterns of information search and purchasing from web statistics [and] search engines" among many other possibilities (ibid., pp. 29–30). This results in a feedback loop, where data is aggregated (particulary from media corporations that own a whole range of media including its content, access, and distribution mechanisms), that can give individual consumers exactly what they ask for (whether they know it or not).

As our definition from Neil Thurman (2011) indicates, the personalization of news can be both "explicit" and "implicit" (p. 397), combining the process of commodification with an extended fragmentation of the audience. In this case, the goal isn't necessarily to commodify the news. Although copyright can still be an important factor, content can be offered for free, such that a more lucrative goal would be the exchange value of the information collected from the individual readers/users. Whereas "explicit personalization uses direct user inputs, implicit personalization infers preferences from data collected, for example, via a registration process or via the use of software that monitors user activity (Gauch et al. 2007)" (ibid.).

In making a version of what Nicholas Negroponte (1996) called "The Daily Me," Thurman (2011) identifies how news content can be produced via "automated editorial processes" that gather information via computer algorithms (explained in Chapter 7) calibrating any number of explicit or implicit feeds. Explicit data collection includes user-registered preferences or associated recommendations for categories of content, types of applications and news feeds, or any other kind of information that can be used to provide "geo-targeted editions" or "profile-based recommendations" (ibid., p. 411). Implicit collection occurs via data collected from matching

PERSONALIZATION OF NEWS

"A form of user-to-system interactivity that uses a set of technological features to adapt the content, delivery, and arrangement of a communication to individual users' explicity registered and/ or implicitly determined preferences" (Thurman, 2011, p. 397).

content preferences and selections with geo-locations, individual computer (IP) addresses, or use of search terms (Thurman & Schifferes, 2012, Tables 1 and 2). This adds another factor to the news in terms of algorithms that seek to identify individual interests and tailor content accordingly, and is a significant factor underpinning changes to the labour of journalism (more on this in Chapter 10) and is fundamental to the development of a surveillance economy (Chapter 12).

This commodication of both content and readers is further complemented in the movement by Google Inc. to digitalize books, as negotiations and disputes arise over who gets to establish what content is free and what content is not. These are only the most current examples of a continuing struggle to control the use value of information (and therefore its access, distribution, and potential to facilitate knowledge and social change), over its exchange value. In the next chapter you will see how this struggle continues with our review of analogue digital media as we trace the development of still and moving pictures.

Key Points

- New technologies continue to create new syntheses, even in the oldest of the mass broadcast media: print.
- Changes in technology are inseparable from changes in labour, content, and ownership.
- We can think of media as products of social relations, such social class, gender, and race.
- Print is important in advancing democracy and social change, and so is the manner in which copyright, monopoly, and oligarchy ownership manage and control it.

Class Discussion

1. Identify the dominant power relations (in terms of social class, gender, and race) that are evident in this history of the press.
2. What do these social relations have to do with how the press developed in Canada, and how (much) have they changed over time?
3. Why is the state so important to media development in Canada, and elsewhere?
4. What are some of the affects of ownership concentration on media? How do these impact what is considered "news"?
5. What are news agencies? Why are they important in agenda setting, gatekeeping, or the framing of news?
6. Why is copyright history significant to the information or knowledge-based society?
7. How does the personalization of news affect content production and the current ability of media to exercise gatekeeping and agenda setting? How might this personalization affect how we identify what is important, and why?

Media on Media

Press Remix

Broccoli, B., Wilson, M. G. (Producers), & Spottiswoode, R. (Director). (1997). *Tomorrow never dies* [Motion picture]. United Kingdom: Eon Productions.

Coblenz, W. (Producer), & Pakula, A. J. (Director). (1976). *All the presidents' men* [Motion picture]. United States: Wildwood.

Finkleman, K., & Peter Meyboom, J. (Producers). (1996–7; 2003–5). *The newsroom* [Television series]. Canada: CBC.

The Living End. (2003). Tabloid magazine. *MODERN ARTillery*. London, UK: EMI. 🖱 www.sing365.com/music/lyric.nsf/Tabloid-Magazine-lyrics-The-Living-End/EA58CE778BAD930F48256DC2002FB3CF

Rachman, T. (2010). *The imperfectionists*. New York: Dial Press.

Rossi, A. (Director). (2011). *Page one: Inside the* New York Times [Documentary]. United States: Participant Media.

ValuSoft. (Developer). (2005). *Tabloid tycoon* [Video game].

Welles, O. (Producer & Director). (1941). *Citizen Kane* [Motion picture]. United States: RKO Radio Pictures.

Wilder, B. (Producer & Director). (1951). *Ace in the hole* [Motion picture]. United States: Paramount Pictures.

Timeline: From Gutenberg to Global News

1440 Johannes Gutenberg invents movable type.

1455 Gutenberg prints his first book, a Latin *Bible*.

1665 The first English newspaper, *The Oxford Gazette*, is founded.

1752 *The Halifax Gazette*, Canada's first newspaper, is published by John Bushnell.

1764 *The Quebec Gazette* is published in Quebec City.

1785 *The Daily Universal Register* is founded; it changed its name to *The Times* in 1788 and is now Britain's oldest surviving newspaper with continuous daily publication.

1793 The *Upper Canada Gazette, or American Oracle* is first published in the new province of Upper Canada (now Ontario).

1796 Lithography, a process enabling the printing of images, is invented by Alois Senefelder.

1806 First use of illustration in *The Times*.

1810 The *Kingston Gazette*, now the *Whig-Standard*, is founded.

1822 Mechanical typesetting is invented by William Church.

1835 Charles-Louis Havas launches Agence Havas—later called the Agence France-Presse (AFP) news agency.

1842 *The Illustrated London News* is launched, and is the first fully illustrated weekly publication.

1844 The Toronto *Globe* is founded by George Brown and later becomes *The Globe and Mail*.

1846 Richard Hoe patents the first rotary press.

1848 The Associated Press news agency is founded in New York.

1849 Paul Julius Reuter uses carrier pigeons to deliver (fly) stock-market prices between Aachen and Brussels.

The London Free Press is founded by William Sutherland.

1851 *The New York Times* is launched.

Reuters News Agency opens in London.

1855 The repeal of the Stamp Act in Britain opens the way for the production of low cost, commercial mass-circulation newspapers.

1858 The *Victoria Gazette* (supported by Sir James Douglas, governor of the Hudson's Bay Company) and *The British Colonist* (operated by Amor de Cosmos) are founded.

1862 Reuters aligns with American Associated Press.

1869 George Desbarats establishes the *Canadian Illustrated News*, which is the first *periodical* newspaper in the world to publish half-tone photographs (previously all illustrations in periodicals were from artist's engravings).

1872 John A. Kenny and William F. Luxton found the *Manitoba Free Press*, which would become the *Winnipeg Free Press*.

1873 The typewriter is invented.

1877 The Southam Company begins, with William Southam's purchase of the *Hamilton Spectator*.

1883 Reuters uses a "column printer" to transmit messages to London.

1892 The *Toronto Star* is founded by C. C. Campbell and Joseph E. Atkinson.

1901 The electric typewriter is invented.

1906 Canadian publishing house McClelland & Stewart is established.

1907 The National Union of Journalists is founded in the UK.

1917 The Canadian Press is founded with the merger of smaller regional wire services with a $50,000 annual grant from the federal government.

1921 Wirephoto, the first electronically transmitted photograph, is introduced.

1922 *Reader's Digest* is launched.

1923 *Time* magazine is launched.

1923   The Canadian Press is restructured as a non-profit cooperative.

1927   Reuters introduces the teleprinter, the forerunner of the telex.

1933   Penguin Press introduces the paperback book.

1934   The Thomson empire begins with Roy Thomson's purchase of the Timmins, Ontario, *Daily Press*.

1936   *Life* magazine is founded.

1939– AFP operates as a French-language anti-Nazi propaganda
1944   unit in London, England.

1944   AFP becomes publicly owned.

1953   *Playboy* magazine is launched.

1959   News agencies United Press and International News Service merge to form United Press International (UPI).

         Free Press Publications is founded with the merger of the Clifton family press and radio holdings with the Bell family media holdings.

1966   Roy Thomson buys *The Times*.

1967   *Rolling Stone* and *New York* magazine are launched.

1969   The Special Senate Committee on Mass Media, chaired by Senator Keith Davey, begins hearings.

1973   Reuters introduces the monitoring of financial markets.

         The *Washington Post* wins a Pulitzer Prize for reporting the Watergate scandal.

1981   The Canadian Royal Commission on Newspapers, chaired by Thomas Kent, releases its report assessing and criticizing the state of concentration in ownership in Canadian newspapers.

1982   The Gannett Company launches *USA Today*, the first newspaper published simultaneously in several cities, via satellite.

1986   *Today*, the first national colour newspaper, is launched by Eddy Shah.

1987   Robert Maxwell launches the *London Daily News*, the first attempt at a 24-hour newspaper in Britain. Publication ceases within a few months.

1992   Knight Ridder establishes the *Detroit Free Press Plus*, an online newspaper.

1994   The Halifax *Daily News* launches an online edition, becoming the first Canadian daily newspaper to do so.

1995   In Sweden, the Modern Times media group launches the world's first *Metro* newspaper, a free newspaper for commuters now published in 64 editions in 91 cities.

1996   The Internet Archive is established as a free digital library (🖳 archive.org/about/).

         Knight Ridder launches 31 news websites based around its daily newspapers.

1997   The National Library of France launches Gallica, an online collection of digitalized books (🖳 *gallica.bnf.fr/*).

1999   The Daily Mail group launches London *Metro* for commuters—in opposition to the Scandinavian product.

2001   *The Globe and Mail* introduces a digital edition of its newspaper through NewsStand, Inc.

2003   Media mogul Conrad Black resigns as CEO of Hollinger, and is subsequently sued by the Hollinger group for $200 million. He is later convicted of fraud and obstruction of justice in a Chicago court and sentenced to six years in jail. Following a successful appeal, he is resentenced, serves 13 months in prison, and is finally released in 2012 and given a one-year temporary residence permit to live in Canada.

2004   Google, in partnership with several universities and libraries, launches Google Print Library Project (later renamed Google Books) in order to digitize the text of books and magazines (🖳 www.google.ca/googlebooks/about/history.html).

2005   Google is sued by The Authors Guild (and other plaintiffs) for copyright infringement of its Google Books initiative. A partial settlement is reached in 2008; the case remains in court as of 2013 (🖳 www.authorsguild.org/advocacy/remember-the-orphans-battle-lines-being-drawn-in-hathitrust-appeal/).

2006   Philips Electronics announces the prototype of a screen-based electronic book.

         Knight Ridder is sold to The McClatchy Company for USD$4.5 billion.

         The Standing Senate Committee on Transport and Communication tables its final report on the Canadian News Media.

2008   The Thomson Corporation and Reuters merge to become the world's largest business media service.

         Europeana launches online, providing access to several European libraries, museums, archives, and audio-visual collections (🖳 www.europeana.eu*)*.

2010   The Canadian Press moves from non-profit cooperative to for-profit news service owned by Torstar Corp., CTVglobemedia, and Gesca (owners of *La Presse*).

         Postmedia Network Inc. is formed by Canwest bondholders and purchases all Canwest newspapers out of bankruptcy.

         Toronto-based company Kobo Inc. releases its Kobo eReader to compete with Amazon's Kindle.

         Random House (owned by Bertelsmann AG) buys the remaining 75 per cent Canadian ownership of McClelland & Stewart from the University of Toronto.

2011   BCE Inc. acquires CTVglobemedia from Torstar, The Woodbridge Company Limited, and the Ontario Teachers' Pension Plan for $1.3 billion.

         The Woodbridge Company Limited acquires Torstar's and the Ontario Teachers' Pension Plan's stakes in *The Globe and Mail*, leading to direct control (85 per cent) of the national paper. BCE retains 15 per cent ownership.

Rupert Murdoch's News Corporation closes its *News of the World* tabloid in the UK; charges of phone hacking, bribery, and internal corruption include subsidiaries in the United States and Australia.

2012 *The Globe and Mail*, as well as four Postmedia newspapers—the Ottawa Citizen, Vancouver Province, Vancouver Sun, and National Post—implement a metered paywall system to charge readers for access to online content.

Douglas & McIntyre Publishers—the largest Canadian-owned publisher—files for bankruptcy.

2013 E-book sales in Canada increase to approximately 17.6 per cent of the book market.

Apple Inc. loses US anti-trust court case for "price-fixing"—colluding with major book publishers to raise the price of e-books to "effectively eliminate price competition in the e-books industry" (El Akkad, 2013, para. 3). Apple will appeal.

Sun Media Corporation, a subsidiary of Quebecor Media, closes 11 newspapers and eliminates 360 positions.

The Canadian Auto Workers union (CAW) and the Communications, Energy and Paperworkers Union of Canada (CEP) merge into one union.

5 Industrial Light and Magic: A Brief History of Still and Moving Pictures

Objectives

After reading this chapter, you should understand the following:

- why the discovery of photography was important for the development of all other forms of mass media as a technology of representation and as an application of convergent technologies;

- how scientific breakthroughs in photography were put to particular social purposes;

- how the technology of moving pictures and synchronized sound are required elements of convergence because they are still the "standard" in terms of capturing the images and audio from the "real" event or performance; and

- the relationship between cinema, social relations, and the state—and the global influence of "Hollywood" content and its economic model as a synonym for American culture and values.

Keywords

- **camera obscura**
- **celluloid**
- **digital technology**
- **half-tone**
- **intellectual property (IP)**
- **patent**
- **photogravure**
- **pixel**
- **realism**
- **trademark**

CELLULOID

Based on the natural polymer cellulose, celluloid is a form of plastic, from which film was originally made in pre-digital times. The word has also become a shorthand way of describing the world of film and its ephemeral character.

The reproduction of images—first on paper, then on film, and now in digital form—has defined mass communication almost as much as the invention of the printing press. Moreover, it has defined the very evolution of our species, as archaeologists identify that the earliest cave drawings were fundamental in the development of the human capacity for memory (Cook, 2013). The ability to record and distribute these images—still, then moving—in printed forms, in celluloid form, over the telephony network, through the air, and in various non-digital and digital wireless forms, continues to influence our cultural expressions. We start here in this part of the chapter with still photography, and consider the ways the still image has etched its way into our understanding of both ourselves—through the family album—and our world.

The second part of this chapter outlines the history of motion pictures from the days of the silent, one-reel comedy to the global movie industry of today. In the first instance, films were made without an electronically recorded soundtrack, and later film stock was manufactured with a special stripe that allowed synchronized sound to be recorded alongside the images. These apparently simple technical innovations, and early examples of technological convergence, have had a profound effect on how culture and social relations are represented worldwide, leading to what some have called the "Hollywoodization" of the world: the almost complete control of the commercial production and distribution "value chain" by the major studios (Cousins, 2004, p. 397). At the same time, this convergence is subject to the dialectic, as still and moving picture technology is made smaller for individual consumers. The compact, hand-held, or pocket-sized cameras and video recorders facilitate both "citizen-journalism" and eyewitness accounts that challenge commercial media and official accounts of events, and amateur videos go viral; the control of technology and labour intersects with the struggle over audio-visual representation.

From "Camera Obscura" to Pixeltopia

In March 2005, Kodak, the multinational communications equipment manufacturer, launched an advertising campaign for its latest digital camera. The company's advertising agency came up with the catchy hook "Welcome to Pixeltopia." The idea behind this slogan was that this new digital camera was so advanced that it would transport the user to some imagined utopian future. There's no doubt that digital cameras are easy to use, almost fool-proof, and less expensive in the long run, but not everyone benefited from the switch from film to pixels.

> **PIXEL**
> A dot that is the smallest single identifiable element of an image or picture. The greater the number of pixels per square inch (PSI), the clearer the image will reproduce.

Just three months before the announcement of the new camera, in December 2004, 360 workers at Kodak's Toronto manufacturing plant were laid-off as part of an overall management plan to reduce up to 15,000 employees from its labour force of 70,000 worldwide (Erwin & Valorzi, 2004). Four years later, Kodak had eliminated over 40 per cent of its workforce, or over 27,000 jobs (Reuters, 2007). Since Kodak's most well-known business was in manufacturing film and cameras for amateur photographers, the lay-offs could be interpreted as the result of the introduction of the "new" media of digital film (Dobbin, 2007). Although the change in technology was certainly a factor—as Kodak literally invented the digital camera (via an employee named Steve Sassen), and deliberately converted to digital film and imaging technology—the decisions that it made concerning its business strategies were arguably more significant to its restructuring (Mendes, 2011). This included moving manufacturing "to a contractor in Mexico" (*Vancouver Sun*, 2008, para. 3), and using its assets to continue its business expansion through vertical integration (buying chemical companies, printing software companies, and printing machine manufacturers, e.g.) to control its product line from the recording device (camera or image screening), to the computer screen, to the printing press, in order to increase its profit margins.

As discussed in earlier chapters, the pressure to become more profitable at any expense in order to compete in the global economy means that the larger the size of the company, the greater the impact on labour, the environment, and the locations and neighbourhoods where it operates, or operated. These "changes to the business model" have a ripple or "trickle-down" effect, felt most acutely by those who were never part of the decision-making process to begin with. For Kodak this included the unemployment of over 27,000 people as well as the devastation of neighbourhoods that were built around the company (Monsebraaten, 2009). In Toronto, the areas that Kodak operated in are part of what is called "the rust belt," due to the closing of factories and abandonment of grounds (ibid.; see also High & Lewis, 2007; and see Figure 5.1, next page); and in Rochester, New York, which is still the company's headquarters, Rochester is coping with one of the highest rates of chemical pollution in the United States (as the processing of film relies on a combination of toxic chemicals; 🖳 www.rochesterenvironment.com and 🖳 www.scorecard.org).

PATENT

A form of private ownership that gives exclusive rights over an invention to the patent owner, whether this invention is a *technology* (a device like film; a machine or any other kind of hardware) or a *technique* (a method—how to do something—as in a software code). In Canada, a patent is defined as "a government grant giving the right to exclude others from making, using or selling an invention. A Canadian patent applies within Canada for 20 years from the date of filing of a patent application" (CIPO, 2010, "Patent").

TRADEMARK

Indicates exclusive ownership of a name, word, symbol, colour, shape or sound, and is represented by the symbol ™. Registration indicates proof of ownership and legal protection of that exclusivity as represented by the symbol ®. In Canada, the government definition of trademark is "a word, symbol or design (or any combination of these features) used to distinguish the wares and services of one person or organization from those of others in the marketplace" (CIPO, 2010, "Trade-mark").

Source: © Paula Johns, 2013

FIGURE 5.1 | **Site of the former Kodak manufacturing plant in Toronto.**

This is the opposite of what is called "supply-side economics," which underpins capitalism and the ideology of neo-liberalism. Its early proponents included former heads of government, including US President Ronald Reagan, British Prime Minister Margaret Thatcher, and Canadian Prime Minister Brian Mulroney, who adjusted national policy and international free trade agreements accordingly. The general idea was that benefits from tax breaks given to the wealthy and to corporations (also called supply-side economics) would eventually trickle down to the workers and the poor, yet it's not the wealth that trickles down. Welcome to Pixeltopia.

Kodak is not the exception here, and its history does indicate a relative concern for its labour force, but it is illustrative of how the process of commodification works. In the first instance, the labour impact was greater because of the overall size of the company itself. It had grown from a business in Rochester to a multinational corporation thanks to an almost monopoly over film (specifically in the United States and Canada) from its first invention in 1875 up until the mid-1970s when Fujifilm became its primary competitor. Kodak was able to secure its initial monopoly via its ownership of the technology through its **patent** as well as its **trademark** of the name of the film (Kodak) and later colour film (Kodachrome). As we review the history of the technology, trademarks and patents are central in understanding its development and use.

Silver Nitrate to Silicon Chips:
The Technology of Photography

The original "camera obscura," invented in Europe in antiquity, was simply a darkened box with a pinprick hole in one face, but the image it generated on the opposite surface was inverted. This created a technical and ethical dilemma for the early experimenters in photography: how to correct for imperfections in the image yet still record a "true" facsimile of the objects in the viewfinder. Until the late eighteenth century, the camera obscura was used to project images on walls and other flat spaces, as an aid to drawing (see Figure 5.2). By the mid-1850s the technology had developed sufficiently to promote a boom in studio photography. During the late nineteenth century, the use of photography was to record everyday life and to provide anthropological information for the study of humans and their history. One of the first significant collections was compiled by Edward S. Curtis (1868–1952), who exposed some 40,000 negatives in his mission to record the life and culture of Native Americans between 1895 and 1928. His work, published in a 20-volume limited edition, is an astonishing mixture of art and anthropology and is currently available online through the US Library of Congress (2010), which adds that the collection is also "controversial" (🖳 memory.loc.gov/ammem/award98/ienhtml/curthome.html).

Critiques of the photographs indicate that Curtis didn't just take the pictures, but sometimes staged the image, removing or adding props and retouching images, some of which drew on and reinforced existing stereotypes of Aboriginal peoples, or left out critical aspects of the impact of colonialism and non-Native governance on their lives (Jacknis, 2000, p. 88). Although specific to this time and photographer, the controversies of photography are endemic to the technology because "context is everything in photography," and a photograph is a *representation* of its subject (p. 89). How someone or something is represented (or recorded), or if they are represented at all, recalls the concepts—from the previous chapter—of agenda setting, gatekeeping, and framing that occur in print. Someone is making the decisions, and those decisions have significant influence on how we view ourselves and our world, particularly if the representations and associated memes are repeated again and again, over time, and in several formats (photography, motion pictures, television programs, and online videos). Compare, for example, representations of Aboriginals as peaceful, spiritual, and living one-with-the-land in contrast to the tribal warrior, the bloodthirsty savage, or the alcoholic "welfare bum" (Harding, 2006).

After 1900, still photography moved in two directions. Manufacturers of cameras

FIGURE 5.2 | Children indoors viewing an outdoor scene with a camera obscura.

Source: © Getty Images / Thinkstock

CAMERA OBSCURA

An ancient form of reprographic technology. Using a pinhole or lens, a lighted image is projected from outside, into a darkened room, allowing the external image to be reproduced on the opposite wall. It is suggested that some of the "Old Masters" who achieved such fine detail in their paintings were assisted by a camera obscura.

and film, while attempting to improve the quality and standards of equipment and materials for professional photographers and cinematographers, also converted the still photograph and the still camera into consumer commodities. This conversion was facilitated via the inventions that were patented by the manufacturers. In 1900 the individual consumer-friendly Kodak Box Brownie camera was released, and in 1906 colour film as well as panchromatic black-and-white film became available. Manufacturing the technology for individual distribution established an almost infinite market as the camera could be owned by anyone who could afford to buy one, and in turn the requisite film for the camera had to be purchased. In 1914, German optics firm Leitz developed a camera using the now standard 24 × 36 mm still frame as well as sprocketed 35 mm movie film. In 1928 Rollei introduced the Rolleiflex twin-lens reflex producing a 6 × 6 cm image on roll film. Advances in film were slower. It not was until 1936 that Kodachrome, a multilayered colour film, was developed. Its technology was patented, and the name was trade-marked, giving Kodak exclusive rights to use, develop, and sell colour film in the United States and through intellectual property agreements between countries such as Canada and Australia. As we reviewed in the previous chapter, copyright is one form of **intellectual property** (IP).

World War II promoted technical developments in cameras, such as the 35 mm single lens reflex (SLR) camera, which were commercialized in the post-war period, with products from Hasselblad and Pentax (1947) and Zeiss (1948). Bypassing the need for laboratory film development, in 1948, the Polaroid Corporation commercialized its SLR camera with the film processing built in: You took a single picture, pulled the negative out of the camera, and waited a few minutes until it developed in front of you. While the negative could not be continually reproduced, the ability to manipulate and process it instantly gave more privacy and control over the product to the individual photographer. The SLR became the standard camera for amateur photographers before the digital age with the current market dominated by a small number of multinational corporations including Nikon, Canon, and Sony.

These corporations emerged as an outgrowth of the invention in 1973 of the C-41 colour negative process, which increased the affordability of colour pictures and led to the opening of photo labs in almost every shopping mall, complete with one-hour photo processing—a concept likely quite alien to the digital camera user. You may consider the family photo album one of the relics of the twentieth century, but it allowed succeeding generations, with their pictures directly in their hands, to see what their forebears looked like. The popularity of digital cameras—and the ease with which data is disposed of—may also mean that it is the twentieth century from which we retain the more enduring images. By 1983, Kodak was marketing photo storage on disks, and a decade later it launched Photo CD. More recently, photos—like any data—can be stored on memory sticks or posted online from a variety of formats (mobile devices, camera phones, personal computers) via Kodak's "Gallery," Google's "Picasa," and Yahoo's "Flickr," for example, the latter of which equates the old family photo album with ageism and technological obsolescence: "The 'album' metaphor is in desperate need of a Florida condo and full retirement" (Flickr, 2013, para. 3; 🖾 www.flickr.com/about/).

It appeared that the days of photographic film were numbered and soon to be over, as the manufacture and processing of film was only able to continue if the company that held its trademarks continued to manufacture it. Thus technology doesn't necessarily become obsolete naturally (due to "inevitable" progress, e.g.) but is subject to consumption, intellectual property control, and corporate decision-making. For example, in 2008, Polaroid ceased manufacture of its film, much to the disappointment of its devotees (Jewell, 2008), and in 2009, Kodak ceased

INTELLECTUAL PROPERTY (IP)

Exclusive private ownership over the products of creative labour. It consists of two components: (1) the *intellectual* component refers to (a) intangible forms (ideas, plans, designs, etc.) and (b) tangible forms (symbols, words, images, sounds) used to communicate these and (2) the *property* component, which indicates private ownership and control over the results of creative labour. IP confers exclusivity of ownership rights as authorized by civil law and international agreements. Patents and trademarks are two types of intellectual property.

to manufacture its trademark Kodachrome film. The trademark "Polaroid" has been continued, however, despite the company's filing for bankruptcy protection in the United States in 2001, as its instant film processing was recently revived (🖥 www.the-impossible-project.com). The revival indicates that despite changes in business decisions and the idea that **digital technology** is both progressive and superior, photographers prefer to retain manual control over the creative process. In a return to the beginnings of photography, Kodak currently manufactures film intended for professional photographers, and otherwise channels imagining to its digital online offerings. Yet, the precarity of online storage is cause for concern because of technological obsolescence. In comparison, the "old" family album—although still subject to physical deterioration over several generations—doesn't take a special program to either store or open, and doesn't require passage through the infrastructure of a multinational corporation, whereas the contents of digital files from just 10 years ago are already inaccessible, never mind what happens if the database goes down or Google decides that in order to see your pictures for free, you have to watch some advertising.

> **DIGITAL TECHNOLOGY**
> A conversion of data (an image, word, or symbol, e.g.) into two electrical states—"positive" and "negative"—that is used to record, store, transmit, and receive data. These conditions of either "on" or "off" are represented by two numbers (digits)— as "one" or "zero"— which is the language of mathematics used in computer technology.

For Real?

Abolish Patents? Polaroid vs. Kodak

Polaroid had several patents out on its camera and film developments, and in discovering that Kodak had been using the technology in its own instant cameras, Polaroid took Kodak to court for wilful patent infringement (Polaroid v. Eastman Kodak, 1986), and after 15 years of legal proceedings, Kodak paid Polaroid USD$925 million (Reuters, 1991). Several years later, Kodak would be back in court, this time to sue other corporations for patent infringement, including Sony, which turned around and sued Kodak for the same reason (Meland, 2004), as well as Apple and HTC (Savitz, 2012). The battle to control and secure private ownership is continually before the public courts and has increased exponentially with digital technology, as both the techniques used and the types of technology converge. The extreme to which the number of patents being filed and the extent to which this is causing more harm than good (whether in terms of technological progress or knowledge development) is argued to be particularly debilitating in software programming as there is more software litigation than in any other area (Bessen, Ford, & Meurer, 2011), and even economists argue that the intellectual (private) property system should be abolished entirely (Bessen & Meurer, 2008).

Discussion Questions

1. What is the difference between a trademark and a patent?
2. Given that you likely use a computer every day, how much of that use (the hardware, the software, the social media sites, the search engines, etc.) is covered by intellectual property rights?
3. Who (or what) owns your photographs when you put them online?
4. Identify arguments for/against intellectual property rights; should intellectual property rights be abolished? Explain why or why not.

The Pictures Make the Page: Photographs and Journalism

The Illustrated London News, a British weekly newspaper, was founded in 1842 by Herbert Ingram, a printer. Successive innovations and the convergence of printing and photographic reproduction technologies enabled the newspaper to thrive. In 1860, hand photo-engraving was employed, and half-tone blocks were used from the mid-1880s onward. The half-tone process enabled the company to launch three new mastheads: the *Sketch* (1893), the *Sphere* (1900), and the *Tatler* (1901). The photogravure process was first employed in 1911. Victorian and Edwardian England—the centre of the British Empire—gave Ingram and his successors the opportunity to showcase the Empire in all its glory. Illustrative of the publication's continuing imperial connections is the fact that it published a special edition in 2002 commemorating the life of Elizabeth, the Queen Mother—a project on which work had begun in the 1970s.

On this side of the Atlantic, in 1880, 24-year-old George Eastman established the Eastman Dry Plate Company in Rochester, New York, and in the same year, the first half-tone photograph was published in the New York *Daily Graphic*, an imitator of the *Illustrated London News* and the *Canadian Illustrated News* (1869–83; Desbarats, 2001, p. 59). The *Daily Graphic* was the first *daily* newspaper in the world to use photographic illustrations, the product of advanced Canadian technology (ibid.). These forerunners to magazines were different in terms of content, timeliness, and length of articles, and (depending on the magazine) may have included a blend of fictional stories with information. The addition of photography made the magazine distinct from newspapers in its size, content, and appearance. The difference was more than aesthetic, however, as the introduction of photography combined a visual art with journalism and made the stories seem more real, and thus more effective, whether in terms of emotional impact or credibility.

The Camera Goes to War

> *Photography was first devoted to portraiture and landscape, but it did not take long for enterprising practitioners to glimpse the possibility of using it to bring news' images to the public. War was always news, and so very quickly after the invention of wet-plate photography, which could be used, if with some difficulty, away from the studio, photographers began to take their apparatus to theatres of war. (John Keegan, cited in Knightley, 2003, p. 6)*

The art of representation via the technology of photography meant that photography could be used to reveal and emphasize—or remove, conceal, or subdue—proving especially useful for propaganda and advertising purposes. Its use by governments is especially evident during wartime when the public is to be convinced of the legitimacy of war or the necessity of the state's engagement. In England, in the 1850s, for example, when the British army was fighting a disastrous campaign against Tsarist Russian troops in the Crimea, a photographer was commissioned to take photographs, but not of images likely to disturb the British public. According to celebrated Australian correspondent and author Phillip Knightley (2003), the work of royal photographer Roger Fenton "established the axiom that although in most cases the camera does not lie directly, it can lie brilliantly by omission" (p. 12). Despite his self-censorship—he apparently refused to take photographs of the dead after the ill-fated and

---

HALF-TONE

A series of black-and-white dots used to simulate grey in the reproduction of black-and-white images. The denser the black dots, the darker that section of the image; the more frequent the white dots, the lighter that section of the image will be when printed.

PHOTOGRAVURE

A mechanical method of printing images whereby a negative of the image is transferred to a printing plate by means of an acid etching process. This process enabled the widespread publication of photographs in newspapers, magazines, and books.

fabled charge of the British Light Brigade—Fenton's work was recognized as an important contribution to "war artistry."

The initial problem with combining photography with press coverage was that, until after the American Civil War, printing technology lagged behind photography, so there was no reliable method of transferring the photographic image to the printed page. But, according to Knightley (2003), by the beginning of the twentieth century "the camera had arrived, and its development, although slow and spasmodic, was now unstoppable" (p. 13). When, through the process of convergence, the newspaper printing press caught up with photography, it created a new wave of interest in the work of photographers. For governments, this included recording their military in action in wartime, which brought it into cooperation with the commercial news media:

> The Canadian War Records Office was established in 1916 by Max Aitken (Lord Beaverbrook). One of its tasks was to secure photographs from the front in order to obtain a permanent and vivid impression of what was happening. . . . Photos of men scrambling over the top of the trenches were acclaimed as accurate portrayals of men at war. In fact, it appears they were taken during combat training or staged far from the front line and later cropped to eliminate any unwarlike paraphernalia. (Tweedie & Cousineau, 2010, para. 27)

Dramatic incidents caught in the glare of a newshound's flash became the staple of the 1920s "yellow press" in America and established the tradition of tabloid news "splashes" on the front page of the daily paper. Ethics were sidelined as the combination of huge headlines, shocking photographs, and gruesome details attracted readers in a formula combining violence with entertainment, and spectacle with sensationalism, one that continues today across all kinds of media including newspapers (e.g., via the Sun Media chain in Canada), radio ("shock-jock" programs like The Howard Stern Show), and television (like *The O'Reilly Factor* on the Fox Network; O'Connor, 2008).

Other dominant representations of American culture were epitomized in *Life* magazine via the art of photo journalism; *Life* published a weekly glossy magazine in a large, almost poster-size format from 1936 to 1972. Founded by *Time* magazine proprietor Henry Luce, it complemented the quintessential weekly news magazine with its high-quality paper and eye-catching art and design, to say nothing of the content, which ranged from political action to pin-up girls. *Life* magazine was to photojournalism what *60 Minutes* was to become to television—a flagship, a populist pulpit, and an exposition of the craft, as well as the source, of some of the most iconic images of the twentieth century. Declining circulation shut *Life* down in 1972, and various attempts have been made to resuscitate it. From 1974 to 1978 it was quarterly, and then monthly from 1978 to 2000; it shut down again until revived in 2004 as a weekly newspaper supplement.

Life's mixture of celebrity, politics, and lifestyle journalism (sound familiar?) became the standard in magazines that blended them all together, or focused on one specific area. *Life*'s iconic status also recognized its effectiveness in providing a specific representation of American culture. Reflecting on these representations in the *American Journalism Review*, journalist Bill Barol (2002) chronicled *Life* magazine's self-perception and its impact on the United States over three decades:

> This is what I know about the world in the years before I was born: In the 1930s foreign governments were either clearly friendly or overtly hostile, and always quaint in their otherness. The early 1940s rumbled with the sound of faraway trouble

ONGOING ISSUES

Media Coverage of Conflict

The controversy over media representation of war is an enduring one. In history, coverage of the US Civil War (1861–65) brought images of death and destruction to a wider audience. Taking cameras in covered wagons onto the battlefields, Mathew Brady and his associates exposed some 7,000 negatives of this conflict. His 1862 exhibition *The Dead of Antietam* was controversial, but it exposed audiences to the raw reality that war is about killing people, in the same way that, a century later, television pictures of the 1968 Tet Offensive in Vietnam would have a profound effect in provoking anti-war opinion in the United States (Hallin, 1989), to the extent that the next time the American military invaded a country, it ensured that it controlled the images via the journalists covering them. This was first practised by the British military in the war in the Falklands (1982), followed by the American military in Grenada (1983), Panama (1989), and the first Gulf War (1991), making it appear to outside audiences that these wars were "casualty-free" and thus reducing criticism of the government, its military, and the exercise of war itself, whether as a state strategy in foreign policy or an act of violence (Cameron, Shin, & Adhikari, 2005).

Government and military management of both the image and the text of journalism has subsequently been managed by "embedding" journalists with "the troops" such that (in theory) the journalist will be more likely to empathize and adopt the view of the soldier and the country that s/he is purportedly "fighting for," again deflecting criticism or questions regarding the legitimacy of the action itself (S. Lewis, 2006). This was practised in the American war on Iraq (2003) and has seen its variants in Canadian media coverage of "the war" in Afghanistan, bringing questions of objectivity and credibility of media to the fore, as the image of Canada's military as "peacekeepers" or "warriors" is manoeuvred via the relationship between the government, its military, and the press (L. Williams, 2010).

The issue is compounded by technological convergence, as the speed at which an event (whether a conflict or environmental or humanitarian disaster) can be recorded and disseminated (i.e., made into "news") may be instantaneous—24/7. This has given rise to what is called "the CNN effect" (named after the Cable News Network; Allan & Zelizer, 2004). The "effect" suggests that the instantaneous broadcast causes a chain reaction whereby the public puts pressure on governments to immediately respond to the crisis, or by its own mass response by sending resources (like donations, e.g.). The theory is that the reaction to the broadcast drives decision-making, decreasing the time (otherwise necessary) to consider the options and make reasoned decisions. The CNN effect has gone beyond the commercial cable networks to the individual with the camera, video recorder, or camera phone, yielding the term *citizen-journalism* (covered in more detail in Chapter 10). Since events can be broadcast via the Internet by anyone with access to the technology to do so, any "professional" or institutionalized editorial control, as well as gatekeeping, agenda setting, and framing, may be bypassed entirely. The extent of the effects will continue to be of issue, not only in defining "what is news" but also in defining what (or who) is trustworthy and, in turn, what actions should (or can) be taken, by whom and when.

Discussion Questions

1. How does a digital media environment affect coverage of conflict?

2. As noted earlier, journalists are often embedded in the militaries of countries (like Canada) who have taken military action in areas of strategic political economic interest (like Afghanistan). How do you think this can influence public understanding of both the Canadian military and the Canadian government's involvement in Afghanistan?

3. Collect some examples of the photographs from commercial media coverage of conflicts in countries other than Canada and the United States. What similarities and differences can you identify in who and what is being represented in these conflicts?

drawing near. In the war years Americans were plucky and defiant, kept their chins up, learned to rivet, saved scraps of soap. The late '40s were years of privation, but a peculiarly American kind in which the new car and the new radio and the long-promised television were not yet in reach, but would be soon. And in the '50s they were, in quantity. The '50s were years of unimaginable abundance, years in which large Caucasian families regularly gathered in the sparsely landscaped yards of their brand-new tract homes to arrange in neat rows exactly a year's worth of canned soup, sewing materials, dungarees and bed linens. . . . The reason I know all this is that I read it in Life *magazine. It's a cliché to think of* Life *as The Great American Magazine, but it was, and the ways it portrayed America are now largely the ways in which we think of America when we look back. Its reach was so vast and deep that it's not at all clear: Did America shape* Life, *or did* Life *shape America?*

It was the significance of being able to mass represent American culture that underpinned some of the arguments that have been used in Canada by a magazine industry seeking government protection from American competition. Concerns over freedom of the press and government "interference" are muted in an industry that has depended on federal government assistance to protect commercial publishers over the last century, whether through *postal subsidies* (preferred rates for Canadian publications), *tariffs* (a duty charged on foreign magazines, making them more expensive than Canadian magazines), or *advertising* (eliminating the tax deduction for Canadian companies that advertise in foreign magazines, thus encouraging advertising in Canadian magazines; Desbarats, 2001, p. 57; Vipond, 2000). As we reviewed in Chapter 4 (a history of the press in England with the stamp tax), accusations of government interference on the basis of "freedom" (whether of corporate enterprise or freedom of the press) can be selective in the media industry depending on whether it is judged to be in its favour or not. Beginning with government patronage and advertising that helped the newspaper industry become established, the history of the communication and cultural industry in Canada is intimately tied to government assistance.

In contrast, with the market size and economy of scale of the United States, the magazine industry has not relied on government support to the extent that it has in Canada. And *Life*, of course, was not the only famous American picture magazine. *National Geographic Magazine* (later abbreviated to *National Geographic*) was first published in 1888; its combination of scholarly articles with brilliant photographs, together with its distinctive yellow border in a book-like size, made it a landmark publication. Unlike *Life*, *National Geographic*, the magazine of the National Geographic Society, has flourished arguably as a result of its non-profit organization that is itself based on research and education. Now being published in over 30 languages, it includes age-specific editions (3–6- and 6–14-year olds), book publishing, home videos, CD-ROM collections, and a subscription television channel (another instance of technological convergence).

In an even smaller portable format, *Reader's Digest* was established in the United States in 1929 and published Canadian editions in both French and English in 1947, and it retains its position as one of the largest paid-circulation magazines, particularly in Canada, but also internationally (■ www.auditedmedia.com/news/research-and-data.aspx). The Reader's Digest Association (RDA) has also converged its publications with its online offerings, and self-reports that it now reaches "140 million consumers in 75 countries and 21 languages through multiple media platforms, including print, online, digital download, books and home entertainment products, and social media" (Reader's Digest, 2013, para. 2; ■ www.rda.com/our-company). Its apparent success has not made it immune to economic decisions, however, since the RDA emerged from bankruptcy protection under US law in 2010 with new ownership and a new board of directors (including executives from other dominant US media corporations including CBS and TimeWarner), only to file for bankruptcy protection again in 2013 (■ www.rda.com/rda-timeline). Earlier, the RDA had gotten itself into ethical and legal proceedings in the United States, as it was taken to court and had to pay USD$6 million for its aggressive and confusing marketing campaigns, which hook people into buying more magazines and merchandise by convincing them to participate in sweepstakes (New Jersey Department of Law and Public Safety, 2001). Again, in 2008, in the United Kingdom, the RDA was charged for violating advertising standards (■ www.asa.org.uk/Rulings/Adjudications/2008/9/The-Readers-Digest-Association-Ltd/TF_ADJ_44924.aspx).

The marketing techniques of the RDA pale in comparison to another American multinational corporation that combined photography with journalism to develop into a worldwide "brand." *Playboy* magazine was launched in 1953 by Hugh Hefner, a purveyor of soft porn. Photographs of nude women are the magazine's staple, even though it has always attempted to claim some of the intellectual high ground by way of news-making interviews with major (usually male) celebrities such as Ralph Nader, Orson Welles, Marshall McLuhan, and Martin Luther King Jr. Although an early adopter of Internet technologies (e.g., its "Cyber Playboy Club"), the overall circulation of *Playboy*'s hard copy edition has been affected by the advent and easy accessibility of online pornography. In a plan to attract younger males to its online content, its current strategy is to "go retro": "Will a journey to the past help the waning Playboy bring in younger readers? It hopes so" (Moses, 2010, p. 6). Hefner has also tried to reach beyond traditional audiences to expand the Playboy brand through reality TV. From 2005 to 2010, Hefner co-produced a reality television show titled *The Girls Next Door* focusing on the lives of his three live-in girlfriends. The show aired on the E! network for six seasons. The original three girlfriends each went on to their own reality TV shows following the stint on *The Girls Next Door* (Wikipedia, 2013b).

Another lifestyle magazine, *Rolling Stone*, was founded by Jann Wenner in San Francisco in 1967 during the so-called "summer of love." Making the cover of *Rolling Stone* was a sign of arrival in the world of popular music. While *Rolling Stone* was famous for its photography and stable of photographers, such as Annie Leibovitz, it was also renowned for its long-time

Case Study

Consumption and the Good Life in Media

Playboy is significant for its marketing strategy because it uses the photographs of naked women to sell the magazine and (re)creates a market based on specific categories of gender (i.e., what a "real woman" looks like, and what a "real man" does). Advertisers in turn tailor their ads towards defining what a real man wants, wears, watches, reads, drives, etc. Heterosexual norms and gender divisions have been reinforced—not challenged—in advertising in particular, however, as women are generally represented as they are in *Playboy*: "supportive and solicitous to men" (Fraterrigo, 2009, p. 5). The formula is similar in "men's magazines" such as *GQ* and *Maxim*, the latter in which pornography is woven into the images in both the articles and the advertising.

   Playboy magazine was also pivotal in visually representing (and arguably set the standard in defining) Western middle-class values with its combination of sexual liberation, consumption, and individualism. This type of convergence reinforces a particular way of thinking about "liberation," or more generally what "freedom" is. As Fraterrigo's (2009) study of *Playboy* suggests, "helped along by advertisers and other spokespersons for the consumer economy, pleasure and self-fulfillment, achieved through the acquisition of material goods or in the form of sexual experience became goals cemented to middle-class life" (p. 5). These "goals" continue to be reinforced in large, glossy photographs of "freedom" and the "good life" (in both the articles and the complementing advertisements), particularly in lifestyle magazines, which suggests that pleasure is only experienced through individual indulgence and consumption. Once you recognize such an ideological formula, you may be able to identify how it is repeated, not only in magazine images but also in advertisements, movies, and music videos in particular.

Discussion Questions

1.   Choose a selection of magazines that are targeted to women and/or girls (such as *Cosmo*, *Cosmo Teen*, *Good Housekeeping*, *Flair*, etc.) and to men (such as *Maxim*, *GQ*, and *Esquire*) over a similar time period (e.g., the last six months).
     a)   How are men and women represented on the cover? For example, what parts of their bodies are showing or accentuated? What racial or ethnic groups are present (or not)?
     b)   What do the headlines indicating the article suggest what is important to women and men? Where do they suggest a woman gets her power from?

2.   Choose a similar selection of magazines targeted towards people of colour (such as *Essence*, *Ebony*, and *Sister 2 Sister*) and repeat Questions 1a and 1b.

3.   Compare the images and text to discuss your findings. How is the process of commodification and social class evident here?

celebrity writer—"Dr. Gonzo" himself—Hunter S. Thompson (1937–2005). In 2006 *Rolling Stone* celebrated its 1000th issue. Its combination of journalism and focus on the music industry has been superseded by magazines and websites that promote the music industry (its artists, its videos, itself) in publications such as *Billboard*, *Vibe*, and *XXL*.

From Film to Digital: Digital Photography in the Public Domain

When terrorists bombed the London Underground rail network in July 2005, some of the most dramatic visions of the event came from passengers who captured pictures on their mobile phones. Such sources, some media commentators said, epitomized the rise of the citizen-journalist. Others, like Mark Glasser at the Annenberg School for Communication and Journalism at the University of California, asked, "Were those quick with the camera phone 'citizen journalists' or 'citizen paparazzi'?"

Citizen-paparazzi is not really a new concept, and the proliferation of cameras has continued unabated since the first point-and-shoot 35 mm cameras took off, right through to cheap digital cameras. But while a few amateur photos might have made it into print magazines in the past, now the Internet is awash with photos and videos taken by amateurs, giving rise to several additional issues. As the term *citizen-journalist* becomes part of mainstream thought—spurred on by entrenched media outlets and relatively new start-ups—what role do these outlets play in encouraging or reining in paparazzi behaviour? Other issues include the encouragement of narcissistic behaviour with the proliferation of "selfies" (pictures taken of yourself, by yourself) posted on social media, or privacy limits as raised by wearable computers (on glasses, helmets, or whatever they can be physically attached to).

Digital photographic technology and the advent of digital cameras in mobile phones and in wearable computers have brought their own ethical dilemmas, and authorities in a number of jurisdictions are now moving to legislate against photography in public places—such as on beaches, and in pool and gym change rooms. Such moves have implications for news photographers, who until now have had no restrictions, except possibly those of taste, on their activities in public places. In Australia, in November 2005, for example, the federal attorney general announced he was considering introducing laws to prevent the unauthorized photography of children in public places, and Surf Life Saving Australia proposed its own ban on people snapping shots of young lifesavers on the beach without permission. Many sporting clubs had by then already introduced similar bans at netball and other junior sporting events (Clark, 2005).

The spectre of terrorism may also threaten to ban or limit photography in public places, as post-9/11 state priorities of "national security" (under the USA PATRIOT Act and the Canadian Anti-terrorism Act, e.g.) provide the authorities with greater latitude as can be exercised over the Canadian Charter of Rights and Freedoms, for example (📷 laws.justice.gc.ca/en/charter/). As you may recall from Chapter 2, the freedom to take photographs in public places is otherwise provided under Section 2(b) of the Constitution Act, 1982, covering all forms of media and communication.

It's not a freedom to take for granted, however, as Canadian history indicates that governments will use the full extent of the law to impose censorship over all kinds of media when it decides it's necessary (Mazepa, 2009). Exactly where future limits can be set will be subject to events and challenges in the courts; meanwhile, in recalling the dialectic, we should remember that this depends on who is taking the pictures, as more cameras are mounted by private security firms and police for surveillance and more images are captured by Google Street View. Identifying what is "private" and what is "public" in consideration of technology is central in questions of surveillance and privacy, and will thus be fully discussed in Chapter 11 when we review the increasing presence of the camera in public and private spaces.

Certainly the technology of photography has come a long way from its origins in the nineteenth century when the subjects had to stand still. We will now consider the technology of moving pictures and the cinema, which from the early twentieth century began to transform leisure time: Entertainment moved out of the home into the cinema, and a new industry was created. As you shall see, like most enterprises in the capitalist economy, it soon developed into a virtual monopoly, dominated by American products, and is now subject to its own dialectic of convergence and fragmentation.

Moving Pictures: Celluloid to Pixels

The house lights went down; fiery letters stood out solid and as though self-supported in the darkness. THREE WEEKS IN A HELICOPTER. AN ALL-SUPER-SINGING, SYNTHETIC-TALKING, COLOURED, STEREOSCOPIC FEELY. WITH SYNCHRONIZED SCENT-ORGAN ACCOMPANIMENT.

"Take hold of those metal knobs on the arms of your chair," whispered Lenina. "Otherwise you won't get any of the feely effects."

The Savage did as he was told. (Huxley, 1965a, p. 128)

This passage from Aldous Huxley's *Brave New World* (as cited in Huxley, 1965a) was written in 1931 when the cinema was still a fairly new industry. The "feelies" prefigure 3D glasses, Dolby surround sound, and digital effects, but "the Savage" begins to get the sensations in his own body, mimicking the action he sees on the screen—two actors kissing: "That sensation on his lips! He lifted a hand to his mouth; the titillation ceased; let his hand fall back on the metal knob; it began again . . . and once more the facial erogenous zones of the six thousand spectators in the Alhambra tingled with almost intolerable galvanic pleasure. 'Ooh . . . '" (p. 129).

The technology to create this virtual sensation would not be invented for another 50 years, but the early cinema was remarkable enough. The technology of cinema is the story of technical advances that enhance the filmgoer's experience. The key innovations have been the advent of sound—the "talkies"—in the late 1920s, the introduction of colour in the 1930s, and the use of digital effects to create special effects from the 1970s onward.

Sound, Colour, and Movement

The first moving pictures ever recorded on film were silent, which, according to Mark Cousins (2004, p. 18), added to their ephemeral appeal and ensured that the birth of the movies was a truly international phenomenon. This idea is confirmed when we examine the invention of moving film and the first "movie" cameras: It occurred almost simultaneously in the UK, Europe, Canada, and the United States in the last years of the nineteenth century (pp. 19–27). In the first years of the twentieth century the modern film industry established itself as the early silent movies took on a more narrative form and began to sell stories, rather than just examine the marvels of the medium. Techniques of lighting and editing also developed a more "artistic" style in this period. By 1912, the Hollywood star system was in place "in all its extravagant, tawdry glory" (p. 43).

The Jazz Singer (1927) is sometimes regarded as the first talkie, but it is largely silent, with Al Jolson making comments in and around his songs. But this new technique proved popular with audiences, and cinemas became more popular. According to Cousins (2004, p. 118), in the first year after sound became widely available, an extra 10 million cinema tickets were sold in the United States. It's also interesting to note, in the light of the success of the Bollywood film industry today, that in the 1930s over 200 films a year were being produced in India (Cousins, 2004, p. 123). The gangster flick *Lights of New York* (1928) was the first film made with sound from beginning to end. The film is poorly plotted, the actors are clearly unaccustomed to film speech, and the film still used the story cards so familiar to silent audiences for scene-setting. One interesting by-product of the talkies was the demise of actors who looked good in silent movies but whose accents grated when they spoke. Stars such as Italian actor Alfonso Guglielmi were expendable in this system. From 1921 to 1925 he was the toast of Hollywood, but he died at the age of 31, and his headstone carried his stage name, Rudolph Valentino. He was the sort of foreign actor who could never be acceptable in an Anglophone Hollywood film that "eroticized and idealized" a constant parade of "beautiful, immature, expendable stars" (p. 135).

The introduction of colour was far more variegated. The looming threat of television—still in black and white—prompted innovations such as Technicolor (1932), CinemaScope (1953) by 20th Century Fox, and Panavision (1959). While the 70 mm format has existed since the earliest days of film, most movies are shot on 35 mm film; one of the exceptions is Steven Spielberg's *Close Encounters of the Third Kind* (1977), in which most of the film was shot on 35 mm but the special effects in 70 mm. The wide, sandy vistas of David Lean's *Lawrence of Arabia* (1962) shows the 70 mm format to advantage, and there was a trend from the 1950s onward to use the 70 mm format because of its superior soundtrack. The advent of digital sound put an end to that, and the last feature film made entirely in the 70 mm format was Kenneth Branagh's *Hamlet* (1996).

While Hollywood, California, is the location most associated with the motion picture industry, the earliest films were made on the east coast of the United States, in New York, New Jersey, and Delaware. One of the first narrative films, Edwin Porter's 10-minute, 14-scene, black-and-white *The Great Train Robbery* (1903), prefigured many of the cinematic techniques that later audiences would find commonplace, including the spatial jumps made possible by sequential editing to collapse time but retain a chronological structure (Cousins, 2004, p. 38). In the final scene, the gang leader faces the camera and fires directly into it. More than a century after the film was made the technique can still surprise the viewer. Porter was a photographer who had worked for the inventor Thomas Edison. Porter directed, filmed, and edited the picture, which was based on a then-recent real-life event. The film used no-name actors—the Hollywood studio system was several decades away. In the early years of the film industry, most movies were shot like stage plays—the action being filmed from front on. It wasn't until the late 1920s, when *The Jazz Singer* ended the era of the silents, that the "classic" age of cinema began to emerge (p. 112).

Early Use and Development of Film in Canada

It was no accident that one of the first ventures into the newest technologies of the 1900s was by the Canadian Pacific Railway (CPR). The company that benefitted from public financing, public land, and cheap labour was looking to attract demand for its supply and ownership of communication—including transportation, telephone, and telegraph services. The CPR well-illustrates the (inter)national reach of vertical and horizontal integration as it owned large parcels of land (particularly in Western Canada) and all major railway and shipping lines across Canada (from tugboats in Vancouver Island, to river boats and ships on the Great Lakes, to transatlantic steamship lines), but what it really needed to become more profitable were goods to transport and consumers to buy the products, buy the land, and buy the tickets to get there. CPR posters and advertisements meant to attract immigrants to Canada ratcheted up considerably with the use of film in promising a new and better life.

Such effective uses of film were not lost on governments at the time. Canadian film historian Malek Khouri (2007, p. 41) identifies the year 1917 as significant given it was the beginning of both the federal and the provincial governments' direct involvement with film production, which was unique to Canada (P. Morris, 1978, p. 127). For the federal government, the year marked the opening of "the first Canadian film studio in Trenton Ontario" (ibid.), and it established what would become the Canadian Government Motion Picture Bureau (1923) and the National Film Board (NFB; 1939). The province of Ontario opened the first public film board and other provinces followed suit. With institutional names like the British Columbia Patriotic and Educational Picture Service, and film titles like *Fishing Just for Fun*, early government films were limited in scope. Similar to the films sponsored by the CPR, the aim was not on developing film as an art form or supporting independent film production, but on using the technology to provide an exchange value for the government and existing Canadian businesses, specifically for the promotion of trade, industry, and tourism (P. Morris, 1978).

Also prioritizing the exchange value of film, in the United States the idea was to develop it as its own industry. Film was thus exhibited as a form of "mass entertainment," something that you paid for individually, but watched together with other people in places initially called movie "palaces" or "theatres"—thereby replicating (and later competing with) the format of live performances and upper-class theatre (ballets, operas, and plays). This kind of structuring included configuring an audience on the basis of commodification and passive viewing; people would pay to sit and watch what was on offer, particularly if the movie theatre was designed to look like a palace and if an escape from the harsher realities of working-class life could be experienced, if even for a short period of time. The commercial success of film thus encouraged its own further development such that escapism (romance, drama, and comedy genres)—as well as a watching, paying audience—was reproduced.

The numbers of movie theatres were expanded to increase audience size to extend both scope and demand, while the distribution networks were correspondingly tightened in order to control supply. The number of people who paid to view a movie thus became equated with its quality, and this in turn became evidence for identifying and justifying what was "popular." Critical theorists, such as Seth Siegelaub (1979), suggest that this equation of the popular with consumption is one that takes the impetus from the public and commodifies it. That is, what is popular is defined by consumption and an industry that encourages and nurtures it for its own ends, leaving little room for either the imagination or the political will for anything outside of consumption.

Today, it is common to subsume the audience in box-office receipts, and the media industry emphasizes how much money a movie makes as evidence of its success and (by association) its quality. However, as we discuss in Chapter 12, it is not the dollar amount that is of the most value to the current industry (as it costs exponentially more to advertise and market a movie than to make it [Epstein, 2010]); rather, it is the information collected about the audience and from the audience that holds the most exchange value (💻 www.boxoffice.com).

Owning the Movies

Initially the extension of control over film production lay in its exhibition and distribution, and it is a significant definer of early film use and development in Canada. Famous Players was established in the United States in 1920, but by 1930 commercially owned theatres (including vaudevilles) were already controlled by American corporations and Famous Players in particular (Morris, 1978, p. 175; Pendakur, 1990, pp. 79–94). Famous Players used its Hollywood connections to aggressively secure its monopoly position across Canada (through price fixing, exclusive distribution, and billing agreements), and managed a nascent media legal system to successfully avoid prosecution (Morris, 1978). Save the one legal challenge, the federal government did nothing to curb American ownership or promote independent domestic production (ibid., p. 179). In fact, the structuring of film into a "market" in Canada was so integrated with the United States that the American producers and distributors considered Canada a small part of its domestic market and still treat it accordingly (Acland, 2003).

Film production would continue in Canada, but its political economy would be significant in how it developed, which included the American corporate monopoly over film and movies, particularly their production, distribution, and exhibition. Government involvement varied accordingly. The provinces still run film-development organizations to this day, but the emphasis is on extending supply-side economics, as provincial governments compete with each other to provide increasing production support (everything from scriptwriting to technical and financial support), including offering tax breaks to attract foreign film production. The incentives range from an astonishing 50–65 per cent tax credit offered by the government of Nova Scotia to the hundreds of millions of dollars that Ontario recently offered video and gaming corporations in attempts to undercut incentives provided by other provinces and US states (E. Chung, 2010). With such government support of the private media industry, and a technology that has no allegiance to place, the provinces are betting the savings of future generations that this kind of economics will eventually fulfill the promise of Pixeltopia.

Cinema and the State

Although the federal government also supports the film industry through Telefilm Canada (formerly the Canadian Film Development Corporation [1967])—tax credits and policies intended to protect Canadian ownership (🖥 www.telefilm.ca/en/telefilm/telefilm/about-telefilm)—its more direct involvement in domestic film production still rests with the National Film Board. Like our discussion of the introduction of the technology of photography, film was initially used by the state to support Canada's 1939 entry and participation in World War II. In addition to convincing Canadians of the legitimacy and impending sacrifices of war, government films made during the war were shown in movie houses as well as community centres across Canada in order to reach working-class women in particular. The films aimed to convince women of their duty (or traditional domestic role) "to keep the home fires burning" while at the same time participating in a workforce increasingly absent of men.

At the end of the war, film was again used to convince women to go back into the home after the men who survived returned (Nash, 1982). This use of media to manipulate gender roles and mobilize labour is significant and calls into question the uses of technology and the relationship of media and the state. In recognizing the work of women outside the home, however, an opening for the dialectic was made, as NFB films countered the dominant hegemony of Hollywood films where women were primarily represented in a subordinate relationship to men (as mothers, wives, sisters, or daughters) rather than as persons in their own right. As Khouri (2007) observes, this meant that

> the hegemonic film discourse on women was being challenged not only on the level of how they were represented, but more importantly, in connection with providing an alternative perspective on the nature of patriarchy. Canadians were confronted with the issue of women's liberation not simply as an ethical or moral question, but as an economic, social and political question that concerned the entire society. (p. 141)

Eisenstein and Stalinism

Making cinema subservient to national aspirations was not unique to Canada or many other nations, but differences in how the medium was used, in terms of its style and content, was historically and contextually distinct. Famous in cinematic history was the "revolutionary cinema" of Russia, developed after the Bolshevik Revolution of 1917 (which resulted in a complete change in political and economic systems—from one based on monarchy to one based on a version of socialism). At the centre of this new cinematic style was the Moscow Film School, led by former fashion designer Lev Kuleshov. The central metaphor for this group of young filmmakers was the rise of the "machine"; their mission was to make propaganda for the Bolshevik Revolution (Cousins, 2004, pp. 102–5). This is most vividly seen in Sergei Eisenstein's *Battleship Potemkin* (1925), which commemorated a revolt by the ship's crew in 1905 during the first Russian revolution against the Tsar. Eisenstein's contribution to film technique lay in his use of montage, an editing of scenes for effect. While under the influence of Stalinism (a way of autocratic governance named after the Russian dictator who distorted socialism accordingly), the ideology of Soviet filmmaking was deemed to be "socialist **realism**," a form of reductionism in which the artistic medium served the purposes and values of totalitarian state power—in short, propaganda. Eisenstein (1898–1948) was nonetheless able to demonstrate a mastery of cinematic technique that emphasized the dramatic image. The most famous sequence in *Battleship Potemkin* is the scene set on the Odessa Steps. This is how Oscar-winning film historian Chuck Workman (1993) described the sequence:

> *This baby carriage—the baby screaming, the mother dead—lurching down Russia's Odessa Steps during the 1905 revolution. The scene is intercut with hundreds of other shots: soldiers killing townspeople, horrified faces, marching feet, crowds of people rushing towards the sea, the army in pursuit, guns firing, bayonets raised, screaming, running, dying. Sergei Eisenstein can probably be called the greatest filmmaker of the silent era, his startling and unique images edited in a complex and inspired counterpoint. (p. 37)*

The sequence is all the more powerful when it is remembered that *Potemkin* is a silent film. Eisenstein made other films: *Strike* (1925); *October* (1927), a film commemorating the tenth anniversary of the Bolshevik Revolution, distributed in the English-speaking world as *Ten Days that Shook the World*; *The General Line* (1929), released as *Old and New* in the United States); and *Alexander Nevsky* (1938). During a hiatus in the United States and Mexico between 1929 and 1932, he failed to make it in Hollywood when David O. Selznick at Paramount rejected his ideas for a film, but Eisenstein shot a huge volume of footage in Mexico, later edited and released by others as *Que Viva Mexico!* (unfinished; 1930–32), *Thunder Over Mexico* (1933), and *Eisenstein in Mexico* (1933). He returned to the Soviet Union when Stalinist paranoia was at its height, and was not permitted to make films again until 1935. A theoretician of film as well as a filmmaker, Eisenstein became engaged in now arcane debates about film theory that thrived in the 1930s in the Soviet Union and were subsequently published in English. His last cinematic work was a series, *Ivan the Terrible* (1945–6), which was unfinished when he died in 1948.

The Hollywood Ten and McCarthyism

It wasn't just in Stalinist Russia that filmmakers were encouraged to be propagandists. In Hollywood, the inevitable commodification of movies also meant the commodification of one of its major inputs: actors. This expressed itself in the star system that prides itself on selling the visual image of the actor while appearing politically neutral. But not everyone in Hollywood was a star and the subject of public adulation. In 1947 a committee of the US House of Representatives, the

REALISM

"A critical notion of realism foregrounds not the 'capture' of the real but its articulation or constitution in representations. The term 'realism' is therefore a useful one . . . because it highlights the argument that any representation, however technologically advanced, is a cultural construction and not the 'real' itself." (Lister, Dovey, Giddings, Grant, & Kelly, 2009, p. 134).

House Committee on Un-American Activities (HCUA), led by ultra-conservative senator Joseph McCarthy, began investigations into alleged left-wing influences in the movie industry. The immediate post-war period—the beginning of the Cold War—saw all progressive politics conflated with the label of "communism." Although the label was both reductive and (over)reactionary, a fear of communism was whipped up by both religious and conservative political protagonists in the United States and Britain as well as in Australia and Canada. Ten of the Hollywood figures interviewed by the HCUA refused to name others who might have had politically "radical" views or associations, citing the Fifth Amendment to the US Constitution, which precluded self-incrimination. It was mainly writers—the Hollywood Ten, as they became known—that were convicted of contempt of Congress and jailed. They, and up to several hundred others, were blacklisted by the studios and forced to write under pseudonyms, work outside of the United States, or move out of the industry. The Hollywood Ten included Ring Lardner Jr. (1915–2000), who later scripted the classic anti-war film *M*A*S*H* (1970), and Dalton Trumbo, who won Oscars for *Roman Holiday* (1953) and *The Brave One* (1956), which he wrote under assumed names.

The persecution of the Hollywood Ten was part of a wider wave of historic anti-communist sentiment that followed the Russian Revolution and later the Russian invasion of Eastern Europe by the USSR at the end of World War II, marking the beginning of what is generally called the Cold War (the term identifies a war of political economy rather than overt military violence or "hot" war). In the United States, both J. Edgar Hoover, director of the Federal Bureau of Investigation, and Senator Joseph McCarthy, as well as Roman Catholic priests such as Father Charles Coughlin, were active and unscrupulous anti-communist crusaders. Michigan-based Coughlin (a forerunner of the shock jocks of today) used the medium of broadcasting and the power of boisterous rhetoric in conducting a weekly radio program, starting in 1926, in which he railed against the evils of communism.

The name given to the overall phenomenon is McCarthyism, but it was not confined to the United States. The media sensationalism and related climate of fear and suspicion that was communicated considered film as particularly effective in spreading propaganda (particularly during war time), such that both the content of film and the filmmakers were subject to suspicion well before McCarthyism.

In Canada, government involvement in film went beyond its production; as early as 1928 the provinces had set up censorship boards to review films shown in theatres. While a majority of films that were censored were classified as morally reprehensible or socially indecent, films that could be construed as critical, radical, or "communistic" were also banned (Mazepa, 2003). Provincial boards could be sporadic in their choices. Manitoba banned *Battleship Potemkin* (J. M. Skinner, 1987, p. 4), while Ontario "banned four Russian films in one year due to 'suspected Communist propaganda'" (Dean, 1981, p. 25) but passed *Ten Days that Shook the World* (a film directly about the Russian Revolution). Even Hollywood films didn't pass the censor if the content could be construed as politically radical in questioning capitalism or war. Such "radical" films included *Of Mice and Men* (1939) and *The Grapes of Wrath* (1940), films based on the novels of John Steinbeck about working-class experiences in the United States during the Great Depression, and *All Quiet on the Western Front* (J. M. Skinner, 1987, p. 4), a film that depicts the mental stress and hardship of military soldiers returning from war. The powers of the provincial censors were not an exception—recall that the federal government had also established censorship committees during both the First and the Second World War (Mazepa, 2011), and even the personnel working for the NFB came under suspicion for being radical infiltrators (Khouri, 2007, pp. 209–19).

Whether in Canada or the United States, the commercial mass media played a significant role in promoting anti-communist hysteria, but not exclusively because of bombastic broadcasts like Father Coughlin's, particularly if freedom of expression is taken as absolute, or because of muted criticisms of government actions during times of perceived crisis, which, as identified earlier, is still a matter for debate. More generally, it was the neglect of the commercial media to investigate and question the very idea that so-called "left" politics was (framed as) threatening and dangerous to the extent that it would naturally lead to violent revolution just like in Russia in 1917, leaving the association in tact despite completely different historical, political economic, social, and cultural contexts. It is thus argued that McCarthyism (or the persistent "red scare") highlighted the extent to which the commercial media maintain, and thus promote, dominant ideology (as discussed in previous chapters), particularly when alternative or oppositional ideas to capitalism (the system on which commercial media rests) are questioned or criticized. This is why the HCUA investigation into Hollywood was aimed at the individual writers themselves and not the general ideas they may have been representing. Alternative ideas were nonetheless discredited in the process via the construction of scapegoats and demonization of them as exceptional threats.

You may well ask, then, how this differs from propaganda and the Soviet Union's policy of "socialist realism" in film and the arts pursued under Stalin in the 1930s; in comparing the results, it doesn't. Both are fundamentally undemocratic and, at the extreme, are totalitarian in nature. Albeit a generalized statement, commercial media engagement with capitalism as the dominant political economic system is of a limited or circumscribed nature in that coverage continues to be focused on its results (poverty, environmental destruction, and social division) rather than considerations of capitalism as cause. The social consequences of framing and media coverage (or lack thereof) are considerably ratcheted up when a group of people are identified as the particular "cause" of a general or complex problem, and grouped as scapegoats—targeted for blame through sensationalism, as is recently evident in stoking the fears of terrorism in association with anyone who can be identified as being from the Middle East (Karim, 2003).

Perpetuation of dominant ideas is not a foregone conclusion, however, whether in making use of image technology or in predicting its reception by audiences, as filmmakers have taken their social responsibilities seriously, pushing them into a dialectical relationship with the commercial media system. In the United States, criticisms of capitalism are evident in the films by Michael Moore, who, while recognizing that his films are one of the few exceptions, suggests that commercial film producers care less about the content as long as the film will make a profit. Given the political economy of film production history in Canada, however, there was more latitude possible in the documentaries of the National Film Board as filmmakers negotiated their relationship between the federal government and their representation and accountability to Canadians.

National Film Board and Social Responsibility

The operations and productions of the National Film Board will continue to be subject to debate as to the extent of government control over the institution and the degree that the production, distribution, and exhibition of film was counter-hegemonic (Druick, 2007; Khouri, 2007). As introduced in Chapter 2, the concept of hegemony suggests that to ask what was "counter-hegemonic" is to ask to what extent did the films counter or oppose dominant ways of thinking about, for example, the "benefits" of capitalism, or the "naturalness" of patriarchy, or even ways of "doing" film (the techniques)—as to what is produced, who produces it, and how it is distributed and exhibited. Careful reviews of films produced prior to the Cold War suggest a number of alternative ways of making and exhibiting film that was accorded to the NFB, partly as a result of its relative independence from government (Druick, 2007), and partly as a result of its direct engagement with the experiences and participation of working-class Canadians (Khouri, 2007).

Focus on Research

The Celluloid Ceiling

It may seem unusual, particularly now, as it appears that anyone can make a film, but factors such as training, equipment, production facilities, and distribution was—and is still—structurally limited. In Canada, it was only in the more recent past, when, for example, women were "given" the opportunity to direct films. In 1974, the NFB established a production facility called Studio D; its mandate was to produce films by, for, and about women. It operated until 1996 when its funding was cut by the federal government (Vanstone, 2007; www.nfb.ca/international-womens-day/).

It also wasn't until the 1970s when First Nations were able to represent themselves in NFB films, and training programs were later established in order to do so. While some national advances in access and representation have been made in such a public, not-for-profit system, the more dominant Hollywood movie system indicates that there is still a substantial "celluloid ceiling" (a variation of the glass ceiling that limits the employment and advancement of women in key decision-making and leadership positions) and a skewed or over-representation of men, particularly Caucasians, who are the actors, writers, producers, directors, and critics—in effect creating a commercial film industry by men, for men, and about men.

Ongoing statistics on commercial media gathered at the University of San Diego (1998–2012) indicate a consistent 25 per cent ceiling for women working in commercial film production, such that for 2012, for example, "women [only] comprised 18% of all directors, executive producers, producers, writers, cinematographers, and editors working on the top 250 domestic grossing films" (Lauzen, 2013a, para. 1). Independent films (those shown at film festivals) have relatively higher representation with "[39 per cent] of women directing independently produced documentaries . . . compared to the [5 per cent] of women directing top grossing films in 2011" Lauzen, 2012, para. 2).

The pattern is repeated consistently across supporting work in film (production—design, managers, sound, editors, etc.; Lauzen, 2011), and extends to journalists writing about films—as women only comprise 25–30 per cent of the film critics in major US newspapers as well as online (Lauzen, 2013b). The representation of women on-screen also hovers around the 30 per cent mark, and is even less for women who are over 40 years old, who only comprise 26 per cent of the roles on-screen (compared to US census data where 45.2 per cent of the population over 40 are women; Screen Actors Guild, 2007, p. 55).

The genre of the documentary itself illustrates how the same technology, in this case film (image and sound), can be developed and distributed in different ways. In contrast to the escapism of Hollywood, in post-World War II Canada this included producing films that directly engaged with working-class experiences at the time, which included addressing labour, education, and issues of collective welfare; acknowledging immigrant and trade union organizations; and recognizing the existence of social movements of the time in questioning the relationship between capitalism, war, and fascism (Mazepa, 2007, 2011). In contrast to the paid movie theatre, for example, films produced by the NFB were shown in schools, community centres, and union halls, and the audience was asked to participate in an interactive format after the film

Race imbalance is also a major factor with 72 per cent of screen roles played by Caucasians (ibid.). This suggests a relationship between labour and representation: it is not only the employment that is restricted but also who is being represented and how.

In contrast, although it is slightly more common to note the number of American industry-based Academy Awards that the NFB has won for its films (12 Oscars, onf-nfb.gc.ca/en/about-the-nfb/publications/institutional-publications/report-on-plans-and-priorities-2013-2014/), its social credits are significant in terms of productions by women, First Nation peoples, and what it calls its Challenge for Change/Société Nouvelle projects initiated in the late 1960s (see Waugh, Baker, & Winton, 2010). The projects emphasized participation and the empowerment of people to bring about social change through a combination of education, motivation, and activism, in and through film (nfb.ca/playlist/challenge-for-change). In considering the democratization of communication, these are important goals and contrast significantly from commercial escapist film, even within an environment of government realism. The future of NFB is in jeopardy, however, as media in general is encapsulated within what may be called a neo-liberal realism (e.g., that the government should only be involved in supply-side economics, and film, like any other media, should be left to the market), while the market is exclusively managed by multinational corporations whether from Hollywood or, its Indian relation, Bollywood. The NFB continues to support independent film production, but its budget, personnel, and organization is restructured to function as a bare minimum operation. While the digitization of film has given it a new life online, at least as Canadians can now access the NFB library of films through its portal (www.onf-nfb.gc.ca/eng/collection/), it remains to be seen if Canadians can visualize something different in the future because of them.

Discussion Questions

1. What are some similiarities and differences between the financing and production goals of the National Film Board and a commercial filmmaker (such as Disney)?

2. Test the research results above with a random sample of your favourite movies. How do you see gender and race represented? Is social class a factor on the genre (kind of movie) produced and for whom?

3. If the people that we see represented on the screen are so disproportionate to reality, how do we understand social relations accordingly?

with questions and discussions of the issues presented in the film (prefiguring the interactive structure attributed to video game technology).

Film discussions offered people further opportunities to raise their own views on the social and political issues of the day. As such, the NFB film circuits opened new venues for interactive communication about the films; they became nuclei for political interaction at the grassroots level. Eventually, this process solidified even further the functionary role of these films as organs for political activism and organization. (Khouri, 2007, p. 98)

While the NFB could be credited with such opportunity, it could also be criticized for it, and it was not immune to the accusations of communism and hostility towards trade unionism and working-class politics, such that the head of NFB (John Grierson) was "encouraged" to resign, and NFB employees were placed under RCMP investigation, later requiring that such government employees require a security clearance in order to work there (Spencer, 2003, pp. 11, 12). Even after the red scare lessened, Zoe Druick (2007) argues that the connection to government still affected documentary film content, resulting in what she characterizes as "government realism."

Focus on Research

Bollywood Films and the South Asian Diaspora in Canada—Identity, Labour, and Commodity

The scale and financial growth of the Indian film industry, often referred to as "Bollywood," rivals the financial power and control of Hollywood in terms of its production, distribution, and extent of associated merchandise (like music; Wasko, 2003). Part of this growth has been in complementing and using similar commodification strategies while (re)presenting what kind of culture is associated with "South Asians." The globalization of the industry not only seeks to connect to the large South Asian population in India, but to link up with diasporic communities around the world, including here in Canada. The importance of the Canadian South Asian diasporic community as a market is significant as demonstrated by the hosting of the International Indian Film Academy Awards in Toronto in January 2011 (CBC News, 2011).

Canadian media scholars like Karim Karim and Faiza Hirji have taken up the particular cultural issues tied into identity construction, diaspora, and Bollywood film in their recent work. Beginning in the early 2000s, Karim, a professor at Carleton University, focused on building a more nuanced discussion of multiculturalism in Canada, arguing for the need to understand the specific cultural norms and patterns of different diaspora within Canada—not as one-way flows of communication from the "old country," but instead as a more complex two-way relationship (Karim, 2003, 2006). His work also highlights the links between transnational media—like film, television, the Internet, and satellite communication—in reinforcing and reforming what are called "diasporic" identities (Karim, 2003). Hirji, an assistant professor at McMaster University, also develops these themes in her work focusing on South Asian youth in Canada and their experience of Bollywood films (see Hirji, 2010). Her work draws attention more specifically to the ways in which Canadian youth of South Asian descent interact with Bollywood (ibid.), and to a critical analysis of gender construction of the Muslim diaspora in Canada (Hirji, 2011). Other scholars studying the South Asian diaspora in North America include Jigna Desai at the University of Minnesota, whose 2004 book entitled *Beyond Bollywood: The Cultural Politics of South Asian Diasporic Film* provides a critical discussion through case studies of several important Bollywood films.

Additional research focuses on explaining the relationship of film production and its social representations to the capitalist mode of production to focus on how labour is structured within

As a branch of government, NFB documentary films reflected the organization and historically dominant practices of governance, such that "almost every film at least implicitly endorses either the federal system or the social policy process by which group identities must be securely fixed before they can be recognized and supported within a larger national context" (Druick, 2007, p. 28). This identifies a significant limitation that contained activism and the more radical uses of film by subsuming social divisions of class, and race and ethnicity, under the rubric of nationalism or "multiculturalism," or treating the working class and elderly as welfare or health issues, for example. Nevertheless, within the programs of the NFB, people who were otherwise marginalized had the opportunity to produce, direct, and self-represent using the medium.

film production, for example. This suggests that within the industry, there is what Miller et al. (2005, as cited in T. O'Regan, 2010) call a "cultural division of labour within Hollywood," which is now "extending beyond the US to a global scale with the advent of geographically dispersed film and television production in so-called 'runaway' productions" (p. 248) where there are significant disparities between the commodified celebrities or "stars" and the millions of other workers used in film production (ibid.), which is duplicated by Bollywood (Gavil, 2005). The emphasis on the relationship between political economy and culture is important here as Garnham (1990, as cited in T. O'Regan, 2010) identifies:

> Political economists find it hard to understand how, within a capitalist social formation, one can study cultural practices and their political effectivity—the ways in which people make sense of their lives and then act in the light of that understanding— without focusing attention on how the resources for cultural practice, both material and symbolic . . . are made available in structurally determined ways through the institutions and circuits of commodified cultural production, distribution and consumption. (pp. 244, 245)

Hence, political economists identify how the film industry in Hollywood works *with* (rather than in direct competition *against*) Bollywood to concentrate the media market across production, distribution, and exchange, and dominate via what Rasul and Proffitt (2010) call a "symbiotic relationship." In this way, the South Asian identity (and any others that can be shown to be profitable) is commodified: "Identities have become marketable, as exhibited by large media corporations seeking to brand multiculturalism and 'sell' Others as products in the global mainstream. As John Fiske writes, 'while the multiculturalist will talk of diversity and difference, the multinational CEO turns the coin over and talks of product diversification and market segmentation'" (Balaji, 2008, p. 24).

Discussion Questions

1. How do you see the dialectic of broadcasting and narrowcasting at work here?
2. What happens to representations of "culture" or "identity" when they are commodified and reproduced worldwide?
3. What kind of ideas (or ideology) do you think the "star" or "celebrity" system reinforces?

Digital Effects

The invention of all technical systems developed since the beginning of the 1950s has been towards reducing the spectator's sense of their "real" world, and replacing it with a fully believable artificial one. (Allen, 1998, p. 127, as cited in Lister et al., 2009, p. 135)

The creation of computer-generated imagery (CGI) techniques added another dimension to the use of "special effects" and the development of technology for movies, evident in earlier productions such as the original *Star Wars* (1977) and *Tron* (1982), for example. CGI allowed a blend of live and drawn action to appear seamlessly on the screen for the first time and was used to great effect to create the "liquid metal" character of the bad-guy assassin in *Terminator 2: Judgment Day* (1991). At the same time, digital technology was also being examined as a means of creating even more commercial convergence in the film industry. In 1992, *Bugsy* (directed by Barry Levinson) was the first full-length feature film to be transmitted electronically from the Sony studios in Culver City, California, to a cinema in nearby Anaheim (Cousins, 2004, p. 457), allowing instantaneous distribution in several different locations. Control over production and distribution over the Internet is what Eli Noam (2009) characterizes as "Hollywood 2.0," illustrating the combination of convergence and fragmentation under a carefully managed distributive network controlled by the six largest film corporations in the United States.

There can be no doubt that digital techniques have altered the creative language of cinema, including the use of 360-degree pans and seamless zoom shots. It has also created an interesting blend of Eastern and Western styles, such as "wire fu"—the use of thin wire supports and harnesses to shoot seemingly impossible fight-action sequences—and also the use of Japanese "anime" styles and sensibilities in mainstream films such as *The Matrix* (1999). *The Matrix* is also interesting as a series of films and in the use of multimedia platforms to fill in pieces "missing" from the cinema releases (Cousins, 2004, pp. 459–60). The use of digital effects has moved from the sci-fi of George Lucas in *Star Wars* (1977) to the fantasy world of Peter Jackson's *Lord of the Rings* (2001) trilogy. Just as Tolkien created new languages to tell his story (appended in *Lord of the Rings*), so Jackson has created a new language for film, which can be seen in his remake of *King Kong* (2005), as well as in *The Matrix* films (1999–2003), in the *Star Wars* prequels (1999–2005), and in *The Lion, the Witch and the Wardrobe* (2005).

Leading the digital effects revolution since 1977 has been George Lucas' company Industrial Light & Magic. The company has won 14 Academy Awards for Best Visual Effects and received 17 Scientific and Technical Achievement Awards. In 2001, the Steven Spielberg film *Artificial Intelligence* used a real-time interactive on-set visualization process that allowed actors to move around virtual sets. The focus on awards for technical prowess and digital effects is an important part of marketing and advertising commercial films. It complements the celebrity focus and fan magazine culture where the fixation is on the image, but in the case of special effects and CGI, it fetishizes the technology itself.

Extending the concept of commodity fetishism, introduced in Chapter 3, suggests a variation on what philosopher and Marxist Guy Debord (1977) called the "society of the spectacle": "In societies where modern conditions of production prevail, all of life presents itself as an immense accumulation of spectacles. Everything that was directly lived has moved away into a representation" (para. 1). This doesn't mean that either the representation or the technology used in making it is thereby rendered independent, but it *appears* as such. This makes it much harder to apprehend that technology is socially constructed in the relationship of production and consumption. "Because the photographic image, it is argued, captures the surface appearance of things, rather than the underlying (and invisible) economic and social relationships, it is always by its very nature ideological" (Comoli, 1980, p. 142, as cited in Lister et al., 2009, p. 142). It is thus an acute version of commodity fetishism, or what we called "technology fetishism"; what we see is the image, what we appreciate as real is what it represents to us, and its credibility is in its *technology* and in what can be immediately grasped via the senses. Its content, and any substantive ideas and representations of social relations or labour fade to the background; in its place we see the attractive and consuming image, the visual effects (marvelling at technological futures, robots, and the things that go "boom"). A sensationalism of the technology encourages a significant shift, not only in the way we think about technology but also in the way we think about communication and our very future.

Conclusion

The photograph is a key component to the understanding of the social construction of media—combining, supplementing, and in some cases supplanting the written word discussed in Chapter 4. The emphasis on the image and technological representation of reality did not begin or end with the photograph, however. The dialectic of technological and economic convergence (in the film industry) and the making of great quantities of audiences were accompanied by convergence in other kinds of media, constructing an audience in places where people lived and worked through the technology of radio and television, to which we now turn to in the next chapter.

Key Points

- Both still and moving pictures are commodified through intellectual property ownership and technological obsolescence.
- Advertising and marketing promote and facilitate the process of commodification.
- The state can influence the development of any medium.
- There are many Canadian examples of the alternative uses (and use values) of film.
- There are many ways to think about media as technologies of representation.

Class Discussion

1. What are the similarities and differences between images produced by a human (as in the earliest cave paintings) and those produced using a camera? Is it possible to separate the image from the image-maker? Why or why not?
2. How is the supply and demand of technology managed through its use and development?
3. How does realism affect our understanding of social relations in film content?
4. What is Telefilm Canada? Why is it necessary (or not necessary)? What is technological fetishism? Provide some examples from current films.

Media on Media

Tunes on Film

The Buggles. (1979). Video killed the radio star. *The Age of Plastic*. Jamaica: Island Records.
    ▣ www.elyrics.net/read/b/buggles-lyrics/video-killed-the-radio-star-lyrics.html
The Kinks. (1968). People take pictures of each other. *The Kinks Are the Village Green Preservation Society*. London, UK: Pye. ▣ www.kindakinks.net/discography/showsong.php?song=302
Paul Simon. (1973). Kodachrome. *There Goes Rhymin' Simon*. United States: Columbia-Warner.
    ▣ www.lyricsfreak.com/p/paul+simon/kodachrome_20105962.html
Yes. (1980). Into the lens. *Drama*. United States: Atlantic.

Pictures on the Pictures

Activision. (Developer). (2005). The movies [Video game].
Burton, T. (Producer & Director). (1994). Ed Wood [Motion picture]. United States: Touchstone.
Caulfield, H. P. (Producer), & Chaplin, C. (Director). (1916). Behind the screen [Short silent film].
    United States: Lone Star. ▣ www.archive.org/details/CC_1916_11_13_BehindtheScreen
Coen, J., & Coen, E. (Producers & Directors). (1991). Barton Fink [Motion picture]. United States:
    Circle Films.
Frei, C. (Producer). (2001). War photographer [Documentary]. Switzerland: First Run Features
    Home Video.
Herzog, W. (Director). (2010). Cave of forgotten dreams [Documentary]. United States: IFC Films.
Vertov, D. (Director). (1929). *Man with a movie camera* [Silent documentary]. Soviet Union.

DVDs

Films Media Group Online. (2007). *DIY TV, where the small screen is the new TV screen*. New
    York, NY: Films Media Group.
Media Education Foundation. (Producer). (2002). *Money for nothing: Behind the business of pop music.*
Media Education Foundation. (Producer). (2007). *Dreamworlds 3: Desire, sex and power in music video.*
Murow, E. R., & Friendly, F. W. (Producers). (2005). *The McCarthy years*. US: CBS News/Docudrama.

Timeline: Celluloid to Pixels—Photography and Cinema

1816 Nicéphore Niépce combines the camera obscura with photosensitive paper.

1826 Niépce creates a permanent image.

1834 Henry Fox Talbot creates permanent (negative) images using paper soaked in silver chloride and fixed with a salt solution, and then also creates positive images by contact printing onto another sheet of paper.

1837 Louis Daguerre creates images on silver-plated copper, coated with silver iodide and "developed" with warmed mercury—the Daguerreotype process.

1841 Talbot patents his process under the name "calotype."

1851 Frederick Scott Archer develops the "wet plate" photography process.

1853 Nadar (Felix Toumachon) opens his portrait studio in Paris.

1854 Adolphe Disdéri develops *carte-de-visite* photography, making professional portrait photography popular and accessible.

1861 The colour separation process is developed by Scottish physicist James Clerk Maxwell.

1861–1865 Mathew Brady and his colleagues cover the American Civil War, exposing 7,000 negatives.

1871 Richard Leach Maddox, an English doctor, proposes the use of an emulsion of gelatin and silver bromide on a glass plate: the "dry plate" process.

1880 The first half-tone photograph is published in the *New York Daily Graphic*.

George Eastman sets up the Eastman Dry Plate Company in Rochester, New York.

1888 "Kodak" registers as a trademark. The advertising slogan "You press the button, we do the rest" is marketed.

1891 The first telephoto lens is created.

1895 The first portable camera is invented.

The French witness the first public screening of projected film by the Lumière brothers in France.

1896 The first public exhibition of motion pictures takes place in Canada (Montreal).

1899 Kodak Canada is founded in Toronto.

1900 The Kodak Box Brownie roll-film camera is introduced, costs $1, and is constructed from cardboard.

1902 Vivaphone, Chronophone, and Kinetophone synchronize sound and film. Georges Méliès, a magician-turned-filmmaker, introduces innovative special effects in the first real science-fiction film, *Le Voyage dans la Lune*, a narrative fantasy of long shots strung together, punctuated with disappearances, double exposures, and other trick photography and elaborate sets.

1903 Edwin Porter directs the *Life of an American Fireman* and *The Great Train Robbery*, the first fictive film form.

1905 The first "nickelodeon" opens in Pittsburgh. The name derives from *nickel*, the price of admission, and *odeon*, the Greek word for theatre. The opening film was Porter's *The Great Train Robbery*.

1906 Panchromatic black-and-white film and high-quality colour separation colour photography are invented.

James Stuart Blackton makes the earliest surviving example of an animated film: a three-minute short, or cartoon, called *Humorous Phases of Funny Faces*.

1907 East coast producers go west in winter as Los Angeles provides cloudless skies, varied locations, low humidity, and lower labour costs.

The entertainment industry trade magazine *Variety* publishes its first film review.

Bell & Howell develop a reliable film projection system.

1908 D. W. Griffith shoots his first film, *The Adventures of Dollie*, for Biograph Studios in New York City.

The Motion Picture Patents Company becomes the first attempt to create a film monopoly, known as "the Trust"; the Company tries to shut out non-members with threats and intimidation.

1909 The first permanent film studio is established in Hollywood by the Selig Polyscope Company.

1910 Thomas Edison demonstrates a talkie using his Kinetophone technology.

The now-forgotten Florence Lawrence, known as the "Biograph Girl," was the first "movie star" created by the Carl Laemmle studio.

1912 Motorized movie cameras supersede hand-cranked machines.

The first true "fanzine," *Photoplay*, spawns the celebrity-gossip magazine culture.

Herbert Kalmus begins experimenting with colour film processes and establishes The Technicolor Motion Picture Corporation.

1913 The name "Hollywood" becomes the official title for the west-coast film industry, which is now bigger than that in New York.

John Randolph Bray's first animated film, *The Artist's Dream* (aka *The Dachshund and the Sausage*), the first animated cartoon made in the United States by modern techniques, is the first to use "cels"—transparent drawings laid over a fixed background.

Live-theatre owners discover cinema. Movie palaces are born. Audiences flock.

1914 35 mm film is developed in Germany by Oskar Barnack at the Leitz optics firm.

1917 Nippon Kogaku K. K., later Nikon, is established in Tokyo.

1918 The Canadian government's Exhibits and Publicity Bureau is established—a forerunner to the Canadian Government Motion Picture Bureau.

1919 *Back to God's Country* (written by Nell Shipman, Canada's first woman film writer and leading actress) is released.

1923 Walt and Roy Disney start an animation studio in Los Angeles.

1924 Leitz markets the Leica, the first high-quality 35 mm camera.

1925 Sergei Eisenstein's *Battleship Potemkin* establishes film montage technique.

1927 Al Jolson's *The Jazz Singer*, the first popular talkie, is released.

Movietone offers newsreels with sound.

The Academy of Motion Picture Arts and Sciences is founded.

German filmmaker Fritz Lang releases the first feature-length science-fiction film, *Metropolis*.

1928 The first Mickey Mouse cartoon airs.

1932 Home movie buffs are introduced to 8 mm film: the precursor technology for home videos and citizen-journalism.

Technicolor comes to the movies as Herbert Kalmus develops an optical and dye three-colour process.

1934 Fuji Photo Film is founded.

1935 Kodak releases Kodachrome colour film *Becky Sharp*, the first all-colour feature-length film.

German filmmaker Leni Riefenstahl releases *Triumph of the Will*, glorifying Hitler and the Third Reich, but displaying new modern techniques of cinematography.

1939   The National Film Act establishes the National Film Board of Canada (NFB).

One of the most popular films of all time, *Gone with the Wind*, starring Clark Gable, is released. Audiences are stunned by the full range of mechanical and optical special effects on display.

1940   Charlie Chaplin's *The Great Dictator* pokes fun at the Nazis and the Italian fascists at the start of World War II.

1941   *Citizen Kane* experiments with flashback, camera movement, and sound techniques.

1947   The House Committee on Un-American Activities investigates alleged communist influences in Hollywood, leading to the blacklist.

The Polaroid camera is invented by Dr. Edwin H. Land.

1948   The Association of Motion Picture Producers and Laboratories of Canada (AMPPLC; a mutual support and lobby organization for independent film production in Canada) is established.

1953   Fox develops CinemaScope, a proprietary widescreen projection technique. Other studios follow with Panavision and Vistavision.

1961   Julian Roffman's *The Mask*, the first Canadian horror film, is distributed by Warner Bros.

1967   The Canadian Film Development Corporation (Telefilm Canada) is established.

1968   NFB (First Nations unit) releases "Battle of Crowfoot" by Willie Dunn

1970   The first feature film directed by a woman in Canada (*Madeleine Is . . .* by Sylvia Spring) is released.

Canadian filmmakers invent the giant projector system IMAX.

1971   The Indian movie industry produces 433 films, making it the largest in the world—Bollywood is born.

1974   The NFB creates Studio D, the first federally funded all-women film unit in the world.

1975   George Lucas founds Industrial Light & Magic.

Sony markets the first Betamax VCR viewer and recorder, followed by JVC with VHS.

1976   Dolby Stereo sound movies are introduced.

1977   *Star Wars* and *Close Encounters of the Third Kind* are released, and are the first of a new generation of films using special effects.

1985   Rupert Murdoch buys 20th Century Fox.

The Canadian Association of Motion Picture Producers merges its membership with the Canadian Film and Television Association (formerly the AMPPLC).

Sony introduces the first chip-based "CAMera/recorder" or camcorder.

1992   Pacific Bell and Sony demonstrate digital cinema with *Bugsy*.

Kodak introduces the Photo CD.

1993   An IMAX 3D digital sound system goes into a New York theatre.

Kodak and Apple release the first digital still camera.

1995   CD-ROMs are able to store full-length feature films.

DV, the file format for digital video, is released.

Toy Story becomes the first completely computer-generated feature film.

1996   NFB's all-women film unit Studio D is shut down amidst sweeping government cuts.

1997   Kodak launches the first point-and-shoot digital camera.

1998   DVDs are introduced.

2000   *The Blair Witch Project* becomes a hit through viral and web marketing.

Ang Lee's *Crouching Tiger, Hidden Dragon* marks the coming of age of Chinese-language cinema in the Western commercial mainstream.

Casio puts a digital camera in a wristwatch.

2003   HDV becomes a registered trademark of JVC, Sony, Canon, and Sharp.

2005   Kodak Canada announces the closure of the 55-hectare Mount Dennis plant (Bozikovic, 2012).

2006   Viacom spins off some media assets to form CBS Corporation.

Disney buys Pixar.

2008   Polaroid announces the end of its instant photography business and will not produce film past 2009 (P. Lyons, 2008).

Blu-ray wins out over HD DVD and becomes the sole high-definition format (Arnold, 2008).

2009   *Avatar* is released—using "stereoscopic" filmmaking (first invented in 1838)—in 2D as well as 3D and 4D formats; audiences wear special glasses for depth perception.

Kodak announces plans to discontinue producing Kodachrome, its oldest colour film stock (C. Thompson, 2009).

2011   Hitachi unveils its glasses-free 3D-projection system at the Combined Exhibition of Advanced Technologies (CEATEC; Toto, 2011).

2012   Disney acquires Lucasfilm for $4 billion and announces plans to release the seventh installation of the *Star Wars* saga in 2015.

Kodak files for bankruptcy protection (De La Merced, 2012).

Kodak exits the digital camera business, and will instead license its name to other camera manufacturers (Pepitone, 2012).

2013   Google Glass provides wearable audio-video cameras to US film students for experimentation, and estimates a commercial release date of spring 2014, with each unit costing USD$1,500.

6

Telegraphy, the Talking Wireless, and Television

Objectives

In this chapter you will begin to see the importance of convergence in the development of the technological forms of telecommunication and the broadcast media based on a combination of sound and image, wires and wireless. In particular, this chapter emphasizes the international and national decision-making on technology and the development of electronic sound and picture recording using both analogue and digital technologies. This chapter makes the following key points:

- the importance of research and innovation in general science that creates the technological and technical platform for the emergence of mass media and global communication;

- how the historical timelines of scientific discovery and commercial application are dialectically related;

- how the industrial development of mass-produced and miniaturized components interacts with the social development of mass communication;

- the important economic links between mass production, the emerging electronic media, advertising, and marketing;

- how the technologies of broadcasting and the cultural forms of radio and television are dialectically related; and

- the importance of the British BBC model in the development of government-funded national television systems like the CBC.

Keywords

- **audience commodity**
- **broadband**
- **broadcasting**
- **Canadian content (Cancon)**
- **common carriage**
- **electromagnetic spectrum**
- **podcasting**
- **reality television**
- **telecommunication**
- **telecommunications common carrier**
- **universal service**

Telegraphy, Telephone, and Telecommunication

This is the age of telegrams. The public is accustomed to the consideration of useful facts set forth in the briefest terms. (Beach, 1873, Preface)

TELECOMMUNICATION

"The emission, transmission or reception of intelligence by any wire, cable, radio, optical or other electromagnetic system, or by any similar technical system" (Public Works and Government Services Canada, 2007, "telecommunication").

BROADCASTING

"Any transmission of programs, whether or not encrypted, by radio waves or other means of telecommunication for reception by the public by means of broadcasting receiving apparatus, but does not include any such transmission of programs that is made solely for performance or display in a public place" (Public Works and Government Services Canada, 2007, "broadcasting").

This 1873 quotation could easily apply to the tweets of today in its evaluation of message brevity; whereas the content may have changed little, the technological change in media is deemed to be more significant, particularly in terms of the contraction of space and time. The early history of communication over distance, or **telecommunication**, involved developing both a *means* and a *mode* of transmission. This includes *what* technology is used (the means) and *how* to encode, record, and transmit as well as how to receive, decode, and respond (together, the mode or technique). The combination of means and modes identifies the technological systems or *networks* used in transmitting messages over distance.

New changes in technology have prompted communication scholars to consider the interrelation between technology and social organization, giving rise to concepts like the "network society" as applied to digital technology (Barney, 2004; Castells & Cardoso, 2005; van Dijk, 2012). This reminds us of the importance of identifying relationships between institutions, organizations, and social relations in our history of telecommunication and **broadcasting**, to which we now turn to identify similarities and differences over time, and to consider not only the technology but also how it is organized, what decisions have been made, and why it has been developed one way versus another.

The tele*graph* (to graph or write) is a means to transmit the mode of communication; in this case, the alphabet, which was translated (and encoded) into a series of dots and dashes with each letter (A–Z), and each number (0–9), being represented by an electronic impulse. Named after its inventor Samuel Morse, Morse code (1837) was adopted as a common electronic language at the International Wireless Telegraph Convention in 1906. Signature states agreed and thus set the standard for its adaptation worldwide, such that, for example, three dots, followed by three dashes and three more dots (...---...) is the international signal for distress (SOS), which any station picking up the signal is obligated to answer (International Wireless Telegraph Convention, 1906, s. 6 (a) XV–XVI; www.earlyradiohistory.us/1906conv.htm#SR6A).

Telegraphy followed the technique of the earliest "semaphore" telecommunication (combining the Ancient Greek *sema* [sign] and *phoros* [bearing or bearer of]), which relied on human visual contact to see physical signs (like smoke signals or flags) sent or relayed between outdoor stations (Encyclopaedia Britannica, 2013, "semaphore"; www.britannica.com/EBchecked/topic/533828/semaphore). The telegraph initially required (1) a human operator to manually press the dots and dashes; (2) the encoding device (similar in size and function to a computer mouse today); (3) a physical wire line to transmit the electronic impulses; (4) another human operator (later mechanical) to receive and decode messages at the other end; and (5) a delivery person to bring the message to the recipient (requiring a "telegraph boy" as messenger; Downey, 2000). Just as the printing press was used to revolutionize communication in terms of distance, speed was the significant distinction in the new media inventions at the end of the nineteenth century, which included the tele*phone* (the electronic transmission of sound over distance).

Although Alexander Graham Bell invented the telephone in Ontario in 1876, he transferred his *patent* (recall from Chapter 5) to his father, Alexander Melville Bell, who used it to develop a private subscription-based service (an exchange value; Babe, 1990). As a commercial enterprise, the patent was eventually sold to the National Bell Telephone Company of Boston (now known as the American Telephone and Telegraph Company, or AT&T). In Canada, the National

Bell Telephone Company was given a monopoly for its service by the federal government in 1880 with the condition that it extend telephone service beyond the urban areas in which it was concentrated, and that it be subject to government regulation in setting its rates to ensure **universal service** (ibid.). In return, Bell had a relatively exclusive customer base and could use public lands to install telephone lines, poles, and transmission lines, facilitating the beginning of the vertical integration of today's Bell Canada Enterprises (BCE Inc.).

Federal government jurisdiction over the telegraph and the telephone was established in 1906 via the Railway Act, which gave the Board of Railway Commissioners authority to regulate the telephone as well as telegraphy. The Board itself had been established two years earlier with a mandate to reduce the extremes that had come about via "market forces" in a relatively "free enterprise" industry. Competition and profit-imperatives in railway transportation had resulted in several disparities across Canada. Where some areas had no rail service, others were controlled by regional monopolies that (since the company controlled supply exclusively) charged much higher rates depending on the customer (particularly if it was in any way a competitor), even though the same weight carried by the railway was to the same destination (Canadian Transportation Agency, 2004a).

As the railway was essential to transportation and the political economic development of Canada (indeed, several provinces joined Canadian federation primarily based on the condition that the federal government guaranteed a railway connection), its government regulation was essential as well. Thus the Board was established as an independent regulatory body to oversee and ensure freight charges and tariffs (at reasonable rates), as well as relatively equitable access or universal service (particularly as the public had already "invested" in the railways via government loans and subsidies, as well as their own hard labour). Moreover, the Board established the principle of **common carriage** so that railway companies could not discriminate between *what* they were carrying and *who* they were carrying it for. The Board also proved necessary in order to ensure worker safety for those who laboured to build and maintain the railway, as death rates (in the hundreds) and injury rates (in the thousands) were significantly high over its construction and maintenance (ibid.).

The inclusion of telegraph and telephone was related to the railways' "rights of way" that allowed the use of public land for the sake of universal service, linking communication lines across the country. Their inclusion was also an outgrowth of market forces, particularly the tendency towards control and monopolization as indicated by the overcharging of rates by telegraph companies. Recall from Chapter 4 the importance of news agencies. In Western Canada, the Canadian Pacific Railway had a monopoly over rail in the region and also operated a telegraph news service. This resulted in its charging competitors increasingly higher rates, and in one case actually "cutting off a newspapers' news-service" that "had published articles critical of the CP" (The Canadian Encyclopedia, 2012). The complaints against such practices resulted in a ruling by the Board to safeguard against such dominance and control over communication, which included making a distinction between transmission and content: "The Board's ruling established a basic principle of Canadian telecommunications—the separation of control of message content from control of transmission. In the telephone industry, a similar principle was used when Bell Telephone, which had a monopoly in a large part of Canada, was prohibited from providing content-based services" (Canadian Transportation Agency, 2004b, para. 52).

Technological refinements to telegraphy followed in time. Automatic, as distinct from manual, transmission of messages began in 1914, teleprinters in 1925, prototypical fax machines in 1927, and telex machines in 1959, which enabled parties to communicate directly without the intermediary of an exchange. Perhaps what is surprising about telegraphy is its longevity in the face of competition from the telephone after 1877. However, it was the advent of data

UNIVERSAL SERVICE

Initially an obligation imposed on the monopoly operator that concentrated on the provision of voice telephony, requiring operators to expand coverage to provide services in remote and underserved areas (ITU and infoDev, 2010). As a principle of government policy, it establishes that communication and other services should be freely available to anyone as a basic necessity or for a reasonable cost.

COMMON CARRIAGE

The principle that the **telecommunications common carrier** cannot discriminate between who pays for the service (any persons of the public) or the content carried.

TELECOMMUNICATIONS COMMON CARRIER

"A person [government, corporate or unincorporated organization or legal representative] who owns or operates a transmission facility used by that person or another person to provide telecommunications services to the public for compensation" (Telecommunications Act, 1993, "telecommunications common carrier").

transmission via computers over the telephony system that was the climate change that turned telegraphy into a dinosaur. Yet during its brief time, telegraphy accentuated the value of speed in communication over distances, what social theorist Henri Lefebvre (1979) called spatialization or the "process of overcoming the constraints of space and time in social life" (as cited in Mosco, 1996, p. 173). As discussed in Chapter 3, spatialization is particularly significant today as information and communication technologies (ICTs) are used to reduce or eliminate differences in both time and space, which itself is a significant indicator and measure of control to those with the capacity and resources to do so.

"Time Is Money"

Today, most of us accept the measurement of time via the 12- or 24-hour clock as a fact of life, but particular decisions were made in order to make it so. The elimination of differences of time underpinned the justification for the standardization of time worldwide, and the use of synchronized clocks was one of the first international agreements made between states. Again, the commercial railway was instrumental as motivation for setting regular and agreed schedules, with Great Britain synchronizing its schedule (as early as 1847) according to Greenwich Mean Time (GMT), which was eventually accepted as the worldwide benchmark at the 1884 International Meridian Conference (see Figure 6.1).

Source: © Robert Kirk / iStockphoto

FIGURE 6.1 | Clock measuring Greenwich Mean Time (GMT) at the Royal Observatory in the UK.

The commodification of time is expressed in what is now considered the common adage "time is money," as made evident in the mid-1880s with the exorbitant rates (even then at USD$10 per word) that telegraph companies initially charged for transmission (Winseck & Pike, 2007, p. 25). Speed as an exchange value was considerably ratcheted up when telegraph reception was automated and machines called "tickers" could deliver information faster than it could be collected (www.earlyradiohistory.us).

The encoded messages were separated into specialized parcels of information meant for specific paying clients. Foremost among these was financial information or "the stock and commodity prices" (Winseck & Pike, 2007, p. 25) from which, for example, Reuters news agency today continues to collect, categorize, sell, and distribute worldwide, reaching well beyond stock prices to link everything from breakouts of disease to predictions of the weather as tied to financial decision- and profit- making (Investopedia, n.d.;   www.investopedia.com/terms/w/weatherfuture.asp). Efforts to increase the amount of data transmitted over the greatest

For Real?

Technological Conditioning?

While we may not think of the clock as a technology or, moreover, an instrument of social control, the standardization of time goes beyond the scheduling of railways to the organization and division of labour, and distinctions made between labour and leisure. Marxist historian E. P. Thompson identified that the standardization of time and the use of synchronized clocks were fundamental to the development of capitalism and industrialism and the corresponding change to a whole way of life. Thompson (1967) called this change "technological conditioning" (p. 80) since it imposes an artificial schedule on what was previously treated as natural or symbiotic time, made collectively by humans in accordance with nature (such as sunlight, ocean tides, and the changing of the seasons).

This technological conditioning and its worldwide standardization may be understood as the founding premise of many kinds of convergence since, as Noel Castree (2009) submits,

> *clock time has the capacity, external to itself, of measuring differences by way of a metrical unity. We now appreciate why clock time is essential if value is to become the dominant measure of wealth in capitalist societies: without it there is no way that the efforts of heterogeneous wage workers could be compared (the competition relation); no way that employers could appropriate surplus value in aggregate or locally (the class relation); and no way that commodities could be sold for money (the exchange relation). (p. 41)*

Such standardization (or convergence?) draws attention to our daily uses of technology, which have become so routine that living without them seems impossible. If we consider, for example, how much time we are in front of a screen, online, attached to our cell phone or BlackBerry, are these connections also a form of technological conditioning?

Class Exercise

Make a list of all the communication and technology devices that you listen to/watch/hear on a daily basis (cell phone, computer, television, radio); next to this list, record the time of day that you do so. Add up the amount of time that you spend connected to communication technology. Estimate how much of it is under your control, and consider what input or control you have over this time and the technology used.

---

distance, and correspondingly decrease the amount of time required for transmission, are common to research and development in telecommunication, with the latest record in transmission speed allowing the "equivalent to beaming 700 DVDs worth of data in a single second" (Mosher, 2011, para. 2).

In the last part of the nineteenth century, the efforts to increase private control over both time and space via telegraphy were efforts by companies aiming to control both the information (the content) and the technology for transmission (the carriage). The telegraph was thus used to extend the processes of commodification and spatialization, and foreshadowed computer networking today. Tom Standage (1998) called this *The Victorian Internet*, and as Winseck and

Pike (2007) explain, by the 1920s, the globe was already divided up by an exclusive and very small interdependent network of news agencies and telegraph companies, illustrating the extent of globalization and first round of global media convergence (pp. 137, 177).

That the telegraph was as important in military affairs as it was in commerce became increasingly clear as war became systematized in the late nineteenth century (McMahon, 2002, p. 384). Indeed, military historians see the telegraph and the railway as two of the defining characteristics of "modern warfare," beginning with the Crimean War (1854–6), when both were used by governments for military purposes (Royle, 2000). As we discuss further in Chapter 9 on state policy, this was made evident in the First World War when liberal democratic governments immediately took control of the telegraph system and many other means and modes of communication were censored, indicating the extent to which political economic imperialism was advanced.

Although we may think of telegraphy as an outdated mode of communication, it is a binary technology—messages were relayed in Morse code, using dots and dashes to form words—and as such, it is a proto-digital technology that established economic and social patterns into which the digital technologies that followed fitted seamlessly. As discussed earlier, it was a technology that assisted the rapid expansion of modern imperialism by facilitating commercial transactions over great distances, and the telegraph was an important component of the global infrastructure needed to build the emerging system of mass industrial development. In the same way that theorists today, such as Manuel Castells, argue that the new information economy is a necessary adjunct to globalization, the telegraph established a "new global information code" (McMahon, 2002, p. 380) that facilitated the circulation of capital (in the form of money) and economic control (in the form of imperialism).

Discovering the Ether

The basics of telegraph technology were further developed when the technology of "wireless telegraphy," or subsequently "radiotelegraphy," was invented, expanding both the scope and the range of communication possible. At the turn of the twentieth century, wireless communication was a convergence of ideas in physics—theorizing the existence of the **electromagnetic spectrum** surrounding the earth (by physicist J. C. Maxwell in 1864)—engineering—identifying electromagnetic "waves" (re)produced and measured by frequencies known as Hertz (after their inventor Heinrich Hertz in 1894)—and finally, an "apparatus" that was used to "transmit and receive them" (as invented by Guglielmo Marconi in 1897; Kern, 2003, p. 211). Whereas telegraphy and the telephone would continue to be used for point-to-point transmission between sender and receiver, wireless telegraphy could be amplified and sent to many receivers, or broadcast over the electromagnetic spectrum (also called "the ether").

> Beginning July 15, 1913, the Weather Bureau is distributing "broadcast" . . . a daily weather bulletin. "Broadcast," as the term is used in the Radio Service, means that the message is fired out into the illimitable ether to be picked up and made use of by anyone who has the will and apparatus to possess himself (sic) thereof. (United States. Superintendent of Documents, 1913; www.earlyradiohistory.us).

The existence of the electromagnetic spectrum indicates that it is a natural and therefore public resource; that is, no one person, business, corporation, or country owns it as it exists independently of human life, but is essential for electronic communication to occur. Its use value is thus one that is shared—the recognition of which wasn't entirely motivated by ethics, but by

---

ELECTROMAGNETIC SPECTRUM

"The range of energy which contains parts or 'bands' such as the visible, infrared, ultraviolet, microwave (radar), gamma ray, x-ray, radio, and which travels at the speed of light. Different parts of the electromagnetic spectrum have different wavelengths and frequencies" (Natural Resources Canada, 2008, "Electromagnetic spectrum").

the physical restrictions of time and space, thus precipitating international agreements over its use value. This is still a fundamental stipulation in international agreements over spectrum frequencies and use, as the Canadian government underscored recently, for example:

> The radio frequency spectrum is vital for national security, public safety, research and individuals making use of the spectrum be it through cell phones, cordless phones or even garage door openers. This natural renewable and finite resource is shared with the world. Finite because the same part of the spectrum can be used again and limited because the spectrum is similar to a highway in that only a certain amount of traffic can be carried depending on the road and weather conditions and the type of traffic on the road. (Government of Canada, 2009, para. 2)

The appreciation of the spectrum as a public resource meant that considerations of its use value and exchange value were paramount in its development. Whereas the latter took precedence in Canada, in the United States, radio was developed as a commercial conduit, and such apparently natural dominance (or hegemony) over the airwaves would later affect the use and development of subsequent broadcasting technologies like television, but it was a hegemony that was a result of a complex process of negotiation and exercise of state and corporate priorities.

Focus on Research

Broadband Networks

> Broadband networks are often described as the utility of the 21st century, as important as water and electricity. (Middleton, 2011a, pp. 4–5)

As Catherine Middleton, Canada Research Chair in Communication Technologies in the Information Society, at Ryerson University aptly notes, **broadband** networks are the most recent iteration of essential telecommunication infrastructure in Canada. Like the telegraph and telephone networks that preceded it, broadband wireless technology has become necessary for citizens throughout the country. In the early days of broadband development (the 1990s), federal government priorities ensured that Canada was a global leader in network development, public adoption, and geographic penetration, but this lead has since waned.

The importance of broadband networks in Canada, like previous telecommunication infrastructure, is in part to link the diverse populations across the country's vast geography nationally and within specific communities. This is particularly valuable in remote communities, as demonstrated in the case of K-Net and Canadian Aboriginal communities (see Fiser & Clement, 2009). Additionally, broadband networks, and in particular wireless networks, offer communities the opportunities to develop their own services and Internet access for their residents, which includes developing the infrastructure, technological skills, and public participation in decision-making in developing this public resource. Several neighbourhoods and municipalities (Fredericton, Toronto, Ottawa, Calgary, e.g.) have done so, by offering, for example, wireless services in public parks and central squares available for use by the public for free.

Middleton contributed to the Community Wireless Infrastructure Research Project (CWIRP)

Continued

BROADBAND

Refers to the (broader) capacity and use of the electromagnetic spectrum (bands) to carry more types of diverse content (sound, text, images, etc.) at increased speeds. This is in contrast to the telegraph, which could only carry one type of signal (Morse code), and the telephone, whose "dial-up" capacity is considerably slower (see Figure 6.2).

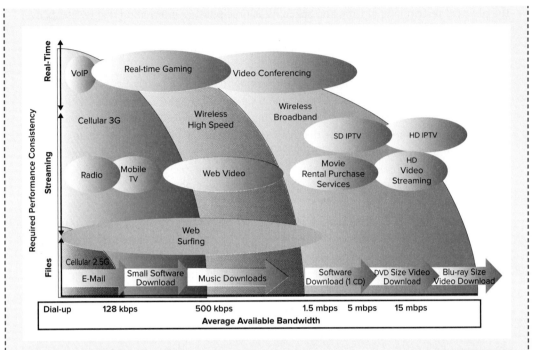

FIGURE 6.2 | Internet applications—bandwidth requirements

Source: CRTC Communications Monitoring Report, September 2012, http://www.crtc.gc.ca/eng/publications/reports/PolicyMonitoring/2012/cmr4.htm#n5. Reproduced with the permission of the Canadian Radio-television and Telecommunications Commission on behalf of Her Majesty in Right of Canada, 2013.

Note: The measurements kbps and mbps indicate the amount of data that can be sent (kilobits or megabits) and the speed that it travels (per second).

whose 2008 "Final Report" identified and evaluated the various community broadband networks and experiments across Canada with comparisons to private networks. It recommended that public infrastructure and supporting policies be a priority for municipal and federal governments alike, as, among other shortcomings, private development does not satisfy or ensure universal service:

> *Infrastructure developed by the private sector does not generally support open network access, or provide users with neutral, non-discriminatory network access. It may not offer ubiquitous service. The private sector does not focus on delivering affordable infrastructure—for-profit companies will charge what the market will bear—nor does it allow for user input into governance or respond directly to its users [sic] needs. This does not mean that the private sector develops bad infrastructure, on the contrary it can offer high quality, reliable, useful, widely available, and secure service. But the needs of the public are not being fully met by infrastructure that is built in response to current market forces. (CWIRP, 2008, p. iv)*

Middleton's work continues to critically engage with issues around access and universal service, specifically their value in developing community communication capacity (Middleton & Bryne, 2011; Middleton & Crow, 2008), and the strengths and weaknesses of relying on market-based approaches to the development of broadband (Middleton, 2011b; Van Gorp & Middleton, 2010). In terms of the latter, Middleton highlights how the slackening of specific policy related to broadband development, along with the shift to greater reliance on market forces in the rollout of the infrastructure, has contributed to Canada's lagging in terms of international adoption of broadband for those functions mentioned previously (Van Gorp & Middleton, 2010). This research should assist the telecommunications industry, government departments, and communities in making informed decisions related to future access for all Canadians to this essential utility.

Discussion Questions

1. What comparisons can you draw between the development of early telecommunications in Canada and broadband technology?

2. Provide examples of broadband wireless services in your own community. What public access is available and where?

3. What is the difference between a publicly owned and managed network and a private network?

4. Why is universal service and public access essential in telecommunications?

Common Airwaves, Different Purposes: Commercial versus Public Radio

> That [radio] broadcasting should develop as a capitalist enterprise, a vehicle for advertising and commercial expansion is not surprising. . . . What is curious is the sequence of steps by which it became so, the twists and turns which took the medium out of the hands of the state and the military and emphasised its universal entertainment value as against its long-distance communication role. (Lewis & Booth, 1989, p. 30)

Peter Lewis and Jerry Booth are talking about the birth of the commercial radio industry in the United States between the end of World War I and the start of World War II. In that 20-year period the radio moved from being a tool for law enforcement and military command to being one of the most widely accepted domestic appliances, services, and social routines of the twentieth century. Today we take radio—or the broadcast of sound—for granted. It's on while we go to work or university; it's in the background at work and in shopping centres. Radio is available almost anywhere, in portable forms—from broadcasting stations, satellite, and over the Internet. We tend to think of the frequent commercials and DJ banter as routine, but radio, like the telegraph, was not exclusively a commercial medium; as a "communications and control" technology it was used in the coordination of international shipping and other forms of transport.

At first, radio's inventor, Guglielmo Marconi (1874–1937), backed by the British and Italian governments, attempted to retain a monopoly over marine communications, but the Germans baulked at the idea, and in 1912, after the "unsinkable" *Titanic* sunk in the North Atlantic, ocean-going vessels were required to carry a radio transceiver as a uniform safety measure (McMahon, 2002, p. 385). Marconi was granted the world's first patent for *wireless* telegraphy (Morse code sent via radio signals, rather than copper cable) in 1896, and in 1897 formed a company to market the new technology. Ironically, Marconi had been supported in his endeavours by the British Post Office, but severed his relationship with the organization when it became clear that it thought the new invention had no real purpose (Weightman, 2003, p. 33). After a series

ONGOING ISSUES

Copper Wire to iPods—Changing Technologies and Ownership of Sound Recording

In 1877 Thomas Edison (1847–1931) produced one of the earliest mechanical devices for reproducing recorded music, the phonograph, which played from cylinders. A decade later the gramophone came on the market and used flat discs to hold the recording. The first electromagnetic tape-recording and playback system was publicly available in 1935. In 1948 the first modern long-playing (LP) discs were developed, and 10 years later the first stereo system was introduced. The short-lived eight-track tape cartridge was introduced in the mid-1960s, but was killed off by the tape cassette in the early 1970s. Compact discs were first marketed in 1982 and were initially very expensive. In the 1990s Sony developed the minidisc recorder and player, and as compression techniques improved and convergence in digital technologies began to move quickly, MP3 files made their first appearance in 1997. This "personalization of music" was further refined as the iPod was released onto the market in 2003 and has quickly replaced the transistor radio and the CD walkman as the mobile music source of choice, particularly with many young people.

The source of the music is a controversial issue that has its origins in the first instance of recorded music as converging issues of labour and copyright carried over from the technology of the printing press. From the very beginning of commercial media, with the change in movies from silent film (where orchestras played live) to the talkies (with recorded sound), many musicians were put out of work. When commercial radio was developed, musicians that had previously been playing live, and largely getting paid accordingly, were now being recorded by studios and radio stations which re-sold their music without compensation to the original artist. Thus in 1896, musicians in Canada and the United States organized themselves into the American Federation of Musicians (of the United States and Canada), defining a "professional" musician as someone who is paid for their services. The union was formed to advance and protect the labour of professional musicians, including their rates of pay, pensions, fair contracts, and related issues of copyright (▣ www.afm.org/about/our-history). As the technology allows a myriad number of ways that the musician's work can be copied, mixed, and replicated into any number of formats, how copyright is legally defined is an issue of labour as well as ownership.

In more recent times, the rights of the musician have been trumped by copyright ownership of the recording industry (even though an artist may have created the work, the ownership of the copyright is more likely the record label). The record labels are protected by powerful industry associations that are always on the lookout for challenges to their ownership and control. Technological change allowing for music downloads and peer-to-peer file sharing, for example, allowed these to be distributed for "free," and a file-sharing website called Napster began facilitating the process in the fall of 1999, thereby circumventing recording industry ownership and control, and challenging the idea of copyright and intellectual property rights. As Enrico Menduni (2007) noted, however, it didn't take long before Napster and its users were sued by the Recording Industry Association of America (RIAA) for copyright just a few months later:

More than 2000 cases have since been brought against Napster and thousands of its users. At first, legal action generated a great deal of publicity for Napster, which had 14 million users by February 2001 but, later, it led to the end of free file sharing by Napster, after a court ruling of September 2001, shortly before September 11. Of course, free file sharing practices continued but Napster went into decline, due both to legal action and to the coming of new players, such as Apple Computers.

There will continue to be challenges in major lawsuits by the multinational recording industry represented by nation-specific associations for the major labels (such as Vivendi SA, Sony, Warner, and EMI) whether in the United States (RIAA), Canada (the Canadian Recording Industry Association, CRIA, renamed Music Canada in 2011) or Great Britain (the British Phonographic Industry, or BPI). Calling music sharing "theft" and "piracy," with claims against individuals called "pirates" and "criminals," file sharing is directly correlated with decreases in industry revenues. In Canada, the recording industry argues that there is no such thing as free music, and it needs to be eliminated. It has an "anti-piracy hotline" to report who may be "infringing sound recordings that are being offered for sale," and it lobbies the Canadian government to strengthen copyright laws and international intellectual property agreements (🔲 www.musiccanada.com).

In contrast, research commissioned by the Canadian federal government via Industry Canada demonstrated that the relationship between downloading and music sales was a positive one, as file sharing actually leads to increased music purchases and other forms of entertainment media (such as movies, concerts, and video games; Anderson & Frenz, 2010; Geist, 2005). The researchers suggested that recording industry claims (that file sharing decreased music sales) exaggerated the negative impacts of file sharing for its own benefit—that is, in order to justify increased ownership and control over content via copyright and other property laws (ibid.). Music Canada (2011) subsequently commissioned its own research to contest and counter the Industry Canada study. While the reliability and validity of the research may be questionable, the tendency for industry exaggerations is not, as it strives to manage the ideas and media frames that support its claims via publishing its own reports relating income to piracy, and by employing its resources to expand its legal proceedings to include advertisers and "piracy sites" (BBC News, 2013b). This includes asking search engines like Google to remove file-sharing sites suspected of copyright infringement. Google has received so many requests that it began publishing a monthly "Transparency Report" (beginning July 2011; 🔲 www.google.com/transparencyreport/removals/copyright/) indicating that, for example, in the first six months of 2013 it had received 100 million requests, the largest number of them from BPI, RIAA (and their member companies), and various film studios such as Warner Bros. (BBC News, 2013a). Reliance on industry research increases as budget cuts to independent government and university research, together with an overall decrease in investigative journalism reduces the public's ability to evaluate industry claims and provide alternatives to the production, distribution and exchange of music. (further discussed in Chapter 10). Nonetheless, since private ownership and copyright is the very foundation on which the industry depends, it will use all of its resources to counter any idea or practice that challenges it. As law is established on precedent, a recent court ruling by a judge in the United States, against the music-sharing service LimeWire and in favour of RIAA, suggests that the line between what is "sharing" and what is "piracy" may soon be eliminated in favour of the latter (Stempel & Adegoke, 2010).

of trials over shorter distances, Marconi made the first intercontinental radio transmission, from Cornwall, England, to St. John's, Newfoundland, in 1901 (The Noble Foundation, 1967).

As an outgrowth of wireless technology, radio (short for electromagnetic radiation) was first referred to as "radiotelegraphy," and it wasn't clear from the outset that its development would correspondingly follow the press and the telegraph in its commodification. In 1920, radio station KDKA in Pittsburgh, Pennsylvania, claimed to be the first commercial radio station in the world. Yet, CFCF in Montreal more accurately holds that title as it was established a year earlier by the Marconi Wireless Telegraph Company of Canada (Nolan, 1986, p. 4; Vipond, 2002). As we cover in the next chapter, just as World War II would give impetus to the development of emerging computer technologies, so World War I had stimulated technical developments and government involvement in radio. It was, however, the convergence of the phonograph, and later the gramophone, with the technologies of radio transmission that gave commercial radio broadcasting its biggest boost. If Britain emerged from World War I decimated, then the United States, which had funded the war, now dominated the world economy.

The 1920s—the Roaring Twenties—was a time of relative prosperity. It was coined the "Jazz Age," and the trumpet and the sax could soon be heard across the United States and southern Canada. It was ushered in by the Radio Corporation of America (RCA), itself a classic example of political economic negotiations between military and corporate power, which resulted in General Electric buying up the assets and patents of the American Marconi company and given an initial monopoly in radio by the American Navy (Winseck & Pike, 2007, pp. 254, 255). The impetus for American commercial development of radio was to counter what was seen as British control over the dominant means of telecommunication at the time, the undersea cable system, and as Mosco (1989) argues "was a direct response to the concern raised by American military and diplomatic interests that the United States could not challenge British Imperialism as long as Britain controlled the undersea cable system" (p. 134). By 1922 there were over 600 licensed commercial radio stations in the United States, and in 1927 two major broadcasting networks were established—CBS (Columbia Broadcasting System), a consortium of private broadcasters, and NBC (National Broadcasting Corporation), a consortium of major US corporations like General Electric, Westinghouse, United Fruit Company, and AT&T (Barnouw, 1966).

In contrast, in 1922 there were 39 relatively separate broadcasting stations across Canada, and six years later, there were 68 (Nolan, 1986, p. 4). By the late 1920s, Canadian stations were facing continental competition from the United States and even integration, as a large number of Canadian stations were affiliates to CBS and NBC (MacLennan, 2005; D. Skinner, 2004). The first effort by the federal government to regulate radio came in 1913 with the Radiotelegraph Act, which "gave the Canadian state power to license the use of airwaves which were considered public property just like other natural resources" (Filion, 1996, p. 119). Attempts were made to stave off the perceived threats of integration of radio from the United States with amendments to the Act in 1923, which failed, and in 1929, with the report of the Royal Commission on Radio Broadcasting (Aird Commission), the federal government took steps to more actively regulate radio with the introduction of the first Radio Broadcasting Act (🖥 www.broadcasting-history.ca/index3 .html?url=http%3A//www.broadcasting-history.ca/politics_regulation_lobbying/The_History_ of_Canadian_Broadcast_Regulation.html).

The Aird Commission marked a very significant time in Canadian broadcasting history in three ways. Firstly, it established a relatively *democratic* model for public participation in the development of communication and cultural policy in Canada through an involved process of Royal Commissions, task forces, and parliamentary committees, all of which include public consultations

(Nesbitt-Larking, 2007, p. 53). Organizations emerging at this time as part of this process were political lobbies for private broadcasting interests as well as those for the advancement of public participation. The Canadian Association of Broadcasters (CAB) was first established in 1926 to advocate on the part of private companies and commercial radio interests, whereas public ownership and participation in radio was principally advocated by an organization called the Canadian Radio League. Headed by (then-journalist) Graham Spry, it was an effective lobby emphasizing the use value of radio and the idea of a national public broadcaster owned by all Canadians.

The strength of these forces bore out in the final report and in the 1932 Act, which created the Canadian Radio Broadcasting Commission (CRBC), the precursor to the Canadian Broadcasting Corporation (CBC), and whose modest mandate at the time was to "decide on the numbers and locations of radio stations in Canada" (Filion, 1996, p. 120). Although the Act prohibited a national commercial network partly due to the recognition that the airwaves are, in fact, a public resource, and that the government-of-the-day saw it as a useful instrument in nation-building, it did allow for private regional chain broadcasting (Vipond, 1994, p. 156). When the CBC was formed in 1936, its programming had a specific mandate as it was supposed to reflect a "Canadian" culture and promote unity across geographical, linguistic, social, and cultural differences. In this way, the public interest was equated with the national interest (Raboy, 1990), rather than supporting a more open politically, socially and culturally diverse, or *democratic* system. In effect, the policy worked to contain and deflect any alternative ideas and practices that challenged the dominant conservative and capitalist political economy of the time; that is, from other immigrant organizations, labour unions or "left" leaning political parties. Similar to the national unity that was promoted in Great Britain at the time of the stamp tax (recall from Chapter 4 early press history), Canadian unity was promoted as a way of countering class divisions and social unrest (Mazepa, 2007, p. 47). Thus for radio, the public system was national in scope, and the CRCB would oversee the whole system, whereas private radio was to operate at the local level.

Secondly, in creating a state-managed system of radio stations, the Commission and the Act that followed demonstrated the primacy of commercial and institutional radio over amateur broadcasters who were experimenting and using the airwaves for all kinds of different (and non-profit) purposes. This grassroots pattern was occurring in the United States as well. As Robert McChesney (2000b) notes, the hobbyists did not give up the ether without a fight, and initially commercial formats were unprofitable (p. 199). In the U.S., the first attempts at regulation came with the introduction of the Federal Radio Commission (FRC) in 1927, and one of its first acts did not favour the amateurs and public experiments, but the allocation of commercial licences that favoured the big companies. As McChesney (ibid.) explains, major corporations like General Electric, Westinghouse, and AT&T (companies that already had well established financial, legal, and technological expertise) were able to draw on these considerable resources to make the case for commercial ownership. Bolstered by existing telecommunication and technological ownership structures (such as patents), they were a formidable force of concentrated and organized opposition in contrast to the relatively under-resourced and unorganized members of the public. These included labour, educational, and religious groups—what McChesney (1995) calls the "broadcast reform movement," which attempted to advance alternative (i.e., non-commercial) uses of the airwaves.

Lastly, in Canada, the Aird Commission and the subsequent Broadcasting Act of 1936 entrenched the key theme of protecting and building national unity and identity through state involvement in communication and culture in Canada, which informed the development of Canadian media and related industries throughout the following century. Graham Spry most aptly coined this theme in his now famous quote that Canadians must choose between the "state and the United States" (as cited in Filion, 1996, p. 120). Absent in most histories of Canadian

Case Study

Technological Change, Ownership, and Government Policy-Making

In early broadcasting history, what Robert McChesney (1995) calls "the battle for the control of US broadcasting" is exemplary of the differences between commercial and public representation in public policy-making, particularly when it comes to the imbalance of resources and advantages of having the momentum of capitalist hegemony. In the U.S. example, further to the financial, legal, and technical resources held by the commercial broadcasters, they held an ideological advantage in presentations before state committees and in convincing the (then-separate) newspaper owners of the financial benefits of a commercial system.

On the government level, American radio historian Nathan Godfried (1997), identifies that the rhetoric used by the commercial broadcasters was highly emotive. Efforts to incorporate state regulation in broadcasting were countered by language wrapped in the rhetoric of patriotism. Equating "freedom of enterprise" with "freedom of speech," state regulation, or any division of the airwaves (which would allow non-profit groups a certain percentage of frequencies) was met with charges of state "interference." This was taken to the extreme in public accusations that regulation would lead to, or be the equivalent of, complete state censorship and thus state control. Although the American government was (and arguably still is) a liberal-democratic one, the argument was meant to invoke fear of "the state" as potentially totalitarian, and to suggest that a government (by, of, and for the people) could become totalitarian simply through the act of regulation. The conflation proved to be an effective deterrent in defense of private ownership (which of course ignores its own totalitarian potential).

Such an appeal was particularly affective in obtaining the support of newspaper owners who sought to protect their own business interests by backing the commercial exploitation of radio. The commercial press supported the view that since "radio was so new," it could only be the "corporations with their resources and efficiency skills who could manage it" (Godfried, 1997, p. 15). In this way, corporations arguing for their own benefit, positioned themselves as the lead decision-makers. These arguments were expanded and used in front of legislators by corporations who thus presented themselves as technological experts and altruistic benefactors who would take it upon themselves to manage the air in order to serve the public good, which government regulation should only thereafter assist. For the commercial broadcasters, Godfried (1997) contends that the cumulative effect of this "manipulation" was "a radio industry and state regulatory agency that defined the public interest as convenience, and necessity in terms of private property rights and profits that had little interest in ensuring equal access to radio facilities for varying views and

broadcasting, however, is the addition that it wasn't just a battle of national jurisdiction or sovereignty, but "a choice between commercial interests and the people's interest" (as cited in McChesney, 1999, para. 20).

The function of the CBC in this early period was twofold: Firstly, it provided national radio service, in both official languages; secondly, it was the regulator of private radio stations. This dual role continued until 1958 at which point the CBC was released from its regulatory role, and the Board of Broadcast Governors (BBG) was created to regulate both public and private broadcasting licences (Nesbitt-Larking, 2007, p. 56). It was at this time in 1958 that Canadian broadcasting regulation options" (p. 77). In accordance with this view, access to radio was considered a privilege, and corporate owners saw the airwaves as their personal property, justifying advertising as only "natural" since the "public was able to listen to it without paying taxes on it" (p. 175).

The commercial broadcasters were thus able to manage both the debate and *the information about the debates* for a public increasingly *becoming used to* entertainment programming, and generally unaware of the arguments put forth by the broadcast reformers. As McChesney (1995) concludes, however, despite a number of potentially insurmountable difficulties that continuously plagued the broadcast reform movement, the movement was able to stave off complete commercial ownership for a period of six years (from 1928–34). With such overwhelming economic and political disadvantages, however, the commercial system was seen as superior and was developed further to the detriment of other alternatives.

Discussion Questions

1. In late 2012, the CBC broadcasting licence was up for renewal. Read the opening remarks by the CBC to the Canadian Radio-television and Telecommunications Commission (CRTC) here: cbc.radio-canada.ca/en/media-centre/2012/11/19a/. Identify where the arguments for public broadcasting are advanced; that is, what is the justification used for its continuance?

2. Also in late 2012, BCE Inc. (Bell) and Astral Media Inc. (Astral) submitted a new proposal to the CRTC that outlined the agreement of Bell's proposed purchase of Astral, which was *denied* by the CRTC (see press release: www.crtc.gc.ca/eng/com100/2012/r121018.htm#.UdxYzW3y2hk) only to be rescinded in June 2013 when the CRTC *approved* the takeover (see press release: www.crtc.gc.ca/eng/com100/2013/r130627.htm#.Udxa_G3y2hk). In comparing these two press releases, identify the following:

    a) What arguments are being made for corporate ownership convergence?
    b) Compare these justifications to those that you identified in Question 1. What are the similarities and differences?
    c) How is Bell/Astral using its broadcasting power to advance its interests? How do these compare to the CBC? Can they be compared?

3. How has the resulting decision by the CRTC affected the Canadian mediascape?

4. What were the alternative (or contrary) arguments put forth by public groups like the Canadian Internet Policy and Public Interest Clinic (https://cippic.ca/Bell_Merger)?

5. How does this example compare with early radio history in Canada and the United States?

formally went from a single public system to a mixed system of public and private radio (and television; Audley, 1983, p. 188). In the 1950s, following two Royal Commissions (Massey-Levesque and Fowler), broadcasting in Canada was amended due to the introduction of television. The importance of this new medium and how it reinforced the concerns about American dominance of Canadian culture led to a commitment for the continuation of a national broadcasting system, although change was evident with the growing importance of local private television stations emerging across Canada, and eventually resulting in commodified rival in the form of privately owned and organized television stations called the Canadian Television Network (or the CTV).

From Public Service to International Broadcasting

Unlike the United States in which "free enterprise" monopolizes the airwaves which creates additional markets for advertising and a commercial music industry, the United Kingdom developed a public service model of radio broadcasting, from which the CBC model was derived. After the First World War, the British government did not open the airwaves to commercial exploitation, but retained control of wireless broadcasting and instituted the BBC as a "public service" network (Lewis & Booth, 1989, pp. 208–10). In Great Britain, already by 1927, the various corporations interested in radio broadcasting, and most certainly in the production and sale of sets on which radio broadcasts could be received, had been allowed to pursue their commercial interests in the equipment necessary for carriage, but were succeeded by a national corporation responsible for the production of radio content.

In contrast to the model adopted in Canada whereby the government-of-the-day allocates the finances of the CRBC/CBC via its annual budget and financial plans (and thus indirectly controls what it can and cannot do), the BBC was funded by a licence fee on every receiver—first radio and later television. The driving force behind the BBC and its philosophy of public service broadcasting was Sir John Reith (1889–1971). For Reith, broadcasting was about creating and preserving cultural capital; it was about education and edification, not entertainment. Such values could only prevail in a broadcaster untrammelled by the need to fund itself by selling airtime to advertisers. It was the model from which the Aird Commission drew for the formation of the CRBC with high (but unrealized) ideals, and was a model that served the British people well, chiefly in "its darkest hour" during the Second World War when broadcasting was essential for information.

Public or private ownership of the airwaves makes for interesting contrasts, particularly in times of crisis when communication to the public by government is considered a necessity. On assuming the US presidency in the Great Depression, for example, Franklin Roosevelt initially used the medium of radio to reassure Americans to sell the New Deal policies, and later to gather support for the US entry into World War II. Known as "fireside chats," these 30 talks between 1933 and 1944 were infamous because they enabled Roosevelt, a Democrat, to avoid the gatekeepers of the mass media—who were largely Republican—and appeal directly to the people. A number of his speeches make the point. In his address of 9 December 1941, following the Japanese attack on Pearl Harbor, Roosevelt said:

> *To all newspapers and radio stations—all those who reach the eyes and ears of the American people—I say this: You have a most grave responsibility to the nation now and for the duration of this war.*

> *If you feel that your Government is not disclosing enough of the truth, you have every right to say so. But in the absence of all the facts, as revealed by official sources, you have no right in the ethics of patriotism to deal out unconfirmed reports in such a way as to make people believe that they are gospel truth. (Roosevelt, 1941, paras. 29–30)*

Notwithstanding what we might think of this today, President Roosevelt's strategy was obviously successful. He was elected to office for four successive terms, and died in office in 1945 in the closing stages of the war. The necessity of broadcasting to/for the public further underscores that control over the airwaves is not without significant ethical and political responsibilities. This responsibility is one that the president had to use his powers of office to emphasize rather than leaving the country to the whims of its commercial owners, meaning that commercial ownership is never politically neutral, despite the claims of an independent media.

Government involvement in media does indicate different kinds of state ownership, particularly when political and economic interests collide internationally. During World War II, the British government used the BBC as a valuable part of Britain's defence infrastructure (Lewis & Booth, 1989, p. 209). Its short-wave service was used as a conduit for the Resistance movements on the Continent, and for British operatives behind enemy lines. The service was also used for propaganda purposes, and state use of the airwaves for international broadcasting is expanded worldwide wherever there are state political and economic interests. Although the BBC was the most well-known international broadcaster, it did not begin its short-wave service until 1932. It was preceded by the Soviet Union in the mid-to-late 1920s (Radio Moscow), and in 1931 by the Catholic Church (Vatican Radio). Other countries followed: Germany (1933), Italy (1935), and later the United States through the Voice of America (VOA; 1942; Taylor, 1997), and, later still, Canada, through Radio Canada International (RCI; 1945; Siegel, 1996; ▣ www.rcinet.ca/).

The use of international broadcasting by governments is an indication of where they have a vested interest through the exercise of so-called "soft power" (Nye, 2004). In this view, international broadcasting is an exercise of persuasion or propaganda that aims to promote a particular way of life and corresponding ideology. This type of communication is in contrast to the exercise of "hard power," which refers to the use of economic sanctions, military force, or other types of violence. Following the worldwide expansion of the VOA for example, ▣ www.voanews.com, one can identify which regions of the world that American governments have vested political economic interests in. While the VOA initially targeted Eastern Europe to denounce communism and promote "prosperity" and "democracy" and thus advance a capitalist way of life (Sussman, 2010), it more recently expanded into the Middle East. The intent is obvious in the naming of the stations such as the satellite channel "Alhurra" ("the Free One"), broadcasting in Arabic, and Radio Farda ("tomorrow") broadcasting in Persian, both established in 2002 just before the US military invasion of Iraq in 2003. The VOA has also been broadcasting in Afghanistan since 1980 (just after the Soviet invasion), and these have been recently updated and supplemented by Radio and TV Ashna (meaning "friend"). It currently broadcasts in over 45 languages and has a budget of over USD$206 million (VOA, 2013).

In contrast, the "Voice of Canada" or RCI was nowhere near as ambitious, but was still vested with political economic interests (J. Hall, 1997). Officially on the air in 1945 it was established partly as Canada's claim on international frequencies, and partly to offer support for Great Britain as its principal ally in the war (in case the BBC facilities were sabotaged; Siegel, 1996). It established a huge transmitter site on the east coast of Canada in Sackville, New Brunswick, which offered time-sharing for other international broadcasters (ibid.). Mainly as a result of perennial budget irregularities and a general lack of political will, its broadcasting mandate has been historically directed to presenting a favourable image of Canada both to immigrants and to businesses abroad. More recently however, the federal government took a renewed interest in international broadcasting by expanding broadcasting into Afghanistan (2004) via the Canadian military through RANA-FM, broadcasting via satellite from Kingston, Ontario, to Kandahar (Mazepa, 2011). RANA-FM used a combination of public service information and commercial music mix similar to commercial radio stations (and this format is increasingly used by the CBC).

As government political economic priorities change, however, so do its decisions on communication. Even prior to the federal government's decision for Canadian military withdrawal from Afghanistan, the usefulness of RANA-FM was also considered to be at an end, when it ceased to broadcast in 2011. RCI was also faced with significant federal budget cuts, resulting in the loss of (unionized) jobs for its employees, so its satellite and short-wave services broadcast around the world—which could be picked up almost anywhere with a relatively inexpensive radio—are now only available online. As of 2013, RCI broadcasting was closed by the federal government, shutting down its Sackville site. RCI still has an existence online and produces podcasts, but the Canadian broadcasting "voice" has been effectively silenced worldwide. A persistent plea is still continued by its (ex-)employees "to protect the international mandate, programs and autonomy of Radio Canada International" (▣ www.rciaction.org/blog/), but it is difficult to promote a public service after government decisions have already been made, especially a service that Canadians may not have even known they had in the first place.

Broadcasting Content: Tunes, Talk, or Advertising?

The question of content is one that has been more central in communication history, largely due to the capabilities of broadcasting (or the "mass media") of reaching large numbers of people with the same content. We are used to hearing, for example, music on the radio or on an iPod, and while it may seem politically benign, as in the case of the American Federation of Musicians and the recording industry, even music is a site of contestation.

The presence of popular music on radio in Canada dates back to its introduction in the 1920s. Private commercial radio stations tended to provide a mix of entertainment content for listeners including music, comedy, and variety shows, yet the majority of them were American. The heavy reliance on foreign, and primarily American, content in music continued in Canadian radio until the 1970s when the CRTC introduced **Canadian content (Cancon)** requirements for radio stations, both public and private, via the Broadcasting Act. Initially the Cancon requirements differed for AM and FM stations, but eventually a uniform Cancon policy was established for both types of stations. What is called the MAPL system was first introduced in the CRTC's 1986 Commercial Radio Policy requiring that at least 35 per cent of music played in a week on Canadian stations be Canadian. The criteria for defining the music selection as Canadian was that, at minimum, a Canadian citizen created two of the following elements: music, artist, production, or lyrics (CRTC, 2009c; ▣ www.crtc.gc.ca/eng/info_sht/r1.htm). The implementation of the Cancon regulation was even contested by the then more commercially successful musicians (like Bryan Adams, who attributed his airtime to his "natural talent"), but it is abundantly clear to the Canadian music industry and fledging Canadian artists that without it (or the public airtime given on the CBC) the primarily commercial (and largely American) dominance of the music industry means that commercial airtime is far less likely.

In the 1970s and 1980s, radio listeners abandoned the AM band for the higher technical quality of the FM band and its initial, comparative freedom from advertising. In the 1990s, however, the AM band bit back with talk radio. Talk radio relies on telephone calls from listeners and the strong—often outrageous—opinions of the presenters. The presenter can then bounce his or her own views against those of the caller. Aided by regulatory changes in the United States in 1987, radio stations were able to be more partisan in the presentation of opinion. One of the most opinionated was Missouri-born Rush Limbaugh, who has a weekly audience variously estimated at between 14 and 20 million listeners. After working in music radio, Limbaugh came to prominence in Sacramento, California, moved to New York, and was syndicated nationally from 1988 onward. In addition to taking calls from listeners, he broadcasts live online, has a "member's only 24/7 club" for online audio/video (▣ www.rushlimbaugh.com/), has made extensive use of email in generating content for his show, and he is of great value to advertisers: "Mr. Limbaugh's fans are fiercely loyal to the host and very responsive to his show's advertisers, media buyers say. 'He is a proven commodity,'

CANADIAN CONTENT (CANCON)

A communication policy requirement of the Broadcasting Act that stipulates the minimum percentage of programming content that is broadcast that must be Canadian (Broadcasting Act, 1991, § 3; ▣ laws-lois.justice. gc.ca/eng/acts/B-9.01/ page-2.html#h-4).

says Mark Lefkowitz, executive vice president and media director at Furman Roth Advertising Inc." (as cited in McBride, 2008, para. 8). Just how much he is valued was written into his latest contract with Clear Channel, which promises him $400 million over eight years (2008–16; ibid.).

In Canada, Limbaugh has his imitators, who are, in the main, politically conservative yet populist presenters. Nationally, Charles Adler, who has a syndicated radio program emanating from the Winnipeg Corus station CJOB, is the most comparable. He has a national audience and presents conservative opinions on current political and public affairs issues. In different regions across Canada there are others who aspire to the same type of programming (see Sampert, 2011). Despite this presence of conservative talk-jocks, Shannon Sampert (2008) argues that the CBC offers some alternative in talk radio, as it hosts programs like Cross Country Checkup (p. 14) and variants like As It Happens (▣ www.cbc.ca/asithappens/).

The rise of shock-jock radio has also grown in Canada, although with more limited success than in the United States. Two reasons why this type of talk radio has been more restricted here are, again according to Sampert (2010), regulatory regimes (covered in Chapter 9) as well as lower ratings. Such examples include the case of Quebec radio station CHOI-FM, which saw the CRTC revoke its licence following a series of listener complaints, and lack of compliance with Commission conditions, of licence. The second case indicates how technological change interacts with content regarding the initially failed attempt to air The Howard Stern Show in Canada in the late 1990s and 2000s. In Stern's case, his program was syndicated by several radio stations in Canadian cities, and within short order, both the CRTC and the Canadian Broadcast Standards Council received numerous complaints about Stern's racist, sexist commentary, including his criticism of the French language (Sampert, 2010; ▣ www.cbsc.ca/). Stern's program was cut from Canadian radio in 2001, but according to Sampert (2008), the decision had more to do with lacklustre ratings than with audience complaints and regulatory action (p. 11). Technological change allowed Stern to circumvent national regulations, however, as the show is now carried by satellite radio via paid subscription, netting Stern a contract worth even more than Limbaugh's at $500 million over five years (McBride, 2008) despite (or because of?) the sensationalism, sexism, and racism that fuels his rants (Soley, 2007).

Talk radio is a close second behind the CBC as far as all radio listening, with the CBC having a 12.4 per cent share of all Canadian listeners and talk radio having 9.8 per cent (Statistics Canada, 2007, Table 2; ▣ www.statcan.gc.ca/pub/87f0007x/87f0007x2007001-eng. pdf). The difference in age groups listening to CBC are more extreme with CBC garnering only 2.6 per cent of the 18–24-year-old listeners compared to 23.8 per cent of the 65-year-old and over listeners (Table 3). These are crucial days for the CBC as it adopts commercial formats (particularly in television) to appeal to a generation with little understanding or appreciation of the importance of public ownership as well as being framed as "an unfair competitor" by the private broadcasters, and targeted by Conservative politicians seeking its elimination (▣ www.friends.ca/ILoveCBC/).

Broadcast to Podcast

> Podcasting might sound like something farmers do with peas but a fast-increasing number of devotees know better . . . (even the Pope has a podcast). (Dudley, 2005)

There's a short note of wry humour in this opening line from Jennifer Dudley's report about the birth and growth of **podcasting**. The term *broadcast* itself has agricultural roots—seed was cast broadly or "broadcast" into the ploughed field. But podcasting today is one of the most

PODCASTING

"Podcasting is a form of distribution of audio contents that can be received periodically on one's computer by subscribing (for a fee) or adding oneself to a list, thanks to special software programmes called 'feeds.' . . . Paying for music is one of the basic premises of podcasting" (Menduni, 2007, p. 14).

important forms of narrowcasting, and it exemplifies the paradigm shift in media as a result of digital convergence.

Podcasting—the word is a combination of *iPod* and *broadcasting*—first became publicly available in 2004 as a way of linking audio to weblogs, and according to Dudley's research, it has become the new wave in Internet downloads. A podcast allows the user to time-shift radio broadcasts that are posted on the Internet by downloading them to an MP3 player and listening to them at their own leisure. The software can also be programmed to automatically check websites for updates and new download material.

Like many innovations in computing, podcasting began as an alternative to the large commercially oriented broadcasters, but it has become a feature on the websites of mainstream broadcasters. In Canada, the CBC has been quick to adopt podcasting as a way to expand the listener base for many of its more popular programs. Alongside free podcasts, the CBC has also begun selling some of its programming on iTunes, such as its radio drama *Afghanada* and certain programs from Ideas. Other than podcasting, the CBC has also made a significant investment in satellite radio. In 2004, the national public broadcaster spent $7.7 million to acquire a 40 per cent share of Sirius Canada (CRTC, 2005, para. 14), which facilitated the acquisition of a satellite radio licence for the American company Sirius Satellite Radio. The investment provided the CBC/Radio Canada with four stations on the satellite service, which could be accessed by subscribers at the same frequency across the country.

The move to a commercial provider marks a significant departure for the CBC from both its programming and its mandate as a public service broadcaster. Whereas RCI was, and CBC is available for free to all Canadians, CBC is now part of a pay-by-subscription or private service, further breaking down historical use values in favour of exchange values. Moreover it ignores the very foundation of broadcasting policy-making given that it is based on ensuring national sovereignty of the airwaves and Canadian ownership, as it now involves a partnership between the public broadcaster and an American commercial business. Despite the early hopes for satellite radio, its success has been slow; in 2009, the CRTC (2010) reported that it along with other new forms of converged radio services available via the Internet received less than 3 per cent of the radio tuning share for an average week (p. 35). This raises a technical question about the delivery of audio over the Internet, either by streaming, podcast downloads, or RSS (Really Simple Syndication) feeds: Is it still radio?

Undoubtedly broadcasting on the Internet retains some of the features of radio—music and spoken word—but it presents a new set of issues concerning culture and political economy. The commercial model for successful podcasting and other forms of digital (non-radio) delivery have yet to be worked out fully, and perhaps it's too early to tell if these new forms will actually replace radio completely. In Canada, most private radio broadcasters continue to profit from the airwaves, however. Although almost all "operating revenues (97.5%) are generated from advertising revenues" (Statistics Canada, 2010b, p. 5; ▣ www.statcan.gc.ca/pub/56-208-x/56-208-x2010000-eng.pdf), there has been a recent drop in revenues for some broadcasters due to a general economic downturn, as the industry is not completely immune from the national economy. In our final chapter we provide a short discussion about the supposed "death" of old media technologies as new ones come along: Is it true that video killed the radio stars, and will podcasting kill the video stars?

Television, Technology, and Cultural Form

Much of the great popular appeal of radio and television has been due to this sense of apparently unmediated access. The real mediations will have to be noted, but again and again they are easy to miss. What is offered is a [television] set with a tuner and a switch; we can turn it on or off, or vary what we are receiving. Throughout its history there has been this popular sense that broadcasting is a welcome alternative to the normal and recognisable social order of communications. (R. Williams, 1978, p. 132)

As cited at the beginning of this book, the dystopian novel *Brave New World* was written in 1932 but set hundreds of years into the future, and Aldous Huxley made use of the television as if it was inseparable from everyday life. In the novel, there is a Bureaux of Propaganda by Television and a television factory at Brentford, near London, England. As the product of convergence in technologies (audio and film recording, the development of broadcast transmission, and, later, video), television is also a cultural convergence that has cannibalized other forms of media, including the stage and music hall variety show, radio news-bulletins, film, and drama (S. Hall, 1996). Although the attention to the screen is shifting from the television to the Internet, given the inordinate amount of time that Canadians spend watching television (28.5 hours per week according to CRTC statistics; CRTC, 2012, para. 3), Huxley was not far off estimating its ubiquity:

> *Despite the availability of content on digital platforms, Canadians spent more time watching television and listening to the radio. On a weekly basis, they watched an average of 28.5 hours of television, up from 28 hours in 2010, and listened to an average of 17.7 hours of radio, up from 17.6 hours the previous year. (ibid.)*

In "Television: Technology and Cultural Form," Raymond Williams (1978) begins by emphasizing the importance of studying cause and effect—the dialectic of contradiction and creative tension—within the relationships between "technology" and "a society," "a culture" and "a psychology." He says these connections are both "theoretical" and "immensely practical." Understanding cause and effect, he says, is the key to asking the right questions about technology. These questions include how it is used; the institutions that bring it into being, and manage and employ it; the impact it has on patterns of work, consumption, and leisure; and the content and form of the medium (R. Williams, 1978, pp. 9–10).

Williams was interested in television because he saw that society generally had come to believe that after just 20 years, television had gained such widespread acceptance and that the medium had "altered our world" (p. 11). Just like any widespread "new" technology, television did appear to have the effect of changing the world forever, but like us, Williams was keen to make the important distinction between those versions of the argument that were technologically determinist and those that understood technologies within a process of change that is "in any case occurring or about to occur" (p. 13). At the same time, Williams is critical of what he calls the "symptomatic" view of technology, where change is caused by events and processes outside the realm of scientific discovery and innovation. This view, he argues, is just as sterile as technological determinism; it is an early form of the cultural determinist argument. The flaw in both cases is that technical innovation and "science" are seen as value-free neutral activities that would take place regardless of social circumstances: "Technology is then as it were a by-product of a social process that is otherwise determined" (p. 12). To escape what he saw as a determinist "trap," Williams introduced the concept of "intention" to the dialectical process of "research and development": Technology is developed consciously "and designed with certain [productive] purposes and [social] practices already in mind" (p. 14).

This insight became clear for Williams in his study of television because it was a technology developed with a clear purpose in mind. Governments, bureaucrats, and business leaders had all learned important lessons over the 150 years of the print media and after nearly 40 years of radio. The mistakes of the past, and the successes, would greatly influence the way in which the technology of television delivered the consequent social impacts that Williams identified and we are still experiencing today. Television can be used or developed to favour a particular kind of content, and to construct or address its viewers as consumers, citizens, or a mixture of both in a clear demonstration of mutual constitution.

Television, the Market, and Citizenship

Television is fascinating. . . . Television fascinates because it embodies the culture it depicts. In a genuine sense, television is culture today: capricious, intemperate and absorbed by a near-religious devotion to consumption. (Cashmore, 1994, p. 2)

Without mass consumption there would be no commercial television, and without the ability of television to influence consumption there would be no market for mass-produced consumer goods. It is often said that "the media have no effects," but if there were no effects, then how does one explain the reason for advertising? There is no doubt that television today exists in, for, and of the market: commercial "breaks" in programming of up to nine minutes; promos and trailers for upcoming programs interrupting dramatic moments; and the endless "brought to you by" and "proudly sponsored" tags that intrude over the end of programs and credits (Wayne, 2003). In many ways, then, television is simply "radio with pictures" (Hilmes, Newcomb, & Meehan, 2012, p. 276; Meehan, 2005, p. 42) or radio with a screen. Now we also have the endless urging and cajoling of presenters and voice-over artists encouraging us to love or hate the house-mate, the wannabe, or the potential lovesick millionaire, enough to call the convenient voting hotlines ($0.55 per call, with a parent's permission), or other developing forms of interactivity that encourage identification with the characters and the products promoted. This is part of the development of what Lee McGuigan (2012) calls "T-commerce," which extends an aspect of narrowcasting to interactive television:

T-commerce refers to home-shopping applications that enable viewers to "click-to purchase" products featured in advertisements as well as items related to or appearing in program content. Advanced advertising describes techniques derived from direct marketing, which allow advertisers to target consumer segments and even individual viewers with personalized solicitations. (p. 289)

As you may well appreciate by now, like development of media that came before it, the key cultural form of television is determined by the social relations of capitalist production: Television is dominated by market relations and by the need to sell both programs and viewers to advertisers (Ehrlich, 1997; McQueen, 1977), and it is understanding how this commodification works that is particularly interesting to political economists. The pattern was established in print media of newspapers and magazines, but was further developed and expanded in commercial radio and then set into television and now the Internet. Recall that the popularity of a film, for example, is thought to be measured by the number of people that go to see it; like film, television has been structured such that the people come to see it—and not just any people, but particular groups of people as "consumers" or "markets." Canadian political economist of communication Dallas Smythe (1977) called commercial media content the "free lunch" offered to audiences for their time and attention sold to advertisers transforming the audience into an exchange value, or the **audience commodity** (pp. 2–3). Indeed, the cost of advertising itself is based on the size and value of the demographic a program intends to attract. With a potential worldwide audience, for example, a 30-second commercial slot during the Super Bowl costs up to USD$4 million with predictions that it will cost $10 million in the near future (Konrad, 2013).

How the size of the audience is estimated underlies not only the cost of advertising but also the kinds of content (and advertisements) produced in order to attract the audiences to them and the kind of business model created in order to do so. We discuss the former relationship further in later chapters, but for now, we can see how a technique that determines content for commercial media began with radio, and has been adapted to fit each change in technology, by identifying the exchange value of the content and its audience based on its *ratings*. As Eileen Meehan (2005) explains,

> advertisers paid for programming and access to networks in the expectation that they would reach bona fide consumers—people with the disposable income, desire, and access to the retail system needed to buy brand names loyally as well as impulsively. With advertisers and consumers as radio's raison d'être, somebody needed to measure the number and quality of consumers attracted to each radio program to see if advertisers were getting their money's worth from networks. (p. 33)

This means that the choice of content by the broadcasters (supply) was directly tied to generating consumption (demand), and it was not *any* listener that the advertisers were interested in, but the attraction and construction of a *particular* kind of listener, what Meehan dubs "the consumer caste" (pp. 34–5). The measuring and monitoring of radio listeners was itself subject to competition between the broadcasters, advertisers, and independent companies as to whose ratings were valid and reliable. Contrary to free-market ideology, which suggests that competition is one fundamental to capitalism, a monopoly was eventually the favoured model to standardize rates and control as accorded to the A. C. Nielsen Company (ACN; Meehan, 2005, p. 39). ACN paid for the development of a device made to record both radio tuning, in terms of which station was selected (the Audimeter), and "when and for how long the radio was on" (the Recordimeter; p. 40). Selected households were initially those with a telephone (which, like the early days of most new technology, was expensive), thus indicating disposable income (or at least a consumption indicator), and included a diary to record demographic data of the household, its time-use, and consumption habits (p. 40). The meters allowed 24/7 monitoring and gave ACN the final advantage over its only competitor to secure a monopoly and contracts with the major American networks (ABC, CBC, NBC), just in time for the new technology of the day—television. "In television broadcasting, [w]hen networks developed new programs, they drew on the genres and character types that had worked on radio. Television was defined as radio with pictures, a view that mitigated attempts to create an aesthetic for television on the basis of the new medium's own abilities and limitations" (p. 42). Thus programs that were "successful" were those that satisfied the interests of the corporations—not necessarily the viewers—in a mutually reinforcing structure: "Rating points earned from old radio households translated into revenues for television networks, access to targeted consumers for advertisers, monopoly for [ACN] and renewals for producers of television programs that appealed to ACN's radio homes" (p. 44). When the radio meters were replaced with the television People Meters in 1987, with which households voluntarily record their viewing habits ([image] www.agbnielsen.net/system/peoplemeters.asp), the structure was extended and entrenched. As you shall see in Chapter 9 on technology and government policy, fundamental changes to government regulation allowing for media ownership convergence means that such a commercial model is applied to content across

AUDIENCE COMMODITY
A concept developed by Canadian political economist Dallas Smythe, referring to the construction and transformation of an audience (their time, attention, and information) into an exchange value.

all media platforms, and is being further refined to measure and monitor increasingly specific "target" or "niche" markets affecting the content choice and longevity of programs accordingly, and a further fragmentation of the public into distinct consumption castes.

Thus, as Meehan (2005) concludes, what appears to be a free choice based on writer creativity, independent (use values) public interests, and decision-making is actually a carefully manufactured attempt and method of media control. This has reached its zenith in television content, particularly in American "reality" television, where social relations are continually represented and cast in stereotypical ways with significant social consequences, as argued by Jennifer Pozner (2010) in *Reality Bites Back: The Troubling Truth About Guilty Pleasure TV* (📺 www.realitybitesbackbook.com/).

The Unreality of Reality TV

Reality TV is also life-changing in the sense that "former reality show contestant" has almost become a career in itself. (K. Murphy, 2006, p. 143)

REALITY TELEVISION

A genre of television drama that purports to be a "fly-on-the-wall" rendering of the activities of non-professional actors in contrived situations. More easily understood as a form of "game show" genre.

What exactly is **reality television**? It turns the mundane into the extraordinary, and ordinary people into instant celebrities. One thing is clear about it: There's very little actual "reality" involved. As soon as a television camera and the enormously expensive process of production are involved, the spectacle loses its most important connections to the "real." It is structured, scripted, and edited according to the wishes of the producers, and their motive is really selling the program to advertisers. When you actually turn off the television and think about it, it's perfectly obvious that so-called reality television is in fact a series of carefully constructed game shows, which are the most lucrative programs to produce, combining, as they do, "low production costs with high audience ratings" (Kilborn, 1994, p. 436, as cited in Penzhorn & Pitout, 2007, p. 74).

Most of them—in fact all of them that are not documentary in style—are competitions: *Survivor*, the *Idol* series, *The Bachelor* and *The Bachelorette*, *The Biggest Loser*, and so on. The people involved—let's call them contestants—are in it for the 15 minutes of fame and the million bucks on offer. In so doing, the show replicates and reinforces particular ideas that suggest a particular way of thinking: that everyone is an individual; that it is part of our innate human nature to compete with each other; and that winning is everything. This view suggests, among other dominant ideas of social relations, that the social world is just like the business world, or moreover that the business world is just like the social world, and that both are entirely natural (and therefore hegemonic) rather than constructed products that—in addition to making material profit—legitimize hierarchy, entrench stereotypes, and personalize conflict in ways that benefit existing power relations. This is, in effect, what Laurie Ouellette and James Hay (2008) argue "teaches" participants (whether as contestants or viewers) how to govern themselves in a way that "sustains the economic structure" (Chaput, 2011, p. 2).

As technology allows more interactivity within the commercial environment of the television, particularly as the number of clicks, views, or preferences, for instance, can be monitored online 24/7/365 (Chapter 12), the cultivation of the audience commodity is both economic and social. As McGuigan (2012) explains, "as commodities, consumers are *both* social actors and information profiles distortedly mirroring economic life. . . . The purposive motion toward the interactive storefront as a prevailing commercial model exposes that advertiser-supported television is organized to produce consumers both as packaged economic data and as social beings necessary to the reproduction and acceleration of capital" (pp. 299, 300).

This dominant economic function of television (and all commercial media) sits in dialectical tension with its public service role as a communication resource that promotes "public dialogue" (Groombridge, 1972, p. 240). Television has definitely been the mass medium of the broadcast age and the arena for both entertainment (mass culture) and political participation. In this climate, what passes for public service broadcasting must also be good for business (Phelan, 1991). Increasingly, this has seen control over programming decisions pass from the media firm to the advertiser, through co-productions and branded formats (McChesney, 2000b, p. 41). These commercial links are only going to expand and strengthen as a result of digital and commercial convergence (Mosco, 1996, pp. 106–7).

Conclusion

In 2012 Canadians marked 60 years of television. In that time the form and content of programming has changed, and the free-to-air model is under threat from "pay-per-view" and Internet-based TV-like series. If the twentieth century was the age of television, the future of broadcasting in the beginning of the twenty-first is uncertain. The dominant commercial structure is again shifting towards new technology; television networks seek to bolster returns as advertising revenues seek to identify where consumer attention can be concentrated and managed, and public service broadcasting is marginalized and stereotyped as unimportant or unrealistic in a commercial and market-based industry. With network television almost saturated with commercials, audiences too look for spaces that suggest more participation and control over viewing, interacting, and contributing to media. The Internet suggests that this space is one without limit, and as you shall see in the next chapter, this too is one under development in its own historical dialectic.

Key Points

- The shift towards narrowcasting and digital convergence is reshaping both the technologies and the cultural forms of broadcasting.

- The development of broadcast technologies follows the now-familiar pattern of technological and commercial convergence.

- Television is a "hybrid" cultural form that borrows from many earlier forms of media and entertainment, such as radio and theatre.

- The technology and the political economy of television are moving the medium away from the "public service" model of broadcasting towards one integrated into the capitalist economy.

Class Discussion

1. Why was the telegraph system called "the Victorian Internet"? What are the similarities and differences between the telegraph and the Internet?

2. Conduct a survey on your own time-use. (Use the data from the Class Exercise in the "For Real?" box in this chapter, where you identified how much time you used communication

technology and media.) If the mechanical clock is a form of technological conditioning, how do these forms of communication also condition your life?

3. How do you make the distinction between labour and leisure time?

4. What is the difference between private and public broadcasting? Why do public broadcasters like the CBC matter to democracy, citizenship, or cultural heritage and development?

5. What is the audience commodity? Provide a variety of examples drawn from your own listening, reading, viewing, or surfing choices.

6. How do ratings shape content? What difference does technological change make if the commercial model is applied to each one of them?

7. How much of reality television is "reality"? Why are reality shows so commercially successful in comparison to, for example, documentaries?

Media on Media

Broadcasting Tunes

Bruce Springsteen. (1992). 57 channels (and nothin' on). *Human Touch*. US: Columbia. 🖥 www.springsteenlyrics.com/lyrics/0/57channels.php

The Clash. (1977). Capital radio one. *Captial Radio*. UK: Neat. 🖥 www.lyricsfreak.com/c/clash/capital+radio+one_20174605.html

Don Henley. (1982). Dirty laundry. *I Can't Stand Still*. US: Asylum.

Elvis Costello and the Attractions. (1978). Radio radio. *This Year's Model*. UK: Radar Records. 🖥 www.lyricsdepot.com/elvis-costello/radio-radio.html

Lady Gaga. (2009). Telephone (ft. Beyonce). *The Fame Monster*. US: Interscope.

Lupe Fiasco. (2011). State run radio. *Lasers*. US: Atlantic Records. 🖥 www.metrolyrics.com/state-run-radio-lyrics-lupe-fiasco.html

Queen. (1984). Radio ga ga. *The Works*. London, UK: EMI. 🖥 www.lyrics007.com/Queen%20Lyrics/Radio%20Ga%20Ga%20Lyrics.html

Red Hot Chili Peppers. (2002). Throw away your television. *By the Way*. US: Warner Bros. 🖥 www.elyrics.net/read/r/red-hot-chili-peppers-lyrics/throw-away-your-television-lyrics.html

Rush. (1980). Spirit of the radio. *Permanent Waves*. UK: Mercury Records. 🖥 www.lyricsfreak.com/r/rush/the+spirit+of+radio_20120011.html

TV, Movies, and Docs

Beveridge, J. (Producer), & Smith, D. A. (Director). (1949). *Canada calling* [Documentary]. Canada: NFB. Retrieved from 🖥 www.nfb.ca/film/canada_calling/

Bevin, T. (Producer), & Curtis, R. (Director & Writer). (2009). *The boat that rocked* [Motion picture]. UK: Working Title Films.

Feldman, E. S. (Producer), & Weir, P. (Director). (1998). *The Truman show* [Motion picture]. US: Paramount.

Gervais, R. (Director & Writer). (2005–7). *Extras* [TV series]. UK/US: BBC/HBO.

Gottfried, H. (Producer), & Lumet, S. (Director). (1976). *Network* [Motion picture]. US: MGM.

Heslov, G. (Producer), & Clooney, G. (Director). (2005). *Good night and good luck* [Motion picture]. US: Warner.

Levinson, B. (Producer & Director). (1998). *Wag the dog* [Motion picture]. US: New Line Home Video.

Salama, H. (Producer), & Noujaim, J. (Director). (2004). *Control room* [Documentary]. US: Magnolia Pictures.

Strong, R. (Producer). (1998–2003). *Made in Canada* [TV series]. Canada: CBC.

Timeline: Telegraphy, the Talking Wireless, and Television

1793 The Chappe brothers establish the first commercial semaphore system between two locations near Paris.

1843 Fax is invented by Scottish physicist Alexander Bain.

1844 The telegraph is invented by Samuel Morse.

1858 Transatlantic submarine cable is laid, connecting Europe and the United States.

1861 The transcontinental telegraph line across the United States is completed.

1866 The first permanent transatlantic telegraph line is established; it is a submarine cable that links Newfoundland and Ireland, and by 1900, there are 18 more, primarily out of Nova Scotia.

1876 Thomas Edison invents the electric motor and the phonograph.

The telephone is invented by Alexander Graham Bell in Brantford, Ontario.

1880 The Bell Telephone Company of Canada is incorporated via a special act of parliament.

Bell Canada installs the first "public" telephone in a Hamilton stationery store.

1881 Bell Canada successfully places the world's first international submarine telephone cable between Windsor, Ontario, and Detroit, Michigan (🖳 www.itu.int/newsarchive/wtsa2000/english/media/timeline.pdf).

1887 The flat record, a horizontal disc developed by Emile Berliner, replaces Edison's cylinder.

1896 Guglielmo Marconi patents the wireless telegraph.

1901 Marconi sends the first transatlantic wireless (radiotelegraph) signal from Cornwall, England, to St. John's, Newfoundland.

1902 Canada's first wireless station is established in Nova Scotia.

1905 The Radiotelegraph Act (Canada's first legislation covering wireless transmission, which includes possible broadcasting activities) is passed. (In 1913 the Act is amended to include radiotelephone.)

1906 Lee de Forest invents the vacuum tube.

The jukebox is invented in Chicago.

The Railway Act provides the federal government with the authority to regulate all telephone tolls, contracts, and agreements of telephone companies. (The Act is amended in 1919.)

1907 De Forest broadcasts music from phonograph records.

Alberta, Saskatchewan, and Manitoba establish provincially owned and operated telephone companies.

1915 Wireless radio service connects the United States and Japan.

1919 The first regular radio broadcast is transmitted from XWA (Experimental Wireless Apparatus) in Montreal—the first private broadcasting station in Canada. (Renamed CFCF AM in 1920.)

The Radio Corporation of America (RCA) is formed.

1920 In England, Marconi creates the first short-wave radio broadcast.

1921 The first commercial radio broadcast of a sporting event (Dempsey vs. Carpentier, heavyweight championship prizefight) takes place.

Wirephoto—the first electronically transmitted photograph—is sent by Western Union.

1922 The first radio advertisement is broadcast in the United States.

The BBC begins radio broadcasting.

1923 Audience measurement company A. C. Nielsen is founded.

Saskatchewan's provincial telephone department provides lines for the first church-service broadcast in Canada (🖳 www.itu.int/newsarchive/wtsa2000/english/media/timeline.pdf).

Reuters uses radio to transmit news.

1924 The first US presidential campaign is broadcast. President-elect buys USD$120,000 in advertising.

1926 US corporate giants RCA, General Electric, and Westinghouse combine to establish the National Broadcasting Company (NBC).

1927 First cross-Canada radio broadcast: Prime Minister Mackenzie King delivers a speech from Parliament Hill.

Philo Farnsworth assembles a complete electronic TV system.

The US Radio Act declares public ownership of the airwaves.

1928 John Logie Baird beams a television image from England to the United States, followed by the first scheduled television broadcast in the United States.

1929 The Columbia Broadcasting System (CBS) is founded by William S. Paley.

The car radio is invented.

1931 The first Canadian private (commercial) television station (VE9EC) goes on air, owned jointly by *La Presse* newspaper and CKAC radio station.

1932 The Canadian Radio Broadcasting Act comes into force, and the federal government establishes a regulation of broadcasting via the Canadian Radio Broadcasting Commission (CRBC).

The CRBC regulates and controls all broadcasting in Canada and provides a national broadcasting service. This involves determining the number, location, and transmission power of radio stations as well as the amount of time that should be devoted to national and local programming. (Reformed in 1936 as the Canadian Broadcasting Corporation [CBC].)

The first Trans-Canada Telephone System (TCTS) is completed (nicknamed "the Copper Highway").

1933 Frequency modulation (FM), a static-free method of transmission, is released.

1934   The US Federal Communications Commission (FCC) broadcasting regulator is established.

1937   The Havana Treaty on radio frequencies is signed in the Americas. Canada gets six unoccupied frequencies.

1938   Orson Welles' broadcast of H. G. Wells' *The War of the Worlds* creates panic in the United States, as listeners believe aliens have invaded. Broadcasting regulations are subsequently amended.

Nielson uses the Recordimeter and the Audimeter to record when and for how long the radio is on, and which station it was tuned into, in private homes. Consumers also record their radio listening via a diary.

1939   Radio Canada's overseas service is launched and broadcasts from England with the Canadian Armed Forces First Division.

1940   The CBS demonstrates colour television in New York.

A single-groove stereo system is developed for phonograph recording.

Regular FM radio broadcasting begins.

1942   The Canadian Association of Broadcasters (CAB) calls on the Association of Canadian Advertisers (ACA) to develop a system for setting the price of advertising airtime, which leads to the creation of the Bureau of Broadcast Measurement (BBM) in 1944.

1946   Radio Canada International (RCI) goes on air, broadcasting from Sackville, New Brunswick, to England and Western Europe (in English, Czech, and German), later adding the languages and range of the Scandinavian countries, followed by the Caribbean, Latin and South America, New Zealand, and Australia.

1947   RCI transmits the United Nations' daily broadcasts.

1948   LP ("long-playing") records, running 25 minutes per side, replace the old four-minute standard 78 rpm.

1949   RCA offers the 45 rpm record and player.

1950   Cable & Wireless Limited and the Canadian Marconi Company become national companies, and a Crown corporation is created: the Canadian Overseas Telecommunication Corporation (COTC).

Pay-per-view television begins in the United States.

Nielsen uses People Meters to track television audiences.

1952   CBC Television is launched (ready a year earlier, but delayed due to the Korean War).

Sony markets a miniature transistor radio.

1953   CKSO is the first Canadian private television station licensed to operate.

1955   The Royal Commission on Broadcasting, chaired by Robert Fowler, is created.

The first issue of *TV Guide* magazine is published.

1958   The revised Broadcasting Act comes into force, creating the Board of Broadcast Governors (BBG), thus creating Canada's mixed broadcasting system and giving the BBG the power to establish regulations requiring stations to promote Canadian programming.

The world's longest microwave network is completed in Canada, and covers over 6,275 km; known as the "electric skyway," it "transports telephone conversations, Teletype messages and television signals" (ITU, n.d., p. 2; www.itu.int/newsarchive/wtsa2000/english/media/timeline.pdf; see Figure 6.3).

CBC launches its Northern Service, expanding radio broadcasting to the Yukon and the Northwest Territories.

1961   Private television consortium launches the Canadian Television Network (or the CTV).

1962   Telstar, the first international communication satellite, makes its first transmission.

Canada launches the Alouette satellite, and is now the third country in the world to have a satellite in orbit.

1964   The Tokyo Olympics are transmitted via global satellite.

The Fowler Committee on Broadcasting is established to define expectations for broadcasting and set objectives for both public and private broadcasting in Canada.

Private radio challenges public radio (BBC) in England.

The first domestic VCR is released.

1966   The first television pictures from the moon are broadcast.

The first satellite television signals are exchanged between the UK and Australia.

Canadian sovereignty over new communication technologies is defined in broadcasting policy.

CBC and CTV begin colour television broadcasting.

1967   Movies are available on video for home use.

US Congress creates the US Public Broadcasting Service (PBS).

1968   The first live televised debate by political party leaders in Canada takes place (a joint CBC/CTV production).

1969   The first "911" system is introduced in Canada (www.itu.int/newsarchive/wtsa2000/english/media/timeline.pdf).

The Telesat Canada Act creates a Crown corporation, and the world's first domestic satellite in geostationary orbit, named "Anik" (which means "little brother" in the Inuit dialect), connects Canadians from coast to coast.

The International Telecommunications Satellite Organization (INTELSAT) is launched, telecasting the American-led *Apollo 11* moon landing, marking the first event to be broadcast to television screens worldwide.

1970   The Gold Leaf Awards for best Canadian artists and groups in music are established, but later renamed the Juneaus (then shortened to the Junos) in honour of Pierre Juneau, chairman of the CRTC, who was instrumental in establishing Cancon regulations.

1971   Cancon regulations are established by the CRTC, providing minimum quotas for Canadian broadcasting content (MAPL).

1972   Sony's Portapak (portable video recorder) signals the start of the camcorder revolution.

HBO begins cable TV.

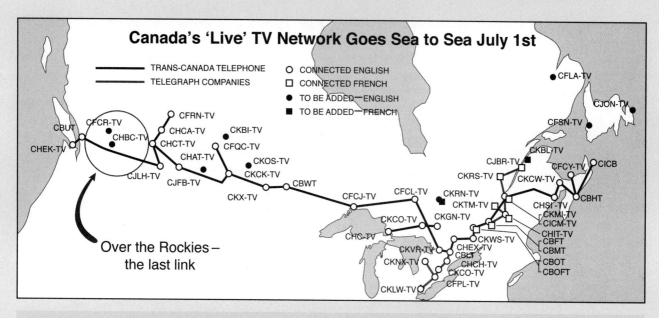

FIGURE 6.3 | A map showing the span of the microwave network by 1 July 1958.

Source: CBC. (2011, June 28). *Canada's electronic skyway* [Web log post]. Retrieved from www.cbc.ca/75/2011/06/the-microwave-network-canadas-electronic-skyway.html

1974   ENG (Electronic News-Gathering) equipment is introduced.

In England, the BBC transmits teletext data to TV sets.

1975   The Canadian Overseas Telecommunication Corporation (COTC) is renamed Teleglobe Canada. Teleglobe is later privatized by the federal Conservative government.

1976   The CRTC's jurisdiction expands; it changes its name to the Canadian Radio-television and Telecommunications Commission but keeps the same acronym.

1980   Ted Turner launches CNN.

1981   MTV (Music Television) launches in the United States as a youth-marketing music video station; variations on the DJ (disc jockey), VJ (video jockey), and later the MVJ (mobile-video jockey) are made.

1982   Alberta Government Telephones introduces the first cellular telephone system to connect Alberta resource industries 🔳 www.itu.int/newsarchive/wtsa2000/english/media/timeline.pdf).

1984   The first specialty television services are licensed by the CRTC, including TSN and MuchMusic. Cancon regulations secure a market for a Canadian music industry (via MAPL). As a condition of its licence, MuchMusic returns a percentage of its revenues to support Canadian independent production. The French version of MuchMusic—Musique-Plus—launches two years later.

SaskTel completes the world's then-largest commercial fibre-optic network, and implements a province-wide relay service for hearing-impaired persons (www.itu.int/newsarchive/wtsa2000/english/media/timeline.pdf).

1985   Nielsen files a content analysis patent (US4677466) for "a method and apparatus for identifying repetitively broadcast programs" (Lert & Lu, 1985, para. 1).

Rupert Murdoch becomes a US citizen to buy more American media outlets.

The Cable Shopping Network is launched in the United States.

1986   The Fox Broadcasting Company (owned by Rupert Murdoch) is established.

1990   The privatization of Alberta Government Telephones (AGT) begins with the establishment of holding company TELUS Communications; AGT sells its remaining ownership to TELUS for $870 million.

1991   The Canadian government amends the Broadcasting Act.

1992   The CRTC allows long-distance competition in the telecommunications industry.

The Government of Canada announces its decision to sell its interest in Telesat Canada to Alouette Telecommunications.

1993   Canadian parliament passes the Telecommunications Act.

1994   DIRECTV launches the first digital TV service via satellite.

1998   BCE Inc. buys 100 per cent of Telesat. Telesat carries Bell ExpressVu and Star Choice as well as more than 200 of Canada's television channels.

1999   US television networks start broadcasting a digital signal.

The Aboriginal Peoples Television Network (APTN), the world's first Aboriginal people's network, is distributed worldwide.

2000 Global Positioning Satellite (GPS) is released as a consumer product.

2002 Research in Motion (Canada) markets the BlackBerry.

2006 The Nintendo Wii (with wireless motion-sensor controls, allowing for full-body video game playing) is released.

VSNL International Canada (owned by Tata Group, India) buys Teleglobe.

2007 The Commissioner for Complaints for Telecommunications Services is established.

The CRTC deregulates the first local telephone markets in Canada.

2008 The iPhone is released.

The first Canadian wireless spectrum auction of the 2 GHz range is held; the sum of winning bids totals roughly $4.25 billion.

Nielsen acquires IAG Research, a company that measures an audience's engagement with commercials and product placement.

2009 The first 3D-TV stereoscopic home movie theatre is released.

2010 CBC broadcasts the first Canadian 3D documentary: *Queen Elizabeth in 3D*.

2011 Nielsen acquires NeuroFocus Inc., "the global leader in neurological testing for consumer research" (Nielsen, 2011, para. 1).

2012 The Canadian government announces that it will cut $115 million in funding to the CBC over three years.

Radio Canada International switches to online-only after budget cuts force it to shut down short-wave transmitters.

2013 The Canadian Space Agency launches its "public-private partnership" satellite CASSIOPE using "the scientific payload ePOP (enhanced polar outflow probe), [to] observe the ionosphere" (Canadian Space Agency, 2013, para. 1), and the telecommunications payload Cascade, which will provide the very first digital broadband courier service for commercial use (www.asc-csa.gc.ca/eng/satellites/cassiope.asp).

7 From Calculation to Cyberia: Computing Over 2,500 Years

Objectives

Every society is an information society. Throughout history, different cultures have adopted different modes of communication, but all are information societies of some kind. . . . The products of the convergence of communications have also meant that contemporary information society is highly dependent on information networks that can distribute images, data and symbols. (Barr, 2000, p. 20)

Trevor Barr is right about society's dependence on images, data, and symbols. These have long been elements of communication. Pictographs on the walls of Stone Age caves, Egyptian hieroglyphics, writing in many languages, and computer code are all tools of communication, each with their own technologies. This chapter begins to flesh out the concept of convergence that is central to the development of digital technology and also to the social conditions in which digital technologies develop. After reading this chapter, you will have a better understanding of the following:

- the long and important history of mechanical and digital calculation that led to the modern computer age;

- what we mean by "convergence";

- how the historical process of convergence has changed over time and why there are clear links between ancient, present, and future technologies;

- why convergence and globalization are social processes, not just the products of technological innovation; and

- the role of the dialectic—as a process of moving history forward—in the social relations of convergence.

Keywords

- **algorithm**
- **bit**
- **computer code**
- **deskilled**
- **Fordism**
- **military–industrial complex**

Convergence: From Calculus to Computing

Convergence is a broad term referring to the interrelation between previously discrete or separate(d) phenomena. It can apply to labour, technology, media, culture, or a particular process (like commodification; Brookey, 2010; Jenkins, 2008; Mosco & McKercher, 2008; Staiger & Hake,

2009). In the context of communications technologies, we're talking about the *coming together* of several discrete technologies to create a hybrid technology. The keys to this modern form of convergence are the microprocessor—the computer chip—and the development of computing algorithms based on binary code. The technologies that are converging rapidly today are telecommunications, computing, and broadcasting (Ostergaard, 1998, p. 95).

ALGORITHM

A specific and finite set of instructions (or formulas, rules, or methods) specifying how to solve a problem. May be represented in mathematical or other types of language and represented by a decision-tree (if "a," do "b"; if not "a," do "c").

As convergence occurs at the level of technologies it does so within the context of the mutual constitution of several other kinds of convergence that also have social impacts and consequences. One of the most important is really a structural *commercial convergence* between media content companies (television and radio networks, and newspaper publishers) and media transmission channels (e.g., film, radio, television, Internet), bringing content and carriage together (recall our media ownership charts in Chapter 3). In the past few decades this has begun to radically reshape the media landscape (Barr, 2000; De Bens & Mazzoleni, 1998, p. 166; Noam, 2009). The major international corporate players continue to seek to control the whole "electronic distribution chain" (Ostergaard, 1998, p. 98), ranging from the production of content through to pay-per-access narrowcast delivery, for example. The consequence, according to Bernt Stubbe Ostergaard (p. 95), is greater concentration of ownership and control, and a situation where regulatory authorities are moving away from addressing questions of content to treat regulation according to the technical means of delivery. In this way, the technology and economics are driving convergence with regulation following, or in some cases just trying to catch up. We return to this theme in Chapter 9, but first a short digression is necessary to understand how technology has been used and developed in facilitating technological and political economic convergence.

In fact we have to travel back in time some thousands of years to really begin with a history of computing in order to see how (and perhaps why) the relationship between technology and humans developed as it did. Indeed, before *computer* meant the machines as we know them today, it simply meant a person employed to do laborious and tedious additions, subtractions, and other sums. A "computer" was a low-paid clerical worker who did calculations day in and day out. That the technology replaced, and is now interfaced with, human labour (via robotics or artificial intelligence, e.g.) means that the relationship between human labour and technology is an enduring challenge of our times.

From Digits to Digital: A Brief History of Counting, Computing, and Convergence

Using a computer thirty years ago [1966], like piloting a moon lander, was the realm of a precious few schooled in the hocus-pocus needed to drive these machines sometimes with primitive languages or none at all (just toggle switches and blinking lights). In my opinion, there was a subconscious effort to keep it mysterious, like the monopoly of the monks or some bizarre religious rite in the Dark Ages. (Negroponte, 1996, p. 90)

In 1996 Nicholas Negroponte was a digital optimist. At the beginning of the digital revolution he believed that computers would make life better for everyone—eventually. But it is his comment about the Dark Ages that draws us to this passage. The Dark Ages was a period from about 500 to 1000 CE in which it is considered that there was very little scientific advance and little in the way of what we might, today, call "progress." Of course this is a very "looking backwards" viewpoint, and through the 500 years of the so-called Dark Ages, human life and history moved forward, though perhaps a little slowly from our perspective. In the vast scale of human evolution, 500 years is not a long time, but when it comes to the evolutionary history

[Handwritten margin notes top: Group work : "Let's Fix CanCon" — CRTC — Brainstorm Policy: Teletithn Canada — Carousel — CanCon Cultural Industries]

*[Handwritten margin notes right: + Convergence / (↳ Telephone / ↳ Television / ↳ Newspaper) / ⇓ / [Content] / Internet / medium ↓ Delivery / one network / ** Regulation / In Canada: / CRTC — regulates / radio + television / + in 1976 / telecommunication / as well. / ↳ (meaning telephone / + possibly internet. / 1999: CRTC rules / no regl'n of / Internet. Why? / – reasons: ① ② ③ / ① not a "broad" / cast technology / ② laws exist to / deal w offensive / content / ③ enough CanCon / on web already]*

of computing, 500 years takes us a long way. In fact it takes us from the first mechanical calculator all the way to the current iPad, but to understand the complete history of computing, we need to go even further back in time to ancient Babylon, 1000 BCE, where objects were assigned a value as a basis for exchange.

In the primitive world, when it came to using objects to represent *numbers* of things, shells, bones, small stones, or seeds could have been used. That the word *calculate* is derived from the Latin word for small stone, *calculus*, suggests that pebbles or beads were the technology used in the first computing devices. By manipulating the beads or stones, it was possible with some skill and practice to make rapid calculations. At the same time, the Chinese were becoming very involved in commerce with the Japanese, Indians, and Koreans. They needed a way to tally accounts and bills, and out of this need the abacus was born. Other historical accounts suggest that the abacus may have been invented in Babylonia (now Iraq) in the fourth century BCE (maxmon.com, 2005a). The abacus is the first true precursor of the adding machines and computers that would follow.

The abacus works by assigning a value to each bead, determined by its position: One bead on a particular wire has the value of one; two together have the value of two. A bead on the next line, however, might have the value of 10, and on the third line a value of 100. The abacus works on the principle of place–value notation: The location of the bead determines its value. In this way, relatively few beads are required to depict large numbers. The beads are counted, or given numerical values, by shifting them in one direction. The values are subtracted by shifting the beads in the other direction. An abacus is really a memory aid for the user making mental calculations, as opposed to the true mechanical calculating machines that were still to come.

Arabic numerals were introduced to Europe in the eighth and ninth centuries, and Roman numerals remained in use in some parts of Europe until the seventeenth century. The Arabic system introduced the concepts of zero and fixed places for tens, hundreds, and thousands, and greatly simplified mathematical calculations. It is not beyond the realm of possibility that the abacus, or a device very similar to it, was invented almost simultaneously in China and the Middle East, or that one followed on the heels of the other. It is consistent with the ways that commerce and trade developed and also with the principles of convergence and simultaneity. It is a common feature of human society that as it becomes more stable, well-off, and complex, its inventiveness will also increase.

Aside from the abacus, early humans also invented numbering systems to enable them to compute, with ease, sums greater than 10. One such numbering system is the decimal numbering system, which is traceable to early Hindu–Arabic influences. This decimal system, with specific digits representing numbers from zero to nine, came into general use in Europe and has survived to the present day.

From Manual to Mechanical Counting

The abacus was a very simple counting apparatus. It is perhaps not even correct to call it a machine, though it did have a few simple moving parts. There was no mechanical power embedded in an abacus; it required the manipulation of the beads on the wire by hand and human interpretation. However, the invention of simple mechanical scales for weighing and measuring helped to move computational technology along. The progress of mechanical calculation was stalled for some time and had to wait for other technologies to catch up, including the development of mechanical clocks, gears, levers, and pulleys. It also had to wait for further advances in mathematics and other sciences, such as astronomy, chemistry, and physics. The primary advances were in mathematics because it was in this field—to help with complex calculations—that mechanical computational devices were of most value. At the same time, other philosophers and inventors were attempting to build mechanical devices to generate proofs of logic. Many of them, like thirteenth-century Spanish theologian Ramon Llull, were attempting, through logic, to prove the absolute truth of statements in the *Bible*. Llull invented a series of discs that rotated around a common centre point. The discs were of various sizes and a series of words or symbols was printed on each. As the discs were rotated, a series of logical sentences or equations would be assembled. Llull's most famous device, the *figura universalis*, had 14 discs and could generate a vast number of possible logical sequences. The Llull device, though not a calculator or computer in a strict sense, did influence later generations of mathematicians, including Gottfried Wilhelm von Leibniz, who invented a mechanical calculator called a Step Reckoner in the seventeenth century (maxmon.com, 2005b).

The next big advances in computation took place in the same century. John Napier (1550–1617), Baron of Merchiston, Scotland, invented logarithms in 1614, which allowed multiplication and division to be reduced to addition and subtraction. A logarithm is simply a mathematical formula, and it quickly became the basis for early, primitive attempts at programming mechanical calculators. In the early 1700s, Napier used logarithms to devise a series of complex multiplication tables, which were inscribed on strips of wood or bone and were a useful tool for mathematicians. This device became known as "Napier's Bones" and was the precursor to the slide rule, which was invented in 1621 by William Oughtred (maxmon.com, 2005c). Napier's logarithms and mathematical genius are also credited with helping to advance early astronomy and helping Isaac Newton with his breakthrough work on the theory of gravitational force (O'Connor & Robertson, 1998b).

Two years later, in 1623, a German mathematician and Lutheran minister, Wilhelm Schickard (1592–1635), built one of the first mechanical calculators; it used a system of cogs and gears modelled after the rules of arithmetic, and was the first calculator that did not require human interpretation (like the abacus or slide rule, e.g.). The machine worked with six digits, and carried digits across columns. It worked, but never made it beyond the prototype stage. When he invented the mechanical calculator, Schickard was a professor at the University of Tübingen, Germany, where he taught and conducted research in mathematics, astronomy, and surveying. Schickard corresponded with many scientists, including renowned astronomer Johannes Kepler, who used Schickard's calculator to help him work out the laws of planetary motion (O'Connor & Robertson, 1996b).

The Pascaline, the First Desktop Calculator

French mathematician, philosopher, and theologian Blaise Pascal (1623–62) built a mechanical calculator, the Pascaline, in 1642. It had the capacity for eight digits, but had trouble carrying numbers, and its gears tended to jam. Pascal was 19 when he built the first machine to help his father, a tax collector in Paris. This is significant in that the technology was developed to meet the political economic requirements of the state. The Pascaline adopted the principles of the abacus but did away with the use of the hand to move the beads or counters. Instead, Pascal used wheels to move the counters.

The Pascaline was based on a design described by Hero of Alexandria (2 CE) to calculate the distance a carriage travelled. The basic principle of Pascal's calculator is still used today in water meters and modern odometers. Instead of having a carriage wheel turn the gear, Pascal made each 10-toothed wheel accessible such that it could be turned directly by a person's hand (later inventors added keys and a crank), with the result that when the wheels were turned in the proper sequence, a series of numbers was entered and a cumulative sum was obtained. The gear train supplied a mechanical answer equal to the answer that is obtained by using arithmetic.

This first mechanical calculator had several disadvantages. Although it did offer a substantial improvement over manual calculations, only Pascal himself could repair the device, and the machine itself cost more than the people it replaced (Dacles, 2005)! Nevertheless, it was intended to replace people, such that the considerations of the social consequences of technology emerged because mathematicians feared for the loss of their jobs (O'Connor & Robertson, 1996a). The principle of Pascal's machine is still being used today, such as in the counters of tape recorders and odometers. Pascal's machine was one of the first mechanical calculating machines. In 1674, von Leibniz made improvements on Pascal's machine; it was now possible for the machine to divide and multiply as easily as it could add and subtract. As well as inventing the Step Reckoner, von Leibniz was also an advocate of the binary system of counting (0, 1), which is a key feature of all modern digital computing (G. O'Regan, 2008).

The Weaving Loom and the Steam Engine: Convergence Aids Calculus and Divides Labour

> *The computer is not as disjunctive from the early history of industrial capitalism as one might imagine; and to see computerisation alone as a new and quite distinct adjunct to surveillance is misleading. . . . This is well illustrated by the example of the work of Charles Babbage in the middle of the nineteenth century. (Giddens, 1995, p. 175)*

When we examine the seventeenth-, eighteenth-, and nineteenth-century developments in mechanical computation it becomes clear that the Industrial Revolution and the digital revolution really began around the same time. It is also obvious that new inventions, like Pascal's counter, borrowed and built on technologies that had been around for some time—in his case a simple distance-counter that had been in use for over 1,400 years. When we come to the nineteenth century, the crossover technologies that spurred research into mechanical calculation were the weaving loom and the steam engine. When the age of industrialization spread throughout Europe, such machines became fixtures in agriculture and manufacturing.

In 1801, a French weaver, Joseph-Marie Jacquard, patented an automatic loom for weaving cloth controlled by punch cards. With the use of cards punched with holes, it was possible for the Jacquard loom to weave fabrics in a variety of replicable patterns. Jacquard's system automated what had, until that time, been an expensive job done by highly skilled weavers. The invention removed control over the process (what control there was to be had) from the skilled worker to the factory owner, which, if you remember the Luddites, was met with protest by the weavers. The punch cards made it possible to record patterns, replicate and reproduce them, on a mass scale; the skilled worker could thereby be **deskilled** to someone whose skill was not in creating the pattern and using the loom to materialize it, but to attend to the machine. In this way, conception (thought and creativity) and execution (carrying out the work) could be separated, creating an imposed (but false) division of labour between mental and manual work (i.e., even though you may tend to a machine, it's not like you shut off your brain in order to do so).

With control over the labour process held by management and the owners of the factories, the formerly skilled workers could be replaced with a relatively unskilled worker, or eliminated entirely. The pattern (pardon the pun) would be consistently repeated in directing technological

DESKILLED

A separation made between conception and execution (or mental and manual work); a practice whereby a worker's skill (ability or expertise in doing a particular task or job) is reduced, downgraded, or eventually eliminated via the combination of technology, management techniques, and the division of labour.

ONGOING ISSUES

Working with Robots

The use of technology—and specifically computer-assisted technology like robotics—in the workplace has been around for centuries. In the latter part of the twentieth century, the use of large-scale expensive robotics equipment on factory floors, and in car manufacturing in particular, is one important feature in the transformation of work and to the transformation in the design of automobiles as well (BBC News, 2012). A central feature of these robots was the scale, precision, and power of the systems, which often required that they were segregated from the human workforce for safety reasons. Thus, the large robotics systems were seen as remote and just another technology on the assembly line.

Rethink Robotics, an American company, is working to change the robot/human relationship with the announcement, in September 2012, of its newest system, Baxter. The benefits of Baxter are that it is more human-like in its actions and appearance. Now, rather than being segregated behind glass, it can work side-by-side with a human. Baxter's computer systems include software to aid it in being better at sensing its environment, stopping to avoid its human co-workers if required (Markoff, 2012). Those who are interested in purchasing Baxter have noted that they will employ the robots in roles that involve repetitive tasks. It was stressed by one corporate executive that the introduction of Baxter would not mean the layoff of human workers, but rather, these people would be "assigned to jobs that require higher-level skills" (ibid., para. 17). From a financial perspective, Rethink is promoting Baxter as a more cost-effective technology, as one Baxter costs only USD$22,000, compared to the hundreds of thousands required prior to previous workplace robotics systems. Also, the company estimates that the robots can work "for the equivalent of $4 an hour" (Kesterton, 2012, para. 1).

Discussion Questions

1. Does the introduction of Baxter signal a shift away from deskilled back to skilled human labour?

2. What impact do you think Baxter will have on the wages of human workers?

3. What other kinds of robots have you heard of? Do you think robots are identified as "threats" to human labour or human existence, or as helpful aids to a range of human deficiencies?

4. Consider the following quotation leading the research of the Institute for Robotics and Mechatronics (n.d.) at the University of Toronto:

    One of the primary innovation engines in technology today is the triumvirate of *Communication—Computation—Information Technologies*. Communication refers to the advent in the last 20 years of widely available communication networks. Computation refers to sweeping advances in processing speed, miniaturization, memory, and power reduction in microprocessors and electrical devices. Information technologies refer to paradigm shifts in software and the Internet, resulting in innovations in the way information is accessed and manipulated. The medium that each of these areas manipulates is information. (para. 1)

    a. What kind of communication is being emphasized here?

    b. What does it suggest is the primary driver of technological change?

    c. What is missing from the definition of this "innovation engine" and thus from the Institute's research?

change in the workplace (from so-called manual labour to machine-driven factory labour) in the mid-eighteenth to nineteenth centuries. It was one of the fundamental changes—along with coal mining, the steam engine, and mass transportation networks like the railway—that mark the beginning of the first Industrial Revolution.

The term *revolution* is not one used lightly; it identifies an almost complete change in the political economy from an agrarian-based and *feudal* system to an industrial-based and *capitalist* system. Feudalism is based on land ownership, monarchist and familial lineage, with a class and labour division between landlords, serfs or peasants, and craft-based work. As discussed in earlier chapters, capitalism is based on private property, both material (like land) and immaterial (like intellectual property), with a division between the workers and the owners of the means of production, and work is distributed (locally and internationally) according to private priorities.

Both systems are based on property ownership, social class, and a division of labour, but the differences are significant. In feudalism, the landowner and monarchist were responsible to all of the people in his/her territory—at least over the human life of the monarch or landowner—whereas in capitalism, this responsibility is left solely with the state. With the transition to capitalism, when corporations were established as legal entities, they were made "humanless" and relatively timeless. A corporation's "life" depends on ceaseless profit-making, and its only legal responsibility is to its shareholders, yet it is granted "the rights, powers and privileges of a natural person" (Canada Business Corporations Act, 1985, § 15[1]) and enjoys these rights without the accountability required of the lord, or landowner. (see Rowland 2012, e.g.) Such changes facilitated a new round of *imperialism*, beginning with a state-led expansion of ownership and control over territories, to one that expands corporate control across the globe. As discussed earlier, processes such as commodification, spatialization, and globalization advance this kind of imperialism, as technology was (and is) used to extend it. It is in this context that the history of technological development is situated.

Case Study

A Classless Society?

With the increasing use of technology in production, the distinction made between manual and mental labour is crucial in managing and controlling workers. It is also vital in understanding the social totality through the creation of a divide between some workers (intellectual labour in management, e.g.) and other workers (manual labour in factory work, e.g.). Throughout the twentieth century, as management techniques and technology were changed, the way labour was organized was characterized accordingly. For example, **Fordism** identifies the top-down, centralized control of factory production practices. It was named after the assembly-line characteristics of the automotive industry and the American who advanced it (Henry Ford). *Post-Fordism* refers to an extension of this kind of managerial control (top-down) and movement from the factory floor to the office building, and the change from industrial (natural resource exploitation) to information or service industries (human resource exploitation). The nature or degree of exploitation is subject to debate in relation to the concept of social class. Where for Karl Marx, there were only the owners of the means of production and those (working class) who were thus forced to sell their labour, differences in production under capitalism also suggested that social class had changed.

Continued

FORDISM
A way of organizing, managing, and controlling capitalist production *and* consumption. Named after its promoter, American Henry Ford, it is based on the division of work into discrete, standardized, and repetitive tasks to allow for industrial mass production (such as in assembly lines in factories) and, correspondingly, mass consumption (goods are made cheaply and priced low enough, and wages are accordingly high enough, so that workers can afford them).

Distinctions were made between the working class, *blue* collar (factory workers paid by the hour or unit produced) or *pink* collar (office workers), and the middle class or *white* collar (semi-professional, management, and salaried employees; Mills, 1956). This included a "new middle class"—people working in media and an industry defined by its use of communication and information technologies (ICTs).

With an emphasis on the increasing use and dependence on ICT, theorists also conceptualized a new social totality to suggest that a fundamental change was occurring from an industrial to post-industrial society (Bell, 1973), and later—with economic, social, and technological convergence—an "information society," and more recently a "knowledge society" (Webster, 2006). In this view, management and the new middle class were now "knowledge workers," and classes would be further differentiated into hierarchies based on their capacity to generate knowledge or innovate and were the new "creative classes" (Florida, 2012).

With the current iteration of economic and technological convergence marking the beginning of the twenty-first century, labour is again being re-conceptualized. The division between manual and intellectual labour is said to be collapsing, as all forms of work and social life increasingly use ICT. The sharing of ideas and the development of knowledge possible through the use of the Internet suggests that the owner/worker, employer/employee, or management/worker division has been broken down in favour of an environment that favours autonomy, collaboration, and cooperation (Hardt & Negri, 2004). This is the purportedly new environment of the networked society, and as you read the rest of this book, you may weigh in on its evaluation and future predictions.

Discussion Questions

1. Review the discussions of social class in Chapter 2. Is the class-based society on the verge of extinction? Has social convergence been added to economic and technological convergence?

2. If wage labour is a defining difference, why are workers in the media or creative industries so different than workers that still toil in the factories? Are such distinctions useful? Why or why not?

COMPUTER CODE

A set of instructions (or a set of symbols arranged according to mechanical and mathematical logic) that are programmed (built) into a computer's operating system, telling it how to perform certain tasks.

The original punch card is important because it is a significant "ancestor of the computer" (Essinger, 2004, p. 281) in terms of establishing a basis for the development of computer codes and the binary system which had both economic and political uses. Weaving patterns (the information) were encoded on the card as a set of instructions into a machine-readable format (e.g., where to place a thread, and where not). In this way, the machine made the "decisions" based on a series of programmable codes. The concept of the punch card was further developed in the work of British mathematician and inventor Charles Babbage (1791–1871), who first conceived of a device to undertake mechanical calculus, which he called the Difference Engine, in 1820 or 1821. At the time Babbage conceived of the Difference Engine, the calculation of logarithms and trigonometric tables (used in astronomy and navigation) was done by hand. Teams of people often called computers would be assembled to perform the necessary calculations. It was very expensive, and the potential for undetected human error to spoil the final results was high. The Difference Engine was designed as a massive steam-powered mechanical calculator to print astronomical tables and thus save time and money, and to be more accurate (O'Connor

& Robertson, 1998a). It was intended to be fully automatic, even to the extent of printing the resulting tables, and was commanded by a fixed instruction program.

In 1823, with the encouragement of the Astronomical Society, Babbage was given a government grant of £1,500 to begin work on the Difference Engine. This "seed money" would typify the development of technology as supported by government political and economic interests, particularly for military purposes. The British government was looking to support the project with the promise that the technology would assist it in its development of navigational tables essential for extending its territorial control (Kopplin, 2002), advancing its imperialism; by February 1830, the government had put nearly £9,000 into the project, but still there was no working machine. Four years later, the government's investment had reached £17,000 and Babbage had sunk £6,000 of his own money into work on the Difference Engine (O'Connor & Robertson, 1998a). Babbage attempted to build a working machine over the next 20 years, only to have the project cancelled by the British government in 1842. However, the work Babbage had put into his device led to his next project, the Analytical Engine (see Figure 7.1).

The Analytical Engine was a mechanical computer that could theoretically solve any mathematical problem. Like the Jacquard loom, the design used punch cards to perform simple conditional operations. The idea of using a punched card to store a predetermined pattern to be woven by the loom clicked in Babbage's mind. He spent many years working on a machine that would be able to perform all types of mathematical calculations, store values in its memory, and perform logical comparisons among values:

Thus it appears that the whole of the conditions which enable a finite machine to make calculations of unlimited extent are fulfilled in the Analytical Engine. The means I have adopted are uniform. I have converted the infinity of space, which was required by the conditions of the problem, into the infinity of time. The means I have employed are in daily use in the art of weaving patterns. (Babbage, 1864/2005, n.p.)

Developing on the concept of the punch cards, Babbage recognized that "the pattern of holes could be used to represent an abstract idea such as a problem statement or the raw data required for that problem's solution" (Kopplin, 2002, para. 5), thus establishing a basis for the development of algorithms now used in computer coding and web search engines.

Babbage realized that punched paper could be employed as a storage mechanism, holding computed numbers for

FIGURE 7.1 | Part of Babbage's Analytical Engine computer, the first ever designed.

Source: © Chris Howes / Wild Places Photography / Alamy

future reference. Because of the connection to the Jacquard loom, Babbage called the two main parts of his Analytic Engine the "Store" and the "Mill," as both terms are used in the weaving industry. The Store was where numbers were held and the Mill was where they were "woven" into new results. In a modern computer these same parts are called the memory unit *and the* central processing unit *(CPU). (para. 6)*

Babbage's work attracted international attention, and he travelled throughout Europe talking to eminent scientists about the Analytical Engine. He had many supporters, including Italian mathematician L. F. Menabrea, who would later become prime minister of Italy. Menabrea and Ada Lovelace wrote a lengthy description of Babbage's ideas and helped to cement his place in the history of computing.

Babbage spent more than a decade working on his invention, investing his own money in workshops and master toolmakers to make his design a reality, but in the end the Analytical Engine was never built. It lacked one thing—electronics. The technology at that time was not capable of building Babbage's dream because electronics were not yet known or even thought of.

Ada Lovelace, the daughter of Lord Byron and the Countess of Lovelace, met Babbage in 1833. She described the Analytical Engine as weaving "*algebraic patterns* just as the Jacquard-loom weaves flowers and leaves" (Menabrea & Lovelace, 1843/2005, n.p.). Lovelace was a remarkable woman who successfully contended with a male-dominated world. She no doubt benefitted from her wealth and title, but that should not diminish her achievements in mathematics and computing. Her published analysis (ibid.) of the Analytical Engine is our best record of its programming potential. In it she outlines the fundamentals of computer programming, including data analysis, looping, and memory addressing. The Analytical Engine was a real parallel decimal computer that would have operated on words of 50 decimals and was able to store 1,000 such numbers. If built, the machine would have included a number of built-in operations such as conditional control, which allowed the instructions for the machine to be executed in a specific order rather than in numerical order.

As Anthony Giddens (1995) notes, Babbage did not succeed for want of trying but was defeated by the lack of appropriate technologies. Babbage was, however, aware of the ways in which his mechanical devices could contribute to the profitability of the emerging industrial system of capitalism through the division of, and control over, labour. In his book, *On the Economy of Machinery and Manufactures*, written in 1834, he was able to make an explicit link between technology, the division of labour in the workforce, and the collection of surplus value by the capitalist; for this he became a "respected" economist. He was one of the first theorists of the Industrial Revolution to predict the coming of so-called thinking machines that could be programmed to do complicated mathematical calculations, leading to improvements in productivity by adapting such machines to the industrial process (Rosenberg, 1997). He thus left the politics of labour (or the moral philosophy of the political economists) by the wayside in favour of economic formulas. Within these formulas, human labour was reduced to a mathematical equation, with the emphasis on ways to gain surplus labour or profit. This would prove very useful in spreading the hegemony of capitalism and propagating the Industrial Revolution with its huge factories and assembly-line work, without much pause to consider what kind of progress this revolution would bring.

The Book of the Machines

How many men at this hour are living in a state of bondage to the machines? How many spend their whole lives, from the cradle to the grave, in tending them by night and day? (S. Butler, 1872/1967, p. 150)

It is also, at this point, worth reintroducing the writing of Samuel Butler, who was an outspoken critic of nineteenth-century British morals and social customs. In his anti-utopian novel *Erewhon*, self-published in 1872, he savagely ridicules what he perceived as the mechanistic treatment of human life in Darwin's theory of evolution. While we now see that Darwin's theory was both valid and reliable, Butler's reworking of evolution in several chapters of *Erewhon* was devoted to an argument against the advancement of machines, and provides an interesting insight into a disturbing nineteenth-century view of the future—our present?

In his "translation" of the Erewhonian "Book of the Machines," Butler provides some startling insights into the future of machine intelligence. There are no machines in Erewhon, the inhabitants having been convinced by the author of the "Book of the Machines" that all mechanical devices, save for the wheel and the lever, should be destroyed. This industrial "counter-revolution," some 200 years before the protagonist (Higgs) arrives in the forgotten land, has left Erewhon in a state of arrested development and stagnation. The name of the land, and novel, is itself significant, as read backwards it is *nowhere* (from the Greek word *ou topos*; Mattelart, 1996, p. 154).

In the chapters devoted to the translation of the "Book of the Machines," Butler lays out some interesting theories about the gradual but inevitable development of machine intelligence. The section culminates in the argument that machines will eventually enslave humans and therefore, to avoid this unpleasant consequence of science, they should be destroyed at once. At one point, there appears a reference to Charles Babbage's work, which Butler no doubt would have been aware of:

> *Have we not engines which can do all manner of sums more quickly and correctly than we can? . . . Our sum engines never drop a figure, nor our looms a stitch; the machine is brisk and active, when the man is weary. . . . May not man himself become a sort of parasite upon the machines? An affectionate machine-tickling aphid? (S. Butler, 1872/1967, p. 148)*

The arguments made in this translation are quite sophisticated, and for readers of *Erewhon* in the late nineteenth century, they would have been recognizable as a commentary on the role of mechanization in the Industrial Revolution. Many of Butler's arguments about the dangers of humans becoming enslaved to machines are arguably similar to those of Marx who, when Butler was writing his satire, was busy working on the main ideas in *Capital*.

Take Butler's example of a railway engine driver who can choose to stop his locomotive "at any moment that he pleases," but in reality can only do so "at certain points which have been fixed for him by others" (ibid.). The locomotive driver has become a part of the machine, and his will is not his own; it is owned by those who own the railway (the engine and the track it runs on). In Volume 1 of *Capital*, Marx makes a similar point: "The automatic mechanism is endowed, in the person of the capitalist, with consciousness and a will" (Marx, 1867/1990, p. 527) that is outside the will of the worker. Like Butler's engine driver, labourers in the industrial factory are incorporated into the machine "as its living appendages" and must work under conditions of "barrack-like discipline" (pp. 548–9). Giddens (1995, p. 124), too, makes a similar argument that the discipline of the factory was reinforced by the mass introduction of machinery, which in turn made mass surveillance of the workforce easier for the factory managers acting as agents of capital.

Despite the hopes of Babbage and others, the Industrial Revolution itself did not directly produce a mechanical computer that worked to any great degree. But it did provide the impetus, both in terms of advances in technology and in terms of the constructed need for such machines, that was to culminate in the successful demonstration of practical computing in the first half of the twentieth century. It was only some 30 years after Babbage's unsuccessful attempts to build the Analytical Engine, on the cusp of the century, that the first commercially viable mechanical calculator was patented and used as the prototype "government engine" for crunching data about people.

Hole-Punched Cards Advance Mechanical Computation

A further and more concrete step towards automated computation was made in 1890 when American engineer Herman Hollerith (1860–1929), working for the US Census Bureau, first successfully applied Babbage's punch-card technique to mechanical computing. The Bureau had taken nearly eight years to complete work on the 1880 census and feared that the 1890 census would take even longer. Hollerith began work on his tabulating machine in 1881 and won a competition sponsored by the Census Bureau (da Cruz, 2004).

Hollerith also adopted Jacquard's punched-card concept. Census data were translated into a series of holes to represent the digits and the letters of the alphabet. The data were then passed through a machine with a series of electrical contacts that were either turned "off" or "on" depending on the position and sequencing of holes in the punched cards. These different combinations of off/on situations were recorded by the machine and represented a way of tabulating the result of the census. What came to be called the Hollerith Code is a set of computer punch cards or paper tapes of telex machines.

Surprisingly, Hollerith said he did not get the idea from the work of Charles Babbage, but from watching a train conductor punch tickets. Of course the big advantage he had over Babbage was the ability to apply the power of electromagnets to the process, while Babbage had only mechanical force (like the Jacquard machine) and the possibility of steam as the driving power.

As a result of Hollerith's invention, reading errors were greatly reduced and work flow increased in the Census Bureau. Importantly, stacks of punched cards could be used as an accessible memory store of almost unlimited capacity; furthermore, different problems could be stored on different batches of cards and worked on as needed.

Hollerith's machine was highly successful. It cut the time it took to tabulate the result of the census by two thirds. Heavily supported by government contracts, it made money for the company that manufactured Hollerith's machine. And in 1911, this company merged with its competitor to form International Business Machines (IBM). From the 1950s onward IBM has been a prominent name in computing and delivered the first mass-market personal computer in the 1970s (for a visual history and commentary on computing, see 🖥 www.computerhistory.org/).

Hollerith's machine, however, was strictly limited to tabulation. The punched cards could not be used to direct more complex computations (Hoyle, 2004). Eventually Hollerith introduced a continuous strip of paper tape with punched holes; when these were passed over a metal drum the presence of a hole allowed an electrical circuit to be made, and the machine would register the data that corresponded to that hole's "position." A series of holes in combination could, in this way, be made to represent more complex data.

Hollerith also invented the first automatic card-feeder mechanism and the key-punch. He is also recognized as a pioneer of programming through the introduction of a switchable wiring panel to his 1906 Type I machine, which allowed it to perform different calculations without having to be rewired. Each of these innovations made a contribution to the rapid development of computing and information processing in the twentieth century (da Cruz, 2004), allowing the collection, storage, and manipulation of information largely to those who controlled the technology and the information gathered by it.

In the 1930s, German civil engineer Konrad Zuse (1910–95), who had already developed a number of calculating machines, released the first programmable computer designed to solve complex engineering equations. His first machine, the Z1, was built in his parents' living room and did not work very well, but it was the first binary machine to use a punched tape, rather than cards, and in that respect prefigured the modern computer. According to his own recollections, Zuse was working independently and had not been following the work of other inventors in the field: "I started in 1934, working independently and without knowledge of other developments going on around me. In fact, I hadn't even heard of Charles Babbage when I embarked on my work" (as cited in O'Connor & Robertson, 1999b).

Zuse pioneered the use of binary math and Boolean logic in electronic calculation. His second calculating machine, Z2, replaced mechanical with electrical components, but it was not completed because World War II interrupted his work. While in the German army, Zuse completed the Z3, which was controlled by perforated strips of discarded movie film. As well as being controllable by these celluloid strips, it was also the first machine to actually work on the binary system, as opposed to the more familiar decimal system. Zuse's work prefigured that of English mathematician Alan Turing in that Zuse's machine was a "general" computer, not one designed to undertake a specific individual function (Redshaw, 1996).

Like much of the historical development of technology, the Z3 was developed for military purposes. It was used by the German Aerodynamic Research Institute to work on problems in the production of military aircraft. The Z3 had over 2,600 electrical relay circuits, and when Zuse proposed to the German high command that he build a computer based on electronic valves, he was told it was not necessary because Germany was close to winning the war (O'Connor & Robertson, 1999b)! After the war, Zuse continued to work on computing problems in the aerospace industry. In 1950 he established his own company, which was eventually incorporated into the giant Siemens electronics firm in 1967. In 1958 Zuse was up to Z22 in his series of computers. It was an early example of a computer that made use of transistors rather than valves.

Binary Code: One Digit/No Digit—On/Off

Zuse's use of binary code was a big step forward in computing technology, particularly when it could be harnessed to an electrical circuit. The binary system is composed of zeros and ones. A punch card with its two conditions—a hole or no hole—was admirably suited to representing things in binary form. If a hole was read by the card reader, it was considered to be a one. If no hole was present in a column, a zero was appended to the current number. The total number of possible numbers can be calculated by putting "two" to the power of the number of bits (2^n) in the binary number. A bit is simply a single occurrence of a binary number—a zero or a one. Thus, if you had a possible binary number of six bits (2^6), 64 different numbers could be generated ($2 \times 2 \times 2 \times 2 \times 2 \times 2 = 64$). Binary representation was going to prove important in the future design of computers, which took advantage of a multitude of two-state devices such as card readers, electric circuits—which could be on or off—and vacuum tubes. Zuse is also remembered for his contribution to computer programming. In 1945 he invented a machine language called "Plankilkül" and was able to design a chess-playing program (O'Connor & Robertson, 1999b).

While Zuse was working on the German war effort, physicist Howard Aiken (1900–73) of Harvard University was working on similar ideas for his Ph.D. Like Zuse and others before him, Aiken wanted to build a machine that would take the drudgery out of the difficult and long mathematical equations that he needed to solve in order to get on with his important work in another field. Aiken fortuitously came across a few parts from Babbage's Analytical Engine that were in storage

BIT

The smallest unit of computerized data, a single binary digit (1 or 0) used to measure data in terms of computer-calculating speed, file capacity, and connection speed rates (usually per second).

at the Harvard science museum and recognized that the technology of 1937 was developed enough to implement Babbage's concept (Ferguson, 1998). With the combined effort of his colleagues at Harvard and IBM, the Automatic Sequence Controlled Calculator (ASCC) was finished in 1944; it cost $200,000 to construct. The ASCC machine weighed 35 tons, held 500 miles of wiring, and could complete an addition to 23 significant places in six seconds, while a division took around 12 seconds.

Also similar to Zuse and others, Aiken used punched paper tapes for instructions and punch cards for the data. IBM donated the machine to Harvard University, and it became known as the Harvard Mark I. Also like the Zuse machines, the Mark I was used in military applications, in this case to calculate the ballistic qualities of heavy-calibre ammunition (O'Connor & Robertson, 1999a). The Mark I had over 760,000 parts and special built-in programs, or subroutines, to handle logarithms and trigonometric functions. It was the first in a series of computers designed and built under Aiken's direction between 1943 and 1952, ending with the Mark IV (Hoyle, 2004; O'Connor & Robertson, 1999a). During this same time, the University of Toronto was also developing its own computers and in 1953 developed a prototype for Canada's first electronic computer, named UTEC (University of Toronto Electronic Computer; web.cs.toronto.edu/dcs/history.htm).

Another researcher of note brought together thinking on computing and mathematical problems with military applications, and was working at the same time as Aiken and his colleagues at Harvard. He was the Hungarian-born John von Neumann (1903–57). Von Neumann immigrated to the United States in 1930 and took up a post at Princeton University, where he pursued an interest in quantum mechanics. He quickly became interested in the work of Aiken and others and also met British mathematician and computing theorist Alan Turing. During World War II, von Neumann worked on the computing needs of the Los Alamos team that was to produce the hydrogen bomb (J. Lee, 2002). After the war, he retained close links to the American military as a member of the Armed Forces Special Weapons Project and then as a member of the Atomic Energy Commission (O'Connor & Robertson, 2003b).

The key aspect of von Neumann's work on computer-related problems is the legacy of the computer infrastructure that is known as the "von Neumann Architecture," which relates to the ability of the machine to store programs and data simultaneously, though in separate parts of its "brain." Before this, computers had to be physically rewired to perform different functions. For example, the Hollerith tabulator used a plug board similar to a telephone exchange, and some machines were hard-wired for only one type of function. Using von Neumann's system, the machine could be much more flexible and could even be self-modifying in a limited way. Von Neumann contributed a new understanding of how practical, fast computers should be organized and built; these ideas, often referred to as the stored-program technique, became fundamental for future generations of high-speed digital computers and were universally adopted.

The primary advance was the provision of a special type of machine instruction called "conditional control transfer" that allowed the program sequence to be interrupted and recommenced at any point, similar to the system suggested by Babbage for his Analytical Engine. If all instruction programs were stored together with data in the same memory unit, instructions could be arithmetically modified in the same way as data. Thus data was the same as program. The stored-program concept quickly became the standard for prototype computers from the late 1940s onward, and in the late 1940s and into the 1950s, von Neumann, Aiken, and others collaborated on several computing projects (J. Lee, 2002). It is for these projects that von Neumann is remembered for his advocacy of the bit as a measurement of computer memory (www.wu.ece.ufl.edu/links/dataRate/DataMeasurementChart.html).

With the success of Aiken's Harvard Mark I as the first major American development, which had now become a computing race as part of wartime, the Americans were working on the next great breakthrough. Their second contribution was the development of the giant machine ENIAC, or Electronic Numerical Integrator and Computer, by John W. Mauchly and J. Presper Eckert. ENIAC was developed for the Ballistics Research Laboratory in Maryland to assist in the preparation of firing tables for artillery. It was built at the University of Pennsylvania's Moore School of Electrical Engineering and completed in November 1945. The ENIAC is believed to be the first electronic digital computer. It had no moving parts, used about 18,000 vacuum tubes, and was able to calculate complex numbers in a few seconds. The vacuum tubes were quite delicate and had to be replaced frequently because they tended to burn out; the storage of all those vacuum tubes and the machinery required to keep them cool took up over 167 m^2 (1,800 square feet) of floor space.

The ENIAC was programmable and had the capability to store problem calculations using words of 10 decimal digits instead of binary ones like previous automated calculators/computers. Nonetheless, it had punched-card input and output and arithmetically had one multiplier, one divider/square rooter, and 20 adders employing decimal "ring counters," which served as adders and also as quick-access (0.0002 seconds) read–write register storage. The executable instructions composing a program were embodied in the separate units of ENIAC, which were plugged together to form a route through the machine for the flow of computations. These connections had to be redone for each different problem, together with presetting function tables and switches. This technique was inconvenient, and brought into question just how far ENIAC could be considered programmable. But it was efficient in handling the particular programs for which it had been designed. ENIAC is generally acknowledged to be the first successful high-speed electronic digital computer (EDC) and was productively used from 1946 to 1955.

The Breakthrough in Britain

> *Perhaps the most remarkable feature of Turing's work on Turing machines was that he was describing a modern computer before technology had reached the point where construction was a realistic proposition. (O'Connor & Robertson, 2003a)*

While Aiken, von Neumann, and others were working at Harvard, over in the United Kingdom, British mathematician Alan Turing (1912–54) wrote a paper in 1936 entitled *On Computable Numbers*, in which he described a hypothetical device that prefigured programmable computers: a "Turing machine" (ibid.). The Turing machine was designed to perform logical operations and could read, write, or erase symbols written on squares of an infinite paper tape. This kind of machine came to be known as a finite state machine because at each step in a computation, the machine's next action was matched against a finite instruction list of possible states.

Turing's purpose was not to invent a computer, but rather to describe problems that are logically possible to solve. His hypothetical machine, however, foreshadowed certain characteristics of modern computers that would follow. For example, the endless tape could be seen as a form of general purpose internal memory for the machine in that the machine was able to read, write, and erase—just like modern RAM (random access memory).

The Technologies of War

Like many of his contemporaries on both sides of the Atlantic, and in both the allied and enemy camps, Turing served as a consultant to the armed forces. The military high command needed powerful machines for calculating complex problems, particularly for ballistics and range-finding. In Britain, Turing worked tirelessly as a government code-breaker and was involved with

"Colossus," a British computer used for code-breaking, that was operational in December 1943. (For an enjoyable insight into the work of code-breakers during the Second World War, we recommend Neal Stephenson's [2002] "what if" novel *Cryptonomicon*). Most of the computing breakthroughs discussed in this chapter began life as military projects. The dialectic of war unleashes both terrible destruction and enormous investment in new technologies by combatant nations (IEEE Virtual Museum, 2005).

The state and private enterprise have had a long-standing and fraught relationship with armed conflict. In the twentieth century this relationship led to two major world wars and many smaller conflicts—from the Crimea to Suez, from Korea to Vietnam, and (from the 1990s onward) Iraq. Such evidence suggests that governments have been willing to gamble with the lives of citizens and with the possible destruction of their entire civil and economic infrastructure for political economic gain. The twentieth century became an era when "total war" (the mobilization of all government, military, and civilian resources towards armed conflict) and the global economy are argued to be built on the back of "war economy" and a never-ending arms race (M. Shaw, 1988, pp. 30–2).

Martin Shaw points to the complete industrialization of warfare in the twentieth century. This relies on the technological development of weapons capable of disrupting the enemy's production of armaments, breaking the distinction between civilians and combatants, and attacking the "socio-economic infrastructure of the enemy." These are the elements of "total war" that led to the development of the giant bomber plane capable of laying waste to entire cities (Dresden, large sections of London, and many other cities in Britain and Europe) and of course the "most important single military research project ever" (ibid., p. 78)—the atomic bomb.

While total war gave the United States the impetus to complete the Los Alamos research project to produce an atomic weapon, it was an idea that first germinated in 1905 when Albert Einstein theorized that splitting an atom would release large amounts of energy. It was also Einstein, in 1939, who urged the American government to begin the top-secret "Manhattan Project" that led to the hydrogen bomb. The project consumed an estimated $2 billion and employed over 120,000 people (IEEE Virtual Museum, 2005). The bomb was the epitome of the progress or end result of science and technology developed for war. Although history has tended to attribute the Manhattan Project to the United States, it was a joint project with Canada and Great Britain (Avery, 1998, p. 176). The atomic research established the basis for technological research and development of the CANDU (CANada Deuterium Uranium) system, and future atomic and nuclear energy development in Canada (ibid., Chapter 7).

This is a poignant example of Shaw's dialectic of war. To build the weapon, a vast amount of capital was diverted from other needs. When the "product" of the research was completed and used, it created even more horror and destruction—the levelling of the Japanese cities of Hiroshima and Nagasaki, resulting in tens of thousands of deaths and billions of dollars worth of destruction of infrastructure and productive capacity. Capital benefits from this destruction of value and profitability is restored through the reconstruction phase, exemplified most recently in the Middle East as presented by Canadian journalist and activist Naomi Klein in her 2008 book *The Shock Doctrine: The Rise of Disaster Capitalism* (🔳 www.naomiklein.org/shock-doctrine). The technological breakthroughs in electronics and computing coupled with the rebuilding of devastated cities and economies were the important contributors to the post-war boom in global capitalism from the late 1940s to the early 1970s.

Radar is another example of how rapid advances in technology are developed to serve the military during war. Radar was expanded in Britain using vacuum-tube technology, but it was the cooperation between British and American scientists working on microwaves that led to the building of about 100 specialized radar systems before the end of 1945. Research into rockets and jet aircraft was also boosted by the need to "weaponize" technologies in aid of the war effort. The technology of the German V-2 rocket, which the Allies captured at the end of World War II, provided the scientific knowledge necessary to launch the "space race" in the 1950s.

Post-World War II Computing and the Military–Industrial Complex

Following the technological and financial boost to computing delivered by the **military–industrial complex** during World War II, researchers in the United States continued their efforts to commercialize computers. Eckert and Mauchly left the Moore School of Electrical Engineering, where they had been academically successful, and started their own computer business. In an ironic twist of fate, their first client was the US Census Bureau, which 50 years earlier had launched Hollerith on the career that would lead to the founding of IBM. Eckert and Mauchly built the UNIVAC (UNIVersal Automatic Computer) for the Bureau, but the effort nearly sent them into bankruptcy, the final cost being close to $1 million. They were eventually bailed out by the Remington Rand Corporation and went on to build and sell 46 UNIVAC machines in direct competition with IBM (Bellis, n.d.). Throughout the 1950s computers became more and more accepted in commercial and bureaucratic applications, and the IBM "seven" series (the 701, 704, and 7090) was successful, renting for around $15,000 a month.

The invention of the transistor at the Bell Telephone Company's laboratories in the mid-1950s was a breakthrough that converged with new computing machines to increase speed and reliability. The smaller and more reliable transistors replaced valves and tubes, the machines thus becoming smaller and more portable. In 1956, John Bardeen, William Shockley, and Walter Brattain won the Nobel Prize in physics for their invention. The development of computer language in the 1950s also created momentum for computing. While working for IBM, "writing programs for computing missile trajectories" (IBM, n.d., para. 6; (🖳 www-03.ibm.com/ibm/history/ibm100/us/en/icons/fortran/), John Backus wrote one of the first high-level programming languages, FORTRAN (FORmula TRANslation), in 1954, and it was commercially released in 1957. FORTRAN significantly reduced the amount of human coding and time that was required, since the software worked with the hardware to generate specific instructions: "The program is, in essence, a compiler: A programmer using Fortran writes only 5 per cent of all instructions, and the program generates (compiles) the remaining 95 per cent for the computer" (para. 4). A second type of computer language, called "assembly language," was also being written at this time. Assembly language uses human words like *add*, but it has to be translated back into machine language—a series of zeros and ones (for "off" and "on")—before a computer can understand it. The third generation of code, HLL (high-level language), uses human syntax and vocabulary, but must be translated for a machine to "understand it." The FORTRAN breakthrough really created the software industry as we know it today, and in 1993, John Backus won the National Academy of Engineering's Charles Stark Draper Prize for the invention of FORTRAN (ibid.).

> **MILITARY–INDUSTRIAL COMPLEX**
> A term used to describe the interdependence of military and business networks and the resulting concentration of power to the extent that the overall political economy relies on armed conflict, surveillance, and security as a necessary condition of its sustenance.

Solid Circuitry to Silicon Chip

What we didn't realize then was that the integrated circuit would reduce the cost of electronic functions by a factor of a million to one, nothing had ever done that before.
(Jack Kilby, as cited in Bellis, n.d.)

There was literally a race between two men and two rival companies to come up with an integrated electronic circuit to replace transistors, resistors, capacitors, valves, and tubes. An integrated circuit allows an almost limitless increase in the number of circuits available for connection on one silicon "chip."

Jack Kilby of Texas Instruments and Robert Noyce of Fairchild Semiconductor both announced the development of an integrated circuit in 1959. In a clever commercial move, the two companies cross-licensed their technologies and created a global market now worth over USD\$1 trillion a year (that's a billion billion dollars). The original integrated circuit had only one transistor, three resistors, and one capacitor. Today they are much smaller and can hold about 125 million transistors (Bellis, n.d.).

In 1957, IBM developed the IBM 704 computer, which could perform 100,000 calculations per second. In 1958, a group of computer scientists met in Zurich and from this meeting came ALGOL (ALGOrithmic Language). ALGOL was intended to be a universal, machine-independent language, but the scientists were not successful because they did not have the same close association with IBM as FORTRAN. A derivative of ALGOL—ALGOL 60—came to be known as C, which is the standard choice for programming requiring detailed control of hardware. After that came COBOL (COmmon Business Oriented Language). Developed in 1960, COBOL was designed to produce applications for the business world and had the novel approach of separating the data descriptions from the actual program. This enabled the data descriptions to be referred to by many different programs. Today there are tens of thousands of computer programs on the market and many thousands of applications that we take for granted. Software has become a global business in its own right.

Don't Forget the State

While it has become hegemonic to associate technological progress with individual entrepreneurs or particular corporations as an example of "private-sector" innovation, few would have become dominant without the research, development, and economic support from government contracts. For example, in the United States, IBM can attribute its financial success to maintaining its ties with the US military, as its 701-series machines were used in atomic research, aircraft production, and the Department of Defense. Indeed, as reported in *Datamation* magazine, by 1961, IBM controlled 81.2 per cent of the computer market (Computer History Museum, 2006b).

Similarly, AT&T gained its dominance not only from its civilian monopoly on telephone and telecommunication services but also from its military contracts during World War I and II (D. Schiller, 2007, p. 129). Although Canada was not involved in the military or space race to the same extent as the United States—whether financially or in terms of credited computer inventions—the Cold War structurally integrated Canadian information and computer technological development into US networks whether through its major corporations (use of IBM machines and IBM branch plants) or through political and economic agreements.

In Canada, government contracts were also the anchor for the parent companies of several technology or "high-tech" firms including Nortel (formerly of Bell Canada's Bell-Northern Research labs), Mosaid Technologies, Mitel, and Corel, among other "spin-offs" (Mosco & Mazepa, 2003, pp. 94–5). The largest and most powerful and custom-designed computers (supercomputers) are still part of a government information ICT system, ranging from military computers, to weather forecasting for Environment Canada, to public hospital and health-related research, to Canada Post (which includes the establishment of postal codes in 1971 designed exclusively for computer readability).

For Real?

A Canadian Military–Industrial *Communication's* Complex (MICC)?

Particularly in the last century, the relationship between military, industrial, and communication and technological development is an intimate one, whether in the United States or Canada. One of IBM's most powerful machines was developed with the US Air Force and called the AN/FSQ-7. It was installed at the Royal Canadian Air Force (RCAF) Station North Bay in Ontario as part of its air-defence facility and its Distant Early Warning (DEW) radar line built across the Canadian north in the 1950s. This was technology meant for the Cold War to identify and track any "enemy" aircraft or munitions, making it "the first large-scale computer communications network" (Computer History Museum, 2006a, para. 2).

The network was an outgrowth of the US military funding of "research into 'command and control'—that is, computing" (Waldrop, 2008, para. 1). The research begat a machine built by MIT known as the "Whirlwind": "the first 'real time' computer capable of responding to events as fast as they occurred" (para. 3). Whirlwind would later become part of a network, or what was called the "Semi-Automatic Ground Environment," or SAGE, system that incorporated what Paul Edwards (1996) identifies as "the first large-scale, computerized command, control, and communications system" (p. 3), known in military lexicon as the 3Cs. It was particularly significant because it made command, control, and communications a *priority* of digital technological development based on "real-time control" 24/7/365. This 24/7/365 high-speed application set both the technical and normative direction for future technological development in general.

The RCAF completed the DEW Line in 1957 as its contribution to NORAD (now called the North American Aerospace Defence Command); and the technology that was used in SAGE and the IBM military projects were foundational for computing today. These included such basics as video and graphic display, techniques for analogue-to-digital and digital-to-analogue conversion, and the basics for network-building (automatic data exchange among different computers; ibid.; see wn.com/Semi_Automatic_Ground_Environment).

Such advances in technology were not limited to the interception of aircraft, but the interception of information transmitted through wireline or wireless. In Canada, the National Research Council (NRC) Examination Unit was established in 1941 to intercept foreign electronic communications and turn raw intelligence into useful intelligence reports. The NRC Communications Branch was later established (1947) to collect "intelligence" and to decipher crypto-graphic messages—to track communication and break any information code via high-speed, complex, and custom-designed computers (or supercomputers; www.cse-cst.gc.ca). It was renamed the Communications Security Establishment (CSE) in 1975 and placed under the Department of National Defence (DND). Today, its mandate includes tracking and monitoring the "global information infrastructure" to supply intelligence and "information technology security" for agencies within the federal government and the federal government itself.

Institutionally separate from the DND and the RCMP (Royal Canadian Mounted Police), the Canadian Security Intelligence Service (CSIS) was established in 1974. Where the CSE is focused on "foreign" intelligence-gathering (monitoring every kind of electronic communication originating and terminating in a country other than Canada), CSIS is focused on threats to the security of Canada, which can include domestic ones (www.csis-scrs.gc.ca/).

Decisions made at the state level have a decisive impact on how technology is developed by industries and what it is used for by both the state and the industries. It also has an impact

Continued

on the growth of specific kinds of businesses to meet government demands and the security requirements of increasingly converged networks. For example, organizations such as the Canadian Association of Defence and Security Industries (CADSI) find its membership numbers increasing as more businesses identify themselves as such in order to advance their business interests and expand their networks and lobbying strength (■ www.defenceandsecurity.ca/). Membership ranges from small, private consulting firms headed by ex-military personnel to large corporations such as IBM Canada and BCE.

Discussion Questions

1. What vision of the future is being advanced here? What is the role of the state in this future?

2. How does the use of the term *MICC* identify the relationship between politics and economics?

3. Considering the concentration of power suggested by the MICC, why do basic political economic questions regarding ownership and control become more important to our citizenship and our social and international relationships?

4. If "defense and security" are government and industry priorities, will the "surveillance society" be the new moniker for the future?

Commercial applications of computing have been driven by the largest banks and insurance companies. These were designed to allow the electronic transmission of records, accounting, as well as electronic trading through the Toronto Stock Exchange (1977). These affected business organization and record-keeping (and surveillance thereof), as well as labour. For example, the Automatic Teller Machine (ATM), introduced in the 1980s, is a historically caustic name for those (mostly women) who were working in banks at the time, considering it replaced the human labour of the bank teller. In addition, office automation would also impact labour and change typewriting to "word processing," and drive the development for compatible software (WordPerfect, Microsoft Word, and Excel) and hardware connections. But, we are getting ahead of ourselves. The Internet had not yet been developed, and its importance today is indisputable; we shall thus turn to it as our main subject in the next chapter.

Conclusion

In the Cold War environment, after World War II, the decision-makers in the United States responded to what they viewed as a "threat" by the looming technological superiority of the USSR, as demonstrated by the successful launch of the *Sputnik* satellite in 1957. During Eisenhower's presidency, the Pentagon poured millions not only into the space race but also into advanced computer research at major universities, such as MIT and Stanford. The Kennedy administration would continue this practice. It was Eisenhower's combined experience as a former military general and president of the United States, however, which caused him to warn of the "military–industrial complex" in his farewell address to the American people in 1961 (■ www.youtube.com/watch?v=8y06NSBBRtY). A less politically and economically charged history focuses on California in 1969 with the first American attempt to network two computers (Hafner & Lyon, 2003, p. 152). It crashed as the scientists entered the letter *G*, the third letter of the log-in sequence (LOGIN). It was an inauspicious kick for a digital revolution that had been two-and-a-half millennia in the making.

From the beginning of the 1960s, and on the foundations laid in the post-war years, computing began to take off at an exponential speed. At the heart of this growth was the silicon chip, which Mary Bellis (n.d.) describes as one of the most important innovations ever. Nearly all of our modern electrical products use some form of chip technology. Through the history outlined here we have discussed the first four generations of computers from the giant hard-wired punch card and tape machines of the Industrial Revolution to the transistor and solid-state circuit commercial machines produced by Remington Rand and IBM in the 1950s. We have also briefly reviewed the close connection between the growing military–industrial complex and computing and communication.

Until the 1960s, computing had been a "stand alone" application used mainly in industrial, military, and pure research settings. The next wave, which some suggest constituted a "Golden Age" of computing, began when computers extended from the laboratories and military installations into the office, the home, and the classroom. In the next chapter we continue the story of computing by looking at particular breakthroughs from the 1980s onward and the innovations of so-called computer "geeks" like Steve Jobs and Bill Gates in places like the now-famous Silicon Valley in central California.

Key Points

- Convergence is not a new idea, but it is one of the key processes that underlies all technological innovation and change.

- The need and desire to develop "thinking machines" has been an integral part of the human story since Neolithic times.

- Technological innovation and change cannot be adequately understood unless we understand the social and historical context in which these changes are taking place and the kind of development that it favours.

- The process of convergence ensures that new technologies in the field of numerical calculation (computing) build on the insights, achievements, and failures of previous generations, which were not random, but selective, in terms of what applications they were developed for and what labour they replaced.

Class Discussion

1. What is your understanding of "progress" and how has it been influenced by technological change?

2. Why is the historical relationship of labour and technology so important in today's working environment?

3. Given the historical development of its technology, is control an inseparable function of the computer? And if so, where is control located: in the programming (code), the operator, the property owner, or the network?

Media on Media

Tuning into Digital?

Brad Paisley. (2007). Online. *5th Gear*. US: Arista Nashville. 🖥 www.cowboylyrics.com/lyrics/paisley-brad/online-22297.html

Ice Cube. (1990). Turn off the radio. *AmeriKKKa's Most Wanted*. US: Priority. 🖥 www.stlyrics.com/songs/i/icecube1889/turnofftheradio89508.html

Movies, Docs, and Videos

Gliner, R. (Writer). (2000). *Time frenzy: Keeping up with tomorrow* [Documentary]. US: Films Media Group.

Spingarn-Koff, J. (Director). (2010). *Life 2.0* [Documentary]. US: PalmStar Entertainment.

Stahl, R. (Producer). (2007). *Militainment Inc.: Militarism & pop culture* [Documentary]. US: Media Education Foundation.

Timeline: A (Modern) History of Computers—Part 1

1801 Joseph-Marie Jacquard patents the automatic loom (the Jacquard loom) for weaving cloth controlled by punch cards.

1837 Charles Babbage invents the Analytical Engine; calculations are completed by the machine by reading, processing, and storing data from punch cards.

1890 Herman Hollerith invents the Hollerith tabulating machine, and adds numbers and letters to the punch card, which are read electronically via a set of electrical on/off contacts. Hollerith gets a contract for processing the 1900 (US) Census using punched cards. His first firm is named IBM in 1924.

1895 Northern Electric and Manufacturing Company (the future Nortel) is founded, a spin-off of Bell Mechanical Department.

1915 Northern Electric designs "telegraphic switching" technology specifically for use by the Canadian military.

1918 German engineer Arthur Scherbius invents and patents the Enigma machine, the first *cipher* machine that encrypts data for transmission and reception.

1936 Alan Turing writes *On Computable Numbers*, and describes the "universal computing machine," or Turing machine.

LATE 1930s German civil engineer Konrad Zuse develops the Z1 model computer, acknowledged as the world's first fully programmable computer using valves. It is followed by the Z3 (1941), which uses binary math and Boolean logic in electronic calculation representing data in zeros and ones (bits).

1939 John V. Atanosoff and Clifford Berry develop the first electronic digital computer.

1941 The Canadian government establishes the National Research Council (NRC) Examination Unit to intercept foreign electronic communications.

1942 The Manhattan Project (US-, UK-, and Canadian-directed research leading to the development of the atomic bomb) begins.

1944 Howard Aiken and a team at Harvard develop the Harvard Mark I computer, also called the Automatic Sequence Controlled Calculator (ASCC).

1945 Vannevar Bush defines hypertext language, the basis of HTML.

The Electronic Numerical Integrator and Computer (ENIAC), the first high-speed electronic digital computer using vacuum tubes, is developed.

1947 Bell Labs' scientists John Bardeen, Walter Brattain, and William Shockley invent the transistor.

The Canadian government establishes the NRC Communications Branch to collect "intelligence," and to detect or decipher code.

1948 Norbert Wiener publishes *Cybernetics* (meaning "steersman" in Greek) based on his experiments using machines to anticipate and predict the course of an airplane based on radar traction; it's used to develop military air-defence systems.

Claude Shannon publishes *The Mathematical Theory of Communication* to construct computer code that could check itself for accuracy after the transmission between computers. The article is later (1963) worked into an influential book (with Warren Weaver) that quantifies information—and by association, communication—as explained via a messaging or transmission model consisting of sender-channel-receiver, feedback and noise.

1951 Remington Rand (a former typewriter and adding-machine company) delivers the first commercial computer to the US Census Bureau, the UNIVAC.

1953   International Business Machines (IBM), later known as Big Blue, enters the computer market with its 701 EDPM model.

1954   Silicon-based junction transistors, replacing vacuum tubes, are produced.

1957   FORmula TRANslation (FORTRAN) programming language is released by IBM.

The first earth-orbiting Russian satellite, *Sputnik*, is launched and transmits the first radio signals from space.

1958   Jack Kilby and Robert Noyce invent the silicon chip—the first integrated circuit.

The Advanced Research Projects Agency (ARPA) is founded by the US government Department of Defense in direct response to the Russian satellite launch, marking the beginning of a "space race."

The laser is invented by Bell Labs' scientists Arthur Schawlow and Charles Townes.

1961   General Motors puts its first industrial robot to use on its assembly line.

1962   MIT students invent SPACEWAR!, the first interactive computer (video) game.

1963   Electronic home-computer kits are commercially available to hobbyists.

1964   Douglas Engelbart invents the computer mouse.

IBM introduces System/360.

1965   The concept of hypertext is conceived: Ted Nelson envisions a "docuverse" in which all documents can be connected to other documents and navigated via links.

1968   UNIX is developed by Ken Thompson and Dennis Ritchie at Bell Labs. UNIX is subsequently trademarked by The Open Group and only available through licensing.

Xerox opens its Palo Alto Research Centre in Santa Clara Valley, California. The area would later be called "Silicon Valley."

1969   The Advanced Research Projects Agency Network (ARPANET) is conceived.

PART III
Re-Emergence of Convergence:
New Century, New Media?

Objectives

The chapters in this section explore the ways in which computers and media technologies have converged in order that we might further tease out the digital dialectic. We identify and examine some myths of the digital age and the legal and regulatory regimes that are struggling with the transition from broadcasting to narrowcasting, and the kinds of decisions that affect how we use technology, and make and participate in media. This section will, we hope, allow you to develop further insights into the issues and keywords raised in its chapters. In particular, you should gain a greater understanding of the following:

- what we mean by "convergence" when we're talking about the digital technologies of communication and media;

- how the concept of convergence is almost as old as technology itself, and how technological change *always* and *only* takes place in a social context;

- *why* we place as much, if not more, emphasis on the social conditions in which digital convergence takes place as we do on the technologies themselves; and

- how the move to digital affects the globalized political economy, and the dynamics of technology and social relations in both utopian and dystopian expressions of convergence.

Keywords

- citizen-journalist
- communication rights
- dot.com crash
- globalization
- Golden Age
- participatory journalism

We begin this section of the book with a chapter that continues to trace the history of computing into the twenty-first century. It's a history that may not be what you are expecting. It's not just a matter of following a long list of technological changes, but with our focus on political economy, we make a particular effort to identify the history of inventions and decision-making in Canada that shape how we use and encounter computer networking and the Internet today. It is a history that is not well known, given the usual American emphasis and claims staked on many inventions, but you may find a number of surprising "firsts" that were invented, experimented, and developed in Canada, as the Chapter 7 Timeline identifies.

It is important in Chapter 8 to consider how computers went from being huge mainframes with buildings and rooms of their own—used and owned by large organizations like the government, military, and business corporations—to the desktop, laptop, or "smart phone" that can be held in your hands. The transition to narrowcast is even evident here as the mainframe computer became the "personal computer"—custom-ordered, custom-fit—made for individual use.

Along the way, of course, we debunk some enduring myths about computer technology and networking, and take you through the constructed frontiers of Cyberia, Silicon Valley, and the global village, and meet its inhabitants: the so-called geeks and hackers, "hacktivists," and techno-gurus—who you may be more familiar with—and the cyber-myths that accompany them—which may not be so well known. One of these myths is the unquestioned association of technology with progress, and how that progress can suddenly reach a crisis and end without warning, while we are left to cope with the fallout well into the future.

In Chapter 9, we take a related tack and consider, in detail, the question of policy convergence in relation to new media, and the dialectic of broadcasting and narrowcasting through a dynamic process of government decision-making. In this chapter (which may take you longer to read if you haven't been introduced to policy before), we want to introduce you to how the process works, and since, as we've already covered, most decision-making on broadcasting and telecommunication is made at the federal government level, we will introduce you to these modes of governance on national and international levels. Even here, we can see that the policy environment is marked by a history of myths that, we argue—and yes, we will put forth several arguments for you to consider here—connect the age of broadcast and narrowcast and still mark decision-making on communication today.

Of all the chapters in this book, Chapter 9 has the most Canadian content (we should apply for a grant!), and, given our earlier caveat, we are now going into some heavier territory. While policy can appear boring or complex, or both (and in practice, it sometimes is), this should perhaps prompt you to question why this is so. Why are we more familiar with all the programs we like on TV, or the latest celebrity gossip, dance, or pet video on YouTube, than we are with the political economic infrastructure and the decision-making that generates it? Complexity shouldn't keep you from learning how something works, and more importantly, when it comes to policy-making, from learning how you can participate in it. If we don't make the effort to inform ourselves about the process, we empower others to do so for us, and since *power* is what policy-making is all about, this should be an exciting and motivating chapter as much as it is demanding.

The final chapter in this section brings the previous readings on press and broadcasting history together with technological and economic convergence to consider the state of journalism today from a political economy perspective. Of course, in order to distinguish what is different today from the past, we need to first take a small trip back in history to follow how—and moreover *why*—changes have been made in the making of media. We thus take up what we started in Chapter 4, from the beginning, when journalism was identified as a "craft," and we move towards how it was made into a "profession," which we may still associate it with today. Along the way we consider issues in news-making like ethics in media and responsibilities of news organizations, governments, and citizens.

You are likely now familiar with the terms *citizen-journalist* or *user-generated content*, which suggest a fundamental change to both journalism and journalists. We consider these in detail in Chapter 10 while centering on both the production of news (as industry, as technology) and the labour of the journalist. It is this latter consideration that is especially food for thought: Has the news been narrowcast? Are we all journalists and entrepreneurs now?

8

The Golden Age of the Internet?

As people once hailed the Telegraph Age, the Age of Electricity, the Age of the Telephone, the Age of Radio, or the Age of Television, we are now said to be in the Age of the Computer. (Mosco, 2004a, p. 2)

This chapter follows the transition from computing technology to the development of computer-mediated communication and computer networking via the Internet. With the benefit of hindsight, this chapter analyzes this transition by comparing past predictions and potentials with existing practices and the social narratives that accompany them. In our review, we also seek to explore some of the myths about the Internet. We take as our starting point Vincent Mosco's argument about the "digital sublime." According to this idea, the digital revolution generates and sustains "important myths about our time" (ibid., pp. 2–3), which support the notion that we are experiencing an "epochal transformation" that overturns our common beliefs about time, space, and power. These myths offer us an "entrance to a new reality," which may be characterized by "the promise of the sublime" (p. 3).

We are particularly interested in what might constitute a "Golden Age" for the Internet, how we might define it and how we might measure both its length (timespan) and its depth (how ingrained the ideological memes that deliver and support the idea may have become in our collective consciousness and in our culture). This means we have to situate our discussion of the Golden Age historically: When did it start? Has it ended yet? How much further into the future might it extend? Is the "Golden Age of the Internet" unfolding, or are we blinded by the offerings of fool's gold?

Objectives

To evaluate these questions and others, in this chapter we want you to consider the following:

- how the development of the Internet, and of digital media, has occurred in phases that have their own distinct material features and their own mythologies;

- how the "dream" of the Internet may be very close to Marshall McLuhan's concept of the "global village," but how the view that the Internet has had (or is having) a Golden Age must be read in a historical context and with critical reflection; and

- if we accept that the reality of the Internet is constituted by the same social relations that sustain inequality in other areas of our lives, shouldn't considerations of money, power, and geographic location also inform our usage and decisions on its future development?

Keywords

- **Cyberia**
- **deus ex machina**
- **dot.com boom**
- **dot.com crash**
- **global village**

- **Golden Age**
- **hacking**
- **new media**
- **personal computer (PC)**

Our journey into and through the Golden Age of the Internet begins with the utopian dreams and technological wizardry of the underground guerrilla armies of the digital revolution. Manuel Castells (2000) documents the "sprawling computer counterculture" associated with the "aftershocks" of the "libertarian/utopian" (p. 49) 1960s as a vital element of the dialectic of convergence. He cites the example from 1978 of how two Chicago students invented the first modem (the "blue box") to send files over the phone so they didn't have to travel in Windy City winter. This ability to create new possibilities using technology lies at the heart of its innovation, but how that technology is used, by whom, and for what purposes is constituted through social struggle and the political economy in which it develops. Given the speed of change and the extent of possibilities using technology—ranging from the enhancement and extension of life itself to its total annihilation—the discourse and predictions that surround it have been equally intense. Keep this in mind as we consider the ways its history is told and our future is predicted.

The Golden Age of the Internet

High technology and high magic are the same thing. They both use tools from inner resources and outer resources. Magic from the ancient past and technology from the future are really both one. That is how we are creating the present; we're speeding up things, we are quickening our energies; time and space are not as rigid as they used to be; the belief system isn't there. Those who did control it have left the plane; they have been forced out because it no longer is their time. Those of us who know how to work through time and space are using our abilities to bend *time and space into a reality that will benefit people the most.*

When Green Fire says all this to your face, believe it or not, it makes sense, especially in a Cyberian context. (Rushkoff, 1994, p. 188)

When reading this passage from Douglas Rushkoff's *Cyberia*, it helps to know that Green Fire is a modern urban witch—a psychic, and probably into serious drugs. But Green Fire is typical of the characters who inhabited the San Francisco Bay Area in the 1980s and 1990s as described in Rushkoff's meandering, journalistic search for the optimistic (rather than the pessimistic) roots of cyberspace. To understand the origins of the sublime myths of the Internet, however, we have to go back further, 20 more years, to the early 1970s.

We deliberately ended the previous chapter in the late 1960s when computing was just beginning to be applied to commercial applications and computer networking was in its infancy. The now almost ubiquitous **personal computer** (PC) was still only a good idea, and the silicon

PERSONAL COMPUTER (PC)
Also called a mini-, micro-, or desktop computer, it was so-named to distinguish it from mainframe computers and servers housed in large businesses and organizations. PCs came of age in the 1980s, as a comparatively low cost and accessible means of processing information by smaller businesses and individuals.

chip had not yet been transferred from the laboratory computer to a commodity of everyday use. As most histories of the computer recount, the "geek," the so-called genius of the digital revolution, was not yet fully formed. In order for this to happen, like the larva of a butterfly, it had to find a safe place to rest in order to fortify and transform, extending from the university lab to experiments in the home garage. Different than the radio hobbyists of the past, however, these techno-geeks sought to capitalize on their inventions and became entrepreneurs, commodifying their wares and starting their own businesses. Most of this geek chrysalis development took place in California, near the desert city of Palo Alto—at the place now called Silicon Valley.

Flowering in the Desert: The Silicon Valley Boom

In the previous chapter we outlined the history of computing from the earliest forms of digital calculation—literally, counting on fingers—to the development of the first prototypes of the modern computer in the early 1960s. We left that story at the time when the high-tech commercial industries located on the fringe of the California desert were beginning to take root. As we commented towards the end of that chapter, the development of "machine language" and computer code has now developed into what Samuel Butler (1872/1967), in the late nineteenth century, predicted would become "a speech as intricate as our own" (p. 147). This development began in the 1940s, but did not really come into fruition until 30 years later, in California. Such an initial time-lag for development is evident in many of the inventions that are now common to the personal computer, but were first demonstrated in laboratories in the 1960s.

While working at the Stanford Research Institute in California in 1968, for example, Doug Engelbart demonstrated the use of a computer "mouse," so named because of its size, shape, and "tail" connections. Four years later, the lab added a word processor, an early hypertext system, and a collaborative application. It was also during this time that the (arguably) most significant development in computer technology was invented—the silicon chip. The chip was invented in 1959 and patented by Robert Noyce who, in 1968, founded the giant silicon chip manufacturer Intel with Gordon Moore.

According to Intel, Moore first predicted that the number of transistors that could be placed on a chip would double every two years (Intel, n.d., para. 2; ■ www.intel.com/technology/mooreslaw/). Given the exponential increase over the last 40 years (from over 2,000 transistors on one chip in 1971 to over 2.5 trillion today), there is a high degree of reliability in this prediction. While it is still arguable whether such a prediction is mathematically accurate, however, what is more significant is the *idea* that accompanies it—that all technological development is similarly relentless (Kaplan, 2011). In this view, both the size and speed of technological change is associated with innovation as the best indicator of *progress*. Accordingly, questions regarding ethics or policy fall by the wayside, or are relatively insignificant compared to the "natural" progression of technology. Primary importance is placed on the technological innovation rather than the political economic and social context of its development and use.

A purely technology-focused history thus lauds the time when American corporation Xerox (perhaps best known for its brand of photocopiers) created its Palo Alto Research Center, or PARC, in southern California, establishing what would become known as Silicon Valley. Yet, there was a lot more going on at the time in terms of social totality. The 1960s were also significant as a sustained challenge to social relations in the movements for civil rights, with protests on the streets and on university campuses against systemic racism, sexism, violence, and war. At the same time as university campuses were sites of activism, technological development moved off campus.

Distinguishing itself from the "low-tech" machines of the factory, this development signalled a transition to a new way of doing things—and was hence dubbed "high-tech" in that digitization (the conversion of information into bits and bytes) was its marker.

As would become common to other high-tech companies, Xerox built its facilities with financial support from the universities (particularly Washington University) and on university lands leased from Stanford—establishing the basis for primarily private ownership of the location and the research centres. As other entrepreneurs and corporations set up shop in southern California, they established what is called a "clustering effect"—and such a model of public support of private development is still promoted as the primary way that innovation occurs (Kukalis, 2010; Ontario Ministry of Tourism and Culture, 2010).

The development of such hardware like the chip would enable the advancement of a number of software applications. In the late 1960s, a Swiss computer scientist, Niklaus Wirth, developed the first of many computer programming languages. His first language, called Pascal, forced programmers to program in a structured, logical fashion and pay close attention to the different types of data in use. He later followed up on Pascal with Modula-2 and 3, which were very similar to Pascal in structure and syntax. Fairchild Semiconductor introduced a 256-bit RAM chip in 1970. It was on the back of these developments, innovations, and new products that Silicon Valley became a booming hub of the digital revolution. In late 1970, Intel introduced a 1-K RAM chip and the 4004, a 4-bit microprocessor. The 8008, an 8-bit microprocessor, came two years later.

Transforming the Computing Machine into the Personal Computer

It was not until the mid-1960s that the third generation of computers came into being. These were characterized by solid state technology and integrated circuitry coupled with extreme miniaturization. A series of events in the early 1970s can, with the benefit of hindsight, be seen as critically important to the myths of the Internet's **Golden Age**. In 1971, Bill Gates and Paul Allen formed Traf-O-Data and found a buyer for their computer traffic-analysis systems. In the same year, Steve Jobs and Steve Wozniak were building and selling blue boxes in southern California. The fourth generation of computers was characterized by further miniaturization of circuit, increased multiprogramming, and virtual storage memory.

In 1971, Intel released the first microprocessor, a specialized integrated circuit that was able to process four bits of data at a time. The chip included its own arithmetic logic unit, but a sizable portion of the chip was taken up by the control circuits for organizing the work, which left less room for the data-handling circuitry. Thousands of hobbyists could now aspire to own their own personal computer. Up to this point, computers had been strictly the preserve of the military, universities, and very large corporations simply because of the enormous size and cost of the machine and its maintenance.

The PC did not naturally enter office and domestic use; it was first marketed to the home hobbyist. In 1975, the cover of *Popular Electronics* featured a story on the "world's first minicomputer kit to rival commercial models . . . Altair 8800." The Altair, produced by a company called Micro Instrumentation and Telemetry Systems (MITS) retailed for $397, which made it easily affordable for the small but growing hobbyist or techno-geek community. The Altair was not designed for your computer novice. The kit required assembly by the owner, and then it was necessary to write software for the machine since none was yet publicly or commercially available. The Altair had a 256-byte memory—about the size of a paragraph, and needed to be coded in machine code—zeros and ones. The programming was accomplished by manually flipping switches located on the front of the Altair.

GOLDEN AGE
The idea that, in looking back, there was a halcyon period in history in which everything was bright and beautiful.

Two young hobbyists were intrigued by the Altair, having seen the article in *Popular Electronics*. They decided on their own that the Altair needed software and took it upon themselves to contact MITS' owner Ed Roberts, and offered to provide him with a BASIC language that would run on the Altair. BASIC (Beginner's All-purpose Symbolic Instruction Code) had originally been developed in 1963 by Thomas Kurtz and John Kemeny, members of the Dartmouth College Mathematics Department. BASIC was designed to provide an interactive, easy method for upcoming computer scientists to program computers. It allowed the usage of statements such as "print 'hello'" or "let b = 10." It would have been a great boost for the Altair if BASIC had been available, so Roberts agreed to pay for it if it worked. The two young hobbyists—Bill Gates and Paul Allen—worked feverishly and finished just in time to present it to Roberts. It was a success. Gates and Allen went on to form Microsoft and produce BASIC and other operating systems for various machines.

Following the introduction of the Altair, a veritable explosion of personal computers occurred, starting with Steve Jobs and Steve Wozniak exhibiting the first Apple II at the first West Coast Computer Faire in San Francisco in 1977. The Apple II boasted built-in BASIC, colour graphics, and a 4,100-character memory for "only" USD$1,298. Programs and data could be stored on an everyday audio-cassette recorder. Before the end of the fair, Wozniak and Jobs had secured the start of a commercial business, selling 300 orders for the Apple II, and from there Apple's business has never looked back; by way of vertical integration it continues to develop technology for commercial growth.

Another lesser-known variant of the home computer was marketed in 1977: The TRS-80 was introduced as a home computer manufactured by Tandy–Radio Shack. In its second incarnation, the TRS-80 Model II, it came complete with a 64,000-character memory and a disk drive to store programs and data on. At this time, only Apple and TRS had machines with disk drives. With the introduction of the disk drive, personal computer applications took off as a floppy disk was a most convenient publishing medium for the distribution of software.

IBM, which up to this time had been producing mainframes and minicomputers for medium- to large-sized businesses, decided that it had to get into the act and started working on the Acorn, which would later be called the IBM PC. This PC was the first computer designed for the home market that would feature modular design so that pieces could easily be added to the architecture. Most of the components, surprisingly, came from outside IBM, since building it with IBM parts would have cost too much for the home computer market. When it was introduced, the PC came with a 16,000-character memory, a keyboard from an IBM electric typewriter, and a connection for a tape-cassette player for USD$1,265.

The PC's *use value* was thus being defined by the commercial development of the technology, and its future trajectory was one based on its exchange value. Via aggressive marketing campaigns, the owners of the means of production—corporations like Microsoft, Apple, and IBM—condensed the mainframe computer and moved the "desktop" computer into homes and businesses. Marketers and advertisers finessed the language of computing and machinery to something more acceptable, less threatening, and less intrusive. This mitigated any reluctance to its use in business, and what might be considered an intrusion of personal space, by deflecting the impersonal language of technology with the language of social relations (Marvin, 1988, p. 154). The micro-computer became the "personal" computer—humanized, intimate, and part of the "family." Similarly, the introduction of the "home office" was encouraged as a positive and desirable change, while further extending relations of production by blurring distinctions between the two. Work done at the office could now be done at home.

Initially, it was a hard sell: The television was the dominant entertainment technology in private homes, and office machines had previously been the purview of accountants and (generally female) secretaries. The adding machine and typewriter had to be replaced with the "spreadsheet" and "word processor"; workers could become more productive or replaced altogether, while the "executive" required training to first accept and then use the computer as the basis for business success.

The acceptance of the computer was negotiated via existing social relations and relationships between commodification and labour, and conception and execution. One of the challenges was to convince middle- and upper-management that using the computer would not disturb the labour hierarchy or reduce managerial control (Mosco, 1989, p. 30). Moreover, it could not be seen as a threat to management such that its use wouldn't indicate that their workers' jobs would be downgraded to secretarial (or women's) work, or, worse still, be reduced to those of manual labourers only tending a machine.

In 1983, supported by its major high-tech advertisers, *Time* magazine substituted its "Man of the Year" issue with the "Machine of the Year" (3 January, Vol. 121, No. 1). The male leaders of technological development or "micro-maestros" were introduced; a "Hacker's Guide" explained the "lingo" used by "computer fanatics," and the editorial told its American readers about the digital sublime—that this was a future everyone desired: "You wished it here because the country was running low on dream time. Which provides equal time. I'm talking social equality. I'm talking freedom with a capital F, like when the railroad first rolled in 150 years ago" (Rosenblatt, 1983, p. 7). Even with such talk of freedom, the editorial added a qualifier—an exchange value was the necessary prerequisite: "There's a New World coming again, looming on the desktop. Oh, say, can you see it? Major credit cards accepted" (ibid.).

This brief overview sets the stage for one explanation of the myth that says the Golden Age perhaps began in Silicon Valley. This was not something that those at the epicentre were necessarily aware of. The seeds of the digital sublime were planted in desert sands and marketed in the commercial press, but they now needed to be culturally tended in order to flourish. This could only happen away from the hothouse atmosphere of Palo Alto and when the PC became more than just a geek toy. To sustain itself and spread, a mimetic myth needs a host organism—in this case a host community. Both of these conditions were met once the chip manufacturers found a way to increase the processing speed and memory-storage capacity and when a market opened up for the new "thinking machines." The host community for the cultural myths of a Golden Age were none other than Rushkoff's "cyberians" and "cybergypsies"—the early adopters of the new technology.

Indra Sinha was an early traveller on the electronic frontier and described himself as a "cybergypsy" in his book *The cybergypsies* (Sinha, 1999). Sinha, in real life an advertising copy-writer, began his exploration of cyberspace in 1984 when the Internet first became publicly available in the UK via a university network known as JANET. Like the cyberians, the cybergypsies were utopian, free-thinking, and disdainful of the commercialization of the developing World Wide Web that was beginning to coalesce around them. The cybergypsies were pioneers of the online gaming world (one vastly different from today). They also haunted the early bulletin boards like Fido and Shades, places where they could entertain each other and hold endless "conversations": "Cybergypsies like free-flowing, live, subtle interaction and internet chat is banal and brutish, compared with the range of expression afforded by Shades or the Fidonet bulletin board" (ibid., p. 59).

Unlike the cyberians of America, Sinha and his cybergypsies mostly lived out their drug fantasies at one remove—they didn't actually ingest any substances, but they felt a strong connection with nineteenth-century writers like Samuel T. Coleridge, who indulged in a heavy opium habit and argued that if you wrote fiction with enough factual referents, the reader would

ONGOING ISSUES

Searching for Freedom in Cyberspace?

Psychedelics appear to be a "given" in Silicon Valley. They are an institution . . . the infrastructure has accommodated them. (Rushkoff, 1994, p. 48)

According to Rushkoff, in the 1980s a list was circulating among the geek crowd alerting them to which Silicon Valley companies had a "cool" attitude towards hard drugs and which ones insisted on urine-testing their staff. He asserts that in the heyday of the Valley, when it was full of innovative young people, the "industry leaders" would turn a blind eye to drug use among their employees because they knew that the "psychedelic-using cyberians" were creating the "computer revolution" at places like Xerox's PARC (p. 49). There was a clear "tug of war" going on in Silicon Valley at that time: on one end of the rope the military–industrial complex and on the other the "heretics"—"pot smokers and psychedelics-users" (p. 50)—who perhaps saw themselves as disassociated from the military–industrial complex because of their lifestyle. But it wasn't just the geeks and nerds who were getting high and putting their extensive creative talents to work. Computers found their way very quickly into the remnants of the hippy underground.

Rushkoff's exploration of **Cyberia** in the Bay Area of San Francisco led him to a secret world of designer drugs that were being manufactured and consumed in order to create a "new designer reality" that more closely resembled the ideal utopian world that the cyberians were trying to create (p. 109). It also had a serious political side. The cyberians were opposed to the tough American drug laws and saw their efforts as a way of developing a counter-offensive about "good drugs and bad drug laws" (p. 145). The psychedelic and "smart" drugs that the cyberians messed around with also had an intimate connection to their travels in cyberspace and their enthusiasm for "virtual reality": "Psychedelics and VR are both ways of creating a new, non-linear reality, where self expression is a community event . . . a kind of technological philosopher's stone, bringing an inkling of the future reality into the present . . . and an active, creative effort by cyberians to reach that future" (p. 84).

We are not, by mentioning this here, encouraging the use of psychedelic drugs. Our purpose is to show how, within the community of cyberians, the mimetic seed of the Golden Age idea began to take root. It was a utopian idea that grew out of the cyberian dissociation from, and dissatisfaction with, what was happening in the "straight" and unconnected world around them. Many of the important carriers of the techno-meme of the Golden Age were people who had grown

CYBERIA

A play on the word *Siberia*—denigrated as a frozen wasteland in Russia—suggesting that the digital future itself is a dystopian wasteland.

"suspend their disbelief" in order to accept the narrative. The cybergypsies' engagement with the online world of gaming, bulletin boards, and fantasy-reality took place in an imaginary landscape, accessed via a modem and a telephone line: "In cyberspace, for the first time, we create imaginary worlds which can truly be shared, in which each of us is fully present, with the power of free and spontaneous action" (p. 131).

Today, the characters who inhabit the online world of the cybergypsies might seem a little quaint, or even downright weird, but 30 years ago they were living out a fantasy of their own Internet Golden Age, complete with cyberspace marriages and honeymoons and even the odd pervert like "Nasty Ned" who traded pornography from his bulletin board, long before pornography took over the Web almost completely—given that now, pornography is second only to up in the Bohemian atmosphere of the 1960s, and they appear—like the "father" of LSD, Timothy Leary—in the pages of *Cyberia*. These characters tell Rushkoff again and again that Cyberia is a new frontier, a seismic tipping point for society at large and a fault line between the old society and the new. Perhaps it was an attempt to extend the civil rights movement into technology, but for the cyberians it is a continuing struggle that involves generating a new reality very different from the constraining real world outside. As described by Rushkoff, it is a new consciousness that is all-embracing "on a personal, theoretical, political, technological, or even spiritual level" (p. 92).

Today, such dreams do not contradict the promises of the marketing campaigns of the high-tech corporations. Appeals to uninhibited recreation and independence still dominate the promise of the "cool jobs" in high technology and the so-called creative class (Florida, 2012). As Gina Neff, Elizabeth Wissinger, and Sharon Zukin (2005) review in their article on "'cool' jobs in 'hot'" industries, the focus on freedom and independence is used to attract employees—particularly young people—to work under "flexible working conditions." Using language borrowed from the ideology of individualism and capitalism, that everyone can (and should) become an entrepreneur together with all the purported creativity, excitement, and the appeal appears to be working. Their research indicated that

> *the common characteristic of new entrepreneurial workers, regardless of their specific activities and rewards, is that they share a more explicit, individualized, profit-oriented risk—a risk that aligns them both economically and culturally with firm founders and employers in a "winner-take-all" society (Frank and Cook 1996). Although not all workers have access to the financial profits, high-profile clients or edgy image of culture industries, the prevalence of these attributes in popular discourse publicizes and promotes the normalization of workers' bearing risk. (Neff, Wissinger, & Zukin, 2005, p. 310)*

We discuss the particulars of work in media specifically in Chapter 10, but for now we want to flag it as an issue to prompt discussion, particularly as labour conditions for youth become more precarious. Richard Maxwell and Toby Miller (2005) ask us to think about what kind of freedom is being offered here as "the casualized work conditions of the cybertarian in jobs that promise freedom" from neckties and hemlines, from established working hours and explicit management hierarchies, also mean freedom from regular paycheques, health benefits, and overtime pay (p. 266).

commercial traffic in worldwide Internet use (TopTenReviews, 2006; 🖼 internet-filter-review. toptenreviews.com/internet-pornography-statistics.html). But in the promise of this imagined community, said Sinha (1999), the line between "reality" and cyberspace appeared permeable and thin; they seemed to "mirror one another" (p. 142). Nevertheless, like the cyberians, the goal had its ethical and normative potentials, as the cybergypsies also recognized its political potential.

Taking Freedom Seriously

The freedom possible with the use of personal computers included a vision to advance progressive social justice. In 1987, Sinha joined one of the first activist web rings in the UK, GreenNet, to campaign on behalf of Iraqi Kurds who had recently been attacked with poison gas by Saddam Hussein's troops in the north of the country. This quickly morphed into a real-life political campaign, and when the Gulf War started at the end of 1990, Sinha began using GreenNet to campaign against government censorship of news. Such optimism for use of the Internet is part of what is now called "social media," and it still exists today even though it can be tempered with the experience of hindsight (Drache, 2008). In 1991, however, it seemed that the Internet was a new tool that would herald a Golden Age of political openness: "I became aware of the enormous power of the internet to subvert and nullify the attempts of governments, corporations and media moguls to stifle free speech" (Sinha, 1999, p. 177).

Equally optimistic forecasts predicted an increasingly democratic future based on the interactive communication and networking afforded by the new technology. Novel terms such as *televoting* (Slaton, 1992), *teledemocracy* (Akerton, 1987), *hyperdemocracy* (Wright, 1995), and *CyberDemocracy* (Poster, 1995) entered academic and media lexicon as indicators of change. Appreciating that each technological change has been accompanied by such potential, political economists of communication continued to underscore that questions of ownership, control, and access were still central in the decidedly undemocratic development and use of information and communication technologies (ICTs). This included the capacity to increase control over political, economic, and cultural resources (Robins & Webster, 1983) as well as people (Gandy, 1988; Harvey, 1989), as intensified by the use of technology for surveillance (Zuboff, 1988). In *The Pay-Per Society*, Mosco (1989) suggested, for example, that the reason why computers were being so closely associated with democracy was largely due to a "common concern about the state of democracy worldwide" (p. 69) and a belief that computers were the **deus ex machina** solution.

The impetus to develop networks through what was then called "computer-mediated communication" (or CMC) was the idea accompanying broadcasting—that its use value was paramount. Just as the broadcasting spectrum is public, access to the spectrum necessary for computer networking to function should also be public. This is considered fundamental to the development of what is called "civil society," particularly for participation in decision-making that could not be subject to repressive government or corporate filtering or control.

Computer networks like GreenNet were supplemented by networks such as PeaceNet, Econet, Women'sNet, and a host of "community freenets" as both evidence and demonstrations of the use of CMC by people dedicated to public action rather than market values (Bonchek, 1995; Downing et al., 1991; Kramarae, 1988; E. Lee, 1997; P. Lewis, 1993). Experiments in progressive computer networking in Canada began very early in the 1980s when the Canadian Union of Public Employees developed the Solidarity Network (or SoliNet), establishing the first national, bilingual computer conferencing system in Canada and the first national labour network in the world (E. Lee, 1997; Mazepa, 1997). Its development was in tandem with the establishment of local computer networks in the 1980s and 1990s in cities across Canada and the United States, in community freenets that provided public access to the Web and email facilities for little or no charge. These were primarily locally based operations (e.g., in Ottawa, the National Capital FreeNet) that depended on the work of volunteers and on the donations of those who could afford to pay for access (J. Weston, 1997). As Brian Murphy (2002) identifies, by 1999, these "autonomous civil society computer networks" (pp. 36–7) were unique to the United States and Canada—with 114 operating in the United States and 67 in Canada, compared to only 10 in the rest of the world—and remain examples of an Internet prior and in opposition to its commodification and commercialization (Kozolanka, Mazepa, & Skinner, 2012b, pp. 13–14).

DEUS EX MACHINA

A phrase from Ancient Greek and Roman drama, it refers to an active agent, "a power or event that comes in the nick of time to solve difficulty" (Sykes, 1982, p. 261).

A Phreaking History

The third important group inhabiting cyberspace during its potential Golden Age were the hackers. In a sense, **hacking** preceded many of the more commercial developments we've been discussing, and in Internet mythology they hold a special and revered place. In 1983, *Time* magazine offered up a benign definition of the term *hackers* to refer to "computer fanatics," which thus deflected and subverted (or at least ignored) hacking's social and political history. Initially, the whole intent of hacking activism (or "hacktivism") was to mess with the system and to undermine the emerging commercial monopolies of the software and telecommunications cartels that were scrambling to make cyberspace like an online shopping mall.

Rushkoff tells the story of one hacker, "De Groot," who had dedicated his life to creating the "Global Electronic Village." According to Rushkoff (1994), De Groot was not "just exploring the datasphere but actively creating the networks that make it up" (p. 51). It wasn't just a hobby. De Groot was actively constructing the future from his equipment-crowded apartment (ibid.). The way Katie Hafner and John Markoff (1991) tell the story, the early hackers began in the 1970s as "phone phreaks"—able to crack into the circuits of the bulk telecom line carriers to make free phone calls. They didn't link up with the world of computers until the early 1980s, but they were already living on the edge of the law. The hacker culture of the first 10 years of the digital revolution represented the "demons" in the myth of the Golden Age. No doubt many of them were involved in criminal behaviour and many went to jail for their crimes, but their significance lies in the ways that the demonization of their activities incited wariness of the new technologies and fearfulness of technological control. As Hafner and Markoff (ibid.) comment, hackers are "the new magicians" who have conquered their own fear of "the machines that control modern life," the subject of occasional hysteria and "sweeps" by law enforcement agencies (pp. 11–12). But when all is said and done, are they a menace to society?

Hackers often see themselves not as criminals but as explorers in "a remarkable electronic world." In the early 1990s the rules of the road for the information superhighway were not clear, and they are still being defined, refined, and rewritten today. Hackers in the early years of the digital revolution represented, in true techno-myth fashion, the "risks" of computer technology and also its "allure" (p. 12). The hacker mythology is also fed through the cyberpunk genre. For example, in *Neuromancer*, Case and Molly enlist the help of the "Panther Moderns," a cross between a terrorist cell and demonic skateboarders: "mercenaries, practical jokers, nihilistic technofetishists" (Gibson, 1993a, p. 75). Case himself is a hacker, a "cowboy hotshot," and a thief who displayed "a certain relaxed contempt for the flesh," even for his own drug-damaged body (p. 12). Neal Stephenson (1992) has drawn similar characters in *Snow Crash*, and they are regular players in many of Gibson's short stories. Many elements of the gritty and dirty world of Gibson's earlier works can be seen as a direct analogy to social phenomena Gibson perceived during the late 1970s and early 1980s. At this time, this included the overpowering influence of globalized corporations, the fear of economic and cultural domination by Asian countries (especially Japan), and the possible impact of emerging technologies such as computer and genetic engineering, to name a few. *Neuromancer* and its sequels take place in a dystopian future—not, however, in an attempt to predict a possible future scenario, but as a metaphor of how the author experienced reality during the time of writing.

Such experiences and clashes with reality challenge the myths that accompany the Golden Age of the Internet. Yet a number of myths endure: constant technological change as the necessary and primary indicator of progress, the perpetual promises of increased productivity and wealth, and the continuing dream of freedom and democracy. Partly based on real events and people,

HACKING

As applied to technology, to change or disrupt the structured design and operating systems of existing technology (whether hardware or software). Hacking can remain at the level of artistry and experiment, or be expanded to deliberately disrupt established computer systems and technologically dependent structures (such as organizations, universities, governments, or corporations).

For Real?

From Hobbyists to Hacktivists to Cypherpunks?

Depending on the extent of time, energy, and resources spent on tapping into "the system," the first hackers were labelled "freaks" since the pursuit of getting into established computer systems, breaking code, and getting at the contents can become increasingly obsessive. The pursuit could be relentless despite personal risks, deteriorating social relationships, suspension from university, loss of employment, or arrest. For the original phreaks, their objectives were twofold. The first was to figure out how such an extensive system (the telephone network) actually worked, and the second was to actually make use of it to make long-distance telephone calls for free, thereby bypassing the monopoly controls that AT&T and Bell had on the networks. This subverted both material and ideological structures—the *private ownership* of the technology itself and the *idea* that private ownership was acceptable (versus a free and public service).

The concept of the hacker extends from two predecessors: the (h)obbyist and the safe cr(acker). While the hobbyist's intent is to figure out how something works and experiment with it, the hacker takes it one step further. More like the safe cracker—someone who discovers or breaks the established (or secret) code to get into the contents of a safe—the hacker breaks into the system, not only to figure it out and change the contents but also to make something new out of what is found there. This can be considered a new and positive creation, or the contents may be altered such that the system is destroyed. It is the latter case where the results may be identified as criminal if the system is broken into in order to steal the contents (such as databases) or even treated as terrorism if the destruction results in the loss of life.

Even if the former is true, that the intent and result of the hacking are both benign, hacking in technology has come to be considered "radical" because of the power relations around the technology, as well as the code, its contents, and the accompanying ideas. Each is made exclusive via the enclosure (metaphorically, the safe), whether through hardware or software design, or other restrictions and limitations due to law or intellectual property rights, such that access and use are limited to varying degrees. Like the hobbyist, the hacker may work to make technology more inclusive, accessible, and shared, but unlike the hobbyist, the goals may include breaking more than just the safe but the entire system that supports or facilitates even the *idea* of safes; that is, the intent is to expose or to break the rules (whatever structure or form they take), not to work within them, since, in this view, the structure otherwise ends up being replicated and perhaps increasingly validated.

It is this action on structure (to disrupt or change it) that yields the term *hacktivist* or *hacktivism*. As hacktivism can be accomplished by one individual or by groups, and the political intent may be unknown or spurious, it is debatable whether all hacktivism can be considered radical or indicative of Castell's "underground guerrilla armies" referred to at the beginning of this chapter. Hacking is defined solely as a "breaking and entering" action; hackers are often employed by governments and are reported to be hacking into other government and military websites as a method of secret surveillance (M. Lee, 2011a). In contrast, some groups self-identify in order to promulgate both their actions and their goals. One of the original hacktivist groups, for example, called themselves the 1984 Network Liberty Alliance (combining Orwell's prescient book with the fictitious rebel faction in the *Star Wars* movie series) in order to draw attention to the combination of corporate and government control of technology. Indeed, given the convergence of, and thus dependence on, computer networking worldwide, such actions can garner significant media attention depending on the extent that the activities are generally disruptive, or the degree of security or importance placed on the organization that was hacked.

As a general rule of thumb, the more powerful the organization is, the more powerful the response will likely be. Cyber "attacks" have been treated as criminal actions; individuals (those who can be caught) have been prosecuted, and specific sites have (been) shut down entirely, whether by government or corporate force, or "voluntarily." For its hacks into the Sony Corporation, the US Senate, and the US Central Intelligence Agency, for example, the hacktivist group called "LulzSec" shut itself down due to "increasing pressure from law enforcement agencies" (Richmond & Bilton, 2011, n.p.). The classification of other groups like "Anonymous"—a current Internet meme—is circulated as much by deed as by debate, since opinion-leaders and media seek to define and explain its actions in terms of "electronic civil disobedience."

Taking another tack, Julian Assange, editor-in-chief of WikiLeaks (discussed in Chapter 10), suggests that it would be more effective for people to build their own safes and access computer networks on their own terms (Assange, Appelbaum, & Muller-Muguhn, 2012). Encryption (writing code) to protect privacy suggests another kind of activism started in the 1990s called "cypherpunk" (www.activism.net/cypherpunk/manifesto.html). Here the goal is to free communication from surveillance (particularly government) such that individuals can communicate with each other in their own secure enclosures.

Discussion Questions

1. Conduct an Internet search of media coverage of "hacktivists," "cyberwarriors," and "cypherpunks" in Canada and the United States. What are the similarities and differences between them? Are the activities considered legitimate, an amusement, or a threat to national security?

2. Is hacktivism and cypherpunking a legitimization of Rushkoff's encouragement to "learn code" (as introduced in Part I of this book)?

3. How effective is this type of activism in terms of advancing political and economic change?

4. Recently, both Microsoft and Facebook have sponsored programs in the United States to encourage children to learn to computer code (www.code.org). Discuss why.

partly based on rich descriptions and embellished fictional accounts, they are the romance of a media-dominant era that continues to resonate. It is thus important to understand why these myths continue and where they are replicated, despite, in some cases, evidence to the contrary.

The Age of Cyber Mythology

Mosco (2004a) writes about the myths of the Internet Age in his book *The Digital Sublime*, describing them as "seductive tales containing promises unfulfilled or even unfulfillable" and as an ideological battle between "feeling" and "reason" (p. 24). Thus, myths contain both positive and negative elements, and when it comes to technological mythology there is both progress and regression; there is both material truth and hyperbole, caught up in a "spiral of hype" (p. 25). Myths can also have a life of their own: They "live" as long as they continue to give meaning to those who subscribe to them and as long as they have the ability to "render socially and intellectually tolerable what would otherwise be experienced as incoherence" (p. 29). Myths also have a naturalizing function: They ideologize certain elements and hide unpalatable truths that contradict the central purpose of mythologizing—the elimination of "complexities and contradictions" (p. 30). According to Mosco, the myths of the Digital Age demonstrate these values by shielding the *ideal* of cyberspace from "the messiness of down-to-earth politics" (p. 31). This is done by a process of "inoculation"—the admission that there are some (relatively minor) problems—in order to protect the myth from more substantial criticism. Inoculation is assisted by the complexity of digital knowledge environments where "linguistic distortions" (a form of ideological meme generation) "obscure and euphemise" the very reality "to which they simultaneously refer" (Hearn, Anthony, Holman, Dunleavy, & Mandeville, 2003, p. 233).

The process of inoculation is further developed through the selective reportage carried in media vectors, what McKenzie Wark (1994) calls an "instantaneous global dialogue" that denies the existence of territorial location and in which events appear to be taking place "on the surface of a strange new virtual geography" (p. viii). Wark names this "telesthesia"—the distanciation of the audience/receptor from real events. Things appear to happen in a never-ending "now," rather than as part of a historically date-stamped flow of events occurring at a particular place and time (p. 83).

Mythology also has another defence mechanism: the denial of history and the constant present of telesthesia (p. 145). This process of denial is aided by the social "dissolution" of the constraints of time and place that occurs within ideologies (Giddens, 1995, p. 91). The ability of an ideology to spread via the mimetic virus of cultural DNA depends, according to Anthony Giddens (1995), on the available "storage capacity": "the retention and control of information or knowledge" that brings with it control over "social power" (p. 94). One power of myths, when seen in this light, is that they can blur the boundaries between "before," "now," and "later." What Giddens calls the "time-space edges" (p. 163) are not clearly defined from one historical period to the next. Techno-myths, supplemented by the vast storage capacity of digital media, have this ability to blur time-space boundaries, and they are able to generate the belief that what happened before the digital revolution is merely "prehistory." Thus, for those who believe in a Golden Age, its beginning, middle, and end points may shift in both time and space, though in a sense such inconvenient facts are irrelevant to the belief system and the purpose of the myth. In this mythic discourse, the Information Age is a product of a revolutionary "rupture" with the past (Mosco, 2004a, pp. 34–5).

Like Mosco, we disagree with the illusion of historical dissonance that accompanies digital myth-making; the whole point of this book is to place convergence and digital technologies *into* an historical context. And we agree with Mosco that there is a need for myth-busters to challenge some of the illusory statements that the cyber-boosters claim as digital truths.

As we discussed earlier with our economic marketing and cultural examples, in order to be propagated as mimetic ideology, myths need champions—carriers—who will spread the word through their public pronouncements, and the Internet has its share of hucksters, boosters, and proselytizers. Mosco (2004a) describes Bill Gates as one of the most powerful myth-makers for the digital revolution, "extolling the transcendent virtues of computer communication as a conqueror of both space and time" (p. 36). Such was the goal of advertisers in 1985, for example, who suggested that AT&T had the "computer with the future built in" (*Time*, 1985, n.p.).

In February 2006, Bill Gates continued delivering his message at the World Economic Forum in Davos, Switzerland. In this instance, the emphasis was on the bottom line: that most companies could expect productivity growth of at least five per cent over the next financial cycle if they were prepared to use interactive electronic transactions (Gottliebsen, 2006). Another early, but powerful, net guru was former US Vice President Al Gore. In the mid-1990s, Gore was milking the benefits of the "information superhighway" as a cure-all for society's many problems. The main criticism of Gore's role in propagating mimetic myths about the Internet is not that they were far-fetched and had not yet been realized, but that by engaging with the myth and giving it legitimacy, Gore helped to make it seem real to those who were listening. During the campaign for the presidency in 1999 (for the 2000 election), Gore claimed to have had a role in inventing the Internet, and he made what Mosco (2004a) calls a "pilgrimage" (p. 39) to Silicon Valley as a way of distinguishing himself from his opponents.

Such examples are not exclusive to the United States, however. In 1994, proponents of computer networking in Canada encouraged the federal government to convene what was called the Information Highway Advisory Council (or IHAC). The council was disproportionately made up of representatives of industry, and its recommendations were heavily influenced by the myth of technological progress and economic success (Dowding, 2002). It subsequently published three reports (between 1995 and 1996) setting out the future policy for Internet development in Canada. As Darin Barney (2005) recounts, it was instigated by the US government's announcement of its plans for a National Information Infrastructure in 1993, which had "generated a considerable urgency for a similar network in Canada" (p. 42). As with telegraphy and broadcasting that came before it, the long-existing tensions between the use value of communication (its democratic potential of public communication via the Internet) and its exchange value (its economic value) became evident in a seismic shift in government policy direction and the assignment of departmental responsibilities.

The existing Department of Communication, which had been responsible for broadcasting *and* telecommunication—following the basic principles confirming the public nature and ownership of communication (as stipulated in the Broadcasting Act)—was dissolved and its responsibilities divided between two divergent departments. The Department of Canadian Heritage became responsible for broadcasting and cultural policy, and Industry Canada was assigned responsibility for telecommunication. As Barney underscores, the government resolved any existing public/private tensions in the mandate of Industry Canada, tying technological—and social—development directly to the economy:

> *Industry Canada's mandate is to help make Canadians more productive and competitive in the knowledge-based economy, thus improving the standard of living and quality of life in Canada. The Department's policies, programs and services help grow a dynamic and innovative economy that . . . [among other such qualifiers] gives consumers, businesses and investor's confidence that the marketplace is fair, efficient and competitive. (Industry Canada, 2002, as cited in Barney, 2005, p. 98)*

This was followed up in 1999 in the CRTC's *Report on New Media*, which withdrew government (and therefore public) participation in Internet regulation: "The CRTC will not attempt to regulate the Internet, leaving the 'Canadian product' to market forces" (CRTC, 1999, n.p.). Indeed, according to Industry Canada (2009), "since IHAC, Canada has been moving aggressively to deal with challenges posed by the Internet, in keeping with its established pro-market philosophy" (Pt. I, para. 9; www.ic.gc.ca/eic/site/wsis-smsi.nsf/eng/00043.html). As we review in subsequent chapters, although the government states that it is not directly regulating the Internet, as evident with other media, it has not left its development to "market forces," but continues to devote substantial government resources (such as time, policy changes, and finances), as the Golden Age always appears to be just around the corner. On each level of governance these resources are redirected: federally (through Industry Canada, the Canada Revenue Agency, the

National Research Council, and direct government purchases of ICT), provincially (through the ministries of health, education, and economic development), and municipally (through changes to property zones, infrastructure support, and taxation). Indeed, the desire to replicate one of the founding myths of the Internet was so strong in Canada in the 1990s that proponents sought to alter the name of the capital city of Ottawa to "Silicon Valley North." As Mosco and Mazepa (2003) indicate, significant federal, provincial, and municipal restructuring and financial support was directed to the high-tech industry and companies located there, which included Corel, Mosaid, and Nortel, among many others.

The myth of the Golden Age also has champions in the commercial media, and Mosco (2004a) describes Internet-boosting journalists as "willing accomplices in the near adulation of cyberspace" (p. 43). The collective noun *digerati* has been coined to describe the main group of digital salesmen and saleswomen who endlessly promote the many benefits of the Internet and convergent new media technologies. These "accomplices" are given plenty of space in newspapers and in other media; many of them are promoters of the latest digital gadgets, and they pop up regularly on lifestyle "infotainment" programs. Some are political figures like Al Gore, or business leaders like Bill Gates; others are intellectuals who have mastered the mythology and work out ways to popularize it through their writing and public appearances. A key figure in this group is Nicholas Negroponte, whose 1996 book *Being Digital* is perhaps one of the most significant books to generate and argue strongly for the mythic representation of cyberspace and digital technologies.

In *Being Digital*, Negroponte (1996) concluded that digital technology would be a "natural force" that could draw people into a sense of "greater world harmony" as "each generation becomes more digital than the preceding one" (pp. 230–1). This is a recurrent theme in the mythology of the Golden Age in which digital technology is described as "the most potent tool of communication ever available to the individual" that will lead to "a new empowerment" and even a return to the utopian "pre-Gutenberg days" (*The Economist*, 1999, para. 28). Individuals will no longer be shackled by space or time, but rather a new **global village** will emerge in which "one man's voice could reach as far as almost any other" (ibid.).

Such utopian visions were escalated by embodying the computer with spiritual powers. These were advanced by some of the most powerful myth-makers of the cyber age—the young misfits who, in the late 1980s and early 1990s, saw the Internet as a means of escape from the drudgery of daily life in the stifling analogue culture of late capitalism. The now world-famous computer magazine *Wired* is to the digerati of the Internet Age what *Rolling Stone* was to the rock generation. Both were originally published in San Francisco and both were trendsetting magazines that became "must read" items for their audiences. One key purpose of *Wired*, though perhaps subconscious on the part of its writers and editors, is the perpetuation of cyber-mythologies. This is illustrated by a series of articles in the December 2002 issue—a time when the world was still reeling from the 2000/2001 **dot.com crash**—that argued for a "new convergence" between technology and religion. One article by "editor-at-large" Kevin Kelly claimed that "God is the Machine" and concluded that "the universe is not merely like a computer, it is a computer" (as cited in Mosco, 2004a, p. 14).

And the Beat Goes On

The current cyberians are cool techno-wizards, individuals who have made millions on inventive uses of technology and social media. This is the heralded dream of the individual entrepreneur, evidence that the Golden Age is still possible, and there's still a lot of money to be

GLOBAL VILLAGE

A term popularized by Canadian media sociologist Marshall McLuhan to describe the social effect of convergent technologies. In essence, a global village would mean that we all get to know each other and interact in some utopian way, as was supposed to be the case in pre-industrial village life.

DOT.COM CRASH

Since the value of stocks can be dependent on how much people are willing to pay, when it became evident that a good number of the dot.com companies weren't worth the investment in the first place, that their value was inflated and the promises were false, the stocks lost their allure, and given the sheer number of them, the market crashed.

made regardless of rising worldwide social and environmental problems. Commercial media sections on technology find never-ending solutions to future and impending hazards, led by the announcements of the latest technologies. Following on major commercial magazines like *Wired*, *InfoWorld*, and the Canadian publications of *Computerworld* (www.itworldcanada.com/publication/computerworld), most newspapers also have dedicated technology reporters, "new media journalists" or "tech-gurus," who are consulted to review and compare the latest technology products and trends. Typically, these sections are a mixture of product news (supplied by company media releases), tips, and hints directed towards the public as consumers, while the more detailed information is reserved for online sections that assume an already tech-savvy audience. These include sites ranging from individual bloggers (e.g., www.sapiensbryan.com/ and allthingsd.com/), to programs such as "This Week in Tech," which aspires to be the "CNN for Geeks" (twit.tv/), to the larger news aggregator and commercial technology promoter CNET (www.cnet.com/). Technology sections of Canadian publications such as *The Globe and Mail* (www.theglobeandmail.com/news/technology/) and the *Toronto Star* (www.thestar.com/life/technology.html) seek to identify and compare the latest commercial technology.

The myth-making efforts of the mass media are supported by the advertising budgets of the major product suppliers that are deployed to build brand awareness and to spread the general message of the digital revolution: "A new age has dawned and we must, in the words of Apple Computer, 'think different'" (Mosco, 2004a, p. 42). There is, in effect, a particular mythic discourse at large that fits within and supports the process of social change that the digital revolution has created. This has particular relevance to the imagined representation of the information society, which is a projection of a "possible state of affairs" (Fairclough, c. 2000, p. 3). Norman Fairclough (c. 2000) suggests that discursive language may play a more significant role in the socio-economic changes wrought by digital convergence than it did in previous changes: "The neo-liberal political project of removing obstacles to the new economic order is discourse-driven" (p. 6).

The scope and penetration of the "neo-political" agenda into digital myth-making is evident in the current federal government's melding of technology to the economy, and thusly co-joined, into the daily lives of Canadians. In the 2010 *Speech from the Throne*, for example, the Government of Canada (2010) committed to "launch a digital economy strategy to drive the adoption of new technology across the economy" (para. 30). This was reinforced in the 2010 *Budget* with an imperative to "enable the ICT sector to create new products and services" (Department of Finance Canada, 2010, p. 84) as purportedly driven by the "digital revolution." The revolution is described as an inescapable, breathtaking process from which there was no alternative: "The relentless pace of technology means that every day there is something newer, faster, better. To succeed in the global economy, Canada must keep step as the world races forward" (Government of Canada, 2010, para. 29).

Accordingly, the global economy is now the *digital economy*, which is defined by the federal government as "the term used to describe the network of suppliers and users of digital content and technologies that enable everyday life" (Industry Canada, 2010a, p. 4). Such a revolution is not only driven by technology, however, but, according to the narrative, "today's consumers—young and old—are demanding instantaneous information, products and services" (ibid.; www.ic.gc.ca/eic/site/028.nsf/eng/00036.html). But if "today's consumers" are "driven by technology," it begs the question, then, of why the government must work so relentlessly to "drive its adoption."

This particular element of myth-making, steeped in the rhetoric of the free market and consumption, is an example of the attempts by many governments to manage and promote the insertion of their national economy into the emerging new world order. The discourse of "no choice" reinforces the myth of adapt or die "on terms dictated by the allegedly impersonal forces of the market" (Fairclough, c. 2000, p. 5). Such speed, such demand, such "reliance on market forces" has, however, not entirely resulted in the realization of a Golden Age. A couple of stark examples serve to illustrate that the Dark Ages may yet be upon us.

The End of Innocence on the Net: September 11, 2001

If there was a Golden Age of the Internet, we think it probably ended—officially—with the events of September 11, 2001. This was when the surveillance society kicked in—in a big way—you couldn't have cybergypsies wandering unsupervised all over the Internet when there might be terrorists lurking. From 9/11 there has been a gradual but continuous rise in the use of electronic surveillance, including digital technologies; there has also been an erosion of civil liberties as governments tighten their controls over many aspects of life that were previously unregulated. In the final chapters of this book, we take up this discussion and outline what we call the surveillance economy that has grown to accommodate new security concerns. Having said that, there's another and slightly earlier end point to the Golden Age that we wish to discuss further—the dot.com crash of 2000. Until that point there had been unquestioned dreams of a promising future for business on the Internet.

The Tech Boom and Bust

From the mid-1990s until mid-2000, any company with .com after its name was a runaway hit on the world's stock exchanges. Thousands of new paper millionaires were created overnight, and it all melted away just as quickly. Through the 1990s there had been an air of technological optimism around the Internet, and it was thought that the new business models that sprang up in response to the declassification of cyberspace could not lose money. This turned out to be a serious miscalculation, and it took several years for economic confidence in the World Wide Web to recover.

In early 2000, international stock markets came crashing down, the biggest collapse in value since "Black Friday" in 1987. According to the market-analysis website Investopedia.com, the high-tech stock index, the NASDAQ, fell a record 78 per cent (Beattie, 2006b). The site also fixes the dates of the dot.com crash as 11 March 2000 to 9 October 2002 (ibid.). In one week, between 7 and 14 April, 2000, American stock markets lost USD$2 trillion dollars, and Bill Gates' personal fortune fell by $30 billion in just a few hours (*The Jobs Letter No. 123*, 2000). Though of course, with a net worth of close to a trillion dollars, you'd have to say he wouldn't really miss it!

The dot.com and telecommunications companies that had led the earlier confident rise in share prices took the hardest hits. Over the next two years (with September 11, 2001, right in the middle) a number of the start-up Internet companies, which on paper were worth billions of dollars, had disappeared entirely. Some of the giants of the copper cable and telecommunications cartel shed around 70–90 per cent of their stock values. Others, such as WorldCom and Global Crossing, were on the edge of bankruptcy; there were huge job losses right across the high-tech sector, and corporate executives were dropping like flies in the face of investigations that showed they'd inflated share prices and profits to lure investors (Mosco, 2004a, pp. 4–5). Mosco makes a wry comment appropriate to the mythical power of the digital revolution: "The only genuine break with history turned out to be the unprecedented collapse of a major industrial sector" (ibid., p. 5).

One of the biggest losers in the dot.com disaster was AOL Time Warner, a (vertically and horizontally integrated) company that had formed through the merger of AOL (a new media company) and Time Warner (an old media conglomerate) only months before, in January 2000. By March 2003, AOL's value had dropped 80 per cent below the merger value; Microsoft Corporation lost just over 50 per cent of its value, and Intel was down 73 per cent. In Canada, the shockwaves hit more than just the tickertape peaks and valleys of the stock market. Mainstays of the high-tech industry like Corel (the maker of WordPerfect and CorelDraw software), Mitel Networks Corporation, and Alcatel drastically cut their workforce. In Silicon Valley North—in the City of Ottawa—the effects were acute as people who had invested their homes, their futures, and their livelihoods in the dream of technology found themselves out of work: "Alcatel cut around 800 local jobs over less than two years. JDS's worldwide workforce shrank from 30,000 to 5,000 and the company moved its headquarters to California. Nortel immediately slashed its workforce in half, carrying out more cuts over the years as its sales sagged and it struggled through a 2004 accounting scandal" (CBC, 2009d).

What was especially telling was the speed of the backlash from the perils of federal government investment in the technology companies. Dell Inc. (one of the leading online computer retailers) shut down its Ottawa call centre in 2008, two years after it had been given $11 million in tax credits in order to create 1,100 jobs (ibid.). As the fallout from Nortel continues to dispense today, the old adage "the bigger they are, the harder they fall" affects more than just the company stock, as the workers are left to fight for their due payments and pensions that they may never see, while Nortel's former executives received million dollar "compensation packages," and its patents (recall from Chapter 5) are transferred to the market based on their exchange value as negotiated by the largest global corporations.

Case Study

Nortel—Government Bailouts, Executive Payouts, and Workers Without Jobs or Pensions?

Nortel's business story begins in 1895 when the Northern Electric and Manufacturing Company incorporated as a manufacturing arm for the vertical integration of the Bell Telephone Company. For the early half of the twentieth century, the company manufactured and distributed a diverse set of products across Canada, ranging from communication devices like telephones and radios to small electrical appliances like kettles and toasters.

Its first boom was a result of government contracts fuelled by the Second World War via the manufacture and sale of radar and radio equipment to the military. Northern Electric prioritized its vertical growth to become Canada's largest developer of communication technology including antennas, satellites, cell phones, and fibre optics. The company continued its expansion globally, setting up manufacturing and research bases around the world, such that, during the 1990s, it was generally seen as the "poster child" of the high-tech industry, leading a purported transition to the "new information economy."

Signs that the Nortel bubble would burst came in October 2000 as it failed to meet its expected revenue targets. A combination of overspending and poor decisions over research and development added to its susceptibility to the dot.com fiasco. The following years were marked

Continued

by huge drops in stock prices, and corporate restructuring and financial losses resulted in massive lay-offs. Despite no less than two federal government bailouts, the downward spiral continued until the company filed for bankruptcy protection in 2009. The huge Nortel campus—the now-empty buildings and vacant grounds—was later bought by the Canadian government with a plan to move the Department of National Defence from its current headquarters in downtown Ottawa to the suburb of Kanata, bringing an ironic close to a history supported by public financing (see Figure 8.1). The geographical location is particularly significant as both an example and a symbol of government support for a much sought-after "high-tech cluster," as Kanata was originally marketed as the "birthplace" of the so-called Silicon Valley North.

Source: Ingram Publishing / Thinkstock

FIGURE 8.1 | Night view of the Nortel Carling Campus Building in Ottawa. The company filed for bankruptcy protection on 14 January 2009.

The aftermath of Nortel's collapse continues to be marked with financial scandal, including the liquidation of its research divisions and properties, and debates over whether or not the company should have had public financing at all. Nonetheless, the piece-by-piece sale of Nortel to the highest (foreign) bidder, and the fall of the "star" of the high-tech industry, is considered a major loss to Canada's contribution and control over ICT research and development. Moreover, Nortel's history illustrates the volatility of the high-tech development and business "growth-at-all-cost" approach, and leaves a questionable track record of government support of this volatile industry, particularly considering the disjuncture between the payouts afforded to its decision-makers and the cost–benefit ratio to Canadian workers and citizens who are left paying the bills.

Timeline: Nortel

1895 Northern Electric and Manufacturing Company is incorporated as a manufacturing arm for the Bell Telephone Company of Canada.

1914 Northern Electric and Manufacturing Company's name is changed to Northern Electric after merging with Imperial Wire and Cable Company.

1929 After years of growth, Northern Electric cuts 66 per cent of its workforce during the economic depression.

1941 Northern Electric experiences major growth when the Canadian government invests $40 million (two and a half times the sales in 1939) for the production of radio and radar equipment to aid the war effort. The company hires 8,000 employees.

1982 By this time Northern Electric has established itself in the United States with 19,000 employees, 14 manufacturing plants, 15 research and development labs, and sales centres in over 100 locations.

1989 The company, now worth USD$5 billion, is established as a global communications giant with plants and labs around the world. Strategic alliances are made with other communication corporations in the UK, France, Japan, and China.

1998 Northern Electric changes its name to Nortel. The new CEO, John Roth, restructures the company to focus on Internet technologies, which is trumpeted as evidence of Canada's transition to the new information economy.

2000 The company value peaks at CAD$250 billion in July with share prices topping out at $124.50 on the TSX. Stock drops 20 per cent in October when Nortel fails to meet revenue targets.

2001 Nortel's workforce is cut in half to 45,000 employees by the end of the year. The company loses USD$23.7 billion. John Roth resigns as CEO and cashes in stock options worth $135 million. In 2010, Roth asks for $1 billion of Nortel assets if he is convicted in legal proceedings.

2003 Export Development Canada, a branch of the Canadian government, gives $750 million bailout to Nortel. The company posts its first profit since 2000, at the end of first quarter, earning USD$54 million. The Canadian government buys the Nortel Skyline Campus in Ottawa for $177 million, only to put it up for sale again in 2007.

2004 Nortel fails to post financial statements for 2003. Stock drops and top-level executives are fired for "financial mismanagement." Nortel sells off its manufacturing plants to Flextronics International in June. US courts begin a formal investigation into Nortel's 2003 accounting scandal in April.

2007 Continued job cuts bring Nortel's total payroll to 31,000, with more jobs transferring to low-cost countries like China, India, and Mexico.

2008 With continued job cuts and losses, new Nortel CEO Mike Zafirovski is given a 21.5 per cent pay increase, to $10.1 million.

2009 Nortel files for bankruptcy protection on 14 January, one day before being forced to pay $107 million in interest payments. The Canadian government offers $30 million for short-term financing. Nortel begins liquidation of patents. Its Wireless Division is sold to Nokia for $650 million in June. The TSX stops trading Nortel shares.

The company pays $14.2 million in compensation to seven of its executives. Seventeen thousand former employees sign a petition to force Nortel to pay their pensions.

2010 Nortel asks a federal judge for permission to remove its insurance coverage for more than 4,000 former employees.

In Ottawa, Nortel's 370 acres and 111 buildings (which used to house 10,000 employees) are bought by the federal government for $208 million, with plans to renovate (at a cost of $790 million) and move military and staff of the Department of National Defence from downtown Ottawa to the suburb of Nepean.

2011 The Ontario government steps in to cover Nortel pension deficits. As of October, compensation claims from former employees remain to be reviewed.

2012 On 16 January, former CEO Frank Dunn and two other executives get set to go to trial for the 2003 accounting scandal and are acquitted in 2013.

Sources: CBC, 2009a, 2009b, 2009c, 2009d; Koskie Minsky, 2009; Montreal *Gazette*, 2010; Nortel Networks Corporation, n.d.; Nguyen, 2013; Pugliese, 2010, 2013; Reuters, 2009; Wikipedia, n.d.

Discussion Questions

1. To what extent is the experience of Nortel exceptional or typical of the high-tech business cycle in Canada? Globally?

2. What are the arguments for and against government/public funding for high-tech businesses?

3. What does this case study suggest in regard to corporate accountability and social responsibility?

Crisis? What Crisis?

The market crash of 2000 may well have been coming anyway—it might not have been just because the high-tech start-ups were inflating their values and hyping their prospects. Capitalism has always been prone to booms and slumps; this is one of the key dialectical fault lines in the system. Political economy tells us that the tendency towards periodic crisis is an inherent feature of commodity production in a capitalist economy because the average rate of profit falls when more capital is invested in a particular sector. This process—the product of an unplanned system of competition and corporate greed—wipes out any advantages that the initial investors may have had. The general collapse in profitability forces the weaker players out of the market, and this process continues until some form of unstable and temporary equilibrium is found. Historically, this process has contributed to the centralization and concentration of capital—the growth of cartels, oligopolies, and monopolies—as an inevitable consequence of the accumulation process (Callinicos, 1987, pp. 128–39). This is precisely what happened during the 2000 dot.com crash: Weaker and less stable companies went to the wall, and those that survived got bigger as they absorbed the remains of their competitors' businesses, thus continually feeding the growth of monopolies and oligopolies.

Capitalist history has a tendency to repeat itself, yet with increasing frequency. As Andrew Beattie (2006a) notes in concluding his survey of market crashes over the past 100 years, "regardless of our measures to correct the problems, the time between crashes has decreased" (para. 3). A market crash often follows what economists call an investment "bubble"—a time when there is plenty of money to be made and new investors are rushing in to grab a share of the action. The bubble period for the new economy stocks based on digital technologies and convergence was probably from about 1996 to the 2000 crash, and over that period the NASDAQ index went from 600 to 5,000 points. There were also signs in early 2000 that the dot.com bubble was going to burst (*The Jobs Letter No. 123*, 2000). Joanna Glasner (2000) wrote in *Wired* magazine about the deflating Internet bubble just days before the NASDAQ demolition derby: "The problem with a stock bubble is you never really know it is one until it pops" (para. 1). Even then, in early April 2000, many digital analysts were talking down the prospect of a real crash, preferring to call it a "correction" to the over-inflated market.

Given the severity of the dot.com crash, it would seem that "market forces" would perhaps be more prudent and less prone to hyper-inflation. Yet another crisis occurred in less than a decade; this time throughout 2008/9, when the US housing market crashed, confirming that the lessons of the dot.com debacle were not well-heeded. In fact, in its attempt to support a failing system, the US government provided bailouts for the largest banks and mortgage companies, continuing to give tax breaks and limit regulation or advancing deregulation to facilitate the capitalist economy, doing—in effect—what market analyst Paul Farrell (2008) calls keeping "the bubble blowing." A bubble always has its breaking point, however, and as Farrell (ibid.) suggests in *MarketWatch*, the bubbles have grown to such a size globally that the Great Depression 2 is looming if market forces continue to inflate stocks, corporate taxes are kept artificially low, and government and public debt continue to rise in direct correlation.

The severity of the fallout remains to be seen. From our perspective, looking at the past, *The Jobs Letter No. 123* (2000) offers a useful explanation of why the dot.com crash and the housing crash happened: "How did things get so over-valued? Most of it has been put down to plain old hype and speculation. But there has also been a powerful new myth at work in financial circles: that the dot.com age [rewrote] the basic laws of economics" (para. 5). Karl Marx called the law of value one of the "iron laws" of history, meaning it is difficult (if not impossible) to rewrite.

From a political economy perspective, the dot.com companies, speculators, and bankers were stopped by this law.

Was There Ever a Golden Age, and Does It Matter?

The aftermath of the crash of 2000 is that the Internet has been brought back to the basics of business. It has been returned to the people with passion. It has been returned to the customers! (Roy, 2000)

As illustrated in this quotation, the dot.com crash did not dent the enthusiasm of the digital boosters too badly. By November 2000, journalist Michelle Roy was predicting that it would all get better, and soon. All the dot.coms had to do to pick themselves up was to refocus on customer service. Roy remained confident, just months after everything went south at speed: "The new economy is more of a new set of rules for businesses that have survived the test of time rather than a new paradigm for brand new companies. . . . Smart companies are still investing in their e-business development strategies" (ibid.).

Roy's vision was common among the people who'd been burned in the blaze of the dot.com crash. In November 2001, information architecture consultant Peter Morville (2001) wrote that the recovery from the crash would position high-tech companies for a more prosperous future: "As we emerge from the ashes during 2001, we will begin to see signs that the Internet industry has come of age" (para. 14). So the new economy came "of age" in the aftermath of the crash of 2000 *and* while the remains of the World Trade Centre complex at "Ground Zero" in New York were still smouldering—a Phoenix-like rise from the ashes of two spectacular disasters.

There's no doubt that the dot.com crash of 2000 dented the Golden Age myth. We have perhaps yet to see if it turns Negroponte's dream of a future digital nirvana into a new technological nightmare of surveillance and cyber-malls. Alex Burns (2001), writing in *Disinformation*, says the crash of 2000 caused many tech-analysts to question the "social mantras" they had been "long conditioned with": "The dot.com disasters glaringly highlight the distance between the chimerical Digital Age and what economist Paul Krugman lucidly calls 'the Age of Diminished Expectations.'"

Despite the heartache and tears, it is hard to write-off the digital myth altogether. It seems it is a necessary condition of the digital age that the myth continues to live in some form. Five years after the crash, Chris Alden (2005) wrote in the *Guardian* that many survivors believed that the shake-out of Internet and other high-tech stocks was a good thing because it cleared the way for a more sensible approach to online business development and a more cautious attitude to the Internet on the part of investors and inventors. This remaking of recent history is part of the inoculation process of myth-making. This is a common view, and many commentators regained their optimism fairly quickly; the signs are now pointing to a resurgence in the digital economy on a more viable platform, pinning predictions on "**new media**" and "social media" as the cash-cows of the future. Early in 2011, for example, *Canadian Business* magazine suggested that the outlook for 2011 was a positive one, predicting a "new **dot.com boom**" based on the current financial worth of new media sites like Facebook, LinkedIn, Groupon (a commercial discount site), and Zynga (a social gaming site; Beer, 2011). Emphasizing the freedom afforded by new technologies, Richard Florida (2010), in *The Great Reset: How New Ways of Living and Working Drive Post Crash Prosperity*, suggests that the "creative class" will lead us all to riches. All is not lost in the faith of the new technologies of tomorrow.

As Mosco (2004a) suggests in *The Digital Sublime*, the Internet and new media technologies really become "important forces for social and economic change" when they move from

NEW MEDIA

Basically a catch-all phrase used to distinguish digital media forms from "old media" forms such as newspapers, magazines, radio, and television.

DOT.COM BOOM

In the second half of the 1990s a significant number of computer companies "went public"; that is, they listed on the stock exchange through a process known as an IPO (initial public offering). They took advantage of the myth of the Golden Age and made their companies look promising for profit-making by adding the ".com" to their names. In doing so, they created fabulous paper profits for those who owned the shares prior to the IPO. Those who cashed in their shares made huge profits. This was known as the dot.com boom.

being the "sublime icons of mythology" and are no longer the source of "utopian visions," but rather enter the "prosaic world of banality" (p. 6). The real power of new technologies does not really emerge in the period when they are highly mythologized, but when they "withdraw into the woodwork" (p. 19). Mosco calls this a shift to "embodied physicality," such as when the microchip was successfully migrated from the mainframe to the desktop and then into a "host of old and new devices" that could be commodified, allowing the power of computing to grow, "while withdrawing as a presence" (p. 21).

This is, in our view, the phase of digital convergence we are now in, and perhaps have been in for the past 10–15 years. There is a certain "taken-for-grantedness" about digital media today. It is no longer a thing to be in awe of, or to fear. Digital devices are now commonplace in Canada, part of the everyday experience of most people. People in their 20s (and younger) today know very little about the pre-digital world (at least from direct experience). Digital technologies are now socially, economically, and culturally embedded in our daily lives. We are living in this "new" economy with "new" media all around us. It may or may not be a new (or enduring) Golden Age, but there's no question that it is now the paradigm for almost everything we do.

Given its importance, we have to ask ourselves how much we are participating in the myriad number of decisions that are constantly being made as we use and work with technology. Whether we see ourselves as consumers or citizens (or a mixture of both), as responsible members of the public we owe it to ourselves and the generations that follow us to learn and familiarize ourselves not only with how to use the latest gadget when it comes out but also to question and understand the relations of both its production and its consumption.

We may all use the Internet, but how many of us are involved in decision-making around the Internet? What are the experiences and issues that have to do with the ubiquity of its use? What is the government's role in shaping its future? And how can we get involved? Such questions are the focus of our next chapter as we review those decisions and identify the issues that chart the media and digital future—a future in which, for better or for worse, we are a decisive part of.

Key Points

- The prevalence of technological "boosterism" is an important element of digital mythologies.
- The role of governments and Silicon Valley as the incubator of consumer-directed digital technologies is important.
- The Golden Age of the Internet—if it ever existed—ended with the dot.com crash of 2000 and the terrorist attacks of September 11, 2001, ushering in the age of digital surveillance.
- Digital mythology continues to generate the memes of an Internet Golden Age that has shifting spatial and temporal boundaries.

Class Discussion

1. In this chapter we have outlined some of the mythology that surrounds digital technologies, particularly the Internet, and we have described what may be the most enduring myth as the Golden Age.

a. How did this chapter suggest that these myths were created? For example, what are the key memes and vectors (recall from Chapter 1) that are associated with spreading the myths about new technology and new media?

b. Identify which (meme or vector) is most familiar to you, and explain why.

2. To aid your discussion in Question 1, collect three advertisements or commercial media text covering the release of the latest technology (new laptop, e-reader, smart phone, computer wristwatch, or other type of individualized consumer device). Compare the images (if any) and text. What promises are offered with its purchase? What myths are drawn on in their promotion? What predictions are made regarding the future?

3. Search recent Canadian federal government press releases or statements by elected politicians regarding "the digital economy" (⬛ digitaleconomy.gc.ca) and identify the language used to describe it and the future. Where does "the public" appear in these statements? Can you identify any myths that are evident or promoted?

4. Identify two or three organizations (besides corporations and governments) that promote "the digital economy" in Canada. Identify why they are promoting it, and how.

5. What possibilities exist to prioritize the use value of the Internet? How are these similar to, or different from, its exchange value?

6. What are some of the types of "hacktivism"? Identify the political economic or social aims of each. How do they compare to groups like "Anonymous," for example?

Media on Media

Tunes on Technology

Corey Smith. (2007). Technology. *Hard-Headed Fool*. US: Undertone Records.
Daft Punk. (2005). Technologic. *Human After All*. UK: Virgin.
Jessie J. (2011). Technology. *Who You Are*. UK: Universal.
Pegasus. (2011). Technology. *Human. Technology*. Zurich, Switzerland: Muve Recordings.
Vengaboys. (2000). Cheekah bow bow (That computer song). *The Platinum Album*. UK: EMI.

Movies, Videos, and DVDs

Badham, J. (Director). (1983). *WarGames* [Motion picture]. US: MGM Pictures.
Films for the Humanities & Sciences (Writer). (2006). *eBay and Napster: Change agents* [Video]. US: MacNeil/Lehrer Productions Inc.
Films Media Group Online. (2005). *Digital dark age? Gambling with humankind's knowledge* [Video]. New York, NY: Films Media Group.
Hughes, A., & Hughes, A. (Directors). (2010). *The book of Eli* [Motion picture]. US: Warner Bros.
Jhally, S. (Producer & Director). (2008). *Capitalism hits the fan: A lecture on the economic meltdown* [Documentary]. US: Media Education Foundation.
Krotoski, Dr. A. (2010). *Virtual revolution: The cost of free* [Documentary]. BBC.
The NewsHour with Jim Lehrer (Producer). (2005). *Microsoft vs. the Justice Department: Playing monopoly* [News segment]. New York: Films Media Group.
Online NewsHour with Jim Lehrer (Producer). (2006). *Computer worms and viruses* [News segment]. US: MacNeil/Lehrer Productions Inc.
Renfroe, J., & Thorsson, M. (Writers & Directors). (2004). *One point O* [DVD]. US: Armada Pictures.
Robinson, P. A. (Director). (1992). *Sneakers* [Motion picture]. US: Universal Pictures.
Silver, J. (Producer), Wachowski, L., & Wachowski, A. (Directors). (1999–2003). *The matrix* [Motion picture trilogy]. US: Warner Bros.
Spielberg, S. (Director). (2002). *Minority report* [Motion picture]. US: 20th Century Fox.

Board Game

de Leon Pereira, R. (Designer). (2009). *Internet tycoon.* 🖥 boardgamegeek.com/boardgame/55625/internet-tycoon

Cyberpunk

Cyberpunk. 🖥 www.cyberpunk.com
The Cyberpunk Directory. 🖥 http:www.cyberpunked.org
The Cyberpunk Project. 🖥 www.project.cyberpunk.ru
Cyberpunks Gaming Podcast. 🖥 www.cyberpunksgaming.com

Timeline: A (Modern) History of Computers—Part 2

1970 Fibre optics are invented.

1971 IBM introduces a program and data storage system: the floppy disk.

The Intel microprocessor—the first computer chip—is released.

Ray Tomlinson uses the @ symbol as part of an electronic messaging system on ARPANET; networked email is facilitated.

1972 Atari is founded by Nolan Bushnell and releases *PONG*, the first commercial video game.

Hewlett-Packard and Texas Instruments release the first electronic calculators.

Motorola demonstrates the cellular telephone to the Federal Communications Commission (FCC). People can call each other without wires.

1973 Robert Metcalfe at Xerox in Palo Alto invents local area networking (LAN), via the Ethernet.

ARPANET goes international.

1974 Barcodes are used in a supermarket in Ohio, and are partly funded by the National Science Foundation (NSF).

Telenet, the first commercially available version of ARPANET, is introduced.

1974–1977 The first PCs come onto the market: IBM 5100, Apple I & II, TRS-80, and Commodore.

1975 Microsoft is founded.

1976 Apple is founded.

1977 AT&T rolls out the world's first commercial fibre-optic system.

The US government adopts IBM's *data encryption standard* as the key to securing the data used by its agencies and unlocking coded messages.

1978 CDs are released by Philips and Sony.

Video laserdiscs are invented.

VisiCalc, a spreadsheet program, becomes the first "killer app."

1979 WordStar word processing software becomes the second "killer app."

The computer "worm" is discovered.

1980 The Organisation for Economic Co-operation and Development (OECD) formulates information privacy principles.

1981 Microsoft brings out the MS-DOS operating system.

The electronic mail system called "Envoy 100" is developed by Telecom Canada.

1983 ARPANET is split into MILNET (military) and ARPANET (civilian) segments. The TCP/IP-based network (the Internet) is released to the public domain.

The GNU operating system is released to the public as a "free alternative" to UNIX (hence the acronym, which stands for "Gnu's Not Unix"), enabling any user to share and change the software (🖥 www.gnu.org/software/).

Paul Mockapetris develops the domain name system.

CoSy, the first COmputer conferencing SYstem, is developed in Canada at the University of Guelph.

1984 The first Personal Digital Assistant (PDA) is released.

Research in Motion (RIM) is established in Waterloo, Ontario.

Michael Dell founds Dell Systems, selling computers by mail order.

The Canadian Union of Public Employees establishes the Solidarity Network (SoliNet).

1985 The Ontario Institute for Studies in Education (University of Toronto) begins offering graduate courses online.

The US government reassigns pieces of ARPANET to the National Science Foundation (NSF), which forms NSFNET.

The first dot.com domain name is registered with the US government and distinguishes itself from five others: .org, .edu, .net, .mil, and .gov.

Microsoft Windows is introduced.

American-Canadian author William Gibson coins the term *cyberspace* in *Neuromancer*.

1987 First global Internet worm infection.

The University of Prince Edward Island registers the first .ca domain name.

1988 Open Source Software Foundation is formed.

1990 Archie, the first Internet search engine, is developed by students at McGill University in Montreal.

The Canadian National Research Council funds CAnet.

Tim Berners-Lee and colleagues at CERN in Geneva invent the World Wide Web, HTML, HTTP, and URLs.

1991 Recordable compact disc drivers, CD-Rs, reach the market.

1992 National Capital FreeNet is founded in Ottawa.

1993 CAnet is enlarged to Canada's Advanced Research and Innovation Network (CANARIE) by the federal government.

Windows Internet Explorer (IE) is released.

1994 Banner ads first appear on the Internet.

First Virtual establishes online banking.

Hewlett-Packard combines printer, fax, and copier into one machine.

1995 Amazon starts selling books online, and expands to sell a range of consumer products online.

eBay offers online shopping and commodity auctions.

Cable modems are introduced.

Sony PlayStation is released.

Java programming language is introduced.

WebTV is formed to combine television and the Internet.

Wiki (What I Know Is), developed by Ward Cunningham, goes online.

1996 DVD technology is demonstrated.

Hotmail is launched; sold to Microsoft in 1998.

Larry Page and Sergey Brin start Google.

1997 Blogging begins.

Google IPO begins as a web search engine.

Philippe Kahn invents the digital camera phone.

Streaming audio and video is available on the Web.

1998 The first satellite phone call is made over the Globalstar system.

The Internet Corporation for Assigned Names and Numbers (ICANN) is established to regulate all domain names.

Microsoft's anti-trust suit begins in United States.

1999 Napster—the first peer-to-peer file-sharing software—is released.

2000 Napster and Bertelsmann AG partner to develop a membership-based music distribution system that would guarantee payments to artists and to copyright holders; Napster is sued by the RIAA and shuts down in 2001.

Dot.com's bubble bursts: The stock market reacts to the end of the "Internet gold rush" (from 1995).

2001 Apple introduces the iPod.

Wikipedia—a free, user-edited online encyclopaedia, is launched by Larry Sanger.

2002 The social networking website MySpace is launched by eUniverse/Intermix, and later bought by News Corp. for over USD$5 million.

2004 Facebook is developed by students at Harvard University.

Flickr, the photo file-sharing site, launches and is purchased by Yahoo! in 2005.

The term *Web 2.0* is coined to describe the increase in social networking and participatory web applications like wikis and blogs.

2005 The first YouTube video is uploaded.

The US Supreme Court holds software distributors liable for copyright breaches.

Google Earth is launched.

2006 The first live webcast is broadcast from the second smallest country in the world, Tuvalu.

Google buys YouTube for USD$1.65 billion.

2008 Apple's iTunes store opens.

2009 Cloud computing is introduced.

Nortel files for creditor protection.

2010 Web 3.0 nomenclature describes an enhanced ability for computers to make connections between stored data independently (also called "intelligent web" or "semantic web").

2011 Microsoft buys Skype for $8.5 billion.

Google offers an opening bid of USD$900 million to purchase Nortel's portfolio of patents. Patents are later sold to a consortium of companies (including RIM, Microsoft, Apple, Sony, and Ericsson) for $4.5 billion (Arthur, 2011).

2013 The US Federal Trade Commission reaches an agreement with Google on its anti-trust investigation.

The US Senate's Permanent Subcommittee on Investigations identifies how major US corporations like Microsoft, Hewlett-Packard, and Apple avoid paying US income taxes on billions of dollars of revenue via transferring income to offshore companies.

9 Policy Convergence: The Government Regulation of Communication

with Sonja Macdonald

In earlier chapters we addressed the history of communication regulation in Canada, and high-lighted different forms of policy and regulation for the press, broadcasting, and telecommunication. We also discussed some of the important political economic, social, and technological conditions that contributed to these regulatory structures in Canada. This chapter moves beyond the history of the distinct forms of communication, press, broadcasting, and telecommunication to address the emergence of policy convergence in Canadian communication. Like the shift from "low-tech" to "high-tech," or from "old" to "new" media, behind this policy convergence are a number of important myths that inform how policy structures enable and constrain public access to, and the use of, communication technology.

This chapter begins with a review of some international aspects of communication policy and the tensions between private and public directions discussed in the previous chapter. It focuses particularly on the dialectic between the legal recognition of communication rights and the effort to expand regimes of global trade liberalization. It details a brief history of the steps taken by the federal government to establish a converged communication policy in Canada and then it highlights important issues and current policy debates, such as ownership, Internet infrastructure, and copyright. The chapter concludes with an assessment of future challenges and opportunities for communication policy in Canada as it sets the context for the final section of this book.

As may become evident, this chapter is likely a more challenging one, as we are less familiar with the language of the governance of communication and technology than we are with the myths surrounding it. This alone should be reason enough for us to pause and question why this is so. Nevertheless, our knowledge of the decision-making processes can better facilitate our participation in them such that neither apathy nor intimidation constrains our agency.

Objectives

After reading this chapter, you should be able to identify and explain the following:

- the different modes of governance employed to regulate the access to and use of new media technologies;
- the international and national contexts for communication policy;
- how the Canadian government is addressing governance of new media; and
- some of the key policy issues currently being debated in Canada.

Keywords

- **communication rights**
- **deep packet inspection**
- **digital content locks**
- **digital rights management (DRM)**
- **globalization**
- **governance**
- **horizontal governance**
- **Internet traffic management practices (ITMPs)**
- **media policy**
- **network neutrality**
- **policy**
- **regulatory capture**
- **vertical governance**

Mythologies: Variations on Theme

It is a theme that we are already familiar with. As each new form of technology is introduced, there are prognostications about how it signals the death of "old" media and how it will transform human society, whether by providing economic gains unforeseen previously or the potential for democratic liberation for all who use it (Mosco, 2004a). The myths surrounding technology that we reviewed in the previous chapter also inform the struggles around the policies and regulations that govern how technologies are used and adapted today. The power of myths is important not only for what they reveal about a society at a particular time but also for what they conceal about the social relations in that era (ibid.). In particular, these myths underscore and support ideological positions, which are articulated in **policy** development. They expose for us what influences policy-makers in their decisions around technological development, and they also illuminate the "common sense" that is communicated by policy-makers around their decisions and resulting policies.

Where Vincent Mosco discusses the general relationships between myth, power, and new media, Robert Babe provides further insight into certain myths that are at the root of communication policy development in Canada. He thus offers us another way to review and connect what we have learned so far about the media environment. In the introduction to *Telecommunication in Canada: Technology, Industry and Government*, Babe (1990) highlights five myths that he argues have long been present throughout the history and development of Canadian communication policy.

The first myth is that of *technological nationalism*, which refers to how Canada as a nation was constructed and connected by technological advances, like the railway and telecommunication networks we reviewed in Chapter 6. Following on the work of Maurice Charland (2004), this myth posits that these technologies are central to keeping Canada united because they physically connect the country's vast geography (Babe, 1990; Charland, 2004). Babe (1990) submits that this is simply not the case, however, as it has been more common that Canadian communication technology has been implemented in aid of continental integration of North America rather than solely directed towards Canadian nation-building (ibid., p. 7; see also Rideout, 2003).

The second myth is what Babe (1990) calls *technological dependence*, which includes two "dueling doctrines" of technological imperative and technological determinism (p. 9). Technological imperative refers to how the necessity of technological progress is subject to little human direction or control (ibid.). Technological determinism refers to the view that all

POLICY

Formal and informal decision-making, where actors with different degrees of power and autonomy participate in the process (Raboy & Padovani, 2010, p. 160).

human phenomena is explainable by the evolution of technology (ibid.). But what this myth obscures, according to Babe, are the decisions made by people, organized in "agglomerations" such as governments, corporations, or citizen groups that encourage the development of certain technologies over others (ibid., p. 12).

The third myth, *technology and industrial structuring*, is founded on three related claims: first, that "efficient and existing industrial structures hinge on underlying technique" (p. 14) such as natural monopolies; second, that each of the forms of communication (radio, television, and telecommunication) constitute separate industries because of unique industrial techniques; and third, that "industrial application of scientific knowledge are now forcing convergence among these industrial sectors" (p. 15). The combination of these three claims that build on the myth of technological dependence highlights how technologies and techniques dominate and drive policy-making rather than human actors involved in the decision-making process. This obscures the actions of policy-makers. As we reviewed earlier, for example, it was government legislation that provided Bell Canada a natural monopoly in telecommunication in exchange for its development of the national telecommunication system. Legislation was also key in the separation of telecommunication and broadcasting as two separate industries (see Babe, 1990; Winseck, 1998).

The fourth myth, the *efficacy of regulation*, is particularly salient in the struggle over the future of communication policy in Canada. This myth advances that regulation has been used throughout Canada's history to protect and promote consumers' interests in the communication sectors. Babe (1990) argues that this is not borne out in a review of policy decisions of the past. He posits that rather than focusing on the consumer, regulatory agencies have been captured by industry interests that come to dominate and form regulatory decisions. This is a myth that is raised again and contested by other Canadian communication scholars such as Liora Salter and Felix Odartey-Wellington (2008), and is evident in our introduction to the founding of IHAC in the previous chapter. This is an issue of **regulatory capture**, which is notably present in CRTC decisions around ownership, as we discuss later in detail.

The final myth that Babe (1990) discusses is what he terms the *gales of creative destruction*, which states that market equilibrium and the protection of the public interest (that are threatened by monopolies) are naturally righted by the gales of creative destruction. These gales are created from "new technologies, capitalistic innovation and the entrepreneurial spirit" (ibid., p. 19). In this case, old monopolies are toppled by the introduction of new technologies and new institutions at the helm of these innovations. Twenty years later, we can still see the propagation of this myth in what Florida (2010) advances in his book *The Great Reset*. This final myth is an extension of the technological dependence myth in that it places the power for change in the realm of new technologies and new uses. Babe (1990) challenges this with a review of the history of telecommunication in Canada, where new innovation was absorbed and controlled by the existing structures of power (p. 20). This is certainly the case, as you will see, with the issues surrounding the regulation of Internet infrastructure.

All of these myths are important in a study of policy development because they tend to assist us in understanding that decisions around communication technology do not just spontaneously appear from the technology itself. It is more likely that these decisions are formed through contentious and political processes, rather than simply as a result of just the invention of a technology that drives its use and development (Freedman, 2008).

Communication policy is quite complex because the sector encompasses two sets of values (introduced in Chapter 2) in the struggle for balance. The first involves the *use value* of communication—the symbolic or normative value of communication in constituting and reinforcing how we think about culture, our communities, and ourselves. The second recognizes that the

REGULATORY CAPTURE

The idea that regulators or operators lost (or never had) the independence to make professional decisions on their merits because of undue influence either from politicians or the regulated monopolies (Melody, 1997, p. 15).

communication sector is dominated by a set of industries grounded in *exchange value* and that, as such, have economic value in their own right. Technological myths often obscure the tension between these values as well as the institutions and actors that are at the core of **media policy**. They obfuscate how these decisions are made, and how it is decided which issues are considered important enough to address by the government and legal system. This is certainly the case at both international and national levels.

Ideology and Policy-Making

Technological myths also tend to obscure their own ideological roots as well as those that are applied to policy development. How can we identify and understand these ideological roots? Communication scholars indicate that a number of ideological approaches underlie policy development (Freedman, 2008; Hackett & Carroll, 2006). We need to know the difference between them to be able to evaluate which approach is being advanced, which prioritizes use values or exchange values, and which affords the public greater or lesser participation.

Des Freedman (2008) argues, for example, that there are two approaches to policy development evident in practice. The first is *liberal pluralism*, where policy is the result of a competitive process of debate and negotiation between various actors. In this view, no one group has full power over policy-making; rather, multiple groups have access to the process, and tensions between use and exchange value can be resolved accordingly. Certainly, existing power imbalances remain (as they are not eliminated by the process), such that private corporate interests may be able to wield certain power over the media system. But, according to liberal pluralism, this can be regulated by public participation in the policy process and through regulatory structures that ensure a diversity of participants have access to the media. Freedman suggests that this ideological approach was the dominant one informing policy-making in communication until around the mid-1980s (ibid., pp. 25–36).

The second approach that Freedman highlights is the *neo-liberal* approach to policy development, which we were introduced to earlier as the one favoured by the several successions of federal government. This approach posits that the communication sector is like any other sector in the economy, and that the best means by which to "regulate" it would be through the so-called free market. In this instance, there is a great deal of skepticism of the state's role in media, and media (like newspapers and broadcasters) are seen as "watchdogs of the state" as an accountability mechanism. The market is viewed as the primary means of regulating consumer choice and determining the future direction of the media system. In this view, state intervention should only occur in instances of market failure. As such, the responsibilities are shifted from accountability, to the "public" (writ large), to the commodified public, to the consumer, the industry, and a capitalist economy. Freedman argues that this approach has become dominant since the 1980s (pp. 36–41).

A third ideological approach, offered by Robert Hackett and Yuezhi Zhao (2005), is the *radical democratic* approach. It is the lesser known and practised of the three and thus you were introduced to it in Part I of this book. In this case, the media system, like all other aspects of society, is marked by structural inequalities—such as gender, race, or class—that limit equal access to resources and to policy structures that regulate those resources. The role of the state is not only to ensure that there is a public forum for discussion and management of the market but also to ensure that the necessary supports exist to create and engender equality in all aspects of life, including participation in media production and policy debates. This means ensuring that those making decisions about the media include people from all walks of life, regardless

MEDIA POLICY
The political economic, legal, as well as social and cultural terms of reference, which are seen to regulate the media environment; there are two main approaches to media policy: On one hand there are *normative positions*, which implicitly or explicitly evaluate the socio-political roles and objectives being served by media use. On the other, there are *institutional arrangements*, which direct the operation of the media to fulfill those roles and objectives. The concept of policy combines these normative and institutional aspects of regulation. It also combines the management of media by both public and private agencies (Hamelink & Nordenstreng, 2007, p. 225).

of capabilities (ibid., pp. 12–13). This approach informs much of the media policy activism that focuses its attention on issues like universal access to communication resources, as well as support for alternative models of media production, as in public and alternative media as we discuss in Chapter 13. As we go through the various examples of Canadian policy-making, see if you can identify when, where, and by whom each one of these approaches is prioritized.

Myth of Globalization

To understand how myth, ideology, and policy are interrelated, it is useful to begin by briefly addressing two broad-reaching myths that shape the direction of policy at both global and national levels, in all aspects of society. These are the myth of **globalization** and the myth of the market; as almost humanless catalysts, each are invoked as entities in their own right, and thus responsible for social change, rather than the results of conscious decision-making made by human beings. We were introduced to the former myth—globalization—in Chapter 2, in economic terms, but it is a more complex and often contentious concept, whose definition encompasses spatial and networked social relations.

There are four types of change that are important in understanding the processes of globalization:

> —First, it involves a *stretching* of social, political and economic activities across political frontiers, regions and continents.
>
> —Second, it suggests the *intensification*, or the growing magnitude, of inter–connectedness and flows of trade, investment, finance, migration, culture, etc.
>
> —Third, the growing extensity and intensity of global *interconnectedness* can be linked to a speeding up of global interactions and processes, as the evolution of world-wide systems of transport and communication increases the velocity of the diffusion of ideas, goods, information, capital, and people.
>
> —Fourth, the growing extensity, intensity and velocity of global interactions can be associated with their deepening impact such that the effects of distant events can be highly significant elsewhere and even the most local developments may come to have enormous *global consequences*. In this sense, the boundaries between domestic matters and global affairs can become increasingly blurred. (Held, McGrew, Goldblatt, & Perraton, 1999, #2)

As Held, McGrew, Goldblatt, and Perraton (1999) note, globalization occurs in part due to, and aided by, the expanding networks of ICTs that underlie the interconnection of global capital and culture. Additionally, ICTs are themselves an industrial sector that is global in scope. The importance of the ICT sector has fuelled international and Canadian economic and industrial policy beginning in the 1970s and continues today. As many scholars contend globalization is not a new phenomenon in the Information Age; the difference now is in how ICTs are used to accelerate the global interconnections (McIver, 2010; Mosco, 2004a; Siochru & Girard, 2002).

In previous chapters we learned that there has always been an international basis for agreements on communication, such as the standardization of time and regulation of the tele-communication and broadcasting spectrum. Nonetheless, the current myth of globalization is

---

GLOBALIZATION

A process (or set of processes) that embodies a transformation in the spatial organization of social relations and transactions, generating transcontinental or interregional flows and networks of activity, interaction, and power (Held, McGrew, Goldblatt, & Perraton, 1999).

having an impact on the power of the nation-state in establishing its own policies related to the development of ICTs and new media.

Throughout the late nineteenth and early twentieth centuries, the power of the nation-state was paramount in decisions related to resources within national geographic boundaries. Since the 1980s there has been a marked shift in this due to two competing approaches to international policy regimes. These include international human rights regimes and global trade systems, leading to models of what is called **vertical governance**.

With respect to communication policy, the UN has been active through its agencies, such as the UN Education, Scientific and Cultural Organization (UNESCO), in establishing a venue for international negotiations around issues such as **communication rights** and cultural diversity. The Department of Canadian Heritage has participated in this forum to advance issues around the protection of Canadian cultural diversity in the global context.

In contrast and in tension with these use values are the trade-related international bodies, like the WTO, which are active in establishing and enforcing international treaties that then inform national policies. These draw the attention of Industry Canada in advancing commodified relations of communication through agreements, such as the Trade-Related aspects of Intellectual Property Rights (TRIPS), that have spurred national copyright reforms. These practices have led many scholars to refer to the lessening of the power of the nation-state and a shift from government to **governance** in the regulation of new media (Castells, 2010; Splichal, 2009).

Arguing that there is still a substantial potential for state power in representing their publics, other scholars such as Saskia Sassen challenge this view of the diminished state. Sassen (2006) does not argue that the nation-state has transformed in light of global governance regimes, but she argues that power still remains at the national level because it's the last, and arguably more important, level of public accountability. As we saw in the previous chapter with the introduction of Industry Canada at the demise of the Department of Communication, Sassen concedes that globalization is indeed changing the state, where the priorities and powers given to certain departments and agencies shift as international issues increasingly influence national government priorities.

From National to Global Policy-Making

"The myth of the market" (Mosco, 2004b, p. 35) refers to a greater reliance on neo-liberal ideology in structuring control over, and access to, communication resources. This shift prioritizes market-oriented processes like commercialization, privatization, liberalization, and financialization, ignoring, distorting, or at least manipulating the use value of communication. The market mythology has led to the adoption of different forms of **horizontal governance**, whereby regulatory responsibility is shifted from sole state responsibility to different arrangements of *co-regulation* or *self-regulation*.

Co-regulation refers to shared responsibility between the state, its agencies, and private-sector actors (Puppis, 2010). In the context of communication policy in Canada, there are a number of bodies where co-regulation is at play. These include the CRTC's co-regulatory arrangements with the privately governed Canadian Broadcast Standards Council (CBSC; www.cbsc.ca/english/) pertaining to broadcasting content. Self-regulation refers to how an industry sector establishes its own set of rules and regulations that come to govern the actions of its membership or industry (ibid.). Often, self-regulatory measures are introduced to protect against the creation of government regulations for an industry. In communications on the international level, the Internet Corporation for Assigned Names and Numbers (ICANN) is an important example given it decides on all IP addresses, while provincial press councils are examples of self-regulation of

VERTICAL GOVERNANCE
The process whereby decision-making has shifted from the internal, unilateral authority of the nation-state up to a series of external regional and international bodies, such as the United Nations (UN) or the World Trade Organization (WTO; Puppis, 2010).

COMMUNICATION RIGHTS
A set of human rights codified in international, regional, and national regulations (such as The Universal Declaration of Human Rights and the Canadian Charter of Rights and Freedoms) that pertain to standards of performance with regard to the provision of information and the functioning of communication processes in society (Hamelink & Nordenstreng, 2007, p. 234). These rights include a right to freedom of expression and opinion; a right to participate in one's own culture and use one's mother language; a right to enjoy the benefits of scientific progress and its applications; a right to information regarding governance and matters of public interest (access to information); a right to protection of the moral and material interests of authorship; a right to privacy, and many others (Raboy & Shtern, 2010, p. 29).

GOVERNANCE

"The rules and procedures that states and other involved parties agree to use to order and regularize their treatment of a common issue" (Mueller, Mathiason, & McKnight, 2004, p. 4).

HORIZONTAL GOVERNANCE

The process whereby decision-making in government has shifted *internally*, from the sole purview of one department with a set mandate to several departments across several mandates, and *externally*, extending government decision-making to include dominant private actors (such as industry associations or corporations) and, to a lesser extent, organizations representing the public.

content in commercial newspapers in Canada (see ▣ www.bcpresscouncil.org, ontpress.com, and ▣ conseildepresse.qc.ca/en, e.g.).

From national to global governance regimes, the struggle between public and private ownership and control, and tensions between use and exchange value, are increasingly acute. Although this has been a historically consistent tension, the consequences of a converged policy environment can subordinate nation-state jurisdiction and thus public ownership and control to decisions made outside the boundaries of national citizenship and accountability.

In liberal democratic and radical democratic approaches to global governance, new media—and particularly the Internet—is approached as a set of shared resources, essential for realizing democratic aims. Thus a set of communication rights—such as access, participation, and universality—must be legally enacted in international treaties and agreements that influence national governments and transnational corporations (TNCs). In contrast, those who view communication as a commodified and private resource also see new media as tradable goods and services just like any others that are subject to international trade regimes. In this view, these information resources should be subject to a "free flow" in trade on a global basis and not protected by national regulatory concerns, such as cultural sovereignty or public interest principles.

Liberal and radical democratic approaches are most apparent in the long-standing struggle of academics, activists, and some national governments and civil society organizations to expand on a set of communication rights for all. This movement began after the Second World War, with the stated goal to end wars and conflict and build a world based on shared and unrestricted communication as the necessary condition for peace. This was articulated in the establishment of the United Nations (with its goal being "to build peace in the hearts of men"), by drafting The Universal Declaration of Human Rights (UDHR), which was adopted in 1948, entrenching the right to freedom of expression (UDHR, 1948, Article 19; ▣ www.un.org/en/documents/udhr/).

Article 19 was an important first step in the push for communication rights, but it marks only the beginning of what is needed. In 1969, Jean d'Arcy, a senior French civil servant, articulated the need for a "right to communicate" that went beyond the protection of freedom of expression, and instead encompassed a greater number of communication rights (Dakroury, 2009; Raboy & Shtern, 2010, p. 31). Thus a long international struggle ensued whereby loose networks of nations, activists, academics, and others coalesced over the next 40 years to pursue a more comprehensive and formalized recognition of communication rights in the ever-changing communication environment.

In the 1970s, the fight for communication rights became prominent as one effort in a larger set of social, political, economic, and cultural movements worldwide. Building on the civil rights movements of the 1960s, these included heightened social unrest related to inequality around issues of race, class, and gender in North America and Western Europe; the growing de-colonization movement throughout the "Global South" in the same period; and economic uncertainly fuelled in part by the OPEC oil crisis in the early 1970s. At this time, a coalition of countries that were not aligned with either the western allies of NATO or the Soviet Bloc countries coalesced into the Non-Aligned Movement (NAM). With increased power due to global events, the NAM countries successfully pushed the UN to open a discussion around a New International Economic Order (NIEO). One aspect of this was the creation of a New World Information and Communication Order (NWICO) under the auspice of UNESCO.

With NWICO, the NAM countries and their supporters were advocating for greater equity in the flow of communication resources globally. They were working against a long tradition of what was seen as "cultural imperialism" in that the flow of information and communication (in both infrastructure and content) was dominated by industrialized countries like the United States and the United Kingdom such that the flow was unidirectional and corporately controlled (recall the "diffusion of innovation" and modernization theories from Chapter 1). In contrast to the NAM position, the United States and the United Kingdom—countries that had long held the balance of power in these communication flows—were advocating for the "free flow of information" based largely on unfettered market forces, entrenching existing control by Western media companies over both communication infrastructure and content. In order to try and reach some consensus, in 1977 UNESCO struck a Commission, which was chaired by Irish Nobel laureate Sean MacBride, to review these issues. The MacBride Commission, as it became known, reported in 1979 with 82 recommendations aimed to bring about "a new more just and efficient world information and communication order" addressing four main areas:

- the development of third-world countries to become truly independent and self-reliant on their own cultural representations. This included building infrastructure, national policy regimes, and (re)distribution of communication resources, such as the Ethernet or spectrum;
- better international news-gathering and better conditions for journalists, involving ethical rules, education, and diverse and multiple news sources;
- democratization of communication, involving access and participation, with the right to communicate as foremost; and
- furtherance of international cooperation via development assistance, support for regional coordination, and support for international research and planning (Carlsson, 2003, p. 46).

The final report recommendations were opposed by the United States and the United Kingdom and ultimately led to their resignations from UNESCO, leading to the eventual demise of this stage of the struggle for communication rights.

World Summit on the Information Society

Despite the inadequacies of both the NWICO and the MacBride Commission, the push for communication rights re-emerged in the early 2000s as part of the United Nations' study of the emerging "information society." The World Summit on the Information Society (WSIS) was launched by the UN and the International Telecommunication Union (ITU) in Geneva in 2003, followed by a second conference held in Tunis in 2005. The process that led up to WSIS was different from NWICO and reflected the shift from government to vertical governance that emerged in global communication policy since the 1980s. Unlike NWICO, which was a process led almost exclusively by nation-states, WSIS, from its inception included participation from corporate interests and from civil society organizations (www.itu.int/council/groups/wsis/index.html). The approach was in response to two changes that had occurred in the 20 years since NWICO was formed. The first was that control and regulation over ICTs had shifted from state control alone to include other forms such as self-regulation, as exemplified by the creation of ICANN, referred to earlier. ICANN is a private US corporation that oversees the allotment of domain names globally. Although it is subject to US corporate laws, ICANN is a private entity with global reach in Internet governance (www.icann.org/). The second change was the growing organization of civil society groups advocating for communication rights globally, exemplified by the campaign for Communication Rights in the Information Society (CRIS), which took a leading role in the WSIS conferences (www.crisinfo.org/).

While the initial mandate of WSIS was supposed to be about an array of issues related to the emerging information society, the actual focus of the Summit narrowed greatly over the number of years of its existence to focus almost exclusively on Internet governance and what role international bodies and national governments would play. This reflected the tensions between who should control the Internet, whether international bodies representing nation-states, or private corporations like ICANN and other corporate entities. CRIS and other civil society groups worked diligently throughout the process to expand the debate around larger questions of communication rights, but with limited success.

The second approach to global communication regulation is found in trade-related international agreements like the North American Free Trade Agreement (NAFTA) or organizations like the WTO that oversee the General Agreement on Tariffs and Trade (GATT), the General Agreement on Trade in Services (GATS), and the already discussed TRIPS (www.wto.org/). In terms of NAFTA and GATT, the main area of attention is in telecommunication and information services, which is significantly unprotected in contrast to other cultural industries, as Canada successfully argued, for example, with broadcasting internationally secured under cultural exemptions.

In illustration of the market-liberal or neo-liberal ideological approach, the GATT Annex Agreement on Telecommunications, for example, calls on its signatory countries to move to a market-oriented regime of regulation, eschewing long-standing public interest principles of access and universality that are entrenched in national legislation. The TRIPS agreement requires its signatory countries to amend their national copyright legislation to incorporate more restrictive rules related to the economic rights of copyright as private property, rather than allowing for a more open system of protections that encourage creative innovation (www.wto.org/english/docs_e/legal_e/legal_e.htm).

Similar to the previous set of international efforts at policy cooperation (NWICO and WSIS), the power of these types of international institutions mark the shift to vertical governance as many of the agreements become binding on member countries like Canada. Yet, these agreements differ from NWICO and WSIS in two important ways. Firstly, as noted by Winseck and Cuthbert (1997), trade-related agreements "served to eviscerate the relationship between communication and human values altogether" (p. 14). Instead ICTs were positioned in terms of their exchange value as tradable goods and services, moving them from the public to the commercial realm. Secondly, these agreements shift the decision-making authority for the regulation of ICTs from the nation-state level, where there is some level of representative democracy and accountability (in Canada at least), to a supra-national level where national citizens have little to no access to decision-making. Related to this, the trade-related agreements also challenge national policies like the protection of cultural sovereignty, an illustration of which is the United States successfully challenging Canada's financial policies in support of the periodical industry in the 1990s through NAFTA and the WTO.

Negotiations in Canadian Communication Policy

The tension between communication rights and market regulation exists at the national as well as the global level. The influence of the myth of the market is certainly at play in the Canadian communication policy arena. This is articulated more pointedly as a tension between public interest principles, such as diversity of ownership, universal access, and fair uses that are normative founding values of Canadian communication policy, and what Hackett and Anderson (2011) call a neo-liberal market orthodoxy that pervades the contemporary re-crafting of communication policy in all areas. While international governance regimes do certainly influence

ONGOING ISSUES

Supporting Public Engagement in the Broadcasting Policy Process?

In the Canadian broadcasting policy environment there is one basic principle that informs the relationship between the public, the government and its agencies (CRTC), and the broadcasting industry; this is that the airwaves over which programs are broadcast are public property. Therefore Canadian citizens, as the owners of the resource, have a right to participate in the decision-making around how these airwaves are used. This is often done through the licencing process of stations at the CRTC, whether by allotting new licences, renewing existing licences, or transferring ownership of licences.

Although public participation in policy has been a basic tenet of the system since before the CRTC, there have traditionally been many impediments to a fulsome engagement of the public in this process, including knowledge of the system, as well as the time and money required to both develop public submissions and/or present before the CRTC at its public hearings. As a result, very few Canadians have participated in this process, despite its impact on their daily lives. Thus the broadcasting policy process has been left in the hands of a select group of participants, including the broadcasters themselves and their lobbyists, government officials, and some public interest groups such as the Public Interest Advocacy Centre (PIAC) or The Centre for Community Study (CCS; 🖥 communitystudy.ca/). These groups have represented the public interest at a myriad of CRTC hearings, but both fully acknowledge that they provide only a portion of the public comments required for a truly democratic policy process. As a result, both of these organizations have recently pursued efforts to improve the avenues for direct public engagement in the broadcasting policy process.

PIAC was chiefly responsible for the creation of the Broadcasting Participation Fund through the CRTC (🖥 www.crtc.gc.ca/eng/archive/2012/2012-181.htm). The Fund emulates a similar one that has been in place for those interested in participating in the public process around telecommunication policy development for decades. The way it works is any public interest and consumer group representing "non-commercial user interests" (CRTC, 2012, no. 6) are eligible to apply to the CRTC for funds to offset the costs of developing and presenting their submissions to the Commission in relation to a specific public proceeding. The Fund was developed through a partnership between Bell Canada Enterprises (BCE) and PIAC as a "tangible" benefit of BCE's re-acquisition of CTVglobemedia in 2011. The details of the Fund are still being developed between the three parties (CRTC, BCE, and PIAC), but the benefits of this Fund for those representing the public interest in broadcasting issues are very important. It is one small step to levelling the playing field when it comes to who has access to the policy process.

Another example of recent efforts to allow for greater public participation in the broadcasting policy process is a new web portal, 🖥 localtelevision.ca, created by the CCS. The purpose of the site is to provide Canadians with current information about the licencing requirements of their local television stations and when these licences are up for renewal. The site provides links to the licences themselves as well as to the public comments process at the CRTC when this is appropriate for each station. The project is in its infancy, and has begun by highlighting the 15 local television markets identified by the CRTC in its Diversity of Voices decision (🖥 www.crtc. gc.ca/ownership/eng/dov_ind.htm). The intent is to expand to all local television markets and eventually into radio as well. The purpose of the site is to provide accurate and approachable information about the CRTC licencing process to encourage more Canadians to participate in the decisions made around their public resources.

Continued

Discussion Questions

1.   Identify and make a list of the television and radio stations that serve the region where you, or your relatives, live in Canada (look for public [CBC], private, and community stations). Visit 🖥 www.crtc.gc.ca and search for the station licences, who owns them, and when they are up for renewal.

2.   Identify the *conditions* of licence for the station and its current programming; write a brief (two- to three- page) commentary about whether or not the station is living up to its requirements.

3.   Share your findings with the class. This can be the basis of a submission to the CRTC when the station licence is next up for renewal.

Canada's policy development, these are not uniform or uncontested. Canada continues to take its own path in policy development, facing successes and challenges.

Policy Convergence and Canada's Digital Future

As we have discussed in previous chapters, convergence is a central aspect of new media, whether it is technological, corporate, or commercial. The policy arena is another place where convergence has been a central theme, going back to the 1970s, when the federal government was trying to figure out how to align its broadcasting and telecommunication legislation in light of the future growth of ICTs. This drive for a unified communication policy for the country builds on the many myths discussed earlier. Most important among these are the myths of technological dependence, arguing that policy action is driven by technology, and of the efficacy of regulation, where the broader public interests of society are incorporated into policy decisions. A review of the last 40 years of policy actions related to the information society demonstrates a shift in the ideological approach to policy from liberal pluralism to neo-liberalism. It also demonstrates a division in the value sets inherent in communication rather than a convergence of goals. Finally, this history exemplifies policy inaction, as the call for policy convergence has been around for decades, yet despite numerous commissions, hearings, and task forces, little has been done to bring the legislation together to map out a clear and balanced direction for Canada's digital future.

The first call for policy convergence came with the Instant World report tabled by the federal government's Telecommission task force in 1971. The task force was responsible for reviewing the development of a telecommunication policy for Canada, including what role these technologies play in the broader lives of Canadians, beyond just economic issues. The final report, according to Marc Raboy (1996), "set the tone for the Canadian approach to communication development in the 1970s: continued public investment in hardware and infrastructure, subsidy and protective regulation of Canadian content, regulatory convergence of broadcasting and telecommunications" (p. 60). The Instant World report suggested a very different kind of policy convergence than what would follow it (🖥 tspace.library.utoronto.ca/bitstream/1807/32119/1/For_Sale_to_the_highest_bidder___Chapter_1.pdf). It was focused on a balance between social and economic considerations. Additionally, it highlighted the importance of public engagement in the communication policy arena, arguing that "those making decisions on fundamental issues of telecommunications policy should have access to all the relevant facts, and should be in a position to hear the views of all concerned so that the effects of their decision may be seen in true perspective" (as cited in Longford, Moll, & Shade, 2008, p. 6).

Very few of the recommendations of the Telecommission's report were adopted by the federal government of its time, however. Notably, a very small step towards policy convergence was taken with moving oversight of the Telecommunications Act to the CRTC in 1976. In the early 1990s, both the broadcasting and the telecommunication legislation were updated, separately. Recall that the Department of Communication was eliminated, and its responsibilities for broadcasting and telecommunication were divided between the Department of Canadian Heritage and Industry Canada, respectively, the result of which was to sever the use value and symbolic aspects of communication from the exchange value or economic aspects of communication, creating a competitive rather than complementary policy environment. What resulted was a move where policy development related to Canada's digital future fell within the purview of Industry Canada with little attention given to the symbolic or public use values of communication.

As we reviewed in the previous chapter, the results of this were exemplified in the establishment of the Information Highway Advisory Council (IHAC) to review and propose a new digital infrastructure policy for the country. Comprised mainly of industry representatives, there were no formal means of public input, such as public hearings, held over the two-year review period. IHAC's reports were very different from Instant World. Unlike its 1970s predecessor, IHAC's final report did not aim to achieve a balance of social and economic considerations, but rather called for an "approach that affirmed the undeniable urgency of facilitating technological development, but in which primary control over the specifics of this development would be handed over to the private sector and market interests" (Barney, 2004, p. 100; www.hc-sc.gc.ca/hcs-sss/ehealth-esante/infostructure/ihac_ccai-eng.php).

While IHAC was meeting and deliberating on Canada's future in the information economy, the CRTC was also reviewing how it would address technological convergence. Beginning in 1995, the Commission held a series of public consultations, seeking input on questions around convergence, content, access, and competitive safeguards, and defining broadcasting (Clement, Moll, & Shade, 2001, pp. 28–9). Clement, Moll, and Shade (2001) argue that, in part, because of the closed-door nature of IHAC, there was a very active public response to the CRTC hearings, where there was broad support for a balanced approach to cyberspace, viewing it, like the radio spectrum upon which it is built, as a public space where commercial and social uses needed to be considered and managed together (p. 29). Despite the public interest and comments, the Commission's final report stayed close to the same tone found in IHAC, focusing on the importance of competition in the communications industry, although it did acknowledge the need for community access as a central pillar of future policies (p. 30).

Another important decision that came from the CRTC in the 1990s was related to how the regulator should address broadcasting in new media. With the increasing use of the Internet for a variety of activities in the late 1990s, the Commission was considering the effects of this on its regulation of Canadian content in broadcasting. Following public consultations, the CRTC released its decision stating that it would not regulate broadcasting in new media because the majority of information available on the Internet was alphanumeric, and therefore outside of the responsibility of the Commission. For those online uses that were within its purview (such as audio/visual content), the CRTC (1999) decided that "regulation is not necessary to achieve the objectives of the Broadcasting Act." As we discussed, this policy was reviewed again in 2009, when the Commission again reiterated that it would not regulate broadcasting content available over the Internet (CRTC, 2009a). At the time of both these policy reviews, the final decisions were widely supported by commercial broadcasters, who wanted to avoid additional regulation of their online activities.

Following the IHAC model, Industry Canada later convened another national task force to review policies related to high-speed Internet access across the country. The National Broadband Task Force (NBTF) reported in 2002, calling on the government to support the expansion of broadband infrastructure across the country through policies and regulation that enabled private-sector investment and innovation, with government subsidizing infrastructure in remote regions (🖥 www.ic.gc.ca/eic/site/smt-gst.nsf/vwapj/C2-574-2001E.pdf/$FILE/C2-574-2001E.pdf). The overall management of the system, according to the report, should be left to the private sector (Barney, 2004, pp. 101–2). Despite the recommendations of the NBTF, no concrete and sustained action followed on the part of the federal government, and there is still no substantive national broadband strategy. Thus, leaving the leadership over these issues to the private sector has led to little action on rolling out universal broadband infrastructure for all Canadians as they jockey for positions in a marketplace dominated by multinational and transnational corporations.

The drive to reform and remake the rules around communication and new media continued throughout the 2000s. The next important action occurred in 2005, when the government convened the Telecommunications Policy Review Panel (TPRP) to "ensure that Canada has a strong, internationally competitive telecommunications industry, which delivers world-class affordable services and products for the economic and social benefit of all Canadians" (as cited in Longford et al., 2008, p. 5). The Panel was composed of three representatives and accepted written submissions throughout 2005, followed by two public fora for public interest and industry groups. The final report was tabled in March 2006, and as Longford et al. (2008) note, although there was at least public input into the process, industry and government concerns far outweighed those of public interest groups by a four to one ratio (p. 6). As Philippa Lawson (2008) notes, the final recommendations for policy change in the TPRP report reflect a "significantly narrower vision of the role of telecommunication in Canadian society" (p. 20; 🖥 www.ic.gc.ca/eic/site/smt-gst.nsf/vwapj/tprp-final-report-2006.pdf/$FILE/tprp-final-report-2006.pdf).

In particular, two of the key recommendations from the TPRP report were a greater reliance on market forces rather than government regulation over the telecommunication sector, which is now a continuing theme. More importantly, however, was its *removal* of any reference to domestic ownership of the telecommunication sector in Canada, thus opening the door for increased foreign ownership of the industry (Lawson, 2008, p. 24). While direct action on the TPRP recommendations were limited due to the Conservative minority government status until May 2011, the overall policy goals articulated in the report signal the direction that the federal government is heading, as you will see in the case study of Globalive detailed later in this chapter.

Despite the rather lacklustre record of implementing recommendations from the series of reports commissioned on how the government should address Canada's digital future, this has not stopped the current government from again aiming to establish a national digital economy policy. As was evident in the Speech from the Throne, this recent effort began in 2010, and the final strategy has yet to be released. There was a public input period in the summer of 2010, and the mandate of the policy review goes even further than the goals of the TPRP in narrowing the scope of communication policy in Canada. As the vision of the forthcoming digital economy policy is stated by Industry Canada (2010b), "by 2020, we see a country that boasts a globally competitive digital economy that is driven by innovation and enhanced productivity and generates enduring prosperity" (para. 2). Gone is any mention of public communication and social goals for our digital future.

This review of the policy history of the attempts by successive governments to design broad-reaching policies to govern the future direction of ICTs in Canada is instructive in many ways. First, it shows that despite broad statements about seeking to balance the public and private aspects of communication, its use and exchange values, and the symbolic and economic aspects of communication in policy convergence, the progress of policy discussion over the last 40 years has veered to neo-liberal market imperatives with less and less attention to considerations of social goals and public communication, as exemplified by the divisions in oversight between Canadian Heritage and Industry Canada.

Second, as Darin Barney (2005) has noted, the processes for how these policies are developed are becoming more and more closed off from our participation—in some cases before the public is even aware that they exist, or before they are cognizant of the high stakes that are in play, or even what the consequences of not participating are. As such, we are becoming more excluded not only from the process but also from the crucial decisions that affect the wider considerations of social, cultural, and even political implications of how technologies help to shape how we work, live, and play.

Third, these processes have exposed the relative ineffectiveness of broad policy pronouncements like IHAC and even the current Digital Economy Policy. This is often due to the policies being too broadly defined, and a lack of action on the part of governments. Finally, these efforts at broad policy change often obscure more particular and incremental actions that are taking place on specific policy issues that are more explicitly framing Canada's digital future (▣ www.scienceadvice.ca/uploads/eng/assessments%20and%20publications%20and%20 news%20releases/digital%20economy/2010-07-12_catalyzing_digital_economy.pdf).

These specific areas are offered in the next section by way of introduction to familiarize you with the current issues in front of decision-makers, and as perhaps an entry point of your participation in them. This participation may be found in three recent areas of policy action: ownership, Internet infrastructure, and copyright reform.

Ownership

Despite calls within policy documents for greater competition in the communication industries, the actual ownership landscape of Canada's media is very small. Even though policy convergence has eluded decision-makers, its corporate counterpart has been wildly successful in Canada, as ownership consolidation has become the norm for the media industries. As Salter and Odartey-Wellington (2008) note, there is "perhaps no issue as thoroughly contested in the Canadian broadcasting system as ownership and control" (p. 685).

There are two general groups of issues related to ownership; the first is ownership concentration within the Canadian communication landscape, including issues around horizontal, vertical, and cross-media ownership, and the second is foreign ownership of Canadian communication companies.

A number of government bodies and acts of Parliament provide the framework for regulation of media ownership in Canada, including the Department of Canadian Heritage, Industry Canada, the CRTC, the Competition Bureau, the Broadcasting Act (1991), the Telecommunications Act (1993), and the Investment Canada Act (1985). The CRTC is responsible for the oversight of ownership and control in the broadcasting and telecommunication sectors, and it is attentive to issues of concentration and foreign ownership. The Commission's responsibility can also reach into print media in situations of cross-media ownership. The CRTC makes decisions about corporate consolidation on a case-by-case basis, and shares this responsibility with the Competition Bureau, which oversees ownership concentration questions in all sectors of the Canadian economy.

Conflicts have arisen between the two agencies, as there are differing parameters by which each measures the impact of concentration within markets. With respect to foreign ownership, the rules are explicitly outlined in sections of both the Broadcasting Act (1991, § 3[1][a]) and the Telecommunications Act (1993, § 16). Additionally, the Investment Canada Act (1985) sets out parameters of foreign ownership of media companies outside the broadcasting and tele-communication sectors.

Ownership Concentration

Corporate ownership concentration of media in Canada is a continually shifting landscape and, as you learned from the previous chapter, not immune to the boom and bust cycles of the capitalist economy. Over the last 15–20 years, there has been an almost constant upheaval in ownership of all types of media properties, many of which have come together, separated, and re-formed in different arrangements. The one constant element of this movement has been a transition from a number of relatively small, regional, and independent media enterprises to far fewer large consolidated media companies.

As discussed in previous chapters, and as Winseck (2002) observed, we are now at the point that "Canada has one of the most consolidated media systems in the developed world and an unrivalled scale of cross media ownership" (p. 798). Armstrong (2010) argues that this consolidation occurs through three forms of industrial concentration: horizontal and vertical concentration and cross-media ownership (p. 209). We introduced these as horizontal and vertical integration in Chapter 3; *cross-media ownership* is where one firm owns more than one property in different media forms in the same market: For example, BCE owns Bell Canada national telecommunication service provider, Bell ExpressVu satellite service, the CTV Television Network, various local radio stations across Canada (previously owned by CHUM and by Astral), and *The Globe and Mail* national newspaper, as illustrated in Figure 3.2.

The purpose of this consolidation is to gain control over communication resources as technological convergence is facilitated. The re-purchase of CTVglobemedia, and recent purchase of Astral by BCE, reflects the move by the telecom company to ensure that they have access to popular content that can then be aired across multiple platforms, such that it owns both the infrastructure and the content. Other benefits of concentration, as articulated by commercial proponents before the CRTC, are that the bigger firms will have the financial wherewithal to deal with technological upgrades, to respond to challenges from new technologies, and they will be able to afford expensive popular programming (Salter & Odartey-Wellington, 2008, p. 688).

There are also real concerns about the levels of concentration in Canada, including how this influences the CRTC. Salter and Odartey-Wellington (2008) caution that large corporate firms are in the position of threatening the balance of the regulatory relationship between the CRTC and its licensees. Thus, they argue that in current CRTC regulations, the threat of "licence suspension" means little when the corporation owns so many media outlets: "When companies reach a size that they need not fear the actions of the regulator, either because they exercise so much clout, or because they pose the only option, or because they have very little to gain from regulation, the bargain collapses. Or rather, one side can dictate the terms" (ibid., p. 690).

A second concern about continued consolidation and the regulator is the Commission's reliance on collecting additional revenues for government from the transfers of ownership of media properties in broadcasting sales. These "tangible benefits" are so large that they generate significant income for the federal government. It thus makes it increasingly difficult for the CRTC to deny the deals when the government can gain so considerably from them.

There are additional concerns about corporate concentration beyond the regulator's ability to retain its authority. These include monopoly power with respect to consumer choice, limited outlets for independent Canadian productions, and limited funding available for Canadian programming, among others (p. 691). Concentration has a decidedly negative effect on the viability of local and community media, including the independence of editorial policies, and it has most significantly led to massive lay-offs and closures of new bureaus as we discuss in the next chapter (Skinner & Gasher, 2005, pp. 53–4; Winseck, 2002, p. 800).

Beyond the negative effects of concentration on the diversity of the media landscape, Skinner and Gasher also challenge the suggested benefits, specifically the greater financial strength that result from these mergers. They highlight that the costs associated with such a pattern of voracious acquisition, as exemplified by Canwest Global in the first decade of the twenty-first century, is

For Real?

The Bigger They Are the Harder They Fall?
Canwest Global Communications

Canwest Global was one of Canada's largest media companies with holdings in print, television, radio, and broadcasting production and distribution (see Figure 9.1). It also owned broadcasting enterprises around the world, such as Australia's Channel Ten. In 2007, Canwest purchased Alliance Atlantis, a national specialty television and distribution company for $2.3 billion. This deal followed another risky and pricey purchase of the *National Post* newspapers, both of

which extended Canwest beyond its means. To afford the Alliance Atlantis deal, Canwest sought the vast majority of its financing from Goldman Sachs Capital Partners in New York. Once the deal was done (and approved by the CRTC), this put Canwest in a very precarious place financially, and gave Goldman Sachs—a foreign equity firm—a 100 per cent equity claim over the Alliance Atlantis properties (G. Taylor, 2007), but not over the majority of Canwest's holdings. When the financial crisis hit in 2008, Canwest's financial gamble failed, leading to its demise. In 2009, after a fire sale of some of its broadcasting properties, Canwest went into bankruptcy protection, and it was divided up and sold off, the print holdings going to Postmedia Corporation, which was comprised of former bondholders. Its remaining broadcasting assets were sold to Shaw Media, for $2 billion, making that company a national player in Canadian broadcasting. The tangible benefits accrued from the Shaw–Canwest deal were approximately $200 million.

Figure 9.1 | The Canwest Global Plaza Tower in Winnipeg.

Source: © Richard Cummins / Alamy

Continued

Discussion Questions

1. How can integration lead to disintegration so quickly?

2. How much do you think financialization (Chapter 2) was a factor here?

3. How is this case similar or different than that of Nortel (Chapter 8)?

4. Where is the accountability to the public . . . and to the former workers of Canwest?

accompanied by crushing debt burdens that "have a detrimental impact on the quality of their content as resource cutback and layoffs invariably follow takeovers" (Skinner & Gasher, 2005, pp. 53–4).

Foreign Ownership

The Canwest–Goldman Sachs deal exposes the second important aspect of media ownership in Canada—that of foreign ownership of the communication industry. The existing regulatory system requires Canadian ownership of broadcasting and telecommunication, yet, as the Canwest deal demonstrates, these policies are not clear-cut. The debate over foreign ownership in Canada is not limited to the communication sector alone. Nor are the implications of foreign ownership of national media a specifically Canadian issue. Existing foreign ownership regulation is being challenged in the telecommunication sector as well as broadcasting, as made explicit in the TPRP report. Additionally, Canada's commitments to the GATT Annex Agreement on Telecommunications calls for the national government to liberalize its telecommunication policies, including eliminating restrictions on foreign investment.

Advocates of lifting restrictions contend that liberalizing foreign ownership rules would keep Canada in line with its international commitments (Moll & Shade, 2008, p. iii), and that this would allow access to foreign capital to expand and upgrade networks (Salter & Odartey-Wellington, 2008, p. 701). Proponents argue that there is no connection between ownership and content, thus existing foreign ownership restrictions are counter-productive (Acheson & Maule, 1999, p. 21). Another argument is that defined as a "small market" country, Canadian cultural industries would be better served internationally with foreign support, rather than trying to go it alone (ibid., p. 7). Additionally, since Canadian companies already own foreign media properties (e.g., the now defunct Canwest, and the global conglomerate Thomson Reuters), it is considered hypocritical for the government not to open the door to foreign ownership here as bolstered by the neo-liberal argument that restrictions are just obscuring a protectionist domestic agenda (Acheson & Maule, 1999; Dornan, 2007, p. 50). Proponents also argue that the "barn door is already open" given past decisions on split-run magazines, grey market satellites (Dornan, 2007; Schultz, 2003), and now the Globalive court decision (see Case Study: Globalive and WIND Mobile). Finally, due to the historically different policies for different Canadian cultural industries, the lack of coherence across media is considered contradictory (Dornan, 2007, p. 54).

There is, however, strong opposition to changes to foreign ownership restrictions. As noted earlier, this would shift Canadian communication policy away from public interest imperatives in favour of market forces. It could also lead to the increased homogenizing of media content and lead to the loss of local particularism (Barney, 2000, p. 252). From the perspective of regulation, it would leave the CRTC with little to no control over the operations of foreign owners (Hannigan, 2001). It is also feared that "removing such restrictions would unleash a tide of transnational consolidations that would make maintaining the regulatory framework and cultural sovereignty across media outlets practically impossible" (D. Skinner, 2008, p. 19). Finally, as exemplified by BCE, with the high level of cross-media ownership in Canada, opponents to foreign ownership raise the alarm that this internationalization would not only open the doors to foreign ownership in telecommunication but also in broadcasting (White, 2008, p. 43).

This discussion of issues related to the consolidation and foreign ownership of Canadian communication is important and is not without its contestation. In terms of concentration, the growing size and scale of the ownership deals could threaten both the stability of the Canadian communication environment and the regulatory power of the CRTC. With respect to foreign

Case Study

Globalive and WIND Mobile

In the summer of 2009 the federal government put 282 wireless-airwave licences in the 105 MHz spectrum band up for sale to wireless operators, both incumbent and new entrants. After two months of bidding, Industry Canada granted licences to 15 companies for a staggering total of $4.25 billion, including the three largest telecommunication carriers—BCE, TELUS, and Rogers—which, combined, account for 94 per cent of the Canadian wireless market. The remaining 12 licences were granted to "new entrants," meaning companies that had not previously been able to provide wireless mobile service. Many of the new entrants were regional companies like MTS (Manitoba Telecom Services) and Eastlink. Globalive, another new entrant, received licences to launch a national wireless service to compete with the incumbents. Prior to the auction, Globalive was providing VoIP (Voice over Internet Protocol) telephone service through its Yak brand, but the new wireless service is offered through WIND Mobile. The company paid $442.4 million for the national licences (Cartt.ca, 2008). While the spectrum auction proved to be a boon for the federal government's coffers, according to some reports, for consumers who would soon be seeing more competitive mobile service plans, it also proved to be another thin edge of the wedge in terms of foreign ownership, due to the Globalive approval.

In order to afford the hefty price tag for the national wireless licences, Globalive had to seek out external financing. According to its founder, Anthony Lacavera, the funding was not forthcoming in Canada; therefore he sought it out beyond our borders, and found support from Egypt's Orascom Telecom Holding. Orascom provided the necessary revenue in exchange for a 65.1 per cent equity stake in Globalive (Castaldo, 2009). Despite this ownership stake, Globalive executives and board of directors were all Canadian. Industry Canada did not show concern about this significant foreign investment in its approval of Globalive's bid for a licence, but the CRTC was not as agreeable. After reviewing Globalive's ownership and financial situation in 2009, the Commission (with the support of the three largest wireless incumbents) denied the licences, stating that Globalive did not meet Canadian ownership requirements. The minister of industry, Tony Clement, then proceeded to overturn the CRTC's decision and let the initial licencing decision stand.

The story does not end here though. Public Mobile, one of the other successful new entrants in the 2009 spectrum auction, filed suit in federal court against the federal government in January 2010. Its main argument was that "the government cannot change the law, only Parliament can

Continued

change the law" (Lam, 2010), meaning that the minister's actions were not lawful because to change the foreign ownership rules the Telecommunications Act needed to be changed, which could only be done by Parliament. In February 2011, the Federal Court ruled, upholding the CRTC's decision to deny Globalive's licence due to its foreign ownership by Orascom. The minister of industry promptly appealed the Court's decision, and in June 2011, the Federal Court of Appeal released its decision, which was to uphold Globalive's licences, arguing that it is a "Canadian owned and controlled company" (I. Marlow, 2011a, 2011b), despite the significant equity stake held by Orascom. Although heralded by many in the mainstream press as a conclusive decision, Public Mobile was continuing its efforts to stop Globalive by appealing this last decision to the Supreme Court of Canada. In 2012 the Supreme Court declined to hear the case, meaning that it had no legal merit (CBC, 2012).

The significance of this saga with Globalive is not simply about a lack of clarity over who owns what, but it demonstrates a number of important issues in the operation of communication policy in Canada.

Discussion Questions

1. Who has the authority to make decisions: the supposedly "autonomous regulator" or the minister of industry?

2. How democratic is the decision-making (and to what extent was Parliament or the public consulted during this deliberation)?

3. How much public input should there be in making legislative change?

4. To what extent does foreign ownership impact decision-making? How important a variable is financial control that resides outside Canadian borders?

5. What does this decision suggest about the three large incumbents' opposition to Globalive's ownership situation? Was patriotism or control over communication the main motivation?

6. What does this case suggest is the state of "competition" in the Canadian communication environment?

7. Where did the $4.25 billion dollars that the federal government made from auctioning off the public airwaves go?

NETWORK NEUTRALITY

"The principle that network service providers treat all traffic on the Internet equally and without discrimination, regardless of source, ownership, content, or destination. . . . Net neutrality provisions prevent service providers (telephone and cable companies) from speeding up, slowing down, or blocking online content or services based on their source, ownership or destination" (Shade, 2009, p. 183).

INTERNET TRAFFIC MANAGEMENT PRACTICES (ITMPs)

Tools "used by Internet service providers to manage the Internet traffic on their networks" (CRTC, 2009b, "Internet traffic management practices"). These "tools" can be technological, economic, or both.

ownership, the recent Globalive decision and the TPRP report signal that we are at a tipping point of transformation for this issue and its implications for the future of a Canadian-owned communications system.

Internet Infrastructure

Ownership issues also influence and inform other current policy debates, namely over how Internet infrastructure is controlled, by whom, and for what purpose. Like other policy debates, this one can be understood through a dialectical relationship of public interests and market forces. In support of the former, advocates seek to preserve the principle of network neutrality, or an open Internet, while the latter position argues in favour of establishing Internet traffic management practices (ITMPs) to measure and monitor usage online. This debate also highlights Babe's (1990) myth about the gales of creative destruction. The issue about the control of Internet infrastructure is in part about the unanticipated uses of the Internet and the abilities of existing incumbent carriers and content providers, mainly consolidated media companies like BCE, to continue to control and profit from how communication resources are deployed and used.

Before explaining the policy debate, it is perhaps helpful to have a cursory understanding (or refresher) of how the Internet works. It is often described as a "universal network of networks" (Solum, 2009, p. 50) that involves many different layers and many different users, creators, and sources. Two of the more general layers of the Internet are between infrastructure, meaning the hardware and software that make the system work, and content, the vast collection of information, images, sounds, and others materials that are available over the network. The current infrastructure can be divided into two layers: (1) the hardware—the computers, fibre optic cables, transmission towers, and other hard infrastructure (mainly telecommunication networks) over which the Internet travels; and (2) the software system that orders how the Internet works. This is made up of three interrelated systems: (1) the transmission control protocol/Internet protocol (TCP/IP) system that organizes, packages, and sends data across the network; (2) the domain name system (DNS) that establishes the addresses to which data is sent; and (3) the IP system that identifies individual computers or servers on the network (Bing, 2009; Solum, 2009). Beyond the infrastructure is the content that flows over the networks, including images, videos, music, news stories, software, games, social networking applications, and much, much more.

Although the Internet is a complex system that is constantly changing, there are certain basic principles that inform the relationship between infrastructure and content that harkens back to older media, specifically railway and telecommunication as discussed in Chapter 6. The main principle is one of network neutrality, which "refers to the founding principle informing the structural design of the Internet that all network traffic be treated equally, regardless of content, ownership, origin or destination" (Milberry, 2012). As Kate Milberry (2012) reminds us, the principle of common carriage that underpin network neutrality in Canada goes back to beginnings of the Railway Act, which ensured that those who owned the rail system could not discriminate against what was travelling the lines. This policy of common carriage was central to the structuring of the Canadian telecommunication system, which is the infrastructure upon which the Internet relies for its operation.

Threatening network neutrality are ITMPs that are technological and economic, for example, as used by those corporations that own the infrastructure supporting the Internet (telecommunication or cable systems). Technological practices restricting traffic include throttling, which is when an Internet service provider (ISP) uses the technique of **deep packet inspection** (that allows the ISP to watch and identify the contents of Internet traffic) and selectively limit the bandwidth it allocates to certain applications (e.g., peer-to-peer [P2P] programs like BitTorrent) at peak times (Stover, 2010, p. 80). Economic practices include usage-based billing (UBB), which allows ISPs to charge a premium for bandwidth and faster service. Ultimately this establishes a two-tiered Internet: one for those who can afford the speed and space of premium service and one for those who cannot. These practices have become more prevalent over the last decade and have led to a push for clearer regulatory decisions in many countries about how to manage the relationship between infrastructure and content. Different models of governance are being followed around the world (see Stevenson & Clement, 2010; Stover, 2010), demonstrating that there are many different approaches to deal with these issues.

In Canada, the push for regulatory action emerged in 2008 following charges made by the Canadian Association of Internet Providers (CAIP) that Bell Canada was throttling Internet

DEEP PACKET INSPECTION
"Refers to a technique that is being imposed on data communications networks in order to probe into the contents of passing traffic. . . . [It] may be performed [with or] without the authority of the sender and[/or] recipient, but also for [state, corporate, or criminal] purposes that are, or at least may be, against the interests of some of the parties" (Clarke, 2009, #1/#7).

traffic on their networks. What followed was a very lively policy process with much public input (see Blevins & Shade, 2010; Milberry, 2012; OpenMedia.ca, 2011), resulting in the CRTC issuing a traffic management policy in 2009 (CRTC, 2009d). Two key aspects of the policy included (1) mandating that ISPs must fully disclose their ITMPs and (2) outlawing the use of deep packet inspection to assist in throttling Internet traffic (Milberry, 2012). One of the main criticisms of the new policy relates to oversight, specifically that the CRTC did not establish regulatory oversight of ISP activities, but rather it relies on consumer-driven complaints to indicate if ISPs are using inappropriate practices (McIver, 2010; Milberry, 2012; 📺 www.crtc.gc.ca/eng/publications/reports/itmp-pgti.htm). This places the onus on the public to monitor providers rather than the CRTC using their resources or regulatory powers to do so. Another limitation of the policy is that it did not restrict economic traffic management practices, which came into use shortly after the decision on technological practices was concluded.

The issues of economic traffic management and specifically UBB are currently being debated in Canada. Similar to the first round of policy discussions on these issues, the UBB debate is all about established conglomerate media companies, such as BCE and Shaw protecting their market dominance. They are attempting to do this by dictating how competitors charge for service, and by trying to freeze out those Internet-based or "over the top" services (e.g., Netflix or Apple TV) that challenge their traditional broadcasting services (Winseck, 2011b). The carriers manage discussion around ITMPs by framing (recall from Chapter 4) the issues according to two specific arguments. The first argument refers to efficiency of service and fairness for consumers by penalizing the so-called "bandwidth hogs" that use more bandwidth than regular consumers. The second refers to protecting Canadian content, and ultimately cultural sovereignty, by blocking Netflix and other web-based broadcasting services. Both of these arguments are questionable. OpenMedia.ca and the Canadian Internet Policy and Public Interest Clinic (CIPPIC) have handily challenged the first in their comments to the CRTC as part of the UBB review process (see OpenMedia.ca/CIPPIC, 2011). Essentially they argue that carriers are penalizing all Internet users through their UBB practices, not just those "bandwidth hogs," and that the negative effects of these practices to maintain market control are a reduction in the usage of the Internet overall, as demonstrated by Bell Canada's net traffic growth numbers, which dropped from 38 per cent in 2009 to 32 per cent in 2010 (ibid.). The second argument marks a complete about-face by the commercial broadcasting industry, whose previous position was to support no government regulation on broadcasting in new media. Instead, by imposing ITMPs, the incumbents are establishing their own self-regulatory system to retain control over the content available both online and off.

The campaign for net neutrality in Canada is being spearheaded by OpenMedia.ca, a national non-profit organization that has been extremely successful in raising the profile of the issue, encouraging citizens to submit comments to the public proceedings at the CRTC, and coordinating support from all sectors of society behind their campaign. Yet even in their campaign, the issues around democratic communication have slipped down the priority list in favour of those related to market issues such as consumer rights, the value of the Internet for innovation, and the growth of the Canadian economy (see OpenMedia.ca, 2011; OpenMedia.ca/CIPPIC, 2011). Less attention is paid to the use of the Internet for democratic, non-market related activities. One reason for this is because OpenMedia.ca is balancing diverse interests as it has created an impressive network of supporters in its efforts that includes commercial, municipal, civil society, and citizen support. Additionally, OpenMedia.ca is working within the set parameters of a policy debate established by the CRTC.

The debate about traffic management and net neutrality is ongoing, yet, in much of the official policy discussion, as well as the organized civil society response in Canada, the discourse has been framed almost entirely within market parameters. ISPs, resellers, and even regulatory agencies have framed much of the discussion around Quality of Service (QoS) issues such as their ability to provide efficient and fast service to the majority of consumers. On the other side of the issue, those advocating for net neutrality are arguing less about the public utility of the Internet (see Barratt & Shade, 2007; Quail & Larabie, 2010) and more about how traffic management practices, like UBB, are detrimental to consumers, innovation, and the economy (see OpenMedia.ca/CIPPIC, 2011).

As far as encouraging public involvement, as Christine Quail and Christine Larabie (2010) have noted, little attention is paid in the mainstream press to the public interest arguments around traffic management and the impact these restrictive practices may have on the democratic potential of the Internet. William McIver (2010) argues that ignoring the fundamental communication rights around net neutrality may have longer-term detrimental effects. He posits that although the current debate is framed around non-critical issues like free access to entertainment services online, ITMPs can have far more detrimental effects on the basic access of communities to critical communication services. He cites the example of the Keewaytinook Okimakanak (KO) First Nations tribal council in Northern Ontario who formed the Kuhkenah Network (K-Net) in the late 1990s "to address major gaps in telecommunications between its communities" (McIver, 2010, p. 158) that had not been addressed by existing telecommunication services. Moreover, McIver argues that as the Internet becomes the central means of communication in society, the issues around net neutrality will become more important.

This debate demonstrates several key issues in communication policy overall. First, as already noted, it is not technology that directs policy action, but people working within and outside of institutional structures that determine how technology is to be used. Second, the debates around communication are not predetermined despite the efforts of certain actors with powerful interests to maintain control over the system. Both the political agency of an organized opposition, like that led by OpenMedia.ca, and the unanticipated uses of technology mean that control is not absolute. Finally, national governments still have the power to decide what policies they wish to follow, and these may differ greatly from country to country.

Copyright

Another open-ended and often contentious policy issue is copyright reform, which, as Sara Bannerman (2010) argues "is often bogged down by conflicting domestic and international demands" (p. 34). Recall our initial discussion of copyright history in Chapter 4, the current move to update Canada's copyright legislation also comes in response to technological change and international obligations. The use of copyrighted material over the Internet and newer digital technologies (e.g., **digital content locks**) has led to the re-writing of copyright provisions nationally and internationally. Practices like the use of peer-to-peer (P2P) downloads for music and other content have spurred the legislative change. Since the mid-1990s, there have been numerous international agreements that have pushed for greater protection of copyright in national legislation, including the WTO's TRIPS agreement (1994), NAFTA (1992), the World Intellectual Property Organization (WIPO) Internet treaties (1996), and two additional agreements that are currently being negotiated: the Anti-Counterfeiting Trade Agreement (ACTA) and the Canada–EU Comprehensive Economic and Trade Agreement (CETA; Bannerman, 2011, p. 40).

The main thrust of all of these agreements is to strengthen the rights of copyright holders over the use and re-use of materials in digital formats and over the Internet or what is called **digital rights management (DRM)** to make tampering with copy-protection measures (e.g., digital

DIGITAL CONTENT LOCKS

"Restrict what people can and cannot do with the media [content, software] and hardware [that] they have legitimately purchased. These locks are variously called digital locks, Digital Rights Management (DRM) or Technological Protection Measures (TPMs)" (EFF, n.d., para. 1).

DIGITAL RIGHTS MANAGEMENT (DRM)

"A catch-all term referring to any of several technologies used to enforce pre-defined limitations on the use and transfer of copyrighted digital content. The content most commonly restricted by DRM includes music, visual artwork, computer and video games and movies, but DRM can be applied to any digital content. First-generation DRM software merely sought to control copying. Second-generation DRM schemes seek to control viewing, copying, printing, altering and everything else that can be done with digital content" (Office of the Privacy Commissioner of Canada, 2006, para. 3).

locks) illegal, and to make the enforcement of rights through notification measures explicit (e.g., Canada's proposed *notice-and-notice system*; Bannerman, 2011; McIver, 2010). The dialectic in copyright reform lies in the tension between the use of digital locks and other means to enclose and bolster the rights of copyright holders, versus the various ways that digital technology and the Internet have expanded access to and use of copyrighted material (e.g., time-shifting, music downloading, and mash-ups).

Different countries have adopted these provisions in different ways in national legislation. For example, in 1998, the United States established the Digital Millennium Copyright Act (DMCA), often referred to as "WIPO+," which some argue imposes "draconian criminal measures, covering not only commercial competitors but also consumers" (Kretschmer, 2005, p. 233; www.copyright.gov/legislation/dmca.pdf). The main difficulty with the DMCA is the anti-circumvention clause that was intended to stop people from getting around blocks intended to stop copyright piracy of music and other materials. The Electronic Frontiers Foundation (EFF), an American non-profit research and advocacy group concerned with these issues, has noted that the anti-circumvention aspects of the DMCA has had multiple unintended consequences since its coming into force (www.eff.org/). Some of the main issues that the EFF highlights are how the DMCA has chilled free expression and scientific research, jeopardized fair uses, and impeded competition and innovation (Van Lohmann, 2010). Beyond its effect in the United States, these elements of the WIPO treaties are included in the numerous free-trade agreements to which the United States is signatory.

Since 2005, there have been three attempts to reform the existing Canadian Copyright Act to incorporate the provisions of the WIPO treaties and other international agreements. The first attempt, in 2005, Bill C-60 closely followed aspects of the US DMCA and was very unpopular. The Bill died on the order papers when the minority Liberal government lost confidence of the House of Commons in 2006. The minority Conservative government that followed reintroduced another bill, C-61, again with stringent anti-circumvention rules, nullifying fair uses in those materials, similar to the rules set out in the DMCA. Additionally, C-61 did allow for certain specific fair uses such as format- and time-shifting in private use, but these were still viewed as overly restrictive (L. Murray, 2010, p. 204). There was considerable public opposition to this Bill, and it, too, died on the order papers when Parliament was prorogued.

The next attempt to revise copyright came following a national public consultation process in 2009 that received over 8,000 submissions and participation in round-tables and town halls (Geist, 2010, p. 1). In 2010, the ministers of industry and Canadian Heritage jointly tabled Bill C-32, which they referred to as a "balanced" response to copyright reform. The new Bill did seek to find a middle ground in a number of areas including expanding fair uses to "creators (parody and satire), educators (education exception, education Internet exception), and consumers (time shifting, format shifting, backup copies)" (p. 2). Additionally, the Bill included a notice-and-notice system for Internet service providers (ISPs), which required providers to monitor uses over their service and notify users of possible copyright infringement. This practice may prove onerous and costly for providers, as well as increase their ability to monitor their users, but in turn, according to Geist (2010), it has been somewhat effective in "discouraging infringement" (p. 3). The one area of the Bill that did not seek balance or compromise, and was the most criticized, was the digital locks rules, which "adopted a foundational principle that anytime a digital lock is used, it trumps virtually all other rights" (ibid.). Significantly, this Bill, like its predecessors and the US DMCA, prioritizes restrictive practices on copyright over fair uses. Bill C-32 did not pass, as it, too, died on the order papers when the minority Conservative government fell in the spring of 2011. When the Conservatives gained a majority government, it was reintroduced in much the same form as Bill C-11, as the Copyright Modernization Act, and it received royal assent in June 2012 (🖥 www.parl.gc.ca/HousePublications/Publication.aspx?Language=E&Mode=1&DocId=5697419).

In response to the more restrictive models pursued in existing government legislation, alternative rights models have developed that recognize moral rights and provide some economic remuneration, all the while keeping a more open approach to fair uses and spurring innovation and creativity. Examples of this include copyleft and Creative Commons. Copyleft is a "general method for making a program (or other work) free, and requiring all modified and extended versions of the program to be free as well" (Free Software Foundation, 2009, para. 1; 🖥 www.gnu.org/copyleft/). The movement is focused mostly on the development of software, particularly Linux software. The idea here is that by sharing the development of software among numerous users and coders, the "final" product will be far more stable than those software applications developed in a more enclosed way. There really is no final product with copyleft software, as coders are continually fixing and upgrading it when bugs and other problems are found. What is essential here though is not just that the initial software is open but that any alterations or changes made to it are also open for all to use.

Creative Commons is an alternative licencing system to traditional copyright, whereby the copyright owner and creator can determine the level of rights protection required: a "some rights protected" approach rather than an "all rights protected" approach, which is the default for traditional copyright (🖥 www.creativecommons.org/licenses/). What these examples show is that even though established regimes of copyright exist that are becoming more restrictive, dialectical responses have emerged and are in regular use, particularly over the Internet to ensure that innovation and creativity remain a dynamic and open process.

Copyright, like regulating Internet infrastructure, demonstrates the complexity of regulating new media. Like the debate around ITMPs, in copyright, technology does not dictate its uses or the policies that govern it. Additionally, people are continually challenging restrictive copyright, whether illegally or legally through alternative options like copyleft and Creative Commons. The most recent attempt at copyright reform demonstrates an approach that may signal a practical willingness for real policy convergence on the part of the federal government. Finally, the most recent history of this reform shows that policy activism is essential to ensure balance is achieved between symbolic and economic values of communication.

Where Are We Going From Here?

The outgoing chair of the CRTC, Konrad von Finckenstein (2011), offered his outlook for the neo-liberal future in a converged communications environment:

> The communications industry has completely restructured itself through digital technology, the Internet and vertical integration. What has not been restructured is the whole public apparatus that governs communications in this country: the legislation, the regulations and the institutions.
>
> So we have a dynamic and evolving industry operating under a regulatory system that was designed for a very different environment. That was the environment of the previous century, before the digital revolution and before the Internet. I think it is now time for you, the leaders of the industry, to get together and tell the powers that be that a major rethinking of the system is necessary, and the sooner the better. . . .
>
> Let's look at the new converged digital world. The Internet has become the nervous system of our planet. Canadians now have multiple choices available for

information, entertainment, communication and interaction. The consumer is in charge; it's a buyer's market. It's an open market. You don't need permission to sell your content in the digital world.

This presents a challenge to some of our long-established regulatory principles. . . .

I believe we need a conceptual rethink of the whole regulatory system.

Currently, we are operating under three separate and very different Acts. Wouldn't it make sense to have a single comprehensive Act to govern all communications? (paras. 3–6, 20–1)

These comments were part of a speech delivered by von Finckenstein following the federal election in May 2011. He was addressing the Telecom Summit, an industry-dominated conference. This is not a radical or new call for policy convergence, but von Finckenstein's comment may have more traction than previous attempts in the past. One of the reasons for this is that there is growing consensus among regulators, politicians, industry representatives, and public and citizen groups that the current system of policies and regulations governing the communication system is not working well.

Several significant policy issues, as we have discussed here, expose the limits and gaps of the current policy structures. The constantly shifting, but precarious, consolidation of private ownership in media presents challenges for the long-term sustainability of a Canadian-owned media system. The "policy by stealth" approach to foreign ownership indicates that there is a desperate need to revisit communication legislation to ensure clarity around who is responsible for what decisions and what approach needs to be prioritized to direct its future considerations. Additionally, significant public reaction to the communication industry's move to meter the Internet and to the government's attempts at copyright reform demonstrate that these policy gaps may be opportunities for those seeking to re-balance the system in favour of both public interest principles and economic viability of the industry. This transformation of the legislation will not be an easy one, nor will it be one that can be done quickly, if the experience of the Copyright Act is any indication. Legislative change is slow, and this is not a bad thing; rather, in following a measured, informed, transparent and consultative approach to policy change, Canada may yet achieve its radical democratic digital future.

Our review of policy convergence was purposely comprehensive to ensure that the future of communication in Canada won't be decided without you. Indeed, as Jean-Pierre Blais (2012), the new chairman of the CRTC suggests, the outlook may be promising:

I have seen numerous comments over the past four months referring to the Commission's "new focus on consumers." This is not entirely accurate. The Commission has always considered consumer issues. What is new is that I have called on the staff and my colleagues to renew their focus on consumers. But, more importantly, our work is not just about Canadians as consumers. The public interest is more complex than that binary analysis. We also have to consider Canadians as creators and citizens. (para. 9; www.crtc.gc.ca/eng/com200/2012/s121029a.htm)

As the last chapter in this section suggests, an additional way of participating in media decision-making is not only to read or study the media but also to *be the media*. A converging media system suggests that there are a number of opportunities to communicate and connect with each other that foreground the citizen (as journalist, e.g.), enlarging our scope of discussion beyond the pages of the textbook. We're not quite ready to go beyond the textbook yet, however; there's a whole set of issues and experiences that we need to consider first, including what it means to be the media and what additional limits and pressures there are in a 24/7/365 world where everyone is watching.

Key Points

- Technological myths have long influenced communication policy development in Canada.

- A disjuncture exists between the goals and practices of communication policy in Canada, as exemplified by the calls for policy convergence beginning in the 1970s and the lack of action on this convergence to date.

- Broad-ranging policies, advanced through government formations such as IHAC and the NBTF, have not been effective in recent years in Canada.

- Instead, the future direction of Canadian communication policy is driven by specific decisions and actions in certain policy areas—for example, in foreign ownership, Internet infrastructure, and copyright.

- Canada's policy development processes have moved away from a balanced approach prioritizing public communication, and incorporating both use value and exchange value, to one dominated by exchange values.

- Policy debates have tended to be led and dominated by neo-liberal goals, yet a growing public activism both internationally and nationally have pushed against this, fighting to preserve public interest principles like universal access to communication resources.

Class Discussion

1. In the previous chapter we reviewed the myths surrounding the history of technology to the present day. Why are myths so important in the study of communication policy-making?

2. In this chapter, we suggested that there are three different ideological approaches to decision-making in Canada. What are the similarities and differences between these approaches? Why are they critical to national and global policy-making?

3. What patterns of decision-making can be discerned from a historical review of communication policy development in Canada?

4. What are some of the reasons for why a broad-ranging digital policy has not developed in Canada?

5. What are some of the concerns about foreign ownership of Canada's media companies? How have these played out the Globalive case study?

6. What are two positions in tension in the regulation of Internet infrastructure? Who represents each position?

7. What are the main reasons for changes to Canadian copyright legislation? What has motivated these changes? Provide concrete examples of policy changes.

8. Are there alternatives to copyright? What are they?

Media on Media

Governing Tunes

Beastie Boys. (2004). This government needs a tune up [B-side]. *To the 5 Boroughs*. US: Capitol.
Nicolette. (1992). No government. *Now Is Early*. Germany: K7.
Perfect Confusion (Cage the Elephant). (2005). Government song. *Perfect Confusion*.
Talking Heads. (1977). Don't worry about the government. *77*. US: Sire.

DVD and Films

Docherty, N. (Writer, Producer, & Director). (2012). *Scandal: Inside the Murdoch empire* [CBC News episode]. Canada: WGBH/PBS Frontline and Cam Bay Productions.
Earp, J., & Killoy, A. (Producers). (2010). *The land is our land: The fight to reclaim the commons*. Northampton, MA: Media Education Foundation.
Films Media Group Online. (2010). *Bill Moyers journal: Bank fraud/net neutrality*. New York, NY: Films Media Group.

Timeline: Canadian Policy—A Recent History, 1971–2013

1971 The Instant World report of the Telecommission Task Force in Canada is tabled.

1979–1980 The New World Information and Communication Order (NWICO) and the MacBride Commission are established.

1992 The North American Free Trade Agreement (NAFTA) comes into force.

1994 The WTO agreement on Trade-Related aspects of Intellectual Property Rights (TRIPS) is enacted.

The Information Highway Advisory Council (IHAC) convenes.

1996 The World Intellectual Property Organization (WIPO) Internet treaties are drafted.

1998 The US Digital Millennium Copyright Act (DMCA) is established.

1999 The CRTC announces its "broadcasting in new media" decision.

2000 The National Broadband Task Force (NBTF) begins in Canada.

The CRTC sets out a licencing structure for digital specialty and pay-television services.

2003 The first World Summit on the Information Society (WSIS) convenes in Geneva, Switzerland.

2005 The second WSIS convenes in Tunis

Bill C-60 revisions to the Copyright Act in Canada, which would bring the WIPO Internet treaties into force, is proposed but not passed.

The federal government establishes the Telecommunications Policy Review Panel (TPRP) to make recommendations on how to update Canada's telecommunication policies.

Canada's first pay-per-subscription radio services are approved.

2006 The Government of Canada directs the CRTC to rely on market forces as much as possible to achieve the policy objectives of the Telecommunications Act.

2007 The CRTC approves Canwest's purchase of Alliance Atlantis, with significant financing from Goldman Sachs.

The CRTC sets 31 August 2011 as the date by which TV stations will broadcast only digital signals.

2008 Bill C-61 revisions to the Copyright Act, which would bring the WIPO Internet treaties into force, is proposed but not passed.

2009 Canwest enters bankruptcy protection; its print holdings are acquired by Postmedia; the remaining broadcasting properties are acquired by Shaw Media.

The 105 MHz spectrum band auction takes place.

Globalive is granted a wireless licence. The decision is then overturned by the CRTC, which in turn is overruled by the minister of industry, Tony Clement.

The CRTC policy on Internet traffic management practices (ITMPs—technological) is established.

The CRTC announces its second "broadcasting in new media" decision.

2010 Bill C-32 revisions to the Copyright Act, which would bring the WIPO Internet treaties into force, is proposed but not passed.

Due to foreign ownership concerns, the Federal Court rules in support of the CRTC's decision to deny Globalive's wireless licence.

Netflix comes to Canada.

The CRTC policy on ITMPs (economic—e.g., usage-based billing [UBB]) is established.

The minister of industry, Tony Clement, overrules the CRTC's decision on UBB following public pressure on the issue.

2011 The CRTC holds hearings into the use of UBB.

The Federal Court of Appeal overturns the Federal Court's decision on Globalive's licence, arguing that the company is Canadian-owned and operated.

2012 (Canadian) Copyright Modernization Act receives royal assent.

CBC/Radio-Canada's 620 analogue transmitters are shut down—no analogue television from 31 July 2012 onward.

The CRTC blocks BCE Inc.'s proposed deal to buy 100 per cent of Astral Media for $3.4 billion, claiming that the merger would "[undermine] 'competition and diversity'" (Campion-Smith, 2012, para. 1) only to change the ruling in 2013 allowing the purchase.

Bill C-11, the Copyright Modernization Act, receives royal assent in June.

BCE Inc. submits another proposal to the CRTC to buy Astral and in early 2013 offers a roughly $175 million tangible-benefits package to advance the deal.

2013 The Canadian Marketing Association asks the CRTC "to relax the rules restricting automatic calls for telemarketing" (LaSalle, 2013, para. 2).

CRTC approves the BCE Inc. purchase of Astral.

10 Who's a Journalist Now? The Expanded Reportorial Community

Objectives

This chapter seeks the answers to a number of questions, the most important perhaps being "Who or what is a journalist in a convergent media world?" After reading this chapter you will have a better understanding of how the Internet, mobile media-enabled technologies, and the shifting social relations of news production and consumption have impacted what we have begun to call the "reportorial community." In particular, in this chapter we discuss the following points:

- how the demarcation lines between journalists, non-journalists, and audience-participants are dissolving, and how this is affecting the production and consumption of news in the twenty-first century;

- how the definitions and roles of journalists have changed over the past 100 years in response to media convergence, changing technologies, and changing social conditions;

- what we mean by the reportorial community and, in particular, how "eyewitness" accounts and interventions in the news-gathering process have been enabled by new media technologies;

- what we mean by "citizen-journalist" and the debates around the impact that so-called "non-professional news-gathering" is having on the old media; and

- what this suggests for the future of published and broadcast news and information.

Keywords

- blogging
- citizen-journalist
- computational journalism
- crowd-sourcing
- ethics
- freelance
- investigative journalism
- journalism ethics
- outsourcing
- participatory journalism
- reportorial community
- robot journalism
- spin
- user-generated content (UGC)
- whistle-blower
- WikiLeaks

Who's Who in the Digital Zoo?

One of the key advances people mention when they talk about all the good things about the Internet is that anyone can now be an author and publisher. The cost of renting a small shopfront on the World Wide Web is negligible (providing one has the income, ability, and access, of course).

A key theme in this section is to address the ways in which the new media are changing the relationship between the producers and consumers of what is broadly defined as "news." Throughout the twentieth century, the functions, character, and class position of journalists all over the world have undergone almost continuous and extensive change (Hargreaves, 2003; Jones & Salter, 2012; Oakham, 2001; Pavlik, 2001; Phillips, Lee-Wright, & Witschge, 2012). It's also fair to say that the modern public relations (PR) industry was established by news reporters and editors who saw they could make more money by advising companies and governments directly. There has always been an unsteady professional relationship between news-gatherers and spin doctors (Ewen, 1996). We often ask our students if the relationship is symbiotic or parasitic: Who is feeding whom?

The new media content providers—whether reporter, marketeer, or PR professional—all hold interesting and relevant positions within the commercial media and communications industries of the twenty-first century. It is important in this context, and in the context of alternative forms of narrowcast media, to have some understanding of the changing character of what we call the **reportorial community** and the ways in which these changes have "disrupted" journalism's traditional focus and practices, which in turn begs the question "What is 'news' itself" (Meadows, 2001)?

Citizen Kane to Citizen-Journalist?

> *Citizen journalism will not make institutional journalism redundant or irrelevant. It is a challenge to the authority of the traditional media, not an alternative. It will make traditional journalism stronger, better, more responsive. Sceptics tend to make you lift your game. (McDonald, 2005, p. 14)*

One of the most volatile fault lines cutting through the world of new media is just who gets to define, shape, edit, and present that bit of content known in the old media-speak as *news*. If one of the ways news is defined is by the act of *dissemination*, the proliferation and use of "videophones" or cell phones—enabling eyewitness recordings in major events and protests such as the Occupy Movement or the social uprisings in the Middle East—have brought public attention to the existence of what has become widely accepted as the **citizen-journalist** (see Figure 10.1, p. 238). It is therefore important to examine the professional, economic, and cultural impacts of such relative power-shifting that has accompanied the widespread introduction of new, affordable, and reasonable-quality means of media production. Can everyone be their own editor and reporter?

In this chapter we examine the recent blurring of boundaries between "professionals" and those who "write" about the news. There are really two dynamics at play in this chapter: On one hand, the rise of the so-called citizen-journalist and, on the other, the changing nature of media work and of traditional journalism in particular as the old media silos of print, radio, television, and online converge or break down further. We should start with some historical accounting and the observation that for more than 100 years the primary demarcation between reporters and amateurs has been the economic relationship (wages and salaries) between the news worker and the employer. There has always been some argument about whether journalism

REPORTORIAL COMMUNITY
Those who "report" in a variety of media, old and new, using traditional journalistic genres and forms: the news story (written inside and outside the inverted pyramid); the feature story; the radio news report; the television news report; the "live cross"; the documentary; the online news story, etc.

CITIZEN-JOURNALIST
An independent person who is not attached to or employed by a media organization who witnesses an event, and then provides an account of that event using traditional and new journalistic forms.

FIGURE 10.1 | Citizen-journalism: A woman holds a tablet to record an anti-fracking protest in London.

Source: © Jay Shaw-Baker / Alamy

is an art form, a craft, or a profession—or even just another form of wage labour. But there has been, until recently, a consensus that reporters, news photographers, and editorial staff were a distinct type of labour, defined by their relationship to both media outlet and audience. This chapter examines the proposition that converging technologies are slowly but surely breaking down this distinction and blurring the boundaries of the community of reporters, and changing (or eliminating?) the wage-labour relationship.

This question of the status of professional journalism is not a new one, yet, as suggested by Suellen Tapsall and Carolyn Varley (2001) in their study of journalists in Australia, for example, making news is usually distinguished from other forms of labour (p. 4). They argued that it is important to have a clear definition of what a journalist is so that consumers of news can tell the difference between "good news, bad news, and no news" (ibid.). As we discuss in this chapter, this suggests a responsibility held by media producers to make such differences evident, yet this can be difficult to distinguish. Tapsall and Varley's research focused on how the journalists themselves viewed their jobs and drew some interesting self-definitions from respondents. In order of frequency, the definitions included "news workers, information workers, gatherers, reporters, entertainers, historians, researchers, explainers, probers and writers." Less frequent responses included "editors, communicators, story-tellers, producers and presenters" (pp. 5–6). One respondent is quoted as saying that journalists are "intermediaries" between audiences and sources and also a "filter" (p. 6). However, that same respondent also added "and that's where the danger lies" (ibid.). Another respondent contributed that an important part of the definition is that reporters and editors analyze information and set events "in context" (ibid.).

Tapsall and Varley note that changing media technologies and changing patterns of media control, production, and consumption can mean that a simple definition—for example, "a journalist is someone employed to report and edit the news"—is no longer as valid as it used to be. From their brief definitional survey it's easy to see how the boundaries can be blurred when it comes to reporting, or information-sharing, in an online environment. It also highlights a difficulty for non-journalists operating in a news-gathering and reporting role. We know that, generally, when it comes to reputable news sources, reporters and editors are filtering the news and putting it into their own contextual framework; we accept that filtering goes on, but can we be sure that the filtering and contextualizing done by "amateurs" is as rigorous, or reliable?

"Constantly successful achievement in journalism requires more judgments on more diverse problems over the working hours than any other occupation" (Rivett, 1965, p. 23). Throughout the twentieth century, during what we might call the age of "industrial journalism," produced for mass consumption like so many "widgets," journalism and journalists changed their characters. At the beginning of the twentieth century, and perhaps up until the end of World War II in 1945, journalism came to be understood as a craft—a vocation to be learned on the job through a system of apprenticeships. The cadet reporter would learn from the master through observation, hard discipline, and patient practice of the art. As the previous quote from the illustrious reporter and editor Rohan Rivett suggests, to be a journalist was to be marked out from the ordinary. According to Rivett, journalism could be distinguished from "every other vocation" by the diversity of the daily routine that demanded, in equal measure, skills, ingenuity, and flexibility on the part of the journalist.

No doubt there's some truth in this statement, but equally we could argue that it is the precociousness and self-absorption of the profession that leads to such statements about the special nature of the journalist and journalism. As you shall see, the definition of the skills may change, and there may, from time to time, be more or less emphasis on "professionalism" versus "craft," but the essential ingredient in most definitions is that reporters and news workers are somehow "different," not like "ordinary" folk, and that the work of journalism demands a particular "type" of personality and dedication to the cause. But does it really?

As we hope we've made clear in the previous chapters, the best way to tackle this question is to examine the situation historically. We pick up our story in the early years of the twentieth century when "muckraking" journalism (the good guys) and the "yellow press" (the salacious, tabloid bad guys) were fighting for circulation in the United States. (Remember our discussion of Upton Sinclair's *The Brass Check* in Chapter 4?) We have a sense of the context of this "fight for circulation" in Canada from this earlier review of the history of print media over what we called the first five periods of the press.

As you may recall, we identified significant changes to several aspects of the journalist's operating environment in Canada, particularly over the last century. These included changes in (1) the structures of ownership (from a partisan press to large commercial businesses and the growth of global news agencies); (2) technology (from shop-printing presses to industrialized production); (3) the journalist's relationship with sources and the location of news (from face-to-face local reporting to an edited, mediated, and expanded collection and distribution network via telegraph, telephone, broadcasting, and satellite); and (4) labour organization (the division of labour, the wage-labour relation, and the development of collective associations and unions)—all affecting the journalist and journalism (i.e., what makes news). We briefly expand on these here to contextualize how these changes are occurring internationally, and identify how they continue to impact journalists and journalism today and, in turn, affect what is considered news.

Journalism in the Twentieth Century: Craft or Profession?

In North America at the beginning of the twentieth century, technological change and the commodification of news already impacted the form and content of journalism, and defined the journalist's job (Hardt & Brennen, 1995). The combination of commercial ownership and mechanization of newspaper production directed the pace and structure of media work: "Time and speed became interwoven within a commercial imperative that machines could deliver news faster to readers, thereby outpacing commercial competition" (Salcetti, 1995, p. 52). As American media historian Marianne Salcetti (1995) recounted, time dependence meant news itself became a "perishable commodity" (ibid.).

Time-Dependent News

Changes were significant in distinctions made between writing and production. The division of labour was organized such that the information would be telephoned in to the office from the field (by the reporter), where it would be composed and typed up as a story (the writer), and together with the rest of the stories of the day, it would be evaluated, corrected, and decided if and where it would be placed in the newspaper (editor and layout) and then sent to be reproduced (the printers). Since the newspaper depended on advertising for revenue, the news would be filled in *after* the advertisements. With advertising, time, and speed as the primary directives, the reporters' and writers' jobs were neither glamorous nor secure. Salcetti (1995) explains that

> *increased speed in newspaper production produced both a division of labor and specialization of labor in newspapers. Reporters were but one widget in this mechanized process, and in spite of the stereotypes of spirited individualism and work freedom, their work life, as characterized by Francis Leupp in 1910, was not so different from that of a railroad worker or iron peddler—workers in other industries whose work was also increasingly driven by machines and speed. (pp. 59–60)*

The Professional Journalist

At the same time, however, Salcetti (1995) recounts that as media labour became "more specialized," so did the expectations for the development of specific skills, such that "the training of reporters for newsroom work was increasingly viewed as occurring within university classrooms" (p. 60). This specialization marked a change in the status of the reporter and writer as combined in the "journalist" as a professional designation distinguished from other kinds of work and apart from other workers. As discussed in our early history of the press, this complemented the commercial goals of the media business, as Canadian political economy scholar Nicole Cohen (2010) emphasizes:

> *While newspaper journalists sought professional status to improve their working conditions, their employers embraced journalistic professionalism as a calculated business strategy. To expand mass readerships in order to increase advertising sales, publishers promoted a vision of professionalism that emphasized objective, detached, unbiased reporting, a vision that pushed reporters to align themselves with publisher's interests rather than with those of other newsroom workers such as printers (Carey 1969; McChesney 2008). (p. 123)*

The emphasis on professionalism, condoned by the owners of the means of production and taught in journalism schools, combined to produce what is arguably two inseparable myths— that of the professional (objective) journalist and that objectivity was a quality and definer of news (in other words, a news value). With the emphasis on professionalism, a "reportorial ethos" emerged and has come to be viewed as the "service ideals of reporters" underpinned by the "notion of sacrifice on behalf of the story, or the public interest as a valued quality" (Salcetti, 1995, p. 55).

The professional journalist-as-citizen gathers news and reports to other citizens and is, in other words, a member of the public responsible to the public. This responsibility and account-ability is managed through legal boundaries (such as libel laws) and its practice is contained within a commercial structure since news is packaged and sold as a commercial product. What may be called the "contradiction of commercial news" was managed by associating the profes-sional journalist with a particular kind of product, tied to what Michael Bromley and Judith Clarke (2012) identify as the "news paradigm" (p. 7). As they explain, this paradigm acts like a template, and is "made up of noted events, news values, journalistic interviewing, the inverted pyramid, a commitment to accuracy, fairness and balance ('objectivity'), and facticity" (ibid.).

The ethos of objectivity, as Robert Hackett and Yuezhi Zhao (1997) argue, has, over the years, been mythologized as defining a high standard of journalism rather than being recognized as a deliberate (re)structuring and repurposing of news. In effect, it de-politicized the news by lessening questions of political economic power, such as those associated with the power of advertisers to influence media content; the power relationship between elites such as politicians, financiers, and media owners; the concentration of ownership in the media industry; and ties to other businesses in terms of conflict of interests. Journalists were to take a neutral position, and present at least two "sides" to an issue or event in order to speak to the widest possible audience and optimize circulation and advertising sales.

The "inverted pyramid" (the organization of news into who, what, where, when, and why—or the five *W*s) was set as the standard for writing content (🔲 www.parl.gc.ca/About/ Parliament/Education/PeopleParliament/newspaper4-e.asp). In this way, the copy was written such that information could be removed in descending order more easily to accommodate advertising (Salcetti, 1995). This affected not only news content but also the work of journalists themselves. Journalists were trained (whether in-house, in college or universities) to write copy in this way—and accept that news values were also exchange values; that is, the ultimate goal was not, for example, to engage, motivate, and activate the public-as-*citizens*, but to sell the news to a reading or listening public-as-*consumer*, and in the process sell themselves and their labour as efficient and disciplined contributors.

This way of making news so alienated some writers (seeing the potential for creativity and originality of writing or critical thinking constrained in a commercial model) that they chose to become freelance (Cohen, 2010). The options, however, are correspondingly limited if one wants to make a living out of writing. The radical freelance writer may reject the wage relationship as controlled by a single employer (or employers) whose profit imperatives can largely determine what can or would be published. As we discuss in Chapter 13, the emphasis on independence and autonomy as a characteristic of what is called "alternative media" is one way in which to oppose or at least negotiate the commodification of media by not making profit the priority in the production of news and information (Kozolanka, Mazepa, & Skinner, 2012a).

Another possibility of negotiating commodification was to form collective organizations, writers' associations, or labour unions in an attempt by media workers to determine the nature and conditions of work, if not the content of the newspaper and other media itself (see Chapter 5;

FREELANCE
Working on the basis of selling a discrete product(s)—in media work, a story, graphics, or editing job—for one or more employers on an impermanent basis.

ETHICS

In general, a moral philosophy whereby human agency is inspired and guided by honesty, mutual respect, and responsibility for the health and welfare of each other and the environment.

JOURNALISM ETHICS

An application of moral philosophy to the practices of journalism that may be formalized in public statements addressing the conduct of the journalist as well as decisions regarding media organizational goals and objectives, content, labour, and other social relations.

Cohen, 2013). Yet another is to work within the structures of commercial media, and associate professional journalism not only by the news paradigm but also as defined by a set of standards or codes that address the conduct of the journalist and the institution that they work for. These standards suggest that the professional journalist is defined by adherence to what is called the **ethics** of journalism.

Case Study

The Ethics of Journalism

Journalism ethics in Canada has its own distinct history and is inseparable from the history of labour union organizing. It is a little celebrated fact that the origins of today's *Toronto Star* was an outcome of a broadsheet produced by writers and printers on strike (Harkness, 1963). In the late 1800s, the editor of what was then called the *Toronto Daily Star* set the newspaper's ethical goals and objectives in support of public service. The newspaper included, for example, early advocacy of social services like unemployment and public health insurance, guaranteed wages for employment and maximum working hours, as well as pensions and social assistance (ibid.). These standards for "progressive journalism" were set by Joseph Atkinson, the editor of the paper for over 50 years (1899–1948). Today, the *Toronto Star* still includes the "Atkinson Principles" as part of its history and guidance:

The editorial principles that Atkinson espoused were founded on his belief that a progressive newspaper should contribute to the advancement of society through pursuit of social, economic and political reforms.

The Atkinson Principles include:

- *A strong, united and independent Canada: Atkinson argued for a strong central government and the development of distinctive social, economic and cultural policies appropriate to an independent country.*
- *Social Justice: Atkinson was relentless in pressing for social and economic programs to help those less advantaged and showed particular concern for the least advantaged among us.*
- *Individual and Civil Liberties: Atkinson always pressed for equal treatment of all citizens under the law, particularly minorities, and was dedicated to the fundamental freedoms of belief, thought, opinion and expression and the freedom of press.*
- *Community and Civic Engagement: Atkinson continually advocated the importance of proper city planning, the development of strong communities with their vibrant local fabrics and the active involvement of citizens in civic affairs.*
- *The Rights of Working People: The Star was born out of a strike in 1892 and Atkinson was committed to the rights of working people including freedom of association and the safety and dignity of the workplace.*
- *The Necessary Role of Government: When Atkinson believed the public need was not met by the private sector and market forces alone, he argued strongly for government intervention.*

These six principles provide the Toronto Star *with an intellectual framework to guide editorial policy and constitute an important part of the newspaper's history. (Torstar, 2011, para. 3ff.; www.torstar.com/html/social-responsibility/Atkinson_Principles/index.cfm)*

While some corporations, like the Toronto Star Newspapers Ltd. and the CBC, formalize ethics codes for all their employees (cbc.radio-canada.ca/en/reporting-to-canadians/acts-and-policies/management/human-resources/2-2-3/), the Canadian Broadcast Standards Council (CBSC) also provides one governing the broadcasting industry, and journalists have formed their own associations to codify ethical standards, such as the Association of Electronic Journalists (RTDNA; www.rtndacanada.com/ETHICS/codeofethics.asp). These codes are set to distinguish the amateur from the professional journalist, and make the responsibility of the journalist to the public clear and relatively accountable; that is, the public can appeal to them whenever they think that ethics have been breached. This suggests a difference that remains between the citizen-cum-professional-journalist as developed in the past, and what we now call the citizen-journalist today.

Plagiarism is a major ethical issue for professional journalists. This is an issue that has affected journalists around the world, including here in Canada. For example, in September 2012, a media issues blog titled *Media Culpa* (2012; mediaculpapost.blogspot.ca/) reported that *Globe and Mail* columnist Margaret Wente was guilty of plagiarizing a 2009 article. The blog post was very quickly picked up by mainstream media, including *Toronto Star* columnist Antonia Zerbisias. Once the claims of plagiarism were confirmed and reviewed by *The Globe and Mail*'s public editor, there was little action on the part of the newspaper against Ms. Wente. The paper's editor, John Stackhouse (as cited in Ladurantaye, 2012), noted the following in response to the plagiarism charges:

> The journalism in this instance did not meet the standards of The Globe and Mail, in terms of sourcing, use of quotation marks and reasonable credit for the work of others," editor John Stackhouse said. "Even in the spirit of column writing, which allows for some latitude in attribution and expression, this work was not in accordance with our code of conduct, and is unacceptable. (para. 4)

Despite the clear indication of plagiarism, the newspaper did not release any information about how or if it intended to discipline Ms. Wente. Rather, the paper provided her with her usual column space on Tuesday 25 September 2012 to counter the charges of plagiarism (Wente, 2012). The only discernible outcome of Ms. Wente's plagiarism was that she was dropped as a regular panelist on the CBC's daily cultural radio program Q. Beyond this and perhaps in light of *The Globe and Mail*'s tame response to these claims of plagiarism, other media watchers and journalists have decried the way the issue has been dealt with and are engaging in an active discussion about plagiarism and how it is being manifest in the new media environment (Alzner, 2012).

Discussion Questions

1. Compare the Atkinson Principles to the CBC's "Procedures and Guidelines: Guiding Principles and Ethics in the Daily Conduct of CBC/Radio-Canada Employees." Tip: Make a point-form list or chart identifying the similarities and differences between them.

2. Now compare your list from Question 1 to the ethical standards of the Association of Electronic Journalists (RTDNA). What additional similarities or differences can you find? What is the significance of these differences?

3. Is a code of ethics in journalism necessary, or even feasible, in today's media environment?

4. What other codes or laws govern public journalism? For example, how does the recent Twitter/BBC libel case impact citizen-journalism (Pfanner, 2012; www.nytimes.com/2012/11/26/technology/26iht-twitter26.html)?

Journalists and Technology: Marriage of Convenience or Potential for Divorce?

In the first half of the twentieth century, the teleprinter, the telephone, and the telegraph all had an impact on news-gathering, and not always for the better. In the latter stages of the twentieth century, the digital revolution was brought about by an expanding arms economy and the exigencies of the Cold War. In the current century, the boom and bust political economy and use of computer algorithms and artificial intelligence are current harbingers of change. We deliberately use the term *impact* here because technology does not simply superimpose itself on a production process: It is imbued with the social relations of production.

The age of media globalization began in effect 150 years ago with the "cable" technology of the telegraph wire, which came to Canada in the 1850s. As introduced in Chapter 4, the news agencies have always been active players in the introduction of new technologies to news-gathering and dissemination. Reuters was instrumental in the laying of telegraph cable in the second half of the nineteenth century and one of the first to take full advantage of satellite technology in the twentieth (Boyd-Barrett, 1998, pp. 32–3). Also, in Chapter 4 we discussed the difference the telephone made to the reporter's job. London *Times* senior reporter Raymond Snoddy (1992) suggests the introduction of the telephone meant that journalists stayed in the office "rather than getting out and meeting the people they're writing about" (p. 144). Of course, in the late twentieth century the fax machine and the Internet strengthened this tendency to gather news from the reporter's room rather than the street. Julianne Schultz (1998) reports studies that showed up to 90 per cent of news was generated from media releases and distributed by fax, or even on videotape (see, e.g., Ward, 1991; Zawawi, 1994).

The use of computers by journalists was incorporated at the same time as other businesses as part of the general office automation in the 1980s, and its use was an improvement over the typewriter. As a word processor, the computer could only help with the task of writing, yet its addition also suggested more than an improvement to the speed and efficiency of writing. A new term, *precision journalism* (Myer 1973), explained the use of the computer as a research tool used for gathering and comparing statistics and other quantitative data. Subsequent editions (Myer, 2002) and similar books followed (Demers & Nichols, 1987) that aimed to assist journalists in the learning and application of research methods used in the social sciences.

The ability to collect and calibrate research enhanced the potential of the investigative reporter, as related to her/his level of experience, access to sources, knowledge of the area, and skill in the craft of writing itself (Rosner, 2011). This was topped off by the journalist's "nose for news," colloquially called the "news-hound," which, for example, Canadian journalist and author Pierre Burton was renowned for (McKillop, 2008). Journalism scholars Sarah Cohen, James T. Hamilton, and Fred Turner (2011) also give credit to the photocopier as a significant technological improvement that allowed journalists to research, or follow, "the paper trail" in hunting down memoranda, documents, and records, as they were passed from "**whistle-blowers**" (p. 67; fairwhistleblower.ca/).

The use of computers was recognized in the early 1990s, extending the "news paradigm" with such prefixes as "computer assisted" or "online" journalism. While these additions point to the computer as a supplementary tool used to enhance journalism, the future suggests one where computer science merges with journalism in what is called **computational journalism** (Cohen, Hamilton, & Turner, 2011). In this model, computer scientists work with public affairs' journalists to identify new research techniques in order to enhance the ability to identify, analyze, and evaluate the complex matrix of information necessary for valid and reliable reporting.

WHISTLE-BLOWER
A person who witnesses or collects evidence of corruption, collusion, illegalities, malfeasance, etc., against an organization, corporation, military or government department, for example, and passes it onto the media or an external public authority for exposure.

COMPUTATIONAL JOURNALISM
The application of computer science to journalism, involving the design and techniques of search engines, algorithms, and data analysis to enhance research and investigative reporting.

ONGOING ISSUES

Investigative Journalism, Access to Information, and the Public's Right to Know

The ability to research and pursue **investigative journalism** is, in large part, dependent on the willingness of the editor and newspaper owner to print stories that challenge concentrated power, whether government, corporate, or social (e.g., class, gender, or race relations). It is also dependent on whether the information needed for an accurate account and evaluation can be accessed. The former has been demonstrated in what is arguably the quintessential film representing investigative journalism in action—*All the President's Men*, based on the non-fiction book by two journalists for *The Washington Post* (Carl Bernstein and Bob Woodward) who helped to expose US president Richard Nixon's culpability in the use of phone tapping and other illegal activities during the 1972 presidential election. The combination of media reports and government and legal investigations prompted Nixon's resignation in 1974, and resulted in significant changes to the US government's Freedom of Information Act and the Ethics in Government Act (Kutler, 1990, 1997).

Since one of the requirements of investigative journalism and a liberal democratic government is transparency, that government documents can now be digitized and made available online, is one of the significant aspects of technological change that can be of benefit both to the public and to the investigative journalist. This is dependent, however, on what the government decides should be available or not. As exemplified by the existence of **WikiLeaks** (an online site that publishes information that is otherwise unpublished—or restricted, classified, or secret), there is a lot of information that is *not* accessible to the public, whether because of media filters or media self-censorship, or because of the withholding of information by powerful agencies (wikileaks.org/). The more powerful the agency, the more the investigative reporter or internal whistle-blower are shown the limits of freedom of expression and information.

These limits to freedom of expression and information have become more acute with digitization and network technology. While in the past, the photocopier was used to amass evidence that could be physically accessed and copied—and was subject to a degree of gatekeeping by the journalist, editor, or newspaper owner (or lawyers thereof) in deciding what (parts) would be published—with digitization, as much information as can be accessed can be uploaded verbatim and distributed worldwide. The sensitivity of the information to governments, in particular, is challenging national and international legal frameworks and questioning whether there are limits to the public's "right to know." As evident in the examples of the trials and tribulations of Julian Assange, who is WikiLeak's editor-in-chief (assange.rt.com), Edward Snowden, who "leaked" US National Security Agency documents to the UK press (Greenwald, 2013), and former US soldier Bradley Manning, who was convicted of "espionage" for passing information to WikiLeaks (Naughton, 2013), there is substantial controversy and debate as to whether they are considered champions of human rights, or traitors (ibid.; CBC News Politics, 2010).

Yet, access to government activities, documents, and records is fundamental to an accountable, democratic, and public government, and in Canada all journalists and all citizens have had this right, federally, since 1983. Beyond classifying or restricting information, however, the government can still manage and curtail this right (according to decisions made by the political party in power). As the Office of the Information Commissioner of Canada (2012) notes,

Continued

INVESTIGATIVE JOURNALISM
In-depth, long-term, sustained, comprehensive research and reporting; finds and reveals information hidden from, or not known to, the public; focuses on the accountability of institutions and individuals wielding power (Philippine Center for Investigative Journalism, 2004).

WIKILEAKS
A non-profit organization that collects and publishes information on its website that is otherwise restricted, classified, or secret, providing anonymity for sources of that information. WikiLeaks proclaims dedication to journalism ethics and Article 19 of the UDHR upholding the right to freedom of information and expression through any media. Since it was launched in 2007, WikiLeaks has published hundreds of thousands of documents regarding US government and military actions, in particular, as well as a wide variety of information from sources and whistle-blowers on a range of corporate, government, and military (in)actions.

there are "some limitations to the information that federal institutions are required to make public. Information such as: Cabinet documents, information that could harm Canada's security or economy, federal–provincial relations or international affairs" (para. 2; 🖥 www.oic-ci.gc.ca/eng/abu-ans-wwd-cqf-brochure.aspx), which is thus subject to a wide range of interpretation.

These limitations to government information and decision-making can also be compounded by the expense and wait periods after a request for access has been made. A study of the reliability of the federal Access to Information Act, sponsored by the Canadian Newspaper Association (CNA) and the Canadian Association of Journalists (CAJ), among others, for example, found that under the current federal Conservative government, "the average wait time for release [from time of request] has risen sharply from 30 to 60 days two years ago to 150 or much more [days] over the past two years" (Tromp, 2008, p. 208). Pertaining to journalism specifically, the CNA and the Canadian Community Newspapers Association (CCNA) publish a yearly audit (via Newspapers Canada) that monitors and records both provincial and federal requests from its media members, indicating widely varying response and increased wait times across Canada (🖥 www.newspaperscanada.ca/public-affairs/freedom-information).

While time is a significant factor in the salience of news, as we discuss further in Chapter 13, government and corporate control over information is also a major factor in the public's and the journalist's ability to participate in decision-making and provide oversight and critical review thereof. Such matters are considered "public affairs," and generally have to do with the underlying political economy, and related government and corporate decision- and policy-making.

Public-affairs reporting is fundamentally different than *public-relations* reporting. Where the latter is a deliberate attempt to manage information for the benefit of the paying client (whether corporate, government, or another organization), the former is considered a necessity for democracy and a well-informed and participative citizenry. The emphasis of the investigative journalist as "watchdog" has tended to focus on the government in particular. As noted before, this side-steps the contradiction of the commercial media industry, where the watchdog can be otherwise occupied or asleep when it comes to criticizing capitalism and corporations, particularly those that own large media holdings.

Discussion Questions

1. Is access to information and decision-making (administrative, legislative, or legal) more or less public with digitalization? Discuss why or why not.

2. How much does information access have to do with information storage (i.e., computing power, algorithms, and search engines)?

3. Access the latest "Freedom of Information Audit" from 🖥 www.newspaperscanada.ca/public-affairs/freedom-information. What changes have been observed over time? Is there a significant difference between government access provincially, federally?

4. What public service(s) does the Office of the Information Commissioner of Canada provide?

5. Is Article 19 of the UDHR absolute? What does WikiLeaks, and the individual examples of Julian Assange, Edward Snowden, and Bradley Manning, suggest about the existing restrictions on communication rights?

While such cooperation suggests several areas of "opportunities" to enhance the work of journalism, government, and public accountability (ibid., pp. 68–70), similar programs have also been under development in public relations since the early 1990s that may work to anticipate or counter investigative gains. As evident in previous chapters of this book, technology designed for one purpose can be used for other applications. In public relations, artificial intelligence (AI), which we first introduced in Chapter 1, for example, is applied as "expert systems" (Cameron & Curtin, 1992) to collect and compare data on human behaviour, opinion formation, and message composition to increase the effectiveness of campaigns directed at specific audiences (ibid., p. 13), in effect narrowcasting the electorate. Message content is designed accordingly, and similar techniques are blurring the distinction between public relations and journalism.

Although all news stories are composed and therefore socially constructed, the public relations' story is one that is deliberately constructed to sell the public a particular way of thinking that benefits the campaign and the client that paid for it. Where ethics of progressive journalism and some professional journalists prioritize public accountability, impacting what and how a story is told, the public relations' story is different. This doesn't mean that the PR industry doesn't also have its own code of ethics, but the priority and accountability is to the client; since PR is a private industry, it—like the commercial media corporations—is, first and foremost, legally accountable to their shareholders.

Prioritizing accountability to shareholders over public accountability in the media industry leads to what could be identified as a conflict of interest that becomes particularly acute with ownership convergence. A recent case in Quebec, for example, was brought against the owners of Quebecor, whose vertical and horizontal ownership extends its control over almost all of the French-language media in Canada (recall Figure 3.3, p. 60–61). Quebecor also owns the Sun Media/Osprey Media chain including 36 newspapers across Ontario and Canada, and most significantly in Quebec where it owns the largest daily newspapers (*The Gazette* and *Le Journal de Montréal*), the largest French-language television network, and more than 80 per cent of the cable network. Quebecor is also vertically integrated as the major Internet service provider in Quebec.

The journalists who work for Quebecor recognized that their work was being impacted by such media convergence and concentration of ownership in two ways. The first had to do with the content of the news itself, and the second with the journalists' control over their own work. Attention was brought to the first by the union representing Quebecor workers at its newspaper *Le Journal de Montréal*. The union—Le syndicat des travailleurs de l'information du Journal de Montréal—suggested that their jobs were becoming more like marketers for the various Quebecor companies rather than as journalists reporting news. As explained by Ted Sprague (2010), according to the union

the media conglomerate's network of publications . . . will effectively blur the line between journalistic reporting and advertisement for Quebecor's empire of commercial printing, cable services, music, books, videos, business telecommunications, and marketing. The union . . . correctly points out [that] under Quebecor's plans, "There would be no way of knowing where the information stops and where promotion and advertising starts. In short, the convergence will override all notions of journalistic ethics." . . . There is no way to know where the reporting stops and where the promotion stops. Thus, effectively what we have is a single voice or single interest expressed in a diversity of outlets. (paras. 1, 3)

Ownership convergence is facilitated through technological convergence and affects the journalist's work in another related way. Content produced for one media is now expected to be flexible enough for all platforms. Content can be standardized, digitized, and distributed throughout the corporation's holdings. Prior to digitization, journalists generally wrote for one type of media. Indeed, the profession still continues to be distinguished by the medium—that is, whether the writing is intended for newspapers, magazines, radio, or television (Baehr & Schaller, 2010; Heyn, 1969; Seldes, 1968), and while journalism schools (both university and college) still train with this distinction in mind, the economically driven practices suggest that this is changing.

While making use of one piece of writing (or other audio-video) work across the various media holdings appears to make for an efficient product and cost-saving sense for the business, the journalists who are producing the work see this as having a negative impact on their jobs, particularly if they are not compensated for it. On one hand is the issue of copyright (see Chapters 4 and 9), whereby the journalist is not paid for work that is duplicated or re-purposed in digital form. Journalists have had to take this to court to legally battle for the rights over their own work, and have won class-action cases in Canada in the past (see Cohen, 2010, p. 126); however, this has arguably resulted in increasingly "restrictive" contracts that "demand multi-platform rights" such that if the writer wants to get published at all, they must assign copyright over their work for any use to the corporation (ibid.). As previously discussed, this is in line with intellectual property practices, but it considerably increases the power of the media conglomerate to determine the terms of the contract and to extract the most surplus value from it, and in turn exploit both the writer and their work (Cohen, 2013, pp. 149–50). Indeed, evidence suggests that this surplus is not being passed down to the writers who created the content to begin with. The last survey of freelance writers in Canada by the Professional Writers Association of Canada (PWAC, 2006, p. 4) indicated that annual after-tax income for writers has actually decreased over a 10-year period, averaging just over $20,000 per year, which puts them close to poverty levels in Canada (Raphael, 2012).

All of the above factors compound the agenda-setting and gatekeeper aspect of journalism discussed in Chapter 4 with media convergence, as some stories are duplicated across many media platforms, whereas others do not make the media at all (see, e.g., Project Censored www.projectcensored.org/the-top-25-index/), or those that do make the media have already been circumvented by public relations or press releases. Technological change and business decisions that combine to reduce both the number of journalists and the time that each reporter has to research negatively impact the ability of the journalist to do investigative reporting. This means that the reporter becomes more reliant on the public relations and press releases. Public-relations reporting has already been discussed in "Ongoing Issues: Investigative Journalism and Access to Information," and press releases are similar in that they are produced in the interest of the organization, institution, or corporation in order to inform, promote, market, advertise, or sell a product or idea, or alternatively counter any negative event or publicity. An annual report from the Pew Research Center, *The State of the News Media 2012*, found that, for example, in the United States this is affecting news particularly at the local level. Technological and business innovation hasn't precipitated any significant change in labour and social relations of power, and may in fact be strengthening already powerful structures:

Newspapers, local TV stations, and local radio stations employ fewer reporters now than they used to, and many of those that have survived have become more like 1930s wire service reporters—filing rapidly and frequently, doing fewer interviews, and spending less time pressing for information. This has resulted in a shift in the balance of power—away from citizens, toward powerful institutions. The watchdog reporter hates a press release; the busy reporter often loves it. (Waldman, 2011, p. 244)

Ownership convergence can also affect what is identified as news. Since 1988, the *Tyndall Report* has been monitoring and tabulating the total number of stories that made the "nightly newscasts" of the three major commercial broadcasters in the United States: ABC (American Broadcasting Company—owned by The Walt Disney Company), CBS (Columbia Broadcasting System—owned by National Amusements [Sumner Redstone]—and includes Viacom, MTV, BET, and Paramount), and NBC (National Broadcasting Company—49 per cent owned by General Electric and 51 per cent owned by Comcast). The report for 2011 indicates that the three top stories were (in order) the "slaying of" former Libyan ruler Moammar Khadafy; the "ousting" of the (former) president (Mubarak) of Egypt; and the American federal government, specifically its "budget, deficit and debt" (*Tyndall Report*, 2011; tyndallreport.com/yearinreview2011/). It also indicates that the Occupy movement did make the top 20 stories (at #18), but was covered substantially less than the British royal wedding (at #11) and several weather or "natural" disasters like the earthquake and tsunami in Japan (at #4) and "winter weather" in general (at #12). The report also observed that this was the first time in 24 years (with the exception of Hurricane Katrina in 2005) that the weather was covered so frequently. The report added that the link between ownership and coverage may have influenced NBC's particular focus on the weather, since NBC is "a corporate sibling of the Weather Channel" (ibid.).

As technologies have been developed, so too have the definitions and duties of journalists. Attention to the content of journalism is but one aspect of our question, "Who is a journalist now?" Another aspect has to do with technological change and business decisions as they affect the labour of journalists. The inspiration of ethical journalism (responsible to the public), combined with the possibility for personal (creative fulfillment) reward and recognition, can still motivate the journalist today. While these are conceivable gains, the political economy of media draws our attention to media work as labour. As part of a commercial industry, it can be treated as just another resource to exploit, similar to natural resources such as land, water, and air. As you shall see, labour is made increasingly expendable as technology is designed to replace the media worker, similar to that which occurred during the time of the Luddites.

Journalism, Technology, and Labour

It is argued that the transition from hard-copy newspapers to online content has resulted in a decrease in readership, a related drop in advertising, and substantial revenue loss (Grover, 2008; Perez Pena, 2009, as cited in McMillan, 2010, p. 820). Newspapers have limited or closed editions, or gone out of business entirely. The Pew Research Center's (2012) study of the *State of the News Media* suggests that, in the United States last year, "when circulation and advertising revenue are combined, the newspaper industry has shrunk 43% since 2000" (p. 4). In Canada, the political economy has also affected the newspaper industry, but given the extent of vertical and horizontal ownership, the bottom line is less affected, and the media industry as a whole continues to be very profitable (Edge, 2011; Statistics Canada, 2012; Winseck, 2010).

The financial conundrum facing the media industry, then, is how else can surplus value (or profit) be extracted? In order to attract online readers, most all of the content from traditional media sources was originally free. This belied the standard business model, because when

For Real?

Watching the Watchdogs?

Given the possibility for increased control of content via ownership concentration in media, together with controls over the message via the combination of advertising, marketing, press releases and public relations, several non-profit organizations have emerged to identify the absences and **"spin"** that can become increasingly prevalent in news (▣ www.cbc.ca/andthewinneris/2012/06/26/spin-cycles-episode-one). These organizations rely on members of the public together with research teams involving communication and journalism faculty and students (like yourself) to assist in the recognition, identification, and source of spin—and publish it via wikis, blogs, or website publications, among other methods. A range of organizations that exist (in the English language) in North America and Europe include NewsWatch (▣ www.newswatch.org), the Center for Media and Democracy (CMD) in the United States (▣ www.prwatch.org and ▣ www.sourcewatch.org), and, in the UK, Spinwatch (▣ www.spinwatch.org) and Media Lens (▣ www.medialens.org), the latter of which identifies but one example of the research process:

> *We check the media's version of events against credible facts and opinion provided by journalists, academics and specialist researchers. We then publish both versions, together with our commentary, in free Media Alerts and invite readers to deliver their verdict both to us and to mainstream journalists through the email addresses provided in our "Suggested Action" at the end of each alert. (Media Lens, 2010, para. 2)*

In Canada, operating from Simon Fraser University in Vancouver, NewsWatch Canada (Hackett & Gruneau, 2000) publishes what it calls *Missing News: The Top 25 Underreported Stories* whenever possible. As funding for such a project is limited—reliant as it is on public or government funding (i.e., no PR, marketing, advertising, or large corporations have sponsored the project in the past)—it is currently compiled by undergraduate students as part of a communications

SPIN

A form of propaganda in which the message is deliberately constructed to positively or negatively manage information about a person, event, institution, or organization. It is usually associated with the public relations industry, but is also part of the advertising, marketing, and lobbying industries. Among other techniques, information can be censored, distorted, manipulated, or exaggerated in favour of the (paying) client.

newspapers first went online, there wasn't a dominant commodified structure already in place. Among other assumptions "about what things should cost on the Internet" (Coughlan, 2010, para. 13) within the industry, it was predicted that the content would pay for itself because the money to be made from advertisers wanting access to readers would be more than the money that could be made by subscription alone.

Offering any content for free had its detractors, however, as in February 2010, the owner of *The Times* in London instituted subscription charges, or "paywalls" for its online content (BBC, 2010; see also Chapter 4). The move is monitored both within and beyond the media industry, not simply as an experiment or measurement of revenue gain or loss, but pivotal to the *idea* of charging for access to *any* information on the Internet. Persuading people that it is normal to pay for content—any content—is fundamental to the process of commodification and essential to capitalism and capitalist ideology in general. Initial reports suggested that there is substantial public resistance to payment as online readership for *The Times* is reportedly down a staggering 90 per cent (Halliday, 2010). As you shall see, this is one example of a continuing struggle to control the use value of information (and therefore its access, exchange, and potential to facilitate knowledge and social change) over its exchange value.

course (📖 pages.cmns.sfu.ca/newswatch). In 2010/11, for example, the top five missing stories (in order) included the Canada–Europe comprehensive economic and trade agreement; Canadian mining companies' lack of accountability; how corporate lobbying is shaping laws; the crisis in long-term health care; and violence against Aboriginal women in Canada (NewsWatch Canada, 2011). This has important consequences for investigation, scrutiny, and public accountability, as the "Executive Summary" suggests:

> These underreported stories were chosen because of their national and international importance and demonstrate issues that are critical to our health, safety, and democracy. Such omissions in major Canadian news media imply that the news provides only a partial reflection of the information citizens need for a functioning democracy, and suggests that we must rethink the role and structure of the large news organizations in Canada. (ibid., para. 1)

Discussion Questions

1. Access the latest Project Censored report. What stories are currently missing from the news? From your general observations (or via an online search), how many of the stories identified by Project Censored were you aware of? Discuss why you were (or were not) aware of them.

2. Consider how your class might do a "news watch" of your own over a specific time period (e.g., last month) in your city, or even in the university. What kind of research would you need to do?

3. *How* is the recognition, identification, and source of spin identified by the organizations listed here? Discuss your findings.

As we discussed in Chapter 3, corporate convergence through vertical and horizontal integration has meant that surplus value has to be extracted from somewhere, however. Revenue needs to service the entire company's holdings and debts incurred in expansion, as well as operating, technology, and labour costs, and especially payments to shareholders. Full-time and part-time staff "reductions" are intended to "streamline" production and reduce costs to the company associated with labour (such as office space, technology and equipment, health and safety, and many other necessities of the working environment), not to mention the "risks" associated with a living labour force that is subject to personal health, familial, community, and commuting responsibilities, and, if unionized, specific contractual obligations for fair and equitable working conditions. The "solution" to cutting costs via staff reductions (also known as early retirement, attrition, or lay-offs) is rarely identified as the elimination of full-time jobs and the "firing" of workers, but this is occurring across the media industries in Europe, the United States, Great Britain, Australia, and Canada, with little exception.

There is never a one-to-one correlation between technology and any form of labour; the introduction and acceptance of new technologies into any field does not always go smoothly. The commercial reality of journalism is that new technology often means a change in the way the work is managed, new and different skill sets being required; in an increasing number of cases, planned reductions in staffing levels; all affect the employment of journalists. Some of these have been attributed to technological change, while others are a direct result of common commercial industry practices that seek to eliminate wage labour as an expense. Attention to the bottom line means that decisions are made to reduce the overall number of employees, outsource parts of the work to other countries with few labour laws or minimum wage requirements, or replace parts of the labour force entirely with technology.

What has become standard practice in other industries, such as manufacturing for example, is also being applied to media industries. These cuts are not just on one or two occasions (see "For Real? The Elimination of Paid Employment in the Media Industry"), but are eliminated overnight as was demonstrated in October 2008 when the former Canwest media company cut 560 employees (CBC, 2008) or when Sun Media/Quebecor cut 600 jobs nine days before Christmas (Shalom, 2008). While there is no accurate cumulative figure for job losses in the media industries in Canada (via Statistics Canada or the CRTC, which rely on corporate statistics), in the United States, the Federal Communications Commission (FCC) study identified "massive job losses—including roughly 13,400 newspaper newsroom positions in just the past four years" (Waldman, 2011, p. 5). As its report on the current media landscape in the United

For Real?

The Elimination of Paid Employment in the Media Industry (January–June 2012, Existing Reports in Media)

Companies

BCE

"Analyst Predicts Job Cuts After BCE Acquires Astral Media"

Vlessing, E. (2012, 22 March). Retrieved from mediaincanada.com/2012/03/22/analyst-predicts-job-cuts-after-bce-acquires-astral-media/#ixzz1xahnZtEb

"Bell Canada Gives Pink Slips to Mississauga Employees"

Talk Radio **AM** 640. (2012, 11 January).

"Bell Canada Lays Off 60 Ottawa Workers"

CBC. (2012, 25 January). Retrieved from www.cbc.ca/news/canada/ottawa/story/2012/01/25/ottawa-bell-canada-layoffs.html

"Serious Layoffs Across the GTA This Week"

McKeown, S. (2012, 12 January). Retrieved from www.citytv.com/toronto/citynews/news/local/article/180180--serious-layoffs-across-the-gta-this-week

Nokia

"Nokia to Cut 10,000 Jobs and Close 3 Facilities"

O'Brien, K. J. (2012, 14 June). Retrieved from www.nytimes.com/2012/06/15/technology/nokia-to-cut-10000-jobs-and-close-3-facilities.html?ref=technology&nl=technology&emc=techupdateema2_20120614

Postmedia

"Job Cuts to Save Postmedia up to $35-million"

Krashinsky, S. (2011, 6 January). Retrieved from www.theglobeandmail.com/globe-investor/job-cuts-to-save-postmedia-up-to-35-million/article572358/

"Postmedia Cuts: Layoffs Expected As Sunday Editions Nixed, National Post Reduces Publication"

The Huffington Post Canada. (2012, 25 May). Retrieved from www.huffingtonpost.ca/2012/05/28/postmedia-cuts-layoffs_n_1551090.html

States suggests, "the media deficits in many communities are consequential. Newspapers are innovating rapidly and reaching new audiences through digital platforms but most are operating with smaller reporting staffs, and as a result are often offering less in-depth coverage of critical topics such as health, education and local government" (ibid.).

Such a precarious environment makes for very volatile working conditions, and the impact on journalists who depend on wage labour is significant. Lise Lareau, former president of the Canadian Media Guild (the union that represents 6,000 media workers, including media free-lancers), pointed out the increased pressure on the employees that do have jobs: Fewer workers are doing more work, there is less time to do creative and investigative research, and owner/management/employee relationships are strained, as workers don't know from one day to the next whether they will be the ones getting an email or phone call telling them not to come to work again (Cohen, Macdonald, Mazepa, & Skinner, 2011, p. 173).

Another way media work and journalism are affected by business decisions and techno-logical change is by the practice of **outsourcing**. The rationale is similar to the elimination of staffing positions, and as media content is increasingly digitized, the work can be distrib-uted worldwide. This is occurring in journalism and across the communication industries. As identified by the Communication, Energy and Paperworkers Union (CEP) in Canada, reasons

> **OUTSOURCING**
>
> Extending the division of labour outside the company such that parts of the product (in the case of journalism, the writing, editing, or layout) are contracted out to a second or third company.

RIM

"RIM Layoffs Could Hit Thousands"

Reuters. (2012, 27 May). Retrieved from business.financialpost.com/2012/05/27/rim-layoffs-could-hit-thousands/

Rogers

"Rogers Cuts 300 Jobs Across Canada"

CBC. (2012, 29, March). Retrieved from www.cbc.ca/news/business/story/2012/03/29/rogers-layoffs.html

Continents/Countries

Australia

"Newspaper Job Cuts Grow at Fairfax Media and News Limited"

Jackson, S. (2012, 1 June). Retrieved from www.theaustralian.com.au/media/newspaper-job-cuts-grow-ay-fairfax-and-news/story-e6frg996-1226379704963

Europe

"Spanish Media Crushed by Economic Crisis"

Agence France-Presse. (2012, 2 May). Retrieved from www.abs-cbnnews.com/business/05/02/12/spanish-media-crushed-economic-crisis

United Kingdom

"140 BBC Journalists to Lose Their Jobs"

Dex, R. (2012, 27 March). Retrieved from www.independent.co.uk/news/media/tv-radio/140-bbc-journalists-to-lose-their-jobs-7593360.html

United States

"Yahoo Layoffs: 2,000 Staff Expected To Go in Latest Shake-Up"

Rushe, D., & Sweney, M. (2012, 4 April). Retrieved from www.guardian.co.uk/technology/2012/apr/04/yahoo-layoffs-2000-staff-go

for outsourcing include reduced operating costs; lower wages; the reduction or elimination of responsibility for employee health and safety; the offloading of payroll taxes; and as a strategy to de-unionize the workforce and avoid labour standards and pension pay-outs, for example (CEP, n.d.; 🖥 www.cep.ca/).

While these may benefit the bottom line in the short-run, the long-term effects on journalists and media content have yet to be fully appreciated (unless you are a journalist currently without a job). The question of who makes the news and where is particularly significant with local news that relies on the journalist's experience and knowledge of the history and context of the area's (town's, city's, or country's) political economy and culture. A particularly surreal instance occurred when the largest newspaper chain in the United States (Gannett) outsourced its writing and copy-editing work to Mindworks Global Media whose home base is in India (Tady, 2008). One of Gannett's community newspapers in Pasadena, California, outsourced its reporting of the municipal council meetings to Mindworks, whose two reporters in India were to watch the proceedings via video camera. When the physical action stepped outside their video screen, however, the reporters were not able to follow and missed the context entirely.

Instances like these illustrate the contradiction between commercial and public service imperatives of journalism, particularly at the local level. Corporate decision-making focused on reducing costs has a direct effect on both the quantity and the quality of journalism, and the communities they are supposed to serve, as a recent finding of the FCC (2011) report underscored: "In many communities, we now face a shortage of local, professional, accountability reporting. This is likely to lead to the kinds of problems that are, not surprisingly, associated with a lack of accountability—more government waste, more local corruption, less effective schools, and other serious community problems" (Waldman, 2011, p. 5).

For media industry experts focused on the bottom line, there are fewer ethical responsibilities to complicate decision-making, but for communities reliant on wage labour and taxes paid by businesses to operate there, not to mention the importance of local news coverage, the reasons do not appear as rational (see, e.g., the reasons why employees at Fairfax Media in Australia, whose editing jobs had been outsourced to New Zealand, were striking [Roberts, 2012]).

The spate of lay-offs and outsourcing are intensified by the use of technology in the newsroom to replace, if not eliminate, human workers almost entirely. It is difficult to estimate how many because the commercial media rarely reports on its own lay-offs. Workers at the CTV broadcasting station in Ottawa, for example, found themselves replaced by what is called the OverDrive Automated Production Control (APC) System as manufactured by Ross Video in Iroquois, Ontario (Cartt.ca, 2012). The Ottawa station CJOH "eliminate[d] 19 full-time and approximately 15 part-time jobs" (ibid., para. 1) since the APC system was able to automate all of the production process except for tending the machine. The APC "enables one person to control the switcher, lighting, audio, video, graphic effects and robotic cameras that would traditionally have taken three to nine other staffers" (para. 4).

Such practices are not limited to the production aspect of journalism but are extending to the work of journalism itself. Called "**robot journalism**," the production of news is no longer left to the sole purview of human decision-making and the investigative and creative writing skills of the journalist; computers can be programmed to select from the entire range of data on the Internet, plus any additional uploads, and write the copy tailored for the intended client, audience, or individual. Engineering and journalism researchers at Northwestern University produced what they called Stats Monkey, a software program that could write stories based on information that it gathered via algorithms (recall our discussion of algorithms in Chapter 7; see also Levy, 2012). From this research project Narrative Science was founded, and Stats Monkey was renamed Quill, which is described by the company as an "artificial intelligence engine that generates, evaluates and gives voice to ideas as it discovers them in the data" (Narrative Science, 2013, para. 1).

The reliance on algorithms turns the way that commercial news has traditionally been identified, produced, and distributed on its head. Or does it? If news is commodified and written to attract the audience as consumer, is it any surprise that the process isn't more refined and narrowcast using technology? The technology is specifically designed to extend the process of commodification: "The algorithms search data to determine what content consumers are seeking, what content advertisers are willing to pay for, and what content can be profitably produced. There are no news meetings. There are no newsrooms. The editorial workforce is freelance, compensated by the piece, at a rate that varies but is never far from skimpy" (Spangler, 2010, p. 51).

Putting the question of the effect on the employment of journalists aside for a moment, what is also significant here is the direct linking of customer to advertiser to content, suggesting the possibility for increased media management and control based entirely on exchange value. What happens to questions of ethics and progressive journalism then? Compare our discussion of audience commodity in Chapter 6 with the "propaganda" model by Edward Herman and Noam Chomsky (1988) in Chapter 4 identifying the five political economic filters of news production. Does robot or client journalism suggest an extension of the audience commodity or an additional filter depending on who or what the customer is? Does it matter if the customer is a government, a multinational corporation, a political party, or a non-profit organization? What happens if the advertiser and the customer are one in the same?

Intensifying and extending the process of commodification heightens the potential for significant manipulation and control over labour, the information, the message, and their distribution, and, as you shall see in the next chapter, requires that priority be placed on identifying who the consumer is, what s/he is watching, listening to, searching for, and purchasing, as well as how and with whom they are interacting online. Returning to how this affects journalism and journalists, however, a new formula for making news is replacing the five *W*s. It's automated news production, and it reads something like a recipe for commodification:

> *2 cups Google-like algorithms to determine popular content*
> *2 cups advertisers who want to appear next to that content*
> *1 tbsp. eBay*
> *1/4 tsp. AOL's in-house editorial staff*
> *Infinite amount of starving writers. (Taylor, 2009, para. 1)*

And just who are those "starving writers"? The enduring popularity of journalism studies in universities has flooded the job market for reporters and increased the competition for scarce jobs. In this context it is legitimate to ask, "What will happen to all the frustrated journalists who cannot find a job? Will they want to express themselves through other means, such as weblogs and social media? And will expressing themselves be enough to put food on the table?"

At the same time as the media industry is reducing its paid labour force, it is capitalizing on the structural change this creates. The professional journalist competes with a reserve army of freelancers, who work for piecemeal—paid by the word, the story, the story's lifespan, or not at all (Cohen, 2013). For some, freelance work means independence from one employer, autonomy (the ability to make one's own decisions, to create what one wants), and freedom of routine obligations, among other attractions. Like the techno-enthusiasts who see all technology as progress, freelance labour is promoted as favourable for the knowledge society today and in the

ROBOT JOURNALISM
News copy and other types of media content compiled, composed, and produced by computers.

future. Indeed, according to urban visionaries like Richard Florida (2002), referred to earlier, we are witnessing the rise of a "creative class," one in which we are all entrepreneurs—self-made, self-employed, and self-marketed.

But this is a distortion of what political economists understand as *social class*, defined in Chapter 2. Creativity is not the issue. Autonomy, independence, and freedom are certainly values of human agency, as is the possibility to control one's own labour and future. This is underscored by the Marxist understanding of social class and the reason it identifies exploitation for what it is—rather than obfuscating it—in order that the conditions can be changed. As Christian Fuchs (2010) underscores, this "concept of class is explicitly normative and political—it aims at the abolition of exploitation and the establishment of participatory democracy" (p. 179). Because such an understanding of social class has a material basis, it asks such fundamental questions of the self-employed, self-educated, self-marketed entrepreneur: Who pays for the training or education necessary to acquire skills? Are there bills incurred during the marketing and advertising of the brand "me"? What happens if I get sick, or I'm disabled? How can I afford to keep up with changing technology? With all this focus on "me," what happens to "us"?

A recent article on freelance writers in the *Ryerson Review of Journalism* addressed this latter point in particular, comparing what the freelance worker needs now to what the freelance worker needed 30 years ago. An abridged version follows; note that despite 30 years of technological change, other aspects have remained constant:

Breaking in then and now

1980
- *Critical communication device: home phone*
- *Essentials: Typewriter, tape recorder*
- *Typical rate for feature article in a major magazine: $1 per word*
- *Gold National Magazine Award value: $1,000 . . .*

. . . 2010
- *Critical communication devices: home phone, cellphone/smartphone, high-speed internet connection;*
- *Essentials: Computer, still more software, more tech support, printer, scanner, photocopier, digital recorder, transcription software, online services (access to databases, etc.)*
- *Typical rate for feature article in a major magazine: $1 per word*
- *Gold National Magazine Award value: $1,000*

(Wilson, 2010, p. 27)

Where creativity may allow some to enter a classless society, the majority are left to compete with each other on increasingly unequal playing fields. This underlies the Occupy Wall Street movements and the student and public-wide strikes in Quebec, where student tuition is seen as directly responsible for rising student debt such that even if one manages to achieve a university education, the time and ability for creativity is dependent on whether you can afford to live without income for long periods of time. Adding to the mix is an opening in commercial media to **participatory journalism**, where the public is invited and encouraged to submit their own creative compositions online—whether these are articles, photographs, or ideas—and you have what might be called a "crisis" in professional journalism.

Participatory Journalism

The impact of technologies and convergence on the practices of journalism has certainly created changes, not the least of which is to the form of journalism and, by implication, journalism education. Automated journalism notwithstanding, the traditional inverted pyramid of print journalism is shaped for the eye, not the ear, so it doesn't transfer very well to electronic media, and this is even the case with web-based news services where "the front-line stories have more in common with radio and television" (Conley, 2002, p. 187). This change in content and form has further consequences for journalists, too: "New-generation media means new-generation journalists" (p. 306). According to David Conley this means that there is even greater pressure on experienced journalists, journalism students, and journalism educators to maintain the distinguishing features of the profession. The Internet, he argues, means that "citizens do not need journalists in the way they once did" (ibid.). We are now seeing this being played out in a million everyday information transactions—emails, weblogs, and SMS instant messaging: "Any literate citizen in any corner of the globe who has a computer or mobile computing device with an internet connection can create his or her own interactive news media" (MacKinnon, 2004, p. 4).

Digital media technologies have given form to a range of new information sources available on the Web. Any number of these can be grouped under the general heading of "participatory journalism." The Internet allows audiences to become more involved in stories, as commentators, sources, and even writers of the news in some cases (Bowman & Willis, 2005). The term *participatory journalism* may, however, be a bit misleading. The idea that anyone can now be a journalist is another one of the enduring myths of the digital age. It is also to some extent a generational question. As a new generation of media consumers embraces a new form of "news" that is "interactive and subject to interrogation, engaging the emotions as much as the brain," older journalists "shudder at this apostasy" (Hargreaves, 2003, p. 220). This proposition leads Ian Hargreaves to challenge our definitions of a journalist. He asks if it is appropriate in the new media environment: "Does it include news presenters, who may be actors rather than people trained in news? Does it include radio talk-show and tabloid TV hosts; does it include someone who sets up a weblog on the internet and shares information and opinion with anyone willing to pay attention?" (p. 227).

What is notable about the definition of *participatory journalism* is that it identifies the public as citizens and not consumers, which begs the question, "Does it matter?" In considering journalism as a commercial product, media theorist John Hartley (1999) suggested that the idea of journalism can be extended a long way past the news media to include "other factual and some fictional forms" (p. 17), even including marketing slogans written on the inside of beer bottle tops to entertain people while they drink. In this postmodern context, Hartley argues, the modernist ideology of journalism and the professional practices associated with it "simply cannot survive unscathed" (p. 27). The "popular and postmodern" forms of journalism that Hartley thinks are capable of democratizing popular culture by broadening the participation of consumers can be found in cyberspace (weblogs, wikis, and personal sites) where the physical terrain of suburbia melts away into the "mediasphere" (Hartley, 1996, 1999). Dan Gillmor, the founder of Grassroots Media Incorporated, also has a very positive view of this media "ecosystem." He argues that "if we're lucky," the electronic media will become a "multidirectional conversation" using a "distributional model" (Gillmor, 2005, p. 11). These predictions may or may not come true, but one thing is clear—on the ground, young reporters and media-savvy individuals are taking up the challenge.

Freelance journalist Bec Fitzgibbon (personal communication, 15 March 2006) describes the casual participant in journalism as a "common correspondent," which she says exists today

PARTICIPATORY JOURNALISM

"'The act of a citizen or groups of citizens, playing a role in the process of collecting, reporting, analysing and disseminating news and information' (Bowman and Willis 2003) to which can be added commenting and publicly discussing same" (as cited in Hermida, 2011, p. 15).

because anyone can broadcast news online: "We don't have to be journalists to make news these days" (ibid.). According to Fitzgibbon, the camcorder has definitely democratized the media as much as weblogs, LiveJournals, and Indymedia (independent media) have. It seems today that do-it-yourself media are infused into every corner of the globe; the little people are making the big news—from Australia to Canada: "We've recently seen a reinvigoration of printed street zines in Tasmania (which I've written about for *The Mercury*); usually edited and published by late teens to mid-20 year olds, there's a distinct air of empowerment with new media for the youth, by the youth. We are all journalists today, definitely. I covet my freelancing magazine work" (ibid.).

We shall cover the production of zines in Canada in our last chapter on politics and alternative media. In the meantime, another way of looking at the "common correspondent" is the concept of the citizen-journalist providing "user-generated" news that the mainstream media is taking seriously (Bowman & Willis, 2005, p. 7). If these new media forms are the work of amateurs, it makes any definition of journalism as a set of codified and structured practices almost meaningless. We have seen a proliferation of news-style sites established on the Web over the past decade, and blogs in particular have become very popular. Some blogs are written by journalists, but are they journalism? Blogs written by professionals in other fields often get quoted in news stories and in other blogs, but are they, strictly speaking, news sites?

New distribution systems, such as "news on demand" and RSS feeds, are also impacting journalism, but more particularly traditional media outlets. It seems we are no longer tied to buying a morning newspaper, or sitting still in front of the television for half an hour in the evenings to get our daily news "fix." The developments in podcasting and news alerts via mobile phones are changing the ways in which we consume news products.

Blog, Blog, Blog. Blog, Blog!

Weblogs are the mavericks of the online world. Two of their greatest strengths are their ability to filter and disseminate information to a widely dispersed audience, and their position outside the mainstream of mass media. Beholden to no one, weblogs point to, comment on, and spread information according to their own, quirky criteria. (Blood, 2006, para. 1)

BLOGGING

An Internet publication of the views and opinions of an individual. The distinctive attribute of blogging is that it is presented as unfiltered by the traditional media "gatekeepers," although not necessarily unmoderated. Purportedly, blogging has created a new flow of opinion, and represents the diversity of opinion characteristic of new media.

Rebecca Blood (2006) is a blogger who has written a handbook on blogging, including a useful chapter on ethics where she makes the sound (in our view) distinction between commercial journalism and blogging: "Individual webloggers seem almost proud of their amateur status" (para. 4). One of the key differences outlined on her site is that, because of their commercial function (selling eyeballs to advertisers), journalists need a rigorous code of ethics. On the other hand, the unstructured and largely unmediated world of blogs is both a strength and a weakness (ibid.). The popularity of blogs means they are unlikely to go away quickly, and we think it's good that Blood has published a handbook. There are other codes of ethics for bloggers that can be found online. The ones we checked all make this important distinction between blogs and journalism, which is not to deny that blogs are, as Blood says, important sources of news and information for many people.

The wild, uncontrolled, and apparently democratic nature of the blogosphere led some, like eminent American media theorist Jay Rosen (2005), to hail blogs as the latest expression of a free press. Rosen argues that blogging turns at least part of the media's power over to those who "want to join the experiment and become, in some sense or another, part of the press" (ibid., p. 27). Today blogs are more than just counterpoint news sites. They can be totally personal, like a diary, or places to express crazy ideas that some people will find amusing enough to return to. There is a certain degree of digital myth-making around the blogging phenomenon, perhaps created by the real challenge that blogs represent to journalism. As Shayne Bowman and Chris Willis (2005) argue, the "hegemony as gatekeeper" role of journalists is now threatened by new technologies and by audiences who are "getting together" (p. 6) to set the news agenda. But we think it is easy, among all the hype, to overstate the case somewhat.

Yet, the existence of blog sites on the Internet today is five times more than what it was just five years ago. In 2011, there were "181 million blogs around the world" (Nielsen Wire, 2012, para. 1). A large proportion of blog sites are run by people who are definitely not journalists and who are not necessarily writing about professional issues in their area of expertise. Can we legitimately argue that these sites are news, or that their authors are working as journalists, even in an amateur capacity? Is it still too early to give a definitive answer to these questions? We may have to reserve judgement for a bit longer. In our view, however, most blogs, wikis, and other amateur sites that contain "newsworthy" material are not the product of journalism, and most bloggers are not journalists. Indeed, Technorati's annual "State of the Blogosphere" identifies that the majority of bloggers are hobbyists (60 per cent), followed by professional bloggers (18 per cent), entrepreneurs (13 per cent), and corporate employees (8 per cent; State of the Blogosphere, 2011). Where the hobbyists are writing personal opinion on a variety of subjects, the latter three write mainly about technology and business. But there is no doubt that blogs and participatory journalism are challenging traditional notions of journalism and can put the "gatekeeper function" of traditional editors into some question (Hermida, 2011).

We don't argue against blogs out of some sort of professional jealousy, or because we necessarily think that the current practices and social relations of journalism are all worth defending. But analytically, the distinction is an important one if we are to maintain any clarity about the terms of the debate, whether for the sake of news or the sake of media labour. That the blogging news site *The Huffington Post* relies primarily on unpaid labour of "volunteers" and freelancers, and is a news aggregator (selects and compiles already-written copy in one place) is a case in point. Its purchase by AOL for $315 million prompted a class-action lawsuit for the "more than 9,000 writers" (Peters, 2011, para. 2) who wrote for the *Post* and were not compensated. As explained by *Globe and Mail* journalist Simon Houpt (2012), "only two full-time employees [are] dedicated to original reporting" (para. 4); the rest are editing already-written copy selected to attract consumers for the advertisements on the site: "You might even say marketing is what HuffPost does best: sampling the highlights of others' work, writing a few original sentences to add context, slapping on a come-hither headline and providing a link to the original article for the convenience of those readers not sated by the summary" (para. 3). While on one end, the writers who contribute to blogs and post freelance work hope that sheer exposure and talent will eventually result in payment—and for some, of course it does—the influx of user-generated content (UGC) provides another reserve army that commercial media can draw on for content.

UGC is likely something everyone reading this has done at least once in their lives, particularly as the definition offered here is very broad. Studies of UGC in the United States and Canada indicate that there is an increasingly wide variety of forms of UGC including

> blogs; micro-blogs (such as those uploaded to Twitter); user reviews (such as product reviews made on Amazon.com); content uploaded to social networking sites (such as Facebook, LinkedIn and Google+); photographs and videos uploaded to file-sharing sites (such as Flickr, SnapFish and YouTube); information uploaded to wikis (such as

USER-GENERATED CONTENT (UGC)
Audio and visual material uploaded and distributed on the Internet, generally voluntary, unpaid, and intended for public viewing.

Wikipedia and Wetpaint); and content uploaded to virtual world websites (such as Second Life). (Glickman & Fingerhut, 2011, p. 49)

The increase in UGC, like early discussions of Internet participation (see Chapter 7), suggests that social media provides a fundamentally new way for the public to participate in the creation of news and information, which is both empowering and democratizing (see, e.g., Benkler, 2006; D. S. Chung, 2007; Shirky, 2008, as cited in Jönsson & Örnebring, 2011, p. 127). Media companies have responded by soliciting input from readers/viewers and listeners on digital editions ranging from asking for occasional input through (1) **crowd-sourcing** (e.g., the *National Post* in Toronto sought input from the public for "eyewitness accounts" and information on a "propane gas explosion in a neighbourhood in Toronto" (Hermida, 2011, p. 20) to (2) blog contributions (see, e.g., the *Calgary Herald*'s "opinion blog" site [www.calgaryherald.com/opinion/blogs/index.html]) to (3) *The Guardian*'s "open journalism" (www.guardian.co.uk/media/open-journalism). Each suggests an opportunity for the public creation of news, wrestling the control over production from the media conglomerates and empowering citizens to participate in a significant way. As *The Guardian*'s Editor-in-Chief Alan Rusbridger announced in launching this kind of journalism as part of its new brand, "open is our operating system, a way of doing things that is based on a belief in the open exchange of information, ideas and opinions and its power to bring about change. . . . The campaign is designed to bring that philosophy to life for new and existing readers" (as cited in Sweney, 2012, para. 5; www.guardian.co.uk/media/2012/feb/29/guardian-tv-ad-open-journalism?intcmp=239).

Such incorporation of the public suggests a change in the journalist's job, to the point where, as Mark Deuze and Christina Dimoudi (2002) advance, the "online journalist" is a distinctly new profession. The "new" is distinguished from the "old" because of the type of media used, the kind of interpersonal communication (computer-mediated), as well as the extent to which public opinion is consulted. While the numbers of public participants are potentially much greater than the past, the relationship of the journalist with them might be argued as returning to the "old" model, wherein journalists were in close contact with their communities. In any case, media organizations that do have publicly stated ethics and policies may include UGC as a source, and the CBC has a special policy to address it:

> CBC *is responsible for all content on its news sites. This policy covers text, image, video or audio contributions from the public which are incorporated into news coverage on any platform.*
>
> *Material that originates from a non-CBC source is clearly identified as such.*
>
> *Before text, image, video or audio is published, its provenance and accuracy is verified.*
>
> *In exceptional circumstances, it may be difficult to authenticate a contribution. There may be times where because of timeliness or if it is in the public interest, we decide to publish without full verification. We are clear with the audience about what we know. The decision to publish material without full authentication must be referred to the Director. (CBC, 2013, paras. 1–4; www.cbc.radio-canada.ca/en/reporting-to-canadians/acts-and-policies/programming/journalism/ugc/)*

Identifying the political economy of UGC indicates that commercial media are incorporating such content in an effort to attract more people to online advertising (McMillan, 2010) and to "rebrand" themselves as new and different (a common marketing strategy), and correspondingly

---

CROWD-SOURCING

Distributed labour, initiated by an online call for participation and collaboration in textual composition (such as journalism), problem-solving, or decision-making; an extension of outsourcing that may (or may not) be financially compensated.

benefit from the "free labour" of UGC with less reliance on paid journalists. As Anna Maria Jönsson and Henrik Örnebring (2011) argue from their literature review and empirical study of online newspaper practices, this is a strategy whereby the contributor to a particular newspaper "is expected to use and identify with that newspaper also in other contexts, thus strengthening the brand. . . . Users are *identified* as consumers but *approached* as citizens" (p. 127), thus suggesting the empowerment of citizens is a "pseudo-power" (p. 141).

In considering the power relations, it is important to identify what has changed exactly. That is, while participation in the production of content has increased, the decision-making and media ownership structures have not.

> *Citizen participation and participatory journalism only allow for users to influence certain stages of the news production process, while other stages are closed for user involvement and/or controlled by journalists. Media professionals control the management of the production process, and this confirms the conclusion that media organizations are not willing (nor institutionally able) to release power over the production process to the user. (p. 128)*

That traditional journalism is nevertheless threatened is an understatement. Our initial question of "Who's a journalist now?" at the beginning of this chapter was also taken up in a recent conference and debate on the question of whether journalists should be distinguished from non-journalists via a formal licencing process. Christine St-Pierre, the former Quebec culture minister, suggested the idea as coming from the Federation of Professional Journalists in Quebec (FPJQ). Such a move would by definition preclude bloggers and amateurs from the category of journalist. This is not a new idea, nor is it unique to Canada (see, e.g., Hirst & Patching, 2005, pp. 118–19), but it has not yet gained any significant "traction" in changing practices here. However, in some countries, including the United Kingdom and New Zealand, tertiary journalism courses are accredited and regulated by an industry body, usually composed of senior editors and educators. The practice may be akin to the inclusion of journalists who are accredited to participate in federal and provincial parliamentary "press galleries" as journalists who have the experience, publications, and media credentials in order to do so (■ press-presse.parl.gc.ca/).

In the meantime, as social media continues to grow, the challenge for professional journalists and journalism will increase accordingly. Currently, however, the Pew Research Center's annual *State of the Media 2012* report concludes that, for now,

> *contrary to what some observers have argued, the rise of social media recommendations at this point does not appear to be coming at the expense of people going directly to news sites or searching for news topics they are interested in. Instead, social media news consumption is supplemental. This expanded behavior also mirrors what we see in the larger report about news consumptions on different digital devices. Smartphones and tablets do not appear to be replacing computers as much as providing additional ways to get news. (Mitchell, Rosenstiel, & Christian, 2012, para. 14)*

The Future of Journalism?

We cannot reverse the trends of history, nor would we necessarily want to. But we can issue a note of caution about the mythical hype surrounding new digital technologies. The argument that podcasting, weblogs, and other forms of interactive information-sharing on the Internet will create a new and more democratic public discourse is seductive, but not all that solid. Certainly digital technology has the potential to reinvigorate democratic debate and certainly it challenges both the old media and our conception of what journalism is. At the same time, breaking down the practice of journalism so that it is "accessible" to everyone, anywhere, anytime, risks collapsing important theoretical and practical distinctions that still have a purpose. We are in favour of radically reforming journalism in a number of ways—increasing the rank-and-file control over newsrooms and exposing the contradiction between profits and public service are two—but we are not in favour of dissolving "journalism" as a particular category of information management that is bounded by certain rules and conventions. In our view, to do so would be to destroy the possibility of a viable independent media capable of reaching and informing vast numbers of people with the potential for mobilization around common experiences and concerns. What is identified or remains of the "common," however, is also subject to the dialectic. In the final section of this book we take up some arguments about the world of narrowcasting that seem ready to take over from the age of broadcasting. We also further tackle some of the more dangerous myths that surround emerging digital media technologies.

Key Points

- What we are calling the "reportorial community" is changing because of the use of new technologies and new commercial methods in the mass media.

- Contemporary journalism education defines and positions journalism, but commercial priorities influence its shape and development.

- There has been a change from traditional—that is, twentieth-century—newsroom organizational structures.

- Different kinds of journalism have emerged, including progressive, professional, online, computational, and robot—as well as participatory journalism, blogging, citizen-reporting, and user-generated content as forms of new media reportage.

Class Discussion

1. To what extent is time a factor in determining what is news? How has the 24/7/365 news-cycle or the focus on instantaneous reporting through social media such as Facebook and Twitter affected how (and what) you think of as news? In turn, how has this impacted the work of the journalist and what you think of as journalism?

2. How effective are organizations such as Spinwatch, Media Lens, or NewsWatch? Are the general public aware that these organizations exist? Why are they important?

3. What is the difference between a professional journalist and a freelance writer?

4. Compare the *Calgary Herald*'s "opinion blogs" (🖳 www.calgaryherald.com/opinion/blogs/index.html) with *The Guardian*'s "open journalism" (🖳 www.guardian.co.uk/media/open-journalism). What are their similarities and differences? Which would you classify as user-generated content and which would you classify as participatory journalism? Why?

Media on Media

Tunes on Work and Journalism

Bob Dylan. (1965). Battle of a thin man. *Highway 61 Revisited*. NY: Columbia Records.

Pete Seeger. (1940). Newspaper men. *Gazette, Vol. 1*. US: Folkways Records.

Placebo. (2000). Slave to the wage. *Black Market Music*. UK: Virgin.

Public Enemy. (1991). A letter to the New York Post. *Apocalypse 91: The Enemy Strikes Black*. NY: Def Jam Records.

Ramones. (1999). It's not my place (in the 9 to 5 world). *Hey! Ho! Let's Go: The Anthology* (Disc 2). UK: Rhino Entertainment, Sire Records.

Rolling Stones. (1967). Yesterday's papers. *Between the Buttons*. US: Decca.

Tom Paxton. (2001). Daily news. *Ramblin' Boy and Ain't That News*. US: Elektra Records.

Movies, DVDs, and Videos

Brooks, J. L. (Director, Producer, & Writer). (2010). *Broadcast news*. US: 20th Century Fox.

Investigative Productions Inc. (Producer). (1988). *The world is watching*. Canada: TVOntario.

Metzgar, E. D. (Director). (2009). *The reporter*. US: Sundance.

Rossi, A. (Director). (2011). *Page one: Inside the New York Times* [DVD documentary]. US: Magnolia Home Entertainment.

PART IV

From Broadcasting to Narrowcasting:
A Surveillance Political Economy

Objectives

In this final section we are looking to the future, but our view is firmly anchored in what's happening today, and builds on our historical survey in earlier chapters. This section is sometimes speculative and gives an indication of what we think some of the possible directions are for media and technology as we identify how narrowcasting is part of the dialectic of convergence. After reading this section you should have a greater understanding of what we mean by "surveillance society" and "surveillance economy" in relation to the following:

- how the mimetic idea of "Big Brother" has come to feature prominently in public debates about the surveillance society;

- how state priorities direct the technological development and growth of surveillance technology;

- how commercial media can legitimize the growing level of commercial and political surveillance over society; and

- how technological convergence can be used to bring business, the state, and its military in closer relationship over concerns of network security.

Keywords

- **alternative media**
- **surveillance economy**
- **surveillance society**

Since you now know enough about government policy-making to participate in it, or at least to appreciate the importance and significance of the process, we invite you to enter the discussions and debates around power as new media and technology is used and developed for surveillance, and—in relation—how it is used to facilitate political continuities and instigate social change.

As we explained in Chapter 9, government decision-making is critical to how we understand and use technology and pivots around questions of power and control. You are all likely well aware of the meme that "9/11 changed the world." The first chapter in this section asks us to consider some of these changes (political, economic, and social) that are being made in its name: Did the world change . . . or just our (or the government's) perception of and reaction to it?

In liberal democracies such as Canada, it is at least expected that our government has always adhered to the Canadian Charter of Rights and Freedoms, even before it was formalized in 1982. As we discuss in Chapter 11, however, particularly in times of "crisis," the government can act in a way that belies this expectation and, in fact, contradicts the very principles that are supposed to give it strength. We identify government decisions in the United States and Canada, in particular, as acutely and inextricably bound with an overarching concern over security that envelops our communication practices and technological development today, and will set it far into the future. We consider how these decisions affect our understandings of public and private space, of freedom of movement (e.g., travel and mobility), and as expressions of ourselves, our experiences, and our relationships with each other. We consider, then, what surveillance has to do with narrowcasting, and how government actions contribute to the perception that we are living, and will always live, in a surveillance society.

In Chapter 12 we develop on these themes of perception, control, and surveillance in greater depth and detail. As Chapter 11 focuses more on the political aspects of surveillance, Chapter 12 zeroes in on its economic aspects as inseparable. Again, this political economic approach may make us feel uncomfortable about our use of technology, our social interactions on the Internet, and maybe even cause us to question our physical surroundings and thus our conceptualizations of privacy, but it is essential both in identifying how convergence leads to narrowcasting and in evaluating our participation in it.

In Chapter 13 we get into the nitty-gritty, roll-up-your-sleeves questions of politics. It's here where we seek to identify how changes in media and technology are being mobilized to entrench or challenge power relations. We have chosen several current examples that are likely closer to your own experience of current events, and consider them in light of larger questions of democracy. These include further considerations of the actions of "citizen-journalists," such as blogging, but much more in terms of how people get together in large numbers, as collective groups, to participate and influence the making of media and technology of the future, and how these groups mobilize to affect meaningful social change.

While this may sound like something made for the imagination, it is an invitation to do so. *Democracy* should not be an already worn-out term, particularly when there are several locations in the world where thousands upon thousands of people are giving their entire lives for the sake of its realization. Considering how people negotiate and resist both convergence and narrowcasting is part of this realization. We thus venture into alternative practices of media— independent and autonomous media—and the people that express them, whether in the form of non-government and community organizations, or joined together in social movements. This is the last section of this book, and in completing your reading, we hope that you will have the time to critically reflect on its content, and that it helped inform, motivate, and empower you to work together and thereby encourage different kinds of convergence.

We Know What You're Doing. . . . The Surveillance Society Has Arrived

Objectives

In this chapter we explore the parameters of the surveillance society. In particular, we explain how the transition from broadcasting to narrowcasting is a symptom and an effect of increasing public surveillance. After reading this chapter you should be familiar with the following:

- what we mean by surveillance society;
- what forms public surveillance can take and what issues are emerging from the use of technology to monitor people;
- how the shift from broadcasting to narrowcasting is symptomatic of the surveillance society; and
- how the commercial media play an important role in legitimizing social surveillance.

Keywords

- **Anti-terrorism Act**
- **CCTV surveillance**
- **lawful access**
- **malware**

- **PIPEDA**
- **spyware**
- **surveillance society**
- **USA PATRIOT Act**

Big Brother Comes to Canada

"Say Hello to Big Brother Government"—Toronto Sun *(Akin, 2012)*

"Online Surveillance Bill Opens Door for Big Brother: Section 34 Gives Orwellian Powers to Government-Appointed 'Inspectors'"—CBC News *(Milewski, 2012)*

"The Threat of 'Big Brother' Internet Monitoring in Canada"—Rabble.ca *(Karlin, 2012)*

All of the headlines above criticized the Canadian federal government's proposed new Bill C-30 entitled An Act to enact the Investigating and Preventing Criminal Electronic Communications Act and to amend the Criminal Code and other Acts, also known as the Protecting Children from Internet Predators Act, or the Lawful Access Bill. This Bill would have extended the powers of law enforcement to access greater amounts of personal information available electronically without a warrant. It would require Internet service providers (ISPs) to store all of their clients' personal information, and make that available, upon request, to the police. There was widespread opposition to this legislation from other political parties, public interests groups, as well as some in the industry, such that the Bill was dropped. However, the requirement still remains in another form under Bill C-12 (An Act to amend the Personal Information Protection and Electronic Documents Act; 🖥 openparliament.ca/debates/2013/3/19/ scott-simms-2/ and www.parl.gc.ca/About/Parliament/LegislativeSummaries/bills_ls. asp?ls=c12&Parl=41&Ses=1), but more on this later.

We have drawn your attention to these articles for two reasons. Firstly, it is typical of the way that George Orwell's dystopian vision of the future, as described in his novel *Nineteen Eighty-Four*, and the character of "Big Brother" in particular, is commonly used to frame discussions about the current world in which we live. Secondly, and perhaps more importantly, it points to the kinds of decisions and justifications (thereof) that governments at all levels are choosing to make that authorizes increased surveillance over the public, their communications and personal information, as well as the uses of ICT.

Such prevalence of Big Brother headlines might tell us something about the state of most newspaper copy, but it's probably also an indication that the concept and image of Big Brother is alive and well in popular culture. Indeed, the first thought and image that may have come to your mind was not the Orwellian novel or the federal bill, but the reality television show *Big Brother Canada*, which we discussed in the Preface of this book. *Big Brother* is a show about surveillance, where the surveillance is voluntary and normalized, where the audience both watches and participates in the surveillance of others. In many senses, then, "Big Brother" has become mimetic, and now has a viral capacity to be used to spread and influence how events and relationships around us are framed and responded to.

The concept of Big Brother is one way of thinking about surveillance and the political economic and social conditions that have contributed to its mimetic spread. Its characterization is usually meant to identify government surveillance over its citizens, and so in this chapter, we shall focus on the more formal "political" aspect, and in the next chapter we will identify the ways that the "economic" privileges surveillance. Together, they mean to address the characterization of the social totality today and predictions of the future as the **surveillance society**. That is, we will consider some of the ways we have come to see surveillance—from the French words *sur* (over) and *veillier* (to watch)—as something that is still defined as "watching deviant or criminal behaviour" (as framed in the proposed Bill C-30), as a normal, or hegemonic, part of our environment, and as a participatory—or perhaps even enjoyable—part of our everyday lives.

> **SURVEILLANCE SOCIETY**
> A way of characterizing the social totality wherein physical and electronic surveillance is commonplace.

I Spy with My Little Eye: Who Was Big Brother?

> *The hostile figure melted into the face of Big Brother, black-haired, black-mustachio'd, full of power and mysterious calm. . . . Nobody heard what Big Brother was saying. It was merely a few words of encouragement, the sort of words that are uttered in the din of battle. . . . At this moment the entire group of people broke into a deep, slow rhythmical chant of "B-B! . . . B-B!"—over and over again . . . a heavy, murmurous sound. . . . It was a refrain that was often heard in moments of overwhelming emotion. (Orwell, 1988, pp. 16–17)*

This is the only physical description we get of Big Brother (B-B), at the beginning of *Nineteen Eighty-Four*. While it is often thought that B-B was modelled on the Russian totalitarian dictator

Joseph Stalin, it could be someone else. When Orwell was writing this novel, in the years immediately after World War II, another European dictator would have been prominent in popular thought; it's just as likely that Orwell's model could have been Adolf Hitler ("black hair and moustache, powerful and mysteriously calm"). Given Orwell's anti-fascist and anti-Stalinist politics, B-B is more than likely an amalgam of the two twentieth-century dictators, just as "IngSoc" (short for "English Socialism") in *Nineteen Eighty-Four* is likely a fusion of the National Socialism of the Nazis and Soviet-style *state capitalism* of the USSR. Throughout the book nobody ever *sees* Big Brother, but he is a constant presence on the telescreen and at the centre of all propaganda efforts by the Inner Party.

The main protagonist, Winston Smith, vaguely recalls first hearing of B-B during the 1960s, but even then B-B's daring exploits and marvellous achievements had been historically re-engineered until "they extended into the fabulous world of the forties and the thirties." Winston tries but cannot remember when the Party was formed, but B-B had always been "the leader and guardian of the Revolution since its very earliest days" (p. 32)—though he has no way of knowing how much of this legend was true and how much invented. For Winston and the other characters in *Nineteen Eighty-Four*, Big Brother had a powerful mimetic presence and helped cement the hegemony of the Inner Party cadre. In effect, people had forgotten how it came to be that power became so concentrated and exercised so fully that they couldn't imagine any alternatives.

Orwell's novel takes place in the fictional nation of "Oceania"—the "newspeak" name for Britain—and it is a frightening rendition of a surveillance society. The telescreens never turn off, and the "Thought Police of the Inner Party" are everywhere. When Winston is struggling to complete the compulsory morning exercise routine, led by a female party member barking through the telescreen, she berates him by name and number—a stark reminder that it is a two-way device, and that she can see him: "'Smith!' screamed the shrewish voice from the telescreen. '6079 Smith W.! Yes, you! Bend lower please! . . . You're not trying. Lower, please! That's better, comrade . . . '" (ibid.).

In Oceania, children are enlisted in a youth organization called the Spies, to spy on their parents and neighbours. When Winston and Julia leave the city to make love in the forest, they have to be careful—there are hidden microphones even in this remote and beautiful place; Big Brother, unseen, but all-powerful, is everywhere. There are some interesting parallels developing between the fictional world of *Nineteen Eighty-Four* and the surveillance society of the twenty-first century.

Nineteen Eighty-Four **Today**

If the surveillance society is defined simply by the quantity of photographs, televisions, camera phones, videos, and security cameras available, there can be no doubt that we're living in a surveillance society, and it's not just in Canada. There is a global shift away from the freedoms we have taken for granted in the past and away from an automatic presumption of privacy (Jensen, 2004). Today it seems that the only place we can have any real *physical* privacy is in our own homes. But even there, we cannot guarantee *electronic* privacy. The telemarketing calls, which never seem to stop, are used to gain information about us that we're not even aware of. Indeed, the Canadian Marketing Association wants the CRTC to allow automated calls to "consumers" with whom companies have "a business relationship" with, such that the calls could be narrowcast directly to the individual (LaSalle, 2013). All these calls are recorded and analyzed to prepare vast data files on our consumption and other habits (O'Harrow, 2005). We are not safe from electronic surveillance if we log on to the Internet, watch cable TV, use the telephone, or use GPS; someone, something, somewhere has access to a record of that transaction. We are leaving electronic fingerprints all over the world, even from the privacy of a computer terminal in a bedroom, or home office.

Not only do we leave a trail all over the Internet, but there is also electronic **spyware** and **malware** that attempts to lodge itself in our computers, unless we're protected behind a network firewall, or have up-to-date anti-virus software installed on our PCs. The situation is worse outside the four walls of our living spaces. In Western societies we have learned to accept a certain amount of surveillance and inconvenience in return for what we perceive to be the security offered by governments. Most people will put up with the minor irritation of longer line-ups and having their stuff searched at sports events, concerts, and airports, but the surveillance society does not necessarily respect local or national boundaries.

As countries like China seek to move into the global economy while retaining a strong grip on the actions and communications of their population, they are able to take advantage of digital surveillance technologies to retain a hold on political power. The case study in this chapter shows how the Chinese government is committed to expanding China's role in the world economy, while trying to maintain a totalitarian grip on civil society. Its political economy is "state capitalist" rather than communist or socialist because their economies are similar in structure to those in the West, despite elements of state ownership of the means of production. Throughout the period that we were writing this book, there were continual updates on growing electronic surveillance measures and deals between the regime in Beijing and international media/communications companies, like Google and Microsoft, which were prepared to accept controls over their products in return for access to the lucrative Chinese market.

SPYWARE

Computer software programs that track a computer's location, contents, and/or online traffic and collect this information without the computer user's knowledge. The information can be used for criminal purposes (like identity theft), for police and state "intelligence gathering," or to narrowcast and advance commodification of the user and their information via targeted advertising and marketing.

MALWARE

Computer software programs that are designed to hack into a computer system to disrupt normal operations and/or gather information. It could be malicious (sent to search and destroy), disruptive, or unnoticeable. Examples include worms, viruses, adware, and spyware.

Case Study

Surveillance on the Internet in China

China's decision to impose further restrictions on internet communication illustrates that the country's economic rise is not being paralleled by a greater tolerance towards freedom of speech. (D. Rosen, 2005, para. 1)

This opening line from journalist Danny Rosen's comment neatly highlights the dialectic at work in the creation of a surveillance society. As China's state capitalist regime is opened up to the globalizing world market, there is a tightening of political surveillance over the population, not, as the laissez-faire theories of economists would have us believe, an accompanying rise in political freedoms. The issues of freedom of expression and Internet access were highlighted globally around the 2008 Olympic Games in Beijing. In order to win the bid for the games, the Chinese government promised it would not restrict access to the Internet, and in the lead-up to the Games it tried to liberalize its rhetoric and tone down the more authoritarian aspects of its global image.

Despite government promises, just prior to the launch of the Games, many international journalists complained of the significant restrictions they faced when trying to access the Internet while reporting from the games (Musil, 2008). This proved to be an embarrassment for the International Olympic Committee, leading to a compromise with the Chinese government once the Games began, such that sites like Amnesty International and BBC's Chinese services were

Continued

unblocked for international visitors, but not for Chinese citizens. Additionally, sites dealing with "sensitive" subjects such as Tibet or Tiananmen Square continued to be blocked for all accessing the Internet from China in this period (Branigan, 2008).

According to Western experts, China wants complete access to the global economy, but cannot afford to open up its political institutions too much, which would challenge or disturb the hierarchical power structure. Peter Goff has highlighted how the dialectic is affecting the use of the Internet in China. There is a contradiction between the regime's desire for economic growth and securing China's place in the world economy, and its fear that allowing too much electronic freedom for citizens will undermine its authority: "The dilemma for the Government is that while the internet is needed to fuel economic growth, the uncontrolled flow of information it brings could undermine one-party rule and the leadership's conservative approach" (Goff, 2005).

In 2011, the government in China continued to violate domestic and international legal guarantees of freedom of press and expression by restricting bloggers, journalists, and (an estimated) more than 500 million Internet users (Human Rights Watch, 2012). Amnesty International and other human rights groups indicate that there are tens of thousands of Chinese police officers whose function is to monitor Internet traffic. Internet cafés are regularly raided or closed down if patrons are found to be surfing on "inappropriate" sites. It seems that the Chinese government is prepared to go even further in trying to control what its citizens can talk and think about. In October 2005, *Newsweek* correspondent Melinda Liu (2005) wrote about how the Net police are now actively participating in chat rooms to put the government's line on controversial topics: "The aim is not simply to stifle dissent or to control the free flow of information, but increasingly to shape public opinion in cyberspace."

The Chinese government continues to ratchet up restrictions on free expression and Internet use today; one reason for this is its response to fears of growing unrest and the potential of the spread of the "Arab Spring" to China. For example, the word *Egypt* was banned in Internet searches in January 2012. Another reason for these growing restrictions was in advance of the 18th Party Congress and leadership change later in 2012. Related to this was the government's blocking of the Bloomberg News website following an investigative report about the massive wealth amassed by Xi Jinping, the (then-rumoured) next president of China (Wan & Richburg, 2012).

The government rules generally restrict searches or access to information on issues that it deems "sensitive" (Human Rights Watch, 2012). It outlaws content that might incite "illegal assemblies, associations, marches, demonstrations or gatherings that disturb social order," and bans content that might help an "illegal civil organization" (Xinhua News Agency, as cited in Liu, 2005). News sites and weblogs are allowed to promote only pro-China views, and they must register with the government as news organizations in order to operate at all (D. Rosen, 2005). Despite this, or perhaps in order to counter the flow of Western social media sites, China has developed its own counterparts to Twitter and Facebook, such as Weibo, with more than 200 million users, which Human Rights Watch (2012) argues "has created a new platform for citizens to express opinions and to challenge official limitations on freedom of speech despite intense scrutiny by China's censors" (para. 14).

When politics meets economics, however, it appears that compromise makes for interesting, and very large, bedfellows. Western technology companies are complicit in much of the censorship and surveillance on the Chinese branch of the Web, as well as other human rights abuses. It has been documented that some firms have been putting content filters in place on Chinese servers at the urging of the government. In 2004, Chinese journalist Shi Tao was arrested and charged for comments he made about Taiwan. He was caught because Yahoo! gave details from his email account to the authorities (D. Rosen, 2005). Apple has faced growing criticism in recent years for the problematic labour conditions of the workers who put together its most popular consumer gadgets such as the iPhone and iPad (Foley, 2012). In June 2005, the global free-speech organization (based in Toronto), the International Freedom of Expression eXchange (IFEX; www.ifex.org/canada/), reported that Microsoft was among the multinational companies hoping to gain commercial favour with the Chinese regime by supplying software that made it easier for authorities to track dissidents over the Web. In tracking what it calls the "authoritarian internationalism," IFEX suggests that the "China model" is being duplicated across countries that seek to control their population and their communications (www.ifex.org/international/2013/03/27/exporting_repression/).

Amnesty International contends that such corporate assistance to the government in efforts to stamp out dissent is a violation of the UN covenant covering "Human Rights Norms for Business," which requires firms to "ensure that the goods and services they provide will not be used to abuse human rights" (as cited in IFEX Communique, 2005; www.amnesty.org/en/library/info/ior42/002/2004). Even Google, which has had a much publicized dispute with Chinese authorities over censorship and its search engine, has acquiesced in a sense. In June 2012, Google announced that it would now warn Internet users that certain search terms might result in blocked content in China (Wines, 2012). On the flip side, RIM, Canada's ailing global technology giant, refuses to manufacture its phones and PDAs in China because of concerns that the Chinese censorship and surveillance laws would significantly compromise its security protections. It is ironic that these protections are one of the key features that ensure RIM's dominance in government contracts here in Canada (Waterman, 2012).

Discussion Questions

1. What is the difference between Google's and RIM's approach to state requirements? Where does it suggest the decision-making power is located: in the state or the corporation (or both)?

2. Why should (or shouldn't) the Chinese (or any other) government be able to control what its citizens do with the Internet?

3. Why does Human Rights Watch or Amnesty International criticize Microsoft and the other companies who are trading in China? Aren't they just protecting their own business interests?

4. Is China's approach to controlling content and traffic on the Internet any different from what we might see in Canada or other Western countries?

5. What possibilities are there for *users* in controlling access or content in cyberspace? What does this case suggest is the possibility for rights to freedom of expression and assembly?

6. Are these rights universal (applicable no matter what a country's political economic system is)?

Surveillance Societies in the West

Since China has a state-run economy and a relatively tightly controlled civil society, we might expect that its government would exercise similar control over all media, including the Internet. In comparison, we could argue that Internet communication is perhaps not so tightly managed in the free-market economies of the West. However, in exercising what we now know about political economy, we would also acknowledge that the term *free market* is a misnomer, and a piece of ideology rather than economic fact. In evaluating private control of the means of production in capitalist economies it is apparent that it also requires a fair degree of government intervention—both in the economy and in the lives of citizens.

The myth of individual liberty and freedom, which derives from both the French and the American revolutions of the eighteenth century—the bourgeois revolutions—tends to disguise the autocratic and rigid class structure of capitalism. Whereas the monarchy may have been "overthrown" in these revolutions, the entire class structure was not. The realization of democracy suggested by revolution has since come to be defined as participation in periodic elections in which we get to "choose" representatives for Parliament or Congress. It is argued that this guarantees our freedoms but only so long as we otherwise agree to collectively live by the rules of the associated "free-" market mythology. This limited understanding of freedom is framed in economic terms, meaning in theory, anyone could be Bill Gates or Rupert Murdoch. We just have to be clever enough to make it as an entrepreneur.

By working hard, saving, and paying for a good education, it is possible for anyone to reach the top. Or so it appears. This is part of the social inequality the Occupy Movement seeks to bring attention to: that the Bill Gates' of the world are symptomatic of a system that favours concentrations of wealth and power (1 per cent) compared with the rest (99 per cent), and that the class system is one that benefits a few at the expense of many. We can't all be entrepreneurs, and the evidence is in the number of people who are working at minimum wage, who are unemployed, and who are living in poverty and hunger (🖥 www.worldhunger.org/us.htm). Canada is no exception, despite being one of the richest countries in the world, and as a member of the Organisation for Economic Co-operation and Development (OECD). OECD statistics indicate that when it comes to poverty, Canada is "worst out of the 31 countries in the OECD, a rich-country grouping. More than 3m[illion] Canadians (or one in ten) are poor; and 610,000 of them are children" (*The Economist*, 2010, para. 1).

Nevertheless, to some degree, all of us have internalized these mimetic surveillance mechanisms of private enterprise capitalism that, despite all its flaws (and mounting evidence thereof), is still touted as the best system (you might ask yourself why you can't think of any alternative, or why it seems tiring to criticize it). Like many reporters working for the commercial media, we may self-censor our hopes, dreams, and frustrations, believing that if we adhere to the myths just a little while longer, we will be all right. Commercial media and popular culture are replete with these myths, and, as we argued in Chapter 2, the memes and viral patterns that these ideological myths create ensure their transmission from person to person, generation to generation. History and current experiences suggest that they are so powerful that anyone who attempts to argue against them is humoured for awhile and encouraged to grow out of it. If that fails, they are shunned and ostracized. Consider recent examples, such as how protesters and activists are framed in commercial media regarding the Occupy Movement, or how students in the Student Movement in Quebec are considered "spoiled brats" (Lagacé & Mason, 2012). If this kind of framing isn't effective, then there have always been ways for sedition laws to deter, silence, or censor.

A Nation of Suspects and Spies?

Since we live in a liberal-democratic country, surveillance, censorship, and sedition are not practices that are usually associated with living in Canada. Human rights, like freedom of expression and assembly, are considered sacrosanct. There is no censorship of communication in Canada! The assumption is that we have *always* had freedom of assembly, association, and communication. . . . But have we?

Before the Canadian Charter of Rights and Freedoms was debated and signed in 1982, human rights in Canada were presumed to be guaranteed by the British North America (BNA) Act (1867). While historical revision has called the BNA Act the "Constitution Act I" (🖥 laws-lois.justice.gc.ca/eng/Const/), it was not ratified by Newfoundland (which was independent at the time) nor were its contents agreed to between the federal and provincial governments. Yet, the BNA Act included two important clauses that are still crucial in government and legal decision-making today. The Act established that the federal government would be governed by the Westminster system, which means that Parliament (the prime minister, the political party in power, and elected representatives) is sovereign. This gives the prime minister (and political majority at the time) the power over "any of the civil liberties, including freedom of political speech [which] can be abolished by the Parliament of Westminster at any time" (Hogg, 1992, as cited in Martin & Adam, 1994, p. 67). The BNA Act also identified the responsibility of government to be "Peace, Order and good Government" (Constitution Act, 1867, § 91). Throughout history—in what we now call "Canada"—federal, provincial, and municipal governments have used the full extent of their powers to keep "peace and order," and, subject to interpretation, have identified individuals or groups who are considered to be disruptive to either part of this combination, or to be threats (Kinsman, Buse, & Steedman, 2000).

One of the many ways that the state has identified who is a threat (or not) is through surveillance. In Canada, this has included opening mail, listening in on communications (telegraph, telephone), monitoring programs and personnel at the CBC and NFB (recall Chapter 5), reading and collecting publications, as well as attending political and cultural meetings, public demonstrations, and protests. People are targeted because of their ethnicity (their family name, the place they live, country or location of origin), their race (whether officially identified or visually by skin colour or dress), their religious affiliation, and/or their political association (socialist, communist, or environmentalist, e.g.). In this way individuals and groups are categorized (according to one or more of the above criteria), stereotyped, and marginalized as separate (as "them" or "others"—different from "us"). Such begins the practice of narrowcasting by the state. Once this way of thinking is established (via speeches by political leaders, government policies, and media framing), people can be demonized (as suspect, as untrustworthy, or as threats) and dehumanized (as "enemies," "monsters," or "aliens"), which makes it easier to justify incarceration (via camps and institutions or prisons) or elimination (via extermination or wars; Mazepa, 2012).

For Real?

Censorship in Canada?

A history of surveillance and Canadian government involvement in censorship and laws made against "sedition" is one that we may be generally unaware of. Even before Canada was a country, mail could be opened by the British Post Office, as it was wary of rebellion and unrest in its colonies (Starr, 2004, p. 95).

The Upper and Lower Canada rebellions of 1837 and 1838 had the press identified as "treasonous or seditious," and censorship of the press in Quebec was experienced most acutely (Hamelin & Beaulieu, 1966). Censorship of the press was exercised explicitly through legislation and charges of treason, followed by subsequent hangings of radical editors and publishers. It was also exercised implicitly by intimidation through such actions, and by threats against individual workers, journalists, and printers (ibid.). While capital punishment for treason (and other crimes) was legally eliminated in 1961, the surveillance of communications and use of censorship was not (Mazepa, 2011).

Throughout Canadian history, governments have taken full advantage of political and legal powers to extend state control over communications including press, association, and assembly. The most poignant examples are those that are exercised in times when the government perceives there is a crisis; while some laws have been meant as "temporary measures" (to address the so-called crisis), the residual legislative and legal effects remain.

In the last century, the declaration of war by the government of Britain in the First World War and the declaration by the government of Canada in the Second World War were decisions that were justified on the basis of fighting against an identified "enemy state" and its allies. While these enemy states were internationally defined and the wars were not fought on Canadian soil, the laws that were passed during these times gave the government the authority to exercise its powers in Canada over all communication, transportation, trade, and people within its own borders. What this meant for every person on Canadian soil was a suspension of any civil liberties (that they might have thought they had), and increased and expanded security and surveillance here.

Prior to the First World War, there were already several other factors that were considered threats to political and economic order. The American and French revolutions indicated that significant social change was possible as can be mobilized by "the people," which undermines the confidence of people in power who are otherwise comfortable with the status quo and their position in it. Ongoing struggles for labour unionization, the development of new "radical" (non-Conservative and non-Liberal) political parties, as well as anti-conscription protests taking place in major cities across Canada were viewed by the government not as democracy in action but as indications of crisis.

As part of its participation in the British-declared war, in 1914, the federal government passed the War Measures Act (WMA; 🖥 www.lermuseum.org/en/canadas-military-history/first-world-war/going-to-war/war-measures-act/). The Act was a clear example of the Westminster system in action as it transferred power from Parliament (elected government) to the Cabinet (chosen by the prime minister). This transfer is critical because it removes public accountability (via Parliament) and places decision-making powers in the hands of members appointed by the prime minister, giving members the power to establish and enforce any law or policy deemed necessary.

In terms of communication, the WMA allowed for government (and later police) telegraph and telephone monitoring; it set up censorship committees, and later acts were extended to contain dissent and criticism of government (Keshen, 1996, p. 66). The WMA first affected people who were already marginalized, such as immigrants, or who were considered radical politically. A range of labour and working-class political and cultural facilities, activities, and publications were thereby declared illegal. These included all publications in so-called "alien" languages (Swyripa & Thompson, 1983, pp. 190–96), a number of English publications (Keshen, 1996), and a number of now "unlawful" cultural organizations (ibid.). While the initial intent was to ensure "peace and order" and dispel criticism of the Canadian government's decision to join the British war, the net was cast even larger to include a wide range of dissent (Mazepa, 2009, pp. 199–202).

Rebellion and social unrest were also some of the catalysts for establishing the Royal Canadian Mounted Police (RCMP) in 1920 as a national police force. (Do you know about the Winnipeg General Strike [www.civilization.ca/cmc/exhibitions/hist/labour/labh22e.shtml]?) The RCMP were given surveillance powers that were exercised throughout the interwar period and through the Second World War before being established officially as a "Special (security) Branch" in the 1950s, and a "Security and Intelligence" directorate in 1962 (CBC News Online, 2005). As Canadian historians Gregory Kealey and Reg Whitaker (1989, 1997a, 1997b, e.g.) have included in the reprint of what the RCMP called *Security Bulletins*, regular reports were provided to the federal government indicating that the RCMP maintained continuous surveillance over a whole range of events, interpersonal communications, publications, radio programs, and public activities across the country.

The WMA was enacted again in World War II and later in what was called the "October Crisis" of 1970 in Quebec (Cohen-Almagor, 2000; Whitaker, 2003; www.cbc.ca/archives/categories/politics/civil-unrest/the-october-crisis-civil-liberties-suspended/trudeaus-war-measures-act-speech.html). Although the WMA has been retired, the "crises" of today—the "War on Terror" or the economic crisis—have yielded comparable responses. Such times of crises bring social relations of power to the fore, such that individuals and groups can find themselves categorized and narrowcast as threats and the resulting actions can be severe. Of the past, you may have heard about the apologies that the federal government advanced to Canadians of Japanese descent for sending thousands to internment camps in the midst of World War II. Internment was not limited to particular ethnic categories (which, at that time, included German, Italians, and Ukrainians, e.g.), but also involved people who were considered radicals, of "left-wing" politics, including specific press publishers and labour and union leaders (Whitaker, 1986). While the policy of internment was somewhat of a "tradition" during the first and second world wars (Bailey, Dubé, & Maryniuk, 2008) and was discontinued, the practices of narrowcasting—of categorizing, marginalizing, and demonizing people—were not.

Such regressive methods are evident today in justifying government actions and decision-making regarding surveillance. For example, after 11 September 2001, then-president George Bush promoted military retaliation in Iraq and Afghanistan when he renounced any criticism thereof, by proclaiming, "Either you are with us, or you are with the terrorists" (The White House, 2001, para. 30; georgewbush-whitehouse.archives.gov/news/releases/2001/09/20010920-8.html). Such a phrase is effective as rhetoric in dividing people between "us" and "them"—ergo, if you are not with us (do not support military action), you are a terrorist, and thus it is legitimate to suspect, watch, interrogate, and perhaps arrest you.

More recently, in Canada, Vic Toews, (then) federal minister responsible for public safety, used similar rhetoric in response to criticism in Parliament of Bill C-30 (allowing surveillance of the Internet), stating that you "either stand with us or with the child pornographers" (CBC News, 2012a, para. 2; www.cbc.ca/news/technology/story/2012/02/13/technology-lawful-access-toews-pornographers.html). One can also look to the passing of Bill 78 initiated by the Parliament of Quebec in 2012 as

Continued

another example. In its title, the Bill made a distinction between legitimate students (those who don't protest) and illegitimate students (those who protest). Entitled An Act to enable students to receive instruction from the postsecondary institutions they attend (■ www.assnat.qc.ca/en/travaux-parlementaires/projets-loi/projet-loi-78-39-2.html), it was compared to the WMA in terms of its breadth and severity (CBC News, 2012d).

Discussion Questions

1. Briefly reviewing these actions by the state in the past, this either/or rhetoric is significant for its management of criticism of the political economy and of the people who may advance it. How is narrowcasting being applied here?

2. How effective is the framing of policy in encouraging or limiting discussion or debate, protest or demonstration?

3. Is protesting a form of public communication? Is it a fundamental freedom guaranteed under the Canadian Charter of Rights and Freedoms?

Permanent Crisis?

It is in periods of crisis when the state's increase in powers may be considered justified. Such history indicates, however, that these times can also be used as somewhat of an excuse in order to increase and solidify its powers. It was also during wartime that other state security agencies were established to monitor "foreign intelligence" and make use of new communication technology in order to do "signals intelligence"—the monitoring and intercepting of signals (such as radio transmissions) crossing the border. As the sovereignty and boundary of the state is marked by its borders, this practice of monitoring communication coming across was put in place long ago when a Customs Office was established in Canada in 1841, allowing the interception and censorship of mail (and later film, photographs, and other media hardcopies).

Similar to the US Federal Bureau of Investigation (FBI) and Central Intelligence Agency (CIA), both made famous via Hollywood and television shows, Canada has its own security establishments. As discussed in Chapter 7, this includes the Communications Security Establishment (CSE—now CSE Canada, or CSEC), established in 1975, which is responsible for foreign and signals intelligence on a permanent basis. Canada also has its own "spy agency," the Canadian Security Intelligence Service (CSIS—an altered version of a now defunct RCMP secret security service). CSIS is afforded extraordinary surveillance and seizure powers over communications and communications technology via the CSIS Act. This Act allows CSIS to monitor a range of activities in Canada that are "directed toward or in support of the threat or use of acts of serious violence against persons or property for the purpose of achieving a political, religious or ideological objective within Canada or a foreign state" (Canadian Security Intelligence Service Act, 1985, § 2).

The CSIS Act and Criminal Code have been amended to address new information and communication technologies (ICTs). These are not temporary measures, existing just during times of crisis, but are a fundamental part of government—both nationally and internationally. The federal (provincial and municipal) government is also tied to several international agreements indicating a policy convergence regarding technology and surveillance. Government surveillance and military integration is made through *intelligence-sharing* agreements between the

United Kingdom, the United States, Australia, and New Zealand; *defence* agreements such as NORAD; and *political alliances* such as NATO (North Atlantic Treaty Organization). These overlap with *economic agreements* such as NAFTA (facilitating commercial trade and large corporate expansion) to become part of the new package of "command, control, communications," or, in military lexicon, C³. More recently, government priorities have added "computers, intelligence, surveillance, and reconnaissance," or C⁴ISR (see, e.g., 🖥 www.c4isrjournal.com). In this way cyberspace is militarized as the new "battle-space." It is no longer limited to the air, ground, or water, as in military strategy past, but has expanded to include the entire electromagnetic spectrum (Mazepa, 2011). This means that the information that is collected on "suspected persons and activities" (which is a very broad parameter) is shared between them. The convergence of data makes it increasingly difficult to sort out what is the exclusive purview of government surveillance and what is not, what information is kept in Canada and what is shared, and, moreover, what information is collected (to begin with) and what it can be used for.

After 9/11, North American state surveillance was considerably ratcheted up in a very short period of time. It took the American government about a month to bring the Uniting and Strengthening America by Providing Appropriate Tools Required to Intercept and Obstruct Terrorism Act into force. This Act, also called the **USA PATRIOT Act**, increased and extended powers of surveillance, including branches of government dealing with law enforcement and immigration, with clauses meant to deal with "domestic terrorism" (🖥 www.fincen.gov/statutes_regs/patriot/index.html). Title II of the Act includes "Enhanced Surveillance Procedures" dealing with communication specifically, which includes wiretapping, information on packet-switching networks used in Internet communications, and access to information on individual and group computer use via Internet service providers. Although there hasn't been another major terrorist attack in the United States in over 10 years, the Act was signed into law by former president Bush in 2006, with some minor modifications, and several key provisions allowing surveillance have been extended by the current president, Barack Obama (🖥 www.cbc.ca/news/world/story/2011/05/26/patriot-act-us.html).

Canada followed suit in less than three months after 9/11, with its own **Anti-terrorism Act**, or Bill C-36: An Act to amend the Criminal Code, the Official Secrets Act, the Canada Evidence Act, the Proceeds of Crime (Money Laundering) Act and other Acts (🖥 laws-lois.justice.gc.ca/eng/acts/A-11.7/index.html). The wording was initially vague enough to capture a whole range of activities as "terrorism," defined as actions that are committed "in whole or in part for a political, religious or ideological purpose, objective or cause . . . with the intention of intimidating the public . . . with regard to its security, including its economic security" (Criminal Code, 1985, § 83.01[1][b]). It basically took the CSIS Act and enlarged and extended the practices across a whole range of government departments and agencies. As evaluated by many legal experts and critics, such a broad definition could include almost anyone (including anyone in the same vicinity as those) protesting or demonstrating against government policies or the capitalist system as a whole, for example (Roach, 2007; see Figure 11.1). This makes it a powerful tool that can be used by government to justify surveillance, and intimidate or silence its critics.

Similar language of "threats" and "terrorism" has recently been applied by the current federal government to refer to "environmentalists" and "anti-capitalists" as "Domestic Issue-based Extremism" (Public Safety Canada, 2012 , p.9; 🖥 www.publicsafety.gc.ca/prg/ns/2012-cts-eng.aspx). Environmental groups like Greenpeace Canada and Sierra Club Canada view this as the Conservative government's response to the criticisms of the federal government's support of the Northern Gateway Pipeline planned to transport oil from the Alberta tar sands across north-western British Columbia (McCarthy, 2012; Stoymenoff, 2012). This linking of

---

USA PATRIOT ACT

Passed by the US Congress in October 2001 following the September 11th bombings of the World Trade Centre in New York City. Requested by (then) president George W. Bush, it is called the Uniting and Strengthening America by Providing Appropriate Tools Required to Intercept and Obstruct Terrorism Act, and authorizes the federal government and its departments to enhance domestic surveillance, and authorizes the interception, surveillance, and seizure of a whole range of communication content and related technology.

ANTI-TERRORISM ACT

Following the passage of the USA PATRIOT Act, the Canadian (Liberal) government passed its own act, which extends the authority and powers of surveillance of the departments and agencies of the federal government. These include increasing government security and surveillance techniques, intelligence-sharing agreements between different states, and restrictions in immigration law, among many others.

FIGURE 11.1 | Police search two young men after they emerge from the subway at Queen's Park during the G-20 in Toronto in 2010. After being documented, they were free to go. A day after mostly peaceful protests turned violent, police were stopping, questioning, and searching many people in the downtown core and around Queen's Park. Some were hand-cuffed while police verified their identities.

dissent with terrorism appears to be a trend in Canadian institutions that do surveillance for the government as the "Focus on Research" box in this chapter identifies.

Lawful Access?

The more technological convergence there is—and the more dependent we become on using computers and computer networking for interpersonal communication, education, governance, and daily functions—the more vulnerable it undoubtedly becomes as an interlocking system. Such is the concept of the dialectic. The possibility of a breakdown (it was thought that the year 2000 would cripple computers or shut down the Internet entirely) or attack (for whatever reason) is also a reality. Remember those hackers discussed in Chapter 8? Such activity is now identified as terrorism under the law. But it depends on who you are working for. The US government in particular has discovered the lack of expertise within their ranks, and so the Department of Homeland Security is actively recruiting high-school students as "web warriors" via security companies that offer games, "cyber-challenges," and scholarships for demonstrations of hacking prowess (Perlroth, 2013).

Cyberspace is managed by the US and Canadian military as "Cyber Command" and subject to continual surveillance. As CSIS (2012) proclaims, the US establishment of Cyber Command is a response to the ubiquity of electronic networks and their increasing vulnerability to attacks, such that "antiterrorist experts in the United States have added hacking and illicit use of the

Focus on Research

Identifying Threats in Canada, from Media Convergence to Narrowcasting

Canadian sociologists Jeff Monaghan and Kevin Walby (2011) analyzed RCMP and CSIS "Threat Assessment Reports" from 2005 to 2011. The reports bring together information (from all levels of policing as well as the Canadian military) to define and identify threats in Canada. This is institutionally possible via national, provincial, municipal, and military "intelligence sharing agreements" and technologically facilitated via databases compiling and comparing the information on particular people and events. Monaghan and Walby's (2011) analysis found a prevalence of "mission creep" (p. 137). That is, they found that the reports extended who or what actions were considered terrorism, in melding terrorism—with extremism—with "ideologically motivated protests" (ibid.). While terrorism (still not adequately defined) may be considered to be extreme violence against members of the public (as opposed to state military violence, e.g.), "'mission creep' resulted in the cataloguing of many left-wing associated groups as threatening, particularly those associated with direct action tactics" (ibid.). Monaghan and Walby observed a fundamental shift in what is considered a threat in Canada: "The primary focus of this new security intelligence hub is the emergence of the global justice movement as a force confronting global capitalism" (ibid., p. 145).

The findings of the research raise several important issues. Firstly, Monaghan and Walby found that the reports are based on an amalgamation of information drawn from previous intelligent reports (that may not be accurate), which includes data drawn from technology, observation, and, significantly, the commercial media (see Boyle & Haggerty, 2009; Daase & Kessler, 2007). Secondly, it suggests that anyone protesting or demonstrating is not considered a citizen exercising their fundamental human rights in a democracy (freedom of expression, association, and assembly) but a threat to "peace and order" and private property. It places a division between the government and the public, and places every member of the public as suspect. As Canadian criminologist Valerie Steeves (as cited in Butler, 2009) suggests,

> "we've inverted the relationship between the citizen and the state." . . . Our governments should be transparent to us, so citizens can hold them to account, she says. Instead, it's citizens who are being made transparent, because we're all viewed as potential risks. "We got it backwards."
>
> The fact that we are increasingly identified as we go about our daily business means anonymity is under threat. . . . "And anonymity is essential if I'm going to be able to exercise free speech and freedom of assembly." (paras. 20–21)

Such an adversarial relationship also divides the public itself into those "passive"(?) people who don't demonstrate or get politically involved and the "activists" who are now narrowcast as considerable "threats." This complements what has been identified as the tendency for the commercial media to frame dissent as a deviant, dangerous, or violent activity, rather than a normal part of democratic action (Boycoff, 2007). Further, the lumping together of protests with terrorism suggests that when terrorism doesn't make itself evident to the public (to legitimize

Continued

all the surveillance activities), then marking protesters as threats means that social movements and "grassroots political opposition receives more scrutiny" (Monaghan & Walby, 2011, p. 42).

Class Exercise and Discussion

To test the research findings of Monaghan and Walby, apply what you know about media framing (recall from Chapter 4) to a study of mainstream commercial newspapers (available online or through the library). Your research plan is to compare how the Canadian commercial media has covered public protests in the Arab Spring, in countries of the Middle East, with public protests in North America (such as the G-20 in Toronto, the Student Movement in Quebec, or the Occupy Movement in various cities across Canada). In communication studies this is accomplished via a content or discourse analysis; decide on a time frame (identifying specific to–from dates to search) and do a select sampling (collect one or two articles from before, during, and after a major event) from a daily newspaper.

   Although there are obvious differences in what the protests are about specifically, what differences or similarities can you identify in how protests are framed in general? In doing your research, consider the following questions:

1.   How are the actors involved identified? What categories or labels are used to identify the participants, the police, and the government?

2.   Are the participants all "citizens," "protesters," or "activists"? Are they representative of "the public" or threats to public safety? Can you identify if there is narrowcasting being applied to the protesters?

3.   How are the police and government framed in each? (For example, do they appear to be operating together or independently? Is the government considered flexible or undemocratic? Is it a defender of public safety, or protector of private property?)

4.   How much importance is placed on the use of cell phones and social media by the protesters? What relationship between technology and democracy is implied?

LAWFUL ACCESS

"Lawful interception of communications and the lawful search and seizure of information, including computer data . . . [as] used by law enforcement and national security agencies, such as the Royal Canadian Mounted Police (RCMP), the Canadian Security Intelligence Service (CSIS) and municipal and provincial police forces, as well as the Competition Bureau" (Government of Canada, 2005, paras. 2, 11).

Internet to their list of weapons of mass destruction. Consequently, on May 21, 2010 US Cyber Command was established, and several other countries have established similar units within their national militaries" (para. 7).

   CSIS also identifies "politically motivated cyber-related attacks" that can be "domestic (resulting from radical opposition to economic summits, political developments or environmental practices) or geopolitical (reflecting the political, economic or military [*sic*] contest between parties in the region)" (para. 5). While such a broad definition again captures a wide range of activities, it can also be used to justify mission creep, bringing more of the Internet and its use under government surveillance.

   In 2010, the federal government (re)introduced a series of bills (C-50, C-51, and C-52) that addressed what it called "**lawful access.**" This would allow the "intelligence" officers and police access to personal information and online communications of online subscribers without warrant. The allowance was significant—as it wouldn't just cover Internet service providers, but other "online intermediaries" involving "mobile service providers, Internet numbering registries, online payment companies, search engines, blog hosting sites, social networking sites, etc." (CIPPIC, 2011, para. 1; www.cippic.ca/index.php?q=fr/node/129187). These are all privately owned entities that collect and transfer massive amounts of information and traffic data every second of every day.

The access to this information on the public in cooperation with the government would mean that every electronic information, communication, and transaction could be monitored, compiling databases of information on individuals and groups. In the United States, for example, the largest cell phone providers (like AT&T, Sprint, and Verizon) reported that in 2010 they have cooperated with 1.3 million government requests for "subscriber information" (Lichtblau, 2012). While the extent of legal access and issues of privacy may be of some "concern" to companies, they have not informed customers that their information has been subject to state scrutiny, or, in the case of AT&T, for example, that the state (i.e., the public) has paid $8.3 million for the privilege (ibid.). Further complications arise since corporations are legally identified as individuals and thus can make choices as to whether they comply with the government requests or not, and thus "corporations have *always* had free discretion to assist law enforcement" (Israel, 2011, n.p.). In the United States, legal precedence was established in 1994 with telephone and broadband companies (such as AT&T) via a government act—the Communications Assistance to Law Enforcement Act (CALEA)—requiring technological design standards with built-in surveillance capabilities allowing immediate search:

> *CALEA was intended to preserve the ability of law enforcement agencies to conduct electronic surveillance by requiring that telecommunications carriers and manufacturers of telecommunications equipment modify and design their equipment, facilities, and services to ensure that they have the necessary surveillance capabilities. Common carriers, facilities-based broadband Internet access providers, and providers of interconnected Voice over Internet Protocol (VoIP) service—all three types of entities are defined to be "telecommunications carriers" for purposes of CALEA section 102, 47 U.S.C. § 1001—must comply with the CALEA obligations. (FCC, n.d., para. 1; transition.fcc.gov/pshs/services/calea/)*

Although in Canada the matter of "lawful access" is still subject to specifics as worked out in changes to government bills, as we discuss further in the next chapter, the potential of combined private (corporate) and government "intelligence sharing" suggests that Big Brother could become Big Data, and any number of classifications and categorizations could be constructed, all without the individual's knowledge. In the meantime, if the electronic record isn't sufficient enough, however, there are always the cameras.

Michel Foucault and the Surveillance Society

French philosopher and sociologist Michel Foucault is credited with some of the first modern writing on the rise of the surveillance society. In his 1979 book, *Discipline and Punish*, Foucault argued that by the turn of the nineteenth century, modern Western capitalism had become a punitive society that relied on prisons and repression to keep populations under control. Discipline and power rose together in the form of the state apparatus, but governments do not only rely on violence to secure compliance. It was possible, Foucault argued, to police society through regimentation, surveillance, and categorizing or differentiating the population into a hierarchy.

This system was perfected in the prison system, where a regime of total surveillance could be instituted and where, to a degree, the prisoners became self-regulating because they could never be sure that they weren't being watched. According to Foucault (1979), the prisoners internalized the surveillance, a system of control that "enables the disciplinary power to be both absolutely indiscreet, since it is everywhere and always alert, and absolutely discreet, for it functions permanently and largely in silence" (p. 177).

A second instrument of power that features in Foucault's writing on discipline and punishment is the use of the examination, which has three functions: (1) to classify objects and people according to some visible means or arrangement, (2) to situate people within socially and ideologically determined fields of "normal" behaviour or performance, and (3) to document an individual's "progress" or "condition" through meticulous record-keeping. This allows individuals to be described and analyzed, compared and, more importantly, corrected if there is deviation from the acceptable norms or standards (p. 190). The racial and psychological profiling techniques that are now popular with law enforcement agencies as a way of identifying potential terrorists are based on these classification techniques that work on all types of gathered data—from phone records to library borrowing transactions, emails, and credit card purchases. The technical, digital means of gathering, sorting, classifying, and building a profile from available data now exist to elevate surveillance abilities "to the level of the science fiction sublime" (T. Lewis, 2003, p. 341).

In the almost 40 years since Foucault wrote *Discipline and Punish*, we have seen the technologies and techniques of surveillance and profiling move out of the prison system and into civil society. Foucault argued that generalizing the modes of surveillance beyond the prison walls has created the social and psychological condition in which all citizens are simultaneously the guards and the guardians. Foucault was not aware of the power of digital technologies when he made these observations, but it is clear today that the convergence of communication and surveillance technologies has made the task of total coverage much easier. According to some estimates, more than 26 million CCTV (closed-circuit television) cameras were installed around the world in 2003, and the market was growing between 40 and 50 per cent each year (Farmer & Mann, 2003, p. 36). Today, there is no reliable figure given the combination of government, police, and private cameras, but there is no question that their use continues to increase in Canada and worldwide.

In identifying how CCTV **surveillance** has spread worldwide, researchers Clive Norris, Mike McCahill, and David Wood (2004) suggest that it occurs through a series of stages. The first is initiated by the banks and retail businesses in installing monitors and cameras in private spaces, particularly shopping malls. The second stage is when CCTV surveillance is used in public institutions such as government buildings and public schools, for example. Traffic control and the monitoring of city streets, sidewalks, and parks are justified as a "crime prevention" measure, marking the third stage. Finally, the last stage is "ubiquity"—surveillance is everywhere (see Lyon, 2002). While these stages aren't necessarily uniform throughout the world, they are instructive in terms of how hegemony works: how practices in one area (banks and shopping malls) are extended to another (government buildings and schools), and how each extension reinforces the previous, and in turn justifies the next (streets and parks; see Figure 11.2). In this example, as surveillance practices are extended to more spaces, the differences between the spaces begin to disappear. That is, there appears to be *no difference* in what is private or what is public space, while the *differences between people* are accentuated: Who is "normal" or "suspect," "criminal" or "innocent"?

CCTV surveillance also indicates the dialectic of convergence and narrowcasting in another way. On one hand, there are now databases in existence that can handle vast amounts of information about individuals and that can run pattern-recognition programs. The tracking of

CCTV SURVEILLANCE

Closed-circuit television and the use of video cameras to monitor and record people and places (businesses, government buildings, airports, shopping malls, public streets, schools, and so on).

individuals via licence-plate identification, facial recognition, and
behavioural patterns is integrated
or accumulated in these databases,
integrating systems from the local
to the national whether in terms of
government, corporate, or private
security surveillance. On the other
hand, as we discuss further in the
next chapter, individuals can now
buy cameras to install on their front
doors, which are networked to continually transmit live feed from the
home to the homeowner's cell phone.

The implication that by owning surveillance technology you too
can control (or at least) monitor your
own space is similar to the argument
that by introducing the personal
computer, cyberspace could be in
your own control. By putting low-
cost surveillance equipment into
the hands of consumers, it somehow "democratizes" the surveillance
society. Is this just another myth of
Mosco's "digital sublime"? Does it

Source: © Paula Johns, 2013

FIGURE 11.2 | A police security camera in Toronto.

create the false sense of "widespread popular empowerment" that grows without substance
in a "spiral of hype" (Mosco, 2004a, p. 25)? Mosco discusses the work of a senior editor at *The
Economist*, Frances Cairncross, who Mosco says has "sounded a mythic triumphalism" about the
ability of the Internet to transcend geographic space and the ability of surveillance to promote
"massive improvements in crime prevention" (ibid., p. 86).

While individual security systems may say something about how people think of property
and the trustworthiness of each other, it is the larger systems that are amassing data (that we
have little to no knowledge of) that have a hegemonic impact on social relations. Even mildly
critical observers are worried about what they see in the future. A decade ago, Maureen Dowd
(2003), a columnist with *The New York Times*, observed that the US government's attempt
to create an all-encompassing, all-seeing database of its citizens is an "attempt to create an
Orwellian 'virtual, centralized grand database,' which could put a spyglass on Americans' every
move, from literally the way Americans move to their virtual moves, scanning shopping, e-mail,
bank deposits, vacations, medical prescriptions, academic grades and trips to the vet" (para. 4).
The Pentagon has argued that no one need fear this new powerful database—it is justified as
a safety precaution in the face of a perceived terrorist threat. However, Foucault might argue
that as power extends its influence and ability to carry out more complex surveillance actions,
it also invents new applications for its new powers. Thus as models of deviant behaviour (such
as a possible propensity for school violence or terrorism) are identified, or created through the
application of technology and technique, the disciplinary and punishing powers are increased
and further deployed (Foucault, 1990, p. 42).

State Surveillance: A Question of Cost and Benefits?

We hear on the news of "domestic terrorism" cases where male individuals have gone on a "killing spree" or "rampage" that can appear to be random until it is discovered that the victims have been chosen specifically because of their gender or race. In Canada in 1989, in what was dubbed the Montreal massacre, 14 women "feminists" were shot (Porter, 2009); in Norway in 2011, gunmen shot 69 people with the intent to kill "Muslims, Marxists and multi-culturalists" (Friedlander, 2011, para. 2), and in the United States in 2012, six Sikhs, who are "frequently confused with Muslims," were killed (Kaur, 2012). The response from government and law enforcement is to increase security and surveillance practices, but as Norris et al. (2004) point out, this response only aggravates and intensifies a surveillance society:

> *The extent to which such measures do anything to protect from further tragedies is questionable, but largely irrelevant. For politicians, there is a need to be seen to be doing something. And as the psychological, social or political conditions that give rise to such incidents are complex, and possibly intractable, technological fixes which promise the appearance, if not the reality of security are highly appealing. When such crises occur, funding will be made available, more sober judgments as to effectiveness and alternative ignored, and legal restrictions and constitutional objections set aside, as it will be argued that the balance between civil liberties and security will have to be tilted in favour of security. (p. 126)*

When confronted with a choice between security and terrorism or crime, public surveillance seems like a small price to pay. Canadian opinion polling suggests that when faced with this as the only(?) choice, most people don't see increased surveillance as a significant public issue or problem—whether via legislation like the Anti-terrorism Act (Mazepa, 2009, p. 214) or via the technology of CCTV, particularly if media coverage suggests that CCTV "will somehow prevent or deter criminal behaviour" (Greenberg & Hier, 2008, p. 479). But it is a price that the public pays for in more ways than one. We cover privacy issues in the next chapter, but in keeping with the relationship of government and surveillance technology, the allocation of state resources suggests a significant shift. The maintenance of the system itself is not cheap, as (already-scarce) public resources are diverted to technology rather than to people. Technology becomes the "problem-solver" rather than social interactions where discussion, prevention, and human judgement are all part of the environment. As the use of surveillance technology increases for security's sake, the more insecure we may feel:

> *The increasing introduction of surveillance systems into every physical and virtual social space subliminally conveys as much the precariousness of safety and order as the actuality of danger and disorder with ever more sophisticated socio-technical devices capturing and portraying the "realities" of chaos and suffering, thus driving, through a self-fulfilling prophecy, a psychological, social and economic demand for other such apparatuses. The central point is that technologies of security produce ontologies of insecurity—their very existence makes real the fragmentation, inequality and uncertainty of everyday life. Paradoxically, the machine (response) is as much the problem as the solution. (Smith, 2009, p. 145)*

Social interaction can be superseded by the camera or compilations of data sets, which can be in error: Does the camera lie? Can a computer make mistakes? The potential for error is evident in an especially poignant example involving Canadian Liberal senator David Smith (any relation to Winston Smith of *Nineteen Eighty-Four*?).

In May 2012, Senator Smith discovered that he was identified as a "potential terrorist" and couldn't board an airplane out of Toronto's city airport because he was on a "no-fly list" originating in the United States (Freeze, 2012). The irony is that Senator Smith was on his way to a "special Anti-terrorism Committee" meeting but had no power to remove himself from the list. As the reporter covering the story from *The Globe and Mail* observed, "The fact that an Ottawa insider—the former chair of the anti-terrorism committee, no less—hasn't a clue how to get his name wiped off a no-fly list does not bode well for ordinary citizens" (ibid., para. 11). While mistakes can happen once or twice, the 70-year old senator has found himself "singled out for added airport screening some 25 times in the past few months" (para. 6), suggesting that the weight and validity of the technological "evidence" and the no-fly list is greater than the actual person.

Public surveillance tends to be identified with crime deterrence, despite controversy and evidence to the contrary. As emphasized by the so-named activist group "Big Brother Watch UK," the city of London, England, has the largest network of CCTV surveillance of any city in the world, suggesting that the "average Londoner is caught on camera more than 300 times every day" (Big Brother Watch, 2012b, para. 6; ▣ www.bigbrotherwatch.org.uk/home; see also O'Brien, 2008). The group compares the extent of surveillance to local crime statistics: "When seen in context of the Met's [the London Metropolitan Police Services'] own research highlighting how 1,000 CCTV cameras solve less than one crime per year in the capital, it is further concern that CCTV is not being used either proportionately or effectively" (Big Brother Watch, 2012a, para. 3). Despite such evidence indicating no reliable correlation between surveillance and crime prevention, and flaws in the way surveillance is used to identify crime, the relationship is still considered a positive one (the reasoning suggests that the more surveillance there is, the less crime there will be; O'Brien, 2008, pp. 29–33). This is myth-building in action, and the commercial media is partly responsible for perpetuating it.

Naturalizing the Surveillance Society

Canadian research from Josh Greenberg and Sean Hier (2008) identifies how the commercial media contribute to public understanding of CCTV surveillance via what kind of coverage it gives surveillance and where the focus of discussion is centred. Through a content and discourse analysis of 11 regional newspapers across Canada over a six-year period (1999–2005), the researchers found that the focus of discussion in over half the newspapers indicated a direct correlation between "the use of video surveillance and crime prevention or deterrence" (Greenberg & Hier, 2008, p. 472), suggesting that

> *the emphasis on prevention partially reflects the efforts of the security and crime control communities to set the definitional parameters within which surveillance is discussed and debated in the media and in other public forums. Advocates of greater surveillance, including but not restricted to police and other law enforcement agencies, often note the deterrent value of CCTV technology as a way to promote its efficacy. (ibid.)*

The reliance on the "security and crime control communities" in turn affects media agenda setting and framing—not only in justifying the use of surveillance (precipitating acceptance by the public) but also in helping to shape public understandings of surveillance of space, and the public in general. Greenberg and Hier (2008) identify the potentials for narrowcasting:

> *News coverage of CCTV surveillance very rarely explores the financial costs, technical efficacy, and reliability of these systems, let alone the ethical implications of what more extensive surveillance might mean for our understanding of notions such as community and trust or the potential of broadcast footage of CCTV images to reproduce existing material inequalities among different categories of citizens. (p. 479)*

However, such social or collective implications are not the focus of media coverage when covering surveillance. It is more focused on *where* the surveillance is occurring—negotiating the spaces deemed legitimate—an indication of how, through stages similar to those Norris et al. (2004) identified, the parameters of "security" are increased and normalized. Greenberg and Hier's (2008) research identified that the most common coverage of CCTV surveillance was of downtown areas (42 per cent of all coverage) followed by workplace surveillance (22.5 per cent; p. 470). Other forms of surveillance at places frequented by the public (such as airports, retail stores, banks, parking garages, and even public schools) received little to no attention, suggesting that surveillance of these places is already considered "normal" (ibid.). This suggests the extent to which hegemony has already taken hold, and how the process of spatialization (from Chapters 3 and 6) is extended.

You've all probably seen CCTV footage of a convenience store or service station hold-up on the local nightly news. Do you ever wonder how and why this material gets into the hands of the television stations? The simple answer is that the police routinely hand it over; it's widely seen as a "public service" role for the media. However, it works the other way, too. Like the cell phone providers discussed earlier, television stations are often compelled, or volunteer, to hand over footage to the police, particularly of demonstrations when the police need to identify "ringleaders" or individuals who commit "violence." On most days you can find local news that is dominated by crime stories and, in some cases, urgings for all of us to contact Crime Stoppers and to report suspicious activity. In academic literature this scaremongering is known as the generation of "moral panics" and often they're hard to avoid if you're at all interested in reading the newspaper or watching television. Since 9/11, the perceived threat of terrorism has created its own forms of moral panic journalism (see Hirst & Schutze, 2004a, 2004b). Uncritical acceptance in the news media also implies that state actions are warranted whether in terms of local crime prevention or international conflict.

The most obvious cases of journalistic self-censorship involving state actions occur during wartime, when "operational security" is used as a catch-all phrase to prevent the release of sensitive or embarrassing information. Military commanders and public affairs officers often rely on the coverage by specific reporters and media companies as a conduit for propaganda (willingly or unwillingly; Allan & Zelizer, 2004). This has become particularly important since 9/11, as the War on Terror has been unfolded and the "enemy" is often no more than a nebulous threat, or vague organizational structure that is hard to pin down (see, e.g., Seymour Hersch's *Chain of Command* for an account of events since 9/11). The media's support for the "terror frame" of analysis often goes unquestioned and unchecked, and there's an unwritten assumption that if the government says something is so, then that's what should be reported (Hirst & Schutze, 2004a, 2004b).

It appears to be the case that, in Canada and the United States, government and corporate support for new and invasive forms of surveillance technology is strong (particularly as its own networks are vulnerable to "cyberattacks"). If media is very supportive of claims—often not backed by evidence—that the new surveillance technologies (whether facial identification, data-mining, or suspect profiling) are going to save lives and protect freedom, then there is less question of their validity. For a number of reasons (discussed in the previous chapter) commercial media may be less inclined to investigate what the accumulated effects may be, a process that supports what the American Civil Liberties Union understands as building the "infrastructure of a surveillance society" (O'Harrow, 2005, pp. 137–8).

Surveillance in our daily lives is also naturalized in media in other ways, most prominently by so-called "reality" television programs, as we discussed in Part I regarding *Big Brother Canada*. Through the entertainment value that these so-called reality television programs generate, the very act of surveillance is naturalized, and we see it rendered in contexts that appear to reduce the intrusive and invasive nature of what we're seeing. In the case of *Big Brother*, our discomfort at essentially spying on the housemates is abated by our knowledge that they're in the house/studio voluntarily, and we can voluntarily participate. These programs and others suggest that surveillance is either necessary or entertaining, and we see surveillance as being somehow normalized and morally acceptable in these terms. Does seeing surveillance as entertaining and participating in it blunt our suspicion or scepticism of monitoring activities?

In addition to moral panic in the news, there are crime dramas on television on most nights of the week, usually two in a row and sometimes on all the commercial networks at the same time. Police procedurals (by Canadian network) include CTV's *Blue Bloods*, *Criminal Minds*, *CSI* (Miami and New York), *Grimm*, *Law & Order: Special Victims Unit*, *The Mentalist*, *Unforgettable*, and *The Listener* (a Canadian production). On Global, you can catch *Bones*, *Chicago Fire*, *Elementary*, *Hawaii Five-0*, *In Plain Sight*, *NCIS* (and *NCIS: Los Angeles*), *NYC 22*, *The Firm* (a Canadian co-production), and *Rookie Blue* (a Canadian production). CBC has less of these types of programs but includes the *Murdoch Mysteries* and the *Republic of Doyle*.

There's an element of what we might call forensic voyeurism about this type of television, and it bears little or no relationship to what's actually happening in the real world, particularly in terms of actual crime statistics. It is compounded when, for example, the current federal Conservative government's "tough on crime" bill suggests that there is an ever-increasing threat and a severe crackdown is warranted. The bill was passed even though Statistics Canada indicates that the crime rate (particularly for violent crimes) is the lowest that it has been since 1972 (▢ www.cbc. ca/news/canada/thunder-bay/story/2012/07/24/crime-stats-canada.html). Called the Safe Streets and Community Act, or Bill C-10, the reach of the "omnibus" bill is so broad (requiring changes to a number of other laws and legislation [▢ openparliament.ca/bills/41-1/C-10/]) that it implies the problem is similarly so wide-reaching that it required immediate government action (CBC News, 2012d; MacCharles, 2011). It's no wonder we feel tense all the time.

Communicating and Normalizing Narrowcasting

Another way to identify how surveillance is incorporated into our lives is through "practices of security" such that surveillance technology comes out of entertainment and the military–industrial complex and into "routines" of human movement, whether on the street, in school, or in travel. As practices become routine, they become less questioned, and as Senator Smith's experience indicates, they become increasingly more difficult to challenge.

As the idea of a surveillance society becomes hegemonic, the practices of narrowcasting affect not only individuals but also (as Greenberg & Hier, 2008, suggested) ways of thinking about each other. In the "routines" of airport security, for example, people enter what Malcolm Feeley and Jonathon Simon (1994, p. 182, as cited in Aas, Gundus, & Lomell, 2009) call a "domain of suspicion," "where everyone seems to be subjected to suspicion and control" (p. 9). The control occurs via the information gathered on each passenger and on their physical passage through the system. Each individual name has been registered via a "Personal Name Record" supplied by all the airlines to Computer Registration Systems or Global Distribution Systems (GDSs). Attending to the process of spatialization and convergence, it is significant that these systems are held by private corporations, three of them in the United States (Bozbeyoğlu, 2011). As the Surveillance Studies Centre (SSC) at Queen's University notes, however, while the GDS controls the traveller's information, neither the airlines nor the passengers have control over this information once it is recorded:

> Since three of the GDS are located in the US and the US has no national law to limit usage and the disclosure of the data, [in Canada] PIPEDA applies but has major issues of enforceability once data moves to these sites. . . . PNR data is also potentially commercially lucrative, and the GDS's own privacy policies give further cause for concern as they do not appear to exclude the renting or licensing of personal data nor their use for marketing analysis. (ibid., p. 3; bold added)

We can see narrowcasting operationalized at the airport. People are also divided into categories whether by physical appearance or by information stored in a database. They can be divided by nationality, ethnicity, religion, gender, race, etc., or via "behaviour recognition patterns" (Bozbeyoğlu, 2011). People at the airport are physically separated via the security line-ups, subject to full-body searches, scans, or various applications of biometric scanning, and thus are excluded from each other. Those who have already subjected themselves to greater scrutiny and pay for the privilege via NEXUS, or by holding an AMEX card, are processed faster, while the rest watch how this "social sorting" (Lyon, 2003) occurs in longer and longer line-ups (www.cbsa-asfc.gc.ca/prog/nexus/menu-eng.html).

Such methods of exclusion and inclusion are not limited to airports, however. As Smith (2009) noted, technologies of security are also technologies of insecurity, since there is an "inherent duality and dialectic between our striving for security and the simultaneous production of insecurity which can result from these efforts" (Aas et al., 2009, p. 1). Research correlates the increase in private security firms with the "privatization of public space" (p. 10), as access to more of the spaces that we take for granted is securitized or restricted. Divisive practices extend into neighbourhoods via "gated communities" and on city streets and sidewalks, with cameras and security guards identifying who is eligible to enter, who can linger, or who is permitted to rest in a public park. It is perhaps telling that, in Canada, there are increasingly more people employed to do "private security" than there are "public police officers" (Li, 2008). People become increasingly segregated, not only on the basis of social relations of class, gender, or race, for example, but also spatially (Kempa, Stenninghand, & Wood, 2004, pp. 564–5, as cited in Aas et al., 2009, p. 10).

As many scholars have realized, this raises the question of whom the security is for exactly, and what "security" is in the first place. Is security located in a camera, the monitoring station, the corporation, the government, or our collective well-being? Is security having access to basic needs such as clean water and air, food, and a roof over one's head? Is security in personal freedom of movement, of expression, of association? When thinking of security in this way, Katja Franko Aas, Helene Oppen Gundhus, and Heidi Mork Lomell (2009) suggest that the technologies and practices that are employed in the name of security are much more than we usually think of. There is always the question of power relations: "Technologies of security and insecurity are significantly also technologies of justice and injustice. The politics of surveillance is a matter not merely of personal privacy but also of social justice" (p. 10).

PIPEDA (PERSONAL INFORMATION PROTECTION AND ELECTRONIC DOCUMENTS ACT)

"Sets out ground rules for how private sector organizations may collect, use or disclose personal information in the course of commercial activities. PIPEDA also applies to federal works, undertakings and businesses in respect of employee personal information. The law gives individuals the right to access and request correction of the personal information these organizations may have collected about them" (Office of the Privacy Commissioner of Canada, 2013a, para. 1; www.priv.gc.ca/leg_c/leg_c_p_e.asp).

We're at a unique time in the history of surveillance: The cameras are everywhere, and we can still see them. Twenty years ago, they weren't everywhere. Even a few years from now, they'll be so small that we won't be able to see them. In addition, several technologies in use or under consideration by governments were not even covered in this chapter, such as national ID cards, digitalization and related privatization of health systems, DNA recordings, embedded micro-chips in human bodies, and many others. There are also alternatives and ways of countering and opposing the use and development of surveillance via strategies like Big Brother Watch UK employs, or participation in government institutions and policy-making (📺 www.priv.gc.ca/resource/fs-fi/index_e.asp) as well as many others (see Lyon, 2006, Part 5, e.g.). Ending with a little instigative scaremongering ourselves, time is limited. Public debates or decisions on them may become moot as soon as surveillance technologies become so ubiquitous that they are able to recognize "you" without you even knowing it.

Key Points

- Big Brother has become a mimetic metaphor for describing, normalizing, and criticizing the surveillance society.

- Communication technologies are being used and developed to exercise surveillance over citizens, a practice that the state is heavily invested in from the local to the international level.

- There is a wide range of examples of how surveillance involves both technological convergence and narrowcasting.

- Narrowcasting is a process involving both structuration (Chapter 12) and spatialization, which entails social and spatial segregation.

- The evidence suggests that the information or knowledge society is more often than not a surveillance society, and the commercial media has a hand in normalizing and legitimizing its acceptance as such.

Class Discussion

1. Count the number of surveillance cameras you can find in one day of your usual activity. Does knowing that surveillance CCTV systems are everywhere make you feel safer, or less safe? Why, or why not?

2. Was Foucault right to think that the increase in surveillance has led to a situation where everyone is both jailer and inmate?

3. Do you agree that the commercial media have played a role in normalizing and legitimizing an increase in surveillance? Are there more ways this can occur in media (other than news coverage of surveillance and entertainment, e.g.)?

4. What options are available (or possible) for people who do *not* want their movements recorded on camera or their communications monitored? Locally, identify what policies are in place in your university, city, or town on CCTV surveillance. What possibilities are there on the provincial or national levels (e.g., 📺 www.ipc.on.ca/, www.oipc.bc.ca/, www.cai.gouv.qc.ca/diffusion-de-linformation/)?

Media on Media

Tunes to Watch By

Earth Crisis. (2000). Mass arrest. *Slither*. US: Victory.
Jill Scott. (2000). Watching me. *Who Is Jill Scott?* US: Hidden Beach.
Lahanna. (2008). Prologue. *Welcome to the Underground*. US: Lahanna L. Demmier.
Rolling Stones. (1974/2009). Fingerprint file. *It's Only Rock n' Roll* [Remastered]. US: Promotone BV (under exclusive licence to Universal International Music BV). www.elyrics.net

Worth Watching

Films Media Group Online. (2006). *Reel bad Arabs: How Hollywood vilifies a people* [Documentary]. New York, NY: Films Media Group.
Films Media Group Online. (2007). *The real Big Brother* [Video]. New York, NY: Films Media Group.
Scott, T. (Director). (1998). *Enemy of the state* [Motion picture]. US: Touchstone.
Timoner, O. (Writer & Director). (2010). *We live in public: Josh Harris* [DVD]. US: Indiepix Films.

Timeline: Surveillance in Canada—Government in Brief

1666 Jean Talon begins a census of residents of New France. This predates similar efforts in Europe and the United States.

1841 Canada Customs is established by the British government.

1842 The first Census Act is passed in Upper and Lower Canada.

1870 Following Confederation (1867), the first Canadian Census Act is enacted, followed by a census conducted in 1871.

1906 The Inquiries Act allows government to investigate government departments and public employees.

1914 The War Measures Act is enacted at the beginning of the First World War.

1915 The Chief Press Censor's Office is created.

1917 Censorship Committee is formed.

Order in Council PC 2381 bans all publications in "alien" languages.

1918 The Dominion Bureau of Statistics, which was responsible for conducting regular censuses in Canada, is created.

1930 Section 98 of the Criminal Code declares any association committed to bringing about government, industrial, or economic change is "unlawful." The law was repealed in 1936 following public and political opposition.

1937 The Padlock Act is introduced in Quebec, allowing for home searches, confiscation of personal property, as well as the confiscation and destruction of any newspaper, periodical, pamphlet, circular, document, or writing, printed, published, or distributed. This Act remained on the books for 20 years following its enactment.

The Alberta Press Act is introduced to attempt to control reporting on the provincial government. The Act stated that any reporting on a government policy or action must be verified as accurate by the government. It was struck down in 11 days following its enactment.

1939 The Defence of Canada Regulations (DOCR) are created, and the War Measures Act is reactivated in advance of the Second World War.

The DOCR gave jurisdiction to the Postmaster General, who was given greater censorship authority over a greater range of media, from postcards to photographs to film.

The Official Secrets Act is created, allowing the federal government to withhold selected information from the public and making it a "serious offence" for any communication with a "foreign power."

1947 The Saskatchewan Bill of Rights includes protection of individual and collective rights by the state, as well as from the state and private institutions.

1960 The Canadian Bill of Rights is introduced, but still limited by the War Measures Act and the Official Secrets Act.

1970 The War Measures Act is re-enacted by Prime Minister Trudeau during the FLQ (or October) Crisis.

1975 The Communications Security Establishment (CSE) is created under the authority of the Minister of National Defence. Its mandate includes a federal communications security task (securing communication internal to government) and a continued "signals intelligence" with commitments to its allies, external to Canada, or foreign "intelligence."

1980 The Privacy Act is enacted, recognizing "the privacy of individuals with respect to personal information about themselves held by a government institution" (Privacy Act, 1985, § 2).

1982 The Canadian Constitution is finally repatriated, including the new Charter of Rights and Freedoms, which provides protection of individuals' rights to freedom of association, assembly, and of the press and other media of communication.

1984   The Canadian Security Intelligence Service (CSIS) is created to replace a discredited branch of the RCMP. CSIS continues to have extraordinary powers of surveillance, but is subject to an independent committee review.

1985   The War Measures Act is replaced by the Emergencies Act, which requires provincial consultation and temporary limits, and it is subordinate to the Charter and the International Covenant on Civil and Political Rights.

The Access to Information Act is enacted, creating, in theory, greater transparency in government information.

2000   The Personal Information Protection and Electronic Documents Act (PIPEDA) is enacted to supplement privacy protection for Canadians beyond what was covered in the Privacy Act. PIPEDA includes all federally regulated public and private companies and ensures personal privacy in how personal information is retrieved, used, and stored electronically.

2001   The Anti-terrorism Act is enacted following 9/11. The Act extends the authority and powers of surveillance of the federal government, including increasing government security, intelligence-sharing agreements between different states, and restrictions in immigration law, among others.

2008   The introduction of "security certificates" and other restrictions to immigration through Bill C-3 increases the criminalization of new immigrants to Canada.

2011   Bill C-12, An Act to amend the PIPEDA, is introduced in the House of Commons, including changes to the exceptions for consent required in the use of personal information. One new exception relates to performing of policing. Yet, "this new exception for policing services appears to add an open-ended and undefined circumstance related to law enforcement to this list. The term *policing services* is not defined in either the Act or the bill" (Lithwick, 2011, §2.3, para. 3). Additionally, the new Bill redefines the concept of *lawful authority, whereby it is no longer limited to* "a subpoena or warrant from a court or to rules of court related to the production of records; this authority appears to be a more general authority that is left undefined" (ibid., para. 4). It's important to note that as of August 2013 this Bill has only passed first reading.

2012   Bill C-30, An Act to enact the Investigating and Preventing Criminal Electronic Communications Act and to amend the Criminal Code and other Acts, also known as the Protecting Children from Internet Predators Act, or the Lawful Access Bill, is introduced. This Act would extend the powers of law enforcement to access greater amounts of personal information available electronically without a warrant. It would require Internet service providers (ISPs) to store greater amounts of their clients' personal information and make that available, upon request, to the police. There has been widespread opposition to this legislation for all opposition parties and public interests groups, as well as the industry.

2013   The federal government passes Bill S-7, An Act to amend the Criminal Code, the Canada Evidence Act and the Security of Information Act, also known as the Combating Terrorism Act, which extends state power over the detention, interrogation, arrest, and imprisonment of any person(s) associated with anyone suspected of terrorism or any terrorist activity.

The Auditor-General's Report is released, and indicates that the Canadian federal government has not accounted for $3.1 billion in anti-terrorism funding.

12 That's the Way the Cookie Crumbles: A Surveillance Economy

SURVEILLANCE ECONOMY
The idea that dominant forces directing economic development are those to do with surveillance and the process of commodification, including that: research and development in an economy has a focus on surveillance or security technologies; capital investment in technologies is in the area of surveillance; recurrent budgets in both the private and the public sector make increasing provision for surveillance; employment growth is related to surveillance and security; and continuing surveillance of the citizenry and border protection are key imperatives in political economic and social structuring.

SURVEILLANCE
"The focused, systematic and routine attention to personal details for purposes of influence, management, protection or detection. . . . [It is] deliberate and depends on certain protocols and techniques" (Lyon, 2006, p. 14).

Objectives

After reading this chapter you will have an understanding of the ways in which a surveillance economy may be emerging as the new mode of development in the global capitalist economy. In particular we hope you become familiar with the following:

- the subtle but important differences between a surveillance *society* and a surveillance *economy*;

- how the recurrent myths surrounding the supposed "death" of old media forms and technologies that underlie a surveillance society condition the growth of a surveillance economy;

- how euphemisms such as "knowledge" or "information" economy disguise the level of commercial surveillance at the heart of economic and social relations of production; and

- where the surveillance economy has come from and some suggestions about where it is heading.

Keywords

- cookies
- creative industries
- dataveillance
- panoptic sort
- Personally Identifiable Information (PII)
- Radio-Frequency Identification Device (RFID)
- search economy
- security economy
- surveillance
- surveillance economy

A *Surveillance Economy*, the Key to a Surveillance Society

This chapter outlines some of the major elements of what constitutes a surveillance economy and how the transition from broadcasting to narrowcasting may contribute to such a development. By identifying how surveillance is being constituted as a fundamental element of the global economy, we can further our understanding of the social relationships in political economy and the concept of Vincent Mosco's "mutual constitution."

In the previous chapter we outlined some of the ways that the emerging surveillance economy is becoming visible as an element of the emerging surveillance society—for instance, in the state as setting technological and security priorities; in the growth of the private security industry; and in crime, security, and surveillance prevalent in the content of commercial media. The previous chapter also laid out the contours of the new surveillance landscape that is having an impact on our cultural, social, and political institutions. This would not be possible, we argue, without some related changes in the economy, whether local, national, or international. In this chapter, our aim is to show how a new mode of development—one that relies heavily on search and surveillance techniques, made possible by digital convergence—is slowly but steadily reshaping the global economy. We hope to demonstrate that a surveillance economy is more than just speculation by documenting how the transition from broadcasting to narrowcasting is constituted by and helps to further develop aspects of surveillance that are now embedded in the economic foundations of global capitalism. We first need to clarify the important distinction between a surveillance society and a surveillance economy. It's not just a matter of semantics, but rather an important theoretical distinction.

A Surveillance Society

In a surveillance society there is a high degree of what we call "social surveillance," by which we mean general surveillance for the purpose of keeping the peace, preventing and detecting crime, and maintaining social order (political surveillance). It is possible to have a surveillance society without a surveillance economy, but a surveillance economy can only develop in societies that have already "accepted" a high degree of social/political surveillance over ordinary life.

Ever since nation-states and governments were developed as separate, or alienated from the majority of the population through social relations and hierarchies of power, rulers have carried out surveillance. Indeed, the origins of the words *censor* and *censorship* come from the ancient Roman world where the censor's mandate was to identify who exactly was in the state's territory (for taxation and military purposes), and to monitor the population according to particular standards of morals and manners. State surveillance was thus formalized through the census and exercised bureaucratically as well as socially (Curtis, 2001).

When the authority of governments is vested in a state's economic and military power, there will always be a suspicion in the minds of the governing elite that someone, somewhere, is hatching a conspiracy to overthrow them. This is why in English common law, and in most judicial systems, there are crimes of sedition and treason, and, as we reviewed in the previous chapter, often with very severe penalties, from imprisonment to execution by hanging or firing squad.

Where states are formalized institutions with generally established territories, set laws, varying types of governments, and identified citizens, they are not fixed or unchanging. The field of international relations and international policy-making well indicates the dynamic flux that can go on within and between borders, whether in terms of trade agreements, or disagreements escalating to conflict or total war. Within a state, governments are also a site of struggle, subject to the pressure created by the contradictions of convergence and narrowcasting that abound in the daily lives of the citizens and democratic governance itself. On one hand, there is the myth that the power of governments is legitimized through popular elections; that is, once elected, governments can act on this power without further consultation with the public. If politicians abuse the existing institutions in the name of the people for the rich and powerful, the more the general populace can be alienated from participating in or perhaps even caring about it. Political and economic power converge as the political institutions become captured by the economic ones, as discussed in Chapter 2. On the other hand is the reality of a system in which voting is, for most people, a ritual of choosing the lesser of two evils rather than a means of direct participation in decision-making.

Further contradictions arise as history suggests that no matter what political party is in power, in pretty much any country in the world that calls itself an electoral democracy, the social relations of power have not been revolutionized. For example, current differences between social classes in many parts of the world are returning to the disparities of the 1850s between the very wealthy and the very poor, and social class divisions continue to be complemented and reinforced by disparities of gender and race, among others. While it may not be on many political parties' agendas, people's every day experiences with economic struggle, subordination, and marginalization in the face of systemic and persistent inequality imply that the end result of narrowcasting is that the individual is completely responsible for their own predicament.

Another contradiction arises with mounting political economic, social, and environmental problems, which can appear too complex, and government and state institutions can be so discredited (whether deliberately or not) that people may think there's nothing they can do about it. As we discuss in the last chapter, apathy or compliance is not the default option, but the strong ideology of self-surveillance and political compliance can have a viral hold on consciousness that can be self-defeating. Dominant rhetoric suggests that everyone gets a "fair go," that anyone can be on top of the pile if they climb the "ladder of opportunity," and that we all "aspire" to be just like those rich, white middle-class confections that we see every day in "television land." But if people's experiences continue to contradict the dream of success, actions taken can threaten existing power relations.

To keep people from collectively expressing their experiences via collective social movements built around class (gender or race), with the progressive aim of eliminating social inequalities, dissent can be also be mobilized, and backlash directed towards narrowcast and minority groups (Mazepa, 2012). As evident in our history of print media (in regard to social class in Chapter 4), dissent can also be diffused or subordinated to regressive constructions of national identity. Nationalism and patriotism can be strong mimetic codes in most hegemonic systems of ideology based on the geographic borders of the nation-state (Jensen, 2004), and linked to race, ethnicity, and gender. These memes have become even more important during the current historical phase—the so-called War on Terror, which bolstered the foundations of the "security state," and narrowcast people as "others" (in representations of Islam and Muslims, e.g.), and they are ever-present in media discourses (Kumar, 2010).

The myth of a society of equals and opportunity is a difficult one to reconcile with experience, however. The reality for many people is unemployment, or eight or more working hours per day and part-time shifts in factories, shops, and offices. This is connected to a whole list of trends: higher taxes for workers; lower taxes for corporations; less but more expensive health care; fewer teachers in public schools; the continual privatization of public resources, including roads, airports, and telecommunications infrastructure and other utilities; and the rob-the-poor-to-feed-the-rich principle of the so-called "user pays" economy.

A Surveillance Economy

Security's third trade-off may involve globalisation an[d] technological change. It is not clear . . . whether globalisation is compounding or extenuating the problems associated with the security economy. One can identify a race between two effects of globalisation. (Brück, 2004, p. 115)

The Paris-based global club of rich nations that Canada belongs to—the Organisation for Economic Co-operation and Development (OECD)—published a report in 2004 called "The Security Economy." It examined the economic consequences of a "changed world situation" since 9/11. The framework of the report was to define and outline the types of issues that began to emerge from the convergence of technologies and the perceived security crisis induced by the now global War on Terror. What the OECD blandly describes as the *security economy* is what we're calling, with much more purpose, the *surveillance economy*.

The definition of the security economy provided by Barrie Stevens (2004) discusses the sharpening focus on security issues and the growing demand for "security-related goods and services" that have given rise to "a wide and varied range of economic activities in both the government domain and the business sector" (p. 8). In previous chapters, we identified how state policies and practices have influenced commercial technology development and the commercialization of technology in general. In 2005, international agreements were forged to link security with economics in a "Security and Prosperity Partnership of North America," and agreements forged between the leaders of Canada (Paul Martin), the United States (George W. Bush), and Mexico (Vicente Fox) relied on private-industry participation in decision-making (e.g., the CEOs of 30 of the largest corporations) to set the policies that would bolster economic agreements such as NAFTA, and facilitate an integrated political (continental security) agreement. While the partnership as defined was not continued past 2009 (due in part to changes in leadership), it has been rejuvenated (or reconfigured) through the current Conservative federal government's "Action Plan" meant to address national and international political economic security and heavily advertised as a benefit to all Canadians (📺 www.actionplan.gc.ca).

Surveillance is a critical part of this top-down, political economic and social construction of security that places more power and control in close relationship between corporations and states. The Internet is a critical site where this relationship is being negotiated and forged for the future. The release of computer networking to the public, and the way it has developed, suggests that it cannot be controlled, that the wealth of networks (Benkler, 2006) is an ever-expanding network of communication and freedom. While this is premised on the possibility of public power and control to use the Internet in non-commodified ways (as evident in the existence of WikiLeaks, e.g.), the Canadian government's decision in 1999 that the Internet could just be left to the market shifted the paradigm to the market (rather than the public), meaning that it should be unregulated, and thus free to be commodified. As far as the state was concerned, it appeared that the future of computer networking would transcend state boundaries, and make them redundant, and that it couldn't be controlled—not so much that it should thus be released for the promotion and development of a participatory democracy, but that the "invisible hand" of the market should (and would) direct its future (Hibbard, 2012, p. 379), thus turning the wealth of networks into networks of wealth. While the previous chapter indicated the extent that the state is otherwise involved in Internet surveillance, as legal experts Michael Birnhack and Niva Elkin-Thoren (2003) submit, since 9/11 there has also been another significant shift to bringing the state back in—in direct relationship with business:

A convergence of interests seems to be developing among players such as copyright owners and service providers on the one hand, and the State's growing interest in the digital environment, on the other hand. Law enforcement agencies seek to enhance their monitoring capacity and online businesses seek to prevent fraud and combat piracy while strengthening their ties with authorities. This convergence might lead to an unholy alliance with potentially troublesome results. The invisible hand turned out to be very useful for the State, and it is now being replaced with a handshake, which, likewise, is invisible. This is the Invisible Handshake. (pp. 2–3)

Convergence of interests is being forged through these practices and through state-industry liaisons that plan for the future. If the government doesn't go far enough in advancing integrated policies, existing industry lobby groups indicate another way to facilitate the surveillance economy. Lobby groups, such as the Information Technology Association of Canada (ITAC), are evidence of the sustained and organized efforts of private industry to influence government policy-making and laws. ITAC was established to benefit the growth of the corporations it represents and promote overall profitability of the industry. Since 2000, for example, ITAC holds a quarterly "Cyber Security Forum" in direct discussions with government, which it identifies as "an industry-government policy roundtable. . . . The Forum is widely regarded as a key venue for industry-government discussion of new and ongoing cyber-security issues and related policies, responses and solutions" (ITAC, 2013, para. 3; ▣ itac.ca/activities/forums-and-committees).

In related forums, the security and prosperity partnership identified previously is forged through the Canadian Association of Defence and Security Industries (CADSI). Its mandate indicates that "it represents Canadian-based for profit enterprises with a common interest in selling goods and services into the domestic and global defence and security markets" (CADSI, 2011, pp. 1–6). CADSI (2013) reports that it represents "950 member companies who are essential contributors to Canada's national defence and security" (para. 2), integrates industry and government decision-making (at all levels—national, provincial, and municipal—through the police, e.g.), and encourages government purchases of industry products through two annual trade shows, CANSEC and SecureTech, for the former of which the 2012 keynote speaker was the former minister of public safety, Vic Toews (▣ www.defenceandsecurity.ca/). It was good timing. Just prior to CANSEC, the minister announced that the federal government had recently made the decision to "invest an additional $155 million over the next five years increasing Canada's cyber security capacity, and reinforcing domestic digital infrastructure," which was "welcomed" by CADSI in its press release (CADSI, 2012, para. 1; ▣ www.defenceandsecurity.ca/index.php?action=news.article&id=198&t=c).

Cybersecurity is prioritized by the federal government as a defense against "cyberattacks," which it broadly defines as

the unintentional or unauthorized access, use, manipulation, interruption or destruction (via electronic means) of electronic information and/or the electronic and physical infrastructure used to process, communicate and/or store that information. The severity of the cyber attack determines the appropriate level of response and/or mitigation measures: i.e., cyber security. (Public Safety Canada, 2010, p. 3; ▣ www.publicsafety.gc.ca/cnt/rsrcs/pblctns/cbr-scrt-strtgy/index-eng.aspx)

While there's no question that cybersecurity is an important issue, questions endemic to political economy mean that we always ask, "Who decides?" and "Who benefits?" Forums such as ITAC and trade shows such as CANSEC fall outside parliamentary (and therefore explicitly public) input, review, and reflection. When the public does enter the discussion, it is as users and consumers, which, as we discovered in the last chapter, can be constructed through surveillance in particular ways—whether through citizen-surveillance (suspects) or as consumers, surveilled for their behaviour and spending habits.

For now we can suggest that in a security economy, the very act of surveillance has become

Case Study

Contradictions in Capitalism? CSIS and Foreign Takeovers of Canadian Businesses

In September 2012, the Canadian Security Intelligence Service (CSIS) tabled in Parliament its 2010–11 Annual Report that included a series of interesting statements related to concerns about "threats to national security" and foreign takeovers. As reported in several Canadian media outlets, the report states:

> "CSIS expects that national security concerns related to foreign investment in Canada will continue to materialize, owing to the increasingly prominent role that (state-owned enterprises) are playing in the economic strategies of some foreign governments." (as cited in Bronskill, 2012, para. 8)

> "Certain state-owned enterprises and private firms with close ties to their home governments have pursued opaque agendas or received clandestine intelligence support for their pursuits here [in Canada]." (as cited in The Globe and Mail, 2012, para. 2)

> "When foreign companies with ties to foreign intelligence agencies or hostile governments seek to acquire control over strategic sectors of the Canadian economy, it can represent a threat to Canadian security interests. The foreign entities might well exploit that control in an effort to facilitate illegal transfers of technology or to engage in other espionage and other foreign interference activities." (as cited in Fekete, 2012, para. 6)

The timing of the report coincides with the news that the second largest energy company in Canada, Nexen, is in the process of a friendly takeover by the China National Offshore Oil Corporation (CNOOC), a Chinese energy company. Concerns have arisen that CNOOC's connection to the Chinese government (it is reportedly state-invested, not state-owned; The Globe and Mail, 2012) make it exactly the kind of company that CSIS is concerned about in its report. The takeover has been approved by Nexen's shareholders but must still be reviewed by Industry Canada under the Investment Canada Act. In this review, it needs to be demonstrated that the deal is a "'net benefit for Canada'" (ibid., para. 1). Similar foreign takeovers have been scuttled in recent years (e.g., BHP Billiton Ltd.'s attempted takeover of Potash Corp. in 2010; see Waldie & Curry, 2010), yet these activities indicate a troubling trend in the Canadian economy—namely, that key businesses in the strategic natural resources sector in the country are being targeted for foreign ownership. While the Nexen deal is by no means done, CSIS' timely report will likely provide ample evidence of legitimate concerns related to foreign takeovers of Canada's strategic resources.

The CSIS report is not the first instance where representatives of the agency have expressed concerns about foreign governments, namely China, influencing Canadian decision-making. In 2010, Rick Fadden, CSIS' director, expressed openly his concerns about the practices of foreign governments in influencing Canadian government policy. Both of these examples raise interesting questions about the scope and reach of foreign state surveillance in Canadian society, particularly as, we introduced in Part I, communication and telecommunication are also considered public resources.

Continued

The government is currently working out how China's Huawei Technologies—one of the largest makers of telecommunications equipment in the world—supplying equipment to Bell, WIND Mobile, and SaskTel, will fit into its security plans (Chase, 2012). As quoted from government documents, obtained by *The Globe and Mail* through the Access to Information Act, this includes identifying "'risk mitigation activities' in connection with the Chinese firm. One briefing note says Canada can't feasibly block foreign technology but recommends routinely inserting computer security requirements into government-purchasing contracts" (ibid., paras. 7–8). Is there something new here?

Discussion Questions

1. What evidence is there of public concern or activism about foreign *states* attempting to influence Canadian policies through the takeover of Canadian businesses?

2. Should this concern or activism be extended to *private* foreign takeovers of Canadian companies?

3. Is the issue at stake one of ownership of existing Canadian businesses or public resources?

4. Do the concerns raised in the CSIS report apply equally to the information and communication industries in Canada? Discuss why or why not.

part of the economic relations of that social formation. By this we mean that some surveillance functions have become commodified, and that in general terms there is a specific set of surveillance functions that support the economy and shape its development. This includes the commodification of both privacy (or lack of it) and personal identity. Mosco (2004a) identifies one of the dialectics at work as being "the struggle for personal privacy," which is also a struggle "against the expanding commodity" (p. 170).

In a surveillance economy, commodified surveillance is not just for the purpose of maintaining good order and weeding out troublemakers, though that still occurs. Surveillance is used to shape and manage consumption patterns, and there are physical, psychological, and emotional manifestations of this in many of the commodities we take for granted today.

One example is the barcodes on products that are routinely scanned at the checkout in nearly all stores and shopping centres. These codes are used to track the merchant's stock and, when tallied at the end of trading, to help manage the restocking of shelves and the reordering of stock through the supply chain all the way back to the manufacturer. This is a fairly benign use of barcodes, and it's easy to see how it increases the efficiency of supply-chain management. It might also be seen as a boon for customers because it means your store is unlikely to run out of your favourite items. The manager always knows when the stock is running low. In fully automated systems the central computer can even alert the supplier and generate an automatic order for regularly stocked items.

But the barcode has other, less benign, uses. Have you ever entered a competition that required you to send in the barcodes from a product—to collect 10 or more barcodes and post them off as the cost of entry into a draw to win fabulous prizes? By entering such competitions and by passing on your carefully hoarded barcodes you are giving the marketing company that's running the competition valuable information about you and your shopping habits. By matching barcodes to your personal details, the marketing company knows where you bought the products, what batches they came from, and the period over which you purchased the products. This can help them work out your spending habits and assess your value as a "loyal" customer for that particular product. As a by-product of this process (collateral damage?), your name is entered into a vast database alongside your customer profile. This will then be used to further target marketing material at you, and it may even be sold to other companies looking for people like you. This is one way that you end up on the mailing or phoning list of a company you've never dealt with before, but who will send you unsolicited advertising for years to come, or who will ring you at the most inconvenient time of the day to see if you're interested in buying what they're selling. The humble barcode may, however, soon be a relic of more benign times. The development of small **Radio-Frequency Identification Device** (RFID) chips could make them completely redundant. Several US-based retailers already implant RFID chips in a range of consumer goods, including groceries and clothing. Once these tracking devices become common there is seemingly no limit to their application: "Virtually everything in the universe could be labelled with a tag containing a unique [identifying] number" (O'Harrow, 2005, p. 286).

The information collected from the tag is used to compile sets of data, not so much on the product that it is attached to, but on the consumer. While RFID tags are one example, the cell phone you hold in your hand is another. Companies like ScanLife and JagTag bring the concept of RFID to your cell phone, in what is called "mobile tagging." Barcodes can be read by a mobile phone's camera to provide more information about products, ads, or newspaper articles, for example, by linking it directly to the user's mobile phone. It can all be recorded, traced, and linked—via your iPad, your computer, your GPS; every click, every query, every visit to a website is being monitored, measured, and compiled, and not usually by just one company but by several—24/7/365. Consumer profiling has become a multibillion dollar worldwide industry in the past decade. This would not have been possible without digital convergence. Personal digital data (everything from personal details to photographs, shopping habits, bank transactions, credit history, medical records, and criminal convictions) has become a very valuable information commodity.

> RADIO-FREQUENCY
> IDENTIFICATION
> DEVICE (RFID)
> "A method of automatic identification in which remote sensors are able to retrieve and store data from transponder devices (or tags). Tags transmit an identification signal every fraction of a second, thus creating vast amounts of data as well as a host of data storage difficulties" (Fitchett & Lim, 2008, p. 142).

Convergence and Surveillance: From Broadcast to Narrowcast

> *The revolution in urban surveillance will reach the next generation of control once reliable face recognition comes in. (*Earth Island Journal*, 2001, p. 34)*

The report to the European Parliament that contains this claim was published in 1998. Today, facial-recognition software is a reality, and along with other biometric surveillance and monitoring technologies, it is already in use. In the United States the BI-LO grocery chain is using digital fingerprint technology to verify customers' ID. One of the leading companies in this field is Biopay of Herndon, Virginia. As Robert O'Harrow (2005) suggests, it is a name like "something out of a cyberpunk novel" (p. 175). The top-secret National Security Agency in Washington, DC, is also using facial recognition to track employees and control access to its secure computer network (p. 176).

Governments spying on their citizens has been going on for a long time. As we identified previously, it's been a fact of political life for centuries. Before the advent of telephones and listening devices, however, surveillance and spying had to be done in close quarters and in a directly physical way. The development of transistors made wiretapping easier because the device could be smaller and less obtrusive; the spy was also at one remove physically and therefore safer. Satellite technology increased the global reach of the spy agencies and exponentially increased the amount of data that could be sampled, stored, and retrieved. The digital stage and even greater convergence has again exponentially increased the amount of surveillance and the volume of information that can be monitored. What is also interesting from our perspective is that many of the same technologies that are used for surveillance are also used in the media to perfect and reproduce the techniques of narrowcasting.

The electronic storage of phone records, text messages, and emails means that data is also retrievable at greater distances of time and space. This echoes what John Thompson (1995) calls the distanciation of communication and is part of the process of spatialization. We now have distanciation of surveillance. This phenomenon of distancing the watcher and the watched has led a professor at the prestigious Massachusetts Institute of Technology (MIT) to argue for a refined definition of surveillance in the age of convergence. Gary T. Marx (2004) says the new definition should include "the use of technical means to extract or create personal data" (p. 20). This new definition (which adds to, not replaces, traditional definitions) takes into account that it's not just the "watching" that constitutes surveillance today, but the additional things that can be done with the data once it's in a digital form. New methods of manipulation and matching make the data far more valuable, to both governments and corporations. According to Marx, the new means of digital surveillance can "extend the senses" of the watcher, but also provide the watcher with "low visibility" or even make them "invisible" to the target; for good measure he adds that such surveillance is likely to be "involuntary." Data collection is also likely to be automated, "relatively inexpensive," mediated "through remote means," and available in real time. Further, he adds that it is "more comprehensive" and can include "multiple measures" (ibid., p. 24).

One interesting and slightly disturbing aspect of the convergence of video technologies with wireless transmission is that many consumers are unwittingly inviting unwanted surveillance into their lives when they purchase home-security video units. In many cases these units operate on low-frequency wireless transmission of the signal back to a video monitor or computer. With the right antenna, anyone can intercept these signals from nearby. When people install these systems to increase their sense of personal security, they are unknowingly giving away their privacy.

This is an example of inadvertent intrusion that is created by flaws in the consumer products that push the surveillance economy into our homes on the pretext of increasing personal security. But this is not the only way we become ensnared in the surveillance economy. We are confident in our argument that suggests that the very transition—from broadcasting to narrowcasting—at the heart of our book is also an important vector for the distribution of the mimetic code that replicates the ideology of a surveillance economy and allows it to enter our minds in a way that almost becomes standard operating procedure.

Why Do We Call It a Surveillance Economy?

There are many theories, descriptions, and names for the current configuration of the global capitalist economy, but do they all fundamentally point to the same thing? The naming of an object, event, or trend is important because the act of naming implies a range of opinions and views about the thing being described. We don't have the space here to launch into a full-scale discussion of the differences in the naming practices that have given us such terms as *knowledge* and *information society/economy*, but we do offer a brief overview and some arguments as to why we prefer to call it a "surveillance" economy/society.

ONGOING ISSUES

Marketing Surveillance as Security

The business of home-security services is a lucrative one. Companies like Chubb, ADT, and AlarmForce are at the top of the sector in Canada and elsewhere, yet they now have competition emerging from Canadian telecommunications companies, such as Rogers.

In August of 2011, Rogers launched its "Smart Home Monitoring" service, providing new smart-touch home security and monitoring to its cable high-speed Internet customers (Chung, 2011). The service "allows [a home]owner to control alarms and sensors from a computer or smartphone" (Johnson, 2011, para. 2). The system functions like most other security systems with a link to a central monitoring station for the alarm function, but provides additional features for the homeowner to be able to not only check but also manipulate household functions via computer or smartphone. The system is equipped with a touchpad installed at the home, as well as an application for computer or smartphone. Additionally, the homeowner can install plug-in sensors for managing everything from turning off a coffee maker to adjusting lights or home temperature. Another "handy" feature is the use of video surveillance (if desired) to record when a resident returns home or if someone is checking out a home (Kapica, 2011).

Rogers is not the only telecommunication service providing this type of service. Verizon in the United States also has a similar sort of service, and Bell Canada briefly offered a similar system but cancelled it in 2008. Companies like AlarmForce have offered two-way voice and video monitoring for years, as a central feature of its security package. In this case though, unlike Rogers, who owns the lines over which the information is travelling, AlarmForce makes use of a homeowners existing telephone service to link communication for its offering. What the AlarmForce system does not currently offer is the ability to manage additional household services like lighting and heating.

While there may be real benefits for those interested in remotely managing their home, there are also some significant concerns around privacy that arise with these systems. Although Rogers has stated that "building privacy into the system was important" (Chung, 2011, para. 12), the Information and Privacy Commissioner of Ontario has noted some issues related to the sharing of information with the central monitoring station (ibid.). Additionally, as this service is provided via Internet, the impact of the Lawful Access Bill (C-30), discussed in the previous chapter, might also apply. Not only could police access your emails and other communications without a warrant, but with the full surveillance of someone's home through this type of service, they may also have access to direct home surveillance.

Discussion Questions

1. What sort of surveillance myths does the Smart Home Monitoring system reinforce?
2. Are there valid privacy concerns that arise with this sort of system?
3. What implications do such systems have on our understanding of private and public space and of social relations in general?

The Knowledge Economy

The concept of "knowledge societies" offers a holistic and comprehensive vision with a clear development-oriented perspective that captures the complexity and dynamism of current changes in the world. (Briet & Servaes, 2005, p. 3)

For the purpose of this review, we have joined "information" and "knowledge" economy/society as their definitions are close and the issues are similar in relation to both. According to Briet and Servaes (2005), a knowledge society is based on four key principles that encompass social well-being and development: "freedom of expression," "universal access to information and knowledge," "respect for human dignity," and "cultural and linguistic diversity" (p. 3). These are admirable principles, but when we examine the reality of the global economy we quickly see that adherence to and action around these principles is hard to measure and hard to find (see, e.g., Gwynne, 2005). The driving forces for change that lead to the knowledge economy are economic globalization, the intensity and density of knowledge embedded in economic activity, and the connectivity of information and communication technologies. The knowledge economy, or the information economy, is named as the "network economy" by Manuel Castells. The network economy is based on the "network enterprise." A network enterprise is one that is able to process knowledge efficiently, adapts to the changing landscape of the global economy, is flexible and innovative, and, above all, "transforms signals into commodities by processing knowledge" (Castells, 2000, p. 188). For Castells and others, the global media and the associated "**creative industries**" are at the core of the network society and the knowledge economy (see, e.g., Hartley, 2005).

A fairly straightforward definition of the knowledge economy simply recognizes that technology (and the knowledge that is embedded in technological objects) is a factor of production. This has been obvious to political economists for over 100 years, but it seems that capitalist economists only discovered this idea in the 1980s when economist Paul Romer published a work proposing that neo-classical economists change their view. In this view, "knowledge" is reinterpreted as a "basic form" of capital, and the argument is put forward that economic growth is driven by the "accumulation of knowledge" (Ernst & Young, 1999).

Upon close examination, however, it is apparent that this formula is another ideological argument that deserves unpacking. It arose mainly in response to the onset of a periodic crisis in profitability and accumulation within the global capitalist economy following the oil crisis of the late 1970s. In a sense the argument presented by neo-classical economists is basically that capital must appropriate as many forms of knowledge as possible in order to commercialize them (what the theory names as the creation of "intellectual capital") and thereby resist the tendency for crisis for a little bit longer. Governments around the world were quick to seize the knowledge economy argument in order to secure a commercial and competitive advantage for their own "national" bits of capital. For example, the British Department of Trade and Industry argued in 1998 that "the generation and exploitation of knowledge play the predominant part in the creation of wealth" (as cited in Ernst & Young, 1999). The key word in this passage, from the perspective of this book, is of course *exploitation*!

The ideology of the knowledge economy is also technologically determinist and relies on ICTs in particular to sustain itself: "Learning means not only using new technologies to access global knowledge, it also means using them to communicate with other people about innovation." The digital-mythic nature of the knowledge economy mantra becomes clear in the following passage: "With the advent of information and communication technologies, the vision

CREATIVE INDUSTRIES

A collective noun that refers to a range of activities and professions associated with media production in the information or knowledge economy. The creative industries include print, radio, and television production; literature and poetry; theatre and film; public relations; journalism; and marketing and advertising.

of perfect competition is becoming a reality" (ibid.). As our political economy approach shows, there is no such thing as "perfect competition" in the global capitalist economy—there is only varying concentrations and exercises of power (via labour and social conflict). The knowledge economy does not shift the balance in favour of labour; it merely reorients the goalposts and changes the rules to ensure the owners of the means of production continue their lucky streak.

This imbalance cannot be ignored in knowledge economy theory. As Briet and Servaes (2005) acknowledge, addressing the "digital divide" is a key question, and the gap "will not easily be reduced" (p. 5). A further important link between definitions of the knowledge or information economy and our preference to call it a surveillance economy is provided by the growing importance of industrial espionage and security. As we noted earlier, this is recognized by governments and inter-governmental agencies like the OECD, which are beginning to name the "security" economy and talk about it.

The "Security" Economy

In recent years security has taken a prominent place on the political and corporate agendas. Organized crime, terrorism, disruption of global supply chains and computer viruses have raised people's awareness of the risks they face in today's world. (OECD, 2004)

According to the OECD discussion paper "The Security Economy" (2004), the global market for security goods and services was then worth over USD$100 billion a year and growing between 7 and 8 per cent each year (🖥 research.microsoft.com/pubs/132691/16692437.pdf). The report supports measures to expand the security economy and acknowledges that commercial and political surveillance is increasing. The only cautionary note is that governments and corporations must ensure that surveillance and security are not misused "Big Brother fashion" (OECD, 2005). We can trace some of the historical outlines of the security economy back to George Bush's "State of the Union" address in January 2002. In that speech President Bush made explicit links between the War on Terror and the American economy and signalled the largest increase in defence spending in over 20 years (CNN.com, 2002). As a result of this unprecedented defence budget, the US Department of Homeland Security now has a mandate to specifically examine security economy issues and to ensure that communications and data storage infrastructure is secured against terrorist threats. More recent reports (2009), commissioned by the European Union, suggest that the United States holds the largest "security market" share in the world with approximately USD$60 billion:

[The] recent "consensus" view is that the global security market is worth some €100bn (2008 figure) with around 2 million persons employed worldwide in the security sector. From a global perspective, North America (mainly the US) is the largest security market, with a current market share of around 40% or more. Europe is ranked 2nd in the global security market, with a market share ranging approximately from 25% to 35%. Despite the financial crisis, global demand for security equipment is expected to grow at a minimum of around 5% per annum, with the fastest growth in coming years expected to be mainly in Asia and the Middle-East. (ECORYS, 2009, p. v)

Of course, like any estimation, numbers indicating economic size can be conflated or inflated depending on what is counted as "security." Even the OECD admits that this is

SECURITY ECONOMY

"Attempts to describe a kaleidoscope cluster of activities concerned with preventing or reducing risk of deliberate harm to life and property. At the broadest level, it could include all matters related to defence and counterintelligence, the public police force, private policing, armed guards, and security technology providers. In a much narrower sense, it might comprise just private spending on personal and corporate security." (OECD, 2005, p. 8)

challenging, but nevertheless, its official definition of security economy indicates just how much is included.

The OECD uses the term *security economy* as a polite way of describing what we define as the surveillance economy. The security economy has grown exponentially over the past decade in response to heightened risk assessment, particularly the threat of terrorism on a global scale. Justification for the US surveillance economy was promoted after 9/11 by the Department of Homeland Security, which encouraged further investment in security technologies by private companies. Such a path can be followed in recent history. For example, in a speech to the American Chamber of Commerce in Singapore in 2005, (then) Homeland Security Chief Michael Chertoff said that new tracking and surveillance requirements for global shipping should be a private-sector responsibility (Lippowicz, 2006). In a highly unstable environment the protection of intellectual property becomes paramount in securing a competitive edge. Hence data security and encryption services are among the fastest-growing sectors in the economy. According to the Computer Science and Telecommunications Board (CSTB) of the US National Science and Technology Council (NSTC), cryptography has always been seen as an essential element of the security society: "In an age of explosive worldwide growth of electronic data storage and communications, many vital national interests require the effective protection of information" (CSTB, 1996).

We think that security economy is a better description than knowledge economy because surveillance and security are key aspects of the new relations of production, consumption, and the political-ideological framework of the network society. This is obvious in what Tilman Brük (2004) describes as the "fifth trade-off" at work in the security economy: "*Security* versus *freedom* and *privacy*."

> *The political decision [is] about the balance of civil rights, privacy and individual freedom versus the possible need to curtail these rights in the pursuit of more security. Internet, computing, mobile and wireless technologies are highly vulnerable to security attacks. At the same time, **these technologies can be used to monitor movements, usage and profiles of individuals or goods**—both those of consumers and those of potential perpetrators of crimes. (p.117; emphasis added)*

In a security economy, the methods of surveillance are much more deeply entrenched in the production and consumption process. Surveillance is, in effect, at the heart of all economic functions and dominates the whole fabric of society. A surveillance economy is a particular stage, period, or epoch in the development of the global capitalist system. As we discussed previously, in our Canadian example, it is also an interesting stage of capitalist economic development because of the close economic and political ties that are developed between capital and the state. O'Harrow's (2005) analysis contains many examples of how the growth of the security economy has been encouraged by huge grants from the American government to private companies to help them develop new technologies, such as facial recognition, RFID chips, and other types of surveillance and data-mining capabilities. The former Bush government created the Homeland Security Advanced Research Projects Agency (HSARPA) along the same lines as DARPA (the agency that built the precursor Internet) to boost research into economic security and surveillance measures, and a senior official at the Department of Homeland Security was explicit in encouraging private investment in a meeting with security industry contractors in 2003:

> *"We want you to recognize the economic opportunity that homeland security represents. It is important for all Americans to remember that when the terrorists*

struck on September 11 2001, one of their goals was to cripple the US economy. We must remember this and change our mindset to make protecting the homeland a mission that moves our economy forward." (Michael McQueary, as cited in O'Harrow, 2005, p. 298)

In our view, the security economy and the surveillance economy are pretty much the same thing. But we have alluded to one important consideration: The security economy is significantly driven by government initiatives that draw in private capital by a process of research grants, commercialization of results, and competitive tendering. The security economy draws the interests of the state and capital even closer, further undermining the "free market" mythology. The security economy, while an important developmental stage of capitalism that highlights the close relationship between state and capital, is only half the picture. There is a purely commercial side to the surveillance economy that has been explored in a recent book called *The Search*, which has the interesting subtitle: *How Google and Its Rivals Rewrote the Rules of Business and Transformed Our Culture* (Battelle, 2005).

The "Search" Economy

As we root around in the global information space, search has become our spade, the point of our inquiry and discovery. (Battelle, 2005, p. 12)

John Battelle calls it the "search" economy because companies like Google recognized a business opportunity in cyberspace and turned it into the fastest-growing business in the history of media. Google was worth $4 billion in 2004 and was estimated to reach $23 billion by 2010 (ibid., p. 34). Current (2012) estimates of its net worth put it at 100 times as much, between $198 and $200 billion (■ www.theirnetworth.com/Businesses/Google/). This puts Google on par with the biggest horizontally and vertically integrated "old media" companies in the world, such as General Electric (worth about $202 billion) and IBM (about $224 billion), yet they all remain well-behind the "new media" mogul, Apple, whose net worth is estimated at $460 billion (Gustin, 2012).

While these figures can boggle the mind, the main reason for Google's meteoric rise, according to Battelle (2005), is that marketing and advertising executives realized that search engines provide an efficient way to capture and exploit new leads, and "marketing leads are the crack cocaine of business" (p. 34). Those new "leads" are your mind and your behaviour. This has led to further commercial convergence between media content providers and search engines, particularly if they are capable of storing an individual's search history for later reference. According to the industry magazine *EContent*, advertisers see this as a valuable "add-on" service. It becomes even more important if the advertiser is able to "follow" a prospective buyer as he or she jumps from site to site (S. Smith, 2005).

The concept of the **search economy** gaining a permanent foothold conceptually, and in practice, was evident in the (2006) Wikipedia entry for "Google economy." Defined as "the concept that the value of a resource can be determined by the way that resource is linked to other resources, it is more complex than search ranking, and broader than interlinked web pages, though it draws meaning from both" (Wikipedia, 2006). 2006 was also the year *Google* was included in the Oxford Dictionary (M. Lee, 2010, p. 914) as both a noun and a verb.

Battelle (2005) painted a convincing picture of a digital future, one in which our television and Internet habits are constantly under surveillance by automatic means to push the most

SEARCH ECONOMY
Battelle (2005) uses this term to describe the economic relations of production that seem to permeate capitalism in the early years of the twenty-first century, epitomized by the ubiquitous presence of Google on the World Wide Web. Bartelle coined the term to emphasize how so much of what constitutes commerce today relies on some kind of search function, particularly forms of electronic commerce.

appropriate (in terms of what we are likely to purchase) advertising content directly at us. He argued that this changes the whole point of online marketing, so that it is no longer merely a conduit for advertising but becomes, in his words, a new and effective "sales channel," which fundamentally changes the economics of marketing in the digital domain: "In the near future, it's quite possible that researchers tracking advertising by medium will have to fold television revenues into interactive [online]—they'll often be one and the same" (Battelle, 2005, p. 171).

Yet, this kind of tracking is only part of the convergence picture. As Canadian surveillance researcher David Lyon (2001) identifies, to understand the extent of surveillance, we should recognize that each and every record of our visits or encounters with computer networking is monitored—not only in terms of government surveillance as citizens or as consumers but also as workers. Employment surveillance has been around since the 1880s, when workers were monitored in "time and motion" studies in order to precisely monitor the time it took to complete specific tasks. The data from this monitoring was then used to manage the timing and organization of the assembly line as calibrated to worker productivity, whether in the factory or the office. Subsequent studies tried to identify all the possible factors in worker productivity in monitoring the effects of electricity on work behaviour (see the Chapter 12 Timeline). With a leap to the future, monitoring computer usage at work is meant to measure your time more precisely (Kiss & Mosco, 2005), as well as tracking your social habits via your email and Facebook entries, which are used to monitor employees and to search and sort job applicants (Brown & Vaughn, 2011).

The monitoring and measuring of workers has continued through a variety of means including camera and computer recording, number of keystrokes entered, phone calls answered, and widgets produced, among many others (Allmer, 2011; ☑ www.amanet.org/training/articles/2007-Electronic-Monitoring-and-Surveillance-Survey-41.aspx). Tracking workers' time is becoming more personal with the introduction of the "finger scan punch clock" already in place at Loblaws grocery stores in Canada, for example (UFCW, 2010), or wearable sensors recording employee movements and conversations as used by the Bank of America Corp. (Silverman, 2013). As Allmer (2011) underscores, surveillance increases in accordance with the necessities of capitalism (recall our discussion from Chapter 2): "In the modern production process, primarily electronic surveillance is used to document and control workers' behaviour and communication for guaranteeing the production of surplus value" (p. 584).

For any number of reasons, but mainly the ones outlined earlier, we prefer the term *surveillance* economy to some of the others. It is more accurate about the core values and processes that are driving it. Surveillance is something empirically concrete that we can currently apprehend with our senses and contextualize, particularly with our senses "working overtime." On the other hand, terms like *knowledge* and *information* economy are less tangible and seem benign, and euphemisms like *security* make it sound a lot safer than it really is.

Surveillance in the Market: Buying and Selling Identity

As Google ventures deeper into the mainstream areas of media and advertising, many of the reigning powers there are watching with a mixture of fascination and fear. (Pfanner, 2006, para. 1)

We most often associate surveillance with a Big Brother-type state apparatus. It seems that governments will spy on citizens in order to maintain the "peace," or alternately, to maintain social control and stabilize power over the dispossessed. For most people this doesn't appear to be a problem; as the old saying goes, "If you've done nothing wrong, you've got nothing to fear." And the FBI and CSIS claim that they only monitor a small percentage of the American and Canadian population, and that there are checks and safeguards to stop the system from being abused. However, as we now know from American history and from the history of RCMP files, police agencies with powers to spy will almost always abuse those powers by indiscriminate wiretapping, physical spying, or undercover surveillance. But what about the prospect of even more commercial surveillance? What about media- and market-based surveillance of our spending, eating, shopping, banking, entertainment, and other habits?

Most of us are blissfully unaware of the snooping that private data companies are doing in our lives, and we probably just chuck unwanted direct mail materials in the recycling bin or delete the varieties of spam in our email. However, to the companies involved, data-mining is a lucrative source of income, and it puts them at the heart of the surveillance economy to the extent that O'Harrow (2005) says data-mining is at the core of the "security–industrial complex" (p. 266). The supporters of free-market data-mining argue that they are only trying to satisfy consumer demand. Bob Weintzen of the US Direct Marketing Association says his members are simply trying to service the needs of the market, and he justifies this by noting that we live in the Information Age.

The sad truth is that today it's harder to be anonymous, not only from political surveillance but also from market surveillance. John Edward Campbell and Matt Carlson (2002) suggest that there has been a shift in thinking as we've moved into the information economy. They call this new paradigm the "commodification of privacy" and say that it has weakened our resistance to surveillance marketing. Privacy has been reconceptualized so that it is no longer seen as a social right or a civil liberty to be exercised by consumers; in the surveillance economy it has become a means of exchange. It has also become what Michel Foucault described as a form of self-discipline and self-surveillance through the unwritten contract that we are assumed to sign when visiting websites, watching cable television, or using email. In a sense we expect to be watched, even though we cannot see the watchers; we must accept this surveillance in order to participate in the narrowcasting world, such as when we do our banking, make a purchase, or view an online news site: "Surveillance has become automated, so that it is now the individual within the marketplace that often initiates the process of data gathering through such mundane activities as visiting an ATM, calling [1] 800 numbers, or making purchases with a credit card" (Campbell & Carlson, 2002, p. 589).

Mining the Mind

The "surrender" of our personal information is made rather casually, considering its importance. While we may not be aware of the RFID tag in the products we purchase, as consumers, we are continually giving our information away for free whenever we are asked for our phone number or postal code, whenever we make a purchase, fill out a warranty card, or enter a contest. If you have a so-called "loyalty" card, this personal information is already on record; what's required is the tracking of your purchases, particularly what you purchase and when. The process is considerably ratcheted up online. As you are likely already aware, the addition of "**cookies**" on your electronic device means that your (or at least your computer's) information is being monitored, measured, and stored for the use of data collection and for sale to marketers and advertisers.

Remember the narrowcasting process started in television and the concepts of the "audience commodity" and "consumer castes" (in Chapter 6)? Well, the process of ratings (tracking who watches and when) via the Nielsen People Meters is a concept that is extended via RFID

COOKIES

"A small data file (up to 4KB) created by a Web site you visit that is stored on your computer either temporarily for that session only or permanently on the hard disk (persistent cookie). Cookies provide a way for the Web site to recognize you and keep track of your preferences" (PCmag. com, 2013, para. 1).

and online monitoring. This data is collected in order to sort people into categories that are commodified (made into an exchange value) for advertisers and marketers. In broadcasting, this categorization was used to aggregate large numbers of people watching or listening, but online, cookies are a mechanism used to narrowcast to the greatest extent—to identify the activities of specific individuals.

> *Using the data from cookies, users are separated into profiles. These profiles provide information such as which websites and products have been viewed, demographics, and when available, personality traits pertaining to the specific individual. Tracking the user is extremely valuable because it allows businesses to narrow their approach and display items that more align with what interests a specific person, based on his or her predilections and search history. (Fuellman, 2011, as cited in Penn, 2012, p. 601)*

In this way, the data amassed can be used to target individuals and direct specific and personalized advertisements to them directly. This data is collected by tracking corporations like DoubleClick whose "propriety technology" collects, compiles, measures, and analyzes every visitor to its more than "11,000 affiliated Web sites" (McClurg, 2003). The data is then used to create individual consumer "data profiles" or **Personally Identifiable Information** (PII).

Data records can be used to follow you (almost) anywhere on the Internet that allows commercial advertising. If you almost purchased that T-shirt, or lingered over those pair of shoes for sale online, the tracking software makes sure that subsequent sites you visit will keep advertising them to you, so you are encouraged and persuaded to buy them. Via a process called "retargeting," as epitomized by a company called FetchBack, this is called "behavioural marketing" as the intent is to use the data collected on your visits, including the time you spent watching, listening, and browsing (i.e., any of your identifiable behaviours), in order to turn it into a purchase. Thus, the intent is to change your "non-purchasing" decision into a purchase (Penn, 2012, pp. 602–4). Behavioural change is closest to the holy grail of advertising. Tracking your online and offline behavioural patterns allows corporations to better predict and manage individual behaviours to their advantage; this targeting, or narrowcasting, online is called "customisation."

> *Customisation can be defined as treating customers differently based on feedback from interactions (Peppers et al 1999). Customisation allowed by new media is the ultimate form of differentiation, as firms can use these tools to tailor products, as well as the ultimate consumption experience based on unique needs (Wind and Rangaswamy 2001).*
>
> *Like [online] interactivity, tailored and customised communications are perceived to be more relevant, credible, and memorable, and therefore are more likely to influence behaviour (Kreuter et al. 1999). . . . New media allow for constant communication with consumers, and provide the opportunities for individuals to give and receive feedback, and thus can serve as a way to encourage behavioural change on a regular basis. (as cited in Hill & Moran, 2011, pp. 822, 824)*

Google—and Ye Shall Find ____?

> *Besides looking for new market segments like [the] local, search companies and new start-ups are focusing on several innovative approaches to monetizing your clickstream. (Battelle, 2005, p. 37)*

PERSONALLY IDENTIFIABLE INFORMATION (PII)

"Information that can be used to distinguish or trace an individual's identity, either alone or when combined with other personal and identifying information that is linked or linkable to a specific individual" (US Memorandum from Exec Office of the President, 2010, as cited in Penn, 2012, p. 604).

Only in the digital age of the surveillance economy could somebody happily spend their working day dreaming up new ways to monetize your clickstream! John Battelle is a founding editor of the cyber age's most influential magazine, *Wired*, so he's been involved in the online business world since the early days of the Internet. In his powerful book *The Search*, he outlines a large shift that is under way in the field of consumer marketing. In 2005, he believed that the shift was still in its "early stages" (Battelle, 2005, p. 167).

According to Battelle's research, Google and other search-engine companies keep tight control over the complex mathematical formulae (algorithms) that determine the results of a search. By keeping track of the number of hits and by carefully screening the keywords and other text on a website, search engines can prioritize the order in which the "organic" links are displayed on a results page. By periodically adjusting its secret algorithms, Google and the other large players can alter the order in which websites are ranked in a search. Google argues that it has to constantly update the algorithm to beat the efforts of spammers and scammers to cheat the search engine by creating false leads that boost a website's rating and push it to the top of the ranking list. Battelle (2005) draws the conclusion—vigorously denied by Google and the others—that this is done in order to maximize the revenue that search engines can generate from paid advertising; "that it helped Google's business can't really be disputed" (p. 165). With Google's purchase of DoubleClick in 2007 for USD$3.1 billion—*cash*—Battelle's prediction was confirmed (🖥 googlepress.blogspot.ca/2007/04/google-to-acquire-doubleclick_13.html).

It's important to recognize that Google's search engines are neither objective nor random, but are constructed and calibrated to provide the results as quickly as possible (🖥 www.google.com/intl/en/corporate/tenthings.html). As M. Lee (2011b) explains, what Google does is "organize information for users," and therein lies its ideology: "While search engines appear to be objective, the decisions behind the design reflect the vision of how information should be organized, presented, and commodified. In turn, the design of the search engine probes users to interact with a search engine in a specific way" (p. 444).

The economic structure of search engines itself is one that follows a traditional formula of convergence and commodification. The consolidation and vertical integration of search engines have significantly reduced the randomness of information available through searches. As Canadian researcher Elizabeth Van Couvering (2010) identifies, where there were 21 search engines operating in 1994, in just over 10 years, there were only six, and these six operate according to a particular "set of practices that emphasize the economic aspects of search engine results to the detriment of other aspects such as public interest aspects" (p. 207, as cited in Mansell, 2011, p. 24). It is no coincidence that these search engines are "systematically biased in favour of commercial sites, popular sites and US-based sites" (Van Couvering, 2004, p. 1). As Canadian political economy of communications' scholar Robin Mansell (2011) adds, "Google and a few other dominant companies are operating within an oligopolistic industry structure that enables them to shape users' encounters with information and to maximize the opportunities for generating advertising revenues" (p. 24). It's also no coincidence that Google's main source of revenue—to the tune of 99 per cent—is from advertising (Google, 2008, as cited in M. Lee, 2010, p. 928).

Google is not just a search engine however, and this is where we get into some significant issues of the surveillance economy, particularly since Google continues to amass a long list of online and offline properties. Its ownership is enormous, of which just a partial list includes software, hardware, operating systems and infrastructure (fibre optics and electricity); email, blogging, and social networking platforms; as well as Google Ads, Google Analytics, Google Apps, Google Books, Google Energy, Google Mobile, Google News, Google Shopping, Google

Translate, Google Voice, and Google Wallet—and don't forget DoubleClick and YouTube. Google has several partners and synergies with other large transnational corporations in telecommunications and other media firms (e.g., Microsoft, Nokia, News Corporation, Universal, Sony, Warner, and Motorola, which it just purchased in 2012). While this is indeed admirable from a business perspective, the amount of power and control being amassed here should be cause for more than a question of how big it is, or how much money it's making.

With this much power under private ownership, when the owners of Google make a decision, like we saw with Kodak (in Chapter 5) and Nortel (in Chapter 8), the public impact can be equally enormous due to the sheer size and scale of its ownership. While Google, like other companies, can decide what advertising it accepts, or not, it can also decide what words and sites it will list and you can access, or not; and what information is available, or not; and this has several significant ramifications. Primarily, it encourages and facilitates the reorganization of information according to economic priorities and places this information under private control, or at least management, according to these priorities. Public information via public websites and libraries is sidelined, dwarfed by the sheer size of ownership; in the process, since Googled information appears free, it appears to be offering a public service. As M. Lee (2010) observes, it "may seem to have replaced the state as the public service provider" (p. 922).

Digital Freedom or Digital Enclosure?

One of the underlying questions in this book is "What is meant by 'free'?" While Google appears free, all the while we are using it, Google is collecting information: Every single click, visit, view, and time spent with Google properties, goes into Google databases. It's no wonder that it makes its money from advertising. "Google does not need customer surveys to understand users' behaviour, it knows users' behaviours more intimately than the users themselves" (M. Lee, 2010, p. 916). Not only is the information it provides compromised accordingly, but the information collected structures its users as commodities—you pay for the content with your information (Mager, 2012, p. 772). This information is "data" and, in a surveillance economy, is known as "**dataveillance**."

As evident in the marginal definition of *dataveillance*, monitoring isn't just something done by Google and other corporations interested in individual consumers, but it also holds the possibility of state surveillance as we discussed in the previous chapter. This has led some researchers to see the Internet not as a vast, free, and open public space but as a privatized, "virtual digital enclosure" (Andrejevic, 2007, p. 296), where the inputs are collected, and where the dystopia envisioned in Orwell's *Nineteen Eighty-Four* is enabled voluntarily through our constant interaction—that is constantly surveilled—online. This includes the data amassed by social networking sites like Facebook as an extension of the audience commodity online, such that users are actually *working for* Facebook, and the surveillance is monetized, given an exchange value (N. S. Cohen, 2008; Fuchs, 2012). Together with the information collected from several sources, including employment monitoring, street and camera monitoring (CCTV), and other combinations of government and corporate information, it is much more difficult to remain independent and "free."

An additional question of the surveillance economy is the result of narrowcasting. Just like Google collects, sorts, and organizes information according to particular criteria it deems important to its economic priorities, so too can the data collected. Generally, without our even knowing it, this data can be used to sort our information, and—by extension—ourselves, as identified by constructed algorithms written for the purposes of those who own and control the data. (Recall our discussion in the previous chapter of Canadian senator David Smith, who found

DATAVEILLANCE

"The systematic monitoring of people's actions or communications through the application of information technology" (R. Clarke, 1988, p. 500). Two types are distinguished: (1) *personal* dataveillance— monitoring one's actions—and (2) *mass* dataveillance— monitoring a group or large sets of populations in order to detect individuals of interest or identify particular patterns of behaviour over time; (Fuchs, Boersma, Albrechtslund, & Sandoval, 2011, p. 1).

himself on the no-fly list.) American political economist of communication Oscar Gandy (1993) identifies the process of this data collection as one in which control is ceded to the technology and the one who owns the data in what he calls the "**panoptic sort**."

To make sense of all this data, a new industry has developed inside the emerging surveillance economy—data-mining. Like all aspects of capitalism, it is rapidly growing into an oligopoly with a handful of giant multinational firms dominating the global market. The inequality of power in the capitalist market system compels us to deal with the data-miners because it is the producers and suppliers, not the consumers, who decide the terms of the contract. In many cases the transaction that results in the delivery of consumer information to the data-mining companies is concealed behind a veneer of consumerism. We willingly comply with requests for personal information online in the (mistaken) belief that we will ultimately benefit from disclosure by gaining convenience and access to a range of otherwise unobtainable commodities. According to Campbell and Carlson (2002), we are "impelled through enticement" and compelled through the threat of exclusion to participate in a "carefully constructed illusion" of a *partnership* between consumers and producers.

The data-mining industry is in the business of selling information. Companies called "data-brokers" collect as much information to sort, organize, and package it according to the requests of its clients who pay for the service. We are currently not allowed to know the uses to which the personal information we hand over will be put (Campbell & Carlson, 2002, pp. 590–91). Even this should be pause for serious consideration given we have no access to the information that is collected on or about us (as Natasha Singer, 2012, a reporter for *The New York Times*, recently tested). There have been some concerns raised in the United States by the Federal Trade Commission (FTC), which opened an investigation into data brokers' "business and privacy practices" (Sasso, 2012, para. 1) in 2012. A year later it issued a "warning" of "possible privacy violations" (FTC, 2013) given the "lack of transparency" when consumers' data was being collected, and how it was being sold or used (ibid.). It isn't yet clear how effective this "warning" will be, particularly given the amount of data that is constantly being amassed.

As far as the data brokers, in 2005, three of the biggest were ChoicePoint, Acxiom, and Experian, and Acxiom bought ChoicePoint in 2006 (Todé, 2008). Along with a few others, data brokerage is a concentrated industry, and the relationships with the state are becoming more complicated. While on one hand, the protection for consumers comes in the form of a government "warning," on the other, these companies are entering into commercial arrangements to also sell data back to the US government, the FBI, and the CIA (▣ www.pbs.org/newshour/bb/business/jan-june05/identity_2-24.html) or, in Canada, to the RCMP (*Ottawa Citizen*, 2006). These data brokers collect, collate, and merge data from many databases. Past managing director of ChoicePoint, Howard Safir, identified this as "his patriotic duty to sell this information back to the US government to help it sift out suspicious behaviour and map profiles of suspected terrorists" (ibid.).

US Attorney General John Ashcroft argued that the FBI should have access to ChoicePoint's data mines so that it could build comprehensive dossiers of potential terrorists by checking everyone's credit cards, travel, and other habits to pinpoint likely suspects for further investigation. The FBI says it only targets criminals, but privacy advocate Chris Hoofnagle says that digital convergence brings with it new risks to privacy. Mike Polime, FBI agent, says the FBI's data warehouse is a necessary anti-terrorism tool in the post-9/11 environment. He argues that this does not infringe on privacy; it just removes the ability of people to remain anonymous. Our acceptance of data-mining seems to be based on a misplaced trust in corporations and governments and relies on the market myth of consumer sovereignty. In reality we surrender control over our personal details with little regard for its importance.

PANOPTIC SORT

A concept identifying the narrowcasting effect of technological data collection. "The panoptic sort is a difference machine that sorts individuals into categories and classes on the basis of routine measurements. It is discriminatory technology that allocates options and opportunities on the basis of those measures and the administration models that they inform" (Gandy, 1993, p. 15).

For Real?

Google Everywhere?

Google recently announced its intentions to expand its local presence in local communities with the Google+ Local offering that builds off its 2011 purchase of the Zagat's restaurant ratings publisher (Bosker, 2011). The move builds on a variety of efforts the search-engine goliath has taken in recent years to expand its services, its data-mining practices, and its capacity for surveillance into local communities around the globe. Other related efforts include Google Places and Google Street View. The Google+ Local service, which is part of the Google Places effort, involves encouraging individuals participating in Google+, the company's social networking service, to share reviews about local restaurants via Zagat's online blog. Another aspect of Google Places is the practice of encouraging local businesses to hire a Google "certified" local photographer to develop a virtual tour of the business' space that would then be posted as part of Google Maps. These elements of Google Places extend Google's reach into local life, leading to Google's oversight of where we eat, as well as of the inner set-up of a business. One of the main ways it is fueling this expansion is through the acquisition of a variety of businesses around the world that offer various types of web-related services from social media analytics to Internet service provision. Of the estimated 113 companies that Google has purchased since 2001, seven are Canadian (Wikipedia, 2012).

The most expansive part of Google's local surveillance reach arrived with the launch of Street View in 2007. Street View is a service that involves a Google vehicle equipped with camera equipment on its roof, travelling through neighbourhoods taking pictures of each building, home, car, person, shrub, and grub on every city street (see Figure 12.1). The information is then posted online as a feature of Google Maps. Although benignly promoted as a "project to photograph the world's streets" (Streitfeld & O'Brien, 2012), Street View has become quite contentious since its introduction. Many European countries, such as Germany, Switzerland, and Greece, have legislated restrictions or outright bans on the gathering of personal information via Street View cameras. For example, in Germany the government ensured that citizens could opt out of Street View by communicating that they wanted their private property and the related images blurred on Google Maps. A large number of Germans chose to opt out, so many that Google decided in 2011 to abandon the service in Germany altogether (D. Murphy, 2011).

More recently, Google Street View has come under international scrutiny for its surveillance practices following a series of national investigations into the type of information that the Street View vehicles were actually gathering. Beginning with an April 2012 report from the Federal Communications Commission (FCC) in the United States, it was revealed that between

FIGURE 12.1 | A Google Maps Street View car. These vehicles travel through neighbourhoods, taking pictures of and mapping city streets.

Source: © DebbiSmirnoff / iStockphoto

2007 and 2010, Street View gathered not only images of everything on local streets but also personal information from Wi-Fi networks, such as emails, passwords, photographs, as well as (in some cases) medical data and information related to financial transactions (Streitfeld & O'Brien, 2012). While the FCC report was highly critical of Google's practices, it only fined the company $25,000 for obstruction throughout the investigation as Google would not release the names of the staff engineers responsible for the creation and oversight of the Street View program, and they also provided a number of redacted documents in response to requests for information from the Commission. The FCC report has led other countries to review Street View's practices within their jurisdictions. For example, the United Kingdom's Information Commissioner's Office (ICO) has launched an investigation into Google's practices of surveillance of personal information in that country.

In 2010, Canada's Privacy Commission conducted an investigation into Google's Street View Wi-Fi data-gathering and found that the company had contravened the Personal Information Protection and Electronic Documents Act (PIPEDA). The findings of the investigation stated that the Commissioner accepted Google's excuse about the data-gathering as a "careless error" of an engineer (OPCC, 2010, para. 2). Despite accepting the error, the Commissioner recommended that Google "ensure it has a governance model in place to comply with privacy laws," that it "enhance privacy training to foster compliance amongst employees," and recommended that it "delete the Canadian payload data it collected" (paras. 15, 16). In 2011, the Office of the Privacy Commissioner of Canada reported that Google agreed to fully adopt all of the Office's recommendations. The Privacy Commissioner also concluded that it would follow up with an independent investigation in 2012 to ensure that the actions had been performed as required. In 2013, in the United States at least, Google conceded that its Street View violated public privacy and has agreed to a settlement of USD$7 million, a mere pittance of the revenue it must be accruing on the data it continues to collect (Streitfeld, 2013; see also "Google Street View Timeline" link in Streitfeld, 2013).

Google's efforts to move into local cities and become a central venue for directions, information, and entertainment has been mixed. On one hand, it contributes to online local information around dining, shopping, mapping, and other activities about a city on the Internet, but on the other, it is encountering both resistance to these efforts from local citizens and competition from locally based or activity specific web services elsewhere on the Internet (e.g., Urbanspoon). As it continues to expand its businesses, its soon-to-be released Google "Glass" (a wearable audio-video camera connected to the Internet) is again raising significant regulatory concerns regarding "ubiquitous surveillance" as expressed in an official letter to Google by "Privacy Commissioner of Canada Jennifer Stoddart and 36 of her provincial and international counterparts" (OPCC, 2013, para. 1). The letter asked Google how it intends to handle the data that is collected and distributed from the device and how it intends to protect that data and the privacy of the people who are captured in its viewfinder. Google responded that "protecting the security and privacy of our users is one of our top priorities" while it is still "actively working" out the details (Office of the Privacy Commissioner of Canada, 2013b, paras. 1, 4).

Discussion Questions

1. What does Google's expansion "in the local" demonstrate in terms of how surveillance and privacy is handled by citizens and their government(s) in different countries?

Continued

2. What distinction can be made between *private* (or personal) space, *public* space, and *commodified* space? Is this distinction no longer valid in a surveillance economy?

3. What does corporate ownership of search engines have to do with privacy or the "fundamental freedoms" guaranteed to citizens under the Canadian Charter of Rights and Freedoms?

4. Why is the Privacy Commissioner asking Google about what it intends to do with the data, rather than Google asking the government (and/or the public) for permission to collect the data in the first place?

A Question of Privacy?

It should be no surprise that one of the major issues emerging from the surveillance economy is the issue of privacy. In Canada, it wasn't until 1980 that there was even a government act that dealt with privacy; it arose as a result of public inquiries into the illegal actions of the federal government and the RCMP (Mazepa, 2009). At that time the Privacy Act recognized "the privacy of individuals with respect to personal information about themselves held by a government institution" and it provided "individuals with a right of access to that information" (Privacy Act, 1985, § 2; 🖥 laws-lois.justice.gc.ca/eng/acts/P-21/index.html). In this case, it identified the information held by government, but since then, as we reviewed earlier, the question of the privacy of individuals collected by commercial entities and via electronic means yields a second act, PIPEDA (🖥 laws-lois.justice.gc.ca/eng/acts/P-8.6/index.html), referred to in the previous chapter and in the "For Real? Google Everywhere?" box.

While our purpose is not to evaluate the Act (although this should be worthy of further investigation and discussion among your friends, family, and classmates), and it is extremely important, it is still incomplete. Specifically, as Levin (2007) identifies, it does not protect the majority of workers across Canada from workplace surveillance and, ironically, may provide a justification for its collection: "Private sector employers are permitted, and perhaps encouraged, by the post 9/11 amendments to *PIPEDA* to collect, use, and disclose personal information on their workers, without their consent or knowledge, if they reasonably suspect their workers of acting against Canada's national interests" (p. 201). In addition, as Valerie Steeves (2011) identifies, it does not adequately address the collection of information from persons under the age of 18 since consent of an adult is required, and when specific sites do have privacy policies, "children report that they are unlikely to read policies because they are long and boring, and when they do read them, they complain that the legal language and the complex structure are intended to take advantage of them because they do not read at a university level" (p. 177). Even those who read at the university level may agree. When is the last time you really read a privacy policy, or cared what it contained?

Although the legal aspects of privacy will continue to be worked out, there are commissioners who are ideally in place for public service, and act as advocates federally (🖥 www.priv.gc.ca/index_e.asp) as well as provincially (e.g., Ontario, 🖥 www.ipc.on.ca, and Quebec, 🖥 www.cai.gouv.qc.ca/diffusion-de-linformation/). However, the issue of privacy is defined (as the Ontario Privacy Commission identifies, e.g.) as focused on the individual in terms of freedom and control, both couched in terms of "choice." This is a hard one to reconcile when it is clear that a lot of information can be collected without such a decision, and it tends to sidestep the structural aspects of political economy that we have been discussing here. It is a particular definition of privacy, one that Christian Fuchs (2012) submits is in keeping with academic studies that "conceive of privacy" in a particular way:

strictly as an individual phenomenon that can be protected if users behave in the correct way and do not disclose too much information. The moralistic tone in these studies ignores how Facebook [for example] commodifies data and exploits users as well as the societal needs and desires underpinning information sharing on Facebook. As a result, this discourse is individualistic and ideological. It focuses on the analysis of individual behaviors without seeing and analyzing how these behaviors are conditioned by societal contexts of information technologies, such as surveillance, the global war against terror, corporate interests, neoliberalism, and capitalist development. (pp. 143–44)

Thus, it is important to follow through and ask ourselves who is collecting the information and why, and what is it used for, as well as to remind ourselves of the questions we began this chapter (and this book) with: Who owns? Who controls? Who benefits? That is, what are the consequences of convergence? What happens when (even with consent) only a few entities control the majority of the information? What happens to the information amassed by Google, for example, if it should go bankrupt (M. Lee, 2010), or its private owners decide to exercise their own politics?

These are also questions of narrowcasting. If the information collected is used to sort people into categories of data, what if your data is either considered so very *important*—to the extent that you end up on a no-fly list (or, worse yet, imprisoned)—or there's no place free of the advertising that is "tailor-made" for you? On the other hand, what happens if you are so very *unimportant* that you are marginalized, identified as unworthy or unnecessary, entrenching divisions in social class, gender, or race or ethnicity, and so on. As Smith-Shomade (2004) identifies, the consequences of the convergence/narrowcasting dialectic as evident in television, for example, are considerably magnified in the "global village" of the Internet where some of us will find ourselves on the outskirts:

Practitioners and scholars admit that the already marginalized (women, the poor, coloreds, inner-city and rural dwellers, and people in underdeveloped countries) will probably find their status moved further in the direction of actual lack. Moreover, as Joshua Meyrowitz and John Maguire (1993) wrote, "information integration heightens the perception of physical, economic, and legal segregation. Television and other media have enhanced our awareness of all the people we cannot be, the places we cannot go, the things we cannot possess. In exposing people to a wider world, television enhances our senses of being unfairly isolated in some corner of it." This new world order may not indeed make everyone feel like we are the world. (p. 79)

Conclusion

We are not yet living in a fully operational surveillance economy, but the signs are there that it is growing in size and appears to be an emerging mode of development within the global capitalist economy. Narrowcasting represents an attempt by global media companies to stay on the crest of this wave. To stretch this metaphor almost to breaking point, our surfing habits—across the Internet and other narrowcast media—will be managed in ways that keep the surveillance economy afloat. Thus, the surveillance economy is not, as some analysts and academics are arguing, something fundamentally different from capitalism; the same laws of value, labour, and capital accumulation apply. Whether we choose to call it the information or the knowledge economy does not alter the basic ground rules of the capitalist mode of production. The digital revolution has already made its mark on the relations of production and the methods of capital accumulation and profit-taking. But the digital revolution and the ongoing process of technological convergence is not a revolution in the same sense as the transition from feudalism to capitalism (for example) was revolutionary. That change was one that radically altered the property and production relations that marked feudalism as a mode of production as distinct from those that had existed before. While profound in many ways, the digital revolution has not displaced capitalism but is a new form of capitalist production relations, perhaps best described as hyper-capitalism, or cyber-capitalism. The process is an extension of the exploitative and alienating relations of production (and all social relations) that distinguish the epoch of global capitalism.

Cyberspace has been tamed; it is still the new frontier, but it is not something separate from the process of accumulation, hegemony, and domination that has characterized capitalism for the past 250 years. These last two chapters may have been a little "heavy," however, the material should not make you feel depressed, or make you think that there's little one can do to change it. We empower ourselves by informing ourselves, getting involved decision making, and making decisions together. In the final chapter we turn our attention to the ways in which the surveillance economy is being re-imagined and normalized in politics and how it may be resisted and changed for the future.

Key Points

- Definitions of the global economy as a knowledge or an information economy are misnomers, and do not take into account the growing importance of both commercial and security surveillance.

- It is more accurate to describe the current formation of global capitalism as a surveillance economy; this involves both a "security" and a "search" economy.

- Narrowcasting is a form of structuring media and social relations that is complementary to and helps sustain the surveillance economy.

- While the roots of convergence are deep, the pace of change and narrowcasting is characteristic of our time, as the dialectic moves inexorably onwards.

Class Discussion

1. Google yourself. See what the Internet tells anyone who cares to look about you. Google your parents and other people you know, perhaps in prominent places in the community. What do you think the evidence suggests about the scope and scale of the surveillance society?

2. Are the distinctions between "knowledge," "security," and "surveillance" economy significant and useful? Explain why or why not.

3. How comfortable are you with the level of commercial and/or political surveillance that now seems to surround our lives, both online and on the street? Name a number of ways that surveillance can be individually or collectively limited.

4. In your own words, how do you understand "privacy" and "security"? Is privacy a feeling? A right? What are some alternative conceptualizations of privacy and security?

Media on Media

Hall & Oates. (1981). Private eyes. *Private Eyes*. US: RCA.
Hates. (2008). Big brother. *30 Years of Hate: 1978–2008*. US: The Hates.
Massive Attack. (1994). Spying glass. *Protection*. UK: Virgin Records.
Police. (1983). Every breath you take. *Synchronicity*. US: A&M.
Rockwell. (1984). Somebody's watching me. *Somebody's Watching Me*. US: Motown.

Watch More Watching and Then Some

BBC and Open University. (Co-Producers). (2010). *Virtual revolution: The cost of free* [TV documentary series]. UK. 🔲 www.bbc.co.uk/programmes/b00n4j0r
Cohen, S., & Gallay, M. (Writers & Directors). (2009). *Tagged*. Montreal, PQ: National Film Board.
Earp, J. (Writer & Director). (2010). *The mean world syndrome: Media violence and the cultivation of fear*. US: Media Education Foundation.
Films Media Group Online. (2007). *Big brother, big business: Data mining and surveillance industries* [Video]. New York, NY: Films Media Group.
Howard, R. (Director). (1999). *EDtv* [Motion picture]. US: Universal Pictures.
MacNeil/Lehrer Productions. (2005). *Internet shopping: Interactive or invasive?* [DVD]. New York, NY: Films Media Group.
Winkler, I. (Director). (1995). *The net* [Motion picture]. US: Columbia.

Timeline: Corporate Surveillance

1878 The phonograph is introduced and used to play and record sounds, sometimes including unknown recordings of conversations, etc. Additionally, the phonograph was touted by its inventor, Thomas Edison, as a means of eliminating the need for human stenographers in dictation, as the technology was more precise (and less editorializing).

1880s Early paparazzi—Portable cameras begin to be used to capture celebrities in different activities (e.g., the governor of Kansas [then a liquor-free state] was photographed having a glass of whisky in a saloon; Lauer, 2012, p. 572).

Frederick Winslow Taylor conducts time studies to measure worker efficiency in completing work-related tasks at the Midvale Steel Company in Philadelphia, with a focus on improving individual performance.

1890 Justices Warren and Brandeis publish *The Right to Privacy*, which was rooted in Warren's own experience of having his personal relationship surveilled by *The Saturday Evening Post* (Holvast, 2009, p. 19).

The first instance of photographs being published without the consent of the subject in the advertisements, prompting the first test case of privacy rights in the United States (Roberson v. Rochester Folding Box Co.; Holvast, 2009, p. 20).

1899 San Francisco newspaper rails against telephone operators for listening in on personal calls and sharing confidential information (Lauer, 2012, p. 577).

1900s The introduction of party lines: shared telephone lines serving numerous homes/businesses, which allow people on the party line to eavesdrop on other members' calls. Party lines are also used to broadcast church services and newspaper readings.

1933 George Elton Mayo conducts a motion study at a Western Electric factory to see the effects of lighting on worker productivity.

1945 RFID technology is first used as an espionage tool by the Soviet Union.

1969 The formation of the first inter-industry organization dealing with the uses and standards of product codes. The organization would become GS1, a global non-profit industry-led organization that creates standards for global "supply chain management systems," including product codes and eventually electronic tracking technologies like RFIDs. A broad range of industry sectors are involved with GS1 including the grocery industry, agriculture, health care, retail, consumer electronics, etc. There are national GS1 organizations in over 100 countries including Canada.

1970s Universal (or Unified) Product Code (UPC) linear barcodes are adopted (GS1 specifications) as universal product identifiers, allowing for products to be scanned and tracked at point of sale.

1973 Smaller, more portable RFID technology is patented at the Los Alamos National Laboratory.

Cameras are installed at Times Square in New York City in an effort to reduce crime—an early use of video surveillance.

1980s CCTV cameras are now commonly used in convenience stores, banks, and shopping malls.

1983 The first patent for the "abbreviated RFID," the precursor to current technology, is issued.

2000s Post-9/11 America sees a marked increase in public video surveillance in major metropolitan areas such as Chicago, Washington, and Boston.

2000 Google launches AdWords, a service that displays particular advertisements to users based on their search keywords.

2003 Google launches AdSense, a service that provides advertisements relevant to specific websites, matching ads to the individual user's interests.

2004 $33 million in US government contracts is given to corporate giants Lockheed Martin, Unisys Corporation, Computer Sciences Corporation, and Northrop Grumman to develop databases that comb through classified and unclassified government data, commercial information, and Internet chatter (Dunn, 2006).

NAFTA clause allows the Canadian federal government to award US-based Lockheed Martin (the world's largest defence contractor) $43.3 million for hardware and software to be used in the 2006 Canadian Census.

VeriChip, a small RFID microchip, is approved by the FDA for implantation into human arms. The chip provides a unique identifier for the individual "wearing" it that can then be linked to personal information, medical data, etc. The VeriChip was discontinued in 2010.

2007 Around half of surveyed American companies use video surveillance to monitor theft, violence, and sabotage; the majority of these companies inform their employees of the monitoring systems in place.

2009 Modern CCTV cameras include motion sensors capable of tracking individuals, facial-recognition technology, and are able to wirelessly transmit data in digital form (IP cameras, PTZ cameras, DSP cameras).

ScanLife and JagTag bring mobile tagging to America. Two-dimensional barcodes can be read by a mobile phone's camera to send more information about products, ads, or newspaper articles, for example, directly to the user's mobile phone.

2010 Foursquare, Facebook Places, and similar services encourage people to "check in" to locations, providing these social media sites (and, indirectly, commercial enterprises and government agencies) information about their whereabouts and habits (www.bizjournals.com/seattle/blog/techflash/2010/08/guest_post_foursquare_government_surveillance_and_privacy.html?page=all).

2011 Facebook's "Like" button generates privacy issues—German state bans federal agencies from using "Like" buttons in order to prevent data from being transferred to US servers (www.thelocal.de/sci-tech/20110819-37073.html#.UV7-uaLvvMo). The presence of "Like" buttons on other websites allows Facebook to gather data and information about user activity, despite not being on Facebook.com, in order to personalize web content and improve services (bits.blogs.nytimes.com/2011/09/27/as-like-buttons-spread-so-do-facebooks-tentacles/?_r=0).

2012 Google reveals "Project Glass," a wearable computer that essentially mounts a camera on a person's head (usatoday30.usatoday.com/tech/news/story/2012-04-04/google-project-glass-augmented-reality/54010466/1).

US Federal Trade Commission (FTC) opens "an investigation . . . into the business and privacy practices of data brokers" (Sasso, 2012, para. 1).

2013 Google admits to privacy breach in the United States and agrees to pay $7 million for violating people's privacy with its Street View mapping project, Maps (www.nytimes.com/2013/03/13/technology/google-pays-fine-over-street-view-privacy-breach.html?pagewanted=all&_r=5&).

The FTC issues a "warning" to data broker companies of "possible privacy violations" (FTC, 2013).

The Privacy Commissioner of Canada sends Google a letter asking how it intends to handle the data that is collected and distributed from Google Glass and how it intends to protect that data and the privacy of the people who are captured in its viewfinder. Google responds that "protecting the security and privacy of our users is one of our top priorities" (Office of the Privacy Commissioner of Canada, 2013b, para. 1).

Google updates its Transparency Report, revealing a 70 per cent increase in government (US and other countries) requests for user data since 2009. Twitter published its first such report in 2012; Facebook has yet to do so (and does not plan to; gigaom.com/2013/01/23/google-releases-new-government-surveillance-data-facebook-stays-mum/).

13 Politics and New Media

with Kirsten Kozolanka

Objectives

There are two aspects to our discussion of politics and the new media. The first is to interrogate the ways that the new media—particularly the shift towards a narrowcasting media environment—may impact the ways in which what we traditionally call "politics" might be conducted. Can we make a case that the shift towards narrowcasting and the surveillance economy makes *participation in politics*, or even what we mean by politics, more problematic? The second aspect is to look at the politics of the new media itself as both an institution and a process. This relates to some of the arguments raised in earlier chapters about *reform of the media* system, in particular around ownership and control, but it also raises questions about the level of public involvement in these changes.

Given its dominance, in this chapter we will concentrate on the first aspect—the conduct of hegemonic politics in the world of narrowcasting. The discussion in this chapter addresses both the ways that new media are being used in the events and institutions of politics as well as the use of new media in political activism. The chapter concludes with a short discussion about media reform through alternative media and alternative media activism. After reading this chapter you should understand the following:

- how the shift towards narrowcasting and digital media platforms might change the nature of political participation, particularly for people who are today just reaching voting age;
- how online media are creating both a new space and a new set of challenges for the conduct of political debate;
- how the shift towards a greater degree of social and political surveillance may alter the broader political landscape;
- how the myths of the digital sublime shape our views of "electronic democracy"; and
- how media and new media tools are central to advancing social and political economic change.

Keywords

- **alternative media**
- **blogroll**
- **branding**
- **democracy**
- **e-democracy**
- **non-governmental organizations (NGOs)**
- **open-source software**
- **prorogation**
- **structuration**
- **Web 2.0**

Web 2.0 Structuration and the End of Politics

One of the more persistent myths throughout the development of communication technology is that it would transform politics as we know it by bringing power closer to the people. (Mosco, 2004a, p. 98)

The supposed democratizing influence of the Internet is indeed a powerful myth of the digital sublime. It is attractive, says Mosco (2004a, p. 99), because it implies that the "fundamental insecurities" deeply embedded in traditional politics can be transcended, just as some believe that the Internet can obliterate the inequities of time and space. Despite the depressing and dystopian dimensions of the digital future possibilities, there are many analysts, commentators, politicians, and academics that make an argument that the Internet offers citizens the capacity to influence the democratic process in previously unforeseen ways (see, e.g., Tsagarousianou, Tambini, & Bryan, 1998).

This argument, about the democratic emancipatory potential of the Internet, highlights three key limitations in understanding traditional politics and new media. First, those who trumpet the Internet as levelling the political playing field limit their discussion of political activity to established political events and institutions, such as political parties and elections. Second, this approach is technologically determinist, as it tends to prioritize the power of the technology to transform or eliminate existing power relations in politics. Finally, it also ignores how use of the Internet for political activity may extend existing power relations and in fact create new ones.

Yet the idea that the Internet will become a revolutionary tool for citizens to control their own destiny still resonates with those who seek answers in response to evidence that young people are turned off by mainstream political bickering (see, e.g., Bryan, Tsagarousianou, & Tambini, 1998). The reality is that there is, in modern society, a shrinking of what communication theorists call a shared "public sphere"—the normatively "open" space where politics and debates about social issues are conducted. Within the capitalist market economy, there is a fundamental contradiction between the formal equality of political participation and the inequalities of income and opportunity that define the relationships of the market (Dahlgren, 1991; Schultz 1989, 1994, 1998). This has a particular impact on the media's relationship with political power—what Julianne Schultz (1998) and others describe as the "Fourth Estate."

The theory of the Fourth Estate suggests that the media can fulfil an unofficial "watchdog" role, in effect acting as a series of checks and balances on those who exercise power. But as we discussed in Chapter 10, this watchdog role has become lost among the "tensions, cracks and contradictions" (Dahlgren, 1991, p. 11) within the media and the broader society. Despite the best efforts of writers like Schultz, any revival of the Fourth Estate seems doomed by the dialectic that has created an unbridgeable fault line between the media's public service role and the profit motive that drives the commercial media (Hirst & Patching, 2005).

Unfortunately, rosy predictions of the "Internet as a revolutionary political tool" represent an idealization of politics and a worldview that denies the centrality of economic power in neo-liberal capitalist states today. In yet another extension of this economic power wielded by the mega-corporations, public politics can be rendered ineffectual (see, e.g., Tiffen, 1989, pp. 178–98). As McChesney's (2000b) political economy analysis suggests, "**democracy**" is tolerated by big business as long as real control is "off-limits to popular deliberation"—"that is, so long as it isn't democracy" (p.111). McChesney argues that those who believe that digital convergence alone can provide a "viable [online] public sphere" are "deluding themselves" (p. 183).

DEMOCRACY

Rule by the people, as distinct from monarchy (rule by a monarch), plutocracy (rule by the rich), oligarchy (rule by a few), and anarchy (the absence of rulers).

Leaps in Logic?

Approaches to democracy can be wide-ranging, and in any case, it is a constant "work in progress," to say the least. In chapters 2 and 9 we discussed neo-liberal, liberal-democratic, and radical-democratic approaches to democracy, and we offer a basic definition in this chapter to distinguish it in terms of where control and decision-making is concentrated. An idealized view of the democratizing power of the Internet is a hopeful prediction; however, it includes some heroic leaps in logic, and a great deal of wishful thinking. Particularly in the United States, such thinking fails to account for the stranglehold that entrenched corporate interests have over the American political system, not just its economic and regulatory system. For example, giant corporations, including all the big media players, bankroll American politicians with millions of dollars in campaign donations, other "in kind" contributions, and through the financing of SuperPACs (privately organized groups that raise money for candidates) that support or oppose candidates at arm's length. And, although the Canadian system of political funding does not currently legalize such donations, there is always pressure on it to open up and be more American in style. In this context, McChesney (2000b) suggests that any view of the Internet as being able to cut through this tangle of interconnected self-interest is "dubious at best" (p. 184). Like much of the rhetoric underpinning digital myths, such a view ignores and glosses over historical political realities, such as the following:

- The Internet is no less susceptible to being manipulated by political parties and sectional interest groups than the current system.
- The issues under consideration in politics online, such as polls and referenda, are still determined by those in power positions and thus do not necessarily address key issues for a broader community.
- Internet-based polling, referenda, or elections will be led by those who are most passionate about a given subject, but may still be largely ignored by the general public.
- The control of sites by those that wish to promote their own interests will greatly diminish the credibility of the polling results within political circles, deflating and undermining those who believe in e-democracy.

Rather than focusing solely and narrowly on political vehicles such as polls and simple votes as "measures" of democracy and a country's political health, we approach political communication using our political economic approach to focus on power relations, including those associated with the use of the Internet for political engagement. This approach aims to avoid the pitfalls of technological and institutional determinism by requiring a more holistic view of the relationship between politics and new media. Additionally, if we are to better understand the changes brought to bear by new media in the political environment, we need to look beyond how it may engage with the existing institutions of political campaigns and elections, and understand how citizen agency can and may alter these institutions, for good or for ill. This can be realized more effectively through an analysis of this relationship through the process of structuration.

In other words, to paraphrase Karl Marx, people make their own history, just not within conditions of their choosing (in Mosco, 2009, p. 185). To help you understand the process of structuration, it may be helpful to consider, for instance, that while you may be a citizen of Canada (or any other country), and thus have some rights accorded to you because of this, both the terms of the citizenship and the resulting rights are structures that were in place before you were born, or before you had the opportunity to participate in the decision-making

E-DEMOCRACY
The use of digital (e = electronic) technologies to enhance the participation of citizens in the democratic process.

STRUCTURATION
"describes a process by which structures are constituted out of human agency, even as they provide the very 'medium' of that constitution" (Mosco, 2009, p. 185).

around them. Yet, structures are not static; they are continually (re)made by humans, and thus are ever-changing. They are not discrete or separate from each other, but are overlapping and dynamic—even though they may not appear as such, particularly when they become hegemonic. Structures may be *formal* (such as laws, policies, regulations, e.g.), *formalized* (in institutions or organizations), or relatively *informal* (via social relations of class, gender or race, e.g.). The degree of agency that one can exercise is dependent on them, but the human ability to exercise this agency means that they can be changed.

A structuration approach is particularly helpful in the study of the relationship between politics and new media, as it allows us to better understand how the agency (or actions) of a diversity of actors—whether politicians, corporations, or social movements, to name just a few—are always working towards shifting power relations. Within this struggle, existing structures can work to both enable and constrain the actions of these actors. New media, such as the Internet and **Web 2.0**, are contemporary tools used in this process.

This chapter begins with a review of politics and how "new media" distinguished by its potential for interactivity is being used within existing structures—such as partisan politics, election campaigns, non-election political campaigns, and government institutions—to both reinforce and transform existing power relations. We then analyze political activism and how different social agents use new media tools in their efforts to change and challenge existing political power relations from outside established structures.

Agenda Setting Online: The Internet as an Election Campaign Tool

We need to recognize the remarkable changes that the interactive tele-communications age is producing in our political system. We need to under-stand the consequences of the march toward democratization. We need to deal with the promise and perils of the electronic republic. . . . In an electronic republic, it will be essential to look at politics from the bottom up as well as from the top down. (Grossman, 1999, p. 282)

How does the Internet—now entrenched in the machinations of Canadian campaigns—play a key role in agenda setting online? As we introduced in Chapter 4, in its most basic form, agenda setting means the transferring of selected or salient issues from and by the media to the public or audiences. Agenda setting is also closely linked to the "gatekeeper" model of the news media: the exercise of "selective control" over the types of items that make it onto the news agenda (Ward, 1995, p. 99). The electronic medium has adopted both agenda setting and gatekeeping and refined the process over many decades. If we can see how this control over the selection and placement of politics in the news occurs today, can we sustain an argument that in the digital world things will be "different," or "better"? Political reporting in most presidential (American) and parliamentary (Canadian) democracies has been reduced to the "sound bite," and for at least the last 20 years, campaign strategies have relied heavily on media management (B. Franklin, 1997, p. 248; Gitlin, 1991; Hargreaves, 2003; Tiffen 1989). Why should we believe that these same problems won't just migrate online?

In Canada, television has been around for just over 60 years and has long occupied a prominent, albeit contentious, place in shaping the country's most important issues. It has played this role for much of the twentieth century and, predictably, will continue to do so in the opening decades of this century. Thus it would be fair to claim that the past half-century, by and large,

---

WEB 2.0

The technological capability of the Internet and World Wide Web used to decentralize communication and facilitate interactivity between citizens, users, and audiences, either individually or in large numbers. "Web 2.0 basically refers to the transition from static HTML Web pages to a more dynamic Web that is more organized and is based on serving Web applications to users. . . . Over time Web 2.0 has been used more as a marketing term than a computer-science-based term. Blogs, wikis, and Web services are all seen as components of Web 2.0" (Webopedia, 2013, para. 1).

belonged to television broadcasting in the dispensing and proliferation of information, news, and entertainment. The traditional news media have always been a "strategic arena" in the "struggle for power" (Tiffen, 1989, p. 7) characterized by political point-scoring and electioneering.

At the emergence of the twenty-first century, though, politicians in Canada, following in the footsteps of their American counterparts, began to embrace the significance and power of using the Internet to reach constituents. The Internet has become an increasingly necessary tool due to its cost efficiency, relative lack of regulation control, production simplicity, and swift narrow-casting via active interaction with the individual, which makes it arguably, and potentially, the most innovative and powerful medium yet for narrowcasting, and for politicians to communicate directly with their constituents. Clearly, the Internet is here to stay, but so too, it seems, are the digital myths that promote the "Internet = democracy" line. We have to conclude, then, that there is some grain of "truth" in these myths that goes some way towards explaining their longevity.

It does not require a great deal of political astuteness to recognize the electoral advantages of catering to the needs of the voters—who may eventually become potential "cyber-voters." This is not so much a matter of being dictated to by the voting public, as it is a case of adapt or perish. Gary Selnow (1998) illustrates this point well when he comments that "we fear being left behind," which may explain why some campaigns got onto the Web by the mid-1990s. Moreover, not without coincidence, by early 1996, America Online (AOL) had announced that it had more than five million subscribers, a tenfold increase in just two years (Casey, 1996). Eric Limer (2011) reports that while AOL was up to five or six million customers in the first decade of the twenty-first century, the number of dial-up subscribers rested at 3.5 million as of late 2011.

In the United States, the Internet and particular social media were marshalled more effectively and earlier than in Canada. In 2008, the US Democratic presidential campaign, "Obama for America" (OFA), very effectively used social media to develop its voter base, engage volunteers at the local level across the country, as well as fundraise from the grassroots (A. Clarke, 2010, p. 2). The same approach was applied in the 2012 presidential election campaign, where President Obama was again using social media as a key fundraising tool. The campaign reported that it raised $114 million in primarily grassroots donations in the month of August 2012 alone (MacAskill, 2012).

In Canada, the uptake of the interactive nature of social media in political campaigns has been slower, particularly at the national level, although Web 2.0 tools like Facebook and Twitter have had a significant impact on local elections. The Calgary mayoral election results in the fall of 2010 are just one example of this. The election was won by a relatively unknown candidate, Naheed Nenshi, who, in the last two weeks of the campaign, surged in the polls and successfully beat out the two front-running candidates for the position of mayor. Much of his success has been credited to his use of social media to engage young voters. What is important to recognize about Nenshi's approach isn't just that he attracted younger voters, but how he did so. He built on existing political networks outside of party politics to engage a previously disengaged voting block. He harnessed his social media campaign by building off of existing city-wide networks committed to issues such as combating poverty, racism, pollution, and urban sprawl, just to name a few (Steward, 2010). The importance of building off these existing networks was that Nenshi's team could develop on the foundation of an already existing shared interest and trust pre-established by those involved with these issues (Finch, Varella, & Walker, 2010). The result was that he engaged those who were politically active, but not in the traditional partisan ways. This led to his victory by more than 28,000 votes (ibid.), and marked a 50 per cent increase in voter turnout (Steward, 2010).

New technologies in election campaigns are not always used to expand the voter base; sometimes they are used to suppress it. It is important to consider that new media tools used to manipulate political outcomes go beyond the Internet as well. This was the case with the results

For Real?

"Pierre Poutine" to the Rescue?

Reports of election irregularities surfaced in 2012 that involved mysterious phone calls to voters on the day of the 2011 general election. As the story unfolded, it merely seemed that election campaigning had made the transition to technology-enabled strategies. But it also revealed how the speed and allure of technology can interfere with the democratic process.

These automated "robocalls" targeted eight ridings in Ontario where Liberal candidates were leading Conservatives by a small margin in the polls. The calls, allegedly from Elections Canada, told voters that a change was made to the polling stations where they were to vote. The calls took place late on election day, which meant that it was too late for some of those who received these calls to vote in all the confusion they caused.

After receiving more than 800 citizen complaints from across the country, Elections Canada began to investigate one of the ridings—in Guelph, Ontario—for what could be a violation of the Canada Elections Act. Elections Canada has this authority as an independent and non-partisan body that reports to Parliament and that has the democratic task of ensuring that Canadians can exercise their rights to vote.

Two investigative journalists from Postmedia, which owned 10 newspapers across Canada, broke the news that Elections Canada was looking into the robocalls made in Guelph. Once their story was printed, about 31,000 more citizens contacted Elections Canada with their concerns about the voting process in their own ridings. Elections Canada even added a button to its home page to "Report a Fraudulent Call." The fact that the robocalls took place in ridings where the governing Conservatives stood to lose seemed to implicate that political party in making the calls. At that point, the Conservatives had two successive minority governments (in 2006 and 2008) and were looking to achieve a majority, and polls showed that Ontario was a key battleground that could give them the few extra victories they needed to form a majority.

Enter "Pierre Poutine."

Someone using the clearly false and insulting name of Pierre Poutine (poutine being a dish of French fries, cheese curds, and gravy that is popular in Quebec) and a false Quebec address implicated a Quebecker in paying a call-service company in Edmonton to produce the robocall messages. "Poutine" used prepaid disposable credit cards and a proxy server in Saskatchewan, which allows users to conceal their identities.

In spring 2012, the Council of Canadians, a public-interest group, launched a legal challenge to overturn the elections in seven of the ridings across the country in which robocalls took place.

of the 2011 federal election and what appeared to be a widespread voter suppression campaign that used electronic telephone systems to undermine the basic precepts of democracy in Canada.

Online Politics and the Reportorial Community

There's more opportunity for DIY communication in cyberspace, lending itself to democratic voices finding an audience. Perhaps it's more democratic online because independent media sources who don't have money for printing can make news without hard copy. (B. Fitzgibbon, personal communication, 15 March 2006)

Democracy Watch, an independent citizen advocacy group, pointed out that Elections Canada had received more than 2,000 complaints since 2004 and called on the commissioner for more transparency and openness by releasing its results and rulings and making it illegal to allow anonymous robocalls. The chief electoral officer appeared before a parliamentary committee, composed of members of Parliament from all parties, to discuss the committee's concerns about the allegations of wrongdoing. Beyond that, since Elections Canada performs its investigations in private, it was unclear when and how this potentially serious breach of the Canada Elections Act would be resolved.

As bizarre as the ongoing saga of the mysterious Pierre Poutine and the robocalls seems, it represents serious issues in how we handle election campaigning that is enabled by technology, but that is also part of the permanent campaign, which has now successfully migrated online with even quicker and broader reach. Although technology may mask them, the issues here are as plain and simple as they were back in the days of the campaigns of Sir John A. Macdonald, but now they're more difficult to identify and resolve. If the current federal government—or any government—uses illegal or underhanded tactics that do not comply with, or even in some cunning way circumvent, the letter of election laws, it is breach of public trust.

The issue of voter suppression, which is what we can call a tactic to prevent citizens from voting, is a curious political tactic at a time when voter turnout in elections is slowly but surely dropping. Levels of voter turnout are usually the highest in federal elections, but decline at lower levels, with municipal politics having the lowest turnout. Nevertheless, federal election turnout is near its lowest ever, at 61.1 per cent in 2011. In the 1992 election, it was 71.8 per cent; in 1962, it stood at 79 per cent. Voter suppression is used in ridings where the party employing the tactic has reached its maximum growth within a political district, yet is still not receiving enough votes to win a race. The losing party then has a choice of either giving up on that political district for the time being or discouraging citizens from voting for the other party's candidate. Running a boring campaign that doesn't electrify the electorate and make citizens want to run out and vote is one tactic and, although a repugnant way to present one's politics, it is technically acceptable by virtue of not being illegal. However, when a candidate uses illegal or unethical means to suppress the vote, as in the robocalls used in the 2011 election—no one denies that such calls took place, just who was behind them—voter suppression cannot be part of a healthy democracy.

Pierre Poutine is one fictional character who doesn't need a sequel.

As we discussed in Chapter 10, there's no doubt that digital media convergence is shifting the borders of the reportorial community. Blogging has become influential in politics and agenda setting and, as Bec Fitzgibbon mentions, do-it-yourself journalism appears to be thriving in cyberspace. Undoubtedly, one of the most significant consequences of online political campaigning is that it has the potential to support a new kind of journalism. However, the projected power of journalists in a Web 2.0 environment needs to be examined carefully. Political journalism already faces many challenges, some related to the state of contemporary media and others related to the process of media-making itself. The mere act of transferring its organizational structures and journalistic norms and practices online will not make political journalism more democratic.

For instance, as Fred Fletcher (in press) notes, in Canada, not much has changed in election coverage by journalists since the 1970s, and recent elections have seen cuts to the amount of money spent by media owners on such costs as the party leaders' cross-country tours. Christopher Waddell (2009) has noted that too much time altogether is spent on following the leaders, which, in effect, then frames the content and non-critical tone of media coverage. In addition, although more coverage of policy has found its way into media stories, reportorial opinion has also increased and focuses on the strategy that lies behind the announcement, rather than on the content, of the political announcements (ibid., pp. 222–4).

Moreover, we cannot simply apply the blueprint of American political journalism and its use of new and social media to the Canadian environment. While the United States has fully integrated these media into its politics, the 2011 general election here saw Facebook and YouTube used by political parties, but mostly for the purpose of fundraising targeted at those already-committed voters, rather than for communicating policy or campaign messaging (Francoli, Greenberg, & Waddell, 2011, pp. 231–3). Using the 2011 election as a gauge, it is clear that Canadian political parties are still learning to cope with the challenge of the two-way interaction that new and social media require, and "netizens" are currently not equal partners engaging in a democratic flow of ideas with political candidates.

In addition, political journalists are dealing with the use of social media by citizens in communicating breaking news to friends, contact lists, and the public. It is especially irksome when citizens report on issues and events that the mainstream media did not know about or choose to report. D. Travers Scott (2008) has identified many political stories that "failed to ignite" (p. 271) the media. These include the risks of e-voting in the United States and the 2004 Iraqi prison-abuse scandal (p. 276). In the London bombings of 2005, those caught in the subway texted and sent photos from their mobile phones, giving us the first accounts of the emergency and its death and destruction. Later in this chapter, we examine alternative media as a vital conduit for bringing untold stories to the attention of the public and the development by those media of new ways of conducting journalism.

Are Bloggers the Future of Democracy?

Individually they may not have many readers, but when you multiply them by several million weblogs, there is a huge audience out there. (Knobel, 2005, p. 54)

While we don't want to underestimate the collective power of "several million" bloggers, as we discussed in Chapter 10, we have to remain a little sceptical about the extent of their influence. If there are, as Lance Knobel says, millions of blogs, there are probably at least hundreds of thousands that are boring, irrelevant, or just plain stupid. There are probably a few hundred that are really influential, and several thousand more that might catch someone's interest, or be focused on politics, but the vast majority will not register with most people.

Nevertheless, there is a vanguard of mainstream journalists who have embraced blogging in different ways, despite the challenge of increasing their daily duties. For example, the *Toronto Star*'s Antonia Zerbisias was an early blogger. She focuses now on selected issues in her current blog, "Broadsides." Her posted list of categories highlights her priority issues, which include politics, reproductive rights, and violence against women. In the tradition of blogger networking, Zerbisias (2012) has also posted a **blogroll** of blogs by "unruly women (and men) I love" and other media sources, including **alternative media** such as *The Tyee* and *Straight Goods*.

BLOGROLL
A sidebar list of favourite, similar, or recommended blogs on a blogger's site.

ALTERNATIVE MEDIA
"Media that try to contribute to emancipatory societal transformation by providing critical media content, content that questions dominative social relations" (Sandoval & Fuchs, 2010, p. 147). This may include challenging or altering other structural conditions of inequality, including the way media is produced and distributed.

CBC journalist Kady O'Malley introduced the concept of "live blogging" to Canadian political journalism. In live blogging, the journalist blogs at the scene of the action and updates every few minutes, so that audiences can get a play-by-play analysis of what is happening in real time. For Parliament-based journalists like O'Malley, live blogging takes place in various venues, including the press gallery in the House of Commons, news conferences at the press gallery and all-party parliamentary committees (many of which sit every day during parliamentary sessions). O'Malley has live blogged on such contentious issues as the government's purchase of F-35 fighter planes, which were much more expensive than the government had publicized, and on citizen problems with getting information from the government under the Freedom of Information and Protection of Privacy Act. She also live blogs at the sessions of the Public Accounts committee, where many government budgetary decisions are discussed.

Live blogging requires an ability to summarize key, but complicated, points on the spot, and convey them in Tweet-length sentences at a rapid pace. It also helps to have a light touch on heavy-duty political issues. For example, one of O'Malley's blog posts was related to the quest by former Liberal MP Borys Wrzesnewskyj to overturn the election results in his former riding due to irregularities in voting related to robocalls. In late 2012, in a close decision, the Supreme Court of Canada voted to uphold the election results. O'Malley (2012b) wrote, "#Borys says that the next election—and elections after that—will be run 'very differently'. As such, he thinks Canadians won. #EtobCtr." On the lighter side, and at a different time, in a post directed at members of Parliament, she wrote, "Rise and shine, MPs! A long day of democracy awaits!" (O'Malley, 2012a).

Twitter is also becoming a source of information for journalists who can tantalize followers with tidbits of information on upcoming issues and stories, while citizens tweet journalists to comment on stories already in the public sphere or to add information, whether relevant or not. For example, Canadian Press (CP) journalist Jennifer Ditchburn tweeted about an ongoing story about misleading calls made to voters in the 2011 general election: "Chief electoral officer says he received 700#robocall complaints." This tweet serves to both give information and stimulate interest in that ongoing political controversy. For the Canadian Press, which is a content provider to other Canadian media, tweets add a personal touch and connection to its readers that would otherwise be absent, since CP is not community based.

New Media, Speed, and the Permanent Campaign

We have been discussing new media in the context of a traditional election campaign. However, over time, election campaigns have changed considerably, especially since the emergence of the Internet as an everyday tool. The Internet has heightened the speed at which society now engages in everything from shopping to private relationships. Naturally, political parties and governments have also felt the impact of speed as an important priority in getting out messages to citizens. In Canada and elsewhere, the length of election campaigns has steadily declined over several decades. In the 1980s, federal election campaigns were between seven and nine weeks long. Our most recent campaigns were only five or six.

Generally, governments call elections at times that favour them and so have an advantage in preparations to go to the polls, such as engaging consultants, booking the airplane for the leader's tour, and arranging for advertising contracts. In fact, it is normal for governments to begin thinking about re-election about halfway through their mandate, which in Canada is no longer than five years. (Naturally, governments can choose to go to the polls more quickly, and often have in recent years.) The halfway point signals the beginning of election preparation

Focus on Research

Did Bloggers Change the Course of Canadian History?

Networked political blogging has a relatively short history in Canada—usually pegged at the time of the 2004 federal election—yet it has already played an important role in our politics. Interestingly, political blogging was first used outside of formal politics, as members of Parliament were slow to blog or use other forms of social media, so political blogging networks grew around MPs, rather than with or through them. But make no mistake, political blogging has always been partisan, linked at least loosely to the ideologies of different political parties. In fact, specific ideological slants are characteristic of political blogging. Not only are political bloggers partisan, but they also tend to network with other like-minded partisan bloggers. One such network, the Blogging Tories, has more than 300 individual sites listed on one blogroll, and has been particularly active and influential—but more on that later.

In addition to their partisan links, political bloggers tend to participate in politics offline and be active in their communities. It is a natural step from activism offline to networking with others online who share one's politics. One explanation for the large number of Blogging Tories is that those bloggers tend to have an individualistic streak that is a prominent feature of conservatism. However, blogging is not a one-way street. It is also a social form of communication that elicits a response and is well-suited to foster political and partisan conversation, dialogue, and debate.

The Conservative Party was the first major party out of the blocks to use blogging as a political tool. In the 2004 campaign, the party sent its media materials to the Blogging Tories to pass on the information through their own links. It is not unusual for the Conservatives to be technologically advanced in campaigning, as they have strong ties with their sister Republican Party in the United States. The latter party is known for an election machine that communicated its views through earlier technological platforms, such as television.

The opposition parties—the NDP, the Liberals, and the Bloc Québécois—followed more slowly, but all parties were making use of blogs and building their own networks by the 2006 election.

Professor Greg Elmer of Infoscape Research Lab at Ryerson University has researched and reflected on the first stage of political blogging in Canada as based on the kind of relationship the partisan bloggers already had with their respective political parties. In 2007, he noted that the Blogging Tories were sensitive to having their views equated with those of the Conservative Party. In contrast, the Liberal bloggers—the Liblogs—wanted to stay in the loop when it came to communications and decision-making in their party, while, according to Elmer (2007), the NDP's first bloggers and the party together formed "a democratic community with a mission of sorts" (p. 18). The NDP bloggers, at first housed within the party website, later diversified into other discussion groups, including blogging on rabble.ca, a non-partisan progressive site. Another blogging site is the Progressive Bloggers, known as "ProgBlogs" (📺 www.progressivebloggers.ca), which is a broad group of those diverse bloggers who see themselves as progressive or "left" of Prime Minister Harper's conservatism.

However, the next stage in networked political blogging grew out of the rising fortunes of conservatism in general and the Conservative Party specifically as the Liberal Party's hold on government, which held majority mandates between 1993 and 2004, was coming to an end. This is when networked partisan blogging made its mark on Canadian history.

In the October 2008 general election, the Conservative Party was re-elected as a minority government with Stephen Harper as prime minister. At the time, the global economy was becoming more fragile, and there were worries that the Canadian economy would be affected. However, the government's post-election economic statement did not address this potentially devastating situation. (A side issue was that the government also announced its intention to end the long-time assistance given to political parties that was considered a democratic equalizer for smaller parties to have a voice.) Two of the three opposition parties, the Liberals and the New Democratic Party, jointly announced that together they intended to form a coalition government. The other party in Parliament, the Bloc Québécois, agreed to vote with them against the government and support (but not join) the coalition.

Although such arrangements are normal in a parliamentary democracy—the UK's coalition government took power in 2010, and Canada has had coalition governments in its history—in a controversial move, Prime Minister Harper prorogued the new parliamentary session rather than lose the vote and have his government fall.

In the days following the fledgling coalition's announcement of its intention, Harper and his government mounted a campaign to stir Conservatives to action, urging them to contribute to a Facebook page, go to rallies, call in to talk shows, sign petitions, and write their MPs to express their opposition (De Souza, 2008). The Prime Minister's Office (PMO) sent an email to its members of Parliament urging them to "use every single tool and medium at [their] disposal," tools that included a package of communications products of their "key messages, talking points for use with local media, talk radio scripts for [their] local activists, a letter to the editor for local media and two 'Just the Facts' documents" (Bryden, 2008, p. 1).

One key Conservative blogger, Stephen Taylor, with a blogroll of more than 300 Conservative sites and ties to Conservative organizations, announced the launch of RallyforCanada.ca. Taylor called for support by email, on Facebook and Twitter, and on the Conservative mainstay of talk radio. To get an idea of how active the Blogging Tories were overall, according to Taylor, posts by Blogging Tories numbered 25,390 in 2008. Within 48 hours of calling for grassroots action, and just after a televised address by the prime minister, Taylor reported more than 127,000 hits on the rally website. Another website reported almost 207,000 names on an anti-coalition petition (🔲 freedomnation.blogspot.com).

Although there is no direct line connecting the PMO campaign and Taylor to what the Blogging Tories were saying, at the same time, the bloggers were talking about the coalition and the rallies—a lot—as well as sharing information from Taylor's website and, more obliquely, from the PMO material. It is believed that about 20 (mostly anti-coalition) rallies were held across Canada within a week. Within days, public opinion research showed the Conservatives' approval ratings were soaring. The success of the rallies themselves speaks to the ability of blogging and other non-traditional media to play a timely role in activating a network at a critical time, both online and offline.

In the midst of this staged upheaval, the prime minister asked for and was granted, in a very controversial decision, the **prorogation** of Parliament by the governor general, thereby saving his government. It is clear from this case that blogs can help construct a political agenda or shape political debate. It also demonstrates how online networks can quickly spread misleading information on how Parliament works. It was a victory for partisan blogging networks, but a worrisome development for parliamentary democracy.

Discussion Questions

1. How is blogging similar to or different from traditional forms of news?

2. Is blogging subject to the same practices of news media, such as agenda setting, gatekeeping, and framing practices that were identified in Chapter 4?

3. Does blogging contribute to convergence or narrowcasting?

4. Why would a government exercise prorogation?

PROROGATION

Ends a parliamentary session, at which time all business comes to a stop. For example, all bills that have not been passed or received royal assent must then be reintroduced in the next parliamentary session. The governor general prorogues Parliament on the advice of the prime minister.

and has been referred to in political-science circles as the beginning of the "long campaign" leading to the formal election period (Clarke, Jenson, LeDuc, & Pammett, 1996).

As discussed in previous chapters, technology of various kinds—from the use of the first complex photocopiers to computer applications that animate and restructure images—has played a role in speeding up the possibilities for political messages to become assembled and disseminated instantly to large groups, as well as to individualized, targeted citizens. The impact of speed in election campaigning now dissolves the boundaries between the formal five- or six-week campaign and the rest of the mandate. Moving beyond the traditional long campaign halfway through the mandate results in what we identified earlier as the "permanent campaign." Other conditions than technology enable this shift as well. Pippa Norris' (2002) research explains that the fragmentation of television audiences into specialized segments, the professionalization of campaign workers, increased and sophisticated marketing tools, and the ever-growing use of the Internet together assisted in making the permanent campaign possible (2002, Ch. 8).

Practically, the permanent campaign, enabled by the Internet, demarcates *quick* responses from *instant* responses in politics. Already using social media for personal use, citizens can now initiate, receive, and react to political messages in real time. Thus the stakes are even higher for political candidates aspiring to win public office. At politically tense moments, such as televised leader debates, it is not only political consultants and assistants to politicians who grab their handheld devices and tweet positive and reassuring messages to cover the gaffe of their candidate or emphasize the foolhardiness in a statement made by the opposing candidate; now citizens can do the same with their own friends and by "talking back" to candidates and political forums through new and social media.

In one of the televised debates in the 2012 election in the United States, for example, presidential candidate Mitt Romney, trying to bolster his support among American women, said that as governor of Massachusetts, he had wanted to see more women in higher positions in the state's government and that his staff had brought him "binders full of women." This wording became the instant subject of a myriad of email memes and videos on YouTube and other social media that produced mash-ups of binders and women together with slogans. Some were raunchy, others were playful and merely funny, but all of them instantly gave many Americans a negative image of the candidate who wanted to be their president. Not only did it indicate the speed of which an image can change but it also indicated how the image itself is prioritized in politics.

The technologically enabled speed of a permanent campaign has other impacts as well that are not directly related to elections, but that have changed politics considerably. When a government engages in permanent campaigning, less time is spent on actually governing. In addition, governing is itself also subject to the permanent campaign in an environment in which instant communication can reap political rewards for governments by framing issues quickly and setting the agenda. During regime changes—that is, when the political party in government changes after an election—the new government wants to set its own course and establish its own rules of engagement, both to differentiate itself from the previous government and to create a positive image for itself.

Since 2006, when the Conservative Party replaced the Liberals as the federal government for the first time in 13 years, the new government has made many changes to establish itself in the minds of Canadians as the natural ruling party. This has included changing the look of government online presence to favour the colour blue, the colour of the Conservative Party, over the colour red, the colour of the Liberal party, which is also the colour of the Canadian flag. The new government also added a blue background to many of its websites, often featuring sky and sea, and often uses the slogan "The True North Strong and Free," a line from our national anthem. In this way, by changing Canada's **branding**, the Conservatives subtly remind citizens that they are now the elected government. The new government also changed the language it used in its communication with the public by calling itself the "Harper government." Although political parties are free to define themselves as they wish, it is unusual for parties in government, where it must serve all citizens, to use public money—as the current government has in advertising programs and services—in such a partisan way.

These and other changes are part of the government's permanent campaign strategy in an effort to become the hegemonic party of Canada. New and social media provide an excellent array of possibilities and means for governments to accomplish such strategies both quickly and deeply, even as they are contentious.

Interactivity and Power: A Strength of the Internet?

For the individual and organizations—public, private, or non-profit—the Internet has created the digital myth that we are empowered with a sense of being in touch with the rest of the community. Additionally, this myth emphasizes that not only can we as netizens be in touch with others in our communities but we can also become more engaged in politics and political activity. Interactivity has the potential of shifting the power of the relationship between politicians and citizens from a mediated one controlled by media companies, and it provides more opportunities for citizens to communicate and participate with elected representatives.

According to the myths of the digital sublime, what better way is there to change "old" politics than to communicate directly with the people via the Internet? A news conference means having your issues mediated by journalists, thus leaving traditional media as the gatekeeper to sift through and interpret the information that seems most salient. The Internet is not only a tool that allows you to determine which issues on your agenda are most newsworthy but it also, better still for politicians, enables you to communicate directly with potential voters any time, anywhere. Never before has a medium been so impressive in its ability to accommodate the ideas and needs of its audience (Paletz, 1999; Parenti, 1999; Selnow, 1998).

Like other aspects of cybermythology, however, we have to interpret these notions with a certain amount of bubble-bursting scepticism. One of our key arguments throughout *Communication and New Media* has been that narrowcasting further fragments the audience of *consumers* for commercial purposes. We can transpose this disaggregating effect onto our discussion of politics to suggest that, far from constituting an active and organized collective, the shift of politics online may further fragment the audience of *citizens*. Some, like Peter Dahlgren (1991), have suggested that this is a positive move that creates "dynamic alternative public spheres" (p. 14) in the vacuum left by the decline of traditional political discourse. Others, such as Neil Postman (1993), argue the opposite: "Bureaucracies, expertise and technical machinery become the principal means by which Technopoly hopes to control information and thereby provide itself with intelligibility and order" (p. 91).

Canadian scholar Darin Barney (2008) develops a more nuanced critique of digital myths relevant to social media and politics. He argues that the traditional concerns about information, communication, and participation are no longer the central power struggles that are facing citizens in a world of an abundance of new media and the information they provide. Social media applications such as Facebook, Twitter, YouTube, Wikipedia, and others allow citizens to like, share, and vote for their support or opposition of a myriad of causes and provide an over-abundance of opportunities for citizens to become informed. What Barney argues is that both being informed and passive participants through these applications do not replace political action or replace

BRANDING

Assigns an entity, such as a business, its own unique identity and attributes, which can then be used to associate that identity positively with the products the business produces. Branding has broadened to include political parties, states, and governments, which can use their brand in their publicity and campaigns to identify them with those positive qualities to gain support from citizens.

judgement and activism, two fundamental principles of radical democratic engagement (ibid., p. 96). He posits that where once issues of information, communication, and participation were (before the new media era) central democratic goals, we are now in a period where we need to develop a more nuanced way of understanding the power relations between what Canadian Jodi Dean (2005) refers to as "communicative capitalism" and its control over these goals and a means of harnessing emerging media technologies in more democratic directions (Barney, 2008, p. 103).

Barney (2008) also draws an important distinction, that we have highlighted here, between *politics*, "understood as partisan competition for the offices of government" (p. 94), and *the political*, "as that which exposes the distribution and operation of power in its myriad forms and relationships and that which opens spaces of judgement, difference and contest" (ibid.), which is thus inherently linked to economics. The digital mythology posits that new media applications can assist in diversifying the actors involved in the former, while also encouraging more citizens to be the latter. One area where this is most apparent is in the claims made about how new media tools can, through e-democracy, overcome space and time to connect a political populace over a large geography.

E-Democracy: A Digital Renaissance?

Can e-democracy overcome the tyranny of distanciation? Much like Americans who lament the distance of tyranny between them and Washington, Canadians are often heard expressing their cynicism about Ottawa's ability, or lack thereof, to relate to the rest of the country. Can the digital myth that the Internet reduces the distance to immeasurably small tolerances overcome the tyranny of separation in a vast country like Canada? The irony is that, according to the myths, in the "electronic age," the Internet has actually bridged distance and time, thus dramatically bringing us closer to those who govern us (Grossman, 1999). This is not a new claim, but one that has been repeated throughout the twentieth century about each emerging technology, whether the telegraph, telephone, television, or Internet.

In recent elections, we have witnessed a disjuncture between the myth of new media overcoming political distance and the policies that govern the electoral process. Specifically, Elections Canada, in order to limit voter influencing, has traditionally forbidden the reporting of election results from Eastern Canada before the polls close in Western Canada. The Internet has challenged this rule, with a number of people posting early results before the polls closed in British Columbia. The concern is that with close to 60 per cent of the seats in the east, knowledge of early results could lead to strategic voting on the part of groups in the west (Teixeira, 2011). In response to recent attempts to get around its rules, Elections Canada instituted staggered voting times in the 2011 federal election, which left only 30 minutes between the closure of eastern and British Columbia polls.

There have been a variety of efforts to harness new media in aid of e-democracy and e-government projects in Canada. The appeal of this is to be able to more effectively provide services to Canadians across the country, while reducing the cost of operating facilities in various remote locations throughout the country. Additionally, e-government projects have taken up a theme of "open government," focusing on efforts to provide citizens with a larger array of government information, as well as provide more opportunities for public participation. At the federal level, the most common e-government application is the widely adopted online tax filing system developed by the Canada Revenue Agency (CRA; Cuddihey & Gordon, 2005).

The take up of e-government initiatives is more developed at both the provincial and the municipal level. Provincially, both Ontario and British Columbia have launched ambitious e-government initiatives with varying degrees of success. In Ontario, the provincial government relaunched its commitment to an e-government strategy for electronic service delivery in May 2011 (Government Services, 2011; 🖥 www.mgs.gov.on.ca/en/IAndIT/STEL02_046918.html).

This followed a rough start with a scandal-plagued effort at developing an eHealth system that digitized the health records of all Ontarians. In British Columbia, the government launched its "Open Government" initiative in 2011, focusing on providing better access to government information, and it has recently opened up "citizen consultation" on "digital service delivery in BC" as tied to its proposed "BC Services Card" (a digitally enhanced identification card; BC Newsroom, 2013) that will likely increase the amount of information that the provincial government (and ergo federal and municipal governments?) may compile and access. There has been more success in the roll out of e-government initiatives at the local or municipal level with efforts to engage citizens more directly in decision-making around infrastructure investments and budgeting. One example of this is in Hamilton, Ontario, where a participatory budget process around decisions about how to spend infrastructure dollars in individual wards has gone online through openbudget.ca.

While there is significant public expenditure at all levels of government around e-government, the scale of influence by citizens into the process remains limited. The information and services available online are still largely determined by governments, not through a more interactive sharing of power with citizens. Rather, the role of citizenship seems to be diminishing as the service provision and information infrastructure development for e-government is contracted out to the private sector. For example, with the CRA's online tax filing, citizens are placed at a greater distance from government, as they are required to purchase commercial tax software to be able to complete their online returns. There are other delays tied to a shift in e-government related to real issues around the transparency of contracting in the development of the systems, privacy protections, and surveillance (A. Clarke, 2010). Finally, although the digital mythology around e-government posits that it will reduce space and time in such a vast country, to date, the greatest successes in e-government applications have been more localized at the municipal level, and there are other significant limitations given that the "assumption that all Canadians are engaged in online activities and accessing online materials" (Middleton, Veenhof, & Leith, 2010, p. 22) is not supported by sustained analyses of individual use (ibid.).

Inequality of Access

> *The question of access is critical to the hopes of the civic networking movement, because, if certain groups either cannot, or simply do not participate in the electronic public sphere—women, the poor, etc.—ICTs will mirror problems of the old media—i.e., exclusion. (Bryan et al., 1998, p. 15)*

It is on this basis that the fallacy of the digital mythology is exposed: Access to the necessary infrastructure is not available to some social groups. In a capitalist world, based on profit rather than need, this is an almost insurmountable problem. If the experts and the media are to be believed, the current situation in Canada is such that information and communications technologies are pervading every stratum of society, to the point that we cannot seem to escape them. Yet if knowledge were to be equated with power, then there are certainly groups in our society who are powerless, for there are some who are not even aware of such technological innovations, let alone possess the knowledge or the means necessary to access them.

According to results published by Statistics Canada, despite the continued strong increases in the growth rates of Internet use in the last few years, there still exists lesser access to technology and a slower uptake among those in the lower income brackets. While the 2010 "Canadian Internet Use Survey" reported that almost 95 per cent of top income (more than $87,000) households used the Internet, less than 60 per cent of lower income ($30,000 or less) households had the same usage (Statistics Canada, 2010a). When assessing which Canadians are more likely to access government services online, there are still significant gaps in access, with less than half of Canadians using these services, among them those who are younger and have achieved the highest education levels (ibid.). As Catherine Middleton, Ben Veenhof, and Jordan Leith's (2010) research underscored, what this demonstrates is that e-government services are not necessarily breaking down traditional barriers to access to information.

In fact, there appears to be a contrary pattern in the Canadian government's approach to government online services. While it has communicated its interest in expanding government services online, it is not interested in ensuring that a greater number and diversity of Canadians have access to those services, as exemplified by the 2012 cuts to the Community Access Program (CAP) that provided funding for Internet access in public spaces like libraries and community centres, particularly in rural and remote Canadian communities (CBC News, 2012b). In addition, the latest federal government's restructuring of online access to government information is meant to reduce the number of access points to the whole range of government departments and channel them through the smallest gateway, with the likely effect of decreasing access to government while increasing its control over surveillance and content (Fekete, 2013).

While access to the Internet and government services online are examples of some of the extended limitations of e-democracy, the question of access itself is important to unpack and to understand in more detail. As Barney (2008) noted above, there is an abundance of information available online, but the question of access to this information continues to plague the mythology of digital democracy. Leslie Regan Shade and Andrew Clement (2000) highlight that we need to consider a more complex and multidimensional definition of access that addresses the features of digital media, such as the ability to receive as well as create content. Shade and Clement argue that we should consider access through the "Access Rainbow" metaphor that involves seven steps, including (1) access to carriage facilities (such as cable or DSL [digital subscriber line]), (2) devices (e.g., computers or mobile devices), (3) software tools (using social media), (4) content and services (as creator and audience), (5) service and access providers (e.g., media corporations such as Bell, Rogers, and Shaw), (6) literacy and social facilitation, and (7) governance. Shortcomings and pitfalls notwithstanding, their argument is that it is crucial for citizens to have access to all these aspects of new media for a level of equality and, in the political context, for the ability to function in an effective democratic way.

One example of political activism that has emerged over the last few years around access has been the campaign to protect network neutrality in Canadian communication policy as reviewed in Chapter 9. OpenMedia.ca, a non-profit organization based out of British Columbia, has successfully taken on the issues of carriage facilities, service and access providers, and governance in their work to engage Canadians to participate in the CRTC review of issues related to network neutrality policy. Part of OpenMedia's success in this campaign has been how it has marshalled new media tools, such as Facebook, to build a national profile for the issue, as well as to encourage Canadians to participate in the regulatory process itself.

Cyberdemocracy: A Digital Myth?

For a politician, the ability to communicate may be a key criterion in determining political success, but equally important is the access to information (Schwartz, 1996). The digital myth suggests that access to and the value of information, hence knowledge, can be equated with power; it then extrapolates from this that the Internet has empowered us both as individuals and as organizations (Flew, 2005, p. 187). This is seen as an embodied feature of digital technology that can steer us towards an era where an entire global network of resources and freedom of information for many appears on the horizon.

The cybermythology also states that the digital media have the power to shrink both time and space (see Cassell, 1993; Giddens, 1995). This implies that the Internet may also become a "place" where our personal ideology; cultural, ethical, and social identities; political structures; and rules are not dictated by the hegemony of the conventional, mainly unilateral, mass media. At the same time, the roll out of "e-democracy" trials in several countries may also contribute to the growth of social surveillance and continued commodification of citizenship. In Europe, the existence of a techno-legal time-gap in the regulation of virtual cities and e-democracy projects has been recognized, particularly around privacy and the distribution of "offensive" material (see Bryan et al., 1998, pp. 14–16). In the British context, the government wants to issue "digital certificates" and "smart cards" to citizens to enable them to participate in e-democracy, but advocates like Ian Kearns (2002) also recognize the digital dialectic and the "potentially serious political consequences" that come with the deployment of more government surveillance technologies that can potentially "undermine privacy" and "threaten equality in new ways" (p. 3). At the same time, he is forced to concede that they are "crucial" to the "security and integrity" of online information (ibid.).

Political Activism, Social Movements, and Democratic Media

The use of new media in politics is one way in which there is a transformation in the relationship between the governed and citizens. Another, as noted earlier, is related to political activism. This is manifest in a number of ways—for example, by using existing commercial (and thus commercially compromised) social networking tools like Facebook and YouTube to inform and coordinate oppositional action (e.g., in Tunisia and Egypt in 2011), and by using these same technologies as forums for political activism in and of themselves. Additionally, new media can be used to facilitate the growth and transformation of alternative media as democratic media. In the case of political activism, digital mythology highlights numerous advantages to be gained from convergence, not the least of which is the much freer, hence more democratic, dissemination of information. It is more democratic because the Internet's very structure is communication from many to many, unlike more traditional media, like newspapers and television, which are from one to many. Democratic media (of which the Internet is undoubtedly a part of) have the potential to be used to broaden the numbers of those producing, sharing, and distributing content, as well as in linking media content with political action.

There are a number of recent examples of the link between democratic media efforts that use the Internet and Web 2.0 technology to develop and advance social movements around the world. While social networking has become an important tool for many organizing social action, there are both benefits and challenges to this form of political action.

Perhaps the most popularized instance of the link between social networks and political activism emerged from the Arab Spring in 2011. Facebook, YouTube, Twitter, and other social networking sites were credited as central instruments in both mobilizing people within Tunisia and Egypt, as well as informing the global community about what was going on in the streets (see Figure 13.1). While in some cases these social networking applications were celebrated as causing the revolutionary change, later assessments were less technologically determinist in their analysis of how Facebook and other networking tools were important in political activism. Writers at the time (Gladwell, 2010, 2011; Pollock, 2011, e.g.) recognized the importance of these tools facilitating and amplifying the causes of the revolutions, but these authors also noted that political activism at this scale "requires deep [community] roots and strong [social] ties" (Gladwell, 2010, 2011, para. 2) and are still subject to existing internal structuring and specific national and local histories of social activism (Bayat, 2002; El-Nawawy & Khamis, 2013). Journalist John Pollock (2011) observed, for example, that, in Tunisia in particular, activists opposing the regime used the Internet as an important tool to communicate their dissent, to create networks of supporters and activists, and subvert existing power structures of the traditional media and state censorship. Nevertheless, the political activism that led to the overthrow of the repressive regime began long before 2011, so it wasn't all down to the new technology (Pollock, 2011).

Yet it is important to recognize that while the dramatic change that came with the overthrow of governments in Tunisia and Egypt in the spring of 2011 was indeed politically revolutionary, the impact and outlook of these changes are slower to develop, and the question of what level of democratic equality will exist in these countries is still being determined, not to mention substantial changes in social relations of class, gender, and race. With respect to political activism and new media, it was not necessarily an equitable forum. While a 2011 report from the Dubai School of Government noted an exponential increase by 29 per cent in Facebook use

Source: © jcarillet / iStockphoto

FIGURE 13.1 | Cairo, Egypt—9 February 2011: A man works on a computer during anti-government demonstrations in Tahrir Square. Social networking and the Internet were useful tools in the Egyptian Revolution.

in the first three months of 2011, this growth was by no means uniform and equal. Barriers in use were evident, as divided by sex, age, and language, for example, as more young males were new Facebook adopters than their female counterparts, and English and French were the main languages of communication used (Haddadi, 2011). Thus, we shouldn't assume that traditional social structures won't be replicated in political activism or the new media environment, or that economic structures will change accordingly.

Case Study

Leadnow.ca—Online Political Activism in Canada

New media has also been harnessed in aid of political activism in Canada. Some recent examples include the Canadians Against Proroguing Parliament (CAPP) campaign that emerged in January 2010 in opposition to the Conservative government's move to prorogue Parliament to avoid a vote of non-confidence that would have seen the government fall. CAPP was primarily organized through Facebook. The premise of the campaign was to organize collective demonstrations across Canada to indicate to federal leaders, including the governor general, the general displeasure with the action of the Harper government. It culminated with rallies in cities across Canada on 23 January 2010, attracting an estimated 21,000 people (Wikipedia, 2013a). This action was followed by similar campaigns, both online and on the streets, around government actions and a more general discontentment with the nature of Canadian democracy.

Leadnow.ca is an organization that emerged following CAPP's rallies to harness the public opposition to the current state of Canadian democracy. Its main activities include highlighting key areas of democratic reform in the country through its website. Issues such as electoral reform, robocall election fraud, and the reimagining of public institutions like the CBC are examples of recent campaigns. Leadnow is essentially a Canadian iteration of what Dick Morris' Vote.com was imagining back in 1999. The main activity of Leadnow is to encourage citizens to sign online petitions related to its profile issues, as well as to attempt to organize some local activism in communities across the country, all of which is coordinated through social media like Facebook and Twitter.

One of the benefits or strengths of these efforts has been to engage a younger segment of Canadians in political action. Yet there are also three significant challenges in Leadnow's model. First, the site does not provide adequate background information on the issues in question to provide citizens with knowledge about different arguments around the issues being profiled or why they are so important. In other words, it assumes a pre-existing knowledge of Canadian politics that may or may not exist among those participating in the petitions. Second, the petitions themselves create some unintended issues around personal privacy protection. Once you have signed the petition, your response is then sent as an email to a variety of political leaders. What has then happened is that many of the political parties in question then capture your personal information and add your coordinates to their communication lists.

So, those who support a specific Leadnow initiative, like Reimagine CBC, may find themselves receiving a plethora of political information from all the different political parties. Finally, perhaps the most troubling of challenges in the Leadnow model is that it embodies, in many ways, Darin Barney's (2008) criticism about superficial political activism through social media.

Continued

Discussion Questions

1. Does signing a Leadnow petition constitute effective political action involving informed decision-making?

2. How is the Leadnow action similar to or different from the online "clicktivism" (evident in the Kony 2012 campaign)?

3. What are the challenges or pitfalls of using social media like Facebook for political activism (▣ stream.aljazeera.com/story/clicktivism-destroying-meaningful-social-activism-0022095)?

4. Will clicktivism actually lead to more apathy in the long term?

The issues that online projects like Leadnow raise about e-democracy are not easy ones with a simple fix. As Roza Tsagarousianou (1998) suggests, it will take much more work in both the real and the virtual worlds for e-democracy to prove itself. The digital dialectic once again asserts itself: "Succumbing to the binary division between optimism and dystopia undermines our ability to comprehend [the] implications and potential [of cyber-democracy]" (p. 176). We agree with Terry Flew (2005) who, after surveying several e-democracy initiatives, concludes that to date there is no clear evidence that they are having the desired effect: "Any assessment of the utilization of the Internet and ICTs for political engagement reveals a decidedly mixed score card" (p. 188).

Alternative Media, Politics, and the Internet

One important aspect of digital mythology is that the Internet is decentralizing the conventional media's power base and structures (Barksdale, 1999; Davis, 1999; Hiebert, 1999; Ogden, 1999). As we have already discussed, in contrast to radio, television, and print media, for example, the Internet has reshaped our current understanding of interactivity and thus an opportunity presents itself. We also underscored, particularly in this last part of the book, that this opportunity appears to be rapidly closing. However, in Canada, we still have relatively general access to the Internet and its technology, and we can determine what information is salient and what information is not—all at our fingertips—almost anywhere. Accordingly, we can choose what to digest and what to reject, and we can decide on the extent that we exercise our agency. The types of information we seek and choose to create and receive are reliant on our subjective perceptions and interpretations, since how we think about the world is directly related to how we act. The benefits of the access to information on the Internet and its relation to interactivity can have a positive impact on the creation and development of different ways of thinking and doing—of creating an oppositional or counter hegemony (recall from Chapter 2).

One of the ways these different ways of thinking and doing are expressed in media is through what is called alternative, autonomous, critical, or independent media. As Kirsten Kozolanka, Patricia Mazepa, and David Skinner (2012a) explain, these media are notoriously difficult to define, and for a good reason. They can include community, ethnic, radical, regressive, and progressive types of media. They can include newspapers, zines, television and radio programmes, films, blogs, websites, posters, graffiti, and many other examples. These media are found at the global, national, and local/community levels, as well as bringing the global to the local and vice versa. They are often linked to social and political movements as a means of communicating the key messages from the movements, as well as communicating alternative issues and perspectives not found in the mainstream press (ibid.). As a whole however, the general intent for its progressive forms is to advance what we identified as a "radical democratic" approach, explained in Chapter 9.

Alternative media tends to challenge dominant (mainstream or commercialized) media in three important and overlapping areas: structure, participation, and activism (ibid.). These areas express the process of structuration identified at the beginning of this chapter. In terms of structure, Kozolanka et al. (2012b) argue that we need to understand how alternative media "both develop out of and are structured into the larger media environment" (p. 15), meaning how they are politically and economically different from "mainstream" media, how they fit within existing policy regimes, and what challenges and opportunities they face in light of the dominant models of media organization. This aims to identify how existing media structures that favour private ownership can be changed to facilitate democracy *of* communication. Participation refers to "the means through which these media extend democracy *in* communication and how this is facilitated (or not) in their internal organization and interpersonal and social practices, as well as their external organization—the extent of information sharing and cooperation with other media and social movements (ibid.). Finally, activism refers to democracy *through* communication, or "how social and political change is advocated and facilitated through the media as connected to external networking" (ibid., p. 16), such as established social movements.

While alternative media are not new, new media have had a profound effect in terms of being used to invigorate them. The Internet sets up an interesting dialectic for alternative media, on one hand, offering greater flexibility in terms of the cost of production and distribution while, on the other hand, potentially "ghettoizing" them among smaller sets of users. As many of these media are not reliant on commercial means of revenue generation (i.e., advertising), they have traditionally struggled with both production costs and building vast distribution networks. The Internet has, in some senses, eased these challenges as the costs of print or audio/visual production are greatly reduced in digital media. In terms of expanding distribution networks, the Internet also provides the potential for greater reach, although it can also, as the dialectic works, lead to these media being ghettoized in like-minded communities, as they do not have the same ability to expand in the Internet as do commercial media with existing interlocking relationships. With this dialectic in mind though, it is useful to look at a few examples of alternative media projects from the global, national, and local levels to get a sense of how they attempt to advance radical democracy.

Following up on our history of alternative developments of computer networking in Chapter 8, one popular example of global alternative media is the global network of Independent Media Center (Indymedia) sites with local chapters based in most nations and large cities dedicated to "the creation of radical, accurate, and passionate tellings of truth" (Indymedia.org, 2006). The movement was initially established in Seattle to support protests at the November 1999 World Trade Organization meeting. The news reports and other content hosted on the various Indymedia sites are generated by volunteers, some of whom are working journalists or students, but all have an activist orientation. The network is decentralized but does have a structure of sorts that can admit new members and provide some sort of collective overview of editorial policy. This generates some friction within and between various Indymedia collectives, but generally relations between individuals and groups are fairly harmonious.

While many Indymedia sites begin as text-only sites, most also carry audio and video files and are updated regularly. While Indymedia only has a limited appeal outside activist circles, this does not take away from its importance in the digital media world. As a global coalition of mostly average people without access to the vast funds at the disposal of the media barons, Indymedia has done well to maintain its presence for nearly a decade. It is not likely to go away, unless there are serious attempts to shut its networks down, and it may build a bigger following over time. Certainly it provides a welcome alternative to what most major media outlets churn out.

It is interesting to note that, historically, Indymedia was a turning point for alternative media activism. Previous online activism was often confined to replicating the same strategies used offline. Although a prominent success for social justice groups such as the Council of Canadians and other **non-governmental organizations** (NGOs) around the world was the defeat of the Multilateral Agreement on Investment in 1997—put forward by the Organisation for Economic Co-operation and Development (OECD) that would have given corporations the legal status of states—as a global online activism model it was limited. Similarly, and also in the 1990s, the successful struggle of the indigenous people known as the Zapatistas for sovereignty over their land in Chiapas, Mexico (which was supported in many countries) was the first Internet-based global struggle. Indymedia, however, upped the ante by using **open-source software** that allowed its justice journalists to be part of the action. This created a huge gathering of activists from around the world in Seattle for a key meeting of the World Trade Organization; in response, it also drew a large gathering of police.

The story of how the Indymedia justice journalists produced counter-accounts of what was happening in tear-gas drenched Seattle in real time is told in several videos, prominent among them is *This Is What Democracy Looks Like*. The key condition that made a difference and became a central part of global organizing that followed the Indymedia breakthrough was the open-source software that enabled the reporting to be not just *networked*, as in previous protests, but *Internetworked* (Scatamburlo-D'Annibale & Chehade, 2004). As activism became globalized, it also became clear that online activism on its own was not as effective as strategies that included both online and offline elements.

In fact, the Internet has had a startling impact on alternative media, as the new medium releases such media from the high costs of distribution that were the cause of many a publication's demise. Although some, like *The Dominion*, still publish print editions while maintaining an online version, many others have made the shift to online-only editions. Some online alternative media are *Rabble* (🖥 rabble.ca/) and *Redwire* (🖥 users.resist.ca/www.redwiremag.com). Others that also maintain a print version are *Upping the Anti* (🖥 uppingtheanti.org), *The Tyee* (🖥 thetyee.ca), *Herizons* (🖥 herizons.ca), *Shameless* (🖥 shamelessmag.com), *This Magazine* (🖥 this.org), and *Our Times* (🖥 ourtimes.ca).

Alternative media have flourished in many regards in Canada. The reasons for this are manifold, including a history of state support of culture and communication through financial and direct policy. Examples of the latter include support for public and community broadcasting, for Canadian periodicals, and for film and television production. These mechanisms have aided both mainstream as well as alternative media over the years. As discussed in our history of film and broadcasting in chapters 5 and 6, for example, Canada has a proud tradition of supporting community broadcasting with the National Film Board of Canada's (NFB) Challenge for Change program (1960s), and government support for community broadcasting in the form of broadcasting policy in the 1970s when the CRTC required cable providers across the country to create and maintain a community television station as a quid pro quo for having a monopoly service in the region served.

The ethos of these early community television stations was a focus on local community content and required community participation not only in content production but also in the

---

NON-GOVERNMENTAL ORGANIZATIONS (NGOs)

Not-for-profit or voluntary groups, NGOs can be single-issue but most often follow broader themes such as the environment or human rights. They monitor, analyze, and provide information to governments and the public. Examples of NGOs are the Council of Canadians and Democracy Watch.

OPEN-SOURCE SOFTWARE

Software that computers can read and users can modify without cost.

operation of the community stations themselves. In recent years, the policies around community broadcasting, both radio and television, have been weakened, leading to greater levels of regionalization and commercialization in the sector and an overall erosion of traditional media options (Lithgow, 2012). In response to this there is a more active push to develop a new model for community media around community media centres that incorporate multimedia options for prosumers in different regions across Canada (e.g., the Canadian Association of Community Television Users and Stations [CACTUS]; cactus.independentmedia.ca/). Another example of state support for alternative media includes state policy and financial incentives to support the Canadian periodicals sector. These policies, which emerged in earnest in the 1970s, were aimed at protecting and promoting the Canadian newspaper and magazines sector, which was perceived to be threatened by American incursion. Since the 1970s, Canadian periodicals, both mainstream and alternative, have received financial support from the federal government for publication and distribution. While the actual policies have changed significantly since the 1970s, due to international trade agreements and neo-liberal shifts within the federal government itself, the current iteration of this support, the Canada Periodical Fund (CPF), continues to financially support small, alternative publications like *Maisonneuve* and *The Dominion*. Again, as in community broadcasting policy, periodicals policy is also being transformed along neo-liberal market parameters privileging the market model.

While some alternative media are funded by the CPF, it is not dedicated to those media only, but includes many different mainstream media. In 2012/13, these included such publications as the *Journal of the Canadian Chiropractic Association*, *Soccer 360*, and *Alberta Outdoorsman* (Canada, 2012a). In addition, the mainstream magazines that were funded consistently received more extensive funding than the alternative magazines. For example, *Briarpatch* received $14,431 and *Canadian Dimension* received $17,064, while *Canadian Cattlemen* got $36,668 and *Canadian Real Estate Wealth* got $60,063 (ibid.). Moreover, some alternative media are not even eligible to apply for program funding if they don't charge for their publication—many alternative publications are free or pay-what-you-can or very low-priced—or if their circulation is less than 2,500, which eliminates many more (Canada, 2012b).

One of the prime motivating factors behind the development of alternative media in Canada is the high level of consolidation in the commercial media sector in the country. As there are fewer and fewer owners of mainstream media throughout the country, there are fewer opportunities for a greater diversity of views and perspectives to be represented. As a result, a number of projects at both the national and the local level have emerged to fill the void left by concentrated media ownership. Many of these are using the Internet as a central tool for their development and dissemination. For example, rabble.ca is a national news website that provides content on a variety of issues tied to more progressive politics in the country or, as their tag line states, "news for the rest of us" (rabble.ca). Funded in part by support from some Canadian unions that are committed to social justice, Rabble is tied into progressive groups and politics within the country and, while successful and respected, does not usually reach a broader Canadian audience.

At the local level there are ample examples of web-based alternative media that have developed to fill the void left by a lack of diversity in media in communities across the country. Many of these sites tend to focus on covering local issues around municipal politics and urban activism, issues that are no longer as prominent in the local daily newspapers. For example, *Spacing*, which has a strong web presence, began as a Toronto magazine/website but now has an "urban blog network" in cities and regions across the country including Vancouver, Montreal, Ottawa, and the Atlantic region.

Case Study

The "Maple Spring" Student Movement and Alternative Media Activism

YouTube is an online medium that, like many other new and social media, requires very little expertise to upload material. Its vibe is contemporary, cutting-edge, and up-to-date; at the same time it is also a dumping ground for old pirated movies, poorly filmed home videos, animal tricks, and much other ephemeral and bizarre content.

In contrast, although the blogosphere also has its share of painful and personal confessional moments, blogging has emerged as a respectable and viable tool for political discussion and activism.

Within the clutter of YouTube, however, lies many opportunities for alternative media activism. The difficulty with YouTube is how to harness its potential for activist campaigning so that political efforts do not remain known only to the groups that post there. Another issue, especially for those who use it for alternative media or other activism, is that YouTube has been a for-profit video broadcasting service owned by Google, the world's second biggest search engine, since 2006. Google funds YouTube through advertising, both in-stream (at the start of the videos themselves) or elsewhere on the site. Although you have ownership rights to material you have uploaded, you may also have agreed to the site's terms when you posted your work, which may have conditions placed on ownership and, as we discussed in chapters 11 and 12, can be subject to additional corporate or government surveillance (or both). In addition, as Curtis Brown (2010) notes, issues that get posted on blogs and YouTube often have limited influence on their own until elite media cover them, "so even if a tree falls in the blogosphere and a reporter hears it crash, it does not actually make a discernible sound until that reporter or his or her editor decides that the public should hear the sound as well" (p. 181).

Brown's point that YouTube needs guides to point the way through the dross towards usable and important content is well-taken. And when a social movement fostered by students in Quebec in early 2012 hit the mainstream media both inside of and outside of the province—and not for the most part with positive depictions of the students—the fledgling student movement knew how to get the public to hear the sound of the tree falling.

The students had already been organizing and strategizing through general assemblies that included any students who wanted to be heard, but the public story began in February 2012 with a massive strike by secondary-school students after the Quebec government proposed a 75 per cent increase in tuition. The government took the view that the increase was justified because the province's tuition was the lowest of all the provinces in Canada. This was true, but the government was not increasing fees to better education but to balance a budget. The strike was called by CLASSE (loosely translated as the Coalition for Student Solidarity and Union), a temporary student organization that brought together 76,000 members across Quebec's universities and colleges. CLASSE took the view that education was a social right that should be accessible to all. To be clear, CLASSE published a manifesto called "We Are Many Youth, But With One Struggle." The manifesto was endorsed by student organizations around the world.

Week after week throughout what some have dubbed the "Maple Spring"—due to the province's high maple-syrup production—the students marched in the thousands. Quebec police reacted strongly to the demonstration by arresting thousands of students, particularly using profiling, a technique that identified the most radical students by their lapel pins made of square pieces of red felt—in French, *carrés rouges*. Many media reports mentioned the high level of police-led violence in response to relatively little infractions by the huge crowds of demonstrating students. CLASSE's strategy involved broadening the strike to include unions and the general public. The tuition hike became law on 18 May, along with strict limitations on the right to assemble (a violation of the Canadian constitution) directed at the student protests, but not before the minister of education resigned. The passage of the law was followed by a march four days later that drew 400,000, which rabble.ca said was "the largest single protest action in Canadian history" (Annis, 2012, para. 2). The demonstrations continued regularly throughout the summer, drawing the same large crowds. Under pressure, the government called an election, which it lost on 4 September. The new premier immediately reversed the tuition hike.

Not only did CLASSE win a tactical victory for students, it drew together both organized groups and ordinary people to support them. An important part of the success was due to how the movement communicated, for instance, through well-attended general assembly meetings where everyone could be heard. In addition, a key role within communication was played by new and social media.

First, the movement communicated by its strong presence at marches. The large crowds not only showed broad support and solidarity for the student strike but they also made for good media coverage, especially on television. Their placards dealt with the freedom to assemble and police violence issues; students carried signs that read "Arrêtez-moi quelqu'un!" ("Someone arrest me!"), which, along with other humorous taunts, were posted on sites like boingboing.net (Doctorow, 2012). Another sign, reading "Je pense donc je désobéis: Descartes contre la loi!" ("I think therefore I disobey: Descartes against Law 78!"), turned up on the Common Dreams website (Zimet, 2012).

More interestingly, CLASSE understood the importance of spectacle—not just in the spectacle of huge numbers protesting, but also in the theatrics of exaggeration, lampooning, and mocking, all with a humorous twist. Over the summer, CLASSE kept spirits up by creating themes for the demonstrations, such as everyone riding bicycles or dressing in costumes or only in their underwear; some took place during the day, some at night. There was even one notorious nude demonstration, although it was unclear if it was officially sanctioned. It was also said that fewer arrests took place on the day of the latter demonstration, as police did not want to handle nude protesters.

Since Law 78 enacted a prohibition on wearing masks, a sympathetic professor masked himself in a full panda costume and became known as "Anarcho-Panda." As a response to the harsh enforcement of the new law, Anarcho-Panda provided disarming humour by embracing police officers and pretending to cry when the hugs were not returned. This particular action negated the mainstream media's frames of chaos and violence.

One particular communication tactic has been credited with assisting to broaden the movement to include the general public. At the demonstrations, the students began to bring kitchen pots and pans to bang on. This is a tactic that has been used in Latin American countries such as Argentina to draw attention to such issues as the disappearance of students and activists that was linked to police forces in those countries. The ear-splitting and joyful cacophony of noise became a turning point in gaining support for the movement, as members of the public joined in. Across Quebec, and later in other provinces, "casseroles" (the French word for *pot*) were organized at universities and on main streets.

Second, the movement made good direct use of social media. As some of the following examples show, even strategies and tactics not expressly intended for social media found their way online. In particular, YouTube became the home for content that was both produced especially for that application and found its way there more informally. Not all the videos were made by

Continued

the students, but they demonstrated the wide appeal of the movement in Quebec society and elsewhere. One animated video shows a police officer in riot gear pummelling a red square. The first stroke breaks the red square into several pieces. As the officer continues to hit those pieces, they too split into more and more pieces. The message of not being intimidated by the violent behaviour of some police and that such behaviour only strengthened the movement is made clearly in only 11 animated seconds. CLASSE also documented itself using popular culture effectively. At one point, its three student leaders appeared on stage with a well-known Quebec band and sang along with the band. The video was posted to YouTube, where it was viewed by large numbers and was forwarded by email to many more. A different video used dance and popular music with a background setting of downtown Montreal, with the camera moving from group to group—one could spot the student leaders in the crowds—through streets and parks and past landmarks. The video expressed both the excitement and the commitment of the students to their goals. It, too, ended up on YouTube. Another video acknowledged that many potential supporters might not understand French, the official language of Quebec, with a voiceover of a speech by one of the leaders in French with an English translation of his words in changing patterns.

After the victory, CLASSE was replaced by the Association pour une solidarité syndicale étudiante (loosely, the Association for Student Solidarity and Union), which represents 66,000 students. A quick look at social media late in November 2012 showed that the student movement under the new association was still active. The most recent post on the new association's website showed that it had 10,212 "likes," while its Twitter account listed 3,708 tweets; 2,433 "following"; and 26,104 "followers" (ASSÉsolidarité, 2012a). Oddly, given the role it played in popularizing the movement and informing the public, only its YouTube account is dormant, with its last post early in 2012—however that post received 103,631 views and the overall website had 150,302 posts (ASSÉsolidarité, 2012b).

Mainstream media coverage outside Quebec was generally not positive, seemingly unable to grasp the significance of the movement as broad-based, and new-media friendly, although there was some take-up on the casserole-led demonstrations. For alternative media, it was a different matter. Rabble.ca and *The Bullet*, a progressive online journal, kept up with the numerous and ongoing events, as well as elaborating on the contexts of the struggle. Interestingly, given the lack of extended coverage by mainstream media, alternative media featured the student movements prominently, even holding up deadlines to ensure coverage was as timely as monthly magazines can be. *Briarpatch*, *Canadian Dimension*, and *New Internationalist* all made the "Maple Spring" a cover story with extended coverage. *Our Schools/Our Selves*, the quarterly journal of the Canadian Centre for Policy Alternatives, devoted its fall 2012 issue to shifts in educational and community activism.

Discussion Questions

1. Did the social-media-led tactics of the Quebec student movement denote new directions for activism, media activism, and student-movement-led media activism?

2. Are alternative media so marginalized in Canada that only a small minority of the public is aware of the breadth and importance of the movement?

3. Comparing your observations in earlier chapters, were dominant frames led by the provincial government retained in commercial media coverage?

These examples are just a very small selection of alternative media available in Canada. There are many others with a more specific focus on different themes, social and political issues. What is compelling about this sector of the media environment is while new media provides greater opportunities to reach larger audiences and produce content in a less costly way, many challenges remain for the sector. These include the changes to state support, in funding and policy, but also challenges tied to specific models of participatory, often volunteer-driven, production and the complexity of actually putting democracy in, of, and through communication in practice.

Conclusion

There is no question that the Internet has been used to propel us into a new era of rapid communication and technological change and that this has had an impact on both politics and political activism in Canada. However, we must continue—as we've attempted in this chapter and in this book—to separate the reality from the mythology. This means we must constantly evaluate the limitations and possibilities in the question "Does the Internet promote democracy?" This is particularly relevant as we shift from a broadcast to a narrowcast communication paradigm.

On the upside, there is no disputing that the Internet has allowed for people to have unrivalled opportunities to obtain information and to encounter a whole new range of views and interactions. The advantages of the medium, as discussed in this chapter, may increasingly reduce our dependence on traditional media and increase our ability to draw our own conclusions about politics and government and get involved in decisions and actions. People at the grassroots level cannot only play a bigger role in political participation but also give the agenda-setting process a whole new dimension. Various Internet tools increasingly make possible the personalization of politics and one-on-one courting of voters. As a new generation shifts its focus more towards online politics—of either the electoral, campaigning, or activist type—it may not necessarily spell *doom* to traditional mass media coverage, as evidenced by the continuing dominance of political and government-related advertising on television; nor will it necessarily affect the large budgets allocated by political candidates to television. But it does raise some important issues that leave room for greater research and sustained consideration.

On the downside, there is every possibility that a move towards online voting and polling will only increase political and social surveillance of citizens by governments. It might also lead to further audience fragmentation and withdrawal from active citizenship as Barney (2008) warns. As we discussed in Chapter 11, while this may be a fairly benign development at the moment, things could be very different in a time of political crisis, or when a government moves from being open and "democratic" to being secretive and authoritarian. In this climate it is important that social movements and alternative media continue to exist and prosper and to remember that government, regardless of its current flaws, is still crucial site for public involvement and change. This is particularly relevant if we are to see the real generation of a "Fifth Estate" in the electronic media that is not beholden to the hegemonic economic and political powers of the day. We can only conclude that our digital future will be determined by the choices we make now as engaged citizens, more so than as engorged or apathetic consumers.

Key Points

- The dialectic of convergence and digital myths create a powerful mimetic effect that portrays the Internet as a great force for democratic change.

- New media can have a transformative effect on the practices of traditional politics, political philosophy, and public policy, but this depends on the existing social and historical context and the process of structuration.

- Interactivity has an agenda-setting and gatekeeping impact on news and information, the importance of net activism, and the potential of bloggers as the town criers of cyberspace.

- Alternative media complements and invigorates activism in developing an oppositional or counter hegemony.

Class Discussion

1. Does the use of the Internet mean a continuance or significant break from dominant forms of framing and agenda setting endemic of commercial newspapers and television for example?

2. Check out alternative media sites in your local area. Do they offer a useful and enjoyable alternative news experience when compared with other news sources that you access? What similarities and differences can you identify in terms of structure, participation, or activism?

3. What do you think is the value of weblogs? Do they offer a good range of alternative opinion? Are all politics simply a matter of opinion?

4. When we are so focused on the politics of new media, what happens to discussions of economics?

5. Does abundance and more diverse types of media and communications technology mean more democracy?

6. How would *you* define democracy and democratic communication?

Media on Media

Tunes—In or Out?

Anti-Flag. (n.d.). Various. 🖥 www.anti-flag.com/
Bruce Cockburn. (1986/2010). Call it democracy. . Canada: True North Records.
Conflict. (1984). From protest to resistance. US: SOS Records.
Gil Scott-Heron. (1970). The revolution will not be televised. US: Flying Dutchman Records. 🖥 //www.gilscottheron.com/lyrevol.html
Leonard Cohen. (1992). Democracy. US/Canada: Sony Music Entertainment.
Le Tigre. (2001). Get off the Internet. US: Le Tigre.
Serj Tankian. (2012). Uneducated democracy. US: Reprise Records.
State Radio. (2006). Democracy in kind. Canada: Nettwerk Productions.

DVD, Videos, and Docs

Hudson Mohawk Independent Media Centre. (Producer). (2003). Independent media in a time of war [Documentary]. US: Media Education Foundation.
Nelson, S. (Director). (1998). Black press: Soldiers without swords [Documentary]. US: Half Nelson Production.

Stahl, R. (Writer & Director). (2011). Returning fire: Interventions in video game culture [Documentary]. US: Media Education Foundation.

Timeline: Activism and New Media Examples

1994 The Zapatista Army of National Liberation uprising in Mexico is the first international example of online activism with the goal of empowering indigenous populations for sovereignty of the Chiapas area.

1997 The Multilateral Agreement on Trade is opposed by activists including the Council of Canadians. It is the first international, Internet-based campaign that exposed secret talks on a proposed international trade treaty that would have given trade rights to corporations, thereby passing and weakening the state. The campaign was decentralized, consensual, and strategically planned, and included basic tools such as emails, website blocking, and electronic mailing lists. Eventually, France withdrew its support and the treaty died. The struggle showed that ICT use in campaigns is most effective when coordinated with networking and activism offline.

1999 Known as "The Battle in Seattle," the Seattle World Trade Organization protests result in the establishment of the Independent Media Center (Indymedia), "a collective of independent media organizations and hundreds of journalists offering grassroots, non-corporate coverage" of the protests (indymedia.org/).

2001 Voter March, an Internet-based organization created by American voters in response to the fracas of the 2000 presidential election, organized a public demonstration in Washington, DC, to protest George W. Bush's inauguration (votermarch.blogspot.com/).

The first annual Media Democracy Day is organized by members of the Campaign for Press and Broadcasting Freedom in Toronto and Vancouver. The event aimed to raise awareness of media reform issues and media democracy in response to increased corporate ownership of the Canadian media (mediademocracyday.org/).

2006 WikiLeaks is founded by Internet activist Julian Assange in 2006 with the goal of bringing secret and classified information and media from anonymous sources to the public. Since 2006, WikiLeaks has posted documents related to the Afghan War (2007), Guantanamo Bay (2011), and the Iraq War (2010), among others (wikileaks.org/).

2010 G-8/G-20 protests begin in Toronto and Huntsville. Protestors gather in downtown Toronto to protest the G-20 meeting and to bring attention to indigenous rights, climate justice, and problems in capitalism. Social media—including Twitter, YouTube, and photo sites—were widely used to document the protests and for the public to express their reactions.

Arab Spring, a series of uprisings and revolutions across North Africa and the Middle East (notably in Syria, Egypt, Tunisia, and Yemen) is caused by issues of dictatorship, human rights violations, corruption, economic decline, and inequality. Social media and the Internet were used to spread awareness of the protests, to communicate, and to network.

2011 Occupy Wall Street is sparked by a blog post by anti-consumerist magazine *Adbusters*, calling for an end to corporate greed and economic inequality. Protestors gather to form a temporary city in Zuccotti Park in New York, as well as in other financial districts around the world, including Canada (occupyto.org/, occupytogether.org/, and therealnews.com [search "Occupy Movement"]).

Chinese pro-democracy protests, initially organized online, take place in cities across China, including Beijing and Shanghai, calling for an end to one-party rule.

2012 SOPA and PIPA online protests erupt against the Stop Online Piracy Act and the PROTECT IP Act (or the Preventing Real Online Threats to Economic Creativity and Theft of Intellectual Property Act), two laws proposed by the US Congress in late 2011 that would undermine online freedom of speech and user-generated content such as free software and YouTube videos. Protests took the form of website blackouts, including Google and Wikipedia.

The Quebec Student Movement (also called the "Maple Spring") begins in response to a proposal to sharply raise university tuition. University students went on strike and held demonstrations in Montreal and across Quebec. The fight for free education is tied to more general experiences of social injustice in Canada, and the students were joined by greater numbers of the public (stopthehike.ca/).

2013 Newspaper censorship protests take place in China. Journalists at *Southern Weekly*, a Chinese newspaper, protest newspaper censorship both online and in the streets.

Glossary

agenda setting Identifying who and what is most important as news of the day, and which stories are subsequently carried forward and for how long.

algorithm A specific and finite set of instructions (or formulas, rules, or methods) specifying how to solve a problem. May be represented in mathematical or other types of language and represented by a decision-tree (if "a," do "b"; if not "a," do "c").

alternative media "Media that try to contribute to emancipatory societal transformation by providing critical media content, content that questions dominative social relations" (Sandoval & Fuchs, 2010, p. 147). This may include challenging or altering other structural conditions of inequality, including the way media is produced and distributed.

Anti-terrorism Act Following the passage of the USA PATRIOT Act, the Canadian (Liberal) government passed its own act, which extends the authority and powers of surveillance of the departments and agencies of the federal government. These include increasing government security and surveillance techniques, intelligence-sharing agreements between different states, and restrictions in immigration law, among many others.

audience commodity A concept developed by Canadian political economist Dallas Smythe, referring to the construction and transformation of an audience (their time, attention, and information) into an exchange value.

bit The smallest unit of computerized data, a single binary digit (1 or 0) used to measure data in terms of computer-calculating speed, file capacity, and connection speed rates (usually per second).

blogging An Internet publication of the views and opinions of an individual. The distinctive attribute of blogging is that it is presented as unfiltered by the traditional media "gatekeepers," although not necessarily unmoderated. Purportedly, blogging has created a new flow of opinion, and represents the diversity of opinion characteristic of new media.

blogroll A sidebar list of favourite, similar, or recommended blogs on a blogger's site.

branding Assigns an entity, such as a business, its own unique identity and attributes, which can then be used to associate that identity positively with the products the business produces. Branding has broadened to include political parties, states, and governments, which can use their brand in their publicity and campaigns to identify them with those positive qualities to gain support from citizens.

broadcasting "Any transmission of programs, whether or not encrypted, by radio waves or other means of telecommunication for reception by the public by means of broadcasting receiving apparatus, but does not include any such transmission of programs that is made solely for performance or display in a public place" (Public Works and Government Services Canada, 2007, "broadcasting").

broadsheet A newspaper format in which each page is approximately A2 size. Traditionally regarded as an upmarket form to distinguish it from a **tabloid (compact)**, which is A3 and downmarket.

camera obscura An ancient form of reprographic technology. Using a pinhole or lens, a lighted image is projected from outside, into a darkened room, allowing the external image to be reproduced on the opposite wall. It is suggested that some of the "Old Masters" who achieved such fine detail in their paintings were assisted by a camera obscura.

Canadian content (Cancon) A communication policy requirement of the Broadcasting Act that stipulates the minimum percentage of programming content that is broadcast that must be Canadian (Broadcasting Act, 1991, § 3; http://laws-lois.justice.gc.ca/eng/acts/B-9.01/page-2.html#h-4).

capital For Karl Marx and for the discipline of political economy, *capital* refers to the accumulation of value (usually expressed in terms of money) that accrues from the exploitation of labour during the production of commodities in a particular set of production relations. In neo-classical economics the term is stripped of any notion of exploitation and refers to the exclusive right of the monied class to own and control the means of production.

capitalism An economic system depending on private ownership of the means of production (capital) and the private accumulation of profits. Capitalist ideology is based on the idea that an unfettered free market is the best way to deliver increased wealth and prosperity for all. The operation of capitalist systems is often characterized by monopoly, oligopoly, and plutocracy; free or wage labour; hyper-consumerism; globalization; and crisis. Capitalism is a class-based system in which two contending classes (labour and capital) are engaged in a constant struggle over resources (use value and exchange value) and the distribution of the production surplus (surplus value).

CCTV surveillance Closed-circuit television and the use of video cameras to monitor and record people and places (businesses, government buildings, airports, shopping malls, public streets, schools, and so on).

celluloid Based on the natural polymer cellulose, celluloid is a form of plastic, from which film was originally made in pre-digital times. The word has also become a shorthand way of describing the world of film and its ephemeral character.

citizen-journalist An independent person who is not attached to or employed by a media organization who witnesses an event, and then provides an account of that event using traditional and new journalistic forms.

commodification The process of turning non-commercial material—goods, services, ideas—into saleable products or commodities; or "the process of transforming use values into exchange values" (Mosco, 2009, p. 129).

commodity A product for sale. According to its etymology, it is from the French word "to benefit," or "to profit," and in a general sense refers to "property possession" (http://etymonline.com/?term=commodity).

commodity fetishism A concept identified by Marx to describe an aspect of capitalism in which material and immaterial commodified products appear to be in relationship with each other rather than as a product of the social relations of labour.

common carriage The principle that the **telecommunications common carrier** cannot discriminate between who pays for the service (any persons of the public) or the content carried.

communication rights A set of human rights codified in international, regional, and national regulations (such as The Universal Declaration of Human Rights and the Canadian Charter of Rights and Freedoms) that pertain to standards of performance with regard to the provision of information and the functioning of communication processes in society (Hamelink & Nordenstreng, 2007, p. 234). These rights include a right to freedom of expression and opinion; a right to participate in one's own culture and use one's mother language; a right to enjoy the benefits of scientific progress and its applications; a right to information regarding governance and matters of public interest (access to information); a right to protection of the moral and material interests of authorship; a right to privacy, and many others (Raboy & Shtern, 2010, p. 29).

computational journalism The application of computer science to journalism, involving the design and techniques of search engines, algorithms, and data analysis to enhance research and investigative reporting.

computer code A set of instructions (or a set of symbols arranged according to mechanical and mathematical logic) that are programmed (built) into a computer's operating system, telling it how to perform certain tasks.

converge To converge means to come together. In the context of communications technologies this means the *coming together* of telecommunications, computing, and broadcasting into one electronic system or field. The key to this modern form of convergence is the microprocessor—the computer chip.

convergence Can be used to identify the bringing together of any number of phenomenon (technological, political, economic, and social); it proceeds dialectically via a series of contradictions among and between phenomenon.

cookies "A small data file (up to 4KB) created by a Web site you visit that is stored on your computer either temporarily for that session only or permanently on the hard disk (persistent cookie). Cookies provide a way for the Web site to recognize you and keep track of your preferences" (PCmag.com, 2013, para. 1).

copyright Provides exclusive rights of ownership "to produce or reproduce a work or a substantial part of it in any form" (Canadian Intellectual Property Office [CIPO], 2013, para. 10; www.cipo.ic.gc.ca/eic/site/cipoint-ernet-internetopic.nsf/eng/h_wr02281.html?Open&pv=1). This may include artistic, dramatic, and musical works (including computer programs) as well as performances, sound recordings, and communication signals (para. 12).

creative industries A collective noun that refers to a range of activities and professions associated with media production in the information or knowledge economy. The creative industries include print, radio, and television production; literature and poetry; theatre and film; public relations; journalism; and marketing and advertising.

crowd-sourcing Distributed labour, initiated by an online call for participation and collaboration in textual composition (such as journalism), problem-solving, or decision-making; an extension of outsourcing that may (or may not) be financially compensated.

Cyberia A play on the word *Siberia*—denigrated as a frozen wasteland in Russia—suggesting that the digital future itself is a dystopian wasteland.

dataveillance "The systematic monitoring of people's actions or communications through the application of information technology" (R. Clarke, 1988, p. 500). Two types are distinguished: (1) *personal* dataveillance—monitoring one's actions—and (2) *mass* dataveillance—monitoring a group or large sets of populations in order to detect individuals of interest (or identify particular patterns of behaviour over time; Fuchs, Boersma, Albrechtslund, & Sandoval, 2011, p. 1).

deep packet inspection "Refers to a technique that is being imposed on data communications networks in order to probe into the contents of passing traffic. . . . [It] may be performed [with or] without the authority of the sender and[/or] recipient, but also for [state, corporate, or criminal] purposes that are, or at least may be, against the interests of some of the parties" (Clarke, 2009, #1/#7).

democracy Rule by the people, as distinct from monarchy (rule by a monarch), plutocracy (rule by the rich), oligarchy (rule by a few), and anarchy (the absence of rulers).

deskilled A separation made between conception and execution (or mental and manual work); a practice whereby a worker's skill (ability or expertise in doing a particular task or job) is reduced, downgraded, or eventually eliminated via the combination of technology, management techniques, and the division of labour.

deus ex machina A phrase from Ancient Greek and Roman drama, it refers to an active agent, "a power or event that comes in the nick of time to solve difficulty" (Sykes, 1982, p. 261).

dialectic The idea that history is shaped by opposing forces. The *predominant* force, idea, movement, or paradigm (the *thesis*) is challenged by an *opposing* force, idea, movement, or paradigm (the *antithesis*), which results in a third *new* force, idea, movement, or paradigm (the *synthesis*). The synthesis, in turn, becomes the new predominant force, idea, movement, or paradigm (the *new thesis*), and the process begins all over again. The dialectic is the process of creation, and the resolution of contradictions.

digital content locks "Restrict what people can and cannot do with the media [content, software] and hardware [that] they have legitimately purchased. These locks are variously called digital locks, Digital Rights Management (DRM) or Technological Protection Measures (TPMs)" (EFF, n.d., para. 1).

digital rights management (DRM) "A catch-all term referring to any of several technologies used to enforce pre-defined limitations on the use and transfer of copyrighted digital content. The content most commonly restricted by DRM includes music, visual artwork, computer and video games and movies, but DRM can be applied to any digital content. First-generation DRM software merely sought to control copying. Second-generation DRM schemes seek to control viewing, copying, printing, altering and everything else that can be done with digital content" (Office of the Privacy Commissioner of Canada, 2006, para. 3).

digital technology A conversion of data (an image, word, or symbol, e.g.) into two electrical states—"positive" and "negative"—that is used to record, store, transmit, and receive data. These conditions of either "on" or "off" are represented by two numbers (digits)—as "one" or "zero"—which is the language of mathematics used in computer technology.

dot.com boom In the second half of the 1990s a significant number of computer companies "went public"; that is, they listed on the stock exchange through a process known as an IPO (initial public offering). They took advantage of the myth of the Golden Age and made their companies look promising for profit-making by adding the ".com" to their names. In doing so, they created fabulous paper profits for those who owned the shares prior to the IPO. Those who cashed in their shares made huge profits. This was known as the dot.com boom.

dot.com crash Since the value of stocks can be dependent on how much people are willing to pay, when it became evident that a good number of the dot.com companies weren't worth the investment in the first place, that their value was inflated and the promises were false, the stocks lost their allure, and given the sheer number of them, the market crashed.

e-democracy The use of digital (e = electronic) technologies to enhance the participation of citizens in the democratic process.

electromagnetic spectrum "The range of energy which contains parts or 'bands' such as the visible, infrared, ultraviolet, microwave (radar), gamma ray, x-ray, radio, and which travels at the speed of light. Different parts of the electromagnetic spectrum have different wavelengths and frequencies" (Natural Resources Canada, 2008, "Electromagnetic spectrum").

ethics In general, a moral philosophy and practice whereby human agency is inspired and guided by honesty, mutual respect, and responsibility for the health and welfare of each other and the environment.

exchange value The value accorded to something based on what it can be exchanged, traded, or sold for; in capitalism, this exchange value is identified by its price, what it costs to buy it.

financialization A process that subordinates use value to exchange value. It concentrates on exchange value as a financial instrument (as money, mortgage, or bonds, e.g.) that is the exclusive currency of financial institutions (such as private banks, venture capitalists, and private equity firms). The process is significant because it concentrates control in these financial institutions and brings more and more decision-making under its logic. Community, not-for profit, government institutions, and other organizations and groups that prioritize use value are made dependent on exchange value since commodification and profit-making become, in effect, dogma leading *all* decision-making.

Fordism A way of organizing, managing, and controlling capitalist production *and* consumption. Named after its promoter, American Henry Ford, it is based on the division of work into discrete, standardized, and repetitive tasks to allow for industrial mass production (such as in assembly lines in factories) and, correspondingly, mass consumption (goods are made cheaply and priced low enough, and wages are accordingly high enough, so that workers can afford them).

framing The context or organizing theme (structural, visual, or textual) that suggests a dominant meaning or way of understanding what or who is being represented in the media and how.

freelance Working on the basis of selling a discrete product(s)—in media work, a story, graphics, or editing job—for one or more employers on an impermanent basis.

gatekeeping Media choices—a selection of whose voices and what messages gets covered in the media.

global village A term popularized by Canadian media sociologist Marshall McLuhan to describe the social effect of convergent technologies. In essence, a global village would mean that we all get to know each other and interact in some utopian way, as was supposed to be the case in pre-industrial village life.

globalization 1) As an idea used in economics, the notion that economic development proceeds best on the basis of a single worldwide market that sources materials and labour from anywhere in the world at the lowest possible cost. As a process, it refers to the ongoing restructuring of corporations, governments, and other institutions to facilitate market integration on a worldwide scale. 2) A process (or set of processes) that embodies a transformation in the spatial organization of social relations and transactions, generating transcontinental or interregional flows and networks of activity, interaction, and power (Held, McGrew, Goldblatt, & Perraton, 1999).

Golden Age The idea that, in looking back, there was a halcyon period in history in which everything was bright and beautiful.

governance "The rules and procedures that states and other involved parties agree to use to order and regularize their treatment of a common issue" (Mueller, Mathiason, & McKnight, 2004, p. 4).

hacking As applied to technology, to change or disrupt the structured design and operating systems of existing technology (whether hardware or software). Hacking can remain at the level of artistry and experiment, or be expanded to deliberately disrupt established computer systems and technologically dependent structures (such as organizations, universities, governments, or corporations).

half-tone A series of black-and-white dots used to simulate grey in the reproduction of black-and-white images. The denser the black dots, the darker that section of the image; the more frequent the white dots, the lighter that section of the image will be when printed.

hegemony A term developed by Antonio Gramsci to explain domination of one social class by another. Gramsci sought to understand how social domination occurs through contest involving both coercion (intimidation, threat, withholding of resources, job loss, or violence) and consent (agreement, compromise, or apathy).

horizontal governance The process whereby decision-making in government has shifted *internally*, from the sole purview of one department with a set mandate to several departments across several mandates, and *externally*, extending government decision-making to include dominant private actors (such as industry associations or corporations) and, to a lesser extent, organizations representing the public.

horizontal integration (Type I) A firm in one line of media buys a major interest in another media operation not directly related to the original business (e.g., Thomson owns newspapers, publishing companies, and broadcasting). (Type II)

Ownership of company is entirely outside of media (e.g., Thomson ownership has included airline, automotive, travel, and oil and gas companies).

idealism The opposite of materialism. Idealism is the worldview in which all manifestations of reality actually stem from the thought-process of human beings, rather than from their material circumstances. Thus, reality is only a construction of the mind; it has no independence from it. In this view, the social construction of language or discourse is crucial since it is seen to determine reality.

ideology A set of ideas joined together that legitimate and facilitate power relations.

intellectual property (IP) Exclusive private ownership over the products of creative labour. It consists of two components: (1) the *intellectual* component refers to (a) intangible forms (ideas, plans, designs, etc.) and (b) tangible forms (symbols, words, images, sounds) used to communicate these and (2) the *property* component, which indicates private ownership and control over the results of creative labour. IP confers exclusivity of ownership rights as authorized by civil law and international agreements. Patents and trademarks are two types of intellectual property.

Internet traffic management practices (ITMPs) Tools "used by Internet service providers to manage the Internet traffic on their networks" (CRTC, 2009b, "Internet traffic management practices"). These "tools" can be technological, economic, or both.

investigative journalism In-depth, long-term, sustained, comprehensive research and reporting; finds and reveals information hidden from, or not known to, the public; focuses on the accountability of institutions and individuals wielding power (Philippine Center for Investigative Journalism, 2004).

journalism ethics An application of moral philosophy to the practices of journalism that may be formalized in public statements addressing the conduct of the journalist as well as decisions regarding media organizational goals and objectives, content, labour, and other social relations.

labour The actual process of work that humans undertake in their interactions with technology and nature (the means of production) to produce the means of subsistence, and the necessities and enjoyment of life. Within any given social formation or economic system, the forms that this labour takes are determined by the relations of production. In the capitalist economy, labour takes a commodity form, which is its price (salary or wage). This is determined not according to its use value or even on the principle of a fair day's pay for a fair day's work (or what may be called a "living wage"), but by the power of capital to impose its conditions of exchange and exploitation on those billions of people who depend on selling their labour for subsistence. Labour is not just an objective market transaction, therefore, but a political process of negotiation and domination evident in the division of labour and social relations of class, gender, and race and ethnicity.

lawful access "Lawful interception of communications and the lawful search and seizure of information, including computer data . . . [as] used by law enforcement and national security agencies, such as the Royal Canadian Mounted Police (RCMP), the Canadian Security Intelligence Service (CSIS) and municipal and provincial police forces, as well as the Competition Bureau" (Government of Canada, 2005, paras. 2, 11).

malware Computer software programs that are designed to hack into a computer system to disrupt normal operations and/or gather information. It could be malicious (sent to search and destroy), disruptive, or unnoticeable. Examples include worms, viruses, adware, and spyware.

materialism The philosophical mode of thought that suggests that events, situations, and relationships in the real, physical world determine, to the largest degree, human consciousness and thinking. Historical materialism, the method of Marx and Engels, posits the theory that human beings' interaction with nature creates the material conditions for the development of social structures and argues that the social force that drives historical change is the struggle between social classes for control of the material world and, in particular, control over the means of production.

means of production An ensemble of the available technologies and natural resources that are combined with human labour (collectively, the means) and within historically specific forms of social relations (such as social class, gender, and race and ethnicity), which are articulated in the organization of work, and of policies and laws regarding labour, to form what political economists call the mode of production.

media policy The political economic, legal, as well as social and cultural terms of reference, which are seen to regulate the media environment; there are two main approaches to media policy: On one hand there are *normative positions*, which implicitly or explicitly evaluate the socio-political roles and objectives being served by media use. On the other, there are *institutional arrangements*, which direct the operation of the media to fulfill those roles and objectives. The concept of policy combines these normative and institutional aspects of regulation. It also combines the management of media by both public and private agencies (Hamelink & Nordenstreng, 2007, p. 225).

meme An application of the reasoning of biology to language and ideas, as coined by geneticist Richard Dawkins in 1976 (Dawkins, 1989). Analogous to biological genes (and pronounced the same way), a meme is an idea (or way of thinking, or piece of information) that is communicated and passed from person-to-person like a virus. It can be socially and historically specific and finite, or it can be reinforced and propagated over time, making it stronger and more difficult to discredit or destroy.

military–industrial complex A term used to describe the interdependence of military and business networks and the resulting concentration of power to the extent that the overall political economy relies on armed conflict, surveillance, and security as a necessary condition of its sustenance.

mode of production The way that humans organize their productive relationships with the natural environment in order to survive and reproduce. A mode of production exists historically as the sum total of the relations of production that govern how society is organized economically, socially, and politically. Feudalism, capitalism, socialism, and communism are all particular modes of production.

network neutrality "The principle that network service providers treat all traffic on the Internet equally and without discrimination, regardless of source, ownership, content, or destination. . . . Net neutrality provisions prevent service providers (telephone and cable companies) from speeding up, slowing down, or blocking online content or services based on their source, ownership or destination" (Shade, 2009, p. 183).

new media Basically a catch-all phrase used to distinguish digital media forms from "old media" forms such as newspapers, magazines, radio, and television.

news agencies Organizations established as the central point of collection, composition, exchange, and distribution of information (text, images, and digital forms). These can be for-profit *commercial* agencies (such as AP, Thomson Reuters, or Canadian Press Enterprises Inc.), *not-for-profit* collectives (like the former Canadian Press/La Presse Canadienne, 1917–2010), or *state-run* (China's Xinhua News Agency or Russia's ITAR-TASS).

non-governmental organizations (NGOs) Not-for-profit or voluntary groups, NGOs can be single-issue but most often follow broader themes such as the environment or human rights. They monitor, analyze, and provide information to governments and the public. Examples of NGOs are the Council of Canadians and Democracy Watch.

open-source software Software that computers can read and users can modify without cost.

outsourcing Extending the division of labour outside the company such that parts of the product (in the case of journalism, the writing, editing, or layout) are contracted out to a second or third company.

panoptic sort A concept identifying the narrowcasting effect of technological data collection. "The panoptic sort is a difference machine that sorts individuals into categories and classes on the basis of routine measurements. It is discriminatory technology that allocates options and opportunities on the basis of those measures and the administration models that they inform" (Gandy, 1993, p. 15).

participatory journalism "'The act of a citizen or groups of citizens, playing a role in the process of collecting, reporting, analysing and disseminating news and information' (Bowman and Willis 2003) to which can be added commenting and publicly discussing same" (as cited in Hermida, 2011, p. 15).

patent A form of private ownership that gives exclusive rights over an invention to the patent owner, whether this invention is a *technology* (a device like film; a machine or any other kind of hardware) or a *technique* (a method—how to do something—as in a software code). In Canada, a patent is defined as "a government grant giving the right to exclude others from making, using or selling an invention. A Canadian patent applies within Canada for 20 years from the date of filing of a patent application" (CIPO, 2010, "Patent").

paywalls Commodifying online content by setting terms of payment for access; paywalls are used to identify restrictions to online content based on the ability and willingness to pay as generally applied to online newspapers.

personal computer (PC) Also called a mini-, micro-, or desktop computer, it was so-named to distinguish it from mainframe computers and servers housed in large businesses and organizations. PCs came of age in the 1980s, as a comparatively low cost and accessible means of processing information by smaller businesses and individuals.

Personally Identifiable Information (PII) "Information that can be used to distinguish or trace an individual's identity, either alone or when combined with other personal and identifying information that is linked or linkable to a specific individual" (US Memorandum from Exec Office of the President, 2010, as cited in Penn, 2012, p. 604).

photogravure A mechanical method of printing images whereby a negative of the image is transferred to a printing plate by means of an acid etching process. This process enabled the widespread publication of photographs in newspapers, magazines, and books.

PIPEDA (Personal Information Protection and Electronic Documents Act) "Sets out ground rules for how private sector organizations may collect, use or disclose personal information in the course of commercial activities. PIPEDA also applies to federal works, undertakings and businesses in respect of employee personal information. The law gives individuals the right to access and request correction of the personal information these organizations may have collected about them" (Office of the Privacy Commissioner of Canada, 2013a, para. 1; www.priv.gc.ca/leg_c/leg_c_p_e.asp).

pixel A dot that is the smallest single identifiable element of an image or picture. The greater the number of pixels per square inch (PSI), the clearer the image will reproduce.

podcasting "Podcasting is a form of distribution of audio contents that can be received periodically on one's computer by subscribing (for a fee) or adding oneself to a list, thanks to special software programmes called 'feeds.' . . . Paying for music is one of the basic premises of podcasting" (Menduni, 2007, p. 14).

policy Formal and informal decision-making, where actors with different degrees of power and autonomy participate in the process (Raboy & Padovani, 2010, p. 160).

political economy "The study of the social relations, particularly the power relations, that mutually constitute the production, distribution, and consumption of resources" (Mosco, 2009, p. 24).

propaganda The systematic repetition and dissemination of a particular set of ideas, views, and/or values.

prorogation Ends a parliamentary session, at which time all business comes to a stop. For example, all bills that have not been passed or received royal assent must then be reintroduced in the next parliamentary session. The governor general prorogues Parliament on the advice of the prime minister.

Radio-Frequency Identification Device (RFID) "A method of automatic identification in which remote sensors are able to retrieve and store data from transponder devices (or tags). Tags transmit an identification signal every fraction of a second, thus creating vast amounts of data as well as a host of data storage difficulties" (Fitchett & Lim, 2008, p. 142).

realism "A critical notion of realism foregrounds not the 'capture' of the real but its articulation or constitution in representations. The term 'realism' is therefore a useful one . . . because it highlights the argument that any representation, however technologically advanced, is a cultural construction and not the 'real' itself." (Lister, Dovey, Giddings, Grant, & Kelly, 2009, p. 134).

reality television A genre of television drama that purports to be a "fly-on-the-wall" rendering of the activities of non-professional actors in contrived situations. More easily understood as a form of "game show" genre.

regulatory capture The idea that regulators or operators lost (or never had) the independence to make professional decisions on their merits because of undue influence either from politicians or the regulated monopolies (Melody, 1997, p. 15).

relations of production   The social ties that bind together the elements (labour, technology, nature) that constitute a mode of production. The relations of production determine how various technologies and labour processes come together to produce goods and services and to reproduce themselves.

reportorial community   Those who "report" in a variety of media, old and new, using traditional journalistic genres and forms: the news story (written inside and outside the inverted pyramid); the feature story; the radio news report; the television news report; the "live cross"; the documentary; the online news story, etc.

robot journalism   News copy and other types of media content compiled, composed, and produced by computers.

search economy   Battelle (2005) uses this term to describe the economic relations of production that seem to permeate capitalism in the early years of the twenty-first century, epitomized by the ubiquitous presence of Google on the World Wide Web. Bartelle coined the term to emphasize how so much of what constitutes commerce today relies on some kind of search function, particularly forms of electronic commerce.

security economy   "Attempts to describe a kaleidoscope cluster of activities concerned with preventing or reducing risk of deliberate harm to life and property. At the broadest level, it could include all matters related to defence and counterintelligence, the public police force, private policing, armed guards, and security technology providers. In a much narrower sense, it might comprise just private spending on personal and corporate security." (OECD, 2005, p. 8)

social class   In Marxian terms, a divisive and conflicting social relation arising as a result of the division of labour; under capitalism, the division is between the owners of the means of production (capitalist class) and those who must sell their labour for a wage or salary (the working class).

spatialization   The process by which time and space are changed (compressed, extended, or almost eliminated) using technology.

spin   A form of propaganda in which the message is deliberately constructed to positively or negatively manage information about a person, event, institution, or organization. It is usually associated with the public relations industry, but is also part of the advertising, marketing, and lobbying industries. Among other techniques, information can be censored, distorted, manipulated, or exaggerated in favour of the (paying) client.

spyware   Computer software programs that track a computer's location, contents, and/or online traffic and collect this information without the computer user's knowledge. The information can be used for criminal purposes (like identity theft), for police and state "intelligence gathering," or to narrowcast and advance commodification of the user and their information via targeted advertising and marketing.

structuration   "describes a process by which structures are constituted out of human agency, even as they provide the very 'medium' of that constitution" (Mosco, 2009, p. 185).

surveillance   "The focused, systematic and routine attention to personal details for purposes of influence, management, protection or detection. . . . [It is] deliberate and depends on certain protocols and techniques" (Lyon, 2006, p. 14).

surveillance economy   The idea that dominant forces directing economic development are those to do with surveillance and the process of commodification, including that: research and development in an economy has a focus on surveillance or security technologies; capital investment in technologies is in the area of surveillance; recurrent budgets in both the private and the public sector make increasing provision for surveillance; employment growth is related to surveillance and security; and continuing surveillance of the citizenry and border protection are key imperatives in political economic and social structuring.

surveillance society   A way of characterizing the social totality wherein physical and electronic surveillance is commonplace.

tabloid (compact)   A newspaper format based on a page size approximately A3. Traditionally associated with journalistic practices such as beat-ups, sensationalist reporting, and photographs of semi-naked women on "Page 3." Also a pejorative term

used to describe poor-quality journalism in any medium.

technological determinism   The idea that technology has the same agency accorded to human beings and that it is independent from human actions and decision-making to the extent that it makes history and leads all social change.

technological obsolescence   The practice of making technology (even though it may still function) outdated, out-of-fashion, useless, or passé—in effect, eradicating its use value.

technology   (1) An object, or system of connected objects, that can be used in a productive process to provide a practical solution to a problem. (2) A process of incorporating knowledge into the production process; in capitalist systems this takes a distinct commodity form.

telecommunication   "The emission, transmission or reception of intelligence by any wire, cable, radio, optical or other electromagnetic system, or by any similar technical system" (Public Works and Government Services Canada, 2007, "telecommunication").

telecommunications common carrier   "A person [government, corporate or unincorporated organization or legal representative] who owns or operates a transmission facility used by that person or another person to provide telecommunications services to the public for compensation" (Telecommunications Act, 1993, "telecommunications common carrier").

trademark   Indicates exclusive ownership of a name, word, symbol, colour, shape or sound, and is represented by the symbol ™. Registration indicates proof of ownership and legal protection of that exclusivity as represented by the symbol ®. In Canada, the government definition of trademark is "a word, symbol or design (or any combination of these features) used to distinguish the wares and services of one person or organization from those of others in the marketplace" (CIPO, 2010, "Trade-mark").

universal service   Initially an obligation imposed on the monopoly operator that concentrated on the provision of voice telephony, requiring operators to expand coverage to provide services in remote and underserved areas (ITU and infoDev, 2010). As a principle of government policy, it establishes that communication and other services should be freely available as a basic necessity or for a reasonable cost.

USA PATRIOT Act Passed by the US Congress in October 2001 following the September 11th bombings of the World Trade Centre in New York City. Requested by (then) president George W. Bush, it is called the Uniting and Strengthening America by Providing Appropriate Tools Required to Intercept and Obstruct Terrorism Act, and authorizes the federal government and its departments to enhance domestic surveillance, and authorizes the interception, surveillance, and seizure of a whole range of communication content and related technology.

use value The value accorded to something because of its social utility.

user-generated content (UGC) Audio and visual material uploaded and distributed on the Internet, generally voluntary, unpaid, and intended for public viewing.

vector In medical science a vector is the pathway or pathways open to pathogens to infect a population. For example, infected chickens may be a vector for avian bird flu to infect humans. In communication studies a vector is a pathway or pathways open for communication, in particular the transmission of ideology via mimetic transfer and mutation.

vertical governance The process whereby decision-making has shifted from the internal, unilateral authority of the nation-state up to a series of external regional and international bodies, such as the United Nations (UN) or the World Trade Organization (WTO; Puppis, 2010).

vertical integration A company extends control over the whole line of production, from supply to delivery, and can be (1) *backward* (e.g., Quebecor buys a pulp and paper plant [for newsprint] or Irving [which owns all the newspapers in New Brunswick] buys pulp and paper plants and property in the Maritimes [supplying the trees for the plant]) or (2) *forward* (e.g., Thomson which owns newspapers, buys broadcasting, satellite, and Internet services).

Web 2.0 The technological capability of the Internet and World Wide Web used to decentralize communication and facilitate interactivity between citizens, users, and audiences, either individually or in large numbers. "Web 2.0 basically refers to the transition from static HTML Web pages to a more dynamic Web that is more organized and is based on serving Web applications to users. . . . Over time Web 2.0 has been used more as a marketing term than a computer-science-based term. Blogs, wikis, and Web services are all seen as components of Web 2.0" (Webopedia, 2013, para. 1).

whistle-blower A person who witnesses or collects evidence of corruption, collusion, illegalities, malfeasance, etc., against an organization, corporation, military or government department, for example, and passes it onto the media or an external public authority for exposure.

WikiLeaks A non-profit organization that collects and publishes information on its website that is otherwise restricted, classified, or secret, providing anonymity for sources of that information. WikiLeaks proclaims dedication to journalism ethics and Article 19 of the UDHR upholding the right to freedom of information and expression through any media. Since it was launched in 2007, WikiLeaks has published hundreds of thousands of documents regarding US government and military actions, in particular, as well as a wide variety of information from sources and whistle-blowers on a range of corporate, government, and military (in)actions.

References

Aas, K. F., Gundhus, H. O., & Lomell, H. M. (Eds.). (2009). Introduction. In *Technologies of (in)security* (pp. 1–18). Abingdon, UK/New York, NY: Routledge-Cavendish.

ABC News Online. (2006). Hitachi claims world's smallest microchip. Retrieved from http://www.abc.net.au/news/newsitems/200602/s1563544.htm

Acheson, K., & Maule, L. (1999). *Much ado about culture: North American trade disputes*. Michigan: University of Michigan Press.

Acland, C. R. (2003). *Screen traffic: Movies, multiplexes, and global culture*. Duke University Press.

Acland, C. R. (Ed.). (2007). *Residual media*. Minneapolis: University of Minnesota Press.

Akerton, F. C. (1987). *Teledemocracy: Can technology protect democracy?* Newbury Park: Sage Publications.

Akin, D. (2012, 14 February). Say hello to Big Brother government. *Toronto Sun*. Retrieved from http://www.torontosun.com/2012/02/14/say-hello-to-big-brother-government

Alden, C. (2005, 10 March). Looking back on the crash. *Guardian Unlimited*. Retrieved from http://media.guardian.co.uk/newmedia/story/0,1434637,00.html [23 March 2006].

Allan, S., & Zelizer, B. (Eds.). (2004). *Reporting war: Journalism in wartime*. New York: Routledge.

Allen, G. (2009). Old media, new media, and competition: Canadian Press and the emergence of radio news. In G. Allen & D. Robinson (Eds.), *Communicating Canada's past: Essays in media history* (pp. 47–77). Toronto: University of Toronto Press.

Allmer, T. (2011). Critical surveillance studies in the information society. *triple, 9*(2), 566–92.

Alzner, B. (2012, 26 September). Wentegate: A roundup of the coverage and commentary. Retrieved from http://j-source.ca/article/wentegate-roundup-coverage-and-commentary

Amis, K. (1960). *New maps of hell: A survey of science fiction*. New York: Ballantine Books.

Anderson, B., & Frenz, M. (2010, March). Don't blame the P2P file-sharers: The impact of free music downloads on the purchase of music CDs in Canada. *Journal of Evolutionary Economics, 20*, 715–74.

Anderson, T. (2003). Method in political economy. *Journal of Australian Political Economy, 54*, 135–45.

Andrejevic, M. (2007). Surveillance in the digital enclosure. *The Communication Review, 10*(4), 295–317.

Annis, R. (2012, 15 June). Quebec students keep up pressure, Charest ponders electoral options. *rabble.ca*. Retrieved from http://www.rabble.ca/news/2012/06/quebec-students-keep-pressure-charest-ponders-electoral-options [21 November 2012].

Armstrong, R. (2010). *Broadcasting policy in Canada*. Toronto: University of Toronto Press.

Arnold, T. K. (2008, 21 February). All Hollywood studios now lined up behind Blu-ray. *Reuters*. Retrieved from http://www.reuters.com/article/2008/02/21/us-bluray-idUSN2118265320080221

Arthur, C. (2011, 1 July). Nortel patents sold for $4.5bn. *The Guardian*. Retrieved from http://www.guardian.co.uk/technology/2011/jul/01/nortel-patents-sold-apple-sony-microsoft

Artz, L. & Kamalipour, Y.R. (Eds.) (2003). *The Globalization of Corporate Media Hegemony*. Albany, NY: State University of New York Press.

Artz, L., Macek, S., & Cloud, D. L. (Eds.). (2006). *Marxism and communication studies: The point is to change it*. New York, NY: Peter Lang.

Assange, J., Appelbaum, J., & Muller-Muguhn, A. (2012). *Cypherpunk: Freedom and the Future of the Internet*. OR Books.

ASSÉsolidarité. (2012a). @ ASSÉsolidarité. Retrieved from https://twitter.com/ASSEsolidarite [20 November 2012].

ASSÉsolidarité. (2012b). Association pour une Solidarité Syndicale Étudiante. Retrieved from http://www.youtube.com/user/ASSEsolidarite [20 November 2012].

Audley, P. (1983). *Canada's cultural industries: Broadcasting, publishing, records and film*. Toronto: James Lorimer and Company.

Avery, D. E. (1998). *The science of war: Canadian scientists and allied military technology during the Second World War*. Toronto: University of Toronto Press.

Babbage, C. (1864/2005). *Pages from the life of a philosopher*. Retrieved from www.four milab.ch/babbage/1pae.html [6 September 2005].

Babe, R. (1990). *Telecommunication in Canada: Technology, industry and government*. Toronto: University of Toronto Press.

Babe, R. (2000). *Canadian communication thought: Ten foundational writers*. Toronto, ON: University of Toronto Press.

Babe, R. (2009). *Cultural studies and political economy*. Lanham, MD: Lexington Books.

Baehr, C. M., & Schaller, B. (2010). *Writing for the Internet: A guide to real communication in virtual space*. Santa Barbara, CA: Greenwood Press.

Bagdikian, B. H. (1997). *The media monopoly* [Third World Traveller version]. Retrieved from http://www.thirdworldtraveler.com/Media/CommunCartel_Bagdikian.html

Bagdikian, B. H. (2004). *The new media monopoly*. Boston: Beacon Press.

Bailey, A., Dubé, N., & Maryniuk, J. (2008). Canada's "tradition" of internment. Centre for Constitutional Studies. Retrieved from http://www.law.ualberta.ca/centres/ccs/issues/internmentfeaturearticle.php

Balaji, M. (2008, spring). Bollyville, USA: The commodification of the other and MTV's construction of the "ideal type" Desi. *Democratic Communique, 22*(1), 23–40. Retrieved from http://journals.fcla.edu/demcom/article/view/76496/74125

Baldasty, G. J. (1993). The rise of news as a commodity: Business imperatives and the press in the nineteenth century. In W. S. Solomon & R. W. McChesney (Eds.), *Ruthless criticism: New perspectives in US communication history* (pp. 98–121). Minneapolis: University of Minnesota Press.

Bannerman, S. (2010). Copyright: Characteristics of Canadian reform. In M. Geist (Ed.), *From radical extremism to balanced copyright: Canadian copyright and the digital agenda* (pp. 17–44). Toronto: Irwin Law.

Bannerman, S. (2011). Canadian copyright: History, change and potential. *Canadian Journal of Communication*, 36(1), 31–49.

Barksdale, J. L. (1999). Ramping up for the Net Economy. In A. Leer (Ed.), *Masters of the wired world*. London: Financial Times Pitman Publishing.

Barney, D. (2000). *Prometheus wired: The hope for democracy in the age of networked technology*. Vancouver: UBC Press.

Barney, D. (2004). The democratic deficit in Canadian ICT policy and regulation. In M. Moll & L. R. Shade (Eds.), *Seeking convergence in policy and practice: Communication in the public interest, vol. 2* (pp. 91–108). Ottawa: Canadian Centre for Policy Alternatives.

Barney, D. (2005). *Communication technology*. Vancouver: UBC Press.

Barney, D. (2008). Politics and emerging media: The revenge of publicity. *Global Media Journal, Canadian Edition*, 1(1), 89–106. Retrieved from http://www.gmj.uottawa.ca/0801/inaugural_barney_f.html

Barnouw, E. (1966). *A tower in Babel: A history of broadcasting in the United States to 1933*. Oxford University Press.

Barol, B. (2002). In my lifes. What began as an impulse buy became a quest to preserve history. And then there was eBay. *American Journalism Review*, 24(10), 18–19.

Barr, T. (2000). *Newmedia.com.au: The changing face of Australia's media and communications*. Sydney: Allen & Unwin.

Barratt, N., & Shade, L. R. (2007). Net neutrality: Telecom policy and the public interest. *Canadian Journal of Communication*, 32, 295–305.

Battelle, J. (2005). *The search: How Google and its rivals rewrote the rules of business and transformed our culture*. Boston: Nicholas Brealey.

Bayat, A. (2002). Activism and social development of the Middle East. *International Journal of Middle East Studies*, 34(1), 1–28.

BBC. (2010, 26 March). Times and Sunday Times websites to charge from June. Retrieved from http://news.bbc.co.uk/2/hi/business/8588432.stm

BBC News. (2012, September 18). Robotic co-worker Baxter joins factory line. Retrieved from http://www.bbc.com/news/technology-19637175

BBC News. (2013a) Google asked to remove 100 million "piracy" links in 2013. Retrieved from http://www.bbc.co.uk/news/technology-23489363

BBC News. (2013b, 27 February). Music piracy "down" as revenues rise for first time since 1999. Retrieved from http://www.bbc.co.uk/news/technology-21601602

BC Newsroom. (2013, 1 August). Public to have its say on digital service delivery in BC [Press release]. Retrieved from http://www.newsroom.gov.bc.ca/2013/08/public-to-have-its-say-on-digital-service-delivery-in-bc.html

Beach, A. E. (1873). *The science record*. New York: S. W. Green.

Beattie, A. (2006a). *Market crashes: Conclusion*. Retrieved from http://www.investopedia.com/features/crashes/crashes10.asp [19 March 2006].

Beattie, A. (2006b). *Market crashes: The dotcom crash*. Retrieved from http://www.investopedia.com/features/crashes/crashes8.asp [19 March 2006].

Beaty, B. (Ed.). (2010). *How Canadians communicate III: Context of Canadian popular culture*. Edmonton, AB: AU Press.

Beer, J. (2011, 14 February). Outlook 2011: The new dot-com boom. *Canadian Business*. Retrieved from http://www.canadianbusiness.com/technology-news/outlook-2011-the-new-dot-com-boom/

Bell, D. (1973). *The coming of the post-industrial society*. London: Harmondsworth.

Bellis, M. (n.d.). *Inventors of the modern computer*. Retrieved from http://inventors.about.com/library/ [21 September 2005].

Benkler, Y. (2006). *The wealth of networks*. New Haven, CT: Yale University Press.

Bennett, W. L. (2007). *News: The politics of illusion*. Toronto, ON: Pearson Longman.

Berman, D. (2013, May). Bye-bye Laverne & Shirley. *The Globe and Mail* Report on Business.

Bessen, J., Ford, J., & Meurer, M. (2011). The private and social costs of patent trolls. Boston School of Law Working Paper No. 11-45. Retrieved from http://docs.vortex.com/costs-of-patent-trolls.pdf

Bessen, J., & Meurer, M. (2008). *Patent failure*. Boston: Princeton University Press.

Big Brother Watch. (2012a). London Met Police spends 4m a year watching CCTV. Retrieved from http://www.bigbrotherwatch.org.uk/home/2012/05/met-cctv-4m-spendin.html

Big Brother Watch. (2012b). The price of privacy. Retrieved from http://www.bigbrotherwatch.org.uk/home

Bilton, N. (2012, 16 November). Apple now owns the page turn. *The New York Times Daily Bits*. Retrieved from http://bits.blogs.nytimes.com/2012/11/16/apple-now-owns-the-page-turn/?smid=fb-share

Bing, J. (2009). Building cyberspace: A brief history of the Internet. In L. A. Bygrave & J. Bing (Eds.), *Internet governance: Infrastructure and institutions* (pp. 8–47). Oxford: Oxford University Press.

Birnhack, M. D., & Elkin-Koren, N. (2003). The invisible handshake: The reemergence of the state in the digital environment. *Virginia Journal of Law and Technology Association*, 6, 2–56.

Blais, J. P. (2012, 29 October). *Speech*. Ottawa, Ontario. Retrieved from http://www.crtc.gc.ca/eng/com200/2012/s121029a.htm

Blevins, J. L., & Shade, L. R. (2010). International perspectives on network neutrality—Exploring the politics of Internet traffic management and policy implications for Canada and the US. *Global Media Journal—Canadian Edition*, 3(1), 1–8.

Blood, R. (2006). *The weblog handbook*. Retrieved from http://www.rebecca-blood.net/handbook/excerpts/weblog_ethics.html [30 March 2006].

Bonchek, M. S. (1995, April 6). *Grassroots in cyberspace: Using computer networks to facilitate political participation*. Paper presented at the 53rd Annual Meeting of the Midwest Political Science Association, Chicago, IL.

Bosker, B. (2011, 11 August). Google buys Zagat: Here's why. *The Huffington Post*. Retrieved from http://www.huffingtonpost.com/2011/09/08/google-buys-zagat_n_953863.html

Bowman, D. (1988). *The captive press: Our newspapers in crisis and the people responsible*. Melbourne: Penguin.

Bowman, S., & Willis, C. (2005). The future is here, but do news media companies see it? *Nieman Reports*, *59*(4), 6–10.

Boycoff, J. (2006). Framing dissent: Mass-media coverage of the global justice movement. *New Political Science*, *28*(2), 201–28.

Boyd-Barrett, O. (1998). "Global" news agencies. In O. Boyd-Barrett & T. Rantanen (Eds.), *The globalization of news* (pp. 19–34). London: Sage.

Boyle, A. (2005, 14–15 May). The human strain. *Weekend Australian*, 28.

Boyle, P., & Haggerty, K. (2009). Spectacular security: Mega-events and the security complex. *International Political Sociology*, *3*(3), 257–74.

Bozbeyoğlu, A. Ç. (2011). *The private sector, national security and personal data: An exploratory assessment of private sector involvement in airport and border security in Canada*. Kingston, ON: Surveillance Studies Centre, Queen's University.

Bozikovic, A. (2012, 22 August). The end of Photography Drive: A city landmark, and an industry, fade out. *The Globe and Mail*. Retrieved from http://m.theglobeandmail.com/news/national/the-end-of-photography-drive-a-city-landmark-and-an-industry-fade-out/article116703/?service=mobile

Branigan, T. (2008, 8 August). China relaxed Internet censorship for Olympics. *The Guardian*. Retrieved from http://www.guardian.co.uk/world/2008/aug/01/china.olympics [20 July 2012].

Briet, R., & Servaes, J. (2005). Introduction: Background and issues for whom and for what? In R. Briet & J. Servaes (Eds.), *Information society or knowledge societies? UNESCO in the smart state*. Penang: Southbound.

Broadcasting Act, S.C. 1991, c. 11. Retrieved from http://laws-lois.justice.gc.ca/eng/acts/B-9.01/page-2.html#h-4

Broccoli, B., Wilson, M. G. (Producers), & Spottiswoode, R. (Director). (1997). *Tomorrow never dies* [Motion picture]. UK: Eon Productions.

Bromley, M., & Clarke, J. (2012). Continuity and change in international news: An introduction. In J. Clarke & M. Bromley (Eds.), *International news in the digital age: East-West perceptions of a new world order* (pp. 3–22). New York, NY: Routledge.

Bronskill, J. (2012, 20 September). Nexen deal: CSIS warns foreign takeover could pose national security threat from China. *Huffington Post Business*. Retrieved from http://www.huffingtonpost.ca/2012/09/20/nexen-deal-spying-china-csis_n_1901701.html

Brookey, R. A. (2010). *Hollywood gamers: Digital convergence in the film and video game industries*. Bloomington: Indiana University Press.

Brown, C. (2010). White noise: The blogosphere and Canadian politics. In S. Sampert & L. Trinble (Eds.), *Mediating Canadian politics* (pp. 173–83). Toronto: Pearson.

Brown, V., & Vaughn, E. D. (2011). The writing on the (Facebook) wall: The use of social networking sites in hiring decisions. *Journal of Business Psychology*, *26*, 219–25.

Brück, T. (2004). Assessing the economic trade-offs of the security economy. In OECD (Ed.), *The security economy* (pp. 101–26). Paris: OECD.

Bryan, C., Tsagarousianou, R., & Tambini, D. (1998). Electronic democracy and the civic networking movement in context. In R. Tsagarousianou, D. Tambini, & C. Bryan (Eds.), *Cyberdemocracy: Technology, cities and civic networks* (pp. 1–17). London/New York: Routledge.

Bryden, J. (2008, 29 November). Tories reverse decision to end public subsidies. *The Toronto Star*, 1.

Brynjolfsson, E., & McAfee, A. (2012, January). *Race against the machine: How the digital revolution is accelerating innovation, driving productivity, and irreversibly transforming employment and the economy*. The MIT Centre for Digital Business.

Bullock, A., & Trombley, S. (Eds.). (2000). *The new Fontana dictionary of modern thought* (3rd ed.). London: HarperCollins.

Burns, A. (2001, 7 January). Dot.com disaster: The new e-poor. *Disinformation*. Retrieved from http://www.disinfo.com/archive/pages/dossier/id333/pg1/ [19 March 2006].

Butler, D. (2009, 5 February). Part I: A very different world. *Ottawa Citizen*. Retrieved from http://www.ottawacitizen.com/Part+very+different+world/1232203/story.html#ixzz1yA440yQs

Butler, S. (1872/1967). *Erewhon. Airmont classic edition*. Clinton, Massachusetts: Airmont Publishing.

Byerly, C. M. (2011). Global report on the status of women in the news media. Retrieved from http://iwmf.org/pioneering-change/global-research-on-women-in-the-news-media.aspx

CADSI. (2011). *Canadian defence and security directory*. Ottawa: CADSI.

CADSI. (2012). CADSI welcomes government actions to support cyber security industries. Retrieved from https://www.defenceandsecurity.ca/index.php?action=news.article&id=198&t=c

CADSI. (2013). Retrieved from https://www.defenceandsecurity.ca/

Callinicos, A. (1987). *The revolutionary ideas of Marx*. London: Bookmarks.

Callinicos, A. (1995). *Theories and narratives: Reflections on the philosophy of history*. Cambridge: Polity Press.

Cameron, G., & Curtin, P. (1992, summer). An expert systems approach for PR campaigns research. *Journalism Educator*, 13–18.

Cameron, G., Shin, J., & Adhikari, D. (2005). What matters in embedded journalism: News sources, news credibility, news control in embedded journalists' reports. *Conference Papers—International Communication Association, 2005*

Annual Meeting (pp. 1–39). New York, NY.

Campbell, J. E., & Carlson, M. (2002). Panopticon.com: Online surveillance and the commodification of privacy. *Journal of Broadcasting & Electronic Media, 46*(4), 586– 605.

Campion-Smith, B. (2012, 18 October). Bell's bid for Astral Media blocked by CRTC. *Toronto Star.* Retrieved from http://www.thestar.com/news/canada/politics/article/1273707--bell-s-astral-bid-blocked-by-crtc [2 November 2012].

Canada. (2012a). Aid to publishers: List of recipients, 2012–13. Canada Periodical Fund. Canadian Heritage. Retrieved from http://www.pch.gc.ca/eng/1344868568577 [19 November 2012].

Canada. (2012b). Minimum average price criteria in 2012–13. Canada Periodical Fund. Canadian Heritage. Retrieved from http://www.pch.gc.ca/eng/1318949749487/#a4 [19 November 2012].

Canada Business Corporations Act, R. S. C., 1985, c. C-44. Retrieved from http://laws-lois.justice.gc.ca/eng/acts/C-44/page-6.html#doc

The Canadian Encyclopedia. (2012). Telegraph. Retrieved from http://www.thecanadianencyclopedia.com/articles/telegraph

Canadian Security Intelligence Service Act, R.S.C., 1985, c. C-23.

Canadian Space Agency. (2013). CASSIOPE: Observing space weather with a hybrid satellite. Retrieved from http://www.asc-csa.gc.ca/eng/satellites/cassiope.asp

Canadian Transportation Agency. (2004a). 100 years at the heart of transportation. Retrieved from http://www.otc-cta.gc.ca/doc.php?did=11&lang=eng

Canadian Transportation Agency. (2004b). All aboard—The Board of Railway Commissioners, 1904 to 1938. Retrieved from https://www.otc-cta.gc.ca/eng/publication/chapter-one-all-aboard-board-railway-commissioners-1904-1938

Carlsson, U. (2003). The rise and fall of NWICO: From a vision of international regulation to a reality of multilevel governance. *Nordicom Review, 24*(2), 31–67.

Carnegie, T. A. M., & Abell, J. (2009). Information, architecture, and hybridity: The changing discourse of public library. *Technical Communication Quarterly, 18*(3), 242–58.

Cartt.ca. (2008, 21 July). $4.3 billion in bids, 282 licenses and 15 companies = a new wireless frontier. Retrieved from http://www.cartt.ca/news/FullStory.cfm?NewsNo=6503&category=Cable-Telecom&title=-4-3-billion-in-bids-282-licenses-and-15-companies-a-new-wireless-frontier

Cartt.ca. (2012, 20 February). The shrinking control room—CTV Ottawa latest to lose jobs to automation. Retrieved from http://www.cartt.ca/news/PrinterFriendly.cfm?NewsNo=13231

Casey, C. (1996). *The hill on the Net: Congress enters the Information Age.* Boston: Academic Press.

Cashmore, E. (1994). *. . . and there was television.* London/New York: Routledge.

Cassell, P. (Ed.). (1993). *The Giddens reader.* London: Macmillan.

Castaldo, J. (2009, 23 November). Globalive, feds ponder options. *Canadian Business, 82*(20), 17–18.

Castells, M. (2000). *The Information Age: Economy, society and culture: The rise of the network society* (2nd ed., Vol. 1). Oxford/Malden, Massachusetts: Blackwell.

Castells, M. (2010). The new public sphere: Global civil society, communication networks, and global governance. In D. K. Thussu (Ed.), *International communication: A reader* (pp. 36–47). London/New York: Routledge.

Castells, M., & Cardoso, G. (Eds.). (2005). *The network society: From knowledge to policy.* Washington, DC: Johns Hopkins Center for Transatlantic Relations. Retrieved from http://www.umass.edu/digitalcenter/research/pdfs/JF_NetworkSociety.pdf

Castree, N. (2009). The Spatio-temporality of capitalism. *Time & Society, 18*(1), 26–61.

CBC. (2008). Canwest cuts 560 jobs Canada-wide. Retrieved from http://www.cbc.ca/canada/story/2008/11/12/canwest-cuts.html

CBC. (2009a). Canada's technology star becomes financial black hole. Retrieved from http://www.cbc.ca/news/business/story/2009/01/14/f-nortel-backgrounder-january09.html

CBC. (2009b). Make Nortel pay our pensions, workers urge Ottawa. Retrieved from http://www.cbc.ca/news/canada/ottawa/story/2009/09/15/nortel-pensioners.html

CBC. (2009c). Nokia deal launches Nortel's liquidation sale. Retrieved from http://www.cbc.ca/news/canada/ottawa/story/2009/06/22/ottawa-nortel-sale-wireless.html

CBC. (2009d). Is Ottawa still Silicon Valley North? Retrieved from http://www.cbc.ca/news/technology/story/2009/06/26/t-tech-silicon-valley-north-ottawa.html

CBC. (2012, 26 April). Globalive wins wireless fight with Public Mobile. Retrieved from http://www.cbc.ca/news/business/story/2012/04/26/scoc-wind-public-mobile.html

CBC. (2013). User generated content (UGC): Verification of user generated content (UGC) in news stories. Retrieved from http://www.cbc.radio-canada.ca/en/reporting-to-canadians/acts-and-policies/programming/journalism/ugc/

CBC News. (2011, 23 June). Indian film awards hit Toronto. Retrieved from http://www.cbc.ca/news/arts/iifaa/story/2011/06/23/iifa-opening-welcome.html

CBC News. (2012a, 13 February). Online surveillance critics accused of supporting child porn. Retrieved from http://www.cbc.ca/news/technology/story/2012/02/13/technology-lawful-access-toews-pornographers.html

CBC News. (2012b, 6 April). Ottawa cuts CAP public web access funding. Retrieved from http://www.cbc.ca/news/canada/calgary/story/2012/04/06/ns-cap-funding-cut.html

CBC News. (2012c, 18 May). Quebec adopts emergency law to end tuition crisis. Retrieved from http://www.cbc.ca/news/canada/montreal/story/2012/05/18/quebec-student-protest-law-bill-78.html

CBC News. (2012d, 6 March). What worries critics about omnibus crime bill.

Retrieved from http://www.cbc.ca/news/canada/story/2012/03/06/f-bill-c10-objections.html

CBC News Online. (2005, 22 June). RCMP: A brief history. Retrieved from http://www.cbc.ca/news/background/rcmp/

CBC News Politics. (2010, 1 December). Flanagan regrets WikiLeaks assassination remark. Retrieved from http://www.cbc.ca/news/politics/story/2010/12/01/flanagan-wikileaks-assange.html

CEP. (n.d.). Telecommunications, regulation and outsourcing [PowerPoint presentation]. Retrieved from http://www.cep.ca/en/publications/telecom-ownership-outsourcing

Chaput, C. (2011). Affect and belonging in late capitalism: A speculative narrative on reality TV. *International Journal of Communication, 5,* 1–20.

Charland, M. (2004). Technological nationalism. In D. J. Robinson (Ed.), *Communication history in Canada* (pp. 28–39). Don Mills: Oxford University Press.

Chase, S. (2012, 21 September). Ottawa casts wary eye on Chinese telecom giant. Retrieved from http://www.theglobeandmail.com/news/politics/ottawa-casts-wary-eye-on-chinese-telecom-giant/article4558259/

Chung, D. S. (2007). Profits and perils: Online news producers' perceptions of interactivity and uses of interactive features. *Convergence, 13*(1), 43–61.

Chung, E. (2010, 14 September). Video game subsidy battle heats up. CBC News. Retrieved from http://www.cbc.ca/news/technology/story/2010/09/08/video-game-incentives-subsidies.html

Chung, E. (2011, 17 August). Smart home security service launched by Rogers. CBC News. Retrieved from http://www.cbc.ca/news/technology/story/2011/08/17/technology-smart-home-rogers.html

CIPO. (2010). A guide to patents—Glossary. Retrieved from http://www.cipo.ic.gc.ca/eic/site/cipointernet-internetopic.nsf/eng/wr00143.html#p

CIPO. (2013). A guide to copyright. Retrieved from http://www.cipo.ic.gc.ca/eic/site/cipointernet-internetopic.nsf/eng/h_wr02281.html?Open&pv=1

CIPPIC. (2011). Agents of the state? The evolving role of online intermediaries in public sector surveillance. Retrieved from https://www.cippic.ca/index.php?q=fr/node/129187

Civil Marriage Act, S.C. 2005, c. 33.

Clark, A. (2005, 16 November). These photos may be illegal. *SMH, 15.*

Clarke, A. (2010). *Social media: Political uses and implications for democracy, Volume 4, No. 2010-10-E.* Ottawa: Library of Parliament Canada.

Clarke, H. D., Jenson, J., LeDuc, L., & Pammett, J. H. (1996). Leading the campaign. In H. D. Clarke, J. Jenson, L. LeDuc, & J. H. Pammett (Eds.), *Absent mandate: Canadian electoral politics in an age of restructuring* (pp. 70–92). Toronto, ON: Gage.

Clarke, L. S. (Ed.). (2007). *Religion, media and the marketplace.* New Brunswick, NJ: Rutgers University Press.

Clarke, R. (1988). Information technology and dataveillance. *Communications of the ACM, 3*(5), 498–512.

Clarke, R. (2009). Deep packet inspection: Its nature and implications. Retrieved from http://www.priv.gc.ca/information/research-recherche/2009/clarke_200903_e.asp

Clement, A., Moll, M., & Shade, L. R. (2001). Debating universal access in the Canadian context: The role of public interest organizations. In M. Moll & L. R. Shade (Eds.), *E-commerce vs. e-commons: Communications in the public interest* (pp. 23–48). Ottawa: Canadian Centre for Policy Alternatives.

Clifford, S., & Hardy, Q. (2013, 14 July). Attention, shoppers: Store is tracking your cell. *The New York Times.* Retrieved from http://www.nytimes.com/2013/07/15/business/attention-shopper-stores-are-tracking-your-cell.html?pagewanted=all&_r=0

CNN.com. (2002). Bush: Prevail in war, defeat.

Cohen, N. (2008). The valorization of surveillance: Towards a political economy of Facebook. *Democratic Communique, 22*(1), 5–22.

Cohen, N. (2010). Negotiating writers' rights: Freelance cultural labour and the challenge of organizing. *Just Labour: A Canadian Journal of Work and Society, 17&18,* 119–38.

Cohen, N. (2013). *Negotiating precarious cultural work: Freelance writers and collective organization in media industries* (Doctoral dissertation). Toronto, ON: York University.

Cohen, N., Macdonald, S., Mazepa, P., & Skinner, D. (2011). Making media public: From discussion to action? *Canadian Journal of Communication, 36,* 169–78.

Cohen, S., Hamilton, J. T., & Turner, F. (2011). Computational journalism: How computer scientists can empower journalists, democracy's watchdogs, in the production of news in the public interest. *Communications of the ACM, 54*(10), 66–71. Retrieved from http://cacm.acm.org/magazines/2011/10/131400-computational-journalism/fulltext

Cohen-Almagor, R. (2000). The terrorists' best ally: The Quebec media coverage of the FLQ Crisis in October 1970. *Canadian Journal of Communication, 25*(2), 251ff.

Collins, I. (1959). *The government and the newspaper press in France 1814–1881.* London: Oxford University Press.

Collinson, R. L. (1973). *The story of street literature: Forerunner of the popular press.* London: Dent.

Computer History Museum. (2006a). *Timeline of computer history: 1958.* Retrieved from http://www.computerhistory.org/timeline/?year=1958

Computer History Museum. (2006b). *Timeline of computer history: 1961.* Retrieved from http://www.computerhistory.org/timeline/?year=1961

Conley, D. (2002). *The daily miracle: An introduction to journalism* (2nd ed.). Melbourne: Oxford University Press.

Constitution Act, 1867, § 91 (1867).

Constitution Act, 1982, § 2 (1982).

Cook, R. F. (2013). Cinema returns to the source: Werner Herzog's Cave of Forgotten Dreams. *Film International, 11*(1), 26-41.

Coughlan, S. (2010, 3 June). The first wave of Internet pay walls. Retrieved from http://news.bbc.co.uk/2/hi/uk_news/magazine/8720282.stm

Cousins, M. (2004). *The story of film.* London: Pavilion Books.

Criminal Code, R.S.C., 1985, c. C-46.

Croteau, D., & Hoynes, W. (2000). *Media/society industries, image and audiences.* Thousand Oaks, CA: Pine Forge Press.

CRTC. (1999). Public notice CRTC 1999-118-1. Retrieved from http://www.crtc.gc.ca/eng/archive/1999/PB99-118-1.htm

CRTC. (2005). Broadcasting Public Notice CRTC 2005-61. Retrieved from http://www.crtc.gc.ca/eng/archive/2005/pb2005-61.htm

CRTC. (2009a). Broadcasting regulatory policy CRTC 2009-329: Review of broadcasting in new media. Retrieved from http://www.crtc.gc.ca/eng/archive/2009/2009-329.htm

CRTC. (2009b). Glossary. Retrieved from http://www.crtc.gc.ca/multites/mtwdk.exe?k=glossary-glossaire&l=60&w=297&n=1&s=5&t=2

CRTC. (2009c). The MAPL system—Defining a Canadian song. Retrieved from http://www.crtc.gc.ca/eng/info_sht/r1.htm

CRTC. (2009d). Telecom regulatory policy CRTC 2009-657. Retrieved from http://www.crtc.gc.ca/eng/archive/2009/2009-657.htm

CRTC. (2010). Communications monitoring report. Retrieved from http://www.crtc.gc.ca/eng/publications/reports/PolicyMonitoring/2010/cmr41.htm#n24

CRTC. (2012a). Broadcasting regulatory policy CRTC 2012-181: Broadcasting participation fund. Retrieved from http://www.crtc.gc.ca/eng/archive/2012/2012-181.htm

CRTC. (2012b, 4 September). CRTC issues annual report on the state of the Canadian communications industry. Retrieved from http://www.crtc.gc.ca/eng/com100/2012/r120904.htm#.Ud8GWW3y2hk

CSIS. (2012). Information security threats. Retrieved from http://www.csis-scrs.gc.ca/prrts/nfrmtn/index-eng.asp

CSTB. (1996). Cryptography's role in securing the information society. National Research Council. Retrieved from http://newton.nap.edu/html/crisis/ [3 April 2006].

Cuddihey, A., & Gordon, G. (2005, January/February). Canada leads the pack in E-government. *CA Magazine*. Retrieved from http://www.camagazine.com/archives/print-edition/2005/january-february/upfront/news-and-trends/camagazine17022.aspx

Curran, J. (1978). The press as an agency of social control: An historical perspective. In G. Boyce, J. Curran, & P. Wingate (Eds.), *Newspaper history from the seventeenth century to the present day* (pp. 51–75). London: Constable.

Curtis, B. (2001). *The politics of population: State formation, statistics, and the Census of Canada, 1840–1875*. Toronto, ON: University of Toronto Press.

CWIRP. (2008). ICT infrastructure as public infrastructure: Connecting communities to the knowledge-based economy & society: Final report of the Community Wireless Infrastructure Research Project. Retrieved from http://www.cwirp.ca/files/CWIRP_Final_report.pdf

Daase, C., & Kessler, O. (2007). Knowns and unknowns in the "War on Terror": Uncertainty and the political construction of danger. *Security Dialogue, 38*(4), 411–34.

Dacles, W. (2005). *The history of computers*. Retrieved from angelfire.com/de3/dacz/index.html [6 September 2005]

da Cruz, F. (2004, September 27). *Herman Hollerith*. Retrieved from www.columbia.edu/acis/history/hollerith.html [14 September 2005].

Dahlgren, P. (1991). Introduction. In P. Dahlgren & C. Sparks (Eds.), *Communication and citizenship: Journalism and the public sphere in the new media age* (pp. 27–57). London/New York: Routledge.

Dakroury, A. (2009). The baron of the right to communicate: Jean d'Arcy (1913–1983). In A. Dakroury, M. Eid, & Y. R. Kamalipour (Eds.), *The right to communicate* (pp. 21–42). Dubuque, IA: Kendall Hunt.

Davies, M., & Ryner, M. (Eds.). (2006). *Poverty and the production of world politics: Unprotected workers in the global political economy*. New York, NY: Palgrave Macmillan.

Davis, D. K. (1999). Media as public arena: Reconceptualizing the role of media for a post-Cold War and postmodern world. In R. C. Vincent, K. Nordenstreng, & M. R. Traber (Eds.), *Towards equity in global communication*. New Jersey: Hampton Press.

Dawkins, R. (1989). *The selfish gene* (2nd ed.). London: Oxford University Press.

DCITA. (2004). *Australia's strategic framework for the information economy 2004–2006*. Canberra: DCITA.

Dean, J. (2005). Communicative capitalism: Circulation and the foreclosure of politics. *Cultural Politics, 1*(1), 51–74.

De Bens, E., & Mazzoleni, G. (1998). The media in the age of digital communication. In D. McQuail & K. Siune (Eds.), *Media policy: Convergence, concentration and commerce*. London: Sage.

Debord, G. (1977). Society of the spectacle. Retrieved from http://www.marxists.org/reference/archive/debord/society.htm

Defense of Marriage Act, Pub. L. No. 104–199, 110 Stat. 2419, 1 U.S.C. § 7 and 28 U.S.C. § 1738C (1996).

De La Merced, M. J. (2012, 19 January). Eastman Kodak files for bankruptcy. *The New York Times*. Retrieved from http://dealbook.nytimes.com/2012/01/19/eastman-kodak-files-for-bankruptcy/

Delbridge, A. (Ed.). (1990). *The Penguin Macquarie dictionary*. Melbourne: Penguin (in association with the Macquarie Library).

Demers, D. P., & Nichols, S. (1987). *Precision journalism: A practical guide*. Newbury Park, CA: Sage.

Department of Finance Canada. (2010, March 4). Budget 2010. Retrieved from http://www.budget.gc.ca/2010/pdf/budget-plan-budgetaire-eng.pdf

Desbarats, P. (2001). The special role of magazines in the history of Canadian mass media and national development. In B. Singer & C. McKie (Eds.), *Communications in Canadian society*, 5th ed. (pp. 57–66). Toronto: Thompson.

De Souza, M. (2008, 4 December). "A slap in the face to all voters": Canadians on the potential Liberal-NDP-Bloc coalition government. The Ottawa Citizen, A4.

Deuze, M., & Dimoudi, C. (2002). Online journalists in the Netherlands: Towards a profile of a new profession. *Journalism, 3*(1), 85–100.

Dobbin, B. (2007, 9 February). Kodak slashes 3,000 more jobs as it turns to digital imaging: Layoffs part of strategy to invest in consumer photography, printing. *Toronto Star*, E4.

Doctorow, C. (2012, 31 May). Arrêtez-moi quelqu'un! Vowing to violate Quebec's anti-protest law. Retrieved from http://boingboing.net/2012/05/31/arretez-moi-quel;quun-vowing.html [20 November 2012].

Dornan, C. (2007). Other people's money: The debate over foreign ownership in the media. In D. Taras, K. Pannekoek, & M. Bajardjieva (Eds.), *How Canadians communicate II* (pp. 47–64). Calgary: University of Calgary Press.

Dowd, M. (2003, 21 May). *Walk this way.* Retrieved from http://www.nytimes.com/2003/05/21/opinion/walk-this-way.html [cited 5 November 2005].

Dowding, M. (2002). Universal access in IHAC and NIIAC: Transforming narrative and meaning in information policy. In M. Pendakur & R. Harris (Eds.), *Citizenship and Participation in the Information Age* (pp. 211–18). Aurora, ON: Garamond Press.

Downey, G. (2000). *Telegraph messenger boy: Labor, technology, and geography, 1850–1950.* New York, NY. Routledge.

Downing, J., et al. (Eds.). (1991). *Computers for social change and community organizing.* London: Haworth Press.

Drache, D. (2008). *Defiant publics: The unprecedented reach of the global citizen.* Polity Press.

Draper, J. (2000). Foreword. In W. Schwartau (Ed.), *Cybershock: Surviving hackers, phreakers, identity thieves, Internet terrorists and weapons of mass disruption.* New York: Thunder's Mouth Press.

Druick, Z. (2007). *Projecting Canada: Government policy and documentary film at the National Film Board of Canada.* Montreal: McGill-Queen's University Press.

Dudley, J. (2005a, 18–19 June). Dial your own future. *Courier-Mail,* 27.

Dudley, J. (2005b, 21–2 May). Ears to the groundswell. *Courier-Mail,* 30.

Duhigg, C., & Kocieniewski, D. (2012, April 28). How Apple sidesteps billions in taxes. *The New York Times.* Retrieved from http://www.nytimes.com/2012/04/29/business/apples-tax-strategy-aims-at-low-tax-states-and-nations.html?_r=0

Dunn, A. (2006). The other domestic spying: Numerous domestic surveillance programs are underway besides the NSA. Retrieved from http://www.thirdworldtraveler.com/Subverting%20_Democracy/US_Surveillance_History.html

Dyer-Witheford, N. (1999). *Cyber-Marx: Cycles and circuits of struggle in high-technology capitalism.* Urbana/Chicago: University of Illinois Press.

Earth Island Journal. (2001). The globalization of repression. *Earth Island Journal.*

The Economist. (1999, December 31). Talking to the world. *The Economist* (Millennium issue), 83–5.

The Economist. (2010, 25 November). Mean streets: The persistence of poverty amid plenty. Retrieved from http://www.economist.com/node/17581844

ECORYS. (2009). Study on the competitiveness of the EU security industry: Final report. Brussels: ECORYS SCS Group. Retrieved from http://ec.europa.eu/enterprise/policies/security/files/study_on_the_competitiveness_of_the_eu_security_industry_en.pdf

Edge, M. (2011). Convergence after the collapse: The "catastrophic" case of Canada. *Media, Culture & Society, 33*(8), 1266–78.

Edwards, P. (1996). *The closed world: Computers and the politics of discourse in cold war America.* Cambridge: MIT Press.

EFF. (n.d.) Digital content locks. Retrieved from https://www.eff.org/sites/default/files/filenode/DRM_pager_FNL.pdf

Ehrlich, M. C. (1997). The competitive ethos in television newswork. In D. Berkowitz (Ed.), *Social meanings of news: A text-reader.* Thousand Oaks, California: Sage.

Eisenstein, E. (1980). *The printing press as agent of change* (Vol. 1). Cambridge: Cambridge University Press.

El Akkad, O. (2013, 20 July). Landmark ruling against Apple changes the game for digital entertainment. *The Globe and Mail.* Retrieved from http://www.theglobeandmail.com/report-on-business/international-business/us-business/judge-says-apple-conspired-to-raise-prices-on-e-books/article13106638/

Elmer, G. (2007, 12 November). Canadian political blogosphere undergoes transition. *The Hill Times,* 12.

El-Nawawy, M., & Khamis, S. (2012). Political activism 2.0: Comparing the role of social media in Egypt's "Facebook Revolution" and Iran's "Twitter Uprising." *CyberOrient, 6*(1). Retrieved from http://www.cyberorient.net/article.do?articleId=7439

Encyclopaedia Britannica. (2013). Retrieved from http://www.britannica.com/EBchecked/topic/533828/semaphore

Engel, M. (1996). *Tickle the public: One hundred years of the popular press.* London: Victor Gollancz.

Engels, F. (1876/1975). *The part played by labour in the transition from ape to man.* Peking (Beijing): Foreign Language Press.

Engels, F. (1888/1976). *Ludwig Feuerbach and the end of classical German philosophy.* Peking (Beijing): Foreign Language Press.

Epstein, E. J. (2010). *The Hollywood economist: The hidden financial reality behind the movies.* Brooklyn, NY: Melville House.

Ernst & Young. (1999, August). *The knowledge economy* [Government report]. Ministry of Economic Development (New Zealand). Retrieved from http://www.med.govt.nz/templates/MultipageDocumentTOC____17256.aspx [3 April 2006].

Erwin, S., & Valorzi, J. (2004, 10 December). Kodak Canada closing Toronto factory; Restructuring claims 360 jobs; Photography giant "adjusting capacity." *Toronto Star,* C01.

Essinger, J. (2004). *Jacquard's web: How a hand-loom led to the birth of the information age.* New York, NY: Oxford University Press.

Ewen, S. (1996). *PR! A social history of spin.* New York, NY: Basic Books.

Fairclough, N. (c. 2000). The dialectics of discourse. Retrieved from www.ling.lancs.ac.uk/staff/norman/2001a.doc [23 March 2006].

Farmer, D., & Mann, C. C. (2003, April). Surveillance nation, Part 1. *Technology Review,* 34–43.

Farrell, P. B. (2008, 19 November). 30 reasons for Great Depression 2 by 2011. *MarketWatch.* Retrieved from http://www.marketwatch.com/story/well-great-depression-2-2011

FCC. (n.d.). Communications Assistance for Law Enforcement Act (CALEA). Retrieved from http://transition.fcc.gov/pshs/services/calea/

Fekete, J. (2012). Spy agency warns of security risks as government reviews Nexen takeover. Retrieved from http://o.canada.com/2012/09/20/114217/

Fekete, J. (2013, 13 March). Critics fear Tory plan to merge websites an effort to cut off access to information. *National Post*. Retrieved from http://news.nationalpost.com/2013/03/28/critics-fear-tory-plan-to-merge-websites-an-effort-to-cut-off-access-to-information/

Ferguson, C. (1998, 9 April). Howard Aiken: Makin' a computer wonder. *Harvard University Gazette*. Retrieved from www. news.harvard.edu/gazette;1998/04.09/HowardAiken/Maki.html [14 September 2005].

Fetherling, D. (1990). *The rise of the Canadian newspaper*. Toronto: Oxford University Press.

Filion, M. (1996). Radio. In M. Dorland (Ed.), *The cultural industries in Canada: Problems, policies and prospects* (pp. 118–42). Toronto: James Lorimer.

Finch, D., Varella, P., & Walker, D. (2010, 23 October). Nenshi, social media and the purple pandemic. *The Calgary Herald*. Retrieved from http://www2.canada.com/calgaryherald/news/theeditorialpage/story.html?id=f1160d0f-2ff4-484a-8a47-11114226f8e7

Fiser, A., & Clement, A. (2009). K-Net and Canadian Aboriginal communities. *Technology and Society Magazine, IEEE, 28*(2), 23–33.

Fitchett, J., & Lim, Ming. (2008). Consumer experiences in the "house of the future": An enquiry into surveillance-based consumer research techniques. *Consumption Markets & Culture, 11*(2), 137–49.

Fletcher, F. J. (in press). Journalism, corporate media, and democracy in the digital era. In K. Kozolanka (Ed.), *Publicity and the Canadian state*. Toronto: University of Toronto Press.

Flew, T. (2005). *New media: An introduction* (2nd ed.). Melbourne: Oxford University Press.

Flickr. (2013). About Flickr. Retrieved from http://www.flickr.com/about/

Florida, R. (2010). *The great reset: How new ways of living and working drive post crash prosperity*. Toronto: Random House.

Florida, R. (2012). *The creative class, 10th anniversary edition*. Basic Books.

Foley, S. (2012, 16 February). Apple admits it has a human rights problem. *The Independent*. Retrieved from http://www.independent.co.uk/news/world/asia/apple-admits-it-has-a-human-rights-problem-6898617.html [20 July 2012].

Forgacs, D. (Ed.). (2000). *The Antonio Gramsci reader: Selected writings 1916–1935*. New York: New York University Press.

Forgacs, D., & Nowell-Smith, G. (Eds). (1985). *Antonio Gramsci: Selections from cultural writings*. Cambridge, Massachusetts: Harvard University Press.

Foucault, M. (1979). *Discipline and punish*. New York: Vintage Books.

Foucault, M. (1990). *History of sexuality* (Vol. 1). New York: Vintage Books.

Francoli, M., Greenberg, J., & Waddell, C. (2011). The campaign in the digital media. In J. Pammett & C. Dornan (Eds.), *The Canadian Federal Election of 2011* (pp. 219–46). Toronto: Dundurn Press.

Franklin, B. (1997). *Newszak and news media*. London: Arnold.

Franklin, U. (2004). *CBC Massey lectures: The real world of technology* (Rev. ed.). Toronto: House of Anansi Press.

Fraterrigo, E. (2009). *Playboy and the making of the good life in modern America*. London: Oxford University Press.

Freedman, D. (2008). *The politics of media policy*. Cambridge, UK: Polity Press.

Free Software Foundation. (2009). What is copyleft? Retrieved from http://www.gnu.org/copyleft/

Freeze, C. (2012, 3 May). Why is a Liberal senator's name on a no-fly list? *The Globe and Mail*. Retrieved from http://www.theglobeandmail.com/news/politics/why-is-liberal-senators-name-on-no-fly-list/article4104653/

Friedlander, B. (2011, 24 July). An interview with a madman: Breivik asks and answers his own questions. *TimeWorld*. Retrieved from http://www.time.com/time/world/article/0,8599,2084895,00.html#ixzz2342gJUER

Friesen, J. (2000). *Aboriginal spirituality and biblical theology: Closer than you think*. Calgary, AB: Detselig Enterprises.

FTC. (2013). FTC warns data broker operations of possible privacy violations [Federal Trade Commission press release]. Retrieved from http://www.ftc.gov/opa/2013/05/databroker.shtm

Fuchs, C. (2009). Information and communication technologies and society: A contribution to the critique of the political economy of the Internet. *European Journal of Communication, 24*(1), 69–87.

Fuchs, C. (2010). Labor in informational capitalism and on the Internet. *The Information Society, 26*, 179–96.

Fuchs, C. (2012). The political economy of privacy on Facebook. *Television & New Media, 13*(2), 139–59.

Fuchs, C., Boersma, K., Albrechtslund, A., & Sandoval, M. (Eds.). (2011). *Internet and surveillance: The challenges of Web 2.0 and social media*. New York: Routledge.

Gandy, O. (1988). The political economy of communication competence. In V. Mosco & J. Wasko (Eds.), *The political economy of information* (pp. 35–47). Madison: University of Wisconsin Press.

Gandy, O. (1993). *The panoptic sort: A political economy of private information*. Boulder: Westview.

Garson, B. (1988). *The electronic sweatshop*. New York: Simon & Schuster.

Geist, M. (2005). Piercing the peer-to-peer myths: An examination of the Canadian experience. *First Monday, 10*(4). Retrieved from http://firstmonday.org/htbin/cgiwrap/bin/ojs/index.php/fm/article/view/1217

Geist, M. (Ed.). (2010). *From radical extremism to balanced copyright: Canadian copyright and the digital agenda*. Toronto: Irwin Law.

Ghosts in the machine. (2005, 23–4 April). *Weekend Australian*, 17.

Gibson, W. (1993a). *Neuromancer*. London: Victor Gollancz.

Gibson, W. (1993b). *Virtual light*. London: Penguin.

Gibson, W. (1995a). Burning chrome. In W. Gibson (Ed.), *Burning chrome*. London: Voyager.

Gibson, W. (1995b). The Gernsback continuum. In W. Gibson (Ed.), *Burning chrome*. London: Voyager.

Gibson, W. (1995c). Johnny Mnemonic. In W. Gibson (Ed.), *Burning chrome*. London: Voyager.

Giddens, A. (1995). *A contemporary critique of historical materialism* (2nd ed.). Houndmills, Basingstoke: Macmillan.

Gillmor, D. (2005). Where citizens and journalists intersect. *Nieman Reports*, 59(4), 11–13.

Ginsburg, J. C., & Kernochan, J. M. (1989). One hundred and two years later: The US joins the Berne Convention. *Columbia–VLA Journal of Law and the Arts*, (13), 1–38.

Gitlin, T. (1991). Bites and blips: Chunk news, savvy talk and the bifurcation of American politics. In P. Dahlgren & C. Sparks (Eds.), *Communication and citizenship: Journalism and the public sphere in the new media age*. London/New York: Routledge.

Gladwell, M. (2010, 4 October). Small change. *The New Yorker*. Retrieved from http://www.newyorker.com/reporting/2010/10/04/101004fa_fact_gladwell

Gladwell, M. (2011, 2 February). Does Egypt need Twitter? *The New Yorker*. Retrieved from http://www.newyorker.com/online/blogs/newsdesk/2011/02/does-egypt-need-twitter.html

Glasner, J. (2000, 14 April). Why the bubble's in trouble. *Wired*. Retrieved from http://www.wired.com/news/business/0,35477-0.html

Glickman, L., & Fingerhut, J. (2011). User-generated content: Recent developments in Canada and the US. *Internet and e-commerce law in Canada*, 12(6), 49–76. Retrieved from http://www.casselsbrock.com/files/file/docs/UGC%20Paper%20in%20IECLIC%20-%20October%202011%20Glickman%20and%20Fingerhut.pdf

The Globe and Mail. (2012). CSIS report raises a question to be asked about the CNOOC-Nexen deal. Retrieved from http://m.theglobeandmail.com/commentary/editorials/csis-report-raises-a-question-to-be-asked-about-the-cnooc-nexen-deal/article4568077/?service=mobile

Goff, P. (2005, 12 October). China rues the sound of one hand tapping. *SMH*, 15.

Gottliebsen, R. (2006, February 4–5). Technology gurus unveil new corporate paradigm. *Weekend Australian*, 32.

Government of Canada. (2005). Summary of submissions to the lawful access consultation. Retrieved from http://www.justice.gc.ca/eng/cons/la-al/sum-res/faq.html

Government of Canada. (2009). Spectrum management policy. Retrieved from http://www.ic.gc.ca/eic/site/ceprc-ccrcp.nsf/eng/00029.html

Government of Canada. (2010, March 3). Speech from the throne. Retrieved from http://www.speech.gc.ca/eng/media.asp?id=1388

Government Services. (2011). e-Government. Retrieved from http://www.mgs.gov.on.ca/en/IAndIT/STEL02_046918.html

Govil, N. (2005). Hollywood effects and Bollywood FX. In G. Elmer & M. Gasher (Eds.), *Contracting out Hollywood: Runaway productions and foreign location shooting* (pp. 92–114). Lanham, MD: Rowman & Littlefield.

Graham, P. (1999). *Hypercapitalism: Political economy, electric identity, and authorial alienation*. Newcastle, UK: Northumbria University.

Graham, P. (2002). Hypercapitalism: Language, new media and social perceptions of value. *Discourse & Society*, 13(2), 228–49.

Greenberg, J., & Hier, S. (2008). CCTV surveillance and the poverty of media discourse: A content analysis of Canadian newspaper coverage. *Canadian Journal of Communication*, 34, 461–86.

Greenpeace. (2010). GMO foods campaign. Retrieved from http://www.greenpeace.org/canada/en/campaigns/ge/

Greenpeace. (2013). Genetic engineering. Retrieved from http://www.greenpeace.org/international/en/campaigns/agriculture/problem/genetic-engineering/

Greenwald, G. (2013, 29 June). Speaking on NSA stories, Snowden and journalism. *The Guardian*. Retrieved from http://www.theguardian.com/commentisfree/2013/jun/29/speech-nsa-snowden-journalism

Groombridge, B. (1972). Television and the people: A programme for democratic participation. In W. van der Eyken (Ed.), *Penguin Education*. Melbourne: Penguin.

Grossman, L. (1999). The electronic republic. In R. E. Hiebert (Ed.), *Impact of mass media: Current issues*. New York: Addison-Wesley Longman.

Grover, R. (2008, 1 August). The news gets worse for newspapers. *Business Week*, 20–23.

Gustin, S. (2012, 10 February). Apple now worth more than Microsoft, Google combined. *Time*. Retrieved from http://business.time.com/2012/02/10/apple-now-worth-more-than-microsoft-google-combined/

Gwynne, B. (2005). Smoke and mirrors: A commentary of prospects for success for the WSIS process and the role of the smart state. In R. Briet & J. Servaes (Eds.), *Information society or knowledge societies? UNESCO in the smart state*. Penang: Southbound.

Habuchi, I. Accelerating reflexivity. In M. Ito, D. Okabe, & M. Matsuda (Eds.), *Personal, portable, pedestrian: Mobile phones in Japanese life* (pp. 165–82). Cambridge, MA: MIT Press.

Hackett, R. A., & Anderson, S. (2011). Research in brief: Democratizing communication policy in Canada: A social movement perspective. *Canadian Journal of Communication*, 36(1), 161–8.

Hackett, R. A., & Carroll, W. K. (2006). *Remaking media: The struggle to democratize public communication*. New York/London: Routledge.

Hackett, R. A., & Gruneau, R. (2000). *The missing news: Filters and blindspots in Canada's press*. Ottawa, ON: Canadian Centre for Policy Alternatives.

Hackett, R., & Zhao, Y. (1997). *Sustaining democracy? Journalism and the politics of objectivity*. Toronto, ON: Garamond Press.

Hackett, R., & Zhao, Y. (2005). Media globalization, media democratization: Challenges, issues and paradoxes. In R. Hackett & Y. Zhao (Eds.), *Democratizing global media: One world, many struggles* (pp. 1–33). Lanham, MD: Rowman & Littlefield.

Haddadi, A. (2011, 30 June). Did social media networks like Facebook and Twitter really influence the Arab Spring? *International Business Times*.

Retrieved from http://www.ibtimes.co.uk/articles/172268/20110701/did-social-networks-likefacebook-and-twitter-really-influence-the-arab-spring.htm

Hafner, K., & Lyon, M. (2003). *Where wizards stay up late*. London: Pocket Books.

Hafner, K., & Markoff, J. (1991). *Cyberpunk: Outlaws and hackers on the computer frontier*. New York: Simon & Schuster.

Hall, J. (1997). *Radio Canada International: Voice of a middle power*. Michigan University Press.

Hall, S. (1996). Techniques of the medium. In J. Corner & S. Harvey (Eds.), *Television times: A reader*. London: Arnold.

Halliday, J. (2010, 20 July). Times loses almost 90% of online readership. *The Guardian*. Retrieved from http://www.guardian.co.uk/media/2010/jul/20/times-paywall-readership?INTCMP=SRCH

Hallin, D. (1989). *The "uncensord war": The media and Vietnam*. Berkeley: University of California Press.

Hamelin, J., & Beaulieu, A. (1966). Aperçu du journalisme québécois d'expression française. *Recherches sociographiques*, *7*(3), 305–48.

Hamelink, C. J., & Nordenstreng, K. (2007). Toward democratic media governance. In E. de Bens (Ed.), *Media between culture and commerce* (pp. 225–42). Changing Media, Changing Europe Series (Vol. 4). Bristol, UK: Intellect.

Hanks, P. (Ed.). (1990). *The Collins concise dictionary plus*. London: Collins.

Hannigan, J. A. (2001). Canadian media ownership and control in an age of the Internet and global megamedia empires. In C. McKie & B. D. Singer (Eds.), *Communication in Canadian society*, 5th ed. (pp. 245–55). Toronto: Thompson.

Harding, R. (2006). Historical representations of Aboriginal people in the Canadian news media. *Discourse & Society*, *17*(2), 205–35.

Hardt, H., & Brennen, B. (1995). *Newsworkers: Toward a history of the rank and file*. Minneapolis: University of Minnesota Press.

Hardt, M., & Negri, A. (2004). *Multitude: War and democracy in the Age of Empire*. New York: Penguin Press.

Hargreaves, I. (2003). *Journalism: Truth or dare?* Oxford: Oxford University Press.

Harkness, R. (1963). *J. E. Atkinson of the Star*. Toronto, ON: University of Toronto Press.

Hartley, J. (1996). *Popular reality: Journalism, modernity, popular culture*. London: Arnold.

Hartley, J. (1999). What is journalism? The view from under a stubbie cap. *Media International Australia Incorporating Culture and Policy*, *90*, 15–31.

Hartley, J. (Ed.). (2005). *Creative industries*. Oxford: Blackwell Publishing.

Harvey, D. (1989). *The condition of postmodernity: An enquiry into the origins of cultural change*. Cambridge, MA: Blackwell.

Hearn, G., Anthony, D., Holman, L., Dunleavy, J., & Mandeville, T. (1994). *The information superhighway and consumers* (Research report). Brisbane: The Communication Centre, Faculty of Business, Queensland University of Technology.

Held, D., McGrew, A., Goldblatt, D., & Perraton, J. (1999). What is globalization? Global transformations. Retrieved from http://www.polity.co.uk/global/whatisglobalization.asp

Henry, F., & Tator, C. (2000). *Racist discourse in Canada's English print media*. Toronto: The Canadian Race Relations Foundation. Retrieved from http://www.crr.ca/index2.php?option=com_content&do_pdf=1&id=256

Herman, E., & Chomsky, N. (1988). *Manufacturing consent: The political economy of the mass media*. New York: Pantheon.

Herman, E., & McChesney, R. (1997). *Global media: The new missionaries of global capitalism*. New York: Continuum.

Hermida, A. (2011). The journalist's relationship with users: New dimensions to conventional roles. In J. B. Singer et al. (Eds.). *Participatory journalism: Guarding open gates at online newspapers* (pp. 13–33). Malden, MA: Wiley-Blackwell.

Heron, C. (1996). *The Canadian labour movement: A short history* (2nd ed.). Toronto: J. Lorimer.

Heyn, H. C. (1969). *Writing for newspapers and news services*. New York, NY: Funk and Wagnails.

Hibbard, C. M. (2012). Wiretapping the Internet. *Federal Communications Law Journal*, *64*, 371–99.

Hiebert, R. E. (Ed.). (1999). *Impact of mass media: Current issues*. New York: Addison-Wesley Longman.

High, S. (2003). Industrial sunset: The making of North America's rust belt, 1969–1984. Toronto: University of Toronto Press.

High, S., & Lewis, D. W. (2007). *Corporate wasteland: The landscape and memory of deindustrialization*. Toronto, ON: Between the Lines.

Hill, R., & Moran, N. (2011). Social marketing meets interactive media. *International Journal of Advertising*, *30*(5), 815–38.

Hilmes, M., Newcomb, H., & Meehan E. (2012). Legacies from the past: Histories of television. *Journal of Communication Inquiry*, *36*(4), 276–87.

Hirji, F. (2010). *Dreaming in Canadian: South Asian youth, Bollywood and belonging*. Vancouver: UBC Press.

Hirji, F. (2011). Through the looking glass: Muslim women on television—An analysis of *24*, *Lost*, and *Little Mosque on the Prairie*. *Global Media Journal*, *4*(2), 33–47.

Hirst, M., & Harrison, J. (2007). *Communication and new media: From broadcast to narrowcast*. Melbourne: Oxford University Press.

Hirst, M., & Patching, R. (2005). *Journalism ethics: Arguments and cases*. Melbourne: Oxford University Press.

Hirst, M., & Schutze, R. (2004a). Allies down under? The Australian at war and the "big lie." In R. D. Berenger (Ed.), *Global media goes to war: Role of news and entertainment media during the 2003 Iraq war*. Spokane, WA: Marquette Books.

Hirst, M., & Schutze, R. (2004b). Duckspeak crusader: Greg Sheridan's unique brand of seculo-Christian morality. *Overland*, *176*, 18–25.

Hollis, P. (1970). *The pauper press: A study in working-class radicalism of the 1830s*. Oxford: Oxford University Press.

Holub, R. (1992). Antonio Gramsci: Beyond Marxism and postmodernism. In C.

Norris (Ed.), *Critics of the twentieth century*. London: Routledge.

Houpt, S. (2012, 12 September). Is the Huffington Post the future of journalism? Retrieved from http://m.theglobeandmail.com/arts/is-the-huffington-post-the-future-of-journalism/article550547/?service=mobile

Hoyle, M. A. (2004, 14 September). *Computers: From the past to the present.* Retrieved from http://www.eingang.org/Lecture/ [6 September 2005].

HRSDC. (2013). Indicators of well-being in Canada: Work–unionization rates. Retrieved from http://www4.hrsdc.gc.ca/.3ndic.1t.4r@-eng.jsp?iid=17

Hudson, I., & Hudson, M. (2003, December). Removing the veil? Commodity fetishism, fair trade, and the environment. Organization Environment, *16*(4), 413–30.

Human Rights Watch. (2012). World report 2012: China. Retrieved from http://www.hrw.org/world-report-2012/world-report-2012-china [20 July 2012].

Huxley, A. (1965a). Brave new world. In A. Huxley (ed.), *Brave new world & brave new world revisited.* New York: Harper Perennial.

Huxley, A. (1965b) [1932]. Brave new world revisited. In A. Huxley (ed.), *Brave new world & brave new world revisited.* New York: Harper Perennial.

IBM. (n.d.). Fortran: The pioneering programming language. Retrieved from http://www-03.ibm.com/ibm/history/ibm100/us/en/icons/fortran/

IEEE Virtual Museum. (2005). War as a technological watershed. Retrieved from http://www.ieee-virtual-museum.org/exhibit [14 September 2005].

IFEX Communique. (2005). Is Microsoft aiding Internet censorship in China? Retrieved from www.ifex.org/ [20 June 2005].

Industry Canada. (2007). *Mobilizing science and technology to Canada's advantage: Executive summary.* Ottawa: Public Works and Government Services Canada.

Industry Canada. (2009). Canada and the information society. Retrieved from http://www.ic.gc.ca/eic/site/wsis-smsi.nsf/eng/00043.html

Industry Canada. (2010a). Improving Canada's digital advantage—Strategies for sustainable prosperity: Consultation paper on a digital economy strategy for Canada. Retrieved from http://www.ic.gc.ca/eic/site/028.nsf/eng/00036.html

Industry Canada. (2010b, 22 November). Minister Clement updates Canadians on Canada's digital economy strategy. Retrieved from http://www.ic.gc.ca/eic/site/064.nsf/eng/06096.html [6 June 2011].

Indymedia.org. (2006). Independent media center. Retrieved from http://www.indymedia.org/en/index.shtml [8 April 2006].

Innis, H. A. (1923). *A history of the Canadian Pacific Railway.* Toronto, ON: University of Toronto Press.

Innis, H. A. (1950). *Empire and communications.* Toronto, ON: University of Toronto Press.

Innis, H. A. (1951). *The bias of communication.* Toronto, ON: University of Toronto Press.

Institute for Robotics and Mechatronics. (n.d.). Our research vision. Retrieved from http://www.mie.utoronto.ca/IRM/research/

Intel. (n.d.). Moore's Law inspires Intel innovation. Retrieved from http://www.intel.com/technology/mooreslaw/

International Wireless Telegraph Convention. (1906). *Service regulations affixed to the International Wireless Telegraph Convention.* Washington, DC: Government Printing Office.

Investopedia. (n.d.). Weather future. Retrieved from http://www.investopedia.com/terms/w/weatherfuture.asp

Israel, T. (2011). Roundtable: The evolving role of cyber surveillance in public sector decision-making. Retrieved from http://www.cippic.ca/uploads/20110602-CyberSurveillance-Roundtable_Agenda.pdf

ITAC. (2013). Cyber security forum. Retrieved from http://itac.ca/program_details/cyber_security_forum1/

ITU. (n.d.). Historical timeline of Canadian telecommunications achievements. Retrieved from http://www.itu.int/newsarchive/wtsa2000/english/media/timeline.pdf

ITU. (2012). Measuring the information society. Retrieved from http://www.itu.int/ITU-D/ict/publications/idi/

ITU and infoDev. (2010). ICT regulation toolkit. Retrieved from http://www.ictregulationtoolkit.org/en/Index.html

Jacknis, I. (2000). Coming to light: Edward S. Curtis and the Native Americans. *Visual Anthropology Review, 16*(1), 87–90.

Jackson, J. (1999). Newspaper ownership in Canada: An overview of the Davey Committee and Kent Commission studies. Retrieved from http://publications.gc.ca/Collection-R/LoPBdP/BP/prb9935-e.htm

Jeffries, S. (2012, 4 July). Why Marxism is on the rise again. *The Guardian.* Retrieved from http://www.guardian.co.uk/world/2012/jul/04/the-return-of-marxism

Jenkins, H. (2008). *Convergence culture: Where old and new media collide.* New York: New York University Press.

Jensen, R. (2004). *Citizens of the empire: The struggle to claim our humanity.* San Francisco: City Lights.

Jewell, M. (2008). Industries frantic to find Polaroid instant film. Retrieved from http://www.manufacturing.net/news/2008/02/industries-frantic-to-find-polaroid-instant-film?menuid=36

The Jobs Letter No. 123. (2000, 12 May). The dot.com crash . . . after Wall St's biggest fall in history. Retrieved from http://www.jobsletter.org.nz/jbl12310.htm [19 March 2006].

Johnson, L. (2011, 31 August). More details of Rogers home security service emerge. SP&T News. Retrieved from http://www.sptnews.ca/Home-Automation/News/more-details-of-rogers-home-security-service-emerge.html#topart

Jones, J., & Salter, L. (2012). *Digital journalism.* London/Thousand Oaks, CA: Sage.

Jones, P., & Holmes, D. (2011). *Key concepts in media and communications.* Los Angeles, CA: Sage.

Jones, S. E. (2006). *Against technology: From the Luddites to Neo-Luddism.* New York, NY: Routledge.

Jönsson, A. M., & Örnebring, H. (2011). User-generated content and the news: Empowerment for citizens or interactive illusion? *Journalism Practice*, 5(2), 127–44.

Josephi, B. (2012). How much democracy does journalism need? *Journalism*, 14(4), 474–89.

Kafka, P. (2013, 5 June). The CIA invests in narrative science and its automated writers. *All Things D*. Retrieved from http://allthingsd.com/20130605/the-c-i-a-invests-in-narrative-science-and-its-automated-writers/?mod=atdtweet

Kapica, J. (2011, 17 August). Rogers introduces web-based home-security system. *Digital Journal*. Retrieved from http://digitaljournal.com/article/310461

Kaplan, J. A. (2011). 45 years later, does Moore's Law still hold true? Retrieved from http://www.foxnews.com/scitech/2011/01/04/years-later-does-moores-law-hold-true/37

Karim, K. H. (Ed.). (2003). *The media of diaspora*. London/New York: Routledge.

Karim, K. H. (2006). Nation and diaspora: Rethinking multiculturalism in a transnational context. *International Journal of Media and Cultural Politics*, 2(3), 267–82.

Karlin, M. (2012, 17 February). The threat of "Big Brother" Internet monitoring in Canada. Rabble.ca. Retrieved from http://rabble.ca/news/2012/02/threat-big-brother-internet-monitoring-canada

Kaur, V. (2012, 8 August). US military open your doors to Sikhs. *The Washington Post*. Retrieved from http://www.washingtonpost.com/blogs/guest-voices/post/us-military-open-your-doors-to-sikhs/2012/08/08/165c634c-e1a0-11e1-a25e-15067bb31849_blog.html

Kealey, G. (1973). *Canada investigates industrialism*. Toronto: University of Toronto Press.

Kealey, G., & Whitaker, R. (Eds.). (1989). *RCMP security bulletins, the war series, 1939–1941*. St. John's: Canadian Committee on Labour History.

Kealey, G., & Whitaker, R. (Eds.). (1997a). *RCMP security bulletins, the depression years, Part IV, 1937*. St. John's: Canadian Committee on Labour History.

Kealey, G., & Whitaker, R. (Eds.). (1997b). *RCMP security bulletins, the depression years, Part V, 1938–1939*. St. John's: Canadian Committee on Labour History.

Kearns, I. (2002). *Code red: Progressive politics in the digital age*. London: Institute for Public Policy Research.

Kern, S. (2003). Wireless world. In D. Crowley & P. Heyer (Eds.), *Communications in history: Technology, culture, society* (pp. 210–13). Toronto: Pearson Education, Inc.

Keshen, J. (1996). *Propaganda and censorship during Canada's Great War*. Edmonton: The University of Alberta Press.

Kesterton, M. (2012, September 23). Does the future of labour involve working alongside robots? *The Globe and Mail*. Retrieved from http://www.theglobeandmail.com/life/facts-and-arguments/does-the-future-of-labour-involve-working-alongside-robots/article4560145/

Kesterton, W. H. (1967). *A history of journalism in Canada*. Toronto: McClelland and Stewart Limited.

Khouri, M. (2007). *Filming politics: Communism and the portrayal of the working class at the National Film Board of Canada, 1939–46*. Calgary, Alberta: University of Calgary Press.

King content. (2006, 21–7 January). *The Economist*, 11.

Kinsman, G., Buse, D. K., & Steedman, M. (Eds.). (2000). *Whose national security? Canadian state surveillance and the creation of enemies*. Toronto, ON: Between the Lines.

Kiss, S., & Mosco, V. (2005). Negotiating electronic surveillance in the workplace. *Canadian Journal of Communication*, 30, 349–54.

Knightley, P. (2002). *The first casualty: The war correspondent as hero and mythmaker from the Crimea to Kosovo*. Baltimore: Johns Hopkins University Press.

Knightley, P. (2003). *The eye of war: Words and photographs from the front line*. London: Weidenfeld & Nicolson.

Knobel, L. (2005). Nullius in verba: Navigating through the new media democracy. In J. Mills (Ed.), *Barons to bloggers: Confronting media power*. Melbourne: Miegunyah Press.

Konrad, A. (2013, 2 February). Even with record prices, expect a $10 million Super Bowl ad soon. *Forbes*. Retrieved from http://www.forbes.com/sites/alexkonrad/2013/02/02/even-with-record-prices-10-million-spot/

Kopplin, J. (2002). An illustrated history of computers: Part 2. Retrieved from http://www.computersciencelab.com/ComputerHistory/HistoryPt2.htm

Koskie Minsky. (2009). Nortel compensation claims process webinar. Retrieved from http://www.koskieminsky.com/upload/090479_WebcastENG_30sep11.pdf

Kozolanka, K., Mazepa, P., & Skinner, D. (Eds.). (2012a). *Alternative media in Canada*. Vancouver: UBC Press.

Kozolanka, K., Mazepa, P., & Skinner, D. (2012b). Introduction to alternative media in Canada. In K. Kozolanka, P. Mazepa, & D. Skinner (Eds.), *Alternative media in Canada* (pp. 1–22). Vancouver: UBC Press.

Kramarae, C. (Ed.). (1988). *Technology and women's voices*. New York: Routledge.

Kretschmer, M. (2005). Trends in global copyright. *Global Media and Communication*, 1(2), 231–7.

Krippner, G. (2005). The financialization of the American economy. *Socio-Economic Review*, 3(2), 173–208.

Kukalis, S. (2010, March). Agglomeration economies and firm performance: The case of industry clusters. *Journal of Management*, 36(2), 453–81.

Kumar, D. (2005). What's good for UPS is good for America. *Television and New Media*, 6(2), 131–52.

Kumar, D. (2010). Framing Islam: The resurgence of Orientalism during the Bush II era. *Journal of Communication Inquiry*, 34(3), 254–77.

Kutler, S. (1990). *The wars of Watergate: The last crisis of Richard Nixon*. New York, NY: Alfred A. Knopf.

Kutler, S. (Ed.). (1997). *Abuse of power: The new Nixon tapes*. New York, NY: Free Press.

Labre, M. P., & Walsh-Childers, K. (2003). Friendly advice? Beauty messages in web sites of teen magazines. *Mass Communication and Society*, 6(4), 379–96.

Ladurantaye, S. (2012, 24 September). Globe takes action on allegations against columnist Margaret Wente. *The Globe and Mail*. Retrieved from http://www.theglobeandmail.com/news/national/globe-takes-action-on-allegations-against-columnist-margaret-wente/article4565683/

Lagacé, P., & Mason, G. (2012, 18 June). Legitimate strikers or self-absorbed brats? *The Globe and Mail*. Retrieved from http://m.theglobeandmail.com/news/politics/quebec-students-legitimate-strikers-or-self-absorbed-brats/article4104939/?service=mobile

Lam, E. (2010, 9 January). Globalive decision sparks lawsuit. Canwest News.

LaSalle, L. (2013, 20 March). CRTC wants public views on automated calls from telemarketers. *Canadian Press*. Retrieved from http://www.ctvnews.ca/business/crtc-wants-public-s-views-on-automated-calls-from-telemarketers-1.1204097#ixzz2P2JgwE1i

Lauzen, M. (2011). The celluloid ceiling: Behind-the-scenes employment of women on the top 250 films of 2011: Executive summary. Retrieved from http://womenintvfilm.sdsu.edu/files/2011_Celluloid_Ceiling_Exec_Summ.pdf

Lauzen, M. (2012). Independent women: Behind-the-scenes representation on festival films: Executive summary. Retrieved from http://womenintvfilm.sdsu.edu/files/2012_Independent_Women_Exec_Summ.pdf

Lauzen, M. (2013a). The celluloid ceiling: Behind-the-scenes employment of women on the top 250 films: Executive summary. Retrieved from http://womenintvfilm.sdsu.edu/files/2012_Celluloid_Ceiling_Exec_Summ.pdf

Lauzen, M. (2013b). Gender @ the movies: On-line film critics and criticism: Executive summary. Retrieved from http://womenintvfilm.sdsu.edu/files/2013_Gender_at_the_Movies_Exec_Summ.pdf

Lawson, P. (2008). Gutting the Telecom Act. In M. Moll & L. R. Shade (Eds.), *For sale to the highest bidder: Telecom policy in Canada* (pp. 17–26). Ottawa: Canadian Centre for Policy Alternatives.

Laxer, J. (2009). *Democracy*. Toronto: Groundwood Books.

Lee, E. (1997). *The labour movement and the Internet: The new internationalism.* London: Pluto Press.

Lee, J. (2002, 9 February). Retrieved from http://ei.cs.vt.edu./~History/VonNeumann.html [6 September 2005].

Lee, M. (2010). A political economic critique of Google Maps and Google Earth. *Information, Communication & Society*, *13*(6), 909–28.

Lee, M. (2011a). A feminist political economic critique of the human development approach to new information and communication technologies. *The International Communication Gazette*, *73*(6), 524–38.

Lee, M. (2011b). Google ads and the blindspot debate. *Media, Culture & Society*, *33*(3), 433–47.

Lepawsky, J. (2012). Legal geographies of e-waste legislation in Canada and the US: Jurisdiction, responsibility and the taboo of production. *Geoforum*, *43*(6), 1194–1206.

Lert, J. G., Jr., & Lu, D. (1985). *US Patent No. 4,677,466*. Washington, DC: US Patent and Trademark Office.

Levin, A. (2007). Big and little brother: The potential erosion of workplace privacy in Canada. *Canadian Journal of Law and Society*, *22*(2), 197–230.

Levy, S. (2012, 24 April). Can an algorithm write a better story than a human reporter? *Wired*. Retrieved from http://www.wired.com/gadgetlab/2012/04/can-an-algorithm-write-a-better-news-story-than-a-human-reporter/all/1

Lewis, J. (2010). Democratic or disposable? 24-hour news, consumer culture, and built in obsolescence. In S. Cushion & J. Lewis (Eds.), *The rise of 24-hour news television* (pp. 81–98). New York, NY: Peter Lang.

Lewis, P. (1993). *Alternative media: Linking global and local*. New York: Oxford University Press.

Lewis, P. M., & Booth, J. (1989). The invisible medium: Public, commercial and community radio. In R. Brunt, S. Frith, S. Niall, & A. McRobbie (Eds.), *Communications and culture*. London: Macmillan Education.

Lewis, S. (2006, 16 March). Nats fear for ads, news in bush. *Australian, 2*.

Lewis, T. (2003). The surveillance economy of post-Columbine schools. *Review of Education, Pedagogy and Cultural Studies*, *25*, 335–55.

Li, G. (2008). Private security and public policing. Retrieved from http://www.statcan.gc.ca/pub/85-002-x/2008010/article/10730-eng.htm#a3

Lichtblau, E. (2012, 8 July). More demands on cell carriers in surveillance. *The New York Times*. Retrieved from http://www.nytimes.com/2012/07/09/us/cell-carriers-see-uptick-in-requests-to-aid-surveillance.html?pagewanted=all

Limer, E. (2011, 3 November). AOL still has 3.5 million dial-up subscribers. *Geekosystem*. Retrieved from http://www.geekosystem.com/aol-3mil-subscribers/ [20 November 2012].

Lippowicz, A. (2006, 30 March). Chertoff: Shipping firms need to invest in tracking systems. Retrieved from http://www.washingtontechnology.com/news/1_1/homeland/28301-1.html [4 April 2006].

Lister, M., Dovey, J., Giddings, S., Grant, I., & Kelly, K. (2009). *New media: A critical introduction*. Routledge.

Lithgow, M. (2012). Transformations of practice, policy, and cultural citizenship. In K. Kozolanka, P. Mazepa, & D. Skinner (Eds.), *Alternative media in Canada: Politics, policies and practices* (pp. 125–44). Vancouver: UBC Press.

Lithwick, D. (2011, 19 October). Legislative summary of Bill C-12: An Act to amend the Personal Information Protection and Electronic Documents Act. Publication Number 41-1-C12E. Retrieved from http://www.parl.gc.ca/About/Parliament/LegislativeSummaries/bills_ls.asp?ls=c12&Parl=41&Ses=1

Liu, M. (2005, 16 October). Big Brother is talking. *Newsweek*, 30–31.

Lohr, S. (2013, 27 February). And now, from IBM, Chef Watson. *The New York Times*. Retrieved from http://www.nytimes.com/2013/02/28/technology/ibm-exploring-new-feats-for-watson.html?pagewanted=all

Lyon, D. (2001). *Surveillance society: Monitoring everyday life: Issues in society*. Maidenhead: Open University Press.

Lyon, D. (2002). Everyday surveillance: Personal data and social classifications.

Information, Communication & Society, 51(1), 1–16.

Lyon, D. (Ed.). (2003). *Surveillance as social sorting: Privacy, risk and digital discrimination.* New York: Routledge.

Lyon, D. (Ed.). (2006) *Theorizing surveillance: The panopticon and beyond.* Portland, Oregon: Willan Publishing.

Lyons, P. (2008, 8 February). Polaroid abandons instant photography. *The New York Times.* Retrieved from http://thelede.blogs.nytimes.com/2008/02/08/polaroid-abandons-instant-photography/

MacAskill, E. (2012, 10 September). Obama campaign outstrips Mitt Romney in August fundraising. *The Guardian UK.* Retrieved from http://www.theguardian.com/world/2012/sep/10/obama-outstrips-romney-august-fundraising

MacCharles, T. (2012, 20 September). Tories roll nine bills into massive crime proposal. *Toronto Star.* Retrieved from http://www.thestar.com/news/canada/politics/article/1056600--tories-roll-nine-bills-into-massive-crime-proposal

MacKinnon, R. (2004). The world-wide conversation: Online participatory media and international news. The Joan Shorenstein Center on the Press, Politics and Public Policy. Working Paper Series. Retrieved from http://shorensteincenter.org/wp-content/uploads/2012/03/2004_02_mackinnon.pdf

MacKinnon, M., & Strauss, M. (2013, 30 May). Underage labour finds a new frontier in Cambodia. *The Globe and Mail,* A1, A8.

MacLennan, A. F. (2005). American network broadcasting, the CBC, and Canadian radio stations during the 1930s: A content analysis. *Journal of Radio Studies,* 12(1), 85–103.

Macnamara, J. (2010, November). Remodelling media: The urgent search for new media business models. *Media International Australia,* 137, 20–35.

Mager, A. (2012). Algorithmic ideology: How capitalist society shapes search engines. *Information, Communication & Society,* 15(5), 769–87.

Mansell, R. (2011). New visions, old practices: Policy and regulation in the Internet era. *Continuum: Journal of Media & Cultural Studies,* 25(1), 19–32.

Marchessault, J. (2005). *Marshall McLuhan.* Thousand Oaks, CA: Sage.

Markoff, J. (2011, 16 February). Computer wins on "Jeopardy!": Trivial, it's not. *The New York Times.* Retrieved from http://www.nytimes.com/2011/02/17/science/17jeopardy-watson.html?pagewanted=all&_moc.semityn.www

Markoff, J. (2012, September 18). A robot with a reassuring touch. *The New York Times.* Retrieved from http://www.nytimes.com/2012/09/18/science/a-robot-with-a-delicate-touch.html?pagewanted=all&_moc.semityn.www

Marlow, I. (2011a, 9 June). Court victory clears way for Globalive. *The Globe and Mail,* B1.

Marlow, I. (2011b, 10 June). Public Mobile wants top court to weigh in on foreign ownership. *The Globe and Mail,* B3.

Marshall, G. (Ed.). (1998). *Oxford dictionary of sociology* (2nd ed.). Oxford/New York: Oxford University Press.

Martin, C. R. (2004). *Labor and the corporate media.* Ithaca, NY: ILR Press/Cornell University Press.

Martin, R., & Adam, G. S. (Eds.). (1994). *The sourcebook of Canadian media law.* Montreal/Kingston: McGill-Queen's University Press.

Marvin, C. (1988). *When old technologies were new: Thinking about electric communication in the late nineteenth century.* New York: Oxford University Press.

Marx, G. T. (2004). What's new about the "new surveillance"? Classifying for change and continuity. *Knowledge, Technology, & Policy,* 17(1), 18–37.

Marx, K. (1867/1976). *Capital: A critique of political economy,* Vol. 1 (B. Fowkes, Trans.). London, UK: Penguin.

Marx, K. (1867/1990). *Capital* (Vol. 1). Penguin classics edn. London: Penguin.

Marx, K. (1884/1990). *Capital* (Vol. 2). Penguin classics edn. London: Penguin.

Marx, K. (1894/1990). *Capital* (Vol. 3). Penguin classics edn. London: Penguin.

Marx, K, & Engels, F. (1872/1973). *Manifesto of the communist party.* Moscow: Progress Publishers.

Mattelart, A. (1983). For a class and group analysis of popular communication practices. In A. Mattelart & S. Siegelaub (Eds.), *Communication and class struggle: Volume 2: Liberation, socialism* (pp. 17–67). New York: International General.

Mattelart, A. (1996). *The invention of communication* (S. Emanuel, Trans.). Minneapolis: University of Minnesota Press.

Mattelart, A. & Siegelaub, S. (Eds). (1979). *Communication and class struggle: Volume.1: Capitalism, imperialism.* New York: International General.

maxmon.com. (2005a). 1000BC to 500BC: The invention of the abacus. Retrieved from www.maxmon.com/1000bc.htm [6 September 2005].

maxmon.com. (2005b). 1274 AD: Ramon Lull's Ars Magna. Retrieved from www.maxmon.com/1274ad.htm [21 September 2005].

maxmon.com. (2005c). 1600 AD: John Napier and Napier's Bones. Retrieved from www.maxmon.com/1600ad.htm [6 September 2005].

Maxwell, R., & Miller, T. (2005, December). The cultural labor issue. *Social Semiotics,* 15(3), 261–6.

Mayer, H. (1968). *The press in Australia.* Sydney: Lansdowne Press.

Mazepa, P. (1997). *The solidarity network in formation: A search for democratic alternative communication* (Master's thesis). Ottawa: Carleton University.

Mazepa, P. (2003). *Battles on the cultural front: The (de)labouring of culture in Canada, 1914–1944* (Doctoral dissertation). Carleton University, Ottawa, Ontario.

Mazepa, P. (2007). Democracy of, in and through communication: Struggles around public service in Canada in the first half of the twentieth century. *Info,* 9(2/3), 45–56.

Mazepa, P. (2009). Rights on paper, but not in practice: A history of press censorship in Canada. In A. Dakroury, M. Eid, & Y. Kamalipour (Eds.), *The right to communicate* (pp. 195–226). Dubuque, IA: Kendall Hunt.

Mazepa, P. (2011). Direct from the source: Canada's integrated system of state propaganda. In G. Sussman (Ed.), *The propaganda society: Promotional culture and politics in global context* (pp. 297–313). New York, NY: Peter Lang.

Mazepa, P. (2012). Regressive social relations, activism and media in Canada. In K. Kozolanka, P. Mazepa, & D. Skinner (Eds.), *Alternative media in Canada: Politics, policies and practices* (pp. 244–63). Vancouver: UBC Press.

McBride, S. (2008, 3 July). Clear channel, Limbaugh ink $400 million new contract. *The Wall Street Journal*. Retrieved from http://online.wsj.com/article/SB121504302144124805.html

McCarthy, S. (2012, 13 March). Ottawa's new anti-terrorism strategy lists eco-extremists as threats. *The Globe and Mail*. Retrieved from http://m.theglobeandmail.com/news/politics/ottawas-new-anti-terrorism-strategy-lists-eco-extremists-as-threats/article2334975/?service=mobile

McChesney, R. W. (1995). *Telecommunications, mass media, and democracy: The battle for the control of US broadcasting, 1928–1935*. New York: Oxford University Press.

McChesney, R. W. (1999). Graham Spry and the future of public broadcasting: The 1997 Spry memorial lecture. *Canadian Journal of Communication*, *24*(1). Retrieved from http://www.cjc-online.ca/index.php/journal/article/view/1081/987

McChesney, R. W. (2000a). The political economy of communication and the future of the field. *Media, Culture & Society*, *22*(1), 109–16.

McChesney, R. W. (2000b). *Rich media, poor democracy: Communication politics in dubious times*. New York: New Press.

McChesney, R. W., & Scott, B. (Eds.). (2003). *The brass check: A study of American journalism*. Urbana/Chicago: University of Illinois Press.

McClurg, A. J. (2003). A thousand words are worth a picture: A privacy tort response to consumer data profiling. *Northwestern University Law Review*, *98*(1), 63–87.

McDonald, D. (2005). Introduction. In J. Mills (Ed.), *Barons to bloggers: Confronting media power*. Melbourne: Miegunyah Press.

McGuigan, L. (2012). Consumers: The commodity product of interactive commercial television, or, is Dallas

Smythe's thesis more germane than ever? *Journal of Communication Inquiry*, *36*(4), 288–304.

McIver, Jr., W. J. (2010). Internet. In M. Raboy & J. Shtern (Eds.), *Media divides: Communication rights and the right to communicate in Canada* (pp. 145–74). Vancouver: UBC Press.

McKercher, C. (2002). *Newsworkers unite: Labor, convergence, and North American newspapers*. Lanham, MD: Rowman & Littlefield.

McKillop, A. B. (2008). *Pierre Burton: A biography*. Toronto, ON: McClelland & Stewart.

McLaughlin, L. (2004). Feminism and the political economy of transnational public space. *Sociological Review*, *52*(1), 156–75.

McMahon, P. (2002). Early electrical communications technology and structural change in the international political economy: The cases of telegraphy and radio. *Prometheus*, *20*(4), 379–90.

McMillan, S. J. (2010). Soap box or box of soap: Consumer understanding of the news, advertising, and funding sources for user-generated content. *Information, Communication & Society*, *13*(6), 820–43.

McQueen, H. (1977). *Australia's media monopolies*. Melbourne: Widescope.

Meadows, M. (2001). A return to practice: Reclaiming journalism as public conversation. In S. Tapsall & C. Varley (Eds.), *Journalism: Theory in practice*. Melbourne: Oxford University Press.

Media Culpa. (2012, 18 September). Margaret Wente: "A zero for plagiarism?" Retrieved from http://mediaculpapost.blogspot.ca/

Media Lens. (2010, 27 September). What is media lens? Retrieved from http://www.medialens.org/index.php?option=com_content&view=article&id=28&Itemid=19

Meehan, E. (2005). *Why TV is not our fault: Television programming, viewers, and who's really in control*. Oxford, UK: Rowman & Littlefield.

Meland, M. (2004, 1 April). Sony sues Kodak over digital camera patents. *Law 360*. Retrieved from http://www.law360.com/articles/1218/sony-sues-kodak-over-digital-camera-patents

Melody, W. H. (Ed.). (1997). *Telecom reform: Principles, policies and practices*. Lyngby, Denmark: Den Private Ingeniørfond.

Menabrea, L. F., & Lovelace, A. A. (1843/2005). Sketch of the Analytical Engine. Retrieved from http://www.fourmilab.ch/babbage/sketch.html [6 September 2005].

Mendes, G. (2011). What went wrong at Eastman Kodak. The strategy tank. Retrieved from http://www.martinfrost.ws/htmlfiles/oct2011/What-Went-Wrong-At-Eastman-Kodak.pdf

Menduni, E. (2007). Four steps in innovative radio broadcasting: From QuickTime to podcasting. *The Radio Journal—International Studies in Broadcast and Audio Media*, *5*(1), 9–18.

Microsoft. (n.d.). Digital inclusion: Empowering people through technology. Microsoft Corporation.

Middleton, C. (2011a). From Canada 2.0 to a digital nation: The challenge of creating a digital society in Canada. In L. R. Shade & M. Moll (Eds.), *The Internet tree: The state of telecom policy in Canada 3.0* (pp. 3–16). Ottawa: Canadian Centre for Policy Alternatives.

Middleton, C. (2011b). Structural and functional separation in broadband networks: An insufficient remedy to competitive woes in the Canadian broadband market. In L. R. Shade & M. Moll (Eds.), *The Internet tree: The state of telecom policy in Canada 3.0* (pp. 61–72). Ottawa: Canadian Centre for Policy Alternatives.

Middleton, C., & Bryne, A. (2011). An exploration of user-generated wireless broadband infrastructures in digital cities. *Telematics & Informatics*, *28*(3), 163–75.

Middleton, C., & Crow, B. (2008). Building Wi-Fi networks for communities: Three Canadian cases. *Canadian Journal of Communication*, *33*(3), 419–41.

Middleton, C., Veenhof, B., & Leith, J. (2010). Intensity of Internet use in Canada: Understanding different types of users. Catalogue no. 88F0006X. Ottawa: Statistics Canada, Ministry of Industry. Retrieved from http://www.statcan.gc.ca/pub/88f0006x/88f0006x2010002-eng.pdf

Milberry, K. (2012). Freeing the net: Online mobilization in defense of democracy. In K. Kozolanka, P. Mazepa, & D. Skinner (Eds.), *Alternative media in Canada* (pp. 226–43). Vancouver: UBC Press.

Milewski, T. (2012, 17 February). Online surveillance bill opens door for Big Brother: Section 34 gives Orwellian powers to government-appointed "inspectors." CBC News. Retrieved from http://www.cbc.ca/news/politics/story/2012/02/16/pol-vp-terry-milewski-bill-c30.html

Miller, J. (1998). *Yesterday's news: Why Canada's daily newspapers are failing us.* Halifax: Fernwood Publishing.

Mills, C. W. (1956). *The power elite.* New York: Oxford University Press.

Milner, A. (1993). *Cultural materialism.* Melbourne: Melbourne University Press.

Mitchell, A., Rosenstiel, T., & Christian, L. (2012). What Facebook and Twitter mean for news. *The State of the News Media 2012.* Retrieved from http://stateofthemedia.org/2012/mobile-devices-and-news-consumption-some-good-signs-for-journalism/what-facebook-and-twitter-mean-for-news/?src=prc-section

Moll, M., & Shade, L. R. (Eds.). (2008). *For sale to the highest bidder: Telecom policy in Canada.* Ottawa: Canadian Centre for Policy Alternatives.

Monaghan, J., & Walby, K. (2011). Making up "terror identities": Security intelligence, Canada's integrated threat assessment centre, and social movement suppression. *Policing and Society.*

Monsebraaten, L. (2009, 26 April). Last chance for Weston, Toronto's rustbelt. *Toronto Star.* Retrieved from http://www.thestar.com/news/gta/2009/04/26/last_chance_for_weston_torontos_rustbelt.html

Montreal *Gazette.* (2010). Nortel criminal trial to begin January 16. Retrieved from http://www.montrealgazette.com/news/Nortel+criminal+trial+begin/5496356/story.html

Morris, P. (1978). *Embattled shadows: A history of Canadian cinema 1895–1939.* Montreal: McGill-Queen's University Press.

Morville, P. (2001). *Lessons learned from the dot.com crash: A passenger's story.* Argus Center for Information Architecture. Retrieved from http://argus-acia.com/strange_connections/strange009.html [19 March 2006].

Mosco, V. (1989). *The pay-per society: Computers & communication in the information age.* Toronto: Garamond Press.

Mosco, V. (1996). *The political economy of communication: Rethinking and renewal.* London: Sage.

Mosco, V. (1999). New York.com: A political economy of the "informational" city. *Journal of Media Economics, 12*(2), 103–16.

Mosco, V. (2004a). *The digital sublime: Myth, power and cyberspace.* Boston: MIT Press.

Mosco, V. (2004b). From here to banality: Myths about new media and communication policy. In M. Moll & L. R. Shade (Eds.), *Seeking convergence in policy and practice: Communications in the public interest, vol. 2* (pp. 23–44). Ottawa: Canadian Centre for Policy Alternatives.

Mosco, V. (2009). *The political economy of communication* (2nd ed.). Thousand Oaks, CA: Sage.

Mosco, V. (in press). The two Marxes: Bridging the political economy/technology and culture divide. In A. N. Valdivia (Ed.), *The international encyclopedia of media studies: Volume 1.* New York: Blackwell.

Mosco, V., & Mazepa, P. (2003). High tech hegemony: Transforming Canada's capital into Silicon Valley north. In L. Artz & Y. R. Kamalipour (Eds.), *The globalization of corporate media hegemony* (pp. 93–112). Albany, NY: State University of New York Press.

Mosco, V., & McKercher, C. (2008). *The laboring of communication: Will knowledge workers of the world unite?* Lanham: Lexington Books.

Moses, L. (2010). Playboy goes retro to reel in readership. *Media Week, 20*(27), 6–31.

Mosher, D. (2011, 1 June). New data transmission speed record set. *TechNews Daily.* Retrieved from http://www.technewsdaily.com/2663-data-transmission-speed-record.html

Mueller, M., Mathiason, J., & McKnight, L. W. (2004, 26 April). Making sense of "Internet governance": Defining principles and norms in a policy context. Retrieved from http://www.wgig.org/docs/ig-project5.pdf

Murphy, B. (2002). A critical history of the Internet. In G. Elmer (Ed.), *Critical perspectives on the Internet* (pp. 27–45). Lanham, MD: Rowman & Littlefield.

Murphy, D. (2011, 10 April). Google abandons street view in Germany. *PC Magazine.* Retrieved from http://www.pcmag.com/article2/0,2817,2383363,00.asp

Murphy, K. (2006). *TV land: Australia's obsession with reality television.* Brisbane: John Wiley & Sons.

Murray L. (2010). Copyright. In M. Raboy & J. Shtern (Eds.), *Media divides: Communication rights and the right to communicate in Canada* (pp. 196–218). Vancouver: UBC Press.

Murray, S. (2005). Brand loyalties: Rethinking content within global corporate media. *Media, Culture & Society, 27*(3), 415–35.

Music Canada. (2011, February). The true price of peer to peer file sharing. CIPC. Retrieved from http://www.music-canada.com/Assets/News/The%20True%20Price%20of%20Peer%20to%20Peer%20File%20Sharing.pdf

Musil, S. (2008, 29 July). Internet censorship plagues journalists at Olympics. CNET. Retrieved from http://news.cnet.com/8301-1023_3-10002097-93.html [20 July 2012].

Myer, P. (1973). *Precision journalism: A reporter's introduction to social science methods.* Bloomington: Indiana University Press.

Myer, P. (2002). *Precision journalism: A reporter's introduction to social science methods* (4th ed.). Lanham, MD: Rowman & Littlefield.

Narrative Science. (2013). What is Quill? Retrieved from http://narrativescience.com/artificial-intelligence-data-engine/

Nash, M. T. (1982). *Images of women in National Film Board of Canada films during World War II and the post-war years, 1939–1949* (Unpublished doctoral dissertation). Montreal: McGill University.

Natural Resources Canada. (2008). Glossary of remote sensing terms. Retrieved from http://www.nrcan.gc.ca/earth-sciences/node/1776

Naughton, J. (2013, 4 August). Bradley Manning case stretches credibility of US computer fraud law. *The Guardian*. Retrieved from http://www.theguardian.com/technology/2013/aug/04/bradley-manning-case-credibility-computer-fraud-law

Neff, G., Wissinger, E., & Zukin, S. (2005, December). Entrepreneurial labor among cultural producers: "Cool" jobs in "hot" industries. *Social Semiotics, 15*(3), 307–34.

Negroponte, N. (1996). *Being digital*. New York: Vintage Books.

Nerone, J. (2012). The historical roots of the normative model of journalism. *Journalism, 14*(4), 446–58.

Nesbitt-Larking, P. W. (2007). *Politics, society, and the media: Canadian perspectives*. Peterborough, ON: Broadview.

Networks of Centres of Excellence of Canada. (2009, 1 December). The Government of Canada makes substantial investment in S&T with the launch of three new research networks. Retrieved from http://www.nce-rce.gc.ca/Media-Medias/news-communiques/News-Communique_eng.asp?ID=33

New Jersey Department of Law and Public Safety. (2001). Reader's Digest enters into multi-state sweepstakes agreement. Retrieved from http://www.nj.gov/oag/ca/press/digest.htm

Newspaper Audience Databank. (2011). Newspaper readership report. Retrieved from http://www.nadbank.com/en/system/files/2011Overviewof Results.pdf

NewsWatch Canada. (2011). Missing news: The top 25 underreported stories. Retrieved from http://pages.cmns.sfu.ca/newswatch/files/2011/11/NewsWatchCanada20111.pdf

Nguyen, L. (2013, 14 January). Ex-Nortel brass get "vindication" after not guilty ruling at Nortel fraud trial. *Canadian Business*. Retrieved from http://www.canadianbusiness.com/business-news/former-nortel-execs-to-learn-fate-in-multimillion-dollar-fraud-trial-2/

Nielsen. (2011, 26 May). *Nielsen acquires NeuroFocus*. Retrieved from http://www.nielsen.com/us/en/insights/press-room/2011/nielsen-acquires-neurofocus.html

Nielsen Wire. (2012, 8 March). Buzz in the blogosphere: Millions more bloggers and blog readers. Retrieved from http://blog.nielsen.com/nielsenwire/online_mobile/buzz-in-the-blogosphere-millions-more-bloggers-and-blog-readers/

Noam, E. M. (2009). *Media ownership and concentration in America*. New York: Oxford University Press.

The Nobel Foundation. (1967). *Nobel lectures, physics 1901–1921*. Amsterdam: Elsevier Publishing Company. Retrieved from http://www.nobelprize.org/nobel_prizes/physics/laureates/1909/marconi.html

Nolan, M. (1986). *Foundations: Alan Plaunt and the early days of the CBC radio*. Toronto: CBC Enterprises.

Norris, C., McCahill, M., & Wood, D. (2004). Editorial: The growth of CCTV. *Surveillance and Society, 2*(2/3), 110–35.

Norris, P. (2002). *A virtuous circle: Political communications in postindustrial societies*. Cambridge: Cambridge University Press.

Nortel Networks Corporation. (n.d.). *Historical timeline*. Retrieved from http://www.nortel-canada.com/about/history/

Nowak, P. (2009, 11 August). Canadian cellphone rates among world's worst. CBC News. Retrieved from http://www.cbc.ca/news/technology/story/2009/08/11/canada-cellphone-rates-expensive-oecd.html

Nye, J. (2004). *Soft power: The means to success in world politics*. Cambridge, MA: Public Affairs, Perseus Books.

Oakham, K. M. (2001). Journalism: Beyond the business. In S. Tapsall & C. Varley (Eds.), *Journalism: Theory in practice*. Melbourne: Oxford University Press.

O'Brien, M. (2008, March). Law, privacy and information technology: A sleepwalk through the surveillance society? *Information & Communications Technology Law, 17*(1), 25–35.

O'Connor, J. J., & Robertson, E. F. (1996a, December). *Blaise Pascal*. MacTutor History of Mathematics. Retrieved from http://wwwgroups.dcs.st-andrews.ac.uk/Printonly/Pascal.html [6 September 2005].

O'Connor, J. J., & Robertson, E. F. (1996b, December). *Wilhelm Schickard*. MacTutor History of Mathematics. Retrieved from www.history.mcs.st-andrews.ac.uk/ Mathematicians/Schickard.html [6 September 2005].

O'Connor, J. J., & Robertson, E. F. (1998a, October). *Charles Babbage*. MacTutor History of Mathematics. Retrieved from http://www-groups.dcs.st-and.ac.uk/~history/Printonly/Babbage.html [6 September 2005].

O'Connor, J. J., & Robertson, E. F. (1998b, April). *John Napier*. MacTutor History of Mathematics. Retrieved from www-groups.dcs.st-and.ac.uk/~history/Printonly/Napier.html [6 September 2005].

O'Connor, J. J., & Robertson, E. F. (1999a, July). *Howard Hathaway Aiken*. MacTutor History of Mathematics. Retrieved from http://www-groups.dcs.st-and. ac.uk/~history/Printonly/Aiken.html [14 September 2005].

O'Connor, J. J., & Robertson, E. F. (1999b, July). *Konrad Zuse*. MacTutor History of Mathematics. Retrieved from http://www-groups.dcs.st-and.ac.uk/~history/ Printonly/Zuse.html [14 September 2005].

O'Connor, J. J., & Robertson, E. F. (2003a, October). *Alan Mathison Turing*. MacTutor History of Mathematics. Retrieved from www.history.mcs.st-andrews.ac.uk/ Mathematicians/Turing.html [6 September 2005].

O'Connor, J. J., & Robertson, E. F. (2003b, October). *John von Neumann*. MacTutor History of Mathematics. Retrieved from http://www-groups.dcs.st-andrews. ac.uk/~history/Printonly/Von_Neumann.html [6 September 2005].

O'Connor, R. (2008). *Shock jocks: Hate speech and talk radio*. AlterNet Books.

OECD. (2004). The security economy. Retrieved from http://www.brookings.edu/press/books/clientpr/oecd/securityeconomy.htm [4 April 2006].

OECD. (2005). Double safe? Retrieved from

http://www.oecdobserver.org/news/fullstory.php/aid/1532/Double_safe_.html [4 April 2006].

Office of the Information Commissioner of Canada. (2012). *Brochure: What is Canada's freedom of information law?* Retrieved from http://www.oic-ci.gc.ca/eng/abu-ans-wwd-cqf-brochure.aspx

Office of the Privacy Commissioner of Canada. (2006). Digital rights management and technical protection measures. Retrieved from http://www.priv.gc.ca/resource/fs-fi/02_05_d_32_e.asp

Office of the Privacy Commissioner of Canada. (2013a). The Personal Information Protection and Electronic Documents Act (PIPEDA). Retrieved from http://www.priv.gc.ca/leg_c/leg_c_p_e.asp

Office of the Privacy Commissioner of Canada. (2013b). Response from Google to data protection authorities regarding Google Glass. Retrieved from http://www.priv.gc.ca/media/nr-c/2013/let_130627_google_e.asp

Ogden, M. R. (1999). Catching up to our digital future? Cyberdemocracy versus virtual mercantilism. In R. C. Vincent, K. Nordenstreng, & M. Traber (Eds.), *Towards equity in global communication.* New Jersey: Hampton Press.

O'Harrow, Jr., R. (2005). *No place to hide.* New York: Free Press.

O'Malley, K. (2012a, 14 March). Orders of the day—Rise and shine, MPs! Another long day of democracy awaits! [Weblog]. Retrieved from http://www.cbc.ca/news/politics/inside-politics-blog/2012/03/orders-of-the-day---rise-and-shine-mps-another-long-day-of-democracy-awaits.html

O'Malley, K. (2012b, 25 October). Supreme Court decision on Etobicoke Centre electoral challenge [Live blog]. Retrieved from http://live.cbc.ca/Event/Liveblog_Supreme_Court_decision_on_Etobicoke_Centre_electoral_challenge?Page=0

Ontario Ministry of Tourism and Culture. (2010). *Ontario's entertainment and creative cluster: A framework for growth.* Toronto: Queen's Printer for Ontario.

OPCC. (2010, 19 October). Google contravened Canadian privacy law, investigation finds [News release]. Retrieved from http://www.priv.gc.ca/media/nr-c/2010/nr-c_101019_e.asp

OPCC. (2013, 18 June). Data protection authorities urge Google to address Google Glass concerns [News release]. Retrieved from http://www.priv.gc.ca/media/nr-c/2013/nr-c_130618_e.asp

OpenMedia.ca. (2011). Casting an open net: A leading-edge approach to Canada's digital future. Retrieved from http://openmedia.ca/news/report-reveals-big-telecom%E2%80%99s-failure-invest-canada%E2%80%99s-digital-economy [27 May 2011].

OpenMedia.ca/CIPPIC. (2011). TNC CRTC 2011-77: Reviewing of billing practices for wholesale residential high-speed access services. Reply comments of OpenMedia.ca. Retrieved from http://www.scribd.com/doc/55599542/OpenMedia-ca-CIPPIC-s-Reply-to-CRTC-2011-77 [26 May 2011].

O'Regan, G. (2008). *A brief history of computing.* London: Springer.

O'Regan, T. (2010). The political economy of film. In J. Donald & M. Renov (Eds.), *The Sage handbook of film studies* (pp. 244–62). London: Sage.

Orwell, G. (1988). *Nineteen eighty-four.* London: Penguin.

Ostergaard, B. S. (1998). Convergence: Legislative dilemmas. In D. McQuail & K. Siune (Eds.), *Media policy: Convergence, concentration and commerce.* London: Sage.

The Ottawa Citizen. (2006, 30 September). RCMP turns to data brokers. Retrieved from http:www.canada.com

Ouellette, L., & Hay, J. (2008). *Better living through reality TV: Television and post-welfare citizenship.* Malden, MA: Blackwell.

Paletz, D. L. (1999). *The media in American politics.* New York: Addison-Wesley Educational.

Parenti, M. (1986). *Inventing reality: The politics of the mass media.* New York: St. Martin's Press.

Parenti, M. (1999). Methods of media manipulation. In R. E. Hiebert (Ed.), *Impact of mass media: Current issues.* New York: Addison-Wesley Longman.

Parliament of Canada. (2011). Cybercrime: Issues. Retrieved from http://www.parl.gc.ca/content/lop/researchpublications/2011-36-e.htm

Parr, J. (1980). *Labouring children. British immigrant apprentices to Canada.* Toronto: University of Toronto Press.

Partington, A. (Ed.). (1997). *The concise Oxford dictionary of quotations.* London: Oxford University Press.

Pavlik, J. V. (1994). Citizen access, involvement, and freedom of expression in an electronic environment. In J. V. Pavlik (Ed.), *People's right to know: Media, democracy, and the information highway.* New Jersey: Lawrence Erlbaum.

Pavlik, J. V. (2001). *Journalism and new media.* New York: Columbia University Press.

PCmag.com. (2013). Encyclopedia. Retrieved from http://www.pcmag.com/encyclopedia_term/0,1237,t=cookie&i=40334,00.asp

Pendakur, M. (1990). *Canadian dreams and American control: The political economy of the Canadian film industry.* Detroit: Wayne State University Press.

Penn, J. (2012). Behavioural advertising: The cryptic hunter and gatherer of the Internet. *Federal Communications Law Journal, 64,* 599–616.

Penzhorn, H., & Pitout, M. (2007). A critical-historical genre analysis of reality television. *Communication, 33*(1), 62–76.

Pepitone, J. (2012, 9 February). Kodak ditches digital camera business. *CNN Money.* Retrieved from http://money.cnn.com/2012/02/09/technology/kodak_digital_cameras/

Perlroth, N. (2013, 24 March). Luring young web warriors is priority. It's also a game. *The New York Times.* Retrieved from http://www.nytimes.com/2013/03/25/technology/united-states-wants-to-attract-hackers-to-public-sector.html?pagewanted=all&_r=0

Peters, J. W. (2011, 12 April). Huffington Post is target of suit on behalf of bloggers. *The New York Times.* Retrieved from http://mediadecoder.blogs.nytimes.com/2011/04/12/huffington-post-is-target-of-suit-on-behalf-of-bloggers/

Pew Research Center. (2012). The state of the news media 2012. Retrieved from http://stateofthemedia.org/overview-2012/

Pfanner, E. (2006, 1 March). Publicis acts to surf the marketing waves of the future. Retrieved from http://www.nytimes.com/2006/03/01/business/media/01adco.html?_r=0 [3 March 2006].

Pfanner, E. (2012, 25 November). Libel case that snared BBC widens to Twitter. *The New York Times*. Retrieved from http://www.nytimes.com/2012/11/26/technology/26iht-twitter26.html?hp&_r=0

Phelan, J. M. (1991). Selling consent: The public sphere as a televisual market-place. In P. Dahlgren & C. Sparks (Eds.), *Communication and citizenship: Journalism and the public sphere in the new media age*. London/New York: Routledge.

Philippine Center for Investigative Journalism. (2004). Investigative journalism. Retrieved from http://www.medienhilfe.ch/fileadmin/downloads/balkanradio/InvestigativeJournalism.pdf

Phillips, A., Lee-Wright, P., & Witschge, T. (2012). *Changing journalism*. New York, NY: Routledge.

Polaroid v. Eastman Kodak, 789 F.2d 1556 (US Ct. App. 1986). Retrieved from https://bulk.resource.org/courts.gov/c/F2/789/789.F2d.1556.86-604.html

Politics & Culture. (2004). Down with digital determinism! *Politics & Culture*, (4). Retrieved from http://www.politicsandculture.org/2010/08/10/down-with-digital-determinism-a-discussion-of-rec-2/

Pollock, J. (2011, 23 August). How Egyptian and Tunisian youth hacked the Arab Spring. MIT *Technology Review*. Retrieved from http://www.technologyreview.com/featuredstory/425137/streetbook/

Porter, C. (2009, 5 December). Lessons of the Montreal massacre: Why women must fight for what they want. *Toronto Star*. Retrieved from http://www.thestar.com/news/canada/article/734817--lessons-of-the-montreal-massacre-why-women-must-fight-to-be-what-they-want

Poster, M. (1995). *CyberDemocracy: Internet and public sphere*. Retrieved from http://www.hnet.uci.edu/mposter/writings/democ.html

Postman, N. (1993). *Technopoly: The surrender of culture to technology*. New York: Vintage Books.

Pozner, J. (2010). *Reality bites back: The troubling truth about guilty pleasure TV*. New York, NY: Seal Press.

Press TV. (2013). Pentagon requests $23 billion for cybersecurity expansion. Retrieved from http://www.presstv.ir/detail/2013/06/17/309507/us-bids-23b-for-cybersecurity-expansion/

Privacy Act, R.S.C., 1985, c. P-21. Retrieved from http://laws-lois.justice.gc.ca/eng/acts/P-21/index.html

Public Safety Canada. (2010). Canada's cyber security strategy. Retrieved from http://www.publicsafety.gc.ca/prg/ns/cybr-scrty/_fl/ccss-scc-eng.pdf

Public Safety Canada. (2012). Building resilience against terrorism: Canada's counter-terrorism strategy. Retrieved from http://www.publicsafety.gc.ca/prg/ns/2012-cts-eng.aspx

Public Works and Government Services Canada. (2007). Archived telecommunications and broadcasting regulation vocabulary—English–French vocabulary. Retrieved from http://www.btb.gc.ca/btb.php?lang=eng&cont=429#b

Puette, W. J. (1992). *Through jaundiced eyes: How the media view organized labor*. Ithaca, NY: ILR Press.

Pugliese, D. (2010, 16 October). DND set to take over Nortel campus. *Ottawa Citizen*. Retrieved from http://www.ottawacitizen.com/business/take+over+Nortel+campus/3680169/story.html

Pugliese, D. (2013, 14 April). Lower cab fares, easier security, among DND reasons for move to ex-Nortel site. *Ottawa Citizen*. Retrieved from http://www.ottawacitizen.com/news/Lower+fares+easier+security+among+reasons+move+Nortel+site/8241817/story.html

Puppis, M. (2010). Media governance: A new concept for the analysis of media policy and regulation. *Communication, Culture & Critique*, 3(2), 134–49.

PWAC. (2006). Canadian professional writers survey: A profile of the freelance writing sector in Canada. Retrieved from http://www.pwac.ca/files/PDF/PWACsurvey.pdf

Quail, C., & Larabie, C. (2010). Net neutrality: Media discourses and public perception. *Global Media Journal—Canadian Edition*, 3(1), 31–50.

Qui, J. L. (2007). The wireless leash: Mobile messaging as a means of control. *International Journal of Communication*, 1, 74–91.

Raboy, M. (1996). Cultural sovereignty, public participation and democratization of the public sphere: The Canadian debate on the new information infrastructure. *Communications & Strategies*, 51–76.

Raboy, M., & Padovani, C. (2010). Mapping global media policy: Concepts, frameworks, methods. *Communication Culture & Critique*, 3(2), 150–69.

Raboy, M., & Shtern, J. (Eds.). (2010). *Media divides: Communication rights and the right to communicate in Canada*. Vancouver: UBC Press.

Raphael, D. (2012). *Poverty in Canada*. Toronto: Canadian Scholar's Press.

Rasul, A., & Proffitt, J. M. (2010). An irresistible market: A critical analysis of Hollywood-Bollywood coproductions. *Communication, Culture & Critique*, 5(4), 563–83.

Reader's Digest. (2013). Our company. Retrieved from http://www.rda.com/our-company

Redshaw, K. (1996, 5 October). *Konrad Zuse*. Retrieved from http://www.kerryr.net/pioneers/zuse.htm [14 September 2005].

Reuters. (1991, 16 July). Kodak pays Polaroid over patent dispute. *Toronto Star*, C3.

Reuters. (2007, 8 February). Kodak adds more job cuts to restructuring. Retrieved from http://www.cnbc.com/id/17044726

Reuters. (2009, 14 January). Timeline: Key dates in the history of Nortel. Retrieved from http://www.reuters.com/article/2009/01/15/us-nortel-timeline-sb-idUSTRE50D3N120090115

Reuters. (2010). Retrieved from www.reuters.com [2010].

Richmond, R., & Bilton, N. (2011, 26 June). Dissolution of hacker group might not end attacks. *The New York Times*. Retrieved from http://www.nytimes.com/2011/06/27/technology/27hack.html?pagewanted=all&_r=0

Rideout, V. (2003). *Continentalizing Canadian telecommunications: The politics of regulatory reform*. Montreal: McGill-Queen's University Press.

Rivett, R. (1965). The press today. In L. Revill & C. Roderick (Eds.), *The journalist's craft: A guide to modern practice*. Sydney: Angus & Robertson.

Roach, K. (2007). Better later than never: The Canadian parliamentary review of the Anti-terrorism Act. *IRRP Choices*, *13*(5), 1–34. Retrieved from http://www.irpp.org/en/research/security-and-democracy/better-late-than-never/

Roberts, G. (2012, 30 May). Fairfax journalists stop work over plan to send jobs offshore. *Herald Sun*. Retrieved from http://www.heraldsun.com.au/business/companies/fairfax-sends-sub-editing-jobs-to-nz/story-fndgp8bl-1226373258712

Robins, K., & Webster, F. (1983). Information technology, Luddism and the working class. In V. Mosco & J. Wasko (Eds.), *The critical communications review: Volume 1: Labor, the working class and the media* (pp. 189–209). Norwood, NJ: Ablex Publishing Company.

Robinson, G. (2005). *Gender, journalism and equity: Canadian, US, and European perspectives*. Cresskill, NJ: Hampton Press, Inc.

Rogers, E. (1962). *Diffusion of innovation*. Glencoe: Free Press.

Roget, P. M. (1979). *Roget's thesaurus. Classic American edition*. New York: Avenel Books.

Roosevelt, F. D. (1941, 9 December). Fireside chat 19: On the declaration of war with Japan. Retrieved from http://www.mhric.org/fdr/chat19.html

Rosen, D. (2005, 4 October). Online curbs in China. *Australian*, *12*.

Rosenberg, N. (1997, January 8). *Babbage: Pioneer economist*. Retrieved from http://www.exeter.ac.uk/BABBAGE/rosenb.html [6 September 2005].

Rosenblatt, R. (1983, January). A new world dawns. *Time*, *121*(1), 6–7.

Rosenstiel, T., & Jurkowitz, M. (2012). *The search for a new business model: An in-depth look at how newspapers are faring trying to build digital revenue*. Washington, DC: Pew Research Center's Project for Excellence in Journalism.

Retrieved from http://www.journalism.org/sites/journalism.org/files/SEARCHFORNEWREVENUEMODEL.pdf

Rosner, C. (2011). *Behind the headlines: A history of investigative journalism in Canada*. Toronto: Oxford University Press.

Rothstein, E. (2003). Utopia and its discontents. In E. Rothstein, H. Muschamp, & M. E. Marty (Eds.), *Visions of utopia*. New York: Oxford University Press.

Rowland, W. (2012). *Greed, Inc.: Why corporations rule the world and how we let it happen*. New York: Arcade Publishing.

Roy, M. (2000). *The phoenix: Back from the ashes of the dot.com crashes*. Expiry Corporation, November 2000. Retrieved from http://www.expiry.com/enet/archive/2000/11-nov-2000-dotcomcrashes.shtml [19 March 2006].

Royle, T. (2000). *Crimea: The great Crimean War, 1854–1856*. New York: St. Martin's Press.

Rushkoff, D. (n.d.). Rushkoff. Retrieved from http://www.rushkoff.com/program-or-be-programmed/

Rushkoff, D. (1994). *Cyberia: Life in the trenches of hyperspace*. London: Flamingo. Used by permission of Douglas Rushkoff.

Rutherford, P. (1978). *The making of the Canadian media*. Toronto: McGraw-Hill Ryerson.

Rutherford Smith, R. (1997). Mythic elements in television news. In D. Berkowitz (Ed.), *Social meanings of news: A text-reader*. Thousand Oaks, CA: Sage.

Salcetti, M. (1995). The emergence of the reporter: Mechanization and the devaluation of editorial workers. In H. Hardt & B. Brennen (Eds.), *NewsWorkers: Toward a history of the rank and file* (pp. 48–74). Minneapolis, MN: University of Minnesota Press.

Salter, L., & Odartey-Wellington, F. (2008). *The CRTC and broadcasting regulation in Canada*. Toronto: Thomson Carswell.

Sampert, S. (2008). *Jock radio/talk radio/shock radio*. Paper presented at the Canadian Political Science Association Conference. Retrieved from www.cpsa-acsp.ca/papers-2008/Sampert.pdf

Sampert, S. (2010). Jock radio/talk radio/

shock radio. In S. Sampert & L. Trimble (Eds.), *Mediations: Making news about politics*. Toronto: Pearson.

Sampert, S. (2011). Verbal smackdown: Charles Adler and Canadian talk radio. In D. Taras & C. Waddell (Eds.), *How Canadians communicate IV: Media and politics* (pp. 295–315). Edmonton, AB: Athabasca University Press.

Sandoval, M., & Fuchs, C. (2010). Towards a critical theory of alternative media. *Telematics and Informatics*, *27*, 141–50.

Sarikakis, K., & Shade, L. R. (Eds.). (2007). *Feminist interventions in international communication: Minding the gap*. Toronto, ON: Rowman & Littlefield.

Sassen, S. (2006). *Territory, authority, rights: From medieval to global assemblages* (Updated edition). Princeton/Oxford: Princeton University Press.

Sasso, B. (2012, 18 December). FTC orders data brokers to reveal business practices. *The Hill* (Hillicon Valley). Retrieved from http://thehill.com/blogs/hillicon-valley/technology/273471-ftc-orders-data-brokers-to-reveal-business-practices

Savitz, E. (2012, 1 October). Kodak sues Apple, HTC for patent infringement. *Forbes*. Retrieved from http://www.forbes.com/sites/ericsavitz/2012/01/10/kodak-sues-apple-htc-for-patent-infringement/

Scatamburlo-D'Annibale, V., & Chehade, G. (2004). The revolution will not be televised, but it might be uploaded. In M. Moll & L. R. Shade (Eds.), *Seeking convergence in policy and practice: Communications in the public interest, vol. 2* (pp. 363–79). Ottawa: Canadian Centre for Policy Alternatives.

Schiller, D. (1999). The legacy of Robert A. Brady: Antifascist origins of the political economy of communications. *Journal of Media Economics*, *12*(2), 89–101.

Schiller, D. (2007). *How to think about information*. Chicago, IL: University of Illinois Press.

Schiller, H. (1969). *Mass communication and American empire*. New York: August M. Keeley Publishers.

Schiller, H. (1976). *Communication and Cultural Domination*. White Plains, NY: International Arts and Sciences Press.

Schiller, H. (1992). *Communication and American Empire*. New York: August M. Kelley Publishers.

Schultz, J. (1989). Failing the public: The media marketplace. In H. Wilson (Ed.), *Communications and the public sphere: Essays in memory of Bill Bonney*. Melbourne: Macmillan.

Schultz, J. (Ed.). (1994). *Not just another business: Journalists, citizens and the media*. Sydney: Pluto Press.

Schultz, J. (1998). *Reviving the fourth estate: Democracy, accountability and the media*. Cambridge: Cambridge University Press.

Schultz, R. (2003). From master to partner to bit player: The diminishing capacity of government policy. In D. Taras, F. Pannekoek, & M. Bajardjieva (Eds.), *How Canadians communicate* (pp. 27–50). Calgary: University of Calgary Press.

Schwartau, W. (2000). *Cybershock: Surviving hackers, phreakers, indentity thieves, Internet terrorists and weapons of mass disruption*. New York: Thunder's Mouth Press.

Schwartz, E. (1996). *Netactivism: How citizens use the Internet*. Thousand Oaks, CA: Songline Studios.

Scott, D. T. (2008). Tempests of the blogosphere: Presidential campaign stories that failed to unite mainstream media. In M. Boler (Ed.), *Digital media and democracy: Tactics in hard times* (pp. 271–300). Cambridge, MA: The MIT Press.

Screen Actors Guild. (2007, winter). A different America on screen. *Screen Actor*, 55–7.

Seldes, G. V. (1968). *Writing for television*. New York, NY: Greenwood Press.

Sell, S., & May, C. (2001). Moments in law: Contestation and settlement in the history of intellectual property. *Review of International Political Economy*, 8(3), 467–500.

Selnow, G. (1998). *Electronic whistle-stops*. New York: Praeger.

Shade, L. R. (2009). Skimming the cream, throttling the tubes, doing the policy laundering, and jiving to the supply-side boogie: Challenges to the right to communicate in Canada. In A. Dakroury, M. Eid, & Y. Kamalipour (Eds.), *The right to communicate* (pp. 177–94). Dubuque, IA: Kendall Hunt.

Shade, L. R. (Ed.). (2014). *Mediascapes: New patterns in Canadian communication*. Toronto: Nelson.

Shade, L. R., & Clement, A. (2000). The access rainbow: Conceptualizing universal access to the information/communications infrastructure. Hershey, PA: Idea Publishing. Retrieved from http://mobilemediaculture.files.wordpress.com/2011/01/clement_shade.pdf

Shalom, F. (2008, 17 December). No holiday cheer at Sun Media; 600 job cuts. "It's really heartless, just nine days before Christmas." *The Gazette* [Montreal, PQ], B3.

Shaw, M. (1988). *The dialectics of war: An essay in the social theory of war and peace*. London: Pluto Press.

Shaw Media. (2012). *The Big Brother phenomenon is coming to Canada* [Press release]. Retrieved from http://shawmediatv.ca/press/read/?1720

Shepard, L. (1973). *The history of street literature*. Detroit: Singing Tree Press.

Siegel, A. (1996). *Radio Canada International*. Oakville, ON: Mosaic Press.

Silverman, R. E. (2013, 7 March). Tracking sensors invade the workplace. *The Wall Street Journal*. Retrieved from http://online.wsj.com

Sinclair, U. (1924/2002). *The brass check: A study of American journalism* (9th ed.). Urbana-Champagne, IL: University of Illinois Press.

Singer, N. (2012, 21 July). Consumer data, but not for consumers. *The New York Times*. Retrieved from http://www.nytimes.com/2012/07/22/business/acxiom-consumer-data-often-unavailable-to-consumers.html?pagewanted=all

Sinha, I. (1999). *The cybergypsies: Love, life and travels on the electronic frontier*. London: Scribner.

Siochru, S. O., & Girard, B. (2002). *Global media governance: A beginner's guide*. Lanham, MD: Rowman & Littlefield.

Skinner, D. (2004). Divided loyalties: The early development of Canada's "single" broadcasting system. *Journal of Radio Studies*, 12(1), 136–55.

Skinner, D. (2008). Television in Canada: Continuity or change? In D. Ward (Ed.), *Television and public policy: Change and continuity in an era of global liberalization* (pp. 3–26). New York/London: Lawrence Erlbaum Associates.

Skinner, D., & Gasher, M. (2005). So much by so few: Media policy and ownership in Canada. In D. Skinner, J. D. Compton, & M. Gasher (Eds.), *Converging media, diverging politics: A political economy of news media in the United States and Canada* (pp. 51–76). Lanham, MD: Lexington Books.

Skinner, J. M. (1987). Clean and decent movies: Selected cases and responses of the Manitoba Film Censor Board, 1930 to 1950. *Manitoba History*, 14, 2–9.

Slaton, C. D. (1992). *Televote: Expanding citizen participation in the Quantum Age*. NY: Praeger.

Smith, A. (1980). *Goodbye Gutenberg: The newspaper revolution of the 1980s*. New York: Oxford University Press.

Smith, G. (2009). Empowered watchers or disempowered workers? In K. F. Aas, H. O. Gundhus, & H. M. Lomell (Eds.), *Technologies of (in)security* (pp. 125–46). Abingdon, England/New York: Routledge-Cavendish.

Smith, S. (2005, January/February). The emerging search economy. Retrieved from http://www.econtentmag.com/Articles/ArticleReader.aspx?ArticleID=7625 [4 April 2006].

Smith-Shomade, B. E. (2004). Narrowcasting in the new world information order: A space for the audience? *Television & New Media*, 5(1), 69–81.

Smythe, D. (1977). Communications: Blindspot of western Marxism. *Canadian Journal of Political and Social Theory*, 1(3), 1–27.

Snoddy, R. (1992). *The good, the bad and the unacceptable*. London: Faber & Faber.

Snow, D. (2005, 1–2 January). The future is running too fast towards us. *SMH*, 35.

Soley, L. (2007). Sex and shock jocks: An analysis of the Howard Stern and Bob & Tom shows. *Journal of Promotion Management*, 13(1/2), 75–93.

Soloski, J. (2012). Collapse of the US newspaper industry: Goodwill, leverage and bankruptcy. *Journalism*, 14(3), 309–29.

Solum, L. B. (2009). Models of Internet governance. In L. A. Bygrave & J. Bing (Eds.),

Internet governance: Infrastructure and institutions (pp. 48–91). Oxford: Oxford University Press.

Sotiron, M. (1992). Concentration and collusion in the Canadian newspaper industry, 1895–1920. *Journalism History, 18*, 26–32.

Sotiron, M. (1997). *From politics to profit: The commercialization of Canadian daily newspapers, 1890–1920.* Montreal/Kingston: McGill-Queen's University Press.

Spangler, N. (2010, November/December). In demand: A week inside the future of journalism. *Columbia Journalism Review,* 51–3.

Spencer, D. R. (1990). *An alternative vision: Main themes in moral education in Canada's English-language working-class press 1879–1910* (Doctoral dissertation). Toronto: University of Toronto.

Splichal, S. (2009). "New" media, "old" theories: Does the (national) public melt into the air of global governance? *European Journal of Communication, 24*(4), 391–405.

Sprague, T. (2010, 3 March). Lockout at the Journal de Montréal: Workers fight back against Quebecor. Retrieved from http://www.marxist.ca/labour/labour-news/536-lockout-at-the-journal-de-montral-workers-fight-back-against-quebecor.html

Stacks, D. W., & Salwen, M. B. (Eds.). (2009). *An integrated approach to communication theory and research.* New York: Routledge.

Staiger, J., & Hake, S. (Eds.). (2009). *Convergence media history.* New York: Routledge.

Standage, T. (1998). *The Victorian Internet: The remarkable story of the telegraph and the nineteenth century's on-line pioneers.* New York: Walker.

Stanford Encyclopedia of Philosophy. (2012). *Max Weber.* Retrieved from http://plato.stanford.edu/entries/weber/

Starr, P. (2004). *The creation of the media: Political origins of modern communications.* New York: Perseus Books Group.

State of the Blogosphere. (2011, 4 November). State of the blogosphere 2011: Introduction and methodology. Retrieved from http://technorati.com/social-media/article/state-of-the-blogosphere-2011-introduction/

Statistics Canada. (2007). Radio listening: Data tables. Retrieved from http://www.statcan.gc.ca/pub/87f0007x/87f0007x2007001-eng.pdf

Statistics Canada. (2009). Perspectives on labour and income: Unionization. Retrieved from http://www.statcan.gc.ca/pub/75-001-x/topics-sujets/pdf/topics-sujets/unionization-syndicalisation-2009-eng.pdf

Statistics Canada. (2010a, 10 May). Canadian Internet usage survey. *The Daily.* Retrieved from http://www.statcan.gc.ca/daily-quotidien/100510/dq100510a-eng.htm

Statistics Canada. (2010b). Radio broadcasting industry, 2009. Retrieved from http://www.statcan.gc.ca/pub/56-208-x/56-208-x2010000-eng.pdf

Statistics Canada. (2012). Table 13.1: Information and cultural industries—Balance sheet and income statement. Retrieved from http://www.statcan.gc.ca/pub/61-008-x/2011003/t012-eng.htm

Steeves, V. (2011). Children's online privacy policy concerns. In L. R. Shade & M. Moll (Eds.), *The Internet tree: The state of telecom policy in Canada 3.0* (pp. 175–86). Ottawa: Canadian Centre for Policy Alternatives.

Stempel, J., & Adegoke, Y. (2010). LimeWire music-sharing service shut down. Retrieved from http://technology.canoe.ca/2010/10/27/15845106.html [28 October].

Stephenson, N. (1992). *Snow crash.* London: Penguin.

Stephenson, N. (2002). *Cryptonomicon.* New York: Avon Books.

Sterne, J. (2007). Out with the trash: On the future of new media. In C. R. Acland (Ed.), *Residual media* (pp. 16–31). Minneapolis: University of Minnesota Press.

Stevens, B. (2004). The emerging security economy: An introduction. In OECD (Ed.), *The security economy* (pp. 7–16). Paris: OECD.

Stevenson, J. H., & Clement, A. (2010). Regulatory lessons for Internet traffic management form Japan, the European Union, and the United States: Toward equity, neutrality and transparency. *Global Media Journal—Canadian Edition, 3*(1), 9–29.

Steward, G. (2010, 26 October). Steward: Young voters elected new Calgary mayor. *The Star.* Retrieved from http://www.thestar.com/opinion/editorialopinion/2010/10/26/steward_young_voters_elected_new_calgary_mayor.html

Stover, C. M. (2010). Network neutrality: A thematic analysis of policy perspectives across the globe. *Global Media Journal—Canadian Edition, 3*(1), 75–86.

Stoymenoff, A. (2012, 11 February). Are Canadian environmentalists a terrorist threat? *Vancouver Observer.* Retrieved from http://www.sierraclub.ca/tar-sands/in-the-news/are-canadian-environmentalists-terrorist-threat

Streitfeld, D. (2013, 12 March). Google concedes that drive-by prying violated privacy. *The New York Times.* Retrieved from http://www.nytimes.com/2013/03/13/technology/google-pays-fine-over-street-view-privacy-breach.html?pagewanted=all&_r=5&%29

Streitfeld, D., & O'Brien, K. J. (2012, 22 May). Google privacy inquiries get little cooperation. *The New York Times.* Retrieved from http://www.nytimes.com/2012/05/23/technology/google-privacy-inquiries-get-little-cooperation.html?pagewanted=all

Suarez-Villa, L. (2012). *Globalization and technocapitalism: The political economy of corporate power and technological domination.* Burlington, VT: Ashgate Publishing Company.

Sussman, G. (2010). *Branding democracy: US regime change in post-Soviet Eastern Europe.* New York, NY: Peter Lang.

Sweney, M. (2012, 29 February). Guardian TV ad kicks off "open journalism" campaign. *The Guardian.* Retrieved from http://www.guardian.co.uk/media/2012/feb/29/guardian-tv-ad-open-journalism?intcmp=239

Swyripa, F., & Thompson, J. H. (Eds.). (1983). *Loyalties in conflict: Ukrainians in Canada during the Great War.* Edmonton: Canadian Institute of Ukrainian Studies, University of Alberta.

Sykes, J. B. (Ed.). (1982). *The concise Oxford dictionary of current English*. Oxford: Clarendon Press.

Tady, M. (2008, November/December). Outsourcing journalism: Localism threatened by offshore reporters and editors. *FAIR Extra!* Retrieved from http://www.fair.org/index.php?page=3705

Tapsall, S., & Varley, C. (2001). What is a journalist? In S. Tapsall & C. Varley (Eds.), *Journalism: Theory in practice*. Melbourne: Oxford University Press.

Taylor, C. P. (2009, 30 November). Aol seeds new journalism model, but will it make journalism wither or flourish? Retrieved from http://www.cbsnews.com/8301-505123_162-43744416/aol-seeds-new-journalism-model-but-will-it-make-journalism-wither-or-flourish/

Taylor, G. (2007). CanWest lands Alliance-Atlantis (with help from big friends). *Media @ McGill: Critical Communication Matters*. Retrieved from http://media.mcgill.ca/en/canwest_lands_alliance_atlantis

Taylor, P. (1997). *Global communications, international affairs and the media since 1945*. New York, NY: Routledge.

Teixeira, D. (2011, 2 May). Reporting the Canadian election results. *BC Business*. Retrieved from http://www.bcbusiness.ca/marketing-media/reporting-the-canadian-election-results

Telecommunications Act, S. C. 1993, c. 38. Retrieved from http://www.efc.ca/pages/law/canada/telecom.html

Thomas, P. (2009). Selling God/saving souls. *Global Media and Communication*, 5(1), 57–76.

Thompson, C. (2009, 22 June). Kodak will retire Kodachrome, its oldest color film stock. *The New York Times*. Retrieved from http://www.nytimes.com/2009/06/23/technology/companies/23kodak.html?_r=0

Thompson, C. (2010, 16 June). What is IBM's Watson? *The New York Times Magazine*.

Thompson, E. P. (1967). Time, work-discipline, and industrial capitalism. Retrieved from http://tems.umn.edu/pdf/EPThompson-PastPresent.pdf

Thompson, J. (1995). *The media and modernity: A social theory of the media*. Oxford: Polity Press.

Thurman, N. (2011). Making "the daily me": Technology, economics and habit in the mainstream assimilation of personalized news. *Journalism*, 12(4), 395–415.

Thurman, N., & Schifferes, S. (2012). The future of personalization at news websites. *Journalism Studies*, 13, 5–6, 775–90.

Tiffen, R. (1989). *News and power*. Sydney: Allen & Unwin.

Tilly, C. (2007). *Democracy*. Cambridge, UK: Cambridge University Press.

Time. (1985, 2 September). *Time*, 126(9).

Todé, C. (2008, 11 July). Acxiom acquires ChoicePoint's database marketing solutions division. *Direct Marketing News*. Retrieved from http://www.dmnews.com/acxiom-acquires-choicepoints-database-marketing-solutions-division/article/112350/#

Toffler, A. (1981). *The third wave*. London: Pan.

TopTenReviews. (2006). Internet pornography statistics. Retrieved from http://internet-filter-review.toptenreviews.com/internet-pornography-statistics.html

Torstar. (2011). Atkinson principles. Atkinson Charitable Foundation. Used with permission. Retrieved from http://www.torstar.com/html/social-responsibility/Atkinson_Principles/index.cfm

Toto, S. (2011, 3 October). Hitachi updates its amazing naked-eye 3D display technology [Weblog message]. Retrieved from http://techcrunch.com/2011/10/03/hitachi-updates-its-amazing-naked-eye-3d-display-technology/?utm_source=feedburner&utm_medium=feed&utm_campaign=Feed: Techcrunch (TechCrunch)

Troianovski, A., Mattioli, D., & Ante, S. E. (2012, 13 September). Is the iPhone 5's "lighting connector" a pain in the neck? *Wall Street Journal*. Retrieved from http://online.wsj.com/article/SB10000872396390443696604577647993201137890.html

Tromp, S. L. (2008). Fallen behind: Canada's Access to Information Act in the world context. Retrieved from http://www3.telus.net/index100/report

Tsagarousianou, R. (1998). Electronic democracy and the public sphere: Opportunities and challenges. In R. Tsagarousianou, D. Tambini, & C. Bryan (Eds.), *Cyberdemocracy: Technology, cities and civic networks*. London/New York: Routledge.

Tsagarousianou, R., Tambini, D., & Bryan, C. (Eds.). (1998). *Cyberdemocracy: Technology, cities and civic networks*. London/New York: Routledge.

Tulloch, S. (Ed.). (1992). *The Oxford dictionary of new words: A popular guide to words in the news*. Oxford/New York: Oxford University Press.

Tweedie, K., & Cousineau, P. (2010). Photography. *The Canadian Encyclopedia*. Retrieved from http://thecanadianencyclopedia.com/articles/photography

Tyndall Report. (2011). Year in review: 2011. Retrieved from http://tyndallreport.com/yearinreview2011/

UDHR, Article 19. (1948). Retrieved from http://www.un.org/en/documents/udhr/

UFCW. (2010). Loblaw companies introduce finger scan punch clock. Retrieved from http://www.ufcw1000a.ca/index.php?option=com_k2&view=item&id=59:loblaw-companies-introduce-finger-scan-punch-clock&Itemid=326

United States. Superintendent of Documents. (1913). *Monthly catalogue, United States public documents, issues 211–22*. Washington, DC: Government Printing Office. Retrieved from http://www.earlyradiohistory.us

Universal Copyright Convention, Article 1. (1952). Retrieved from http://portal.unesco.org/en/ev.php-URL_ID=15381&URL_DO=DO_TOPIC&URL_SECTION=201.html

Upbin, B. (2013, 8 February). IBM's Watson gets its first piece of business in healthcare. *Forbes*. Retrieved from http://www.forbes.com/sites/bruceupbin/2013/02/08/ibms-watson-gets-its-first-piece-of-business-in-healthcare/

Van Couvering, E. (2004, July). *New media? The political economy of Internet search engines*. Paper presented to the International Association of Media and Communication Research Conference, Porto Alegre, Brazil. Retrieved from http://www.academia.edu/1047079/New_media_The_political_economy_of_Internet_search_engines

Van Couvering, E. (2010). *Search engine bias: The structuration of traffic on the World-Wide Web* (Unpublished doctoral dissertation). London School of Economics and Political Science.

Vancouver Sun. (2008, 11 December). Merry Christmas! Oh, here's your pink slip. Retrieved from http://www.canada.com/story_print.html?id=b0256b17-6446-4243-8afe-0a0596e2f9a3&sponsor=

van Dijk, J. (2012). *The network society.* Thousand Oaks, CA: Sage.

Van Gorp, A. F., & Middleton, C. (2010). The impact of facilities and service-based competition on Internet services provision in the Canadian broadband market. *Telematics & Informatics, 27*(3), 217–30.

Van Lohmann, F. (2010). *Unintended consequences: Twelve years under the DMCA.* San Francisco: Electronic Frontier Foundation.

Vanstone, G. (2007). *D is for daring: The women behind the films of Studio D.* Toronto, ON: Sumach Press.

Vipond, M. (1994). The beginnings of public broadcasting in Canada: The CRBC, 1932–1936. *Canadian Journal of Communication, 19*(2). Retrieved from www.cjc-online.ca

Vipond, M. (2000). *The mass media in Canada* (3rd ed.). Toronto: James Lorimer & Company Ltd.

Vipond, M. (2002). *The mass media in Canada* (3rd ed.). Toronto: Lorimer.

VOA. (2013). Fast facts. Retrieved from http://docs.voanews.eu/en-US-INSIDE/2013/03/07/7643c1bf-2af4-4978-a9ca-f9cc1cb7b004.pdf

von Finckenstein, K. (2011, 5 May). CRTC. Reproduced with the permission of the Minister of Public Works and Government Services Canada, 2013 Speech. Cambridge, ON. Retrieved from http://www.crtc.gc.ca/eng/com200/2011/s110505.htm

Waddell, C. (2009). The campaign in the media 2008. In J. Pammett & C. Dornan (Eds.), *The Canadian Federal Election of 2008* (pp. 217–56). Toronto: Dundurn Press.

Wagman, I., & Urquhart, P. (Eds.). (2012). *Cultural industries.ca: Making sense of Canadian media in the digital age.* Toronto: James Lorimer & Company.

Waldie, P., & Curry, B. (2010, 3 November). Potash ruling casts doubt on foreign takeovers. *The Globe and Mail.* Retrieved from http://www.theglobeandmail.com/globe-investor/potash-ruling-casts-doubt-on-foreign-takeovers/article1316275/

Waldman, S. (2011). The information needs of communities: The changing media landscape in a broadband age. Retrieved from http://transition.fcc.gov/osp/inc-report/The_Information_Needs_of_Communities.pdf

Waldrop, M. (2008). DARPA and the Internet revolution. Retrieved from http://itlaw.wikia.com/wiki/DARPA [see "External reading: Mitch Waldrop, 'DARPA and the Internet Revolution' (full-text)"].

Walker, R. B. (1976). *The newspaper press in New South Wales, 1803–1920.* Sydney: Sydney University Press.

Wan, W., & Richburg, K. (2012, 29 June). US urges China to respect Internet freedom after Bloomberg web site is censored. *Washington Post.* Retrieved from http://www.washingtonpost.com/world/asia_pacific/us-urges-china-to-respect-internet-freedom-after-bloomberg-web-site-is-censored/2012/06/29/gJQAQ5hOCW_story.html

Ward, I. (1991). Who writes the news? Journalists as hunters or harvesters. *Australian Journalism Review, 13*(1/2), 52–8.

Ward, I. (1995). *Politics of the media.* Melbourne: Macmillan.

Wark, M. (1994). *Virtual geography: Living with global media events.* Bloomington: Indiana University Press.

Wasko, J. (2003). *How Hollywood works.* London: Sage.

Waterman, S. (2012, 12 July). BlackBerry eschews China for security reasons. *The Washington Times.* Retrieved from http://www.washingtontimes.com/news/2012/jul/12/blackberry-eschews-china-security-reasons/

Waugh, T., Baker, M., & Winton, E. (Eds). (2010). *Challenge for change: Activist documentary at the National Film Board of Canada.* Montreal/Kingston: McGill-Queens University Press.

Wayne, M. (2003). Marxism and media studies: Key concepts and contemporary trends. In M. Wayne & E. Leslie (Eds.), *Marxism and culture.* London: Pluto Press.

Weber, M. (2001). *The Protestant work ethic: The spirit of capitalism* (T. Parsons, Trans.). New York: Routledge.

Webster, F. (2006). *Theories of the information society.* London/New York: Routledge.

Webopedia. (2013). Web 2.0. Retrieved from http://www.webopedia.com/TERM/W/Web_2_point_0.html

Weightman, G. (2003). *Signor Marconi's magic box: How an amateur inventor defied scientists and began the radio revolution.* London: HarperCollins.

Wente, M. (2012, 25 September). Columnist Margaret Wente defends herself. *The Globe and Mail.* Retrieved from http://www.theglobeandmail.com/commentary/columnist-margaret-wente-defends-herself/article4565731/

Weston, G. (2012). Canada "at risk" from Chinese firm, US warns. Retrieved from http://www.cbc.ca/news/politics/story/2012/10/09/huawei-canada-weston-interview.html

Weston, J. (1997). Old freedoms and new technologies: The evolution of community networking. *Information Society, 13,* 195–201.

Whitaker, R. (1986, spring). Official repression of Communism during World War II. *Labour/Le Travail, 17,* 135–66.

Whitaker, R. (2003). Keeping up with the neighbours? Canadian responses to 9/11 in historical and comparative context. *Osgoode Hall Law Journal, 41*(2/3), 241–65.

The White House. (2001). Address to a joint session of congress and the American people. Retrieved from http://georgewbush-whitehouse.archives.gov/news/releases/2001/09/20010920-8.html

White, J. (2008). Keeping Canadian culture: Why Canadians need self-determination of our telecom policy. In M. Moll & L. R. Shade (Eds.), *For sale to the highest bidder: Telecom policy in Canada* (pp. 37–54). Ottawa: Canadian Centre for Policy Alternatives.

Wikipedia. (n.d.). Nortel. Retrieved from http://en.wikipedia.org/wiki/Nortel

Wikipedia. (2006, 23 March). Google economy.

Retrieved from http://en.wikipedia.org/wiki/Google_economy [4 April 2006].

Wikipedia. (2012). Google. Retrieved from http://en.wikipedia.org/wiki/Google

Wikipedia. (2013a). 2010 Canada anti-prorogation protests. Retrieved from http://en.wikipedia.org/wiki/2010_Canada_anti-prorogation_protests

Wikipedia. (2013b). The girls next door. Retrieved from http://en.wikipedia.org/wiki/The_Girls_Next_Door

Wilde, W. (2006). Crossing the river of fire: Mark's gospel and global capitalism. Peterborough, ON: Epworth.

Williams, K. (1997). *Get me a murder a day! A history of mass communication in Britain*. London: Arnold.

Williams, L. (2006, 11–12 February). Every move they make, mum's watching. *SMH*, 1, 2.

Williams, L. (2010). Maneuvering the peacekeeping myth: The Canadian Press and the misrepresentation of the Canadian Forces (Master's thesis). Toronto: York University.

Williams, R. (1978). Television: Technology and cultural form. In J. Benthall (Ed.), *Technosphere*. London: Fontana.

Williams, R. (1980). Base and superstructure in Marxist cultural theory. In R. Williams (Ed.), *Problems in materialism and culture: Selected essays* (pp. 31–49). London: Verso.

Williams, R. (1983). *Towards 2000*. London: Chatto & Windus.

Williams, R. (1989). *Keywords: A vocabulary of culture and society* (3rd ed.). London: Fontana Press.

Willison, D. J., & MacLeod, S. M. (2002, 6 August). Patenting of genetic material: Are the benefits to society being realized? *Canadian Medical Association Journal*, 167(3), 259–62.

Wilson, M. (2010). Battle ready freelance writers march into war. The cause: Increased rates, rights and respect. The enemy: Publishers like Transcontinental. Who will retreat first? *Ryerson Review of Journalism*, 25–31.

Wines, M. (2012, 1 June). Google to alert users to Chinese censorship. *The New York Times*. Retrieved from http://www.nytimes.com/2012/06/02/world/asia/google-to-alert-users-to-chinese-censorship.html

Winseck, D. (1998). *Reconvergence: A political economy of telecommunication in Canada*. Cresskill, NJ: Hampton Press.

Winseck, D. (2002). Netscapes of power: Convergence, consolidation and power in the Canadian mediascape. *Media, Culture and Society*, 24, 795–819.

Winseck, D. (2010). Financialization and the "crisis of the media": The rise and fall of (some) media conglomerates in Canada. *Canadian Journal of Communication*, 35(3), 365–93.

Winseck, D. (2011a). The political economies of media and the transformation of the global media industries. In D. Winseck & D. Y. Jin (Eds.), *The political economies of media: The transformation of the global media industries* (pp. 3–48). New York, NJ: Bloomsbury.

Winseck, D. (2011b, 18 April). The struggle for the future of media in Canada. *The Globe and Mail*. Retrieved from http://www.theglobeandmail.com/news/technology/digital-culture/dwayne-winseck/the-struggle-for-the-future-of-media-in-canada/article1989836/

Winseck, D. (2014). The political economies of media and the transformation of the global media industries. In D. Winseck & D. Y. Jin (Eds.), *The political economies of media: The transformation of the global media industries* (pp. 3–48). New York, NY: Bloomsbury Academic.

Winseck, D., & Cuthbert, M. (1997). From communication to democratic norms: Reflections on the normative dimensions of international communication policy. *Gazette*, 59(1), 1–20.

Winseck, D., & Pike, R. (2007). *Communication and empire: Media, markets and globalization, 1860–1930*. Durham/London: Duke University Press.

Winter, J. (1997). *Democracy's oxygen: How corporations control the news*. Montreal: Black Rose Books.

Workman, C. (1993). Lasting impressions. *Modern Maturity*, 36(1), 36–9.

Wright, R. (1995, 23 January). Hyperdemocracy. *Time*, 145(4), 40–46.

Zanish-Belcher, T., & Leigh, P. R. (2011). Documenting and digitizing the student experience: A collaboration between Iowa State University's Carver Academy and the University Archives. Association for Advancement of Computing in Education, E-Learn 2011. Honolulu. Retrieved from http://lib.dr.iastate.edu/speccoll_conf/1/

Zawawi, C. (1994). Source of news: Who feeds the watchdogs? *Australian Journalism Review*, 16(1), 67–72.

Zerbisias, A. (2012). Broadsides. *The Toronto Star*. Retrieved from http://thestar.blogs.com/broadsides/ [19 November 2012].

Zimet, A. (2012). Arrêtez-moi quelqu'un! (Someone stop me!). Retrieved from https://www.commondreams.org/further/2012/06/01-3 [20 November 2012].

Zuboff, S. (1998). *In the age of the smart machine: Future of work and power*. Butterworth-Heinemann Ltd.

Index